The Mark of Nicholas Kegg

Volume II A-K

Research and Compilation by

Debbie Alexander

Copyright © 2023, Debbie Alexander

ALL RIGHTS RESERVED.
No part of this publication may be reproduced, stored in a retrieval system, or transmitted in any form or by any means whatsoever, whether electronic, mechanical, magnetic recording, or photocopying, without the prior written approval of the Copyright holder or Publisher, excepting brief quotations for inclusion in book reviews.

Published by:

Janaway Publishing, Inc.
732 Kelsey Ct.
Santa Maria, California 93454
(805) 925-1952
www.janawaygenealogy.com

2023

Library of Congress Control Number: 2023941660

ISBN: 978-1-59641-474-7 Volume 2
Other volumes in this set:
978-1-59641-473-0 Volume 1
978-1-59641-475-4 Volume 3

Cover artist Chelan Hawk Shumacher (8th great grandson of progenitor Nicholas Kegg) artistically depicts the contents of this book. He includes the Mark of Nicholas Kegg carved into the family tree. The actual mark shown above was taken from a court document dated March 5, 1778 whereas Nicholas cursed the new law, damned the congress, money and those who made it. Unable to read or write, Nicholas made his mark with the letter N. It is all that remains by the hand of the progenitor.

Edited by Jenna Meeker Alexander Published by Janaway Publishing Inc., Publisher of Barbara Jean Walling Sistler (6th great granddaughter of Nicholas Kegg) along with her husband Byron H. Sistler, books.

Special thanks to more than 250 cousins who provided the photographs contained in this book.

DISCLAIMER: Within the following pages, the total number of children born to an individual includes only those who have been proven without a shadow of doubt. The utmost care has been taken to ensure the genealogical accuracy of this publication, however, that does not mean there can't be mistakes. You should always verify and do your own research.

Made in the United States of America

THE PROGENITOR

Gazing toward the ridge that separates Friends Cove from the Black Valley, one can only imagine the exact location where a barn, with its cow and two horses stood on the 100 acres that had been improved by the sweat of Nicholas Kegg and, wonder what his life might have been like. In 1772, Colonial discontent prompted Samuel Adams to appoint a 21-man group which he called the Committee of Correspondence. They were to provide leadership and aid intercolonial cooperation. The committee would communicate the rights of the Colonists as men, as Christians and as subjects. Within two years they were the body of delegates who called themselves the First Continental Congress and according to history acted collectively for the people of the colony. However, they must not have acted in behalf of the then 40 year old Nicholas who remained discontented as reflected in the 1778 court document that was described in Vol. I.

There I was, in Central Pennsylvania unable to find the unmarked grave of Nicholas Kegg, an early pioneer who after the start of the Revolutionary war had settled at the western base of Tussey's mountain. I was not alone; many have unsuccessfully searched. His remains are said to rest in what was once a farm plot near Ott Town in Colerain Township. It had only taken three generations before time seemingly erased any memory of Nicholas Kegg (1732 – 1800) a 68-year-old Bedford County man who supposedly had been buried there.

Few records remain, giving way to conjecture. The Allegany County Maryland courthouse caught fire on January 5, 1893, destroying records that might provide evidence otherwise however, from what I have gathered; Nicholas is likely the first of the Kegg family line to be born in what was known as the thirteen British colonies on the Atlantic coast. It appears that Nicholas shares the same birth year as George Washington, the first American president and Commander of the Continental Army. Although there is no record that Nicholas was called to serve in the Revolutionary war. He was however, called to serve for six days in the Maryland Militia under the Muster of Captain John White's Company during the French and Indian war as evidenced on page 95 in Colonial Soldiers of the South, 1732-1774 by Murtie June Clark . Ms. Clark gives her source for the Capt. White Muster Roll as MHS:375 Maryland Historical Society, Baltimore, MD, Manuscript Division, French and Indian War Account Books.

Evidence also suggests Nicholas was twice married. Neither wife has ever been identified by name. He was the father of eight known children. Five sons were born to his first wife in Washington County, Maryland which included Henry, Sebastian, John, William, and Andrew. Two daughters and a son were born to the second wife in Bedford County, Pennsylvania including Peter and his two sisters. It remains unknown what first names were given to the two daughters born to the second wife of progenitor

Nicholas Kegg. Roy believed the oldest daughter may have married a Diehl who lived in Whipp's Cove. The youngest daughter likely married Christopher Myers of Londonderry Twp.,

The ancestral origin of the progenitor Nicholas Kegg is a conundrum. Evidence of who his parents were remains unknown. At this time, it's impossible to prove without a shadow of a doubt where the ancestral immigrants specifically came from. Evaluating inconclusive evidence includes William G. Cutler's History of the State of Kansas Part 17 Osage County states that the great grandson of Nicholas Kegg whose name was **Nicholas Alexander Knouf** 1824 – 1888 was a member of the German Reformed Church. The Bedford County obituary of his great granddaughter **Catherine (Kegg) Diehl** [77] 1812 – 1905 states that she was a most devoted Christian woman and a constant reader of her German Bible. **Christina (Diehl) Kegg** 1819 – 1902 wife of John Kegg Jr. whose German family Bible remains in the possession of Marjorie (Talcott) Mack is not enough to presume a German heritage. However, if you believe oral tradition (meaning information that is transmitted by word of mouth through successive generations) the answer would be this Kegg line originates in Holland.

Following migration, the predominant early settlers of Bedford County, Pennsylvania came from a German settlement 71 miles away that had been made near Hagerstown, Maryland in the early 1700's. Those Bedford County settlers were known as Pennsylvania Dutch, an American corruption of the word "Deutsche" meaning Germans as an ethnic group. Was this oral tradition a misunderstanding to the successive generations or did they literally mean the Dutch from Holland? One might look to science for the answer. Many descendants have submitted DNA tests that show Western Europe. However, it should be noted that it is not possible to reliably distinguish between, British Isles, Scandinavia and the region known as Western Europe.

Etymology
According to Manx Names by Arthur William Moore London Elliott Stock, 62, Paternoster Row, E.C. 1906; The Kegg surname originates from a Scandinavian Viking known as Mac Taidhg (meaning Tadg's son). The name underwent a kind of phonetic corruption that was Celticised in form during the eighth century when the Vikings settled on the Isle of Mann. By 1408 considered a Manx name and spelled Mac Kyg, 1511 Mac Kegg, and Mac Coag and by 1623 Keage and Kegg.

More recent spelling variations in U.S. records weren't any better. The name was spelled Keg, Kegg, Keggs, Cegg, Keck, Kagg and Cagg. Sometime around 1810, Kegg became the dominant spelling connecting the consanguineous group.

[77] Bedford Gazette (PA) Oct 27, 1905

There are three exceptions, the most recent is KEG, the result of a birth certificate with an undetected spelling error.

- John Cagg (1789-1870) a grandson of the progenitor, whose parents were William and Susannah (Koontz) Kegg, and his successive generations continue to use the CAGG spelling.

- David Sanford Keggs (1824 – 1876) a great-grandson of the progenitor, whose parents were Solomon and Elizabeth (Shuman) Kegg, and his successive generations continue to use the KEGGS spelling.

Regardless of how you spell it, the direct descendants of Nicholas Kegg continue to reside in both Washington and Allegany County, Maryland where the progenitor is first recorded. They also live in all 50 states and Canada. Unfortunately, it was impossible to obtain a photograph of everyone and/or permission of use for such a large family therefor, those thousands of direct descendants without a photograph are alphabetically listed on the following pages. The Mark of Nicholas Kegg is a story about a farmer, who is the common ancestor connecting the descendants contained in the three volumes to each other.

1. Source Citation 1732-1763 Maryland Militia
Nicholas Cagg listed line 31; Muster of Captain John White's Company for 6 days service
2. Source Citation 1779 Colerain, Bedford County spelled Nicholas Kegg
Pennsylvania Historical & Museum Commission; Records of the Office of the Comptroller General, RG-4;Tax & Exoneration Lists, 1762-1794; Microfilm Roll: 315
3. Source Citation 1781 Colerain, Bedford County spelled Nicholas Keck
Pennsylvania Historical & Museum Commission; Records of the Office of the Comptroller General, RG-4;Tax & Exoneration Lists, 1762-1794; Microfilm Roll: 315
4. Source Citation 1782 Colerain, Bedford County spelled Nicholas Keck
Pennsylvania Historical & Museum Commission; Records of the Office of the Comptroller General, RG-4;Tax & Exoneration Lists, 1762-1794; Microfilm Roll: 316
5. Source Citation 1783 Colerain, Bedford County spelled Nicholas Kegg
Pennsylvania Historical & Museum Commission; Records of the Office of the Comptroller General, RG-4;Tax & Exoneration Lists, 1762-1794; Microfilm Roll: 316
6. Source Citation 1785 Colerain, Bedford County spelled Nicholas Kegg
Pennsylvania Historical & Museum Commission; Records of the Office of the Comptroller General, RG-4;Tax & Exoneration Lists, 1762-1794; Microfilm Roll: 316
7. Source Information 1786 Colerain, Bedford, PA spelled Nicholas Kegg
Ancestry.com. Pennsylvania, Septennial Census, 1779-1863 [database on-line]. Provo, UT, USA: Ancestry.com Operations, Inc., 2012
8. Source Citation 1790 Bedford Census Pennsylvania spelled Nicolas Cegg
Year: 1790; Census Place: Bedford, Pennsylvania; Series: M637; Roll: 9; Page: 237; Image: 134; Family History Library Film: 0568149 (Census shows Nicholas living with 3 free white females/total in household 4)
9. Source Information 1800 Colerain, Bedford, PA spelled Nicholas Kegg
Ancestry.com. Pennsylvania, Septennial Census, 1779-1863 [database on-line]. Provo, UT, USA: Ancestry.com Operations, Inc., 2012

ABBOTT

BENJAMIN ABBOTT Seventh great grandson of progenitor Nicholas Kegg. **CHRIS ABBOTT** Sixth great grandson of progenitor Nicholas Kegg. **CINDEE ABBOTT** Sixth great granddaughter of progenitor Nicholas Kegg. **CONNIE ABBOTT** Fifth great granddaughter of progenitor Nicholas Kegg. **CRAIG ABBOTT** Sixth great grandson of progenitor Nicholas Kegg. **DEAN VERL ABBOTT** Fifth great grandson of progenitor Nicholas Kegg. **DOROTHA ELMA ABBOTT** (1915 – 1997) daughter of John and Sarah (Gray) Abbott married William Elton Berry with whom she was mother of (4). **DOUGLAS ABBOTT** Sixth great grandson of progenitor Nicholas Kegg.
EARL DALE ABBOTT [2609] (1924 – 1985) son of John and Sarah (Gray) Abbott married Helen Hall with whom he was father of (3). Earl was employed as a plumber. **FINN ABBOTT** Seventh great grandson of progenitor Nicholas Kegg. **GENEVIEVE ELEANOR ABBOTT** Fifth great granddaughter of progenitor Nicholas Kegg **GERALD FRANKLIN ABBOTT** (1937 – 2015) son of Hugh and Violet (Boswell) Abbott married Loretta Mae Larson. Gerry owned Abbott's Big Sky Ranch where he raised Llama's. **HUGH FRANKLIN ABBOTT** [2610] aka "Franklin" (1912 – 1971) son of John and Sarah (Gray) Abbott married twice, first to Violet Belle Boswell with whom he was father of (3). Later, he married Elsa Helena Eichhorst. Franklin was a good horseman. He had one special horse, he called Babe and a matched team he called Doc and Dan. Franklin was a fast runner who had a love for sports and saw to it that his sons had baseballs, bats and gloves to play with. He was a farmer. He enjoyed woodworking and made family members beautiful cake trays. **JACKSON H. ABBOTT** Seventh great grandson of progenitor Nicholas Kegg. **JAYNE ABBOTT** Fifth great granddaughter of progenitor Nicholas Kegg. **JENNA ABBOTT** Sixth great granddaughter of progenitor Nicholas Kegg. **JERRY WAYNE ABBOTT** Fifth great grandson of progenitor Nicholas Kegg. **KAREN ABBOTT** Fifth great granddaughter of progenitor Nicholas Kegg. **KELLY ABBOTT** Sixth great granddaughter of progenitor Nicholas Kegg. **LISA ABBOTT** Fifth great granddaughter of progenitor Nicholas Kegg. **LUCILLE AGNES ABBOTT** (1919 – 1965) daughter of John and Sarah (Gray) Abbott married Everard Stark with whom she was mother of (1). **MORGAN ABBOTT** Seventh great granddaughter of progenitor Nicholas Kegg. **NANETTE ABBOTT** Fifth great granddaughter of progenitor Nicholas Kegg. **ROBIN ABBOTT** Sixth great granddaughter of progenitor Nicholas Kegg.
ROLAND JOHN ABBOTT [2611] (1917 – 1995) son of John and Sarah (Gray) Abbott married twice, first to Lorrene Hazel Ingraham with whom he was father of (3). Later, he married Albina Anna Pomykal. **RONALD DWAINE ABBOTT** [2611A] aka "Ron" (1938 – 2015) son of Roland and Lorrene (Ingraham) Abbott, married Noreen Tower with whom he was father of (3) Ron enjoyed spending time on his farm with his cows and friends. **THELMA ELLEN ABBOTT** [2612] (1910 – 1990) daughter of John and Sarah (Gray) Abbott married Homer D. Ridler with whom she was mother of (5). Thelma was a member of the Seventh Day Adventist church. **TIMOTHY ABBOTT** Sixth great grandson of progenitor Nicholas Kegg. **VELTA NANCY ABBOTT** [2613] (1913 – 2001) daughter of John and Sarah (Gray) Abbott married Floyd William Price with whom she was mother of (1). Velta loved to take trips down memory lane recalling her growing up years and special family events. She learned sewing skills from her mother and loved to sew clothes, quilts, toys and pillows. Velta enjoyed gardening and canning. **VERLE GALE ABBOTT** [2614] (1924 – 2011) son of John and Sarah (Gray) Abbott, married Alnora R. Christensen with whom he was father of (4). Verle served his country in the United States Army during W.W. II as a Quarter Master. He participated in Campaigns in France, Germany and Belgium and landed on Normandy Beach two days after the D-Day Invasion. He was a farmer for a couple of years, when he became an iron worker and joined the Des Moines Iron Workers Union Local 67. His iron working years found him involved in many major construction projects including the Vets Auditorium, the nuclear plant at Palo, IA, and the SAC missile silos at the Offutt Air Force Base in Omaha and the Lincoln (NE) Air Force Base. In his free time, Verle enjoyed fishing, dancing, crafts, and he loved to play cribbage.

[2609] p.7A The News (Northfield, MN) June 13, 1985 [2610] p.185- Adair County Iowa Sesquicentennial Edition 1851-2001 written by Duane Abbott [2611] p. 2B- Prescott Daily Courier (AZ) Jan. 19, 1995 [2611A] Watson-Armstrong Funeral Home [2612] Adair Co. Free Press (IA) 1990 [2613] Sun Newspapers (MN) Aug 22, 2001

WAYNE ELMER ABBOTT [2614] (1922 – 2012) son of John and Sarah (Gray) Abbott, married Ruth Bolger with whom he was father of (2). He served in the Medical Corp during World War II in Australia, New Guinea and The Philippines from 1942 to 1945. After he was discharged from the military, the family moved several times in the Midwest following Wayne's work as an engineer. Wayne enjoyed woodworking, gardening, riding his bicycle and taking walks. **WILHELMINA MAIE ABBOTT** (1965 – 1965) daughter of Verle and Alnora (Christensen) Abbott. **YVONNE MARLENE ABBOTT** Fifth great granddaughter of progenitor Nicholas Kegg.

ABE

CAROL JANE ABE 5th great granddaughter of progenitor Nicholas Kegg. **JEFFREY LYNN ABE** Fifth great grandson of progenitor Nicholas Kegg. **JOEL JAMES ABE** Fifth great grandson of progenitor Nicholas Kegg.

ACHABAL

AMORITA ACHABAL Seventh great granddaughter of progenitor Nicholas Kegg.
CLETO YGNACIO ACHABAL Sixth great grandson of progenitor Nicholas Kegg.

ACUFF

FAYE ACUFF Fifth great granddaughter of progenitor Nicholas Kegg. **LYNDA ACUFF** Fifth great granddaughter of progenitor Nicholas Kegg. **TERRY FRED ACUFF** Fifth great grandson of progenitor Nicholas Kegg. **WESTON ACUFF** Sixth great grandson of progenitor Nicholas Kegg.

ADAMCZYK

ASHLEY ADAMCZYK Seventh great granddaughter of progenitor Nicholas Kegg.
JESSE SCOTT ADAMCZYK Seventh great grandson of progenitor Nicholas Kegg.
KATRINA ADAMCZYK Seventh great granddaughter of progenitor Nicholas Kegg.
RYLIE MCKENZIE ADAMCZYK Eighth great granddaughter of progenitor Nicholas Kegg.

ADAMS

AMY ADAMS Sixth great granddaughter of progenitor Nicholas Kegg. **ASHLEY ADAMS** Eighth great granddaughter of progenitor Nicholas Kegg. **CHRISTOPHER ADAMS** Sixth great grandson of progenitor Nicholas Kegg. **DANNY LEE ADAMS** [2615] (1969 – 2007) son of Danny and Kathy (Reed) Adams was a graduate of Ottawa Hills High School and near completion of a business associate degree at Owens Community College. He was employed as an Area Sales director for Ohio Referral Association, Inc. Dan enjoyed classic cars, camping, jet skiing, golfing, music, and was an avid Pittsburgh Steelers and Ohio State Buckeye fan. The majority of his life was spent as a man of strong faith in Jesus Christ. Amongst his most rewarding experiences was participating in a missionary trip to Russia. Danny was a kind-hearted, soft-spoken man and a great father figure.
DEBORAH A. ADAMS Sixth great granddaughter of progenitor Nicholas Kegg.
DUSTIN ADAMS Seventh great grandson of progenitor Nicholas Kegg. **EMILY M. ADAMS** Seventh great granddaughter of progenitor Nicholas Kegg. **JAMISON ADAMS** Seventh great grandson of progenitor Nicholas Kegg. **KEN ADAMS** Sixth great grandson of progenitor Nicholas Kegg. **KURTIS ADAMS** Seventh great grandson of progenitor Nicholas Kegg.

[2614] Steen Funeral Homes (IA) [2615] Toledo Blade (OH) Aug 25, 2007, obtained by D. Sue Dible

MARC L. ADAMS Sixth great grandson of progenitor Nicholas Kegg. **MARISSA ADAMS** Seventh great granddaughter of progenitor Nicholas Kegg. **MARY CATHERINE ADAMS** Seventh great granddaughter of progenitor Nicholas Kegg. **MEGAN R. ADAMS** Seventh great granddaughter of progenitor Nicholas Kegg. **NEIL J. ADAMS** Sixth great grandson of progenitor Nicholas Kegg. **NICHOLAS ADAMS** Seventh great grandson of progenitor Nicholas Kegg.
NORMA JEAN ADAMS [2616] (1937 – 1995) daughter of Earl and Edith (Diehl) Adams married Joseph Walker Yurechko with whom she was mother of (1). **ROBERT LEON ADAMS** Sixth great grandson of progenitor Nicholas Kegg. **STEVEN ADAMS** Sixth great grandson of progenitor Nicholas Kegg. **STEVEN ADAMS** Seventh great grandson of progenitor Nicholas Kegg. **TODD ADAMS** Sixth great grandson of progenitor Nicholas Kegg. **WALKER ADAMS** Seventh great granddaughter of progenitor Nicholas Kegg.

ADAMSON

MARLA K. ADAMSON Sixth great granddaughter of progenitor Nicholas Kegg.

AESCHLIMAN

JASON DAVID AESCHLIMAN [2617] (1974 – 1982) son of Terry and Ann (Werder) Aeschliman. Jason had been attending first grade at Stryker Elementary School. He also attended the Poplar Ridge Church of the brethren. **ZANDER ANN AESCHLIMAN** Seventh great granddaughter of progenitor Nicholas Kegg.

AGAMALIAN

ALEXA AGAMALIAN Seventh great granddaughter of progenitor Nicholas Kegg.
GRANT AGAMALIAN Seventh great grandson of progenitor Nicholas Kegg.

AGNEW

BRIAN NEAL AGNEW Sixth great grandson of progenitor Nicholas Kegg. **DAWN MARIE AGNEW** Sixth great granddaughter of progenitor Nicholas Kegg. **MICHELE DENISE AGNEW** Sixth great granddaughter of progenitor Nicholas Kegg.

AGUILAR

ERIC AGUILAR Seventh great grandson of progenitor Nicholas Kegg.
JASON AGUILAR Seventh great grandson of progenitor Nicholas Kegg.

AHMAD

AZMAI AHMAD Seventh great grandson of progenitor Nicholas Kegg
INFANT AHMAD (2003 -2003) son of Iftikhar and Angela (Nelson) Ahmad.

AIKEN

NICHOLE ELIZABETH AIKEN Seventh great granddaughter of progenitor Nicholas Kegg.
RYAN DONOVAN AIKEN Seventh great grandson of progenitor Nicholas Kegg.

[2616] p6B San Antonio Express-News (TX) Feb. 3, 1995 [2617] p 3 The Bryan Times (OH) May 17, 1982

AINLEY

LESLIE ANN AINLEY Fifth great granddaughter of progenitor Nicholas Kegg.
ROBERT KENT AINLEY Fifth great grandson of progenitor Nicholas Kegg.

AKE

CATHERINE L. AKE [2618] (1924 – 2012) daughter of Pearl and Margaret (Cessna) Ake, married Clifford Walter Blackburn with whom she was mother of (6). **MARIAN W. AKE** (1921 – 1999) daughter of Pearl and Margaret (Cessna) Ake.

AKERS

ALLEN ANDREW AKERS Sixth great grandson of progenitor Nicholas Kegg. **CAYLIN DAWN AKERS** Eighth great granddaughter of progenitor Nicholas Kegg. **DEBORAH L. AKERS** Sixth great granddaughter of progenitor Nicholas Kegg. **GREGORY CARTER AKERS** Eighth great grandson of progenitor Nicholas Kegg. **GREGORY L. AKERS** [2618A] (1962 – 2010) son of Charles and Leona (Calhoun) was employed at Grove Manufacturing for 21 years in maintenance and recently at Fairfield Inn by Marriot in Winchester, Va. Greg enjoyed hunting, fishing, working outdoors and spending time with his dogs. - **AARON ALEXANDER** 7th great grandson of progenitor Nicholas Kegg. **HOPE RENE AKERS** Eighth great granddaughter of progenitor Nicholas Kegg. **JASON AKERS** Seventh great grandson of progenitor Nicholas Kegg. **JOANNE AKERS** Sixth great granddaughter of progenitor Nicholas Kegg. **LISA KAY AKERS** Sixth great grand- daughter of progenitor Nicholas Kegg. **OLIVIA ROSE AKERS** Seventh great granddaughter of progenitor Nicholas Kegg. **RANDY E. AKERS** Sixth great grandson of progenitor Nicholas Kegg. **ROGER L. AKERS** Sixth great grandson of progenitor Nicholas Kegg. **ROGER L. AKERS JR.** Seventh great grandson of progenitor Nicholas Kegg. **SCOTT LYNN AKERS** Seventh great grandson of progenitor Nicholas Kegg. **STEVEN C. AKERS** Sixth great grandson of progenitor Nicholas Kegg. **STEVEN TROY AKERS** Seventh great grandson of progenitor Nicholas Kegg. **TREVOR ALLEN AKERS** Seventh great grandson of progenitor Nicholas Kegg.

ALBATER

GINA ALBATER Fifth great granddaughter of progenitor Nicholas Kegg.

ALBRIGHT

THOMAS HAROLD ALBRIGHT [2619] (1936 – 2006) son of Harold and Laura (Beegle) Albright. Thomas was an avid Cubs fan.

ALDERSON

DYLAN ALDERSON Seventh great grandson of progenitor Nicholas Kegg. **KEN ALDERSON** Sixth great grandson of progenitor Nicholas Kegg. **MACKENZIE LYNN ALDERSON** Seventh great granddaughter of progenitor Nicholas Kegg. **STACEY ALDERSON** Sixth great granddaughter of progenitor Nicholas Kegg.

[2618] Pittsburgh Post-Gazette (PA) June 24, 2012 [2618A] Akers Funeral Home (PA) [2619] The Times (IN) Dec. 17, 2006

ALDRICH

ABIGAIL ALDRICH Seventh great granddaughter of progenitor Nicholas Kegg.
BENJAMIN ALDRICH Seventh great grandson of progenitor Nicholas Kegg.
BRIAN ALAN ALDRICH Sixth great grandson of progenitor Nicholas Kegg.

ALDRIDGE

AMY ELIZABETH ALDRIDGE Seventh great granddaughter of progenitor Nicholas Kegg.

ALFORD

BROCK WILLIAM ALFORD Seventh great grandson of progenitor Nicholas Kegg.
TYLER L ALFORD Seventh great grandson of progenitor Nicholas Kegg.
ZACHARY CLAY ALFORD Seventh great grandson of progenitor Nicholas Kegg.

ALGE

AMANDA LYNN ALGE Seventh great granddaughter of progenitor Nicholas Kegg. **ASHLEY ALGE** Seventh great granddaughter of progenitor Nicholas Kegg. **CARSON ALGE** Seventh great grandson of progenitor Nicholas Kegg. **CATI ALGE** Seventh great granddaughter of progenitor Nicholas Kegg. **CHRISTINA SUE ALGE** Seventh great granddaughter of progenitor Nicholas Kegg. **COURTNEY BROOKE ALGE** Seventh great granddaughter of progenitor Nicholas Kegg. **DOUGLAS L. ALGE** Sixth great grandson of progenitor Nicholas Kegg. **KALEIGH ALGE** Seventh great granddaughter of progenitor Nicholas Kegg. **RYAN MICHAEL ALGE** Seventh great grandson of progenitor Nicholas Kegg. **SUSAN E. ALGE** Sixth great granddaughter of progenitor Nicholas Kegg.

ALKIRE

COREY E. ALKIRE Sixth great grandson of progenitor Nicholas Kegg. **ERICK R. ALKIRE** Sixth great grandson of progenitor Nicholas Kegg. **JENNIFER R. ALKIRE** Sixth great granddaughter of progenitor Nicholas Kegg. **KENNETH TYLER ALKIRE** Sixth great grandson of progenitor Nicholas Kegg. **MEREDITH A. ALKIRE** Sixth great granddaughter of progenitor Nicholas Kegg.

ALLAN

LAURA ALLAN Sixth great granddaughter of progenitor Nicholas Kegg. **MARTIN W. ALLAN** Sixth great grandson of progenitor Nicholas Kegg. **MICHAEL KASH ALLAN** Sixth great grandson of progenitor Nicholas Kegg. **ROBERT ALLAN** Sixth great grandson of progenitor Nicholas Kegg. **SCOTT ALLAN** Sixth great grandson of progenitor Nicholas Kegg. **TERRY L. ALLAN** Sixth great grandson of progenitor Nicholas Kegg.

ALLEMAN

LAUREL ALLEMAN Seventh great granddaughter of progenitor Nicholas Kegg.
LOGAN ALLEMAN Seventh great grandson of progenitor Nicholas Kegg.

ALLEN

BERTHA E. ALLEN (2620) (1880 – 1968) daughter of Frank and Etta (Green) Allen. Bertha was employed as a librarian at Andrews University. **BRITTANY ALLEN** Seventh great granddaughter of progenitor Nicholas Kegg. **CHRISTOPHER JAMES ALLEN** Seventh great grandson of progenitor Nicholas Kegg. **JEANNE LUCRETIA ALLEN** (2620A) (1923 – 2013) daughter of Glenn and Lou (Bowers) Allen, married Donald Harry Shafer Jr., with whom she was mother of (2). Jeanne sang in the church choir until age 83. She was co-owner and operator of Shafer's. **LINDSAY ALLEN** Eighth great granddaughter of progenitor Nicholas Kegg. **SARA ANNE ALLEN** Seventh great granddaughter of progenitor Nicholas Kegg.

ALLISON

BRITTANY SUE ALLISON Seventh great granddaughter of progenitor Nicholas Kegg. **JACE ALLISON** Seventh great grandson of progenitor Nicholas Kegg. **JASMINE NICOLE ALLISON** Seventh great granddaughter of progenitor Nicholas Kegg. **JENNIFER DAWN ALLISON** Seventh great granddaughter of progenitor Nicholas Kegg. **JOSHUA BRADY ALLISON** Seventh great grandson of progenitor Nicholas Kegg. **MISTI ALLISON** Seventh great granddaughter of progenitor Nicholas Kegg.

ALLSUP

ANGELA ALLSUP Seventh great granddaughter of progenitor Nicholas Kegg.
BRIAN KURT ALLSUP (2620B) (1963 – 2013) son of Kenneth and Rita (Woodson) Allsup was twice married first to Pamela Thomas with whom he was father of a daughter. Second, he married Helen Pearce. Brian worked in the construction business for many years living in Florida, Texas and New York before settling in Stuart. He enjoyed playing competitive games of golf, bowling, pool and cards. He was an avid outdoorsman that loved hunting and fishing. **CARRIE ALLSUP** Seventh great granddaughter of progenitor Nicholas Kegg. **CHAD ALLSUP** Seventh great grandson of progenitor Nicholas Kegg. **CHRISTOPHER WAYNE ALLSUP** (2621) (2002 – 2013) son of Scott and Jane (Fitch) Allsup. Christopher loved school, enjoying basketball, track and playing tag at recess. He was a member of the Earlham Church of Christ and just joined the Boy Scouts of America. Christopher was a very bright-eyed, energetic little boy. He enjoyed riding go-carts, playing with his animals, fishing, and hunting, but most of all he enjoyed spending time with his family. **DANIEL WAYNE ALLSUP** (2622) (1964 – 2019) son of Kenneth and Rita (Woodson) Allsup was father of (4). Danny worked as a heavy equipment operator for many years and in many states including Texas, California, Florida, and Missouri before settling in Iowa. He enjoyed the outdoors and especially enjoyed fishing. He also enjoyed spending most spring days in the woods looking for morel mushrooms. **JOSH ALLSUP** Seventh great grandson of progenitor Nicholas Kegg. **KENDALL ALLSUP** Seventh great granddaughter of progenitor Nicholas Kegg.
KEVIN LEE ALLSUP Sixth great grandson of progenitor Nicholas Kegg.
MEGAN ALLSUP (2623) (2002 – 2014) daughter of Penny Allsup and Lloyd Lee.
MICHAEL ALLSUP Seventh great grandson of progenitor Nicholas Kegg. **NICOLE ALLSUP** Seventh great granddaughter of progenitor Nicholas Kegg. **PENNY ALLSUP** Sixth great granddaughter of progenitor Nicholas Kegg. **RANDY ALLEN ALLSUP** Sixth great grandson of progenitor Nicholas Kegg. **SCOTT ALLSUP** Sixth great grandson of progenitor Nicholas Kegg. **TYLER ALLEN ALLSUP** Seventh great grandson of progenitor Nicholas Kegg.

(2620) p10 - Benton Harbor News Palladium Mar 16, 1968 (2620A) Johnson Family Funeral Home (2621) Athens Messenger (OH) Aug 25, 2013 (2621B) Johnson Family Funeral Home (IA) (2622) Creston News Advertiser (IA) Feb 26, 2019 (2623) Des Moines Register (IA) May 30, 2014

ALT

JAMES CLINTON ALT Sixth great grandson of progenitor Nicholas Kegg.
SUSAN REBECCA ALT Sixth great granddaughter of progenitor Nicholas Kegg.

ALTMAN

CHRISTINA MARIE ALTMAN Seventh great granddaughter of progenitor Nicholas Kegg.

AMBROSIER

ANNA ARLENE AMBROSIER (1954 – 1956) daughter of Arlo and Ellen (Fetterolt) Ambrosier.
ARLAINE ANN AMBROSIER Fifth great granddaughter of progenitor Nicholas Kegg.
ARLO ARTHUR AMBROSIER [2623A] (1917 – 2007) son of James and Nellie (Knouf) Ambrosier married Ellen Fetterolt, with whom he was father of (3). Arlo worked for R. C. Williams, where he was manager, retiring in 1985. He belonged to the First Christian Church, Liberal. **CHARIS AMBROSIER** (1949 – 1949) Fifth great granddaughter of progenitor Nicholas Kegg.
DALICE LUCILLE AMBROSIER [2623B] (1921 – 2000) daughter of James and Nellie (Knouf) Ambrosier married twice, first to Oscar Marty with whom she was mother of (2). After his death she married John Schmitt. She was a member of the VFW Auxiliary and the Eagles Lodge. Dalice was a homemaker most of her life. She worked as a waitress at the Fort Sidney Motor Lodge in Sidney and at Nettie's Cafe in Gurley. Her hobbies included crocheting, garage sales, bird watching, gardening and spending time with her family. **EUGENE CLAYTON AMBROSIER** [2624] (1938 – 2010) son of James and Dorothea (Hopkins) Ambrosier married Betty Louise Bass. **FAYLENE AMBROSIER** Fifth great granddaughter of progenitor Nicholas Kegg. **GEORGE HENRY AMBROSIER** [2625, 2626] (1909 – 1964) son of James and Nellie (Knouf) Ambrosier, married Helen M. Narum with whom he was father of (4). **GLODIE OLIVE AMBROSIER** [2626A] (1907 – 1998) daughter of James and Nellie (Knouf) Ambrosier was twice married, first to Elmer Jackson with whom she was mother of (2). After his death she married John Hull. Glodie was a waitress for many years and a member of the American Legion Auxiliary, VFW Auxiliary and Eagles Auxiliary. **JAMES CLAYTON AMBROSIER, JR** [2626B] aka "Jim" (1911 – 1999) son of James and Nellie (Knouf) Ambrosier was twice married, first to Dorothea Hopkins with whom he was father of (3). Jim was a former member of the Hill City city council. He was a truck driver and had worked for the railroad. **JOSEPH WARREN AMBROSIER** Fifth great grandson of progenitor Nicholas Kegg. **KAYLENE AMBROSIER** Fifth great granddaughter of progenitor Nicholas Kegg. **LANA AMBROSIER** Sixth great granddaughter of progenitor Nicholas Kegg. **MARTHA MAE AMBROSIER** [2626C] (1903 – 1996) daughter of James and Nellie (Knouf) Ambrosier, married Joseph Colson with whom she was mother of (3) Martha was a homemaker. At one time she sold Avon products. She worked as a telephone operator on McCleary's first phone systems, worked summers at a tree nursery for Weyerhaeuser at Mima Mounds and worked in a cannery in Olympia. She was active in McCleary Alliance Church and always took food to the sick and elderly. Martha liked working in her garden and used to sew a lot. She enjoyed traveling and visiting relatives. She collected rocks during her travels and marked where each was from.
MICHAEL TIMOTHY AMBROSIER Fifth great grandson of progenitor Nicholas Kegg.
LONNIE L. AMBROSIER Sixth great grandson of progenitor Nicholas Kegg.
PAUL WARREN AMBROSIER Sixth great grandson of progenitor Nicholas Kegg.
RHONDA AMBROSIER Sixth great granddaughter of progenitor Nicholas Kegg.
ROBERT LEE AMBROSIER [2627] (1925 – 1997) son of James and Nellie (Knouf) Ambrosier married

---

[2623A] Hutchinson News (KS) Nov 3, 2007 [2623B] Southwest Daily Times (KS) Feb 20, 2000 [2624] p 4 - Benton County Daily Record (AR) Mar 4, 2010 [2625] p 27 - Minneapolis Morning Tribune Aug 24, 1964 [2626] Minneapolis Star Tribune Jan 25, 1984 [2626A] p A2 - Hays Daily News (KS) Feb 22, 1998 [2626B] p A8 -Hays Daily News (KS) June 11, 1999 [2626C] p C2 - Olympian (WA) April 20 1996 [2627] Hutchinson News (KS) May 7, 1997

and was father of (1). He later married Jean Patrick Hines and Clara Fuller. Robert served in the military for more than 25 years and worked for Stran Steel. He attended Gallaway Park Church of God, La Grange. He was a U.S. Army veteran of World War II, Korean War and Vietnam, serving in the European and African theater campaigns. He won four Bronze Stars, WWII Victory medal, Purple Heart, Good Conduct with four oak leaf clusters, Korean Campaign medal, Vietnam Service medal and Campaign medal. Robert retired as a master sergeant in 1970 and remained in the Georgia National Guard.
ROLLAND JAMES AMBROSIER [2628] (1942 – 2011) son of James and Dorothea (Hopkins) Ambrosier was father of (4). Rolland was a truck driver for many years with Clear Creek Trucking.
ROLLAND JAMES AMBROSIER, Jr. Sixth great grandson of progenitor Nicholas Kegg.
SCOTT JOSEPH AMBROSIER Sixth great grandson of progenitor Nicholas Kegg.
SHARON LEE AMBROSIER (1953 – 2004) daughter of Robert Lee Ambrosier married twice. First to Bobby Leaton Shocklee with whom she was mother of (1). Later, she married Charles Edward Abercrombie. **TIMOTHY MICHAEL AMBROSIER** Sixth great grandson of progenitor Nicholas Kegg.

AMICK

BEVERLY AMICK Fifth great granddaughter of progenitor Nicholas Kegg. **COREY ELLIS AMICK** Seventh great grandson of progenitor Nicholas Kegg. **DAVID BRIAN AMICK** Sixth great grandson of progenitor Nicholas Kegg. **JAN AMICK** [2629] (1947 – 2005) daughter of Arthur and Geraldine (Heeter) Amick, married Lynn Carter II. Jan was the owner/operator of Showcase Designs, specializing in interior design and oriental jewelry. She was well-known for her design and taste. She was a member of the Greenmeadows Book Club. For several years, she sponsored a child through the Christian Children's Fund. **MATTHEW LLOYD AMICK** Seventh great grandson of progenitor Nicholas Kegg.
TED EMORY AMICK Fourth great grandson of progenitor Nicholas Kegg. **TOM AMICK** Fourth great grandson of progenitor Nicholas Kegg.

AMMONS

KELLY AMMONS Sixth great granddaughter of progenitor Nicholas Kegg.

AMOS

CHEVANN DANAE AMOS Cheyann Danae Eighth great granddaughter of progenitor Nicholas Kegg.
SANIYAH RENAE PATTON AMOS Eighth great granddaughter of progenitor Nicholas Kegg.

AMSPACHER

ASHLEE AMSPACHER Sixth great granddaughter of progenitor Nicholas Kegg.
DUSTIN AMSPACHER Sixth great grandson of progenitor Nicholas Kegg.

ANDERS

ALEC ANDERS Eighth great grandson of progenitor Nicholas Kegg. **ARLAND LAVON ANDERS** [2630] (1931 – 1993) aka "Andy", son of Robert and Lucille (Rice) Anders married twice, first to Beverly Jean Stellhorn with whom he was father of (9). He later married Bonita Schuller. Andy served in the Air Force from 1951-52. A pattern maker at General Motors Central Foundry Division for 32 years, he was a former member of the Pattern Maker League of Fort Wayne and was a member of the St. Mark Lutheran Church, the Elks, and the Grand Lodge of F&AM of Indiana.

[2628] Rindt-Redman Funeral Home (KS) [2629] The Union Leader (NH) Jan 11, 2005, obtained by D. Sue Dible [2630] p5 - Crescent-News (OH) April 26, 1993

CARY BRIAN ANDERS Fifth great grandson of progenitor Nicholas Kegg. **EVAN ARLAND ANDERS** Fifth great grandson of progenitor Nicholas Kegg. **JEFFREY K. ANDERS** Fifth great grandson of progenitor Nicholas Kegg. **JUDITH C. ANDERS** Fourth great granddaughter of progenitor Nicholas Kegg. **LESLEY KAY ANDERS** Fifth great granddaughter of progenitor Nicholas Kegg. **MAHALA LEA ANDERS** Sixth great granddaughter of progenitor Nicholas Kegg. **MARK PRESTON ANDERS** Fifth great grandson of progenitor Nicholas Kegg. **PAMELA GAIL ANDERS** Fifth great granddaughter of progenitor Nicholas Kegg. **STEVEN SCOTT ANDERS** Fifth great grandson of progenitor Nicholas Kegg. **TIMOTHY CRAIG ANDERS** [2631] (1954 – 2004) son of Arland and Beverly (Stellhorn) Anders married twice; first to Denise Marie Hall with whom he was father of (1). Later, he married Tammy with whom he was the father of (2). Tim was an avid outdoorsman and appreciated the pristine beauty of Montana where he enjoyed hunting and fishing.
VICKY S. ANDERS Fifth great granddaughter of progenitor Nicholas Kegg.

ANDERSON

ANDREW ANDERSON Sixth great grandson of progenitor Nicholas Kegg.
ASPEN GLENN ANDERSON Seventh great grandson of progenitor Nicholas Kegg.
CHARLES ALFRED ANDERSON Fifth great grandson of progenitor Nicholas Kegg.
CHERI ANDERSON Sixth great granddaughter of progenitor Nicholas Kegg. **CHRIS ANDERSON** Sixth great grandson of progenitor Nicholas Kegg. **CHRISTINE ANDERSON** Sixth great granddaughter of progenitor Nicholas Kegg. **CRAIG FRANK ANDERSON** Fifth great grandson of progenitor Nicholas Kegg. **CURTIS RUDY ANDERSON** Fifth great grandson of progenitor Nicholas Kegg. **DARRYN ANDERSON** Seventh great grandson of progenitor Nicholas Kegg.
DAVID BROWN ANDERSON Fifth great grandson of progenitor Nicholas Kegg.
ERIC THOMAS ANDERSON Sixth great grandson of progenitor Nicholas Kegg.
GLEN CHARLES ANDERSON [2631A] son of Andrew and Bernice (Rice) Anderson, married Delores Berka with whom he was father of (4). Glen was employed in law enforcement.
GLENN K. ANDERSON III aka "Buddy" Sixth great grandson of progenitor Nicholas Kegg.
JEFFREY MICHAEL ANDERSON Sixth great grandson of progenitor Nicholas Kegg.
JESSICA ANDERSON Sixth great grand- daughter of progenitor Nicholas Kegg.
JOHNNY JAMAAL ANDERSON Eighth great grandson of progenitor Nicholas Kegg.
KAYLEE ANDERSON Eighth great granddaughter of progenitor Nicholas Kegg.
KIMBERLY ANDERSON Sixth great granddaughter of progenitor Nicholas Kegg.
KYLE ANDERSON Sixth great grandson of progenitor Nicholas Kegg.
LARRY MARVIN ANDERSON [2632] (1958 – 1959) son of Glen and Delores (Berka) Anderson.
LARRY WAYNE ANDERSON [2633] (1957 – 1957) son of Glen and Delores (Berka) Anderson.
LINDA MARIE ANDERSON Sixth great granddaughter of progenitor Nicholas Kegg.
MARILYN ANDERSON Fifth great granddaughter of progenitor Nicholas Kegg.
MICHELE ANDERSON Sixth great granddaughter of progenitor Nicholas Kegg.
RHONDA ANDERSON Sixth great granddaughter of progenitor Nicholas Kegg.
SARAH ANDERSON Eighth great granddaughter of progenitor Nicholas Kegg.
TRACY ANDERSON Seventh great granddaughter of progenitor Nicholas Kegg.

ANDREWS

JACOB ANDREWS Seventh great grandson of progenitor Nicholas Kegg. **JUDY LYNN ANDREWS** Sixth great granddaughter of progenitor Nicholas Kegg. **JULIE MARIE ANDREWS** Sixth great granddaughter of progenitor Nicholas Kegg. **LIBBY ANDREWS** Seventh great granddaughter of progenitor Nicholas Kegg.

[2631] Independent Record (MT) June 29, 2004 [2631A] Omaha World-Herald (NE) May 15, 1955 [2632] p12B Omaha World-Herald (NE) Apr 05, 1959 [2633] p32 Omaha World-Herald (NE) Dec 26, 1957

ANSLEY

ADAM ANSLEY Seventh great grandson of progenitor Nicholas Kegg.

ANTHONY

CRAIG LINCOLN ANTHONY Seventh great grandson of progenitor Nicholas Kegg.
KATHLYN FAITH ANTHONY Sixth great granddaughter of progenitor Nicholas Kegg.
KEITH LOUIS ANTHONY Seventh great grandson of progenitor Nicholas Kegg.
KRISTIN LOUISE ANTHONY Seventh great granddaughter of progenitor Nicholas Kegg.
MELISSA JOY ANTHONY Sixth great granddaughter of progenitor Nicholas Kegg.

ARCHER

AUTUMN ARCHER Sixth great granddaughter of progenitor Nicholas Kegg. **SCOTT ARCHER** Sixth great grandson of progenitor Nicholas Kegg. **SHANNON ARCHER** Sixth great granddaughter of progenitor Nicholas Kegg.

ARD

KAIDEN ARD Eighth great grandson of progenitor Nicholas Kegg. **KENNETH WAYNE ARD** Seventh great grandson of progenitor Nicholas Kegg. **KENSON ARD** Eighth great grandson of progenitor Nicholas Kegg. **SARAH ELIZABETH ARD** Seventh great granddaughter of progenitor Nicholas Kegg. **ZOEY ARD** Eighth great granddaughter of progenitor Nicholas Kegg.

ARIAS

ADRIAN LUIS ARIAS Seventh great grandson of progenitor Nicholas Kegg.
AGUSTIN LORENZO ARIAS Seventh great grandson of progenitor Nicholas Kegg.

ARMIGER

BROOKE ARMIGER Seventh great granddaughter of progenitor Nicholas Kegg.
GRACE ANN ARMIGER aka" Gracie", Seventh great granddaughter of progenitor Nicholas Kegg.
JOELLE MARIE ARMIGER Sixth great granddaughter of progenitor Nicholas Kegg.
LOUIS EARL ARMIGER aka "Earl" Fifth great grandson of progenitor Nicholas Kegg.
LOUIS SCOTT ARMIGER Sixth great grandson of progenitor Nicholas Kegg.
MARY LOU ARMIGER Fifth great granddaughter of progenitor Nicholas Kegg.
SEAN ARMIGER Seventh great grandson of progenitor Nicholas Kegg.

ARMSTRONG

ARTHUR LEE ARMSTRONG (1916 – 1971) son of Arthur A. and Mabel Naomi (Baer) Armstrong married Kathryn Goodwin, with whom he was father of (3). **CAROL ANN ARMSTRONG** Sixth great granddaughter of progenitor Nicholas Kegg. **CHANDLER DEAN ARMSTRONG** Seventh great grandson of progenitor Nicholas Kegg. **CINDI LOU ARMSTRONG** Sixth great granddaughter of progenitor Nicholas Kegg. **GEORGE STEMEN ARMSTRONG JR.** Fifth great grandson of progenitor Nicholas Kegg. **JAMES E. ARMSTRONG** Sixth great grandson of progenitor Nicholas Kegg. **JAMES LEE ARMSTRONG** [2633A] (1948 – 2015) aka "Jim", son of John and Mary Louise (Schoettler) Armstrong was an accomplished Marine Top Gun fighter pilot and made a career as a pilot for Delta Airlines. **JEFFREY LEE ARMSTRONG** [2634] (1972 – 2002) son of Laurence and Harriet (Allen) Armstrong, married Jennifer Lynn Frederick with whom he was father of (3). Jeff was an Eagle

Scout, an alumnus of Appalachian State University, and member of Alpha Phi Omega service fraternity.
JENNIFER KATHLEEN ARMSTRONG aka "Jennie" Sixth great granddaughter of progenitor Nicholas Kegg. **JOHN PAUL ARMSTRONG** Fifth great grandson of progenitor Nicholas Kegg.
LAURA ARMSTRONG Seventh great granddaughter of progenitor Nicholas Kegg.
LAUREL ANN ARMSTRONG Sixth great granddaughter of progenitor Nicholas Kegg.
LAUREN KYLEIGH ARMSTRONG Seventh great granddaughter of progenitor Nicholas Kegg.
LINDA LOU ARMSTRONG Fifth great granddaughter of progenitor Nicholas Kegg.
LORALEE JEANNE ARMSTRONG Fifth great granddaughter of progenitor Nicholas Kegg.
MARIE DORA ARMSTRONG Sixth great granddaughter of progenitor Nicholas Kegg.
MARK ALLEN ARMSTRONG Sixth great grandson of progenitor Nicholas Kegg.
MARY ELISABETH ARMSTRONG [2635] (1920 – 2009) aka "Lee" daughter of Frederick and Mollie (Russell) Armstrong, married Fay Vernon Raymond with whom she was mother of (2). Lee traveled by train to Siskiyou County at 7 days of age to be adopted by Fredric and Mollie Armstrong. She grew up on farms in Gazelle, Grenada and Big Springs and developed a lifelong love of Mt. Shasta. After graduating from Yreka High School in 1938, she moved to Sacramento and attended Sacramento Jr. College. She worked for her board and room and while buying groceries at Arata Bros. Grocery in Oak Park met her future husband, Fay Raymond. Just after Pearl Harbor, they began their 55-year marriage. Lee worked for the Dept. of Food and Agriculture for over 25 years and was a 25-year club member. She also joined many organizations as Blue Bird and Camp Fire Girl Leader, Cub Scouts Den Mother, President of CSEA Chapter #145, Noble Grand of Oak Park Rebekahs Lodge, President of Bret Harte PTA, bowling leagues, Toastmasters and REPA member. She enjoyed gardening, reading, crossword, crytoquote and jig-saw puzzles, neighborhood watch and bowling. **RANDALL JAY ARMSTRONG** Sixth great grandson of progenitor Nicholas Kegg. **STEPHEN DEAN ARMSTRONG** Sixth great grandson of progenitor Nicholas Kegg. **THOMAS ARMSTRONG** Fifth great grandson of progenitor Nicholas Kegg.
VICTORIA ASHLEY ARMSTRONG Seventh great granddaughter of progenitor Nicholas Kegg.
WADE D. ARMSTRONG Sixth great grandson of progenitor Nicholas Kegg.

ARNOLD

ANDREW ARNOLD Seventh great grandson of progenitor Nicholas Kegg. **ANGIE ARNOLD** Sixth great granddaughter of progenitor Nicholas Kegg. **ANTHONY DAVID ARNOLD** aka "Tony" Sixth great grandson of progenitor Nicholas Kegg. **BETH MARIE ARNOLD** [2635A] (1966 – 2022) daughter of Derrill and Julia Lee (Hinkle) Arnold married Matthew Terrance Shanahan with whom she was mother of (2). Later, she married Lee Alan Hardesty with whom she was mother of (3). Beth earned her bachelor's degree in Fashion Merchandising from BGSU. Beth led an active life as a school volunteer on both the PTO Board at Donnell and the Ohio Reads Program, was a club soccer team manager and an ALS advocate in Washington D.C. She had been the Operations Manager at the Lions Store, a client relationship manager and I9 Sales Rep at ADP, and a recruiter for TriWorth. Beth enjoyed watching her kids play sports, traveling (especially anywhere that included a beach), reading, playing the piano, listening to her son and mother play the piano, tailgating with the college kids at their universities, taking walks hand in hand with her husband, helping others, being with family on any vacation, going to church or sharing a glass of wine with her girlfriends. **DANIEL ARNOLD** Seventh great grandson of progenitor Nicholas Kegg. **ELIZABETH ARNOLD** Seventh great granddaughter of progenitor Nicholas Kegg. **GREGG LEE ARNOLD** Sixth great grandson of progenitor Nicholas Kegg.
JANET ELAINE ARNOLD Sixth great granddaughter of progenitor Nicholas Kegg.
JENNIFER ARNOLD Seventh great granddaughter of progenitor Nicholas Kegg.
JOHN GREGG ARNOLD Seventh great grandson of progenitor Nicholas Kegg.
LESTER EDWIN ARNOLD JR. [2636] (1939 – 2017) son of Lester and Evelyn (Pennell) Arnold married

---

[2633A] Clairemont Mortuary (San Diego, CA) obtained by D. Sue Dible [2634] News & Observer (Raleigh, NC) Nov 13, 2002 [2635] The Sacramento Bee (CA) Oct 28, 2009 [2635A] Coldren-Crates Funeral Home (OH) Nov 23, 2022 [2636] Buffalo News (NY) Feb. 7, 2017

Ingrid S. Andersen with whom he was father of (5). Lester was an Industrial Engineer and received his bachelor's degree in industrial engineering from Johns Hopkins University and his MBA from the University of Buffalo. **LEZLEY NICOLE ARNOLD** Sixth great granddaughter of progenitor Nicholas Kegg. **PENNY SUZANNE ARNOLD** Sixth great granddaughter of progenitor Nicholas Kegg. **RACHEL HELEN ARNOLD** Seventh great granddaughter of progenitor Nicholas Kegg.
SARAH LEANN ARNOLD Seventh great granddaughter of progenitor Nicholas Kegg.
SETH DAVID ARNOLD Seventh great grandson of progenitor Nicholas Kegg.
STEVEN M. ARNOLD Seventh great grandson of progenitor Nicholas Kegg.
STILLBORN ARNOLD (1891 – 1891) Child of Thomas and Sarah (Kegg) Arnold.
TERESA ARNOLD Sixth great granddaughter of progenitor Nicholas Kegg.

ARNOTT

DAVID W. ARNOTT Fifth great grandson of progenitor Nicholas Kegg.
DIANA ARNOTT Fifth great granddaughter of progenitor Nicholas Kegg.

ARPAN

AMY ARPAN Fifth great granddaughter of progenitor Nicholas Kegg. **CHERIE ARPAN** Fourth great granddaughter of progenitor Nicholas Kegg. **JORDON ARPAN** Fifth great grandson of progenitor Nicholas Kegg. **JUSTIN ARPAN** Fifth great grandson of progenitor Nicholas Kegg. **LAURA ARPAN** Fifth great granddaughter of progenitor Nicholas Kegg. **NATHAN RYAN ARPAN** Fifth great grandson of progenitor Nicholas Kegg. **PIPER ARPAN** Fifth great granddaughter of progenitor Nicholas Kegg. **RANDALL BROOKS ARPAN** Fourth great grandson of progenitor Nicholas Kegg. **THEA ARPAN** Sixth great granddaughter of progenitor Nicholas Kegg. **WILLIAM SETH ARPAN** [2637] (1974 – 1994) Randall and Susan (Eberle) Arpan, married Brooke Willeane Morrison with whom he was father of (2). William worked in the shipping and handling department of the Irwin Corporation in Wilmington. **WILLIAM SETH ARPAN II** Sixth great grandson of progenitor Nicholas Kegg.

ARRANTS

ELEANOR MAE ARRANTS Sixth great granddaughter of progenitor Nicholas Kegg.
FLORENCE ARRANTS (1932 – 1972) daughter of Everett and Helen (Norman) Arrants married George Oscar Carlson. **GRACE ANN ARRANTS** Sixth great granddaughter of progenitor Nicholas Kegg. **MARYLYNNE ARRANTS** Sixth great granddaughter of progenitor Nicholas Kegg.
NOMA WINONA ARRANTS Sixth great granddaughter of progenitor Nicholas Kegg.
PATRICIA ARRANTS Sixth great granddaughter of progenitor Nicholas Kegg.

ARTHUR

JOANNE ARTHUR Sixth great granddaughter of progenitor Nicholas Kegg.
LELAND JAMES ARTHUR Sixth great grandson of progenitor Nicholas Kegg.
RHYS MORGAN ARTHUR Sixth great grandson of progenitor Nicholas Kegg.
RYAN ARTHUR Seventh great grandson of progenitor Nicholas Kegg.
WILLIAM ARTHUR Seventh great grandson of progenitor Nicholas Kegg.

[2637] p 2 - The Record Herald (OH) Feb 25, 1994

ARTINO

JEANNIE RENE ARTINO Seventh great granddaughter of progenitor Nicholas Kegg.
JODY LIN ARTINO Seventh great granddaughter of progenitor Nicholas Kegg.
JOHN LEE ARTINO Seventh great grandson of progenitor Nicholas Kegg.

ARTIS

CHERYL BROCKMAN ARTIS Fifth great granddaughter of progenitor Nicholas Kegg.
JAMES P. ARTIS Fifth great grandson of progenitor Nicholas Kegg.

ASCH

TRAVIS LEE ASCH Seventh great grandson of progenitor Nicholas Kegg.

ASCHERMANN

BRIAN JEFFREY ASCHERMANN Sixth great grandson of progenitor Nicholas Kegg.
DAVID LEE ASCHERMANN Fifth great grandson of progenitor Nicholas Kegg.
ERIK MICHAEL ASCHERMANN Sixth great grandson of progenitor Nicholas Kegg.
GARRETT LEE ASCHERMANN Sixth great grandson of progenitor Nicholas Kegg.
JOHN BUCKLEY ASCHERMANN Sixth great grandson of progenitor Nicholas Kegg.
JOHN S. ASCHERMANN Fifth great grandson of progenitor Nicholas Kegg.   **JOY ASCHERMANN** Sixth great granddaughter of progenitor Nicholas Kegg.   **MATTHEW JOHN ASCHERMANN** Sixth great grandson of progenitor Nicholas Kegg.   **ROBERT LEWIS ASCHERMANN** Sixth great grandson of progenitor Nicholas Kegg.   **SCOTT PAUL ASCHERMANN** Sixth great grandson of progenitor Nicholas Kegg.

ASCHMAN

CARL ASCHMAN III Sixth great grandson of progenitor Nicholas Kegg.
HARALD ASCHMAN Sixth great grandson of progenitor Nicholas Kegg.

ASHBY

GERTRUDE SUSAN ASHBY Sixth great granddaughter of progenitor Nicholas Kegg.

ASKEW

LUKE CESSNA ASKEW Eighth great grandson of progenitor Nicholas Kegg.
SARAH CARLYLE ASKEW Eighth great granddaughter of progenitor Nicholas Kegg.

AST

DEREK C. AST Seventh great grandson of progenitor Nicholas Kegg.
MARCELLA LYNN AST Seventh great granddaughter of progenitor Nicholas Kegg.

ASTON

BRIAN C. ASTON Seventh great grandson of progenitor Nicholas Kegg.

ATCHISON

CHAD DOUGLAS ATCHISON Fourth great grandson of progenitor Nicholas Kegg.

ATHEY

AMANDA ATHEY Seventh great granddaughter of progenitor Nicholas Kegg.
AMINTA ATHEY Seventh great granddaughter of progenitor Nicholas Kegg.
JAMES ATHEY Seventh great grandson of progenitor Nicholas Kegg.
PAGE ATHEY Eighth great granddaughter of progenitor Nicholas Kegg.

AUDLEY

DAVID B. AUDLEY Seventh great grandson of progenitor Nicholas Kegg. **JAMES C. AUDLEY** Seventh great grandson of progenitor Nicholas Kegg. **MICHAEL R. AUDLEY** Seventh great grandson of progenitor Nicholas Kegg. **PETER ALAN AUDLEY** [2638] (1940 – 2003) aka "Pete", son of Robert and Marjorie (Crooke) Audley. Pete served in the United States Navy and spent his entire working career with Trans World Airlines. Pete was a pilot (holding private, commercial and instructors' licenses for both fixed wing aircraft and helicopters), a photographer and a model train enthusiast among his many interests. A longtime member of the First Presbyterian Church of Burlingame, he was a member of its Chancel Choir. **ROBERT RICHARD AUDLEY** Sixth great grandson of progenitor Nicholas Kegg.

AUGUST

TERRY JAMES AUGUST Sixth great grandson of progenitor Nicholas Kegg.

AUMILLER

CHRISTINE AUMILLER Sixth great granddaughter of progenitor Nicholas Kegg.

AUTRY

JACKSON AUTRY Seventh great grandson of progenitor Nicholas Kegg.
SPENCER AUTRY Seventh great grandson of progenitor Nicholas Kegg.

AXLINE

JOSHUA AXLINE aka "Josh" Sixth great grandson of progenitor Nicholas Kegg.
LUCAS ISAIAH AXLINE Seventh great grandson of progenitor Nicholas Kegg.

AXTON

AUBREY MARIE AXTON Eighth great granddaughter of progenitor Nicholas Kegg.
CODY AXTON Eighth great grandson of progenitor Nicholas Kegg. **CORY AXTON** Eighth great grandson of progenitor Nicholas Kegg.

[2638] Alameda Times Star (CA) Mar 31, 2003

AYALA

ANTHONY AYALA aka "Tony" Sixth great grandson of progenitor Nicholas Kegg.
CATHY AYALA Sixth great granddaughter of progenitor Nicholas Kegg. **CHARLES AYALA** aka "Chuck" Sixth great grandson of progenitor Nicholas Kegg. **CHRISTY AYALA** Sixth great granddaughter of progenitor Nicholas Kegg. **DAVID AYALA** Sixth great grandson of progenitor Nicholas Kegg. **GABRIEL DAVID AYALA** Seventh great grandson of progenitor Nicholas Kegg. **GENE AYALA** Sixth great grandson of progenitor Nicholas Kegg. **JACKIE JOE AYALA** Sixth great grandson of progenitor Nicholas Kegg. **JESSE AYALA** [2639] (1955 – 1976) son of Jesse and Marijean (Gordon) Ayala was a US Navy veteran serving in Vietnam. **MARY P. AYALA** Sixth great granddaughter of progenitor Nicholas Kegg. **MIGUEL ANGEL AYALA** Seventh great grandson of progenitor Nicholas Kegg. **PAUL AYALA** Sixth great grandson of progenitor Nicholas Kegg. **TANYA AYALA** Seventh great granddaughter of progenitor Nicholas Kegg.

AYLESWORTH

ALYCIA AYLESWORTH Seventh great granddaughter of progenitor Nicholas Kegg.
SHANNON AYLESWORTH Seventh great granddaughter of progenitor Nicholas Kegg.

AYRES

BILLY LEE AYRES Sixth great grandson of progenitor Nicholas Kegg.

AZEVEDO

NICOLE MORANDA AZEVEDO Sixth great granddaughter of progenitor Nicholas Kegg.
RENEE FRANCES AZEVEDO Sixth great granddaughter of progenitor Nicholas Kegg.

AZPARREN

DOLORES JEANETTE AZPARREN [2640] (1932 – 2012) aka "Jeanette," daughter of Martin and Ruth (Schrengohst) Azparren married Michael Matthew Matovina with whom she was mother of (3). Jeanette's favorite memories were camping trips with family and friends, the many bowling leagues and various clubs in Reno and Yerington to which she belonged. **MARTIN AZPARREN** Fifth great grandson of progenitor Nicholas Kegg. **MITCHELL AZPARREN** Fifth great grandson of progenitor Nicholas Kegg.

BABCOCK

JOSHUA BABCOCK aka "Josh" Sixth great grandson of progenitor Nicholas Kegg.
ZACHARY ANDREW BABCOCK Seventh great grandson of progenitor Nicholas Kegg.

BACHMANN

ELIZABETH M. BACHMANN Fifth great granddaughter of progenitor Nicholas Kegg.
KATHE BACHMANN Fifth great granddaughter of progenitor Nicholas Kegg.

[2639] Greeley Daily Tribune (CO) May 9, 1977 [2640] Reno Gazette-Journal (NV) Dec 21, 2012

BACIGALUPI

MARTIN WAYNE BACIGALUPI Seventh great grandson of progenitor Nicholas Kegg.
MARVIN JAY BACIGALUPI Seventh great grandson of progenitor Nicholas Kegg.
MARY KATHLEEN BACIGALUPI Eighth great granddaughter of progenitor Nicholas Kegg.
MEGAN COLLEEN BACIGALUPI Eighth great granddaughter of progenitor Nicholas Kegg.

BACORN

AYRABELLA GRACE BACORN Seventh great granddaughter of progenitor Nicholas Kegg.

BADEN

JACOB BADEN Seventh great grandson of progenitor Nicholas Kegg.
LACIE BADEN Seventh great granddaughter of progenitor Nicholas Kegg.

BAEHLER

CASSANDRA LYNAE BAEHLER Sixth great granddaughter of progenitor Nicholas Kegg.
CHAD N. BAEHLER Sixth great grandson of progenitor Nicholas Kegg.
CONNIE EASTER BAEHLER Fifth great granddaughter of progenitor Nicholas Kegg.
DIANA JEAN BAEHLER Fifth great granddaughter of progenitor Nicholas Kegg.
DONNA LEE BAEHLER (1948 – 1992) daughter of James and Katie (Graham) Baehler married Joseph W. Wilson with whom she was mother of (1). **JAIME M. BAEHLER** Sixth great granddaughter of progenitor Nicholas Kegg. **JAMES CHRIS BAEHLER** Fifth great granddaughter of progenitor Nicholas Kegg. **JOLENE ELIZABETH BAEHLER** Sixth great granddaughter of progenitor Nicholas Kegg.

BAER

ALVIN WEBSTER BAER [2640A] aka "Bud" (1889 – 1955) son of Alvin and Emma (Parent) Baer, married Alfield Alice Anderson with whom he was father of (2). Bud was associated with Douglas Aircrafts, El Segundo, Calif., he was chief inspector for the Navy Bureau of Aeronautics Representatives there. **ALVIN WEBSTER BAER JR.** Fourth great grandson of progenitor Nicholas Kegg.
ARTHUR LAWRENCE BAER (1892 – 1953) son of Alvin and Emma (Parent) Baer worked as a watchman after having served in the Navy during WWI. **CYNTHIA ANN BAER** Fifth great granddaughter of progenitor, Nicholas Kegg. **DOUGLAS ALAN BAER** (1947 – 2014) son of Alvin and Elizabeth (Wyman) Baer, married Lynne Powell with whom he was father of (3).
ERIC JONATHAN BAER (1947 – 1996) son of John and Aeleen Aroon (Davis) Baer married Meryl Beth Lande. **GEORGINA BAER** Fifth great granddaughter of progenitor Nicholas Kegg.
JOHN ALLEN BAER Fifth great grandson of progenitor Nicholas Kegg. **JOHN ARTHUR BAER** [2641] (1919 – 1999) son of Alvin and Alfield (Anderson) Baer married Aeleen Aron Davis with whom he was father of (2). John worked for NASA's quality control department. He previously worked as a chief weapons inspector for 20 years, including at Lockheed Aircraft in Burbank, McDonnell-Douglas in ElSegundo and General Dynamic Convair in San Diego. He enjoyed prospecting for gold, uranium, tungsten and rare-earth metals. He also enjoyed collecting stamps and coins. **JULIE A. BAER** Sixth great granddaughter of progenitor Nicholas Kegg. **MABEL NAOMI BAER** [2642] (1887 – 1930) daughter of Alvin and Emma (Parent) Baer married three times, first to Thomas Prugh McCrea, then to

---

[2640A] p2 - Fort Wayne Journal Gazette (IN) Sep 10, 1955 [2641] Press-Enterprise (CA) Oct 4, 1999 [2642] p 4 - Fort Wayne News Sentinel (IN) May 14, 1930, obtained by D. Sue Dible

William Otto Danke with whom she was mother of (1). Later she married Arthur A. Armstrong with whom she was mother of (4). **MATTHEW D. BAER** Sixth great grandson of progenitor Nicholas Kegg. **PAUL FRANK BAER** [2642A] (1894 – 1930) son of Alvin and Emma (Parent) Baer. Paul was an excellent pilot, having obtained his training in a French flying school during the World War as a member of the famous Lafayette Escadrille. During the war his plane was forced to descend behind German lines and was taken prisoner at Gradenz, West Prussia. After the war, Paul had been actively engaged in commercial flying with more than 3,500 flying hours to his credit. Paul had been working for the China National Aviation Corporation, owner of the plane, only two months when he was killed when the amphibian plane which he was flying struck the mast of a Chinese junk on the Yangtze River as he was taking off. **ROBIN JEAN BAER** (1957 – 1957) daughter of Alvin W. and Betty (Wyman) Baer Jr. **SANDRA CHRISTINE BAER** Sixth great granddaughter of progenitor Nicholas Kegg. **SHERRY LYNNE BAER** Sixth great granddaughter of progenitor Nicholas Kegg. **VICKI E. BAER** Sixth great granddaughter of progenitor Nicholas Kegg.

BAERLIN

DAVID LEWIS BAERLIN Sixth great grandson of progenitor Nicholas Kegg. **LAURALEE ANN BAERLIN** Sixth great granddaughter of progenitor Nicholas Kegg. **MICHAEL LAVON BAERLIN** aka "Mikey", Sixth great grandson of progenitor Nicholas Kegg. **SETH CHANDLER BAERLIN** Seventh great grandson of progenitor Nicholas Kegg.

BAGLEY

BRANDI BAGLEY Sixth great granddaughter of progenitor Nicholas Kegg. **BRENT BAGLEY** Sixth great grandson of progenitor Nicholas Kegg. **BRIAN BAGLEY** Sixth great grandson of progenitor Nicholas Kegg. **GERALD LEE BAGLEY** [2643] (1938 – 2001) aka "Jerry", son of Glen and Elizabeth (Bowers) Bagley married Alacia J. Tulley with whom he was father of (3). Jerry was a veteran of the U.S. Army. Retired Water Superintendent for the City of Gahanna. Worked as Head of Construction Inspections for E. M. H. & T. Member of Jersey Baptist Church and Choir. **JACK L. BAGLEY** (1933 – 1968) son of Glen and Elizabeth (Bowers) Bagley. **MARGARET A. BAGLEY** [2644] aka "Peggy" daughter of Linton and Mary Ellen (Brilhart) Bagley married Thomas D. Fancher with whom she was mother of (1). Although the runways of Europe were calling her name, this self-driven former fashion model managed to graduate with honors from Johnson County Community College and go on to become an Executive with United Telecom (now Sprint). With a natural eye for fashion, Margaret also worked as a personal stylist for many in the Kansas City area. Margaret was quite the adventurer. She absolutely loved to travel and share stories of her times spent abroad in France, Italy, and England. She loved fast cars and looked beautiful in them. Golfing, waterskiing, and bowling were a few of her favorite things to do. Also, she was an avid fan of the Kansas City Chiefs and the Kansas City Royals. She was over the moon when her "boys in blue" won the World Series. **SUSAN BAGLEY** Fifth great granddaughter of progenitor Nicholas Kegg.

BAILEY

KAREN L. BAILEY Sixth great granddaughter of progenitor Nicholas Kegg.

BAIR

BRANDON GLENN BAIR Seventh great grandson of progenitor Nicholas Kegg. **DAVID BAIR** Sixth great grandson of progenitor Nicholas Kegg. **DEBORAH E. BAIR** aka "Debby" Sixth great granddaughter of progenitor Nicholas Kegg. **JENNELL NICOLE BAIR** aka "Jen" Seventh great granddaughter of progenitor Nicholas Kegg. **STEVEN G. BAIR** Sixth great grandson of progenitor Nicholas Kegg.

BAIRD

BARBARA JOY BAIRD Sixth great granddaughter of progenitor Nicholas Kegg.
BEVERLY JEAN BAIRD Sixth great granddaughter of progenitor Nicholas Kegg.
CARY L. BAIRD Sixth great grandson of progenitor Nicholas Kegg. **GREGORY A. BAIRD** Sixth great grandson of progenitor Nicholas Kegg. **KEVIN R. BAIRD** Sixth great grandson of progenitor Nicholas Kegg. **LAURA PATRICIA BAIRD** (1922 – 1995) daughter of Lyman and Eunice (Kegg) Baird married Joseph Connolly Jr. with whom she was mother of (1). **RODNEY WAYNE BAIRD** Sixth great grandson of progenitor Nicholas Kegg. **SHARON BAIRD** Seventh great granddaughter of progenitor Nicholas Kegg.

BAKER

ALVIN ROY BAKER (1902 – 1958) son of John and Susan (Smith) Baker married Effie Edna Troutman with whom he was father of (1). Alvin was employed as a truck driver for City Transfer.
ANITA ROLINE BAKER Fifth great granddaughter of progenitor Nicholas Kegg. **ANNA M. BAKER** Sixth great granddaughter of progenitor Nicholas Kegg. **ARLENE RUTH BAKER** [2644A] (1924 – 2008) daughter of Alvin and Effie (Troutman) Baker married James Howard Leslie Arlene was in the United States Navy Waves. In 1944, after leaving the Navy, she attended college at Louisiana State, receiving her teaching degree. She taught in Saudi Arabia for two years. Upon coming back to the United States, she taught in Big Bear, Calif. At the age of 53 she retired and moved to Orofino. She touched so many lives. **ARRYN QUINN BAKER** Eighth great grandson of progenitor Nicholas Kegg.
CAROL BAKER Fifth great granddaughter of progenitor Nicholas Kegg. **CHARLES P. BAKER** Fifth great grandson of progenitor Nicholas Kegg. **CHEVON BAKER** Seventh great granddaughter of progenitor Nicholas Kegg. **CLETTUS DWAINE BAKER** (1911 – 1966) son of John and Susan (Smith) Baker, married Clela Belle Hartman. Later, he married Evelyn Parsons with whom he was father of (1). He then married Margaret Ellen Bashore with whom he was the father of (3).
CRISTAIN BAKER aka "Cris," Seventh great grandson of progenitor Nicholas Kegg.
DOUGLAS BAKER Sixth great grandson of progenitor Nicholas Kegg. **ETHYN QUADE BAKER** Eighth great grandson of progenitor Nicholas Kegg. **GEORGE DUANE BAKER** [2645] (1940 – 1994) son of Clettus and Margaret (Bashore) Baker. **JEAN BAKER** Fifth great granddaughter of progenitor Nicholas Kegg. **JEREMIAH BAKER** Seventh great grandson of progenitor Nicholas Kegg.
JHAYDANN BAKER Eighth great granddaughter of progenitor Nicholas Kegg. **JOHN EDWARD BAKER** [2646] (1937 – 2021) aka 'Ed," son of Clettus and Evelyn (Parsons) Baker, married Joyanne Gundram with whom he was father of (3). Enlisting in the Marine Corps, Ed was stationed in Hawaii and after marriage moved to Sitka where he was very active in the community. Ed volunteered for the Douglas Fire Department, eventually becoming the Chief during the 70's. He was also a member of the Elks Club and an avid bowler. Ed worked as a meatcutter for Foodland in Juneau. **JOHN EDWARD BAKER JR.** Sixth great grandson of progenitor Nicholas Kegg. **JOHN M. BAKER** Fifth great grandson of progenitor Nicholas Kegg. **KAITLYN LOUISE BAKER** Sixth great granddaughter of progenitor Nicholas Kegg. **KELCEE BAKER** Eighth great granddaughter of progenitor Nicholas Kegg. **KOLTON BAKER** Eighth great grandson of progenitor Nicholas Kegg. **KRYSTA BAKER** Eighth great granddaughter of progenitor Nicholas Kegg. **LEIGHANNA GRACE BAKER** Ninth great granddaughter of progenitor Nicholas Kegg. **MARK JAMES BAKER** (1971 – 1972) son of Alfred and Candace (Tindle) Baker. **NICOLE ANDREA BAKER** Seventh great granddaughter of progenitor Nicholas Kegg. **O.T. BAKER** [2647] (1908 – 1985) son of John and Susan (Smith) Baker married twice, first to Mary Delphine Shafer with whom he was father of (1). Later, he married Alice E.

[2642A] San Antonio Express (TX) Dec 10, 1930 [2643] Ohio Obituary and Death Notice Archive - Page 997 [2644] Kansas City Star (MO) Feb 2, 2016 [2644A] Lewiston Tribune (ID) Jan 17, 2008 [2645] Sturgis Daily Journal Transcribed by Maudie Carole Sturgis Public Library [2646] Juneau Empire (AK) Apr. 1, 2021 [2647] The South Bend Tribune (IN) Apr 3, 1985

(Bowman) Mecklenburg. O.T. retired in 1969 from Citizens Lumber Co., and he was a farmer. He was a member of St. James Episcopal Chapel, Howe   **PAMELA A. BAKER** Seventh great granddaughter of progenitor Nicholas Kegg.   **SHANA ANNE BAKER** Sixth great granddaughter of progenitor Nicholas Kegg.   **SHARON L. BAKER** Fifth great granddaughter of progenitor Nicholas Kegg.   **THELMA I. BAKER** aka "Nina" (1909 – 1920) daughter of John and Susan (Smith) Baker.   **THOMAS C. BAKER** Sixth great grandson of progenitor Nicholas Kegg.   **TONYA BAKER** Sixth great granddaughter of progenitor Nicholas Kegg.   **TRINA SUE BAKER** Sixth great granddaughter of progenitor Nicholas Kegg.   **WAYLAND J. BAKER** Seventh great grandson of progenitor Nicholas Kegg.

BAKERINK

DELL ARTHUR BAKERINK [2647A] aka "Butch" (1947 – 2013) son of Gail and Ruby (Means) Bakerink, was twice married, first to Cindy Robinson, then to Kathlene Maly with whom he was father of a daughter. Butch served as a medical corpsman in the U.S. Army during the Vietnam era, was employed by the Santa Fe Railroad and as truck driver for Smart and Final Foods. He was known as a devoted father and a lover of animals.   **GAIL ARCHIE BAKERINK** aka "Archie" 5th great grandson of progenitor Nicholas Kegg.   **JAY ALAN BAKERINK** Sixth great grandson of progenitor Nicholas Kegg.   **JEFFREY SCOTT BAKERINK** [2647B] (1957 – 2013) son of Rex and Sandra (Diddens) Bakerink married Monique Lujan with whom he was father of (2). Jeff was recognized and honored as being one of the hardest working and successful trial attorneys in Southern California when he was selected as the top Civil Defense Trial Attorney of the Year in 1994. At that time Jeff was the youngest attorney ever to be selected to receive this very prestigious award. Jeff is a member of the prestigious American Board of Trial Advocates, the State Bar of California, the Association of Southern California Defense Counsel, the American Bar Association, the Los Angeles County Bar Association, the Orange County Bar Association and the San Diego County Bar Association. Jeff also had an entrepreneurial spirit, which was inspired by his father Rex. He was well rounded and had many different business ventures. He was an attorney, counselor, mentor, and consultant. His goal was to always build people up and add value to their lives. He merged his law experience, business knowledge and his love for people and relationships and used it to consult for many different types of businesses. Although very accomplished, he was a humble man.   **JULIA BROOKE BAKERINK** Seventh great granddaughter of progenitor Nicholas Kegg.   **KATIE BAKERINK** Seventh great granddaughter of progenitor Nicholas Kegg.**KIMBERLY ELIZABETH BAKERINK** Sixth great granddaughter of progenitor Nicholas Kegg.   **MICHELLE KRISTEN BAKERINK** Seventh great granddaughter of progenitor Nicholas Kegg.   **NICHOLAS BAKERINK** Seventh great grandson of progenitor Nicholas Kegg.

BALDOSSER

AVERY DREW BALDOSSER Seventh great granddaughter of progenitor Nicholas Kegg.   **DARYL GLEN BALDOSSER** (1947- 2017) [2648] son of Willis and Aura (Hersheiser) Baldosser married Marilyn June Weiker with whom he was father of (4). **DARYL GLEN BALDOSSER JR.** Sixth great grandson of progenitor Nicholas Kegg.   **EMME GLEN BALDOSSER** Seventh great granddaughter of progenitor Nicholas Kegg.   **LINDA ARLENE BALDOSSER** Fifth great granddaughter of progenitor Nicholas Kegg.   **MARTHA ELLEN BALDOSSER** Fifth great granddaughter of progenitor Nicholas Kegg.   **MARY ELIZABETH BALDOSSER** Sixth great granddaughter of progenitor Nicholas Kegg.
MELODY ANN BALDOSSER Sixth great granddaughter of progenitor Nicholas Kegg.
RUTH ELLEN BALDOSSER Sixth great granddaughter of progenitor Nicholas Kegg.
THOMAS EUGENE BALDOSSER [2649] aka "Tom" (1945 – 2019) son of Willis and Aura (Hersheiser) Baldosser married Carlene Bland. Tom had a passion for trucks, nature, especially star gazing in the early

[2647A] Tracy Press (CA) May 2, 2013 [2647B] Murrieta Valley Funeral Home (CA) [2648] The Advertiser-Tribune (OH) Oct 28, 2017 [2649] Advertiser-Tribune (OH) May 11, 2019

morning and traveling the open roads. He was remembered for his story telling, humor and caring personality.

BALDWIN

KATIE SUE BALDWIN Sixth great granddaughter of progenitor Nicholas Kegg.
KIMBERLY A. BALDWIN Sixth great granddaughter of progenitor Nicholas Kegg.

BALES

CAROLINE DIANA BALES Eighth great granddaughter of progenitor Nicholas Kegg.

BALINT

PAUL J. BALINT IV Seventh great grandson of progenitor Nicholas Kegg.

BALLANTINE

AMBER G. BALLANTINE Eighth great granddaughter of progenitor Nicholas Kegg. **CHRISTOPHER G. BALLANTINE** Eighth great grandson of progenitor Nicholas Kegg. **DANIEL A. BALLANTINE** Seventh great grandson of progenitor Nicholas Kegg. **DAVID G. BALLANTINE** Seventh great grandson of progenitor Nicholas Kegg. **DYLAN BALLANTINE** Eighth great grandson of progenitor Nicholas Kegg. **GEORGE M. BALLANTINE** Seventh great grandson of progenitor Nicholas Kegg. **GEORGE MILFORD BALLANTINE** Sixth great grandson of progenitor Nicholas Kegg. **JULIE ANNE BALLANTINE** aka "Jewell" Seventh great granddaughter of progenitor Nicholas Kegg. **KERI ANN BALLANTINE** Eighth great granddaughter of progenitor Nicholas Kegg.
MEGAN J. BALLANTINE Eighth great granddaughter of progenitor Nicholas Kegg.
MORGAN BALLANTINE Eighth great granddaughter of progenitor Nicholas Kegg.
ROBERT A. BALLANTINE JR. Seventh great grandson of progenitor Nicholas Kegg.
ROBERT A. BALLANTINE III. Eighth great grandson of progenitor Nicholas Kegg.
THOMAS W. BALLANTINE Sixth great grandson of progenitor Nicholas Kegg.
TORI N. BALLANTINE Eighth great granddaughter of progenitor Nicholas Kegg.
WAYNE EDWARD BALLANTINE Seventh great grandson of progenitor Nicholas Kegg.
WILLIAM ALEXANDER BALLANTINE JR. aka "Punky" Sixth great grandson of progenitor Nicholas Kegg.

BANGSTON

MATTHEW BANGSTON Seventh great grandson of progenitor Nicholas Kegg.
THOMAS BANGSTON Seventh great grandson of progenitor Nicholas Kegg.

BANISTER

JERED ARLO BANISTER Seventh great grandson of progenitor Nicholas Kegg.
JOSHUA BANISTER aka" Josh", Seventh great grandson of progenitor Nicholas Kegg.

BANKS

MICHAEL BANKS Sixth great grandson of progenitor Nicholas Kegg.

BANKSTON

CRYSTAL BANKSTON Eighth great granddaughter of progenitor Nicholas Kegg.
DEANNA BANKSTON Seventh great granddaughter of progenitor Nicholas Kegg.

BANSEN

TIMOTHY JACOB BANSEN aka "Jake" Seventh great grandson of progenitor Nicholas Kegg.

BARATTA

LISA BARATTA Sixth great granddaughter of progenitor Nicholas Kegg.
TINA BARATTA Sixth great granddaughter of progenitor Nicholas Kegg.

BARKELL

FLORENCE ELOISE BARKELL [2650] (1903 - 1977) daughter of George and Cora (Myers) Barkell married James Love Hamilton with whom she was mother of (3). Eloise was a former past Matron of Eastern Star in Penn **WAYNE ROBSON BARKELL** (1910 – 1957) son of George and Cora (Myers) Barkell married Katherine Maxine Barnes with whom he was father of (2). Wayne was a veteran having served as SGT. 8th Army Infantry 4th Division decorated with Bronze Star Medal with Oak Leaf Cluster.

BARKER

KELSEY LANE BARKER Eighth great granddaughter of progenitor Nicholas Kegg. **LEAH BARKER** Eighth great granddaughter of progenitor Nicholas Kegg. **LINDSEY ERICKA BARKER** Eighth great granddaughter of progenitor Nicholas Kegg.

BARKLEY

CATHERINE JEANNE BARKLEY Seventh great granddaughter of progenitor Nicholas Kegg.
DAYE DAWN BARKLEY Fourth great granddaughter of progenitor Nicholas Kegg. **GREGORY LEE BARKLEY** Fourth great grandson of progenitor Nicholas Kegg.

BARKMAN

ANDREW C. BARKMAN Seventh great grandson of progenitor Nicholas Kegg. **SHAUN L. BARKMAN** Sixth great grandson of progenitor Nicholas Kegg. **TAMMY BARKMAN** Seventh great granddaughter of progenitor Nicholas Kegg.

BARLOW

DANIEL JAMES PATRICK BARLOW Sixth great grandson of progenitor Nicholas Kegg.
SHAWN CHRISTOPHER BARLOW Sixth great grandson of progenitor Nicholas Kegg.

BARNES

AIDAN BARNES Eighth great grandson of progenitor Nicholas Kegg. **ANDREA DEE BARNES** Sixth great granddaughter of progenitor Nicholas Kegg. **ALEXANDER A. BARNES** Sixth great grandson of progenitor Nicholas Kegg. **BARBARA JEAN BARNES** [2651] (1935 – 2020) daughter of

---

[2650] Fort Lauderdale News (FL) Jan 3, 1977 [2651] Arbaugh Pearce Greenisen Funeral Home (OH)

Albert and Lena Margaret (Kegg) Barnes married Glenn Atlee Bates with whom she was mother of (7). Barbara spent a lifetime enjoying her family. She enjoyed traveling many miles to attend sporting and musical events. Barbara loved the glow of a fire and the many camping trips with family and friends. Barbara enjoyed reading, her puzzle books, watching birds, and was a collector of many things. **BELVA LOUISE BARNES** Fifth great granddaughter of progenitor Nicholas Kegg. **BETTY MAE BARNES** Fourth great granddaughter of progenitor Nicholas Kegg. **BONNIE S. BARNES** Fifth great granddaughter of progenitor Nicholas Kegg. **BRAD M. BARNES** Sixth great grandson of progenitor Nicholas Kegg. **BRANTLEY BARNES** Eighth great grandson of progenitor Nicholas Kegg. **CAYLA ALEXIS BARNES** [2652] (2008 -2010) daughter of Sean and Jessica (Moffitt) Barnes. **CHARLENE BARNES** Fourth great granddaughter of progenitor Nicholas Kegg. **CONSTANCE JAYNE BARNES** Sixth great granddaughter of progenitor Nicholas Kegg. **CHRISTINA BARNES** Sixth great granddaughter of progenitor Nicholas Kegg. **DANE SEAN BARNES** Eighth great grandson of progenitor Nicholas Kegg. **DAVID BARNES** Sixth great grandson of progenitor Nicholas Kegg. **DAWN NADINE BARNES** Sixth great granddaughter of progenitor Nicholas Kegg. **EDWARD LARRY BARNES JR.** [2653] (1959 – 2014) aka "Ted" son of Edward and Lorna (Hamilton) Barnes married Cheryl A. Parke with whom he was father of (1). Later, he was the father of (2). Ted was a Christian Disc-Jockey for WKCL (We Know Christ Lives) Radio, in Ladson/Charleston, South Carolina; He also owned and operated a taxi-van service in the Greater Charleston area. Ted was awarded the prestigious and coveted Microsoft "Most Valuable Professional" Award for 3 consecutive years for his involvement in 7 forums and for authoring 31 tutorials. Later, he returned to his native Ohio and worked as a truck driver for AWL Transport in Mantua, OH hauling steel. **EDWARD LARRY BARNES** [2654] (1940 – 1993) aka "Jake" son of Albert and Lena (Kegg) Barnes married Lorna Hamilton with whom he was father of (2). Jake was a chief naval officer in the U.S. Navy for 25 years. He was a graduate of Western Reserve High School and a member of the Square Wheels Square Dance Club. **JAMES BARNES** Fifth great grandson of progenitor Nicholas Kegg. **GRANVILLE S. BARNES** [2654A] aka "Barney" (1931 – 2007) son of Sherman and Anna (Diehl) Barnes, married Mildred Shoemaker with whom he was father of (1). Barney was a wounded Korean War veteran. His hobbies were fishing and coin collecting. He enjoyed football, NASCAR and blue grass. He retired from Hedstrom Corp. **JAMES ALBERT BARNES** [2655] (1931 – 1986) son of Albert and Lena (Kegg) Barnes married Carol J. Stitle with whom he was father of (2). James retired from the Stitle and Barnes Construction Co. in Salem. He was a member of the Demascus Methodist Church, and a past counselor of the United Commercial Travelers of America Council 590. He was also a member of the Hope Cemetery Board and the Goshen Ruritan Club. He was a veteran of the Korean conflict and during the 1950s and 1960s was an outstanding softball player in the Salem Industrial League. **JESSABELLE ANN BARNES** [2655A] aka "Jessica" (1983 – 2015) daughter of Keith and Thelma (Scott) Barnes. Jessica was mother of Kea Marie Barnes, and later married Michael Giarth with whom she was mother of a son. Jessica and her children passed through the Heavenly Gates together after a tragic fire at their home. **JOSEPH JAMES BARNES** Sixth great grandson of progenitor Nicholas Kegg. **KAREN BARNES** Sixth great granddaughter of progenitor Nicholas Kegg. **KEA MARIE BARNES** [2655A] (2005 – 2015) daughter of Jessica Ann Barnes and Jo Hose. **KEITH G. BARNES** Sixth great grandson of progenitor Nicholas Kegg. **KRYSTAL LYNN BARNES** Sixth great granddaughter of progenitor Nicholas Kegg. **KYL LEE LOGAN BARNES** Seventh great granddaughter of progenitor Nicholas Kegg. **LAWRENCE JAMES BARNES** [2656] (1939 – 2019) son of Sherman and Anna (Diehl) Barnes marries Helen Viola College with whom he was father of (5). Lawrence retired from Gannett Fleming, and after retirement worked at Wal-Mart. He was a member of Red Lion Bible Church. **LEE RANDALL BARNES** [2656A] (1939 – 2019) son of Albert and Lena (Kegg) Barnes, married Joyce Eileen Harmon with whom he was father of (4). He was a self-employed carpenter. He enjoyed being outside hunting, fishing,

---

[2652] Citrus County Chronicle (FL) July 24, 2010 [2653] Gednetz-Ruzek Funeral Home, obtained by D. Sue Dible [2654] p. 2 - Salem News (OH) Aug 17, 1993 obtained by D. Sue Dible [2654A] Timothy Berkebile Funeral Home (PA) [2655] p. 42 - The Vindicator (OH) July 2, 1986 [2655A] Bedford Gazette (PA) Jan 22, 2015 obtained and contributed by Bob Rose [2656] York Daily Record (PA) Aug. 5, 2019 [2656A] Salem News (OH) Apr 15, 2019

and trapping. Lee was very well known for catching and preparing snapping turtles for soup. There were many folks in the area who would deliver him large turtles. Lee was All-State Basketball his sophomore year with Berlin Center. He also enjoyed college football and followed Ohio State. The tractor pulls at Bunker Hill was a favorite place to visit. **LILLY ALEXIS BARNES** Eighth great granddaughter of progenitor Nicholas Kegg. **LINDA C. BARNES** Sixth great granddaughter of progenitor Nicholas Kegg. **LISA RAE BARNES** Fifth great granddaughter of progenitor Nicholas Kegg. **LORI BARNES** Fifth great granddaughter of progenitor Nicholas Kegg. **MICHAEL KENNETH BARNES** Fifth great grandson of progenitor Nicholas Kegg. **MICHAEL RAY BARNES** [2656B] (1989 – 2016) son of Michael and Melissa (Miller) Barnes was a self-employed construction worker. He enjoyed fishing and spending time with family and friends. **MICHELE RAI BARNES** Fifth great granddaughter of progenitor Nicholas Kegg. **MIKAELA JO BARNES** Sixth great granddaughter of progenitor Nicholas Kegg. **NORITA A. BARNES** Fourth great granddaughter of progenitor Nicholas Kegg. **PAMELA SUE BARNES** [2657] (1960 – 1999) daughter of Lawrence and Helen (Colledge) Barnes. Pamela was a resident of the Community Services Group Inc. in York and worked for Shadowfax Corp., also in York. **PATSY LEE BARNES** Fifth great granddaughter of progenitor Nicholas Kegg. **RANDOLPH BRADLEY BARNES** [2658] (1942 – 2020) aka "Duke", son of Sherman and Anna (Diehl) Barnes married Beverly Joann Eshelman with whom he was father of (3). Randolph worked at O'Neil Steel Company in Conshohocken, Pa., then was later employed at a horse ranch. After retiring, he moved back to Everett. He enjoyed planting flowers at the senior home where he lived. In the fall and winter, he loved feeding the birds and squirrels. **RAYMOND ROY BARNES** [2659] (1944 – 2006) son of Albert and Lena (Kegg) Barnes, married Georgia Lynn Flynn with whom he was father of (2). Raymond retired following 38 years of service as a conductor for the Norfolk-Southern Railroad. He was an honorably discharged U.S. Navy veteran. **RODGER EDGAR BARNES** [2660] (1943 – 2020) son of Sherman and Anna (Diehl) Barnes married Gerlinde Reindl with whom he was father of (2). Rodger served in The United States Army for 22 years until his retirement. He was a life-long member of The Fort Bedford V.F.W. Post #7527. **ROXANNA BARNES** Fifth great granddaughter of progenitor Nicholas Kegg. **SCOTT RANDALL BARNES** Fifth great grandson of progenitor Nicholas Kegg. **SEAN BARNES** Seventh great grandson of progenitor Nicholas Kegg. **SUSAN BARNES** Fifth great granddaughter of progenitor Nicholas Kegg. **TAMMY D. BARNES** Sixth great granddaughter of progenitor Nicholas Kegg. **TIMOTHY BARNES** Fifth great grandson of progenitor Nicholas Kegg. **VICKY BARNES** [2661] (1950 – 2011) daughter of Sherman and Anna (Diehl) Barnes, married Lee Phillips with whom she was mother of (2). Vicky worked in nursing homes in the area, until retiring due to a car accident. **WAYNE STANLEY BARNES** Fifth great grandson of progenitor Nicholas Kegg. **WILLIAM BARNES** Fifth great grandson of progenitor Nicholas Kegg. **ZACKREY PAUL BARNES** Seventh great grandson of progenitor Nicholas Kegg.

BARNETT

BRAZEN BARNETT Eighth great grandson of progenitor Nicholas Kegg. **BRUCE RONALD BARNETT** Seventh great grandson of progenitor Nicholas Kegg. **HAEVYN BARNETT** Eighth great grandchild of progenitor Nicholas Kegg. **LONNIE BARNETT** Seventh great grandson of progenitor Nicholas Kegg. **RAYMOND COLDIRON BARNETT JR.** aka "Ray" Sixth great grandson of progenitor Nicholas Kegg. **ROBERT CHARLES BARNETT** Seventh great grandson of progenitor Nicholas Kegg. **TIMORA ROSE BARNETT** Seventh great granddaughter of progenitor Nicholas Kegg. **TIMOTHY RAY BARNETT** Sixth great grandson of progenitor Nicholas Kegg.

[2656B] James Funeral Home (OH) [2657] Bedford County Historical Society, bk 82, p 3 obtained by D. Sue Dible [2658] Bedford Gazette (PA) Dec 21, 2020 obtained by Bob Rose [2659] http://www4.vindy.com/ [2660] Bedford Gazette (PA) Dec. 6, 2020 obtained by Bob Rose [2661] p. 8 - Bedford Inquirer (PA) March 11, 2011, obtained by Bob Rose

BARNEY

JARRYD BARNEY Fifth great grandson of progenitor Nicholas Kegg.

BARNHILL

DUSTIN BARNHILL Seventh great grandson of progenitor Nicholas Kegg.
EMILY BARNHILL Seventh great granddaughter of progenitor Nicholas Kegg.

BARONE

TYLER BARONE Seventh great grandson of progenitor Nicholas Kegg.

BARRAVECCHIO

NICO BARRAVECCHIO Sixth great grandson of progenitor Nicholas Kegg.
VITO BARRAVECCHIO Sixth great grandson of progenitor Nicholas Kegg.

BARRON

FRANCIS DIANE BARRON Sixth great granddaughter of progenitor Nicholas Kegg.
JILL DENISE BARRON Sixth great granddaughter of progenitor Nicholas Kegg.
LINDA L. BARRON Sixth great granddaughter of progenitor Nicholas Kegg.

BARRONER

ARLA J. BARRONER Fifth great granddaughter of progenitor Nicholas Kegg.
DANIEL FRANCIS BARRONER (1965 – 1965) infant son of Francis and Annabelle (Wolf) Barroner.
DAVID HARRY BARRONER Fifth great grandson of progenitor Nicholas Kegg.
JUSTIN D. BARRONER Sixth great grandson of progenitor Nicholas Kegg.

BARRY

DAVID BARRY Sixth great grandson of progenitor Nicholas Kegg. **DAWN BARRY** Sixth great granddaughter of progenitor Nicholas Kegg. **DEBBIE BARRY** Sixth great granddaughter of progenitor Nicholas Kegg. **JOHN BARRY** Fifth great grandson of progenitor Nicholas Kegg.
KENNETH OLIE BARRY (1937 – 1981) son of Olie and Daisy (Kegg) Barry. **LINDA LEE BARRY** [2661A] (1947 – 2015) daughter of Olie and Daisy (Kegg) Barry married twice, first to Robert David Popa with whom she was mother of (2). Later, she married Alan Michael Graham. Linda worked as an executive secretary for Chrysler for a number of years. She was an excellent typist with a speed in excess of 130 wpm. She then became a small business owner of Office Helper Secretarial Services which she had taken pride in operating for many years. One of Linda's most favorite activities was gambling in Cripple Creek with her friends. She was a talented pianist and square dancer. **ROBERT BARRY** Sixth great grandson of progenitor Nicholas Kegg. **RONALD FREDERICK BARRY** [2662] (1940 - 1980) son of Olie and Daisy (Kegg) Barry, married Christine with whom he was father of (5).
SHELLY BARRY Sixth great granddaughter of progenitor Nicholas Kegg.

[2661A] The Gazette (CO) Sep 20, 2015 [2662] Detroit Free Press (MI) Feb 20, 1980

BARTELS

EUGENE K. BARTELS Sixth great grandson of progenitor Nicholas Kegg.

BARTH

ANDREW THOMAS BARTH [2663] (1992 – 2014) son of Tim and Rhonda (Sullivan) Barth worked for his family at Modular Powerhouse, then went on to own MPH Landworks. Andrew loved the outdoors, especially fishing until that fatal Memorial Day when multiple gunshots were fired from another vehicle at 1:15 p.m. There was an altercation with occupants of a dark-colored minivan. A black man in his 20s got out of the van and opened fire. The man returned to the van and then fled in the van, which was driven by another suspect. Andrew's pickup crashed into a parked car. He sought help at a residence where he collapsed. **ANDREW THOMAS BARTH** Sixth great grandson of progenitor Nicholas Kegg.
JOHN THOMAS BARTH Sixth great grandson of progenitor Nicholas Kegg.
JONATHAN THOMAS BARTH Seventh great grandson of progenitor Nicholas Kegg.
KATHERINE ANN BARTH aka "Katie", Seventh great granddaughter of progenitor Nicholas Kegg.
TIMOTHY THOMAS BARTH Sixth great grandson of progenitor Nicholas Kegg.

BARTHOLOW

JOHN O. BARTHOLOW Fifth great grandson of progenitor Nicholas Kegg.
KATHY BARTHOLOW Sixth great granddaughter of progenitor Nicholas Kegg.
NANCY EILEEN BARTHOLOW [2663A] (1944 – 2018) daughter of Leo G. and Anna Dean (Kidd) Bartholow married Douglas Fochtman with whom she was mother of (2) Nancy retired from and was employed as a hostess at the Landmark Restaurant in Bedford. She also worked at the Sewing Factory in Everett and provided babysitting for several families over the years. She enjoyed watching the Western Channel, the Andy Griffith show, and game shows. Nancy was an avid reader and loved her beloved kitties. Most importantly she enjoyed spending time with her family, especially her grandchildren.
TERESA BARTHOLOW Sixth great granddaughter of progenitor Nicholas Kegg.

BARTLETT

CHRISTOPHER ANDREW BARTLETT JR. Sixth great grandson of progenitor Nicholas Kegg.

BARTLEY

QUINTON CHASE BARTLEY Eighth great grandson of progenitor Nicholas Kegg.

BARTO

JAXON BARTO Seventh great grandson of progenitor Nicholas Kegg.

BARTON

DAISY VIOLA BARTON [2664] (1902 – 1979) daughter of Watson and Lucinda Ettie (Bussard) Barton, married Fred G. Akers. **SIMON MCCLELLAN BARTON** (1906 – 1965) son of Watson and Lucinda Ettie (Bussard) Barton married Edna Pearl Walters.

[2663] Midland Daily News (IL) May 29, 2014 [2663A] Bedford Gazette (PA) Jan 16, 2018, obtained and contributed by Bob Rose [2664] p.3 - Bedford Inquirer (PA) Mar 29, 1979

BARTOR

LAUREN JEAN BARTOR Seventh great granddaughter of progenitor Nicholas Kegg.

BASHAW

MASON VIRGINIA BASHAW Seventh great granddaughter of progenitor Nicholas Kegg.
TRAVIS SCOTT BASHAW Seventh great grandson of progenitor Nicholas Kegg.

BASOM

ADIA BASOM Seventh great granddaughter of progenitor Nicholas Kegg. **CHARLOTTE BASOM** Seventh great granddaughter of progenitor Nicholas Kegg. **JACK BASOM** Seventh great grandson of progenitor Nicholas Kegg.

BASTIAANS

CHLOE BASTIAANS Eighth great granddaughter of progenitor Nicholas Kegg.
JOHN BASTIAANS Eighth great grandson of progenitor Nicholas Kegg.

BATES

BRADY LEE BATES Fifth great grandson of progenitor Nicholas Kegg. **CLARABELLE BATES** [2664A] (1928 – 2004) daughter of Kenneth and Gladys Fern (Knouf) Bates, married William Ronk with whom she was mother of (3). Clarabelle was a League President, Vice-President, Players Agent and Team Mother at Park View Little League in Chula Vista. She enjoyed this so much she continued as President even after her children were out of baseball. **CLAYTON EVANS BATES** Sixth great grandson of progenitor Nicholas Kegg. **CRAIG ALBERT BATES** Sixth great grandson of progenitor Nicholas Kegg. **DARLENE BATES** Fifth great granddaughter of progenitor Nicholas Kegg. **DAVID CARL BATES** Fifth great grandson of progenitor Nicholas Kegg. **ERIC SCOTT BATES** Sixth great grandson of progenitor Nicholas Kegg. **FRANCES ELNORA BATES** [2664B] (1930 – 2016) daughter of Kenneth and Gladys Fern (Knouf) Bates, married Amos Duane Swartz with whom she was mother of (4). Frances worked 21 years for the State of Iowa. She was a faithful member of her church for many years and loved singing in the choir and being a part of the United Methodist Women. **LONNA BATES** Fifth great granddaughter of progenitor Nicholas Kegg. **SCOTT ALLEN BATES** Fifth great grandson of progenitor Nicholas Kegg. **TERRI BATES** Fifth great granddaughter of progenitor Nicholas Kegg. **TRISHA BATES** Fifth great granddaughter of progenitor Nicholas Kegg.

BATZEL

BETTY LEE BATZEL [2664C] (1932 – 2016) daughter of George Percy and Dorothy Louise (Fickes) Batzel married Samuel Leroy Graffious, with whom she was mother of a son. **DAVID ANTHONY BATZEL** Fifth great grandson of progenitor Nicholas Kegg. **MARY LORRAINE BATZEL** [2665] (1927 – 2002) daughter of George and Dorothy (Fickes) Batzel, married William Lewis Figard with whom she was mother of (6). Mary was a member of Round Knob Church of God, where she taught Sunday and Bible School and served on the Church Council. She graduated from high school at age 16 and went to work as a cryptologist at the Pentagon and later at the IRS. After her marriage she was employed by Bedford Memorial Hospital as an insurance clerk for over 20 years. Mary and her husband

---

[2664A] San Diego Union-Tribune (CA) Mar 11, 2004 [2664B] Des Moines Register (IA) Sept. 4, 2016 [2664C] Bedford Gazette (PA) Sep 27, 2016, obtained and contributed by Bob Rose [2665] Bedford Inquirer (PA) Nov. 29, 2003, contributed by Bob Rose

enjoyed traveling and horse racing. **PATRICIA L. BATZEL** [2666] (1931 – 2021) daughter of George and Dorothy (Fickes) Batzel, married H. Glenn "Pete" Ford with whom she was mother of (3). Patricia enjoyed traveling with her husband, working jigsaw puzzles and reading. She liked to take her walks in the woods, sitting on the porch and gardening. **SARAH LOUISA BATZEL** Fifth great granddaughter of progenitor Nicholas Kegg.

BAUER

BRANTLEY BAUER Eighth great grandson of progenitor Nicholas Kegg. **CHRISTOPHER BAUER** Seventh great grandson of progenitor Nicholas Kegg. **CHRISTY BAUER** Fifth great granddaughter of progenitor Nicholas Kegg. **COLTON BAUER** Eighth great grandson of progenitor Nicholas Kegg. **GREG BAUER** Fifth great grandson of progenitor Nicholas Kegg. **JESSICA BAUER** Seventh great granddaughter of progenitor Nicholas Kegg.

BAUGHMAN

ADELE BAUGHMAN Eighth great granddaughter of progenitor Nicholas Kegg. **JANICE BAUGHMAN** [2666A] (1936 – 2007) daughter of Roy and Grace (Kegg) Baughman married James Gwin with whom she was mother of (3). Janice started Homestead Oaks Inc. with her husband, James, in 1989 on the Conneaut Lake Road, Meadville, and still was involved with the business. She previously had been employed for 22 years at Northwest Bank which became First Seneca and later became Mellon, working in the loan department in Clarion and Oil City. Janice will be remembered as a loving mother and a devoted grandmother whose greatest joy came from being with her family and taking care of her grandchildren. **JENNIFER BAUGHMAN** Seventh great granddaughter of progenitor Nicholas Kegg. **JOHN DOUGLAS BAUGHMAN** [2667] (1945 – 2020) son of John (Keys) Baughman and Martha Olympia, married Christin Jeanne Conner with whom he was father of (3). **JUSTIN DOS REIS BAUGHMAN** Seventh great grandson of progenitor Nicholas Kegg. **KAHLIN BAUGHMAN** Eighth great grandson of progenitor Nicholas Kegg. **LUCIA BAUGHMAN** aka "Lulu" Eighth great granddaughter of progenitor Nicholas Kegg. **MATTHEW GRANT BAUGHMAN** Seventh great grandson of progenitor Nicholas Kegg. **SANDRA LEE BAUGHMAN** Sixth great granddaughter of progenitor Nicholas Kegg. **WESTON DAVID BAUGHMAN** Seventh great grandson of progenitor Nicholas Kegg. **WILLIAM DALE BAUGHMAN** Sixth great grandson of progenitor Nicholas Kegg.

BAUMAN

CHASE BAUMAN Sixth great grandson of progenitor Nicholas Kegg. **GABBI BAUMAN** Sixth great granddaughter of progenitor Nicholas Kegg. **NOAH BAUMAN** Sixth great grandson of progenitor Nicholas Kegg.

BAYNE

ALEX BAYNE Seventh great grandson of progenitor Nicholas Kegg.
SUSIE BAYNE Seventh great granddaughter of progenitor Nicholas Kegg.

BEACH

DWAYNE C. BEACH Sixth great grandson of progenitor Nicholas Kegg. **EMILY IRENE BEACH** Sixth great granddaughter of progenitor Nicholas Kegg. **HEATHER L. BEACH** Seventh great granddaughter of progenitor Nicholas Kegg. **JAMES D. BEACH** Sixth great grandson of progenitor

---

[2666] Bedford Gazette (PA) March 29, 2021 [2666A] The Derrick (Oil City, PA) May 16, 2007 [2667] Star Advertiser (Honolulu) Aug 2020

Nicholas Kegg. **REBECCA SUE BEACH** Sixth great granddaughter of progenitor Nicholas Kegg. **ZACHARY SCOTT BEACH** Seventh great grandson of progenitor Nicholas Kegg.

BEARD

DAWN E. BEARD Sixth great granddaughter of progenitor Nicholas Kegg.
DOUGLAS K. BEARD Sixth great grandson of progenitor Nicholas Kegg.

BEATY

ALICE FAYE BEATY Sixth great granddaughter of progenitor Nicholas Kegg. **BONNIE LOU BEATY** Sixth great granddaughter of progenitor Nicholas Kegg. **CONNIE SUE BEATY** Sixth great granddaughter of progenitor Nicholas Kegg. **LAUREN BEATY** (2004 – 2004) daughter of Gregory and Tamra (Easton) Beaty, Seventh great granddaughter of progenitor Nicholas Kegg. **MARCUS BEATY** Seventh great grandson of progenitor Nicholas Kegg. **MITCHEL BEATY** Seventh great grandson of progenitor Nicholas Kegg. **SANDRA KAY BEATY** aka "Sandy" Sixth great granddaughter of progenitor Nicholas Kegg. **SARA LEE BEATY** Sixth great granddaughter of progenitor Nicholas Kegg.

BEAULIEU

BRIAN BEAULIEU Seventh great grandson of progenitor Nicholas Kegg. **KARLYN BEAULIEU** Eighth great granddaughter of progenitor Nicholas Kegg. **MEGAN BEAULIEU** Seventh great granddaughter of progenitor Nicholas Kegg.

BEAUPRE

ELLIE BEAUPRE Seventh great granddaughter of progenitor Nicholas Kegg.
TODD M. BEAUPRE Sixth great grandson of progenitor Nicholas Kegg.

BEAVER

ALBERT A. BEAVER (1853 – 1935) son of Nicholas and Sophia (Fickes) Beaver, married Anna Maria Turner. **BESSIE F. BEAVER** [2668] (1888 – 1973) daughter of Isaac and Emma (Suter) Beaver married George Edwin Schofield with whom she was mother of (2). **BETTY BEAVER** [2668A] (1923 – 2005) daughter of George and Madge (Brown) Beaver married James Espey Sherrard with whom she was mother of (4). Betty was a nurse. **CAROLE BEAVER** Fifth great granddaughter of progenitor Nicholas Kegg. **CARRIE BELL BEAVER** (1869 – 1869) daughter of Nicholas and Sophia (Fickes) Beaver. **CHARLES R. BEAVER** [2669] (1877 – 1941) son of William and Annie (Garlinger) Beaver. **CHARLES S. BEAVER** (1919 – 1919) son of Rev. Perry and Daisy (Smith) Beaver. **CHARLES WASHINGTON BEAVER** [2670] (1892 – 1930) son of David and Sarah (Fritz) Beaver. **DAISY BELLE BEAVER** [2671, 2672] (1884 – 1962) daughter of Isaac and Emma (Suter) Beaver married Charles Augustus Sellers with whom she was mother of (3). **DAVID BEAVER** Fifth great grandson of progenitor Nicholas Kegg. **DAVID FRANKLIN BEAVER** [2673] (1859 – 1927) son of John and Sarah (Nicodemus) Beaver, married Sarah Ellen Fritz with whom he was father of (2). **DELAINE LAVERNE BEAVER** [2674] (1916 – 1965) son of George and Madge (Brown) Beaver Jr., married Mary Lou Anderson with whom he was father of (2). Delaine was head funeral director at the Kraeer funeral home, Pompano Beach. He was graduated from Cincinnati College of Embalming in 1951

[2668] Bedford Gazette (PA) Dec 1, 1973 [2668A] Evening Standard (PA) Oct 6, 1941 [2669] ancestry message board posted by June M. Napora [2670] Bedford Gazette (PA) Apr 25, 1930 [2671] Bedford Gazette (PA) Feb 15, 1907 [2672] Frieden's Lutheran Cemetery, Somerset County, PA [2673] Bedford Gazette (PA) Mar 18, 1927 [2674] p21 Connellsville Daily Courier (PA) Apr 28, 1965

and received the Bowsher Medal for proficiency in the restoring arts and "enthusiasm and outstanding spirit for funeral services." He was a member of the First Christian Church and Fayette Lodge No. 228, F. & A.M. of Uniontown, the National and Florida Funeral Directors Assns., and the International Order of the Golden Rule.   **EDWIN H. BEAVER** [2675] (1878 – 1913) son of Mary Ellen Beaver married Naomi W. Smith with whom he was father of (1).   **EFFIE KATHERINE BEAVER** [2676, 2677] (1875 – 1965) daughter of William and Annie (Garlinger) Beaver, married Thomas Huston Rock with whom she was mother of (3).   **ELIZA ANN BEAVER** daughter of Nicholas and Sophia (Fickes) Beaver.
FLORA JANE BEAVER daughter of Nicholas and Sophia (Fickes) Beaver.
FRANKLIN SOMERS BEAVER [2678] (1880 – 1969) son of William and Annie (Garlinger) Beaver married Virginia Dare Bowser. Frank was a retired salesman for the National Biscuit Company.
GEORGE C. BEAVER [2679] (1864 – 1929) son of John and Sarah (Nicodemus) Beaver, married Louisa Dempsey with whom he was father of (2). George had worked as a coal miner for many years.
GEORGE RUSSELL BEAVER [2680] (1891 – 1978) son of George and Anna (Douglas) Beaver married Madge B. Brown with whom he was father of (2).   **GEORGE W. BEAVER** (1856 – 1929) son of Nicholas and Sophia (Fickes) Beaver married Anna E. Douglas with whom he was father of (3).
GERTRUDE VIOLA BEAVER [2681] (1880 – 1965) daughter of George and Anna (Douglas) Beaver, married Samuel Duran Hough with whom she was mother of (2).   **HARVEY D. BEAVER** (1887 – 1891) son of George and Anna (Douglas) Beaver. **HENRY BEAVER** (abt. 1830 -) son of John Peter and Elizabeth (Kegg) Beaver.   **ISAAC WILLIAM BEAVER** (1859 – 1936) son of Nicholas and Sophia (Fickes) Beaver married Emma Elizabeth Suter with whom he was father of (2).   **JOANNA BEAVER** [2682, 2683] (1855 – 1894) aka "Annie", daughter son of John and Sarah (Nicodemus) Beaver married John H. Williams with whom she was mother of (5).   **JOHN S. BEAVER** (1822 – 1880) son of John and Elizabeth (Kegg) Beaver married Sarah Nicodemus with whom he was father of (6).
KATHRYNE BELLE BEAVER [2684] (1882 – 1962) daughter of George and Anna (Douglas) Beaver married Professor Thomas Gemmill Estep with whom she was mother of (1). Kathryne was a member of the Alexandria Presbyterian Church and the Alexandria Book Club.
MARIAH CATHERINE BEAVER [2685] (1851 – 1913) aka "Maria" daughter of William and Hannah (Egolf) Beaver married Charles A. Dannaker. Maria was a woman of noble parts and winning personality. She had the gifts, not simply of winning friends, but the gift rarer of retaining them and causing this friendship to grow deeper with the passing years.   **MARIAN A. BEAVER** [2686, 2687] (1923 – 2012) daughter of Rev. Perry and Daisy (Smith) Beaver, married Mr. Jenkins with whom she was mother of (1). Later she married Fred J. Hillebrecht, then William Leon Boen and last, to Merrill Rudolph Kalloch.
MARTHA ALICE BEAVER [2688] (1859 – 1930) aka "Mattie" daughter of William and Hannah (Egolf) Beaver married Edmund Garlinger Luken with whom she was mother of (2). Mattie came to Schellsburg when about 5 years of age, her mother having brought her family here after the death of the father in the Civil War. She spent her girlhood here until her marriage to Edmund G. Luken when she went to Kansas to make her home. As Mattie A. Beaver she taught school in Schellsburg, New Paris, Pleasantville and Fishertown and many of the older men and women will remember her as their teacher. Her parents both were from this place but moved to Iowa earlier in their life.   **MARY ELLEN BEAVER** [2689] (1851 – 1925) aka "Ellen" daughter of Nicholas and Sophia (Fickes) Beaver was mother of (1).
NANNIE E. BEAVER [2690] (1872 – 1936) daughter of William and Annie (Garlinger) Beaver married John M. Culp with whom she was mother of (1).   **NICHOLAS BEAVER** [2691] (1824 – 1914) son of John and Elizabeth (Kegg) Beaver married twice, first to Elizabeth Devore and later to Sophia Fickes with whom he was father of (7). On August 17, 1862, he enlisted in Company E., 138th Pa. Vol. and was

---

[2675] Bedford Gazette (PA) Feb 21, 1913 [2676] Morrisons Cove Herald Nov. 13, 1903 obtained by Carol Eddleman [2677] p2 Bedford Gazette (PA) Jun 10, 1949 [2678] Bedford Inquirer (PA) March 13, 1969 [2679] Johnstown Tribune (PA) Dec 19, 1929 contributed by D. Sue Dible [2680] Fort Lauderdale News (FL) March 7, 1978 [2681] Pittsburgh Post Gazette (PA) May 26, 1965 [2682] Tribune Democrat Marriage Index [2683] p1 Bedford Gazette (PA) May 4, 1900 [2684] Daily News (Huntingdon, PA) March 12, 1962 [2685] Bedford Gazette (PA) May 16, 1913 [2686] Times-Advocate Sep 7, 1971 [2687] Find A Grave#26010768 maintained by Haley Cook [2688] Bedford Gazette (PA) Sep 12, 1930 [2689] bk 44, pB26 Bedford County Historical Society contributed by D. Sue Dible [2690] Johnstown Daily Tribune (PA) Jan 3, 1936, contributed by D. Sue Dible [2691] p4 Bedford Gazette (PA) Feb 27, 1914

a brave and good soldier, ever ready to do his duty. He was present at the battles of Winchester, Antietam, Petersburg, Appomattox and the surrender of General Lee. He had two brothers in the Civil War. John S. Beaver, the father of Nicholas, was five years in the War of 1812. Mr. Beaver was a member of the reformed Church and a Republican. He was a good citizen, honest and upright in all his dealings. He was a weaver by trade and the saying "Nicholas Beaver, the coverlid weaver," was often heard. **PAUL ELMAN BEAVER** Fourth great grandson of progenitor Nicholas Kegg.
PERRY FRANKLIN BEAVER [2692] (1889 – 1974) son of David and Sarah (Fritz) Beaver married Daisy Ruth Smith with whom he was father of (6). Perry retired from the Kopper's Company plant in Green Springs, W. Va., in 1952. While employed there he served as a part-time minister in West Virginia Methodist churches. After retiring, he became pastor of both the Moorefield and St. George circuits of United Methodist churches. **REBECCA JOSEPHINE BEAVER** [2693] (1856 – 1921) daughter of William and Hannah (Egolf) Beaver married Professor Cyrus Jeffries Potts with whom she was mother of (2). **ROSE BEAVER** [2694] (1896 – 1896) daughter of George and Louisa (Dempsey) Beaver.
RUSSELL MEYERS BEAVER (1904 – 1904) son of William and Mary (Meyers) Beaver.
RUTH ELIZABETH BEAVER Fourth great granddaughter of progenitor Nicholas Kegg.
SIMON J. BEAVER (1847 – 1878) son of William and Hannah (Egolf) Beaver. **SOPHIA BEAVER** (1838 – 1860) daughter of John and Elizabeth (Kegg) Beaver. **SOPHIA CATHERINE BEAVER** [2695] (1856 – 1949) daughter of John and Sarah (Nicodemus) Beaver married Augustus Lightningstar with whom she was mother of (2). **SUE ANN BEAVER** [2696] (1938 – 1999) daughter of Delaine and Mary Lou (Anderson) Beaver married three times, first to Donald Edward Benefield with whom she was mother of (1). Later she married James R. Dennis and last, married Dr. Clyde Thurston Stoner.
VIOLET BEAVER [2697] (1896 – 1899) daughter of George and Louisa (Dempsey)Beaver was playing around the kitchen when she fell into and upset a bucket of scalding water over herself, which virtually parboiled her legs and back. Dr. I. E. Sloan was summoned, but Violet was beyond medical assistance, and the most he could do was to partially relieve the terrible agony which she suffered. Interment being made at Hooversville, Mrs. Beavers former home. Little Violet was the only living child of the couple, her twin sister having died at the age of a few weeks from cholera infantum. **VIOLET DOROTHY SMITH BEAVER** [2698] (1903 – 1996) daughter of Edwin and Naomi (Smith) Beaver married Robert Catanese with whom she was mother of (5). **WILLIAM BEAVER** [2698A] (1827 – 1862) son of John and Elizabeth (Kegg) Beaver married Hannah Egolf with whom he was father of (5) was the first man from Cedar County, Iowa to fall in battle. He enlisted in Co. A, 5th Iowa Inf. June 24, 1861, at Tipton, Ia. Shot in the breast by Confederate pickets while on a scouting mission March 4, 1862, near New Madrid, Mo. He survived until March 5, 1862, when he died in enemy hands. The rebels buried him and placed a headboard on his grave that read, "William Beaver, Welcome here, Here lies one who not satisfied with letting other folks alone would insist on being buried a "Lincolnite". On inside of headboard was, "This Yankee said he belonged to the 5th Iowa." Grand Army of the Republic Post 110 in Tipton, Iowa was named after him. **WILLIAM BROWN BEAVER** Fifth great grandson of progenitor Nicholas Kegg.
WILLIAM HARRY BEAVER [2699] (1848 – 1922) son of William and Hannah (Egolf) Beaver, married Annie E. Garlinger with whom he was father of (5). William was a loyal member of the I.O.O.F.
WILLIAM FRANKLIN BEAVER aka "Bill" Fourth great grandson of progenitor Nicholas Kegg.
WILLIAM HENRY BEAVER [2700] (1850 – 1942) son of John and Sarah (Nicodemus) Beaver married Mary J. Meyers with whom he was father of (1). William went to Akron, O., where he was employed for a time in making pottery. He then returned to Bedford County and from 1884 until 1887 carried mail by horseback from Schellsburg to Stoystown. Removing to Johnstown about 18888, he made his home here ever since. At the time of the 1889 flood, he was employed at the Hawn Brick Yard and assisted in rescue work at the Stone Bridge and in reconstruction work after the disaster. Mr. Beaver then entered the

---

[2692] Cumberland News (MD) Dec 17, 1974 [2693] Bedford Gazette (PA) Sep 9, 1921 obtained by Bob Rose [2694] Johnstown Daily Tribune (PA) Aug 10, 1896 obtained by D. Sue Dible [2695] Johnstown Tribune (PA) Dec 10, 1949 [2696] Sun Sentinel (FL) Sep 8, 1999 [2697] Johnstown Daily Tribune (PA) Dec 11, 1899 obtained by D. Sue Dible [2698] p4 Cumberland Times News (MD) Dec 2, 1996 [2698A] A Topical History of Cedar County, Iowa 1910 Sec IX Military History [2699] Bedford Gazette (PA) June 30, 1922 obtained by Bob Rose [2700] Johnstown Tribune (PA) Dec 23, 1942, obtained by D. Sue Dible

employ of the Old Cambria Iron Company and remained with that firm and later the Cambria Steel Company, Midvale Steel & Ordnance and Bethlehem Steel Company for 32 years. In 1923, shortly after the steel mill was acquired by Bethlehem, he was placed on pension at the age of 73. At the time of his retirement, he was working in the mill as a blacksmith and boiler tender. After coming to this city, Mr. Beaver made his home for some time on David Street, Dale, and for the last 35 years had resided at 612 Bedford Street. An ardent fisherman, he made annual fishing trips to Bedford County until he was about 78 years old. The nonagenarian was a member of the Beulah Evangelical Church and the Brotherhood Bible Class of the church.

BECHTEL

ANDREW BECHTEL Seventh great grandson of progenitor Nicholas Kegg. **DAVID BECHTEL** Seventh great grandson of progenitor Nicholas Kegg. **JENNIFER BECHTEL** Seventh great granddaughter of progenitor Nicholas Kegg. **MATTHEW BECHTEL** Seventh great grandson of progenitor Nicholas Kegg.

BECK

CLARENCE W. BECK JR. [2700A] son of Clarence and Bernice (Diehl) Beck. Clarence was an army veteran and was employed as a payroll manager and head of the trust department at First Fidelity Trust, Philadelphia. **J. WILLIAM BECK** Eighth great grandson of progenitor Nicholas Kegg.
KENDRA ESTELLE BECK Seventh great granddaughter of progenitor Nicholas Kegg.
LEILA BECK Seventh great granddaughter of progenitor Nicholas Kegg. **NANCY BECK** [2700B] (1941 – 2015) daughter of Clarence and Bernice (Diehl) Beck married Jose Luis Florez Estrada with whom she was mother of (2), a Ph.D., associate professor of Spanish, Nancy was the recipient of numerous awards that recognize her expertise in teaching, as well as her dedication to working with students as the Spanish Club advisor, the International Club and as director of the International Academic Village. Additionally, she worked as a Spanish/ESL instructor and translator for General Foods Corp. in Madrid, Spain. **PARKER JAMES BECK** Seventh great grandson of progenitor Nicholas Kegg.
SEAN WILLIAM BECK Seventh great grandson of progenitor Nicholas Kegg.
VIVIAN BECK Seventh great granddaughter of progenitor Nicholas Kegg.

BECKER

DAVID BECKER Eighth great grandson of progenitor Nicholas Kegg.

BECKLEY

DEBORAH BECKLEY Sixth great granddaughter of progenitor Nicholas Kegg. **DONALD BECKLEY** Fifth great grandson of progenitor Nicholas Kegg. **RICHARD BECKLEY** [2701, 2702] (1913 – 1991) son of Richard and Olive (Beegle) Beckley, married Matilda Mae Tittermary with whom he was a father of (2). Later, he married Evelyn Natatia Obuchowski with whom he was father of (3).
RICHARD BECKLEY (1939 – 1939) son of Richard and Matilda Mae (Tittermary) Beckley.
RICHARD BECKLEY Fifth great grandson of progenitor Nicholas Kegg. **RICHARD BECKLEY** Sixth great grandson of progenitor Nicholas Kegg. **ROBERT BECKLEY** Fifth great grandson of progenitor Nicholas Kegg. **STEVEN BECKLEY** Sixth great grandson of progenitor Nicholas Kegg.
WILLIAM BECKLEY Fifth great grandson of progenitor Nicholas Kegg.

[2700A] p.D13 - Philadelphia Inquirer (PA) Sept 22, 1991 [2700B] Snyder Funeral Service (PA) Jan 19, 2015, obtained and contributed by D. Sue Dible [2701] The Philadelphia Inquirer (PA) April 26, 1984 [2702] Pittsburgh Post Gazette (PA) May 14, 2013

BEEBER

ALEXANDRA BEEBER aka "Alex" Sixth great granddaughter of progenitor Nicholas Kegg. **AMBER NICOLE BEEBER** Sixth great granddaughter of progenitor Nicholas Kegg. **BRENDA GAIL BEEBER** Fifth great granddaughter of progenitor Nicholas Kegg. **DAVID M. BEEBER** Sixth great grandson of progenitor Nicholas Kegg. **DONALD DEAN BEEBER** [2703] (1929 – 1999) son of John and Iva (Smith) Beeber married Judith Parmely with whom he was father of (5). Donald worked in Code 135 at Puget Sound Naval Shipyard for 30 years. He also served as a volunteer deputy sheriff in Mason County. **DONALD ERVIN BEEBER** [2703A] (1950 – 2009) son of Donald and Judith (Parmely) Beeber, married Vanessa Lynn Cheplak with whom he was father of (2). Donald was a cement mason for 25 plus years before retiring. He was a practical joker and could light up any room with his sly smile. He enjoyed hunting, fishing, was an avid John Wayne and NASCAR fan. He loved his personally restored 1965 Mustang Fastback which he won many local car show awards with. He was a great animal lover, but most of all he was a dedicated family man. **DONNA RAE BEEBER** Sixth great granddaughter of progenitor Nicholas Kegg. **DEBBIE BEEBER** Sixth great granddaughter of progenitor Nicholas Kegg. **DENISE BEEBER** Sixth great granddaughter of progenitor Nicholas Kegg. **DOUGLAS LLOYD BEEBER** Sixth great grandson of progenitor Nicholas Kegg. **FRANK C. BEEBER** (1910 – 1930) son of John and Mary (Knouf) Beeber. **GEORGE H. BEEBER** [2704] (1887 – 1893) son of John and Mary (Knouf) Beeber. **GRACE LOUISE BEEBER** [2704A] (1956 – 2016) daughter of Marlin and Mary (Ochoa) Beeber, was twice married, first to Roger Clark with whom she was mother of (2), later she married Noil Elgin Breedlove. **GRACE MAXINE BEEBER** (1920 – 2011) daughter of Noah and Grace (Jones) Beeber married three times, first to Fred Leclair, later to Everett E. Darling with whom she was mother of (5). Later, she married Frank Pensoneau. **GWENDOLYNN SUE BEEBER** Fifth great granddaughter of progenitor Nicholas Kegg. **HAZEL LYDIA BEEBER** [2705] (1903 – 1991) daughter of John and Mary (Knouf) Beeber married John William Kittel with whom she was mother of (2). Hazel was a homemaker and worked as a practical nurse in Salinas, Calif. Later, she worked as a volunteer with the Retired Seniors Volunteer Program in Grand Junction, completing 5,000 hours of service. She enjoyed crafts, needlework, traveling and playing cards. **HERON NOAH BEEBER** [2706] (1919 – 1996) aka "Bud" son of Noah and Grace (Jones) Beeber married twice, first to Agnes L. Black with whom he was father of (2). Later, he married Vivian Margaret Moffitt. **JESSE L. BEEBER** (1896 – 1899) son of John and Mary (Knouf) Beeber. **JOHN ABRAHAM BEEBER** (1892 – 1954) son of John and Mary (Knouf) Beeber married Iva Myrtle Smith with whom he was father of (1). **KAREN LYNN BEEBER** Fifth great granddaughter of progenitor Nicholas Kegg. **KATHRYN L. BEEBER** aka" Kathy" Fifth great granddaughter of progenitor Nicholas Kegg. **MARLIN LLOYD BEEBER** [2706A] aka "Pat" (1924 – 2006) son of Noah and Grace (Jones) Beeber, married Mary Louise Ochoa with whom he was father of (5). Marlin was a member of the United States Marine Corp. and served honorably in WWII and the Korean Conflict. He was a member of Carpenters Local 743 for 33 years and an ordained So. Baptist Minister. **MARVIN BOYD BEEBER** (1924 – 2000) son of Noah and Grace (Jones) Beeber married Anitra Lillian Macrobert. **MARVIN LLOYD BEEBER** [2706B] aka "Marv" (1938 – 2019) son of Heron and Agnes (Black) Beeber, married Joan Sanders with whom he was father of (4). Marv was a union plasterer retiring in 1997. He loved to travel and was especially fond of central Oregon. For approximately 10 years Marv coached Little League, Babe Ruth and high school baseball teams. Marv loved his family, his other love being a lifelong Yankees fan. **NICHOLAS B. BEEBER** Sixth great grandson of progenitor Nicholas Kegg. **NICHOLAS BOYD BEEBER** (1954 - 1995) son of Marlin and Mary Louise (Ochoa) Beeber married twice, first to Brenda D. Cobb with whom he was father of (2). Later, he married Rhonda Lynn Bell with whom he was father of (1). **NOAH LLOYD BEEBER** Fifth great grandson of progenitor Nicholas Kegg.

[2703] Kitsap Sun (WA) Aug 6, 1999 [2703A] Bremerton Sun (WA) Mar 4, 2009 [2704] Solomon Valley Chronicles/Hill City Republican (KS) Sep 30, 1893 [2704A] McAlester News-Capital & Democrat (OK) March 2, 2016, obtained and contributed by D. Sue Dible [2705] The Daily Sentinel (Grand Junction, CO) Aug 7, 1991 [2706] p.21 Oregonian (OR) May 1, 1956 [2706A] Bakersfield Californian April 4, 2006 [2706B] Orgonian (OR) Oct 23, 2019

NOAH NICHOLAS BEEBER (2707) (1898 – 1971) son of John and Mary (Knouf) Beeber married Grace Edith Jones with whom he was father of (4). Noah was a retired construction worker.
ORLANDO C. BEEBER (1886 – 1886) son of John and Mary (Knouf) Beeber.
PATRICIA A. BEEBER Fifth great granddaughter of progenitor Nicholas Kegg.
RUTH MARIE BEEBER (2707A) (1956 – 2012) daughter of Marlin and Mary (Ochoa) Beeber married three times, first to Jessie Murch with whom she was mother of (2). **STACEY D. BEEBER** Sixth great granddaughter of progenitor Nicholas Kegg. **TORI LYNN BEEBER** Sixth great granddaughter of progenitor Nicholas Kegg. **VICTORIA BEEBER** Sixth great granddaughter of progenitor Nicholas Kegg. **WILLIAM ALEXANDER BEEBER** (1890 – 1964) son of John and Mary (Knouf) Beeber.
WILLIAM LEONARD BEEBER (2708) (1939 – 1978) son of Heron and Agnes (Black) Beeber married Carole Anita Molloy with whom he was father of (1).

BEEGLE

ADA LOUISE BEEGLE (2709) (1918 – 2001) daughter OF Isaiah and Mary (Robinson) Beegle married Chalmer Ivan Barkman with whom she was mother of (1). Ada was a member of the Black Valley Federated Church, where she had formerly been a member of the Ladies Aid of the church. In 1939, she graduated from Everett High School, but worked primarily as a homemaker.
ADA REBECCA BEEGLE (2710) (1886 – 1965) daughter of Isaiah and Sarah (Smouse) Beegle, married George Lloyd Price with whom she was mother of (3). **ADAM BEEGLE** Sixth great grandson of progenitor Nicholas Kegg. **AGNES HELEN BEEGLE** (2711) (1908 – 1987) daughter of Roy and Sarah (Hall) Beegle married twice, first to Warren Sylvester Fickes, later to Ralph Charles Stickler.
ALENE OLIVE BEEGLE (2712) (1922 – 2007) daughter of Harvey and Violet (Bennett) Beegle married Wayne Edwin Surrena with whom she was mother of (1). Alene retired after 18 years as a teller from Mellon Bank of Grove City. After retirement, she was employed by McDowell Bank, also Grove City. Mrs. Surrena belonged to Holy Trinity Lutheran Church and was a former member of Order of the Eastern Star Chapter 86, both Grove City. **AMY BEEGLE** Fifth great granddaughter of progenitor Nicholas Kegg. **ANGELA BEEGLE** Seventh great granddaughter of progenitor Nicholas Kegg.
ANN E. BEEGLE (2712A) (1939 – 2014) daughter of Glen and Mary Elizabeth (Kegg) Beegle, married Jewell McLain Tate with whom she was mother of (2). Ann held various jobs over her working life and, most significantly, spent the past 28 years in faithful service at York Technical Institute (YTI). Ann was a greatly respected and loved associate at YTI. She was one of the first recipients of the Beacon Award, an annual recognition given to the person that best exemplifies the values and mission of the school. The "Ann Tate Commitment to Externship Excellence Award" has been established in Ann's name and will be awarded to a deserving student each term. **ANNA JEAN BEEGLE** (2712B) aka "Jeanne" (1938 – 1975) daughter of Clarence and Mildred (Bussard) Beegle was mother of (1). **ANNA LOUISE BEEGLE** Fifth great granddaughter of progenitor Nicholas Kegg. **ANNIE ALDA BEEGLE** (1887 – aft 1916) daughter of William and Sarah (Friedline) Beegle. **ANNIE R. BEEGLE** (2713) (1862 – 1937) daughter of Emanuel and Rebecca (Kegg) Beegle married Peter T. Bowser with whom she was mother of (5).
BARBARA ANN BEEGLE (2714) (1960 – 2012) daughter of Philip and Geraldine (Beasley) Beegle married Jerry Paul Lambert with whom she was mother of (2). Barbara was an active volunteer and fundraiser for numerous organizations dedicated to fighting breast cancer. Barb attended Pace Academy and Vanderbilt University. **BARBARA BEEGLE** (2714A) (1960 – 2012) daughter of Philip and Geraldine (Beasley) Beegle, married Jerry Paul Lambert with whom she was mother of (2). Barbara was an active volunteer and fundraiser for numerous organizations dedicated to fighting breast cancer.

(2707) San Martin News (CA) May 6, 1971, contributed by D. Sue Dible (2707A) McAlester News Capital (OK) July 4, 2012 (2708) p2 Oregonian (OR) Feb 22, 1962 (2709) Bedford Inquirer (PA) Feb 23, 2001 (2710) Bedford County Historical Society Pioneer Library; book 101, p 121 obtained by D. Sue Dible (2711) Bedford County Genealogical Society obtained by D. Sue Dible (2712) The Herald (Sharon, PA) Mar 14, 2007 (2712A) Bedford Gazette (PA) July 8, 2014, obtained and contributed by Bob Rose (2712B) p.6 Everett Press (PA) June 5, 1975 (2713) p.3-The Canton Repository (OH) Dec 29, 1937 (2714) Atlanta Journal-Constitution (GA) Mar. 14, 2012 (2714A) Atlanta Journal-Constitution (GA) Mar. 14, 2012

BARBARA A. BEEGLE (2715) (1919 – 2004) daughter of Charles and Barbara (Steck) Beegl, married Ward Winchester Rowe with whom she was mother of (2). Barbara had been a dental assistant in Galesburg, a secretary at Poland China Association and worked in dietary at the former Galesburg Research Hospital. **BARRY EUGENE BEEGLE** Sixth great grandson of progenitor Nicholas Kegg. **BARRY L. BEEGLE** Fifth great grandson of progenitor Nicholas Kegg. **BAYLEE ANN BEEGLE** Ninth great granddaughter of progenitor Nicholas Kegg. **BEATRICE JANE BEEGLE** (2716) (1933 – 1991) daughter of William Frank and Gussie (Foor) Beegle. **BEAU BEEGLE** Seventh great grandson of progenitor Nicholas Kegg. **BETH BEEGLE** Sixth great granddaughter of progenitor Nicholas Kegg. **BETH ANN BEEGLE** Sixth great granddaughter of progenitor Nicholas Kegg. **BETSY BEEGLE** Fifth great granddaughter of progenitor Nicholas Kegg. **BETTY ANN BEEGLE** Fifth great granddaughter of progenitor Nicholas Kegg. **BEVERLY RAE BEEGLE** Fifth great granddaughter of progenitor Nicholas Kegg. **BRENDA LEE BEEGLE** Sixth great granddaughter of progenitor Nicholas Kegg. **BRIAN L. BEEGLE** Sixth great grandson of progenitor Nicholas Kegg. **BRIAN S. BEEGLE** aka "Scotty" Seventh great grandson of progenitor Nicholas Kegg.
BRIAN SCOTT BEEGLE Sixth great grandson of progenitor Nicholas Kegg.
BRYAN EUGENE BEEGLE (2717) (1959 – 1994) son of Eugene and Patricia (Weaver) Beegle married Sandra Carson with whom he was father of (2). Bryan was a postdoctoral fellow in Comparative Medicine at the University of Tennessee, Memphis, and a 1988 graduate of University of Tennessee College of Veterinary Medicine. **BUCKY BEEGLE** Seventh great grandson of progenitor Nicholas Kegg. **CALVIN JAMES BEEGLE** Ninth great grandson of progenitor Nicholas Kegg.
CARL DEAN BEEGLE (2717A) (1939 – 2005) son of Dale and Virginia (Carl) Beegle, married Margaret Feather with whom he was father of (6). Carl owned and operated Jay Blackburn and Sons Hardware Store. **CARL G. BEEGLE** (1934 – 1934) son of Herbert and Emma (Good) Beegle.
CARLA DEANNE BEEGLE Sixth great granddaughter of progenitor Nicholas Kegg.
CASSANDRA L. BEEGLE Seventh great grandson of progenitor Nicholas Kegg.
CHARLES FLECK BEEGLE (2718) (1889 – 1969) son of Isaiah and Sarah (Smouse) Beegle married Barbara Nellie Steck with whom he was father of (2). **CHARLES WILLIAM BEEGLE** Sixth great grandson of progenitor Nicholas Kegg. **CHERYLDELEE BEEGLE** (2718A) aka "Cheryl" (1950 – 2015) daughter of William and Evelyn (Young) Beegle was married twice. Cheryldelee worked at Design T as a registered CAN. **CHRISTINE A. BEEGLE** (2718B) aka "Sis" (1948 – 1993) daughter of Calvin and Margaret (Smith) Beegle married Mr. Miller with whom she was mother of (3). Later, she married James Reid. **CHRISTOPHER EMANUEL BEEGLE** Fifth great grandson of progenitor Nicholas Kegg.
CLAIR CALVIN BEEGLE (2719) (1912 – 1985) son of Emanuel and Grace (Diehl) Beegle married twice, first to Phyllis Romaine Collins with whom he was father of (2), later he married Vada Pearl (Martin) Talbott. Clair was a retired truck driver for Continental Trucking Company, and a veteran of World War II. **CLARENCE FEASTER BEEGLE JR.** (1940 – 1940) son of Clarence and Mildred (Bussard) Beegle. **CLARENCE WALTER BEEGLE** (1898 – 1902) son of William and Sarah (Friedline) Beegle. **CLAYTON CLARENCE BEEGLE** Fifth great grandson of progenitor Nicholas Kegg. **CLETUS H. BEEGLE** Fifth great grandson of progenitor Nicholas Kegg.
CONNIE LEE BEEGLE Sixth great granddaughter of progenitor Nicholas Kegg.
CORY JAMES BEEGLE Eighth great grandson of progenitor Nicholas Kegg.
DALE SHANNON BEEGLE (2720) (1914 – 1982) son of Emanuel and Grace (Diehl) Beegle married H. Virginia Carl with whom he was father of (5). **DANA N. BEEGLE** Sixth great granddaughter of progenitor Nicholas Kegg. **DAREL LINN BEEGLE** Sixth great grandson of progenitor Nicholas Kegg. **DAVID LESTER BEEGLE** Fifth great grandson of progenitor Nicholas Kegg.

[2715] p.B5-Peoria Journal Star (IL) Nov 2, 2004 [2716] Bedford Gazette (PA), BCHS book 74, p 9 obtained by D. Sue Dible [2717] Commercial Appeal (Memphis, TN) Nov 27, 1994 [2717A] p.12 - Bedford Gazette (PA) July 1, 2005 [2718] Bedford County Historical Society (PA), book 1, p 282 obtained by D. Sue Dible [2719] Bedford County Genealogical Society obtained by D. Sue Dible [2718A] Bedford Gazette (PA) April 10, 2015, obtained and contributed by Bob Rose [2718B] Bedford Inquirer (PA) Dec 10, 1993, obtained and contributed by Duke Clark [2720] p.10 – Bedford Gazette (PA) Feb 16, 1982

DEVON KAYNE BEEGLE Eighth great grandson of progenitor Nicholas Kegg. **DIANA BEEGLE** aka "Dee" Sixth great granddaughter of progenitor Nicholas Kegg. **DONALD CRAIG BEEGLE** Sixth great grandson of progenitor Nicholas Kegg. **DONALD LESTER BEEGLE** [2721] (1919 – 1985) son of Emanuel and Grace (Diehl) Beegle, married Eula Grace Bennett with whom he was father of (6). Donald was a retired truck driver for Hall's Motor Freight Company. **DONALD W. BEEGLE** [2722] (1931 – 1973) son of William Frank and Gussie (Foor) Beegle was father of (2). Donald was a member of Union Lodge 48, A. F. & A.M. of Elkton and served with U.S. Air Force during the Korean War. He was employed by the U.S. Postal Service in Delaware. **DONNA BEEGLE** Fifth great granddaughter of progenitor Nicholas Kegg. **DONNA LEE BEEGLE** [2723] (1938 – 1994) daughter of Herbert and Emma (Good) Beegle. **DENIVAN ISAIAH BEEGLE** (1919 – 1919) on of Harry and Louise (Peak) Beegle. **EDWARD A. BEEGLE** (1906 – 1939) son of Edward and Flora Belle (Clark) Beegle. **EDWARD GUMP BEEGLE** (1872 – 1925) son of George and Rebecca (Diehl) Beegle, married Flora Belle Clark with whom he was father of (6). **ELLEN LOUISE BEEGLE** Fifth great granddaughter of progenitor Nicholas Kegg. **EMANUEL LESTER BEEGLE** [2724] (1891 – 1952) aka "Lester", son of Shannon and Mary (Smouse) Beegle, married Grave Verda Diehl with whom he was father of (6). **ERIC BEEGLE** Sixth great grandson of progenitor Nicholas Kegg. **ERIC BEEGLE** Seventh great grandson of progenitor Nicholas Kegg. **ERIC GEORGE BEEGLE** Fifth great grandson of progenitor Nicholas Kegg. **EUGENE S. BEEGLE** [2724A] (1931 – 2018) son of Glenn and Mary Elizabeth (Kegg) Beegle, married Patricia Weaver with whom he was father of (3). Eugene owned and operated Beegle's Sporting Goods in Bedford from 1951-1970 before moving to Tennessee in 1970. He graduated from Christ for the Nations Bible College in Dallas, Texas. **EVA CATHERINE BEEGLE** [2725] (1881 – 1945) daughter of George and Rebecca (Diehl) Beegle married George Ross Lutz with whom she was mother of (2). **FAYE BEEGLE** Fifth great granddaughter of progenitor Nicholas Kegg.
FLOYD BEEGLE Fifth great grandson of progenitor Nicholas Kegg. **FRANK REESE BEEGLE** (1880 – 1925) son of William and Sarah (Friedline) Beegle. **GARY W. BEEGLE** Fifth great grandson of progenitor Nicholas Kegg. **GEORGE EARL BEEGLE** [2726] (1889 – 1924) son of Shannon and Mary (Smouse) Beegle, married Alma Christine Horne with whom he was father of (4).
GEORGE EARL BEEGLE [2727] (1937 – 1994) son of Emanuel and Grace (Diehl) Beegle married twice first to Judith Ann McGuire, later to Lorraine Anita Calcott with whom he was father of (5). George was a former truck driver. **GEORGE EARL BEEGLE** Fifth great grandson of progenitor Nicholas Kegg. **GEORGE THURMAN BEEGLE** [2727A] (1888 – 1921) son of George Henry and Rebecca (Diehl) Beegle, married Valera Smith with whom he was father of (3). **GEORGE THURMAN BEEGLE JR.** [2727B, 2727C] (1920 – 2007) son of George and Valera (Smith) Beegle married Margaret Fox Pedrick with whom he was father of (3). George was a veteran of WWII. **GEORGE THURMAN BEEGLE III** Fifth great grandson of progenitor Nicholas Kegg. **GLADYS LEONE BEEGLE** [2727D] (1921 – 2013) daughter of Robert and Nora (Wolfe) Beegle was twice married, first to Guy Franklin Kegg with whom she was mother of (4). A widow, she later married George W. Henderson. Gladys was a registered nurse at Sipes and Timmons Hospital in Everett. She was the school nurse at Colerain Elementary for 24 years. She worked at Clites Rest Home. She was a member of the Conemaugh Valley Memorial Hospital Alumni Association, St. Mark LCW and was a lifetime member of St. Mark Lutheran Church.
GWEN BEEGLE Fifth great granddaughter of progenitor Nicholas Kegg.
HARRIET JANE BEEGLE Fifth great granddaughter of progenitor Nicholas Kegg.
HARRY S. BEEGLE [2728] (1883 – 1970) son of Isaiah and Sarah (Smouse) Beegle married Louise D. Peak with whom he was father of (4). **HARRY VERNON BEEGLE** [2729] (1886 – 1925) son of George and Rebecca (Diehl) Beegle married Bessie Mae Bequeath.

[2721] Bedford County Genealogical Society obtained by D. Sue Dible [2722] p.6A- Cecil Whig (MD) Nov 21, 1973 [2723] Bedford Gazette (PA) Apr 14, 1994 [2724] Bedford Gazette (PA) June 4, 1952 [2724A] Bedford Gazette (PA) July 20, 2018, obtained and contributed by Bob Rose [2725] p.10 - The Bedford Gazette (PA) Sept 14, 1945 [2726] Bedford Gazette (PA) Jan 4, 1924 [2727] Bedford Gazette (PA) Jun 11, 1994 BCHS book 76, p. 23 obtained by D. Sue Dible [2727A] p. 8 -Bedford Gazette (PA) July 28, 1916 [2727B] p.6 - Cumberland Evening Times (MD) March 1, 1943 [2727C] Bedford Gazette (PA) Jul 3, 1947 [2727D] Bedford Gazette (PA) Sept 14, 2013, obtained and contributed by Bob Rose [2728] Calgary Herald (Alberta, Canada) Sep 15, 1970 [2729] p.1 - Bedford Gazette (PA) June 19, 1925, obtained by Bob Rose

Harry was a father of (2) foster daughters Janette and Mildred. He was a faithful and trustworthy employee of the J. H. Laher ice-cream factory. Harry was a member of Fort Bedford No. 90, and Knights of the Ku Klux Klan.   **HARVEY WILLIAM BEEGLE** [2730] (1892 – 1965) son of Shannon and Mary (Smouse) Beegle married Violet Marguerite Bennett with whom he was father of (4). He was a member of the St. Mark's Lutheran Church in Friends Cove and a farmer in that area.
HATTIE IRENE BEEGLE [2730A] (1881 – 1995) daughter of William and Sarah (Friedline) Beegle was twice married, first to Charles Ross Diehl with whom she was mother of (4). A widow, she later married Harry Hinish. Hattie was a member of Everett Gospel Hall Tabernacle.
HAZEL FLORIENE BEEGLE [2730B] (1921 – 1988) daughter of Lester and Grace (Diehl) Beegle, married Willard Jesse Colledge with whom she was mother of (2).   **HEIDI BEEGLE** Seventh great granddaughter of progenitor Nicholas Kegg.   **HEATHER BEEGLE** Seventh great granddaughter of progenitor Nicholas Kegg.   **HELEN CATHERINE BEEGLE** [2730C] (1916 – 1998) daughter of Harvey and Violet (Bennett) Beegle, married Robert Lee Cessna with whom she was mother of (12). Helen was a member of the Yeager Lutheran Church and was president of the Rainsburg Senior Citizens. She was a former member of the Order of the Eastern Star, Bedford Springs Chapter 41. She was primarily a homemaker but had formerly been employed by the Record Club of America in York for 12 years. She was an avid gardener and loved cooking for her family. **HERBERT ELLIS BEEGLE** [2731] (1912 – 1994) son of Isaiah and Mary (Robinson) Beegle married three times, first to Emma May Good with whom he was father of (3), he then married Gladys Lewis Ash with whom he was father of (1), last he married Annie Custer Shimer.   **HERBERT ISAIAH BEEGLE** [2732] (1944 – 1983) aka "Herbie" son of Herbert and Gladys (Lewis) Ash Beegle. Herbie was a member of the Cherry Lane Church of the brethren, had attended Everett High School, and was working as a construction supervisor in Tamarac. **IMOGENE C. BEEGLE** [2732A] (1917 – 2005) daughter of Charles and Barbara (Steck) Beegle, married Merle Whitney Nelson with whom she was mother of (4). Imogene was a cashier at Arlan's for 10 years and also worked at Sudsy's for 2 years and Leighton's Sundries for 8 years. She lived most of her life in Galesburg and graduated from Galesburg High School. She was a member of Faith United Methodist Church.   **ISAAC FRANKLIN BEEGLE** [2733] (1877 – 1955) aka "Franklin" son of George and Rebecca (Diehl) Beegle married Ida Elizabeth French.   **ISAIAH BEEGLE** (1857 – 1890) son of Emanuel and Rebecca (Kegg) Beegle, married Sarah Elizabeth Smouse with whom he was father of (5). **ISAIAH SCOTT BEEGLE** [2734] (1890 – 1970) aka "Bunt" son of Isaiah and Sarah (Smouse) Beegle married Mary E. Robinson with whom he was father of (2). Bunt was a long-time maple syrup producer in Black Valley.   **JACK DIEHL BEEGLE** [2734A] (1931 – 2010) son of Lester and Grace (Diehl) Beegle, married Vera Maxine Leppert with whom he was father of (3) Jack was an active member of Point United Methodist church where he served as a trustee, taught Sunday School, was a member of the pastor parish relation committee and was a Deacon of the Church. He was a member of the Bedford Masonic Lodge F&AM # 320. Jack started his career at Howard Johnson at the age of 12. He worked as a restaurant worker, truck driver and eventually worked his way to the title of distribution manager. He won the prestigious Howard Johnson District Manager of the Year award. One of his greatest achievements was winning a car for his outstanding work performance with Howard Johnson. Together with his wife, he owned and operated the JaVa Mobile Home Park in Bedford. Upon retiring from Howard Johnson after 40 years of service, he found joy in working at Walmart for the next eight years. Jack enjoyed the time he spent with his friends sharing a cup of coffee at McDonald's in Bedford. He also enjoyed attending auctions and adding to his collection of antique toys. **JACK GEORGE BEEGLE** (1923 – 1978) son of George and Alma (Horne) Beegle married Dorothy A. Peifer with whom he was father of (4).   **JACQUELINE BEEGLE** Fifth great granddaughter of progenitor Nicholas Kegg.

[2730] p.2 - Bedford Gazette (PA) Feb 17, 1965 [2730A] p.2 - Bedford Gazette (PA) Nov. 15, 1955 [2730B] Bedford County Historical Society (PA), book 70, page 30 obtained and contributed by D. Sue Dible [2730C] Bedford Inquirer (PA) March 27, 1998 obtained and contributed by Bob Rose [2731] Bedford Inquirer (PA) Nov 25, 1994 [2732] Bedford County Genealogical Society Bk40 p93 contributed by D. Sue Dible [2732A] Hinchliff-Pearson-West Galesburg Chapel (IL) [2733] p.28- Altoona Mirror (PA) Jan 11, 1955 [2734] Bedford Gazette (PA) Dec 23, 1970, obtained by Mary Hall Miller [2734A] Geisel Funeral Home (PA)

JAMES BEEGLE Sixth great grandson of progenitor Nicholas Kegg. **JANE MAY BEEGLE** Fifth great granddaughter of progenitor Nicholas Kegg. **JANET BEEGLE** Fifth great granddaughter of progenitor Nicholas Kegg. **JEANNE NORMA BEEGLE** [2735] (1933 – 2008) daughter of Emanuel and Grace (Diehl) Beegle married Thomas H. Lukowski with whom she was mother of (2).
JEFFREY LYNN BEEGLE [2736] (1958 – 2001) son of Stanley and Donna (Dunkle) Beegle, married Brenda S. Farrow with whom he was father of (2). Jeff was an Air Force veteran. He was employed with Eastern Communications as a tower technician. He spent most of his career with Aycock Tower Company. **JENNIFER BEEGLE** Sixth great granddaughter of progenitor Nicholas Kegg.
JODIE LYNN BEEGLE Sixth great granddaughter of progenitor Nicholas Kegg.
JOHN IRA BEEGLE [2737] (1894 – 1916) son of William and Sarah (Friedline) Beegle. John was a flagman for the railroad. **JOHNATHAN STORM BEEGLE** Eighth great grandson of progenitor Nicholas Kegg. **JORDAN BEEGLE** Seventh great granddaughter of progenitor Nicholas Kegg. **JORDAN MICHAEL BEEGLE** Sixth great grandson of progenitor Nicholas Kegg.
JOSEPH BEEGLE Sixth great grandson of progenitor Nicholas Kegg. **JOSHUA BEEGLE** aka "Josh" Seventh great grandson of progenitor Nicholas Kegg. **JOYCE DIANE BEEGLE** Sixth great granddaughter of progenitor Nicholas Kegg. **JUDITH ANN BEEGLE** aka "Judy" Fifth great granddaughter of progenitor Nicholas Kegg. **KAELEIGH BEEGLE** Seventh great granddaughter of progenitor Nicholas Kegg. **KAREN BEEGLE** Sixth great granddaughter of progenitor Nicholas Kegg. **KATHERINE MARGARET BEEGLE** Fifth great granddaughter of progenitor Nicholas Kegg. **KATHLEEN BEEGLE** Sixth great granddaughter of progenitor Nicholas Kegg.
KATHLEEN CARSON BEEGLE Sixth great granddaughter of progenitor Nicholas Kegg. **KATHRYN ODELIA BEEGLE** [2738] (1917 – 2006) daughter of George and Valera (Smith) Beegle married Thomas Andrew Christopher with whom she was mother of (6). Kathryn had been employed with Lion Manufacturing in Everett as a presser operator for more than 43 years. She enjoyed family gatherings, painting, crocheting, and quilting. **KATHY LEIGH BEEGLE** Sixth great granddaughter of progenitor Nicholas Kegg. **KENNETH M. BEEGLE** [2739] (1915 – 2002) son of Robert and Nora (Wolfe) Beegle married Margaret Pearl Koontz with whom he was father of (6). Ken was a member of St. Marks Lutheran Church where he served on the church council in various offices. He was a member and former treasurer of St. Marks Cemetery Association. He was a lifetime supporter of Bedford County dairy shows and 4H clubs. Mr. Beegle retired as a lifelong farmer. **KENNETH WILLIAM BEEGLE** [2740] (1951 – 2000) son of Donald and Eula Grace (Bennett) Beegle. Ken was a veteran having served in the Navy. He had been employed at Corrine's Beauty Salon. **KIMBERLY BEEGLE** Sixth great granddaughter of progenitor Nicholas Kegg. **KIMBERLY DAWN BEEGLE** Fifth great granddaughter of progenitor Nicholas Kegg. **LARRY R. BEEGLE** Seventh great grandson of progenitor Nicholas Kegg. **LAURA JEAN BEEGLE** [2741] (1913 – 2009) aka "Jeanne" daughter of George and Alma (Horne) Beegle married Harold W. Albright with whom she was mother of (1).
LIAM ALEX BEEGLE Eighth great grandson of progenitor Nicholas Kegg.
LINDA CAROLYN BEEGLE [2742] (1948 – 1954) daughter of Clair and Phyllis (Collins) Beegle.
LISA GAYE BEEGLE Sixth great granddaughter of progenitor Nicholas Kegg.
LOIS JANE BEEGLE [2742A] (1944 – 1988) daughter of Clarence and Mildred (Bussard) Beegle was twice married, first to Roger James Clark with whom she was mother of (1) She later married John Kidwell. Lois was employed by Faxon in Herndon, VA., as a coordinator for pre-order services.
LUTHER BEEGLE Sixth great grandson of progenitor Nicholas Kegg.
LUTHER WILLIAM BEEGLE [2743] (1910 – 1968) son of Robert and Nora (Wolfe) Beegle married Ora E. Diehl with whom he was father of (4). Luther was a farmer and trucking contractor.

[2735] Bedford Inquirer (PA) May 9, 2008, obtained by Bob Rose [2736] Savannah Morning News (GA) Sept. 24, 2001 [2737] Bedford County Genealogical Society obtained by D. Sue Dible [2738] p.3 - Bedford Inquirer (PA) Sept 22, 2006 obtained by Bob Rose [2739] Bedford Gazette (PA) Jan 21, 2002 obtained by Sheryl Kelso [2740] The Repository (Canton, OH) June 11, 2000 [2741] The Times (IN) July 20, 2009 [2742] Bedford Gazette (PA) Dec 30, 1954 [2742A]) bk 70, p85 Bedford County Historical Society obtained and contributed by D. Sue Dible [2743] Bedford County Historical Society obtained by D. Sue Dible

MABEL DE HART BEEGLE [(2744)] (1912 – 1972) daughter of Harry and Louise (Peak) Beegle married William Carl Kelso. **MABEL FLORENCE BEEGLE** [(2745)] (1918 – 1990) daughter of George and Valera (Smith) Beegle married Ralph Carlyle Wells with whom she was mother of (4).
MARIETTA BEEGLE Fifth great granddaughter of progenitor Nicholas Kegg. **MARK BEEGLE** Fifth great grandson of progenitor Nicholas Kegg. **MARK EDWARD BEEGLE** Sixth great grandson of progenitor Nicholas Kegg. **MARY ADA BEEGLE** (1918 – 1983) daughter of Edward and Flora Belle (Clark) Beegle married Leroy Fritz Bonham with whom she was mother of (1).
MARY ELIZABETH BEEGLE Fifth great granddaughter of progenitor Nicholas Kegg.
MARY ANN BEEGLE [(2745A)] (1971 – 2023) daughter of Calvin and Margaret Irene (Smith) Beegle.
MARY CHARLOTTE BEEGLE [(2746)] (1926 – 1927) daughter of Harvey and Violet (Bennett) Beegle.
MARY E. BEEGLE [(2747)] (1859 – 1923) daughter of Emanuel and Rebecca (Kegg) Beegle married Samuel Naugle with whom she was mother of (4). Her jovial disposition and hospitality won for her many friends. Mary was a member of Grange No. 698 and a charter member of Camp 134 P.O.S. of A both of Charlesville. **MARY EMMA BEEGLE** [(2747A)] (1935 – 2013) daughter of Herbert and Emma (Good) Beegle married Joseph H. Gochnour with whom she was mother of (1). Mary Emma worked at Pennwood Nursing Home for a while and also cleaned and cared for others in their home throughout the years. She enjoyed crossword puzzles, crocheting and walking her dog "Benji".
MATTHEW S. BEEGLE aka "Matt" Seventh great grandson of progenitor Nicholas Kegg.
MAYNARD SHANNON BEEGLE [(2748)] (1918 – 2002) son of Harvey and Violet (Bennett) Beegle married Catherine V. Shaffer with whom he was father of (2). Maynard was a mechanic and owner-operator at Friends Cove Garage for 54 years. He was a member of the Friends Cove United Church of Christ, the Improved Order of Redman Wambic Tribe #507, Everett, and the Bedford Moose Lodge #480.
MERTLE ELLEN BEEGLE [(2749)] (1877 – 1946) daughter of William and Sarah (Friedline) Beegle married twice, first to David Franklin Imler with whom she was mother of (1), later she married Frederick Haller. **MICHAEL BEEGLE** [(2749A)] (1950 – 2016) son of Calvin and Margaret (Smith) Beegle, married Jane Louise Kidd. Mike was employed at Everite Door Company for forty-one years until his retirement. He enjoyed woodworking, spending time with family and friends and shooting pool.
MICHAEL D. BEEGLE Fifth great grandson of progenitor Nicholas Kegg.
NANCY LOUISE BEEGLE [(2749B)] (1936 – 2011) daughter of Dale and H. Virginia (Carl) Beegle, married Bernard J. Rock with whom she was mother of (3) Nancy was a homemaker who dedicated her life to her family. **NICHOLAS BRYAN BEEGLE** Sixth great grandson of progenitor Nicholas Kegg.
NICOLE BEEGLE Sixth great granddaughter of progenitor Nicholas Kegg. **OLIVE B. BEEGLE** Fourth great granddaughter of progenitor Nicholas Kegg. **OLIVE ROMANE BEEGLE** (1884 – 1945) daughter of William and Sarah (Friedline) Beegle married twice, first to Richard R. Beckley with whom she was mother of (1). Later, she married George Terry. **PAMELA ANN BEEGLE** Fifth great granddaughter of progenitor Nicholas Kegg. **PATRICIA ANN BEEGLE** Fifth great granddaughter of progenitor Nicholas Kegg. **PATRICK BEEGLE** Sixth great grandson of progenitor Nicholas Kegg. **PAUL ALLEN BEEGLE** Sixth great grandson of progenitor Nicholas Kegg. **PAUL E. BEEGLE** Sixth great grandson of progenitor Nicholas Kegg. **PEARL MARY BEEGLE** (1918 – 1976) daughter of George and Alma (Horne) Beegle, married Eugene Peters with whom she was mother of (2).
PHILIP HAROLD BEEGLE [(2749C, 2749D)] (1924 – 2016) son of Lester and Grace (Diehl) Beegle, married Geraldine Beasley with whom he was father of (3) Philip joined the Army Air Corps and served in World War II as a Bombardier. He flew a mission on D Day in France. After the war, he completed flight training and was assigned as a pilot in the Strategic Air Command. The Army Air Corp was transferred to the newly formed US Air Force. His was the first class to graduate in the USAF, after which he was assigned to a division in charge of building the Strategic War Plan. This was in the time of the Cold War

---

[(2744)] Edmonton Journal (Alberta, Canada) Jan 7, 1972 [(2745)] p.9C- Bucks County Courier Times (PA) Jan 23, 2005 [(2745A)] Bedford Gazette (PA) Jan 13, 2023 [(2746)] The Bedford Gazette (PA) Dec 16, 1927 [(2747)] Bedford Gazette (PA) July 20 1923 [(2747A)] Akers Funeral Home (PA) [(2748)] Bedford Inquirer (PA) Sept 6, 2002 obtained by Bob Rose [(2749)] p.2- Altoona Mirror (PA) May 9, 1946 obtained by D. Sue Dible [(2749A)] Akers Funeral Home (PA) [(2749B)] Louis Geisel Funeral Home (PA) [(2749C)] "My Life...So Far" By Col. Philip H. Beegle, Sr., USAF (Ret.) [(2749D)] The Newnan Times-Herald (GA) Dec 12, 2016

and SAC kept crews on alert. He was sent to the Air War College and by the time he graduated, he was promoted to Lt. Colonel. He was put in charge of the computer division, which provided support to the war planning staff. This was to prepare him for his post-military life. In 1967, he retired from the Air Force, having risen to the rank of Colonel. He went into business in Atlanta with a former Air Force contemporary and formed NDC, National Data Corporation, the first company to have a nationwide data collection system with real time response. After retiring from that business, he formed a real estate business and sold and managed office buildings and farmland. He found a large tract of land in middle Georgia and called it 5B Ranch. He and Geri spent many happy times on "the farm". Phil enjoyed playing tennis, joining ALTA, with his daughter as his mixed-doubles partner. **PHILIP H. BEEGLE JR.** Fifth great grandson of progenitor Nicholas Kegg. **PHILIP H. BEEGLE III** Sixth great grandson of progenitor Nicholas Kegg. **PHILIP H. BEEGLE IV** Seventh great grandson of progenitor Nicholas Kegg. **PHYLLIS A. BEEGLE** [2749E] (1943 – 2022) daughter of Maynard and Catherine (Shaffer) Beegle, married Rickie L. Bollman with whom she was mother of (1). **RANDY LEE BEEGLE** Fifth great grandson of progenitor Nicholas Kegg. **RAYMOND C. BEEGLE** (1911 – 2000) son of Edward and Flora Belle (Clark) Beegle married Muriel Beverly Watson with whom he was father of (1). **RENEE BEEGLE** Eighth great granddaughter of progenitor Nicholas Kegg. **RHIANNON BEEGLE** Seventh great granddaughter of progenitor Nicholas Kegg. **RICKY EDWARD BEEGLE** Sixth great grandson of progenitor Nicholas Kegg. **ROBERT CARY BEEGLE** Fifth great grandson of progenitor Nicholas Kegg. **ROBERT LEWIS BEEGLE** [2749F] (1879 – 1947) son of George and Rebecca (Diehl) Beegle, married Nora Myrtle Wolfe with whom he was father of (4) Robert was a well-known Bedford County farmer, and member of St. Marks Lutheran church. **ROBERT LOUIS BEEGLE** (1911 – 1983) son of Edward and Flora Belle (Clark) Beegle married twice, first to Harriet Mary Brackney with whom he was father of (3), later he married Mildred M. Rose. **ROBERT LOUIS BEEGLE II** (1936 – 2010) son of Robert and Harriet (Brackney) Beegle married Eileen L. Manning with whom he was father of (2). **ROBERT LOUIS BEEGLE III** Sixth great grandson of progenitor Nicholas Kegg. **RODNEY NEAL BEEGLE** Fifth great grandson of progenitor Nicholas Kegg. **ROY E. BEEGLE** [2749G] (1941 – 2013) son of Donald and Eula (Bennett) Beegle, married Shirley Weiser with whom he was father of (3) Roy served in the United States National Guard. Roy was employed at New Enterprise Stone and Lime for more than 36 years as a superintendent until his retirement. **ROY ROBERT BEEGLE** [2750, 2751, 2752] (1890 – 1957) son of William and Sarah (Friedline) Beegle married twice, first to Sarah Jane Hall with whom he was father of (2). He married Minnie May Layton and together adopted a daughter. Roy was employed as an inspector for the B&O Railroad. **RUSSELL E. BEEGLE** Sixth great grandson of progenitor Nicholas Kegg. **RUTH ELIZABETH BEEGLE** [2752A] (1915 – 2011) daughter of Harry and Louise (Peak) Beegle, married Ellis John Stange with whom she was mother of (3). **SALLY ANN BEEGLE** [2752B] (1950 – 2011) daughter of Dale and H. Virginia (Carl) Beegle. Sally was a member of St. Mark's Church Bedford. **SAMUEL ALLEN BEEGLE** Fifth great grandson of progenitor Nicholas Kegg.
SAMUEL M. BEEGLE [2753] (1934 – 2022) son of Glenn and Mary Elizabeth (Kegg) Beegle married Mary Catherine Mowry with whom he was father of (4). Sam proudly served his country in the US Army during the Korean War. Sam worked as a Telecom Technician for Texas Eastern. He also was a part-time farmer. Sam was a real outdoorsman and enjoyed gardening. He greatly enjoyed golfing and in his spare time could be found on a golf course. Sam was a hardworking and kind man.
SANDRA MARIE BEEGLE Sixth great granddaughter of progenitor Nicholas Kegg.
SARAH BEEGLE [2754] (1852 – 1919) daughter of Emanuel and Rebecca (Kegg) Beegle married Winfield Scott Fickes with whom she was mother of (6). **SARAHANNE BEEGLE** Sixth great granddaughter of progenitor Nicholas Kegg. **SAUNDRA LEE BEEGLE** [2754A] (1941 – 1995) adopted

---

[2749E] Bedford Gazette (PA) July 20, 2022 obtained by Bob Rose [2749F] Bedford Gazette (PA) May 15, 1947 contributed by Bob Rose Obtained by thedetars@comcast.net [2749G] Bedford Gazette (PA) Jan 24, 2013 obtained and contributed by Bob Rose [2750] p.12 – Bedford Gazette (PA) July 13, 1972 [2751] Bedford County Historical Society bk134p3 obtained by D. Sue Dible [2752] Bedford Gazette (PA) Jan 21, 1944 [2752A] Wombold Family Funeral Homes Wetaskiwin, Alberta, Canada [2752B] Louis Geisel Funeral Home (PA) [2753] Bedford Gazette (PA) March 7, 2022 [2754] Bedford Gazette (PA) Feb 7, 1919 [2754A] Bedford Inquirer (PA) May 9, 1995, obtained and contributed by Duke Clark

daughter of Roy and Minnie May (Layton) Beegle, married William R. Smith. Saundra was a member of the Bedford Lodge Women of the Moose, was the previous owner and operator of Jim's Sandwich Shop and was a licensed pilot. **SCOTT ALAN BEEGLE** Sixth great grandson of progenitor Nicholas Kegg. **SHANE F. BEEGLE** Sixth great grandson of progenitor Nicholas Kegg. **SHANNON B. BEEGLE** [2755] (1886 – 1951) son of Emanuel and Rebecca (Kegg) Beegle married Mary Catherine Smouse with whom he was father of (3). Shannon was a well-known retired lumber dealer and farmer of Friends Cove. **STACIE ELIZABETH BEEGLE** Sixth great granddaughter of progenitor Nicholas Kegg. **STANLEY ROBERT BEEGLE** [2755A] (1938 -2008) son of Kenneth and Margaret (Koontz) Beegle, married Donna Lee Dunkle with whom he was father of (3) Stanley served in the U.S. Army for two years. One of his greatest hobbies was attending his grandchildren's sporting events. **STEPHANIE LYNN BEEGLE** Sixth great granddaughter of progenitor Nicholas Kegg. **STEPHEN BEEGLE** Sixth great grandson of progenitor Nicholas Kegg. **STEPHEN KENNETH BEEGLE** Fifth great grandson of progenitor Nicholas Kegg. **STEVE BEEGLE** Eighth great grandson of progenitor Nicholas Kegg. **STEVEN BEEGLE** Seventh great grandson of progenitor Nicholas Kegg. **STEVEN BEEGLE** Fifth great grandson of progenitor Nicholas Kegg. **SUSAN BEEGLE** Fifth great granddaughter of progenitor Nicholas Kegg. **TARA JAYNE BEEGLE** Eighth great granddaughter of progenitor Nicholas Kegg. **TERRI LYNNE BEEGLE** Sixth great granddaughter of progenitor Nicholas Kegg. **TERRY BEEGLE** Sixth great grandson of progenitor Nicholas Kegg. **THEODORE BEEGLE** Fourth great grandson of progenitor Nicholas Kegg. **TIARRA BEEGLE** Sixth great granddaughter of progenitor Nicholas Kegg. **TIMOTHY ALAN BEEGLE** (1943 – 1966) son of William and Barbara (Barnes) Beegle. **TRICIA SUZANNE BEEGLE** Sixth great granddaughter of progenitor Nicholas Kegg. **TRISTAN MATTHEW BEEGLE** Seventh great grandson of progenitor Nicholas Kegg. **VANESSA NOELLE BEEGLE** Sixth great granddaughter of progenitor Nicholas Kegg. **VICKI BEEGLE** Fifth great granddaughter of progenitor Nicholas Kegg. **VIOLET GRACE BEEGLE** [2755B] (1903 – 2000) daughter of Robert and Nora (Wolfe) Beegle, married Joseph Earl Hunt with whom she was mother of (2). Grace worked at G.C. Murphy in Everett and as a waitress at Howard Johnson's at South Midway. **WALTER HEWITT BEEGLE** [2756] (1882 – 1899) son of Isaiah and Sarah (Smouse) Beegle. Walter was a boy of good moral principles, kindhearted and industrious and highly respected by all who knew him. **WALTER K. BEEGLE** [2757] (1922 – 2007) son of Harry and Louise (Peak) Beegle. **WANDA JANE BEEGLE** Fifth great granddaughter of progenitor Nicholas Kegg. **WANETTA SUE BEEGLE** Sixth great granddaughter of progenitor Nicholas Kegg. **WILLIAM BEEGLE JR.** [2758] (1928 – 1994) son of William and Ida Grace (Zinn) Beegle married Evelyn Eloise Young with whom he was father of (2). **WILLIAM F. BEEGLE** [2759] (1854 – 1902) son of Emanuel and Rebecca (Kegg) Beegle married Sarah Friedline with whom he was father of (8). In 1892 William went to Hollidaysburg and while there joined Company C., Fifth regiment, National Guard of Pennsylvania. He remained one year at Hollidaysburg and moved from that place to Westmoreland County. He was employed at the steel works at Ligonier for two tears. He then returned to Friends Cove and engaged in farming. William was an industrious, honest and upright man and had a large circle of friends. **WILLIAM FRANK BEEGLE** [2760] (1907 – 1972) son of Roy and Sarah Jane (Hall) Beegle married Gussie Viola Foor with whom he was father of (2). **WILLIAM H. BEEGLE** (1909 – 1960) son of Edward and Flora Belle (Clark) Beegle married Dorothy Mae Barnes with whom he was father of (1). **WILLIAM ROYDEN BEEGLE** [2761] (1883 – 1955) son of George and Rebecca (Diehl) Beegle, married Ida Grace Zinn with whom he was father of (1).

[2755] The Bedford Gazette (PA) Aug 6, 1951 [2755A] p.3 - Bedford Inquirer (PA) May 30, 2008 [2755B] Bedford County Historical Society obtained and contributed by D. Sue Dible [2756] Bedford Gazette (PA) Jan 5, 1900 [2757] p.3 - Bedford Inquirer (PA) July 13, 2007 obtained by Bob Rose [2758] Arizona Republic (AZ) Aug 20, 1994 [2759] Bedford Gazette (PA) Dec 5, 1902 [2760] p4 Bedford Gazette (PA) June 27, 1930 [2761] Arizona Daily Star (Tucson, AZ) April 19, 1955

BEEM

BESSIE LEAH BEEM [2762] (1902 – 1984) daughter of Carroll and Bessie (Snavely) Beem married twice, first to Ernest Jennings Christiansen with whom she was mother of (1). Later she married Frank E. Hawkins.   **BURTON CARROLL BEEM** Fifth great grandson of progenitor Nicholas Kegg. **GEORGE CARROLL MCCLELLAN BEEM** (1899 – 1944) aka "Carroll" son of Carroll and Bessie (Snavely) Beem married Emma Caroline Root with whom he was father of (2).
JESSIE MARGARET BEEM [2763] (1893 - 1981) daughter of Carroll and Bessie (Snavely) Beem, married Ralph Leroy Jones. Jessie was a member of the G.A.R. Auxiliary, Eastern Star, White Shrine, Veterans of Foreign Wars Auxiliary and American Legion Auxiliary.   **KENT DOUGLAS BEEN** Sixth great grandson of progenitor Nicholas Kegg.   **MARILYN JANICE BEEM** [2764] (1932 – 1980) daughter of George and Emma (Root) Beem, married Lowell Adolph Trede.

BEEMAN

JAMES BEEMAN Fifth great grandson of progenitor Nicholas Kegg.
META BEEMAN Fifth great granddaughter of progenitor Nicholas Kegg.

BEEMILLER

CHAD R. BEEMILLER Fifth great grandson of progenitor Nicholas Kegg.
MATTHEW BEEMILLER Sixth great grandson of progenitor Nicholas Kegg.

BEEN

AMY BEEN Seventh great granddaughter of progenitor Nicholas Kegg.   **JAMES MARVIN BEEN** (1915 – 1917) son of William Harley and Leona (Saltzman) Been.   **JONEL BEEN** Sixth great granddaughter of progenitor Nicholas Kegg.   **LAURA J. BEEN** Sixth great granddaughter of progenitor Nicholas Kegg.   **MAC SALTZMAN BEEN** [2764A] (1919 – 2000) son of Harley and Leona (Saltzman) Been, married Nila Kitchen with whom he was father of (3). Mac worked for the City of Goodland for 25 years as an electrical lineman. He was a Sunday school teacher, 4-H leader and Little League coach. Mac was a member of the United Methodist Church in Goodland and had been a member of the Elks Lodge, Veterans of Foreign Wars and Lions Club.   **MARDELL EVA BEEN** [2764B] (1925 – 2010) daughter of Harley and Leona (Saltzman) Been, married Donald Donner with whom she was mother of (1). Mardell loved to crochet afghans and give them to hospitals, teachers, and POW organizations. She was an avid crafter. Nothing was more important to her than the time she spent with her great-grandchildren.   **MARGARET ELNORE BEEN** [2764C] (1916 – 2004) daughter of Harley and Leona (Saltzman) Been, married Charles Dutton with whom she was mother of (3) Margaret spent many hours working with her hands making crafts which she shared with family and friends. Among her many attributes she had a listening ear and a loving heart.   **MARILYN ELOISE BEEN** [2765] (1923 – 1999) daughter of William Harley and Leona (Saltzman) Been married Max H. Tindle with whom she was mother of (2). Marilyn was owner of her own beauty shop.   **MARK EMERY BEEN** [2766] (1918 – 2001) son of William Harley and Leona (Saltzman) Been, married Lillian. Mark was a retired watchmaker and a Navy veteran of World War II.   **MARRABELL EDNA BEEN** [2766A] (1921 – 2013) daughter of Harley and Leona (Saltzman) Been, married Lawrence Schulz with whom she was mother of (2) Marrabell was a member of the American Legion Auxiliary and VFW Auxiliary, Beautiful Savior

---

[2762] p.20- Des Moines Register Dec 7, 1955 [2763] Des Moines Tribune (IA) Jan 14, 1981 [2764] p7 Des Moines Register (IA) Sep 23, 1980 [2764A] The Goodland Daily News (KS) Dec 15, 2000 obtained and contributed by D. Sue Dible [2764B] Augusta Chronicle (GA) July 4, 2010 [2764C] Roland Funeral Home (IA) [2765] Lenox Time Table (IA) March 10, 1999 [2766] St. Petersburg Times (FL) Feb 26, 2001 [2766A] Corvallis Gazette-Times (OR) March 3, 2013

Lutheran in Lebanon and Family of Christ Lutheran Church in Vancouver. Marrabell loved to crochet and made afghans for everyone. She enjoyed patio gardens. She loved to cook and enjoyed anything tasty. **MAUDEENE ELIZABETH BEEN** [2766B] (1920 – 2013) daughter of Harley and Leona (Saltzman) Been, married Charles Oliver Swinehart with whom she was mother of (2) Maudeene worked as a mail clerk for the State of Iowa until retirement. She also enjoyed cooking, dancing, crocheting, crafting and spending time with her family. **MELODY BEEN** Sixth great granddaughter of progenitor Nicholas Kegg. **MERLE C BEEN** [2766C] (1933 – 2005) son of Harley and Leona (Saltzman) Been, married Doris Johnson with whom he was father of (3) Merle entered the armed forces during the Korean conflict. After service, Merle entered into various positions in Des Moines related to the printing industry, until he decided to "venture" off and start his own printing career. In 1965 he purchased the Town & Country Advertiser of Wesley, Iowa and started The Reminder in Belmond, this led to the beginning of Printing Services Inc. One of Merle's favorite mottos was "Nothing Ventured, Nothing Gained" as was evident throughout his life. Merle enjoyed being a part of and serving his community. A member of the Midwest Free Community Papers, where he served as board member and treasurer for over twenty-seven years. Through this organization he was honored with the highest award, Past Presidential Memorial Award and was honored with a Merle C. Been night, where he was given an annual scholarship to be awarded in his name. Over the years Merle helped many people get started in ventures of their own and will be missed as a mentor and contributor to the community. **MILO HARLEY BEEN** [2766D] (1929 – 2017) son of Harley and Leona (Saltzman) Been, married Naomi Minnick with whom he was father of (1) Milo worked for Firestone Retread Plant in Des Moines as a Plant Manager until his retirement Milo's most favorite pastime of all was the planning and travelling with family and friends. Mention where you might be heading and Milo would have instructions and mileage for you in a minute, with the help of his favorite book, "The Road Atlas!" Everyone enjoyed Milo's "bringing to life" the stories of their adventures. No way can we not mention his love of his computer. This little technological wonder enabled Milo to send humorous stories and jokes to everyone. **NEAL JAMES BEEN** (1959 – 1977) son of Mac and Nila (Kitchen) Been. **RODNEY BEEN** Sixth great grandson of progenitor Nicholas Kegg. **STEVEN MICHAEL BEEN** Sixth great grandson of progenitor Nicholas Kegg.

BEHRENDS

MARIAH BEHRENDS Seventh great granddaughter of progenitor Nicholas Kegg.
SARAH BEHRENDS Seventh great granddaughter of progenitor Nicholas Kegg.

BELCHER

GERALD EUGENE BELCHER 5th great grandson of progenitor Nicholas Kegg.
GERALD EUGENE BELCHER JR. Sixth great grandson of progenitor Nicholas Kegg.
JAMIE LYNN BELCHER Sixth great granddaughter of progenitor Nicholas Kegg.
JASON S. BELCHER Sixth great grandson of progenitor Nicholas Kegg. **JONATHAN MICHAEL BELCHER** Sixth great grandson of progenitor Nicholas Kegg. **LEXI MAE BELCHER** Seventh great granddaughter of progenitor Nicholas Kegg. **PAIGE LEE ANN BELCHER** Seventh great granddaughter of progenitor Nicholas Kegg. **PATRICIA A. BELCHER** [2766E] (1964 – 2010) daughter of Timothy and Barbara (Kegg) Belcher was twice married, first to Anthony Wade Oyler with whom she was mother of (1), later she married Daniel Warner with whom she was mother of (3).
TIMOTHY BELCHER Sixth great grandson of progenitor Nicholas Kegg.

[2766B] Des Moines Register (IA) July 19, 2013 [2766C] p24 Des Moines Register (IA) May 12, 2005 [2766D] Des Moines Register (IA) Sept. 1, 2017, obtained and contributed by D. Sue Dible [2766E] Raven-Choate Funeral Home (IN)

BELEW

MADELINE BELEW Seventh great granddaughter of progenitor Nicholas Kegg.
ROLAND BELEW Seventh great grandson of progenitor Nicholas Kegg.

BELKEN

KAYLA MARIE BELKEN Seventh great grandchild of progenitor Nicholas Kegg.
KRISTINA A. BELKEN Seventh great granddaughter of progenitor Nicholas Kegg.

BELKNAP

DONALD GERALD BELKNAP Sixth great grandson of progenitor Nicholas Kegg. **JENNIFER ROSE BELKNAP** Seventh great granddaughter of progenitor Nicholas Kegg. **JESSICA GRACE BELKNAP** Seventh great granddaughter of progenitor Nicholas Kegg. **JOHN ROBERT BELKNAP** Seventh great grandson of progenitor Nicholas Kegg. **JUDITH ANN BELKNAP** Sixth great granddaughter of progenitor Nicholas Kegg. **MARY KATHRYN BELKNAP** Sixth great granddaughter of progenitor Nicholas Kegg. **ROBERT E. BELKNAP JR.** Sixth great grandson of progenitor Nicholas Kegg. **ROBERT EMMETT BELKNAP** [2767] (1931 – 1981) son of Raymond and Ruth (Gump) Belknap, married Bennie Fazzino with whom he was father of (4). Robert was head accountant for the city Treasurer's Office, a member of the Tom Dooley Knights of Columbus Council 5492, of St. Gemma Catholic Church's education committee and of the board of directors of St. Gemma's men's club, and vice-president of St. Gemma's credit union. He also was a board member of the Parent-Teacher TV A 124 Association at Bishop Borgess High School and a member of the alumni association of Sam Houston State University, Huntsville, Tex.

BELL

BREANNA KEGGS BELL Sixth great granddaughter of progenitor Nicholas Kegg.
BRITTANY KEGGS BELL Sixth great granddaughter of progenitor Nicholas Kegg. **CHAD BELL** Fourth great grandson of progenitor Nicholas Kegg. **CHRISTIAN BELL/BEEMER** Seventh great grandson of progenitor Nicholas Kegg. **DANIEL LEE BELL** Seventh great grandson of progenitor Nicholas Kegg. **DAVID A BELL** Seventh great grandson of progenitor Nicholas Kegg.
DAVID C BELL Sixth great grandson of progenitor Nicholas Kegg. **DAVID D. BELL** Third great grandson of progenitor Nicholas Kegg. **DONALD S. BELL** Third great grandson of progenitor Nicholas Kegg. **ELAINE ALMA BELL** Third great granddaughter of progenitor Nicholas Kegg.
GILBERT EUGENE BELL Fifth great grandson of progenitor Nicholas Kegg.
JAMES MICHAEL BELL, aka "Mike" Sixth great grandson of progenitor Nicholas Kegg.
JARRETT BELL Fourth great grandson of progenitor Nicholas Kegg. **JENNIFER BELL** Sixth great granddaughter of progenitor Nicholas Kegg. **JERRY LEE BELL** [2767A] (1931 – 2018) son of Lee and Ruth (Karns) Bell married Mary Ann Baker with whom he was father of (2) His life was simple but extraordinary, revealed through his leadership in youth groups, singles ministries, scout troops, non-profit organizations, and his local church. A career with the former Southwestern Bell Telephone Co., and AT&T would lead to 18 moves across Oklahoma, New York City, and New Jersey. When working in New York in the 1960's the Wall Street Journal wrote a feature article about Jerry and the changes he experienced moving from Oklahoma to one of the largest cities in the world. He retired from a corporate career in his mid-fifties, joining Scope Ministries where he worked as a counselor for another 28 years.
JESSICA BELL Seventh great granddaughter of progenitor Nicholas Kegg. **JESSICA ANN BELL** Seventh great granddaughter of progenitor Nicholas Kegg.

[2767] p7 Detroit Free Press (MI) Oct 30, 1981 [2767A] Mercer-Adams Funeral Home (OK)

JULIANNE BELL Sixth great granddaughter of progenitor Nicholas Kegg.
MATTHEW WARREN BELL Seventh great grandson of progenitor Nicholas Kegg.
PIERSON MICHAEL BELL Seventh great grandson of progenitor Nicholas Kegg.
TIMOTHY LEE BELL aka "Tim" Sixth great grandson of progenitor Nicholas Kegg. **URIAH BELL** Seventh great grandson of progenitor Nicholas Kegg. **URIETTA ANN BELL** Sixth great granddaughter of progenitor Nicholas Kegg. **WINIESHA PATRIECE BELL** Seventh great granddaughter of progenitor Nicholas Kegg.

BELT

JAMES RUSSELL BELT Sixth great grandson of progenitor Nicholas Kegg. **JANE BELT** Sixth great granddaughter of progenitor Nicholas Kegg. **JENNIFER LEE BELT** Sixth great granddaughter of progenitor Nicholas Kegg. **JUDITH ELIZABETH BELT**, aka "Judy" Sixth great granddaughter of progenitor Nicholas Kegg.

BELTZ

DALE LELAND BELTZ Fourth great grandson of progenitor Nicholas Kegg.
JOE LELAND BELTZ Fifth great grandson of progenitor Nicholas Kegg.

BENEFIELD

ALLISON PAIGE BENEFIELD Seventh great granddaughter of progenitor Nicholas Kegg.
DEBORAH JANE BENEFIELD Sixth great granddaughter of progenitor Nicholas Kegg.
INFANT TWINS BENEFIELD (1977 – 1977) children of Martin and Patricia (Beeber) Benefield.
JUSTIN BENEFIELD Seventh great grandson of progenitor Nicholas Kegg.
MARTIN W. BENEFIELD aka "Marty" Sixth great grandson of progenitor Nicholas Kegg.
PATRICK JAMES BENEFIELD Seventh great grandson of progenitor Nicholas Kegg.

BENEIGH

CONNIE BENEIGH [2767B] (1945 – 2017) daughter of Julius and Rosann (Grier) Beneigh, married Roger P. Schwab with whom she was mother of (2). **JUDITH ANN BENEIGH** Fifth great granddaughter of progenitor Nicholas Kegg. **JULIUS ARTHUR BENEIGH** (1909 – 1968) son of William and Minnie (Turner) Beneigh married twice, first to Ruth Baumgardner and later, to Rosann Grier with whom he was father of (3). **THELMA DARLENE BENEIGH** Fifth great granddaughter of progenitor Nicholas Kegg.

BENGE

CAROLYN SUZANNE BENGE [2767C] (1955 – 2010) daughter of Frank and Peggy (Fredrick) Benge married Don Burrell with whom she was mother of (2) Carolyn was a long-time violinist in the orchestras of Houston First Baptist Church and the Lake Charles Symphony, violinist & vocalist in The Daystar Project, as well as teaching and playing in many local orchestras and other musical organizations.
FRANK STEVEN BENGE Fifth great grandson of progenitor Nicholas Kegg.
JORDON BENGE Sixth great grandson of progenitor Nicholas Kegg.

[2767B] Tribune-Democrat (Johnstown, PA) Dec 11, 2017 [2767C] Woodlawn Funeral Home (TX)

BENNETT

ALYSSA RENEE CARROLL BENNETT Eighth great granddaughter of progenitor Nicholas Kegg.
ASHLEY BENNETT Seventh great granddaughter of progenitor Nicholas Kegg.
BEVERLY BENNETT Sixth great granddaughter of progenitor Nicholas Kegg.
CATHERINE LYNN BENNETT Sixth great granddaughter of progenitor Nicholas Kegg.
CHASE JORDAN BENNETT Seventh great grandson of progenitor Nicholas Kegg.
CHRISTINE LOUISE BENNETT Sixth great granddaughter of progenitor Nicholas Kegg.
DEANNA BENNETT Fifth great granddaughter of progenitor Nicholas Kegg.
EDWARD MARTIN JAY BENNETT Sixth great grandson of progenitor Nicholas Kegg.
EMMA BENNETT Eighth great granddaughter of progenitor Nicholas Kegg.
ERIN BENNETT Seventh great granddaughter of progenitor Nicholas Kegg. **EVONNE BENNETT** Seventh great granddaughter of progenitor Nicholas Kegg. **JEFF A. BENNETT** Sixth great grandson of progenitor Nicholas Kegg. **JOHN MARK BENNETT III** [2767D] (1967 – 1985) son of John and Darlene (Hipp) Bennett, a senior at Johnstown Area Vo-Tech. Member of First Lutheran Church, Johnstown **KEEGAN BENNETT** Seventh great grandson of progenitor Nicholas Kegg.
KELCIE BENNETT Sixth great granddaughter of progenitor Nicholas Kegg.
LARRY C. BENNETT Sixth great grandson of progenitor Nicholas Kegg. **LEXI BENNETT** Eighth great granddaughter of progenitor Nicholas Kegg. **MIKEY BENNETT** Seventh great grandson of progenitor Nicholas Kegg. **PHILLIP BENNETT** Sixth great grandson of progenitor Nicholas Kegg. **RICHARD BENNETT** Sixth great grandson of progenitor Nicholas Kegg. **TARAH BENNETT** Seventh great granddaughter of progenitor Nicholas Kegg.

BENSON

JEFF BENSON Sixth great grandson of progenitor Nicholas Kegg.
SCOTT BENSON Sixth great grandson of progenitor Nicholas Kegg.

BENTON

ANDREW PAUL BENTON Seventh great grandson of progenitor Nicholas Kegg.

BENTZ

DANIEL BENTZ Sixth great grandson of progenitor Nicholas Kegg.
JACK BENTZ Sixth great grandson of progenitor Nicholas Kegg.

BEQUEATH

CARLA SUE BEQUEATH Sixth great granddaughter of progenitor Nicholas Kegg.
ELTON MARSHALL BEQUEATH [2768] (1917 – 2003) son of Marshall and Naomi (Hockenberry) Bequeath married Helen R. Weight with whom he was father of (1). Elton served in the United State Marine Corps during World War II as a Private First Class, working as a mechanic. Previously, he was employed at the Earlston Planing Mill for 31 years, and then was employed at Everett Hardwood Lumber for 19 years until retiring. Elton enjoyed woodworking and gardening. **ELTON M. BEQUEATH** [2768A] aka "Sonny" (1938 – 2011) son of Elton and Helen (Weight) Bequeath, married Helen Deanne Keebaugh with whom he was father of (3). Sonny proudly served full time at the Dorseyville missile site and retired from the Army National Guard after 42 years of service. He worked as a dispatcher and

---

[2767D] Johnstown Tribune-Democrat (PA) Jan 2, 1986, obtained by D. Sue Dible [2768] Bedford Inquirer (PA) July 25, 2003, obtained by Bob Rose [2768A] Fox Funeral Home (Saxonburg, PA)

mechanic for the Kenneth E. Bauman Bus Co. He retired from Wayne Sell Trucking, where he was a diesel mechanic. Sonny enjoyed hunting, woodworking, watching football, NASCAR and listening to classical music. **REBECCA A. BEQUEATH** aka "Becky", Sixth great granddaughter of progenitor Nicholas Kegg. **ROBIN BEQUEATH** Sixth great granddaughter of progenitor Nicholas Kegg.

BERGEMAN

DOROTHY BERGEMAN [2768B] (1916 – 2003) daughter of Samuel and Leapha (Thompson) Bergeman, married Stanley Walgast Morgan. **NINA E. BERGEMAN** [2769] (1913 – 2006) daughter of Samuel and Leapha (Thompson) Bergeman, married Daniel Wesley Roberts with whom she was mother of (3).

BERGSTEIN

ANDREW T. BERGSTEIN Fifth great grandson of progenitor Nicholas Kegg. **NAN REED BERGSTEIN** [2770] (1961 – 1997) daughter of Milton and Elizabeth (Reed) Bergstein. Nan enjoyed singing in the choir and reading to others. She also worked at the Copper Tree Work Center at Martha Lloyd.

BERGSTROM

HEZEKIAH BERGSTROM Seventh great grandson of progenitor Nicholas Kegg.
MATTHIAS BERGSTROM Seventh great grandson of progenitor Nicholas Kegg.

BERKEBILE

JEFFREY ALLEN BERKEBILE Sixth great grandson of progenitor Nicholas Kegg.
JENNIFER BERKEBILE Seventh great granddaughter of progenitor Nicholas Kegg.
JOHN ABRAHAM BERKEBILE Fifth great grandson of progenitor Nicholas Kegg.
MADISON ANNE BERKEBILE Seventh great granddaughter of progenitor Nicholas Kegg.
MARIANN BERKEBILE Fifth great granddaughter of progenitor Nicholas Kegg.
WILLARD W. BERKEBILE Fifth great grandson of progenitor Nicholas Kegg.

BERKEBILL

SHANNON BERKEBILL Seventh great granddaughter of progenitor Nicholas Kegg.

BERKEY

HELEN BERKEY Fifth great granddaughter of progenitor Nicholas Kegg. **LINDA BERKEY** Fifth great granddaughter of progenitor Nicholas Kegg. **ROBERT WILSON BERKEY** (1923 – 1975) son of Robert and Geneva (Kerr) Berkey. **SALLY BERKEY** Fifth great granddaughter of progenitor Nicholas Kegg. **WILLIAM GRANT BERKEY** [2771] (1922 – 2002) aka "Red", son of Robert and Geneva (Kerr) Berkey married twice, first to Anna C. Kasper with whom he was father of (3). Later, he married Mildred Buchanan. Red was a World War II Army veteran. He retired from Bethlehem Steel, Johnstown.

[2768B] Arizona Republic (AZ) May 30, 2003 [2769] Denver Post (CO) Oct. 17, 2006 [2770] www.joycetice.com/clippings/tcobit97.htm [2771] Daily American (PA) Nov 25, 2002 Meyersdale Library obtained by Patty Millich

BERKHEIMER

DAVID LEON BERKHEIMER [2771A] (1942 – 1967) son of Samuel and Violet (Foor) Berkheimer, married Fern J. Patterson. **DONNA LOUISE BERKHEIMER** [2771B] aka "Skip" (1932 – 2001) daughter of Samuel and Violet (Foor) Berkheimer, married Albert O'Dellick with whom she was mother of (1). Skip worked as a cutter at the Altoona Shoe Company, then as a receptionist for Drs. Rosch and Kron and finally as a cashier for BiLo Foods, Orchard Plaza until she retired. She enjoyed collecting panda bears, crafts and spending time with her grandchildren. **HAROLD LEWIS BERKHEIMER** [2771C] (1929 – 1963) son of Samuel and Violet (Foor) Berkheimer, married Betty Hammel with whom he was father of (3) was employed as a machinist at the westbound repair yards of the Pennsylvania Railroad. Mr. Berkheimer was a veteran of the Korean War, a member of the Duncansville V.F.W., Hollidaysburg American Legion and of the Lutheran faith. **JOY BERKHEIMER** Sixth great granddaughter of progenitor Nicholas Kegg. **LINDA SUE BERKHEIMER** [2772] (1954 – 2005) daughter of Harold and Betty (Hammel) Berkheimer was mother of (2). Linda Sue was employed with Employment Security Commission. **MILDRED IRENE BERKHEIMER** [2772A] aka "Midge" (1931 – 2018) daughter of Samuel and Violet (Foor) Berkheimer, married Joe Floyd Davis with whom she was mother of (2) Midge was Co-Owner and Co-Operator of Davis Hardware in Camp Hill for many years. She was also a sports fanatic who played basketball and softball for the Air Force. She was a member of Camp Hill United Methodist Church. **RUBY REBECCA BERKHEIMER** [2773] (1935 – 2020) daughter of Samuel and Violet (Foor) Berkheimer married Thomas R. Strayer with whom she was mother of (2). Ruby retired as a machine operator from Cove Shoe. She enjoyed playing cards and her animals. **SAMUEL BERKHEIMER** Sixth great grandson of progenitor Nicholas Kegg. **SAMUEL T. BERKHEIMER** [2774] (1905 – 1979) son of Ira and Anna (Naugle) Berkheimer married Violet V. Foor with whom he was father of (5). Samuel retired as a car repairman from the Pennsylvania Railroad. He was a life member of the Transport Workers Union.

BERNARD

CODY BERNARD Seventh great grandson of progenitor Nicholas Kegg. **KATHRYN BERNARD** aka "Kathy" Sixth great granddaughter of progenitor Nicholas Kegg. **KORY E. BERNARD** Sixth great grandson of progenitor Nicholas Kegg. **ZACHARY BERNARD** Seventh great grandson of progenitor Nicholas Kegg.

BERNARDS

ANTHONY EBVERETT BERNARDS aka "Tony" Sixth great grandson of progenitor Nicholas Kegg.
DONNA BERNARDS Sixth great granddaughter of progenitor Nicholas Kegg.
IVAN EMIL BERNARDS JR. Sixth great grandson of progenitor Nicholas Kegg.

BERNAS

PAIGE BERNAS Eighth great granddaughter of progenitor Nicholas Kegg.

[2771A] Altoona Mirrror (PA) Aug 9, 1967 [2771B] p.6 – Altoona Mirror (PA) Jan 14, 2001 [2771C] Altoona Mirror (PA) Aug. 31, 1963 [2772] South Carolina Obituary and Death Notice Archive - Page 266 [2772A] Jeff Coat Trant Funeral Home (AL) [2773] Leslie Miller Funeral Home (PA) contributed by D. Sue Dible [2774] Bedford County Genealogical Society BK1 p351, obtained by D. Sue Dible

BERNAT

BRENDA LOUISE BERNAT aka "Bibi" Sixth great granddaughter of progenitor Nicholas Kegg.
JUNE ELIZABETH BERNAT aka "Betsy", Sixth great granddaughter of progenitor Nicholas Kegg.
REBECCA LYNN BERNAT Sixth great granddaughter of progenitor Nicholas Kegg.

BERNET

DANIEL CHRISTIAN BERNET Sixth great grandson of progenitor Nicholas Kegg.
JEANNINE LAUREN BERNET Sixth great granddaughter of progenitor Nicholas Kegg.
KIMBERLY JORDAN BERNET Sixth great granddaughter of progenitor Nicholas Kegg.

BEROLO

DEBORAH JEAN BEROLO (1952 – 1983) daughter of Angelo and Florence Belle (Schoepflin) Berolo married twice, first to Mark G. Marquard and later to Billy James Seabourn.
MICHAEL ANGELO BEROLO (1953 – 1953) son of Angelo and Florence Belle (Schoepflin) Berolo.

BERRY

ALFRED LLOYD BERRY (1958 – 1991) son of William and Rose (Warneke) Berry.
B. BRADLEY BERRY Sixth great grandson of progenitor Nicholas Kegg.
CHRISTIAN EVAN BERRY Eighth great grandson of progenitor Nicholas Kegg.
DENISE IRENE BERRY (1963 – 1982) daughter of William and Rose (Warneke) Berry.
DIANE KAY BERRY Sixth great granddaughter of progenitor Nicholas Kegg.
DONALD DOUGLAS BERRY Sixth great grandson of progenitor Nicholas Kegg.
EDWARD ALLEN BERRY Sixth great grandson of progenitor Nicholas Kegg.
GEORGE PATRICK BERRY Fifth great grandson of progenitor Nicholas Kegg.
HAROLD DEAN BERRY Fifth great grandson of progenitor Nicholas Kegg.
HOWARD GENE BERRY (1955 – 2011) son of Alpha Andrew and Ellen Alice (Williams) Berry.
HUNTER MARIE BERRY Eighth great granddaughter of progenitor Nicholas Kegg.
IVAN EUGENE BERRY (1935 – 1991) son of William and Dorotha (Abbott) Berry, married Wilma Elaine Scott with whom he was father of (1). **JOYCE CAROLYN BERRY** Fifth great granddaughter of progenitor Nicholas Kegg. **KRISTINE LEE BERRY** Sixth great granddaughter of progenitor Nicholas Kegg. **LINDA JEAN BERRY** (1953 – 2016) daughter of Alpha and Ellen (Williams) Berry married Karl Joseph Trimble Hopkins. **LINDA LOU BERRY** Fifth great granddaughter of progenitor Nicholas Kegg. **LYDIA A. BERRY** Fifth great granddaughter of progenitor Nicholas Kegg.
MARVIN LEROY BERRY [2774A] (1938 – 2018) son of William and Dorotha (Abbott) Berry, married Theresa Ann Warneke with whom he was father of (4) Marvin was an avid sports fan and continued attending games throughout his life. Marvin was always a hard worker. He hauled canned milk to local creameries in his youth. He drove transit bus in Minneapolis and school bus in Isle for quite some time. Marvin loved to spend his summers traveling with carnivals where he spent many years working on different rides and doing electric work. He also drove for Anderson Trucking Service and earned driver of the year with his wife Theresa. He greatly enjoyed working with his hands and riding the snowmobile.
RAYMOND ANDY BERRY Fifth great grandson of progenitor Nicholas Kegg.
ROBERT RANDOLPH BERRY Sixth great grandson of progenitor Nicholas Kegg.
ROGER ELTON BERRY (1968 – 1968) son of William and Rose (Warneke) Berry.
ROY MARVIN BERRY Sixth great grandson of progenitor Nicholas Kegg.
VICKY LYNN BERRY Sixth great granddaughter of progenitor Nicholas Kegg.

[2774A] MilleLacs Messenger (MN) March 27, 2018

WILLIAM ANDREW BERRY Sixth great grandson of progenitor Nicholas Kegg.
WILLIAM ELTON BERRY JR. (1940 – 1979) aka "Billy" son of William and Dorotha (Abbott) Berry married Rose M. Warneke with whom he was father of (2). An Army veteran, Billy served in Vietnam.

BEST

ELLIOT BEST Seventh great grandson of progenitor Nicholas Kegg. **HENRY BEST** Seventh great grandson of progenitor Nicholas Kegg. **TRISH BEST** Seventh great granddaughter of progenitor Nicholas Kegg.

BETSWORTH

DORIS J. BETSWORTH Fifth great granddaughter of progenitor Nicholas Kegg.
ELLA MAE BETSWORTH [2775] (1924 – 2001) daughter OF James and Mary (Rice) Betsworth married Holmer Guy Parrish with whom she was mother of (2). **EUGENE ROBERT BETSWORTH** [2775A] (1921 – 1988) son of James and Mary (Rice) Betsworth, married Virginia Mally with whom he was father of (4); Eugene was on duty at the naval air station at Pearl Harbor when the Japanese attacked December 7, 1941, the navy storekeeper first class survived. **JOANNE BETSWORTH** Fifth great granddaughter of progenitor Nicholas Kegg. **KATHY BETSWORTH** Fifth great granddaughter of progenitor Nicholas Kegg. **MARGARET ALICE BETSWORTH** [2775B] (1922 – 2007) daughter of James and Mary (Rice) Betsworth, married John Harding with whom she was mother of (2). Margaret was a registered nurse having served in the Army Nurse Corps. Her nursing career took her to Virginia Mason Hospital and then on to Swedish Hospital, where she worked until retirement. She was active as a troop leader with the Girl Scouts, and later in life became an avid sports fan, supporting the Seattle teams. In addition, she spent many hours knitting, quilting, reading mysteries, and doing crossword puzzles.
ROBERT L. BETSWORTH Fifth great grandson of progenitor Nicholas Kegg.

BETTS

CAROL ANN BETTS [2776] (1953 – 2000) daughter of Herbert and Virginia (Martin) Betts married twice, first to Mr. West with whom she was mother of (1), later she married Gary Wainuskis. Carol was a molder with Hartville Plastics. **WILMA L. BETTS** Fifth great granddaughter of progenitor Nicholas Kegg.

BETZLER

FLORENCE E. BETZLER [2776A] (1903 – 1970) daughter of Henry and Florence (Kegg) Betzler was twice married, first to Horace Murfin, and then to Norman Erpelding with whom she was mother of (1). Florence was a member of Railroad Yard Masters Ladies Auxiliary. **HARRY P. BETZLER** [2776B] (1918 – 2006) son of Henry and Florence (Kegg) Betzler, married Esther Shade with whom he was father of (1) Harry spent a lot of time duck and pheasant hunting, fishing for Salmon in Puget Sound, Trout fishing in the rivers and lakes. Harry golfed for 50 plus years. He even had a hole in one.
HARRY PHILLIP BETZLER [2776C] aka "Bud" (1939 – 2020) son of Harry and Esther (Null) Shade Betzler, married Judith Faye Goings with whom he was father of (4). Bud was employed as an automotive technician and retired from Vern Sims Ford Ranch. Bud was an avid fisher and duck hunter. Bud also enjoyed watching his grandkids sporting events. Over the last few years, he worked part time for Tom-n-Jerrys Boat Center and spent lots of time visiting with friends at the sport store.
KATHY R. BETZLER Fifth great granddaughter of progenitor Nicholas Kegg.

[2775] Hood River News (OR) Oct 20, 2001 [2775A] p.3 - The Orgonian (OR) March 6, 1944 [2775B] Seattle Times (WA) Feb 14, 2007 [2776] pg. 2 - Alliance Review (OH) July 26, 2000, contributed by D. Sue Dible [2776A] Tacoma News Tribune (WA) Apr 13, 1970, obtained and contributed by D. Sue Dible [2776B] News Tribune (WA) Jan 15, 2006 [2776C] Skagit Valley Herald (WA) Oct. 1, 2020

MAMIE R. BETZLER [2777] (1912 – 1996) daughter of Henry and Florence May (Kegg) Betzler married Roy Monroe Booth with whom she was mother of (2).   **MARY HENRIETTA BETZLER** [2778] aka "Etta" (1910 – 2011) daughter of Henry and Florence (Kegg) Betzler, married Howard S. Harmon with whom she was mother of (3) Mary was a master flower arranger of bouquets, corsages and wedding arrangements. She participated in the activities of the McKinley Hill Friends Church and the Olympic View Friends Church, where she taught children's classes and sang soprano in the choir.
MICHAEL SCOTT BETZLER Fifth great grandson of progenitor Nicholas Kegg.
PEARL IRENE BETZLER (1904 – 1993) daughter of Henry and Florence (Kegg) Betzler, married Extra Edwin Rothmiller with whom she was mother of (2).   **RICHARD PHILLIP BETZLER** [2778A] aka "Ricky" son of Harry and Judith (Goings) Betzler, was employed with Chinook Enterprised until the age of 40 when he retired. Ricky enjoyed cars, music, camping and family **ROBIN L. BETZLER** Fifth great granddaughter of progenitor Nicholas Kegg.

BEURY

MICHAEL BEURY JR. Eighth great grandson of progenitor Nicholas Kegg.
SHAYLA BEURY Eighth great granddaughter of progenitor Nicholas Kegg.

BEVENS

DARWIN KIRK BEVENS [2779] (1924 – 1993) son of Theodore and Lila (Sanders) Bevens, married Thelda Nellie Goode with whom he was father of (2). Darwin was a retired child development specialist. Darwin served in the U.S. Navy during World War II. He received a citation for bravery during the South Pacific campaign. Darwin was a charter member of the Prospect Lions Club. He also was a member of Phi Delta Kappa and Elks Lodge 1371 in Bend.   **JERALD KIRK BEVENS** Fifth great grandson of progenitor Nicholas Kegg.   **MARNELLE EMMA BEVENS** [2779A] (1923 – 2012) daughter of Dolph and Emma (Sanders) Bevens, married Eugene Leonard Hutchins with whom she was mother of (1). Marnelle studied theatre at Pasadena City College, where she performed in several plays, including a performance with Jack Webb. She followed her dream and moved across the country to New York City, where she worked as a page at NBC's Radio City Music Hall during World War II. A highlight of her experience in NYC was celebrating the end of the War in Times Square. She enjoyed playing golf, gardening, and traveling.   **MICHAEL FRANKLIN BEVENS** Fifth great grandson of progenitor Nicholas Kegg.

BEVERIDGE

CHAD ROBERT BEVERIDGE [2780] (1975 – 2020) son of Cleo and Gloria Jean (Phipps) Beveridge worked for Robert Dydball, Walsh Door Company, and as a countertop installer for Jon Top. He loved fishing and mushroom hunting. He had a kind heart. Chad never knew a stranger and was always willing to help anyone in need.   **CLEO ROBERT BEVERIDGE JR.** aka "Bob" [2781] (1950 – 2022) son of Cleo and Audrey (Roach) Beveridge married Gloria Jean Phipps with whom he was father of (2). Later he married Pamela Joy DeKoning. Bob was employed at Meredith Printing/RR Donnelly for 33 years until the company closed in 2002. He then worked various jobs until he retired. Bob belonged to GWTA and enjoyed attending rallies on his motorcycle across the USA. Fishing, whether ice or summer, was a favorite hobby. Bob s enjoyed working with his hands, tinkering and repairing small engines. Bob had a strong faith in God. **ELLA BEVERIDGE** Seventh great granddaughter of progenitor Nicholas Kegg.
JULIA BEVERIDGE Seventh great granddaughter of progenitor Nicholas Kegg.

[2777] Tacoma News Tribune (WA) Mar 25, 1996 [2778] Skagit Valley Herald (WA) Jan 3, 2012 [2778A] Skagit Valley Herald March 31, 2011 [2779] Oregonian (OR) Mar 8, 1993 [2779A] San Luis Obispo Tribune (CA) Jan 31, 2013 [2780, 2781] Hamilton's Funeral and After Life Services (Des Moines, IA)

STEVEN CRAIG BEVERIDGE Fifth great grandson of progenitor Nicholas Kegg.
TRAVIS AARON BEVERIDGE Sixth great grandson of progenitor Nicholas Kegg.

BIBLE

RODNEY WAYNE BIBLE Fifth great grandson of progenitor Nicholas Kegg.
SHIRLEY ANN BIBLE Fifth great granddaughter of progenitor Nicholas Kegg.

BICKFORD

HAILEE MARIE BICKFORD Seventh great granddaughter of progenitor Nicholas Kegg.

BIDDLE

ALBERT RUSSELL BIDDLE [2782] (1894 – 1977) son of Francis and Mary Jane (Stuckey) Biddle married Mary Martha Stiffler with whom he was father of (1). Albert was a retired farmer in the Friends Cove area. **ANDREW DAVID BIDDLE** (1970 – 1970) son of William and Donna (Daniels) Biddle. **ANDREW GLYDEN BIDDLE** [2783] (1887 – 1967) aka "Andy", son of Francis and Mary Jane (Stuckey) Biddle, married Ella Marie Imler with whom he was father of (3). Andy was a Bedford Township farmer. **BINNIE JEANE BIDDLE** [2783A] (1926 – 2006) daughter of Francis and Ethel (Moore) Biddle, married Elmer L. Landis with whom she was mother of (3). Binnie was a member of Trinity Lutheran Church, D.A.R., Bedford American Legion Auxiliary, Ladies of the Moose, and was an RSVP volunteer who knitted several hundred sets of caps and mittens for Head Start Children over the years. She was also a member of several bridge clubs and enjoyed bowling. **CAROLYN MARIE BIDDLE** Fifth great granddaughter of progenitor Nicholas Kegg. **CATHERINE J. BIDDLE** [2784] (1916 – 2001) aka "Kate", daughter of Robert and Bridget (Gillum) Biddle, married Thomas L. Wear with whom she was mother of (2). Kate was a teacher for the Tuscarora Intermediate Unit for 21 years. She was a member of the First United Methodist Church in Mount Union, where she was a member of the choir for 40 years, taught Sunday School for 30 years, and was the first female lay leader of the church. She was a past worthy matron of the Order of the Eastern Star, Chapter 280, Mount Union; was a former and first female member of the Mount Union Borough Council; and volunteered for J.C. Blair Memorial Hospital in Huntingdon. **CHARLES ORIN BIDDLE** [2784A] (1931 – 1998) son of Francis and Ethel (Moore) Biddle, married Lillian Miller with whom he was father of (2). Charles retired from Florida Steel Corp., Tampa. He was a Marine veteran of the Korean War. He was a volunteer for Florida Blood Services and a member of the North Bay Community Church, the Golf League, the North Pinellas Bowling League and Elks Lodge 2275, Dunedin. **DOROTHY E. BIDDLE** [2785] (1918 – 1991) daughter of Robert and Bridget (Gillum) Biddle, married Wendell W. Wear with whom she was mother of (2).
DOROTHY ELLEN BIDDLE [2786, 2787] (1921 – 1984) daughter of Francis and Ethel (Moore) Biddle married twice, first to Arthur L. Knisely. Later, she married Jack David Lehman with whom she was mother of (3). **FRANCIS ORIN BIDDLE** [2788] (1889 – 1961) son of Francis and Mary Jane (Stuckey) Biddle married Ethel M. Moore with whom he was father of (4). F. Orin was a retired milk hauler.
GEARY MARSHALL A. BIDDLE [2789] (1895 – 1958) son of Francis and Mary Jane (Stuckey) Biddle married Kathryn Sipe. Geary was employed by Schmidt and Ault Paper Company until he retired. A veteran of World War I, he was a member of Bedford Post 113, . American Legion, and Pleasureville Fire Company. **GLORIA JEAN BIDDLE** Fourth great granddaughter of progenitor Nicholas Kegg.
HARRY JAMES BIDDLE [2789A] (1917 – 2005) son of Andrew and Ella (Imler) Biddle, married Carrie Marie Anderson with whom he was father of (5). Harry was a lifelong farmer and a former Bedford

---

[2782] obituary clipping contributed by Glenn Biddle [2783] p.3 -Bedford Inquirer (PA) Feb 23, 1967 [2783A] p.3 - Bedford Inquirer (PA) May 5, 2006 [2784] Huntingdon Daily News/GenealogyBuff [2784A] St. Petersburg Times (FL) July 10, 1998 [2785] p.2 - Huntingdon Daily News (PA) May 13, 1991 [2786] p.6 - Bedford Gazette (PA) Jan 6, 1950 [2787] p.3 - Bedford Inquirer (PA) Aug 5, 1977 [2788] p.5 - Bedford Gazette (PA) Oct19, 1961 [2789] p.30 Gazette and Daily from York (PA) Feb 24, 1958

Township Supervisor for 30 years. He was a member of St. James Lutheran Church, and the Bedford Grange. **HARRY RALPH BIDDLE** Fifth great grandson of progenitor Nicholas Kegg.
HARRY WILIAM STUCKEY BIDDLE [2790] (1881 – 1906) son of Francis and Mary Jane (Stuckey) Biddle. Harry was appointed mail carrier on Route No. 4, Bedford, and attended to his work faithfully and well until failing health compelled him to resign his position. He then secured a position in the Hershberger planning mill where he worked for about a year. **HAZEL LOUISE BIDDLE** [2791, 2792] (1914 – 1997) daughter of Robert and Bridget (Gillum) Biddle married James Albert McDonough with whom she was mother of (1). **HUNTER JOSEPH BIDDLE** Seventh great grandson of progenitor Nicholas Kegg. **JAMES SCOTT BIDDLE** Sixth great grandson of progenitor Nicholas Kegg. **JULIE BIDDLE** Fifth great granddaughter of progenitor Nicholas Kegg.
MAKAYLA GRACE BIDDLE Seventh great granddaughter of progenitor Nicholas Kegg.
MARIE BIDDLE [2793] (1900 – 1988) daughter of Francis and Mary Jane (Stuckey) Biddle married Glenn C. Trail with whom she was mother of (7). Marie was a member of the Trinity Lutheran Church of Bedford and a former member of the American Legion Auxiliary of Bedford. **MARY JANE BIDDLE** [2794] (1914 – 2003) daughter of Andrew and Ella Marie (Imler) Biddle married Joseph Emory Dibert with whom she was mother of (4). Mary was a member of the Pleasant Hill Reform Church and the Ladies Aid of the Church. **MARY MARGARET BIDDLE** 5th great granddaughter of progenitor Nicholas Kegg.
MARY MARGARET BIDDLE (1890 – 1977) daughter of Francis and Mary Jane (Stuckey) Biddle, married Benjamin Harrison Eshelman with whom she was mother of (7).
MAUDE BLANCHE IRMA BIDDLE [2795] (1880 – 1963) daughter of Francis and Mary Jane (Stuckey) Biddle married Joseph Franklin Reighard with whom she was mother of (3). Maude was a member of the St. James Lutheran Church and one of the oldest members of the Bedford Grange.
MICHAEL O. BIDDLE Fifth great grandson of progenitor Nicholas Kegg. **NELLIE E. BIDDLE** [2796] (1884 – 1964) daughter of Francis and Mary Jane (Stuckey) Biddle married George B. Fetter. Nellie was a member of the United Church of Christ of Friends Cove. **OWEN JAMES BIDDLE** Seventh great grandson of progenitor Nicholas Kegg. **PAMELA SUE BIDDLE** Sixth great granddaughter of progenitor Nicholas Kegg. **ROBERT IRA BIDDLE** [2797] (1885 – 1948) son of Francis and Mary Jane (Stuckey) Biddle married Bridget May Gillum with whom he was father of (3). R. Ira had been employed by Penelec company for 28 years and was foreman of the gas department at the Huntingdon plant for 22 years. **RUTH BIDDLE** [2797A] (1923 – 2018) daughter of Francis and Ethel (Moore) Biddle, married Kenneth Wilson with whom she was mother of (2). Ruth retired from the Bedford Area School District and also worked for the Bedford County Courthouse in addition to volunteering at the Bedford County Humane Society to relocate pets into new homes. **RUTH HELEN BIDDLE** [2798] (1927 – 2000) daughter of Andrew and Ella Marie (Imler) Biddle married William F. Mowry with whom she was mother of (2). **SUSAN LOUISE BIDDLE** Fifth great granddaughter of progenitor Nicholas Kegg.
TAMMY MARIE BIDDLE Sixth great granddaughter of progenitor Nicholas Kegg.
VIRGIL EARL BIDDLE [2799] (1886 – 1960) son of Francis and Mary Jane (Stuckey) Biddle married Jennie Grace Diehl. Virgil was a veteran of World War I. **WILLIAM ANDREW BIDDLE** [2799A] aka "Bill" (1943 – 2021) son of Harry and Carrie Marie (Anderson) Biddle married Donna Jean Daniels with whom he was father of (4). Bill retired from New Holland Concrete (Kilcoin Blocks) after 30 years of service. Bill was an active hunter and enjoyed working on the family farm.

[2789A] p.8 - Bedford Inquirer (PA) March 11, 2005 obtained and contributed by Bob Rose [2790] Bedford Gazette (PA) June 1, 1906 [2791] p.8 - Daily News (PA) March 24, 1945 [2792] Huntingdon Daily News (PA) March 11, 1975 [2793] p.3 - Bedford Inquirer (PA) Sep 23, 1988 [2794] p.8 - Bedford Inquirer (PA) April 11, 2003 obtained by Bob Rose [2795] Bedford Gazette (PA) Jan 23, 1963 [2796] p.10 - Bedford Gazette (PA) Nov 7, 1964 [2797] p.3 - Daily News (PA) Aug 27, 1948 [2797A] Bedford Gazette (PA) May 21, 2018 obtained and contributed by Bob Rose [2798] Bedford Gazette (PA) Oct. 21, 2000 [2799] Altoona Genealogical Society obituary clipping obtained by D. Sue Dible [2799A] Bedford Gazette (PA) June 3, 2021

BIERWIRTH

AMY LYNN BIERWIRTH Sixth great granddaughter of progenitor Nicholas Kegg.
ELLEN RENEE BIERWIRTH Sixth great granddaughter of progenitor Nicholas Kegg.
GARY D. BIERWIRTH [2799B] (1951 – 2017) son of Glen and Ellen (Clark) Bierwirth, married Judy Arrowood with whom he was father of (2). Gary honorably served in the United States Navy during the Vietnam era and was stationed aboard a submarine. During his time in the Navy, Gary was afforded the opportunity to travel the world. He worked as a Control Operator for Dresden Generating Station for over twenty-five years until his retirement. In his free time, he enjoyed fishing and playing harmonica. Gary always had a desire to learn and loved doing research. **JOANN M. BIERWIRTH** Fifth great granddaughter of progenitor Nicholas Kegg. **LARRY GLENN BIERWIRTH** [2799C] (1942 – 2000) son of Glen and Ellen (Clark) Bierwirth, married Linda Oedewaldt Bennett with whom he was father of (2). A Vietnam Army veteran, he was honorably discharged with the rank of Specialist 4. He was a teacher at Limestone Community High School for 33 years where he taught Industrial Arts and Vocational Training. During those years he was the assistant coach for the boy's track and field. He was also a member of the Core team and designed, constructed and painted backgrounds and sets for numerous plays and Madrigal dinners. He was recently awarded Who's Who Among America's teachers, being nominated by a former student he had influenced during his teaching career. He was also a Patent draftsman for Caterpillar Tractor, Inc. Larry served as the Mayor of Mapleton from 1970 to 1980. Mr. Bierwirth was a member of the Church of the Brethren in Peoria He was a member of the Bartonville Jaycees and played softball for Stahl Brothers. He was a member of the S'More Dancers for 7 years. He was an avid gardener, artist and woodworker. **LORI BIERWIRTH** Sixth great granddaughter of progenitor Nicholas Kegg.
MARLENE F. BIERWIRTH Fifth great granddaughter of progenitor Nicholas Kegg.
MELISSA ANN BIERWIRTH Sixth great granddaughter of progenitor Nicholas Kegg.
ROBIN BIERWIRTH Sixth great granddaughter of progenitor Nicholas Kegg.
ROGER LEE BIERWIRTH [2800] (1935 – 2008) son of Glenn and Ellen (Clark) Bierwirth married twice, first to Janice Schoon and later to Mary J. (Horn) Homann with whom he was father of (2). Roger worked for Keystone Steel & Wire Co. in Bartonville for 43 years, retiring as a wire drawer.
TIMOTHY L. BIERWIRTH aka "Tim" Sixth great grandson of progenitor Nicholas Kegg.

BIGAM

GARY BIGAM Sixth great grandson of progenitor Nicholas Kegg. **JASE BIGAM** Seventh great grandson of progenitor Nicholas Kegg. **JOSHUA BIGAM** aka "Josh" Sixth great grandson of progenitor Nicholas Kegg.

BIGGINS

BRIAN SHANE BIGGINS [2801] (1963 – 2003) son of Elwin and Martha (Shoemaker) Biggins married Bernadette Denise Tonning. Music was a major part of his life. **MICHAEL BIGGINS** Fifth great grandson of progenitor Nicholas Kegg. **SHARON LORRAINE BIGGINS** [2802] (1959 – 2017) daughter of Edwin and Martha (Shoemaker) Biggins married Patrick Anton.

[2799B] The Herald-News (IL) Dec. 28, 2017 [2799C] p.7 The Pantagraph (Bloomington, IL) Oct 10, 2000 [2800] Peoria Journal Star (IL) Oct 24, 2008 [2801] Grand Rapids Public Library obituary obtained by D. Sue Dible

BIGGS

BETSY BIGGS Sixth great granddaughter of progenitor Nicholas Kegg. **BRETT BIGGS** Sixth great grandson of progenitor Nicholas Kegg. **CARLA MARIE BIGGS** Sixth great granddaughter of progenitor Nicholas Kegg. **CATHERINE A. BIGGS** (1926 – 1927) daughter of Edward and Marie (Soucik) Biggs. **CATHERINE ROSE BIGGS** [2802A] (1946 – 2009) daughter of John and Mary (Kepenach) Biggs, married James Lavon Hudson with whom she was mother of (3). Catherine was a gracious woman who put her children first. She instilled great values in her children which are carried on today as her legacy. Catherine enjoyed her friends and family and opened her home and her heart to all and enjoyed a great laugh. **CHARLES FREDERICK BIGGS** [2803] (1917 – 1975) aka "Red" son of William and Elsie (Metcalf) Biggs married Mary Gertrude Kelley with whom he was father of (1). Red worked at Oak Rubber as manager of operations for three years, at McNeil of Akron as a master mechanic. He also worked at Seiberling Tire & Rubber 19 years as a plant engineer. He was a member of Barberton Elks # 982, and a veteran of WWII Army. **CHELSIE LYNNE BIGGS** Sixth great granddaughter of progenitor Nicholas Kegg. **CLEE CHARLES BIGGS** [2804] (1887 – 1970) son of Peter and Eva (Keggs) Biggs, married Violet Nancy Morrison with whom he was father of (2). Clee was a retired farmer. **DAVID BIGGS** Fifth great grandson of progenitor Nicholas Kegg.
DEBORAH JO BIGGS Fifth great granddaughter of progenitor Nicholas Kegg.
EDWARD CLARK BIGGS (1907 – 1928) aka "Eddie" son of William and Elsie (Metcalf) Biggs married Marie Pauline Soucik with whom he was father of (2). A merchant marine, Eddie was lost at sea.
ELAINE E. BIGGS Fifth great granddaughter of progenitor Nicholas Kegg.
JOHN CHARLES BIGGS Fifth great grandson of progenitor Nicholas Kegg. **JOHN CLEE BIGGS** [2805] (1914 – 1970) son of William and Elsie (Metcalf) Biggs, married Mary Kepenach with whom he was father of (3). **KAREN SUE BIGGS** Fifth great granddaughter of progenitor Nicholas Kegg.
KATHRYN BIGGS aka "Katie" Sixth great granddaughter of progenitor Nicholas Kegg.
MARK ALLEN BIGGS Fifth great grandson of progenitor Nicholas Kegg. **MICHELLE L. BIGGS** Sixth great granddaughter of progenitor Nicholas Kegg. **MOLLIE BIGGS** Sixth great granddaughter of progenitor Nicholas Kegg. **MORRIS LEE BIGGS** [2805A] (1914 – 1991) son of Clee and Violet (Morrison) Biggs, married Olive Lucille Kendall with whom he was father of (2). Morris was a U.S. Army veteran serving in WWII and was employed at Columbia Gas of Wooster (OH) for 38 years, retiring in 1978. He was a member of Riplay Church of Christ. **PAUL WORLEY BIGGS** [2806] (1912 – 1972) son of William and Elsie (Metcalf) Biggs married twice, first to Clara Louise Chirkoski with whom he was father of (1). Later, he married Elizabeth Ruth (Farkas) Jurich. **PAUL WORLEY BIGGS JR.** Fifth great grandson of progenitor Nicholas Kegg. **RICHARD SCOTT BIGGS** [2807] (1961 – 2004) son of Richard and Ida Mae (Hoskins) Biggs married Roxanna B. Blankenship. After high school, R. Scott joined the Air Force and spent the rest of his life in Tampa. **RICHARD ALLEN BIGGS** (1935 – 1979) son of Clee and Violet Nancy (Morrison) Biggs, married Ida Mae Hoskins with whom he was father of (4). **ROBERT BIGGS** Fifth great grandson of progenitor Nicholas Kegg.
ROSA C. BIGGS [2808] (1874 – 1961) daughter of Peter and Eva (Keggs) Biggs married William Glen Morgan with whom she was mother of (1). Rosa was a member of Clinton Grange in Shreve and Ripley Church of Christ. **ROSA CATHEREN BIGGS** [2808A] aka "Catherine" (1906 – 1974) daughter of William and Elsie (Metcalf) Biggs married Roy Kennedy Dobbs. Catherine was an index clerk in the Ohio House of Representatives and a researcher in the Ohio Legislative Library and become the only woman mayor of the city of Barberton, Ohio, she built her political career on a platform designed to appeal to the woman voter. Women, she observed, "know that they must have candidates for public office

---

[2802] Grand Rapids Press (MI) July 9, 2017 obtained by D. Sue Dible [2802A] Springfield News-Sun (OH) Aug 19, 2009 [2803] Akron Beacon Journal (OH) Dec 10, 1975 obtained by D.Sue Dible [2804] p.2 Wooster Daily Record (OH) Nov 9, 1970 obtained by D.Sue Dible [2805] Akron Beacon Journal (OH) Feb 11, 1970 obtained by D. Sue Dible [2805A] p.C12 Wooster Daily Record (OH) Sep 3, 1991 obtained and contributed by D. Sue Dible [2806] Akron Beacon Journal (OH) Aug 14, 1972 obtained by D.Sue Dible [2807] Daily Record (OH) Dec 28, 2004 [2808] p2 Wooster Daily Record (OH) Oct 24, 1961 obtained by D.Sue Dible [2808A] Akron Beacon Journal (OH) Jan 2, 1974 obtained and contributed by D. Sue Dible

that will campaign for the Moral Health of our Great Nation." Early in her political career, she was campaigning against corruption and pornography, and experienced enormous success. She started her political career by running for the Ohio Senate. Running as a Democrat, she won the seat, the first woman ever to do so and only one of eight women in the nation to serve in any state Senate. Ohio had two women in its state Senate. **RUSSELL MARION BIGGS** [2809] (1898 – 1916) son of William and Elsie (Metcalf) Biggs. Russell was a cartoonist of considerable ability. He was drowned in Long Lake while out canoeing with two other young men. Biggs went out in a canoe with Glenn Durrin and Roy Stitznof, strangers to him. Near the middle of the lake the canoe upset. Biggs was caught under the canoe and drowned before he could be rescued by bathers. The other men were rescued. The lake was dragged for the body, which had not been found. **SHERMAN EARL BIGGS**, (1899 – 1915) son of William and Elsie (Metcalf) Biggs. **SHERRY LEE BIGGS** Fifth great granddaughter of progenitor Nicholas Kegg. **WILLIAM SHERMAN BIGGS** [2810] (1874 – 1918) of Peter and Eva (Keggs) Biggs married Elsie Metcalf with whom he was father of (7). William was a man of exceptional talents. He conducted business in Shreve for a short time. He was for a considerable period employed by W.E. Jones, of Loudonville (OH) as a piano salesman. He was light-hearted, jovial, looked upon the bright side of life, and mastered many of the difficult problems that confront a father and husband in life.
WILLIAM SHERMAN BIGGS Fifth great grandson of progenitor Nicholas Kegg.

BILLINGSLEY

CIENDA RENE BILLINGSLEY Sixth great granddaughter of progenitor Nicholas Kegg. **JORDAN ARTHUR BILLINGSLEY** Sixth great grandson of progenitor Nicholas Kegg.

BING

BETTIE ONEILL BING [2810A] (1920 – 2011) daughter of Horton and Helen (O'Neill) Bing, married Arlo Ray Thompson with whom she was mother of (1). **HELENA MAY BING** (1914 – 2002) aka "Evalina" daughter Of Horton and Helen (O'Neill) Bing, married Julian Franklin Johns with whom she was mother of (1).

BINGAMAN

GLENN ALSTON BINGAMAN [2810B] (1988 – 2008) son of Glenn and Leanne (Eby) Bingaman Jr. Glenn loved working on his cars, playing Xbox and playing sports including golf, disc golf, paintball, bowling, baseball, volleyball, football and track. **GLENN ERVIN BINGAMAN** Fifth great grandson of progenitor Nicholas Kegg. **MICHAELA BINGAMAN** Sixth great granddaughter of progenitor Nicholas Kegg. **NANCY LEE BINGAMAN** [2811] (1947 – 2019) daughter of Glen and Kathryn (Smith) Bingaman married Jimmie Glen Johnson with whom she was mother of (3). Later she married John Allen Niswonger. **PAMELA IRENE BINGAMAN** Fifth great granddaughter of progenitor Nicholas Kegg. **RYAN G. BINGAMAN** Sixth great grandson of progenitor Nicholas Kegg.
SHEILA MAE BINGAMAN [2811A] (1944 – 1968) daughter of Glenn and Kathryn (Smith) Bingaman married David L. Hunt with whom she was mother of (3) Sheila was a member of the Salvation Army.

[2809] Loudonville Democrat (OH) Aug 14, 1916 obtained by D.Sue Dible [2810] Loudonville Democrat (OH) Mar 14, 1918 obtained by D.Sue Dible [2810A] Lawrence Journal World (KS) Oct 11, 2011 [2810B] The Elkhart Truth (IN) Mar 23, 2008 [2811] Billings Funeral Home (Elkhart, IN) obtained by D. Sue Dible [2811A] p11 Elkhart Truth (IN) Jan 23, 1968

BINGHAM

ADA ALICE BINGHAM [2812] (1886 – 1944) daughter of Henry and Eva (Diehl) Bingham married Harry H. Diehl with whom she was mother of (4). **ALLISON BINGHAM** Seventh great granddaughter of progenitor Nicholas Kegg. **AMANDA REBECCA BINGHAM** (1873 – 1881) daughter of Henry and Eva (Diehl) Bingham. **BARBARA ANN BINGHAM** [2812A] (1938 – 2022) daughter of Charles and Martha (McGee) Bingham married Thomas R. Shippey with whom she was mother of (2). Barbara was a homemaker and was also a Tax Auditor. **BERNARD WILLIAM BINGHAM** Fifth great grandson of progenitor Nicholas Kegg. **BETHANY RAYNEV BINGHAM** Sixth great granddaughter of progenitor Nicholas Kegg. **BRIAN GEORGE BINGHAM** [2812B] (1980 – 2000) son of H. Cyril and Christina (Storm) Bingham. Brian had served with the 82nd Airborne at Fort Bragg, N.C., and had worked on the assembly line for JLG Industries. **BRIAN LLOYD BINGHAM** Sixth great grandson of progenitor Nicholas Kegg. **CAROL ANN BINGHAM** Fifth great granddaughter of progenitor Nicholas Kegg. **CARRY MAY BINGHAM** [2813] (1880 – 1944) daughter of Henry and Eva (Diehl) Bingham. **CHARLES EDWARD BINGHAM** [2813A] (1916 – 1976) son of Franklin and Julia (Williams) Bingham, married Martha Jane McGee with whom he was father of (3). Charles had been a Bedford Borough Police Officer. He was one of the early gas and steam engine enthusiasts in this area, he had pioneered the local Fort Bedford association, and played a significant role every autumn in the association's annual display during Fall Foliage Festival Days. Known for his interest over a wide area, he was also a member of the Williams Grove Steam Engine Association, among others. Active in the Bedford Loyal Order of Moose 430, he was also a member of Bedford Elks Lodge 1707, the Redmen of Everett, the Liberty Fire Company in New Berlinville, Pa., the Fort Bedford CB Club, the Fraternal Order of Police, the Lazy Bee Campers Club, and the American Association of Retired Persons. He was of the Protestant faith. **DANIEL CYRIL BINGHAM** 5th great grandson of progenitor Nicholas Kegg. **DESIREE BINGHAM** Seventh great granddaughter of progenitor Nicholas Kegg. **DIXIE L. BINGHAM** Fifth great granddaughter of progenitor Nicholas Kegg. **DONALD OSCAR BINGHAM** Fifth great grandson of progenitor Nicholas Kegg. **DONALD RAYMOND BINGHAM** aka "Doc" (1933 – 1992) son of Franklin and Julia Elizabeth (Williams) Bingham, married Mary lou Brown with whom he was father of (1). **DONNA FAYE BINGHAM** [2814] (1961 – 1965) daughter of Harry and Lois (Shaffer) Bingham. Donna was a member of the Sunday School Nursery Class of Bald Hill Lutheran Church. **DUSTIN BINGHAM** Sixth great grandson of progenitor Nicholas Kegg. **DWAYNE WILMONT BINGHAM** Sixth great grandson of progenitor Nicholas Kegg. **FRANKLIN EDWARD BINGHAM** [2815] (1889 – 1976) son of Henry and Eva (Diehl) Bingham married Julia Elizabeth Williams with whom he was father of (5). **FREDERICK LEWIS BINGHAM** [2816] (1914 – 1986) aka "Fred" son of Isaac and Carrie (Little) Bingham married Eleanor Mary Marsh with whom he was father of (2). Fred was proprietor of Bingham's Milkshake Inn. **GARY W. BINGHAM** [2817] (1950 – 2014) son of Harry and Lois (Shaffer) Bingham married twice, first to Kathy Virginia Rose with whom he was father of (2). Later, he married Debra Stark with whom he was father of (1). Gary was the owner of Bingham Heating and Plumbing. He attended Sugar Loaf Church. **H. CYRIL BINGHAM** [2817A] (1902 – 1973) son of Isaac and Carrie (Little) Bingham married three times, first to Clarice Neidermyer with whom he was father of (1), then to Leah Robinson with whom he was father of (1). H. Cyril Bingham, one of the most experienced and respected Justices of the Peace in the State of Pennsylvania, and a civic, municipal and fraternal leader in Bedford for 40 years. During his varied and colorful career, he achieved distinction as an outstanding football player, an accomplished musician, and an able law enforcement officer.

[2812] pg. 2 - The Bedford Gazette (PA) July 14, 1944 obtained by Bob Rose [2812A] Bedford Gazette (PA) Oct 10, 2022 [2812B] Bedford Inquirer (PA) Dec 15, 2000 obtained by Bob Rose [2813] p.7 - The Bedford Gazette (PA) May 5, 1944 [2813A] Bedford County Genealogical Society obtained and contributed by D. Sue Dible [2814] p.8-Bedford Gazette (PA)Mar 23, 1965 obtained by Connie Detar contributed by Bob Rose [2815] Spielman Collection Bedford Genealogical Society obtained by D. Sue Dible [2816] The Bedford Gazette (PA) March 1, 1954 [2817] Bedford Gazette (PA) July 24, 2014 obtained by Bob Rose [2817A] Bedford County Genealogical Society obtained and contributed by D. Sue Dible

HARRY WILMOT BINGHAM [2818] (1919 – 1966) son of Franklin and Julia (Williams) Bingham married Lois Marietta Shaffer with whom he was father of (6). Harry was treasurer of the Bedford Merged School District. He had been a driver for the Blackburn-Russell Company for 15 years and also was a member of Bedford Lodge 480, Moose. **HOBY BINGHAM** Fifth great grandson of progenitor Nicholas Kegg. **IDA CATHERINE BINGHAM** (1876 – 1881) daughter of Henry and Eva (Diehl) Bingham. **ISAAC WITMORE BINGHAM** [2819] (1878 – 1953) aka "Ike" son of Henry and Eva (Diehl) Bingham married three times. First to Carrie M. Little with whom he was father of (2), he then married Sarah Alwilda Moser and Ella Davenport Salkeld. Ike had a long record as a businessman for 40 years or more and is rivaled by few persons. After starting his business career with a small grocery, he opened Bingham's Milks Shake Inn on February 22, 1920. In more than 33 years in serving the Community and Bedford's many visitors, the restaurant achieved a wide reputation for wholesome food served in generous portions. "Ike" Bingham, as he was known to just about everyone in Bedford, was a familiar and well-liked figure in the community. His infectious laugh brought many a smile and chuckle to fellow movie-goers at the Pitt Theatre, for he believed in enjoying good fun to the fullest, and his general attitude was contagious for all who met him. **JANET BINGHAM** Fifth great granddaughter of progenitor Nicholas Kegg. **JEREMIAH BINGHAM** Sixth great grandson of progenitor Nicholas Kegg. **JOANN BINGHAM** Fifth great granddaughter of progenitor Nicholas Kegg. **JOHN BINGHAM** Sixth great grandson of progenitor Nicholas Kegg. **JUNE ELIZABETH BINGHAM** [2819A] (1918 – 2016) daughter of Franklin and Julia Elizabeth (Williams) Bingham, married John Raymond Evans with whom she was mother of (4). June was employed at the Dairy Dell in Everett and then as a cook for the Everett Area School District at Everett Elementary for many years until her retirement. After retirement she went to work through the Green Thumb Program with placement at Old Bedford Village and Pennknoll Village working well into her 80s. She enjoyed gardening, flowers, and being with family. **KENNETH C. BINGHAM JR.** Sixth great grandson of progenitor Nicholas Kegg. **KENNETH C. BINGHAM** [2820] (1929 – 2003) son of H. Cyril and Clarice (Neidermyer) Bingham, married Charlotte Ohrin with whom he was father of (1). Ken served with the U.S. Army during the Korean War, having served twice, once during his last year of high school and then being recalled when the war started, and was wounded while serving there. **LAWRENCE E. BINGHAM** [2821] (1941 – 2016) son of Charles and Martha Jane (McGee) Bingham. Lawrence served in the U.S. Navy, and enjoyed tending his flower garden, and going to the Williams Grove Steam Engine shows. **LEAH BINGHAM** Fifth great granddaughter of progenitor Nicholas Kegg. **MATTHEW BINGHAM** Sixth great grandson of progenitor Nicholas Kegg. **MELANIE BINGHAM** Sixth great granddaughter of progenitor Nicholas Kegg. **MICHELLE BINGHAM** Sixth great granddaughter of progenitor Nicholas Kegg. **MITCH BINGHAM** Sixth great grandson of progenitor Nicholas Kegg.
NORMA JEAN BINGHAM Fifth great granddaughter of progenitor Nicholas Kegg. **NORMAN JAY BINGHAM** Fifth great grandson of progenitor Nicholas Kegg. **OLIVIA BINGHAM** Seventh great granddaughter of progenitor Nicholas Kegg. **QUINN BINGHAM** Sixth great grandson of progenitor Nicholas Kegg. **ROBERT BARRON BINGHAM** Fifth great grandson of progenitor Nicholas Kegg. **ROBERT HENRY BINGHAM** [2822] (1921 – 2004) son of Franklin and Julia (Williams) Bingham married Romaine M. Evans with whom he was father of (5). Robert was an Army veteran of World War II and served in the Pacific Theater. He was a member of the Bedford Masonic Lodge No. 320, F&AM, Bedford American Legion Post No. 113, Fort Bed-ford Honor Guard, Bedford VFW Post No. 7527, lifetime member of North American Hunters Association and former member of the Lazy Bee Campers Club. He retired in 1984 from New Enterprise Stone and Lime Co. as a truck driver and drove the cart van for Area Agency on Aging until 2003. **ROGER BINGHAM** Fifth great grandson of progenitor Nicholas Kegg. **RONALD LEW BINGHAM** Sixth great grandson of progenitor Nicholas Kegg.

[2818] pg. 13 - Cumberland Evening Times (MD) Dec 31, 1965 [2819] Bedford Gazette (PA) Aug. 19, 1953 [2819A] Bedford Gazette (PA) Feb 27, 2016, obtained and contributed by Bob Rose [2820] p.3 - Bedford Inquirer (PA) Apr 25, 2003, obtained by Bob Rose [2821] Bedford Gazette (PA) March 15, 2016, obtained by Bob Rose [2822] p. 3 - Bedford Inquirer (PA) Nov 26, 2004, obtained by Bob Rose

RONALD W. BINGHAM (2822A) son of Robert and Romaine (Evans) Bingham married twice, He was father of (4) with his 1st wife and father of (2) with his 2nd wife Delaine R. Hernandez. Ronald was an Army veteran who served during the Vietnam War. He worked at Cannondale for many years and also enjoyed farming, being outdoors, hunting and fishing. He was an avid motorcycle enthusiast, and his passion was demonstrated by the two motorcycles he proudly rebuilt and rode. He was also a member and past commander of the Bedford American Legion Post No.113. **SABRINA BINGHAM** Seventh great granddaughter of progenitor Nicholas Kegg. **THOMAS BINGHAM** (2822B) (1952 – 2017) son of Harry and Lois (Shaffer) Bingham, married Diane Allison with whom he was father of (3). Tom was a very hard worker and provided for his family by working in the coal mines for eight years doing underground wiring. He worked for 27 years in the maintenance department at Kennametal. Tom enjoyed traveling abroad to assist in setting up machines for Kennametal in China, Russia, Poland and South Africa. For several years, Tom served as a past president for Kennaford Credit Union, he served on the board for Thrivent Financial for Lutherans, and he was a board member of the Bedford Township Municipal Authority. Tom was a true family man, and his best times were spent with his loved ones. He enjoyed camping and vacationing with his family, watching football and tinkering in his garage with his antique cars. Tom was a jack-of-all trades and no task was too hard for him as he took great pleasure working around the house on many projects. **TIFFANY A BINGHAM** Sixth great granddaughter of progenitor Nicholas Kegg. **WENDY BINGHAM** Sixth great granddaughter of progenitor Nicholas Kegg. **ZACHARY BINGHAM** Seventh great grandson of progenitor Nicholas Kegg.

BINKLEY

ANN LOUISE BINKLEY Sixth great granddaughter of progenitor Nicholas Kegg.
SUSAN FAY BINKLEY Sixth great granddaughter of progenitor Nicholas Kegg.
STANLEY ROBERT BINKLEY (2822C) (1929 – 2017) son of Howard and Sara (Millin) Binkley married Fay Louise Trautman with whom he was father of (2). Stanley was a proud U.S. Marine Corps Veteran. Stanley was a teacher retiring from Hempfield High School after thirty-five years of service. Stanley was a member of Emmanuel Lutheran Church for eighty-two years. He was also a member of the American Legion Post #185, Lancaster County Conservancy, National Rifle Association, Pennsylvania Association of School Retirees and he was a former member of the Red Rose Rod and Gun Club. Stanley loved fishing, hunting, gardening, and woodworking.

BIRCH

JACK CHARLES BIRCH JR. Fifth great grandson of progenitor Nicholas Kegg. **RANDY BIRCH** Fifth great grandson of progenitor Nicholas Kegg. **RIC BIRCH** Fifth great grandson of progenitor Nicholas Kegg.

BIRD

ALEX BIRD Seventh great granddaughter of progenitor Nicholas Kegg. **BRANDY BIRD** Seventh great granddaughter of progenitor Nicholas Kegg. **JAMES ALLEN BIRD** (2822D) aka Jim (1959 – 2012) son of Jerry and Frances (Lee) Bird, married Lana Marie Richards with whom he was father of (4). Jim served in the U.S. Army. He worked as a carpenter and also cooked. **JAYDREE KAY BIRD** Seventh great granddaughter of progenitor Nicholas Kegg. **JEFFREY MICHAEL BIRD**, aka "Jeff" Sixth great grandson of progenitor Nicholas Kegg. **JENNIFER BIRD** Seventh great granddaughter of progenitor Nicholas Kegg. **JEREMY BIRD** Seventh great grandson of progenitor Nicholas Kegg.

(2822A) Bedford Gazette (PA) Feb 3, 2017, obtained and contributed by Bob Rose (2822B) Bedford Gazette (PA) Feb 21, 2017, obtained and contributed by Bob Rose (2822C) LNP (Lancaster, PA) Dec 28, 2017 (2822D) Powers Funeral Home (IA)

JERRY BIRD Sixth great grandson of progenitor Nicholas Kegg. **JESSICA BIRD** Seventh great granddaughter of progenitor Nicholas Kegg. **JOEL DAVID BIRD** Sixth great grandson of progenitor Nicholas Kegg. **SHAYLEE BIRD** Seventh great granddaughter of progenitor Nicholas Kegg.
TROY BIRD Seventh great grandson of progenitor Nicholas Kegg.
WILLIAM MICHAEL BIRD Seventh great grandson of progenitor Nicholas Kegg.

BISBERG

ALEXANDER JARED BISBERG Seventh great grandson of progenitor Nicholas Kegg.
EMMA ROSE BISBERG Seventh great granddaughter of progenitor Nicholas Kegg.

BISH

BRANTLEY WILLIAM BISH Seventh great grandson of progenitor Nicholas Kegg.

BISHOP

DAVID W. BISHOP Sixth great grandson of progenitor Nicholas Kegg. **KEVIN W. BISHOP** Sixth great grandson of progenitor Nicholas Kegg. **MATTHEW BISHOP** Seventh great grandson of progenitor Nicholas Kegg.

BITHELL

BERNICE BITHELL Fourth great granddaughter of progenitor Nicholas Kegg.

BITTER

ARTHUR HOWARD BITTER JR. [2823] (1923 – 1979) son of Arthur and Beatrice (Howard) Bitter. Arthur worked at the aeronautics division headquarters at Capital Airport in Springfield.
BARBARA BITTER Fifth great granddaughter of progenitor Nicholas Kegg.
BETTE JANE BITTER [2823A] (1921 – 2016) daughter of Arthur and Beatrice (Howard) Bitter, married Robert Thomas Cadwallader with whom she was mother of (3). Bette was a Research Analyst in the Military Intelligence Division in the Pentagon, remaining until the conclusion of World War II. She was an accomplished pianist, loved to sing and dance, and was convinced her frequent bridge games kept her young. **SARA ELIZABETH BITTER** Fifth great granddaughter of progenitor Nicholas Kegg.
SUSAN BITTER Fifth great granddaughter of progenitor Nicholas Kegg.
WILLIAM EDWARD BITTER [2824] (1925 – 2020) son of Arthur and Beatrice (Howard) Bitter, married Martha Schubert with whom he was father of (3). William was a graduate of the University of Missouri and a veteran of World War II. He retired from the JCPenney Company.

BITTNER

ALESIA JORDAN BITTNER Sixth great granddaughter of progenitor Nicholas Kegg.
DUANE BITTNER Sixth great grandson of progenitor Nicholas Kegg. **JOSH BITTNER** Sixth great grandson of progenitor Nicholas Kegg.

[2823] p.5 State Journal-Register (Springfield, Illinois) May 19, 1979 [2823A] The News & Observer (NC) Sept. 28, 2016 [2824] Courier-Journal (KY) Aug. 9, 2020

BIXEL

ALLEN P. BIXEL Fifth great grandson of progenitor Nicholas Kegg. **GREGORY C. BIXEL** Fifth great grandson of progenitor Nicholas Kegg. **KRISTINE E. BIXEL** Fifth great granddaughter of progenitor Nicholas Kegg. **SHAUNA BIXEL** Sixth great granddaughter of progenitor Nicholas Kegg. **STEVEN C. BIXEL** Fifth great grandson of progenitor Nicholas Kegg.

BLACK

BRIAN KEITH BLACK Sixth great grandson of progenitor Nicholas Kegg. **CAROL A. BLACK** Fifth great granddaughter of progenitor Nicholas Kegg. **CONNIE BLACK** Fourth great granddaughter of progenitor Nicholas Kegg. **ERIC V. BLACK** [2825] (1949 – 1951) son of Galen and Betty (Kegg) Black. **JEREMY BLACK** Eighth great grandson of progenitor Nicholas Kegg. **JOHN ALLEN BLACK** Sixth great grandson of progenitor Nicholas Kegg. **KELLYN BLACK** Sixth great granddaughter of progenitor Nicholas Kegg. **LINDY D. BLACK** Fourth great grandson of progenitor Nicholas Kegg. **MARY JANE BLACK** Fourth great granddaughter of progenitor Nicholas Kegg. **MATTHEW BLACK** Sixth great grandson of progenitor Nicholas Kegg. **MEGAN COURTNEY BLACK** Sixth great granddaughter of progenitor Nicholas Kegg. **SHANNON LEIGH BLACK** Sixth great granddaughter of progenitor Nicholas Kegg. **TERRY LEE BLACK** Fourth great granddaughter of progenitor Nicholas Kegg.

BLACKBURN

ALLISON BLACKBURN Sixth great granddaughter of progenitor Nicholas Kegg. **BARBARA BLACKBURN** Fifth great granddaughter of progenitor Nicholas Kegg. **BETH ANN BLACKBURN** Fifth great granddaughter of progenitor Nicholas Kegg. **CATHERINE E. BLACKBURN** [2826] (1832 – 1913) daughter of William and Julianna (Kegg) Blackburn. She was noted for her kindly, generous disposition. **CATHERINE VIRGINIA BLACKBURN** [2827] aka "Cass," (1928 – 2022) daughter of William and Carrie (Imler) Blackburn married Norman A. Cessna with whom she was mother of (2). was a very talented oil painter and taught oil painting for 20 years. Catherine was a member and former Deacon and Elder of the Bedford Presbyterian Church. She was also a member of Chartiers Hill United Presbyterian Church, Washington County, Pa. She was a lifelong lover of nature and enjoyed all things outdoors. Catherine was a kind-hearted and generous lady. **CLIFFORD WAYNE BLACKBURN** Fifth great grandson of progenitor Nicholas Kegg. **GUY CHRISTOPHER BLACKBURN** Fifth great grandson of progenitor Nicholas Kegg. **IIVARENE E. BLACKBURN** [2828] (1917 – 2008) daughter of Simon and Ethel (Smith) Blackburn married Philip L. Mankin. **JAMES WILLIAM BLACKBURN** Fifth great grandson of progenitor Nicholas Kegg. **JANICE ELAINE BLACKBURN** Fifth great granddaughter of progenitor Nicholas Kegg. **JESSICA BLACKBURN** Sixth great granddaughter of progenitor Nicholas Kegg. **JOHN BRIGHT BLACKBURN** Fifth great grandson of progenitor Nicholas Kegg. **JUDITH ANN BLACKBURN** Fifth great granddaughter of progenitor Nicholas Kegg. **KAREN BLACKBURN** Fourth great granddaughter of progenitor Nicholas Kegg. **LYNN ELAINE BLACKBURN** Fifth great granddaughter of progenitor Nicholas Kegg. **MARK TRAVIS BLACKBURN** Sixth great grandson of progenitor Nicholas Kegg. **MAUD LESLIE BLACKBURN** [2829] (1882 – 1962) daughter of William and Charlotte Minerva (Hull) Blackburn married William James Shoenthal with whom she was mother of (5). Maud assumed management of the Shoenthal Country Store in 1933, noted throughout the area for the quality and variety of its merchandise. The Shoenthal family donated between two and three acres of land for a community park in New Paris.

[2825] p.9 - Daily News (PA) Jan 22, 1951 [2826] Bedford Gazette (PA) Aug 1, 1913 [2827] Bedford Gazette (PA) March 7, 2022 [2828] Akron Beacon Journal (OH) Jan 1, 2009 [2829] obituary clipping obtained by Duke Clark

MICHAEL DUANE BLACKBURN Fifth great grandson of progenitor Nicholas Kegg.
NICHOLAS BLACKBURN (1835 – 1862) son of William and Julianna (Kegg) Blackburn.
RICHARD IMLER BLACKBURN [2830] (1920 – 1994) son of William and Carolina (Imler) Blackburn married twice, first to Grace Della Hengst with whom he was father of (2). Later, he married Vera Evelyn Houck. Richard was employed for 38 years at Bedford Rural Electric, where he retired in 1985 as line superintendent. He was a U.S. Army Air Corps veteran of World War II, having served in the Pacific Theater; a life member of Trinity Lutheran Church, Bedford, where he served on the Church Council and was a Sunday school teacher for many years. Mr. Blackburn was a member and treasurer of the Bedford Area School Board for 32 years, member and chairman of the Bedford Water Authority, member and treasurer of the Central Pennsylvania Unit of Wally Byam Caravan Club International, and a member of Bedford Elks Lodge 1707 and Bedford American Legion Post 113. **ROBERT BLACKBURN** Sixth great grandson of progenitor Nicholas Kegg. **ROBERT F. BLACKBURN** [2830A] aka "Turk" (1923 – 2017) son of William and Carrie (Imler) Blackburn, married Audrey Miller with whom he was father of (2). Turk served in the U.S. Army. He was employed at Kennamental in Bedford for over 30 years. Turk enjoyed hunting and loved baseball, both as a player and a spectator. He was an avid Pittsburgh Pirates fan. **SARAH BLACKBURN** (1837 – 1839) daughter of William and Julianna (Kegg) Blackburn.
SARAH ELLEN BLACKBURN [2830B] aka "Ella" (1874 – 1961) daughter of Thomas and Mary (Coplin) Blackburn, married Jackson Andrew Crissman with whom she was mother of (3).
SIMON ROSS BLACKBURN [2830C] (1875 – 1948) son of Thomas and Mary (Coplin) Blackburn, married Ethel Smith with whom he was father of (2). He was employed by the Goodyear Rubber Co.
SIMON ROSS BLACKBURN JR. [2831] (1910 – 1948) aka "Ross" son of Simon and Ethel (Smith) Blackburn. **SKYE BLACKBURN** Fourth great granddaughter of progenitor Nicholas Kegg.
THOMAS KEGG BLACKBURN [2831A] (1840 – 1925) son of William and Julianna (Kegg) Blackburn, married Mary Coplin with whom he was father of (3). Thomas received a good common school education and studied surveying. He was known everywhere as an enterprising merchant and a valuable citizen.
TRAVIS JEFFREY BLACKBURN Seventh great grandson of progenitor Nicholas Kegg.
WILLIAM ELSWORTH BLACKBURN [2831B] (1877 – 1961) son of Thomas and Mary (Coplin) Blackburn, married Carolina Imler with whom he was father of (3). William worked as a liveryman, hauling people. **WILLIAM JAMES BLACKBURN JR.** Sixth great grandson of progenitor Nicholas Kegg. **WILLIAM R. BLACKBURN** Fourth great grandson of progenitor Nicholas Kegg.
WILLIAM THOMAS BLACKBURN [2832] (1845 – 1916) son of William and Julianna (Kegg) Blackburn married Charlotte Minerva Hull with whom he was father of (1). William was a farmer by occupation and was noted for his honesty in dealing with his fellowmen. He was elected and held the office of school director in the borough of New Paris.

BLACKSTONE

AMANDA MARIE BLACKSTONE Eighth great granddaughter of progenitor Nicholas Kegg.
SAMANTHA SHYANN BLACKSTONE Seventh great granddaughter of progenitor Nicholas Kegg.
STEPHANIE NICOLE BLACKSTONE Eighth great granddaughter of progenitor Nicholas Kegg.

BLADES

APRIL BLADES Seventh great granddaughter of progenitor Nicholas Kegg.
SHANE BLADES, aka "Nebraska", Seventh great grandson of progenitor Nicholas Kegg.

[2830] p.12 - Bedford Gazette (PA) Aug 23, 1994 [2830A] Bedford Gazette (PA) Feb 21, 2017, obtained and contributed by Bob Rose [2830B] p.5 - Bedford Gazette (PA) Feb 7, 1961 [2830C] p.2 - Bedford Gazette (PA) March 4,1948 [2831] Akron Beacon Journal (OH) Feb 14, 1948 [2831A] History of Bedford, Somerset, and Fulton Counties, Pennsylvania With Illustrations and Biographical Sketches of Some of its Pioneers and Prominent Men" (pub date 1884) [2831B] Altoona Mirror (PA) June 29, 1961, obtained and contributed by Michael S. Caldwell [2832] Bedford Gazette obituary obtained by Bob Rose

BLAHA

JAMES JAIME BLAHA Seventh great grandson of progenitor Nicholas Kegg.
LENA DELL BLAHA Eighth great granddaughter of progenitor Nicholas Kegg.

BLAISING

DANIELLE BLAISING Sixth great granddaughter of progenitor Nicholas Kegg.

BLAKE

ANGELA MICHELLE BLAKE Sixth great granddaughter of progenitor Nicholas Kegg.
CHARLENE MARIE BLAKE Sixth great granddaughter of progenitor Nicholas Kegg.

BLANCHARD

CLAUDINE NOEL BLANCHARD Sixth great granddaughter of progenitor Nicholas Kegg.
DENNIS LEE BLANCHARD Fifth great grandson of progenitor Nicholas Kegg.
PHILIP BROOKS BLANCHARD Fifth great grandson of progenitor Nicholas Kegg.
TERRI ANN BLANCHARD [2832A] (1961 – 2016) daughter of Philip and Carol (Bontrager) Blanchard served in the U.S. Navy in Patuxent River, Md. She earned a bachelor's degree from UNLV and worked in computer operations for EG&G for 20 years. Terri was gentle, engaging, spirited and fearless, always eager to try new experiences. She loved to laugh, loved life, her friends and her family. She was caring and giving and unselfishly spent time thinking of and doing things to improve the lives of others.

BLANK

CHRISTOPHER BLANK Seventh great grandson of progenitor Nicholas Kegg.
GLENN M. BLANK Fifth great grandson of progenitor Nicholas Kegg.   **JONATHON BLANK** Seventh great grandson of progenitor Nicholas Kegg.   **MARY BLANK** Fifth great granddaughter of progenitor Nicholas Kegg.   **ROBERT A. BLANK** Fifth great grandson of progenitor Nicholas Kegg.

BLANKLEY

ANGELA RENE BLANKLEY aka "Angie", Sixth great granddaughter of progenitor Nicholas Kegg.
BRAD ANDREW BLANKLEY Sixth great grandson of progenitor Nicholas Kegg.
BRAYDEN MARSHALL BLANKLEY [2833] (2002 – 2021) son of Brad and Beth (McNutt) Blankley graduated from Jeff Tech in Reynoldsville, PA. He enjoyed the outdoors, riding four wheelers and dirt bikes, and fishing.

BLATNICA

CLAUDINE RENEE BLATNICA Sixth great granddaughter of progenitor Nicholas Kegg.
SCOTT DAVID BLATNICA Sixth great grandson of progenitor Nicholas Kegg.

BLEAKNEY

JOSEPH LEROY BLEAKNEY Fifth great grandson of progenitor Nicholas Kegg.
NANCY ANN BLEAKNEY Fifth great granddaughter of progenitor Nicholas Kegg.

[2832A] Las Vegas Review-Journal (NV) Dec 16, 2016 [2833] Chapel Hills Funeral Home and Cemetery Hardage-Giddens (FL) Nov 12, 2021

THOMAS JOSEPH BLEAKNEY Sixth great grandson of progenitor Nicholas Kegg.

BLENDY

JONATHAN MICHAEL BLENDY Sixth great grandson of progenitor Nicholas Kegg.
MICHELLE NICOLE BLENDY Sixth great granddaughter of progenitor Nicholas Kegg.

BLOCHER

CHRISTOPHER BLOCHER Fifth great grandson of progenitor Nicholas Kegg.
EMMA JEAN BLOCHER Fourth great granddaughter of progenitor Nicholas Kegg.
JOHN V. BLOCHER JR. Fourth great grandson of progenitor Nicholas Kegg.
MICHAEL BLOCHER Fifth great grandson of progenitor Nicholas Kegg.
PATRICIA BLOCHER Fourth great granddaughter of progenitor Nicholas Kegg.

BLODGETT

DAVID WARREN DONALD BLODGETT [2834] (1970 – 2018) son of William and Sheryl Ann (Richardson) Blodgett married and was father of (3). He had a big heart and touched many people's lives with joy. David enjoyed music and was a talented poet and artist. He filled the lives of all who knew him with happiness by acting silly and making people laugh. David was a hard worker who was always willing to help others in need. His biggest joy was his family, and he adored his grandsons. David loved animals and people alike and made friends wherever he went. **JACOB BLODGETT** Eighth great grandson of progenitor Nicholas Kegg. **KATELYN BLODGETT** Eighth great granddaughter of progenitor Nicholas Kegg. **LACEY BLODGETT** Eighth great granddaughter of progenitor Nicholas Kegg. **MICHAEL RICHARD BLODGETT** Seventh great grandson of progenitor Nicholas Kegg.
RICKY JOE BLODGETT Seventh great grandson of progenitor Nicholas Kegg.
SANDRA LEE BLODGETT [2834A] (1950 – 2013) daughter of Basil and Marguerite (Childers) Blodgett was twice married, first to Richard Moll, then to Johnny Parkerson with whom she was mother of (2). Sandra was Miss Palm Springs from 1969 to 1970. She enjoyed quilting, gardening, baking and spending time with her grandchildren. She was a very loving and caring person. Faith and family were the most important things in her life. **WILLIAM RICHARD BLODGETT** [2835] (1948 – 1977) aka "Billy" son of Basil and Marguerite (Childers) Blodgett married Judy D. Kirby. Later, he married Sheryl Ann Richardson with whom he was father of (3). Billy was a construction worker and a member of Easton Baptist Church.

BLOMQUIST

ANNE BLOMQUIST Sixth great granddaughter of progenitor Nicholas Kegg.
DONALD LEROY BLOMQUIST [2835A] (1934 – 2015) son of Herbert and Inez (Rice) Blomquist, married Rosalie Alice Nelson with whom he was father of (3). Don enjoyed fishing and hunting, watching old cowboy movies and playing with his grandkids. **JOHN BLOMQUIST** Sixth great grandson of progenitor Nicholas Kegg. **KAREN KAY BLOMQUIST** Fifth great granddaughter of progenitor Nicholas Kegg. **MARK BLOMQUIST** Sixth great grandson of progenitor Nicholas Kegg.

[2834] Hamilton's Crematory (Des Moines, IA) [2834A] Tyler Morning Telegraph (TX) May 14, 2013 [2835] Des Moines Tribune (IA) Sep 26, 1977 [2835A] Crawford-Bowers Funeral Home (TN) obtained and contributed by D. Sue Dible

BLOOM

ALEXIS NICOLE BLOOM Sixth great granddaughter of progenitor Nicholas Kegg.
CHRISTOPHER C. BLOOM Sixth great grandson of progenitor Nicholas Kegg.
ROY LEE BLOOM [2835B] aka "Lee" (1938 – 2013) son of Roy and Margaret (Hough) Bloom married Dorothy Taylor with whom he was father of (2). Lee earned a degree in Pharmacy from the University of Pittsburgh. He graduated from the Chicago College of Osteopathic Medicine. Lee practiced hematology and oncology until 1998, when heart disease forced him into early retirement. An avid fly fisherman, Dr. Bloom was a lifetime member and onetime president of Trout Unlimited, as well as president of the Erie Casting Club. Dr. Bloom was also a fan of auto racing and competed as a member of the SCCA in the early 1970s. He was known for his passion for Alfa Romeo sports cars. He loved big band jazz and classical music and was a longtime supporter of the Erie Philharmonic.
OWEN BLOOM Seventh great grandson of progenitor Nicholas Kegg.

BLOSSER

BRENT LEE BLOSSER Sixth great grandson of progenitor Nicholas Kegg. **JAMES BLOSSER** Fifth great grandson of progenitor Nicholas Kegg. **JOANNA MAE BLOSSER** (1944 – 1944) daughter of Roy and Lillian (Eigsti) Blosser. **KEITH BLOSSER** Fifth great grandson of progenitor Nicholas Kegg. **MABEL BEULAH BLOSSER** [2836] (1919 – 2004) daughter of Samuel and Maggie (Stichter) Blosser married Royal Evert Miller with whom she was mother of (8). Mabel was a homemaker. **MARTHA S. BLOSSER** [2837] (1911 – 1994) daughter of Samuel and Maggie (Stichter) Blosser. **MICHAEL S. BLOSSER** Seventh great grandson of progenitor Nicholas Kegg. **OSCAR BLOSSER** (1929 – 1929) son of Samuel and Maggie (Stichter) Blosser. **ROY S. BLOSSER** [2837A] (1913 – 1991) son of Samuel and Maggie Lucretia (Stichter) Blosser, married Lillian Eigsti with whom he was father of (3).

BLOUGH

JEFFREY BLOUGH Sixth great grandson of progenitor Nicholas Kegg. **JOEL T. BLOUGH** Fifth great grandson of progenitor Nicholas Kegg. **KIERAN JAMES BLOUGH** Seventh great grandson of progenitor Nicholas Kegg. **KRISTINA LEIGH BLOUGH** Sixth great granddaughter of progenitor Nicholas Kegg. **LAUREN LEE BLOUGH** Sixth great granddaughter of progenitor Nicholas Kegg. **MARTIN LEE BLOUGH** Fifth great grandson of progenitor Nicholas Kegg. **STEVEN R. BLOUGH** aka "Steve" Sixth great grandson of progenitor Nicholas Kegg.

BLUE

AMBER BLUE Eighth great granddaughter of progenitor Nicholas Kegg. **MOLLY BLUE** Eighth great granddaughter of progenitor Nicholas Kegg. **SHANE BLUE** Eighth great grandson of progenitor Nicholas Kegg.

BLUNT

JASON BLUNT Eighth great grandson of progenitor Nicholas Kegg.

[2835B] Tribune Democrat (PA) Dec 31, 2013 [2836] Goshen News (IN) Oct 28, 2004 [2837] pA4 - South Bend Tribune (IN) Aug 13, 1994 [2837A] The Pantagraph (IL) Feb 24, 1991

BLYTHE

CORY GAGE BLYTHE Seventh great grandson of progenitor Nicholas Kegg.
CORY GAGE BLYTHE JR. Eighth great grandson of progenitor Nicholas Kegg.
PAUL RICHARD BLYTHE JR. aka "Ritchey" Sixth great grandson of progenitor Nicholas Kegg.

BOBBITT

BRIANNA GRACE BOBBITT Seventh great granddaughter of progenitor Nicholas Kegg.
ELLIOTT ALDEN BOBBITT Seventh great grandson of progenitor Nicholas Kegg.
SAMUEL JOSEPH BOBBITT Seventh great grandson of progenitor Nicholas Kegg.

BODE

BAMBI BODE Sixth great granddaughter of progenitor Nicholas Kegg. **KOLTEN BODE** Sixth great grandson of progenitor Nicholas Kegg. **LACY N. BODE** Sixth great granddaughter of progenitor Nicholas Kegg. **LAKOTA BODE** Seventh great granddaughter of progenitor Nicholas Kegg.

BODEL

GEORGE W. BODEL [2838] (1872 – 1938) son of Samuel and Matilda (Kegg) Bodle married twice, first to Bertha F. Galloway with whom he was father of (1). **MERILL DEWEY BODEL** [2839] (1898 – 1962) son of George and Bertha (Galloway) Bodel, married Sarah Elizabeth Keffer.

BODEN

BILLIE JEAN BODEN Sixth great granddaughter of progenitor Nicholas Kegg. **BONNIE LYNN BODEN** Sixth great granddaughter of progenitor Nicholas Kegg. **BRANDY SUE BODEN** Sixth great granddaughter of progenitor Nicholas Kegg. **BRUCE W. BODEN** [2840] (1954 – 2017) son of Sherwood and Maxine (Kerr) Boden. A father of (3), Bruce was an active hunter and fisherman, sharing his love outdoors with his family and friends. He was a skilled craftsman who shared his talents with those around him. **CAROL JEAN BODEN** Fifth great granddaughter of progenitor Nicholas Kegg. **DAVID R. BODEN** Fifth great grandson of progenitor Nicholas Kegg. **JAMES S. BODEN** Fifth great grandson of progenitor Nicholas Kegg. **ROBERT S. BODEN** Fifth great grandson of progenitor Nicholas Kegg.

BODENSTEINER

BRITTANY SAGE BODENSTEINER Seventh great granddaughter of progenitor Nicholas Kegg.
MICHAEL BODENSTEINER Sixth great grandson of progenitor Nicholas Kegg.
MYA BODENSTEINER Seventh great granddaughter of progenitor Nicholas Kegg.

BODLE

ELIZABETH ANN BODLE [2841] (1868 – 1944) aka "Lizzie" daughter of Samuel and Matilda (Kegg) Bodle married Joseph Gilmore Nelson with whom she was mother of (8). **HAZEL J. BODLE** (1903 – 1967) daughter of John and Charlotte (Heitmiller) Bodle, married Vernard L. Miller with whom she was

---

[2838] Elkhart Weekly Review (IN) Sept 15, 1897 [2839] Coal Valley News (WVA) Nov. 13, 1962 obtained by D. Sue Dible [2840] Centre Daily Times (PA) Mar 29, 2017 [2841] "The Life of Joseph Gilmore Nelson: His Ancestors and Descendants," by Celia Bell Richardson Yoder, Blackwell, OK, 1998

mother of (2).   **JOHN MELVIN BODLE** (2842) (1865 – 1945) son of Samuel and Matilda (Kegg) Bodle married Charlotte Elizabeth Heitmiller with whom he was father of (2). John was a member of the Tillamook County Pioneer Association and the Masonic lodge of Bay City from which organization he received his jewel commemorating a 50-year membership. He was also active on the city council and the school board at Bay City.   **MARY K. BODLE** (1861 – aft 1920) daughter of Samuel and Matilda (Kegg) Bodle married three times, first to Charles F. Johnson, then to Calvin Mack and later to George S. Jacobs.   **ORVAL RICHARD BODLE** (1925 – 1995) son of Orval and Rosemary (Conner) Bodle married Dorothy Elizabeth (Matley) Brady.   **RICHARD MONTGOMERY BODLE** (1874 – 1945) son of Samuel and Matilda (Kegg) Bodle. Richard was employed as a carpenter.   **SAMUEL ELTON BODLE** (2843) (1877 – 1940) son of Samuel and Matilda (Kegg) Bodle, married Ina Mary McMillan.   **SARAH JANE BODLE** (2844) (1860 – 1932) daughter of Samuel and Matilda (Kegg) Bodle married Thomas E. Smith with whom she was mother of (10).

BODTKE

DAWN J BODTKE Sixth great granddaughter of progenitor Nicholas Kegg.
ELIZABETH ANN BODTKE Fifth great granddaughter of progenitor Nicholas Kegg.
JESSE PAUL BODTKE Sixth great grandson of progenitor Nicholas Kegg.   **PAUL DAVID BODTKE** (2844A) (1949 – 2013) son of David and Jeanbelle (Fisher) Bodtke was twice married, first to Lynn Dore with whom he was father of (1), then to Evelyn Lindsey with whom he was father of (1) His pottery was a favorite with locals and tourists passing through town. Paul combined his love of pottery and fishing when he created ceramic fish pressings using molds of fish he caught in Oregon and Mexico. He was well known for his annual Seconds Sale held on July 3, where crowds would gather for a good deal on pottery, a free gin and tonic and a big dose of Paul's enthusiasm and love for life. Paul loved nature and his biggest passion in life was fishing, making Port Orford the perfect spot for him. He was always just minutes from a beautiful beach or river where he could fish for perch, stripers or salmon with one of his fishing buddies or with one of his beloved canine companions Singer, Bessie, Maya or Buddy. When the wind blew from the south and the ocean was flat, he would run down to the dock with his kayak and paddle out to catch rockfish. For Paul, life could not get better than this! Paul was always interested in learning new things and finding new ways to express himself. He played the harmonica and standup bass with the Hensley Hillbillies and other friends in town. He also was a woodworker, wove rugs on a loom, gardened and made glass art.   **ROSEMARY BODTKE** (2844B) aka "Rusty" (1946 – 2013) daughter of David and Jeanbelle (Fisher) Bodtke, married William Morawski. Rusty was a total "Navy Brat" who grew up on military bases all over the country. Her career path was in Human Resources and she successfully worked her way to a director position in an engineering firm before being diagnosed with ALS, more commonly know as Lou Gehrig's disease. But Rusty never let that keep her from living life fully. Her astounding adventures continued, doing just what she wanted to do, like roughing it in a van trip through the Alaska wilderness, crabbing off the Oregon coast, and flying to Italy to do Tuscany with her sister. She was brave and unyielding becoming, after 23 years of treatment, the longest surviving female ALS patient at Johns Hopkins Hospital in Baltimore, Maryland

BOE

GERALD FREDERICK BOE Fifth great grandson of progenitor Nicholas Kegg.
KENNETH ALLEN BOE Fifth great grandson of progenitor Nicholas Kegg.

[2842] Headlight-Herald (OR) July 12, 1945 obtained by D. Sue Dible [2843] p16 Orgonian (OR) Dec 5, 1940 [2844] Fort Wayne News Sentinel July 7, 1932 obtained by D. Sue Dible [2844A] Ventura County Star (CA) June 8, 2013 [2844B] Maryland Gazette (MD) Feb 9, 2013

BOES

CHRISTY BOES Sixth great granddaughter of progenitor Nicholas Kegg. **MICHAEL BOES** Sixth great grandson of progenitor Nicholas Kegg. **NICHOLAS BOES** Sixth great grandson of progenitor Nicholas Kegg.

BOETCHER

BRADLY BOETCHER Seventh great grandson of progenitor Nicholas Kegg.
ARLENE LORETTA BOETTCHER Fourth great granddaughter of progenitor Nicholas Kegg.
MAHLON ERNST BOETTCHER [2845] (1940 – 2002) son of Ernst and Hazel (Kegg) Boettcher married Carol Anne Sayor with whom he was father of (1). Mahlon was employed for 30 years by Met-Ed as a mechanic. Mahlon was a U.S. Army veteran. He was a member of Shiloh American Legion Post 791, East Berlin VFW, Hawk Gunning Club and the 12th Ward and 13th Ward political clubs.
SCOTT ALLEN BOETTCHER Fifth great granddaughter of progenitor Nicholas Kegg.

BOGEN

BRYNN BOGEN Fifth great granddaughter of progenitor Nicholas Kegg.

BOGERT

DANIELLE MARIE BOGERT Seventh great granddaughter of progenitor Nicholas Kegg.
JUSTIN RICHARD BOGERT Seventh great grandson of progenitor Nicholas Kegg.
SAMANTHA BOGERT Eighth great granddaughter of progenitor Nicholas Kegg.

BOHMONT

JANICE MAY BOHMONT Fifth great granddaughter of progenitor Nicholas Kegg.
LYNETTE BOHMONT Fifth great granddaughter of progenitor Nicholas Kegg.

BOISSENET

BEVERLY JOAN BOISSENET [2846] (1931 – 2006) daughter of Floyd and Edith (Tretheway) Boissenet married Billy Carl Casey with whom she was mother of (4). Beverly was a housewife. **BYRON C. BOISSENET** (1919 – 1919) son of Charles and Edith (Blackburn) Boissenet. **CHARLES HIRAM BOISSENET** [2847] (1896 – 1982) son of Louis and Ada (Parent) Boissenet married twice, first to Edith Rose Blackburn with whom he was father of (3). Later, he married Gladys M. Schell. Charles retired in 1961 as president of White Cross Beauty Supply Co. in Fort Wayne after 30 years. He also was associated with Business Brokers for 17 years. **CHARLES WILLIAM BOISSENET** [2848] (1924 – 2002) son of Charles and Edith (Blackburn) Boissenet married Mary Lou Neith with whom he was father of (2). The Fort Wayne native retired in 1992 after 34 years as a realtor and broker. He served in the Air Force during World War II and was a member of Masonic Lodge 170, Scottish Rite, Mizpah Temple and Fort Wayne Board of Realtors. **CHARLIE PAUL BOISSENET** Fifth great grandson of progenitor Nicholas Kegg. **CHARLIE PAUL BOISSENET JR.** aka "Chuck" Sixth great grandson of progenitor Nicholas Kegg. **ERIK O'NEILL BOISSENET** Sixth great grandson of progenitor Nicholas Kegg.
FLOYD ARTHUR BOISSENET (1901 – 1972) son of Louis and Ada (Parent) Boissenet married twice, first to Esther Beahrs with whom he was father of (1). Later, he married Edith J. Tretheway with whom he

---

[2845] York Dispatch (PA) Aug 27, 2002 [2846] Arkansas Democrat-Gazette: Northwest Edition (AR) Dec 3, 2006 [2847] Fort Wayne Journal Gazette (IN) Nov 10, 1982 obtained by D.Sue Dible [2848] p 7A - News-Sentinel (IN) March 4, 2002

was father of (2). **FLOYD C. BOISSENET** (1924 – 1939) son of Floyd and Esther (Beahrs) Boissenet. **GOLDA PAULINE BOISSENET** (1900 – 1984) daughter of Louis and Ada (Parent) Boissenet married twice, first to William Clayton Herring with whom she was mother of (1). **LAURENA BOISSENET** [2849] (1895 – 1901) daughter of Louis and Ada (Parent) Boissenet.
LEIF BOISSENET Seventh great grandson of progenitor Nicholas Kegg.
PAUL ARTHUR BOISSENET aka "Tink" Fourth great grandson of progenitor Nicholas Kegg.
PAULETTE ANGELIA BOISSENET [2850] (1958 – 2015) daughter of Paul and Cecile (Ruff) Boissenet married Stephen Wayne Watkins with whom she was mother of (1). Paulette was a homemaker who enjoyed being a florist, crocheting, china painting, and she loved spending time with her grandchildren.
RENEE L. BOISSENET Fifth great granddaughter of progenitor Nicholas Kegg.
VICKI LYNN BOISSENET Fifth great granddaughter of progenitor Nicholas Kegg.
VIVIAN LOVAN BOISSENET [2851] (1918 – 2003) daughter of Charles and Edith (Blackburn) Boissenet married Carl Edward Wert with whom she was mother of (6). Vivian was a homemaker.

BOLANDER

ANDREW K BOLANDER Seventh great grandson of progenitor Nicholas Kegg.
ANGELA L. BOLANDER Seventh great granddaughter of progenitor Nicholas Kegg.
DANIEL BOLANDER Seventh great grandson of progenitor Nicholas Kegg.
DAVID CHARLES BOLANDER Seventh great grandson of progenitor Nicholas Kegg.
DEBRA JEAN BOLANDER Sixth great granddaughter of progenitor Nicholas Kegg.
DOUGLAS J. BOLANDER [2852] (1960 – 2021) son of Elmer and Patsy Ann (Hindall) Bolander, married Vicki M. Robinson with whom he was father of (2). Douglas enjoyed preaching and being with his church family. He also enjoyed playing basketball, softball, bowling, and fishing.
JAMIE R. BOLANDER Seventh great grandson of progenitor Nicholas Kegg.
JOHN ARTHUR BOLANDER Sixth great grandson of progenitor Nicholas Kegg.
NICHOLAS A. BOLANDER Seventh great grandson of progenitor Nicholas Kegg.
ROSS DANIEL BOLANDER Seventh great grandson of progenitor Nicholas Kegg.
STEVEN ALAN BOLANDER Sixth great grandson of progenitor Nicholas Kegg.

BOLDEN

EMROY DECORSEY BOLDEN aka "Skipp" Fifth great grandson of progenitor Nicholas Kegg.
JASON EDWARD BOLDEN Sixth great grandson of progenitor Nicholas Kegg.
JEFFRIES DAWSON BOLDEN Fifth great grandson of progenitor Nicholas Kegg.
MARY DECOURSEY BOLDEN Fifth great granddaughter of progenitor Nicholas Kegg.

BOLDT

KIM L. BOLDT Sixth great granddaughter of progenitor Nicholas Kegg. **KRISTIN BOLDT** Sixth great granddaughter of progenitor Nicholas Kegg. **RYAN BOLDT** Sixth great grandson of progenitor Nicholas Kegg.

BOLDURIAN

ANTHONY JOHN BOLDURIAN Seventh great grandson of progenitor Nicholas Kegg.

[2849] Elkhart Daily Review (IN) Nov 25, 1901 [2850] Amarillo Globe News (TX) June 1, 2015 [2851] Chino Champion (CA) July 12, 2003 [2852] Brewer & Sons Funeral Homes & Cremation Services (FL) obtained by D. Sue Dible

BOLINGER

KEVIN M. BOLINGER Sixth great grandson of progenitor Nicholas Kegg.   **LEISA BOLINGER** Sixth great granddaughter of progenitor Nicholas Kegg.   **TERRY BOLINGER** Seventh great grandson of progenitor Nicholas Kegg.   **WILLIAM LEWIS BOLINGER** aka "Willy" Seventh great grandson of progenitor Nicholas Kegg.

BOLLES

CHARLES WALTER BOLLES JR. (1965 – 2000) son of Charles and Lois (Daley) Bolles.

BOLLINGER

ROSEMARY BOLLINGER Fifth great granddaughter of progenitor Nicholas Kegg.

BOLLMAN

AMBER BOLLMAN Sixth great granddaughter of progenitor Nicholas Kegg.   **ALBERT EDWARD BOLLMAN** Fifth great grandson of progenitor Nicholas Kegg.   **BLANCHE ELMIRA BOLLMAN** [2853] (1914 – 1985) daughter of Albert and Flora (Smith) Bollman married Clyde R. Fisher with whom she was mother of (2).   **ELLA MAE BOLLMAN** (1933 – 2009) daughter of James and Mae (Diehl) Bollman married Jackson Francis Knisely with whom she was mother of (3).   **ERIC ROBERT BOLLMAN** Seventh great grandson of progenitor Nicholas Kegg.   **JAMES EDGAR BOLLMAN** [2954, 2855] (1913 – 1971) son of Albert and Flora (Smith) Bollman married three times. First, to Mae Sarah Diehl with whom he was father of (2), he married Clemmie Gertrude Harding and later married Jacqueline Yvone Gearhart with whom he was father of (1). James was a member of Fitzgerald Lodge No. 299, F. & A. M., the Scottish Rite and Samis Grotto.   **JUNE VICTORIA BOLLMAN** [2856] (1916 – 2004) daughter of Albert and Flora (Smith) Bollman married Charles A. Weicht with whom she was mother of (4). June was a homemaker who enjoyed cooking and baking, always remembering her family and friends' birthdays and special occasions.   **LINDA BOLLMAN** Fifth great granddaughter of progenitor Nicholas Kegg.   **MARC BOLLMAN** Seventh great grandson of progenitor Nicholas Kegg.   **MARINA GISELE BOLLMAN** Sixth great granddaughter of progenitor Nicholas Kegg.   **MARK GIRARD BOLLMAN** Sixth great grandson of progenitor Nicholas Kegg.   **PAMELA M. BOLLMAN** Sixth great granddaughter of progenitor Nicholas Kegg.   **ROBERT E. BOLLMAN** Sixth great grandson of progenitor Nicholas Kegg.   **RUTH MAE BOLLMAN** [2857] (1918 – 2002) daughter of Albert and Flora (Smith) Bollman married Grant Ulysses Steach with whom she was mother of (5).   **SHERRY L. BOLLMAN** Sixth great granddaughter of progenitor Nicholas Kegg.

BOLTON

ARABELLA JADE BOLTON Seventh great granddaughter of progenitor Nicholas Kegg.
CARTER THOMAS BOLTON Seventh great grandson of progenitor Nicholas Kegg.
MADISON KAY BOLTON Seventh great granddaughter of progenitor Nicholas Kegg.

BOLYARD

BRANDI BOLYARD Sixth great granddaughter of progenitor Nicholas Kegg.
KYLE CHARENCE BOLYARD Sixth great grandson of progenitor Nicholas Kegg.

[2853] p.16 - Bedford Gazette (PA) Sept 16, 1985 [2854] p.6 – Huntingdon Daily News (PA) June 21, 1933 [2855] obituary clipping obtained by Duke Clark [2856] Bedford Inquirer (PA) Oct 8, 2004, obtained by Bob Rose [2857] p.3 - Bedford Inquirer (PA) June 14, 2002, obtained by Bob Rose

BOMER

JAMES DALE BOMER Sixth great grandson of progenitor Nicholas Kegg. **LINDA MAE BOMER** [2857A] (1945 – 2009) daughter of James and Wilave Leona (Kane) Bomer married Howard Norman McDaniel with whom she was mother of (2). Later, she married Donald Alan Laudermith **MARVELLA MONA BONA** (1951 – 1983) daughter of James and Wilave Leona (Kane) Bomer married Gary Kokaisel with whom she was mother of (2). **WILLIAM CHESTER BOMER** [2857B] (1949 – 2011) son of James and Wilave Leona (Kane) Bomer.

BONDONI

BRIANA BONDONI Eighth great granddaughter of progenitor Nicholas Kegg.
GINA ANN BONDONI Seventh great granddaughter of progenitor Nicholas Kegg.
JAMES ALTON BONDONI [2858] (1953 – 2018) aka "Jim" son of James and Janet (Fickes) Bondoni married Debra Akins with whom he was father of (2). Jim was employed as a mechanic at Joel's Garage. He enjoyed stock car racing, Nascar racing, bowling, and especially loved watching his granddaughters play sports and other activities. Jim was a 4th Degree Member of the Knights of Columbus Council #557 and a member of the Christopher Columbus Society. **JAMES ALTON BONDONI JR.** Seventh great grandson of progenitor Nicholas Kegg. - **JANETTE MARIE BONDONI** Sixth great granddaughter of progenitor Nicholas Kegg. - **JOSEPH L. BONDONI** Sixth great grandson of progenitor Nicholas Kegg. - **JULIANNE BONDONI** Sixth great granddaughter of progenitor Nicholas Kegg. **JUSTINE LOUISE BONDONI** Sixth great granddaughter of progenitor Nicholas Kegg. **MARISSA JO BONDONI** Eighth great granddaughter of progenitor Nicholas Kegg.

BONDY

DEEGAN BONDY Eighth great grandson of progenitor Nicholas Kegg.

BONHAM

CLARALEE ROSE BONHAM Fifth great granddaughter of progenitor Nicholas Kegg.

BONNETT

JOHN CLARKE BONNETT Sixth great grandson of progenitor Nicholas Kegg.
STEPHANIE MICHELLE BONNETT Sixth great granddaughter of progenitor Nicholas Kegg.

BONNEY

ALLAN BONNEY Sixth great grandson of progenitor Nicholas Kegg. **BRYN LAUREN BONNEY** Seventh great granddaughter of progenitor Nicholas Kegg. **SHANLEY DEIRDRE BONNEY** Seventh great granddaughter of progenitor Nicholas Kegg. **TARA BROOKE BONNEY** Seventh great granddaughter of progenitor Nicholas Kegg. **WILLIAM LEE BONNEY** Sixth great grandson of progenitor Nicholas Kegg.

[2857A] Find A Grave Memorial# 33609414 [2857B] Kansas City Star (MO) Sep 20, 2011, obtained by D. Sue Dible [2858] The Alliance Review (OH) Dec 1, 2018, obtained by D. Sue Dible

BOOCHER

MICHAEL BOOCHER aka "Mike" Seventh great grandson of progenitor Nicholas Kegg.
SUSAN BOOCHER Seventh great granddaughter of progenitor Nicholas Kegg.

BOOR

HAROLD EMANUEL BOOR [2859, 2860] (1912 – 1942) aka "Shine" son of Cromwell and Arvilla (Rose) Boor. He received his nickname because John "Shine" Cortazzo, former Cumerland Colt was his baseball idol. Harold was a well-known ballplayer, having been an outfielder of note and played with Corrigansville, Cumberland and Frostburg teams. Joining the Air Corps., Shine was stationed in the South Pacific serving as a mechanic. **LINDA BOOR** Fifth great granddaughter of progenitor Nicholas Kegg. **MARK BOOR** Fifth great grandson of progenitor Nicholas Kegg. **STANLEY MORRELL BOOR** Fifth great grandson of progenitor Nicholas Kegg. **WILLIAM BOOR** Fifth great grandson of progenitor Nicholas Kegg. **WINSTON BOOR** Fifth great grandson of progenitor Nicholas Kegg.

BOORE

ELIJAH BOORE Sixth great grandson of progenitor Nicholas Kegg. **ERIC BOORE** Sixth great grandson of progenitor Nicholas Kegg. **JASON BOORE** Sixth great grandson of progenitor Nicholas Kegg. **RACHEL BOORE** Sixth great granddaughter of progenitor Nicholas Kegg.
STACY BOORE Sixth great granddaughter of progenitor Nicholas Kegg.
WILLIAM CONRAD BOORE Sixth great grandson of progenitor Nicholas Kegg.

BOOSE

ANNA MARY BOOSE [2861] (1918 – 1976) daughter of Howard and Charlotte (Good) Boose married John Johnston Houser with whom she was mother of (2). **ANNAMARIE BOOSE** Fourth great granddaughter of progenitor Nicholas Kegg. **BUDD B. BOOSE** [2862] (1887 – 1947) son of John and Anna (Turner) Boose married Bertha Weimer. After graduation from Somerset High School, Budd was employed for several years by the Farmer's National Bank of Somerset. He ended that employment to prepare himself for the legal profession, receiving his LL. B. degree from the University of Michigan in 1915. After graduating he became the first secretary of the Somerset County Coal Operators Association. A short time later he entered military service in World War I. He was honorably discharged Mar. 1, 1919. After his admission to practice at the Somerset County bar, in 1919, and later to the Federal Appellate Court of Western Pennsylvania, he joined his brother, Norman T. Boose, in practice. The partnership of Boose & Boose was dissolved in 1930 when Norman T. Boose was elected to the bench. After that attorney Budd B. Boose practiced alone, until the close of World War II, when his nephew, Capt. Robert I. Boose returned from service and became affiliated with him using the old firm name of Boose & Boose. Attorney Boose was a director of the Somerset Trust Company, a trustee of Trinity Lutheran Church and of S.S. Crouse American Legion Post of Somerset. **EARL LYNN BOOSE** [2863] (1903 – 1964) son of Harvey and Nora (Fike) Boose married Agnes Rachel Landon with whom he was father of (2) Earl was a dentist. He was a graduate of Sunnyside High School and the Pacific Northwest Dental College in Portland. he was a member of the Seattle and Washington State Dental Societies, Psi Omega, dental fraternity, and the University Presbyterian Church. **ELIZABETH ANN BOOSE** [2864] aka "Beth" (1957 – 2012) daughter of John and Opal (Bennett) Boose married three times, first to Asem Zulfic with whom she was mother of (1), She was mother of (2) with her 2nd husband. Last, she married

---

[2859] Hagerstown Daily Mail (MD) Sep 2, 1942, obtained by Bob Rose [2860] Huntingdon Daily News (PA) Sep 5, 1942 [2861] Daily American (PA) Jan 3, 1977 [2862] Meyersdale Republican (PA) Oct 2, 1947 [2863] p.53 - Seattle Daily Times (WA) March 16, 1964 [2864] Peoria Journal Star (IL) Nov 21, 2012

Roy Chappel. Beth could find beauty in anything and bring it out for the world to see. She had a gift for making people feel special. **HAROLD ALSTON BOOSE** [2865] (1907 – 1986) son of Harvey and Nora (Fike) Boose married Anna Blanche Chambers with whom he was father of (2). After graduation, Harold managed the DeSoto Creamery in Sunnyside. Later he was employed by the Milk Product Co., the Yakima City Creamery and Maple Leaf Creamery in Toppenish. The family moved in 1950 to Grandview, where he worked for the Grandview School District. He was a past member and officer of the Grandview Lions Club, the PTA, the Public-School Employees Union and the Lower Valley Rock and Mineral Club. He was a member of the Grandview Bethany Presbyterian Church and the Sunnyside Pioneers Association. He was an avid fan of the Grandview Greyhounds, and often drove buses carrying the teams to athletic events. **HARVEY ALLEN BOOSE** [2866] (1873 – 1958) son of John and Anna (Turner) Boose married Nora Fike with whom he was father of (5). Harvey always made good use of his opportunities, qualified for teaching, which profession he took up in Pennsylvania. He devoted nine years to teaching, six years of which were passed in his native state and three in Illinois. He came to Washington in 1900, settling at Sunnyside, and there purchased wild land. He developed and improved a fine farm of forty acres, at which time there was no town here. In 1907, however, he became identified with the banking interests of Sunnyside but still made his home upon the farm. Harvey is a man of genuine personal worth as well as business ability, and his many sterling traits of character and his loyalty in citizenship have gained him an enviable place in the regard of his fellow townsmen. **HEATHER BOOSE** Fifth great granddaughter of progenitor Nicholas Kegg. **HOMER EDISON BOOSE** (1884 – 1892) son of John and Anna (Turner) Boose. **HOWARD RUSSELL BOOSE** [2867] (1880 – 1971) son of of John and Anna (Turner) Boose, married Charlotte Pearl Good with whom he was father of (5). Howard held a position in the auditing department of the Somerset Coal Company.
HOWARD RUSSELL BOOSE II [2868] (1914 – 2001) son of Howard and Charlotte (Good) Boose married Peggy Specht with whom he was father of (3). Howard grew up in Somerset and remained in the area until he entered the Army just prior to World War II. He returned briefly after the war and founded Boose and Hawke Concrete Products. In 1946 he decided to return to the Army. He was a retired Army colonel and former civilian intelligence officer and an Arlington real estate agent. He had maintained a home in Arlington since the 1950s. Col. Boose attended both Gettysburg College in his native Pennsylvania, and Ohio State University. He served in the Civilian Conservation Corps before receiving and Army commission about 1940. During World War II, he served in this country with armored units. He later spent much of his uniformed career in intelligence. Fluent in Turkish, he also served for a time as an adviser to the Turkish army. His last assignment, before retiring from active duty in 1961, was in a Pentagon intelligence post. He served with Army intelligence in a civilian capacity from 1961 to 1976, then became an Arlington real estate agent. He worked for the Arlington realty firms of Better Homes and George Mason Green before founding his own firm, Neighborhood Realty, which he operated in the 1980s before retiring altogether. Col. Boose was a 40-year member of St. Ann's Catholic Church in Arlington, where he had served as a Eucharistic minister. He was a past president of the Arlington Optimist Club. **HOWARD RUSSELL BOOSE III** Fifth great grandson of progenitor Nicholas Kegg. **IRA C. BOOSE** (1878 – 1891) son of John and Anna (Turner) Boose. **JEAN ERNA BOOSE** Fourth great granddaughter of progenitor Nicholas Kegg. **JENNIE B. BOOSE** [2869, 2870] (1891 – 1987) daughter of John and Anna (Turner) Boose married Jerome Stufft Good with whom she was mother of (1). Jennie had been employed as a teacher in the Somerset schools. **JOHANNA JANE BOOSE** Fourth great granddaughter of progenitor Nicholas Kegg. **JOHN RALPH BOOSE** aka "Jack", Fourth

---

[2865] p.11A -Yakima Herald Republic Apr 24, 1986, obtained by D. Sue Dible [2866] The History of the Yakima Valley, Washington Volume II, page 105 [2867] p.6 - The Daily Courier (PA) May 12, 1909 [2868] Daily American (PA) May 23, 2001 [2869] p.2 - Daily Courier (PA) Nov 14. 1918 [2870] Daily American (PA) June 11, 1987

great grandson of progenitor Nicholas Kegg. **JOHN W. BOOSE** Fifth great grandson of progenitor Nicholas Kegg. **JULIA A. BOOSE** aka "Toni" Fourth great granddaughter of progenitor Nicholas Kegg. **JULIE BOOSE** Fifth great granddaughter of progenitor Nicholas Kegg. **LARRY EDWARD BOOSE** Fifth great grandson of progenitor Nicholas Kegg. **LINDA BOOSE** Fourth great granddaughter of progenitor Nicholas Kegg. **LOUIS ANDREW BOOSE** [2871] (1868 – 1908) son of William and Margaret (Turner) Boose. **LYNN ALLEN BOOSE** Fifth great grandson of progenitor Nicholas Kegg. **MARGARET BOOSE** aka "Maggie" Fifth great granddaughter of progenitor Nicholas Kegg. **MARGARET BOOSE** (1920 – 1920) daughter of Norman and Mary (Miller) Boose died a result of premature birth. **MARY A. BOOSE** Fifth great granddaughter of progenitor Nicholas Kegg. **MAURICE VERNON BOOSE** [2872] (1908 – 1982) son of Harvey and Nora (Fike) Boose married twice, first to Lola R. Nelson with whom he was father of (2). Later, he married Marie Mitchell. Maurice owned and operated his own meat market from 1938 to 1972 in Sunnyside. Maurice was a member of Masonic Lodge No. 138 of Sunnyside, Yakima B.P.O.E. No. 318, Fraternal Order of Eagles Lodge No. 289 of Yakima and the William Wharton Post VFW No. 379. **MERIDITH JANE BOOSE** Fourth great granddaughter of progenitor Nicholas Kegg. **MILES A. BOOSE** Sixth great grandson of progenitor Nicholas Kegg. **MILLICENT GAIL BOOSE** Fourth great granddaughter of progenitor Nicholas Kegg. **NANCY BOOSE** [2873, 2874] (1917 – 1980) daughter of Howard and Charlotte (Good) Boose married George Park Gourley with whom she was mother of (1). **NORALEE BOOSE** aka "Noni" Fifth great granddaughter of progenitor Nicholas Kegg. **NORMAN T. BOOSE JR.** (1915 – 1920) son of Norman and Mary (Miller) Boose. **NORMAN T. BOOSE** [2875] (1876 – 1965) son of John and Anna (Turner) Boose married Mary E. Miller with whom he was father of (3). Norman obtained his public-school training in Brothersvalley and Elk Lick Townships and Rockwood Borough. Later he studied at West Chester Normal School and then entered the University of Michigan where he obtained his law degree in 1902. He was the first native-born judge of Somerset County to have a law degree. After completing his law course at the University of Michigan, he spent several years in Ohio, Indiana and Michigan, and was admitted to the bar in each of those states. He returned to Somerset County where he was admitted to practice law Feb. 20, 1905. For a number of years, he maintained his own law office, but after his younger brother, the late Budd B. Boose returned from the armed service after World War I, they formed the law firm of Boose & Boose. The firm was dissolved in 1930 when Judge Boose assumed his duties on the bench. He served as president judge of Somerset County Courts for 20 years—longer than any other judge in the history of the county. He first was elected in 1929 and was reelected in 1939, the first time a judge won reelection in the county. Judge Boose left the bench in 1950 after bidding unsuccessfully for a third term. **ORLO J. BOOSE** (1899 – 1899) son of Harvey and Nora (Fike) Boose. **PEGGY BOOSE** Fifth great granddaughter of progenitor Nicholas Kegg. **R. ANDREW BOOSE** Fifth great grandson of progenitor Nicholas Kegg. **RICHARD MAURICE BOOSE** [2876] (1936 – 1941) son of Maurice and Lola (Nelson) Boose. The five-year-old, riding in the backseat of a car, was killed instantly when he opened the door and fell out while the machine traveled about forty miles an hour. **ROBERT I. BOOSE** Fifth great grandson of progenitor Nicholas Kegg. **ROBERT ISAIAH BOOSE** [2877] (1915 – 2000) son of Howard and Charlotte (Good) Boose married Lillias B. Barilar with whom he was father of (3). Robert received his B.S. degree in 1939 and law degree in 1941 from Ohio

---

[2871] Rockford Republic (IL) Jan 16, 1908 [2872] Yakima Herald Republic (WA) Feb 1, 1982 [2873] p.2 - The Daily Courier (PA) Feb 25, 1937 [2874] Daily American (PA) May 13, 1980 [2875] p.21 - Daily Courier (PA) Oct 6, 1965 [2876] p8 - Seattle Daily Times (WA) Mar 14, 1941 [2877] Daily American (PA) March 21, 2000

State University. He has been a member of the Somerset County Bar Association since 1941. His practice of law was interrupted by his enlistment in the U.S. Air Force in December 1941, and he served in the armed forces until August 1945, when he was separated from the service with the rank of captain. While in the service, he was pilot of a P-38 fighter aircraft and assigned to the First Fighter Group, 94th Fighter Squadron. He flew 50 combat missions in the North African Theater of operations during World War II, and later served as a test pilot at the Air Force Proving Ground Command at Eglin Field, Florida. He received the Air Medal with seven Oak Leaf Clusters and was awarded the Distinguished Flying Cross. He practiced law, first with his uncle Budd R. Boose, and subsequently with Fike, Cascio and Boose. Robert he was past commander of the American Legion; past president of the Somerset Country Club Board of Directors; past president of the Somerset Bar Association and served on the board of directors. He was an avid golfer. **STACY LYNN BOOSE** Fifth great granddaughter of progenitor Nicholas Kegg. **VIDA MAY BOOSE** [2878] (1900 – 1965) daughter of Ellis and Emma (Miller) Boose married Leland Woy Walker with whom she was mother of (2). Vida was prominent in civic affairs. **WILLIAM R. BOOSE** Fourth great grandson of progenitor Nicholas Kegg.

BOOTH

ADDISON RENAE BOOTH aka "Addie" Seventh great granddaughter of progenitor Nicholas Kegg. **ALICIA BOOTH** Sixth great granddaughter of progenitor Nicholas Kegg. **D.J. BOOTH** Sixth great grandson of progenitor Nicholas Kegg. **DANIEL BOOTH** Sixth great grandson of progenitor Nicholas Kegg. **DAYTON RYME BOOTH** Seventh great grandson of progenitor Nicholas Kegg. **DEBBIE BOOTH** Fifth great granddaughter of progenitor Nicholas Kegg. **DEVIN BOOTH** Sixth great grandson of progenitor Nicholas Kegg. **DIRK BOOTH** Sixth great grandson of progenitor Nicholas Kegg. **DUSTY RAY BOOTH** Fifth great grandson of progenitor Nicholas Kegg. **EDWARD BOOTH** Fifth great grandson of progenitor Nicholas Kegg. **GLORIA BOOTH** Fourth great granddaughter of progenitor Nicholas Kegg. **JACOB BOOTH** Seventh great grandson of progenitor Nicholas Kegg. **JAMES FLOYD BOOTH** [2879] (1953 – 1964) aka "Jim" son of Edward and Iona (Rice) Booth. Jim attended the Clarks Public School where he was a member of the 6th grade class. He attended Sunday School and Vacation Bible School at Clarks Methodist Church. **JEFFREY BOOTH** Sixth great grandson of progenitor Nicholas Kegg. **JESSICA BOOTH** Seventh great granddaughter of progenitor Nicholas Kegg. **JORDON BOOTH** Seventh great grandson of progenitor Nicholas Kegg. **LARRY BOOTH** Fifth great grandson of progenitor Nicholas Kegg. **ROBERT BOOTH** Sixth great grandson of progenitor Nicholas Kegg. **ROGER BOOTH** Fifth great grandson of progenitor Nicholas Kegg. **SUE BOOTH** Fifth great granddaughter of progenitor Nicholas Kegg. **THOMAS SCOTT BOOTH JR.** (1996 – 1996) son of Thomas and Leann (Johnson) Booth. **WILLIAM BOOTH** Sixth great grandson of progenitor Nicholas Kegg.

BOPP

CHELSEA BOPP Seventh great granddaughter of progenitor Nicholas Kegg.
HATHERLEIGH BOPP aka "Hattie" Seventh great granddaughter of progenitor Nicholas Kegg.
JAY MORGAN BOPP Sixth great grandson of progenitor Nicholas Kegg.
LAURIE KAY BOPP Sixth great granddaughter of progenitor Nicholas Kegg.
SUE ANN BOPP Sixth great granddaughter of progenitor Nicholas Kegg.

[2878] p.2 - The Daily Courier (PA) Sept 3, 1965 [2879] The Clarks News (NE) Oct 1, 1964

BORDER

ALBERT WEBSTER BORDER (1860 – 1883) son of William and Maria (Hopkins) Border. **ALONZO DAVID BORDER** [2880] (1842 – 1941) aka "Lon" son of William and Maria (Hopkins) Border, married Anna Elaine Roberts with whom he was father of (4). **BERNICE E. BORDER** (1893 – 1956) daughter of William and Emma (Smith) Border married Forrest Wherry Clark with whom she was mother of (1). **BIRDIE ESTELLE BORDER** (1879 – aft 1932) daughter of John and Elizabeth (Lane) Border married William Tidball Hoffman. **CAROLINE BORDER** (1828 – 1904) daughter of David and Catherine Myers (Kegg) Border married Simon Silver Stuckey with whom she was mother of (9). Caroline was a woman highly esteemed by all in the community a few miles northeast of Altona, Walnut Grove, Knox County, Illinois. It was here that she settled on a farm in 1855. The welfare of her children was always paramount with her and they in turn all loved and cherished her. **DAVID BORDER JR.** (1818 – 1893) son of David and Catherine Myers (Kegg) Border married Rosana Barrick with whom he was father of (4). **DAVID OSCAR BORDER** (1862 – 1931) son of John and Elizabeth (Lane) Border married twice, first to Maria L. Grayble with whom he was father of (1). Later he married Sarah C. Duffy. David was employed as a plasterer contractor. **EVA AUGUSTUS BORDER** [2881] (1864 – 1958) daughter of William and Maria (Hopkins) Border married Leonard W. Traver with whom she was mother of (2). Eva was a member of Mt. Hood Order of Amaranth and was past state president of the Degree of Honor. **ISABELL BORDER**, (abt 1856 – bef 1903) daughter of David and Rosana (Barrick) Border. **KATHERINE BORDER** [2883] (1841 – 1903) daughter of David and Rosana (Barrick) Border married George Brinton Sleek. Katherine became a member of the Lutheran church at an early age and in 1869 was received as a member of the M.E. church and remained such till death. **KATHRYN E. BORDER** (1892 – 1967) daughter of Alonzo and Anna (Roberts) Border married twice, first to Chester Walter Patterson and later to Merwin John Weber. **LEILA A. BORDER**, (1881 – 1935) daughter of Alonzo and Anna (Roberts) Border married John Washington Turnham. **NORRIS BORDER** (1853 – 1862) son of David and Rosana (Barrick) Border. **OLIVE GERTRUDE BORDER** (1867 – 1880) daughter of John and Elizabeth (Lane) Border died a result of Scarlett Fever. **ROSE E. BORDER** (1884 – 1926) daughter of Alonzo and Anna (Roberts) Border married Clarence C. Clelland. **SAMUEL G. BORDER** (1877 – bef 1910) son of John and Elizabeth (Lane) Border. **VIVIAN A. BORDER** (1886 – 1971) daughter of Alonzo and Anna (Roberts) Border, married John Jack Buedell. **WILLIAM AUGUSTUS BORDER** [2884, 2885] (1825 – 1919) son of David and Catherine Myers (Kegg) Border married Maria Hopkins with whom he was father of (3). William was always ready to lend a helping hand to others, and more than one owes his start in life to encouragement received from William A. Border. As a boy a teacher was engaged by his father to come to the house and instruct the children, and neighbors' children were allowed the privilege of attending this little private school. Later he took a course in the Bedford high school and was a 1847 graduate in a business course. At the same time, he engaged as a contractor on a railroad. In 1848 he entered the coal and iron mines at Lonaconing, Md., where he had charge of outside work for twenty-seven years. William was a member of the Republican Party and a firm believer in the wisdom of its principals as applied to the government of the nation. In religion he identified with the Episcopal Church. Local matters have engaged his attention to a large degree, and although not desirous of office he has frequently consented to accept positions of local trust and importance. Among such offices is that of city councilman, which he held for four terms; another position was that of school director, which he filled for two terms. William dated his residence in Oregon from 1875 and his arrival at Myrtle Point occurred during the same year. For two years he devoted much of his time to travel, thus acquiring a thorough knowledge of the state at the same time being impressed with the magnitude of its resources. Beginning in 1877, he spent ten years engaged in the hotel business, but with that exception he has given his time largely to the care and development of his large farm adjoining town.

[2880] p.26- Oregonian (OR) Aug 5, 1941 [2881] p.11- Oregonian (OR) Apr 12, 1958 [2882] [2883] Bedford Gazette (PA) June 12, 1903 [2884] p.770-771 Portrait and Biographical Record of Western Oregon Chapman Publishing Co. Chicago 1904 [2885] p.17- Oregonian (Portland, Oregon) March 19, 1919

WILLIAM BRANWELL BORDER [2886] (1850 – 1905) son of David and Rosana (Barrick) Border married Emma Smith with whom he was father of (1). William was a highly esteemed merchant of Cuming Street, who died from pneumonia. He was an elder of the church and a member of the Knights of Pythias and of the Macabees

BORDNER

ANNE K. BORDNER Sixth great granddaughter of progenitor Nicholas Kegg. **EUGENE ELSWORTH BORDNER** (1914 – 1981) son of Ira and Dorothy (Cagg) Bordner married twice, first to Lucille June Hart and later, to Myrtle Louise (Stewart) Chaffin. **IRMA ARDELTHEA BORDNER** [2886A] (1909 – 1991) daughter of Ira and Dorothy (Cagg) Bordner was twice married, first to Louis James White with whom she was mother of (7). Irma retired from White Castle Corp.

BORGQUIST

CINDY BORGQUIST Sixth great granddaughter of progenitor Nicholas Kegg. **HEIDA BORGQUIST** Sixth great granddaughter of progenitor Nicholas Kegg. **JOSEPH J. BORGQUIST** Sixth great grandson of progenitor Nicholas Kegg. **PATRICK J. BORGQUIST** Sixth great grandson of progenitor Nicholas Kegg. **SANDY BORGQUIST** Sixth great granddaughter of progenitor Nicholas Kegg. **WENDY BORGQUIST** Sixth great granddaughter of progenitor Nicholas Kegg.

BORKOSKY

AUSTIN ROBERT BORKOSKY Seventh great grandson of progenitor Nicholas Kegg.
JOSEPH ALLEN BORKOSKY Seventh great grandson of progenitor Nicholas Kegg.

BOSLEY

BETHANY NICOLE BOSLEY Sixth great granddaughter of progenitor Nicholas Kegg.

BOSSLER

BETTIE MAE BOSSLER (1918 – 1973) daughter OF Edwin and Louise (Hite) Bossler married William Francis Dwyer with whom she was mother of (3).
GERTRUDE JUNE TAYLOR BOSSLER [2887] (1918 – 1998) daughter of Louise Hite/ adopted by Edwin Bossler. Gertrude served as Lieutenant U.S. Army WWII, Korea and Vietnam.
JENNIFER LEE BOSSLER Sixth great granddaughter of progenitor Nicholas Kegg.
MARY LOUISE BOSSLER Sixth great granddaughter of progenitor Nicholas Kegg.
MICHAEL JESSE BOSSLER (1964 – 1977) son of Thomas and Patricia (Rerko) Bossler died a result of non-Hodgkin's lymphoma. **PATRICIA ANN BOSSLER** Sixth great granddaughter of progenitor Nicholas Kegg. **THOMAS HITE BOSSLER** [2887A] (1931 – 2010) son of Edwin and Louise (Hite) Bossler was twice married, first to Patricia Rerco with whom he was father of (5). a retired chemical engineer at U.S. Steel who lived in an underground home that he and his son built. Tom had few hobbies beyond science; he was the type who considered a book on quantum mechanics to be light reading. At U.S. Steel's Clairton Coke Works in the 1970s, his family said, he was instrumental in developing new ways to process coke oven gas and treat wastewater at a time when pollution controls were just being implemented. He never lost the drive to learn. He was an incredibly curious person.
THOMAS RERKO BOSSLER Sixth great grandson of progenitor Nicholas Kegg.

[2886] p.2 Omaha World Herald (NB) Oct 25, 1905 [2886A] Arizona Daily Star (AZ) Feb 16, 1991 [2887] p.B5 - Pittsburgh Post-Gazette (PA) Jun 2, 1998 [2887A] Pittsburgh Post Gazette (PA) Jan 6, 2011

BOST

KEITH BOST Seventh great grandson of progenitor Nicholas Kegg.

BOSTON

ALYSEN BOSTON Eighth great granddaughter of progenitor Nicholas Kegg.
MANDI MARIE BOSTON Eighth great granddaughter of progenitor Nicholas Kegg.

BOUCHARD

ABBY SUZANNE BOUCHARD Seventh great granddaughter of progenitor Nicholas Kegg.
DREW MICHAEL BOUCHARD Seventh great grandson of progenitor Nicholas Kegg.

BOUDREAU

JANET JANE BOUDREAU Sixth great granddaughter of progenitor Nicholas Kegg.
PEGGY JOYCE BOUDREAU Sixth great granddaughter of progenitor Nicholas Kegg.

BOULGER

MADDIE MAE BOULGER Eighth great granddaughter of progenitor Nicholas Kegg.

BOURNE

BERNICE BOURNE Sixth great granddaughter of progenitor Nicholas Kegg.
GEORGE DAVID BOURNE [2888] (1964 – 2014) son of David and Bertha Louise (Kelso) Bourne. George was a man of great depth, a deep thinker and philosopher of life and the universe. He enjoyed favorite pastimes such as playing board games like D & D and Lord of the Rings and online games such as poker. George was a graduate of the Northern Alberta Institute of Technology where he studied Biology Sciences, specializing in Environmental Protection. George was a National Construction Safety Officer. In addition, George was a Commercial Chef where he graduated from the Kelsey Institute in Saskatoon, Saskatchewan. **IDA BOURNE** Sixth great granddaughter of progenitor Nicholas Kegg.
JENNIFER LEE BOURNE Seventh great granddaughter of progenitor Nicholas Kegg.
MARY BOURNE Sixth great granddaughter of progenitor Nicholas Kegg.

BOWE

ASHLEY NICOLE BOWE Eighth great granddaughter of progenitor Nicholas Kegg.

BOWERS

ALLISON LEON BOWERS [2889] (1874 – 1965) son of Thomas and Harriett (Cagg) Bowers married Margaret Keplar with whom he was father of (9). Allison was a member of the First Christian Church. Nelsonville, and was a retired coal miner. **BILLIE MAE BOWERS** [2890] (1935 – 1996) daughter of William and Mabel (Garbe) Bowers married Noel Kirben Ott with whom she was mother of (4). **BONNIE LEE BOWERS** [2891] (1931 – 2014) daughter of William and Mabel (Garbe) Bowers married Robert M. Ell with whom she was mother of (1). **CHARLEIGH BOWERS** Seventh great

[2888] Parkland Funeral Home and Crematorium Red Deer, Alberta Canada [2889] p2 Logan Daily News (OH) Nov 2, 1965 [2890] Columbus Dispatch (OH) Dec 17, 1996 [2891] The Columbus Dispatch (OH) Aug. 29, 2014

granddaughter of progenitor Nicholas Kegg. **CYNTHIA BOWERS** 6th great granddaughter of progenitor Nicholas Kegg. **DEBORAH BOWERS** Sixth great granddaughter of progenitor Nicholas Kegg. **DONNA MAE BOWERS** Fifth great granddaughter of progenitor Nicholas Kegg.
DOW LORENZO BOWERS [2892] (1879 – 1938) son of Thomas and Harriett (Cagg) Bowers married Bertha Wilson Verity with whom he was father of (4). Dow and his brothers were associated in the operation of the Bowers Bros Mine at Murray City. He was a member of the Nelsonville civil service commission. **DUANE B. BOWERS** aka "Buck" Fifth great grandson of progenitor Nicholas Kegg.
ELIZABETH MAY BOWERS (1911 – 1985) daughter of Allison and Margaret (Keplar) Bowers married Glen L. Bagley with whom she was mother of (2). **EUGENE SCOTT BOWERS** (1882 – 1951) son of Thomas and Harriett (Cagg) Bowers was a coal miner. **GARY BOWERS** Sixth great grandson of progenitor Nicholas Kegg. **GLADYS LOUISE BOWERS** (1900 – 1981) daughter of Allison and Margaret (Keplar) Bowers. **GLADYS RUTH BOWERS** [2893] (1933 - 2003) daughter of Roy and Ruth (Stevens) Bowers married Roy Westley Coey Jr., with whom she was mother of (4). Gladys was a member of Fairfield Christian Church and the Women American Bowling Congress.
HARRIET FRANCES BOWERS (1912 – 1966) daughter of Allison and Margaret (Keplar) Bowers married Kenneth Leroy Pryfogle with whom she was mother of (2). **INFANT BOWERS** (1942 – 1942) son of William and Mabel (Garbe) Bowers died of exhaustion a result of premature birth.
JAMES BOWERS, aka "Jim" Sixth great grandson of progenitor Nicholas Kegg.
JAMES EUGENE BOWERS (1939 – 1988) aka "Butch" son of Roy and Ruth (Stevens) Bowers married twice, first to Carolyn J. Gray and later to Holly E. Shadwick. **JAMES GAILEN BOWERS** [2894] (1908 – 1976) son of Allison and Margaret (Keplar) Bowers married Doris M. Buck with whom he was father of (4). **JEAN BOWERS** [2894A] (1936 – 2017) daughter of Roy and Ruth (Stevens) Bowers was married, first to Earl Purcell with whom she was mother of (1). Later, with her companion, Clyde Mahan she was mother of (1). Jean retired from National City Bank after more than 30 years of service. Jeans favorite job was working at 35 Raceway in Frankfort in the pit office.
JEFFERSON PEARL BOWERS [2895] (1876 – 1968) son of Thomas and Harriett (Cagg) Bowers married twice, first to Margaret Francis with whom he was father of (2). Later he married Varenia Rebecca Stimmel. Jefferson was a retired coal miner and a member of the First Christian Church.
JEFFREY ALLEN BOWERS 6th great grandson of progenitor Nicholas Kegg.
JOSEPH WILLIAM BOWERS [2896] (1915 – 1973) aka "Joe" son of William and Hazel (Turner) Bowers married Dorothy Mavis Miller with whom he was father of (2). **JUDITH A. BOWERS** Fifth great granddaughter of progenitor Nicholas Kegg. **KAREN BOWERS** Fifth great granddaughter of progenitor Nicholas Kegg. **KATHLEEN BOWERS** Sixth great granddaughter of progenitor Nicholas Kegg. - **KEVIN RAY BOWERS** Fifth great grandson of progenitor Nicholas Kegg.
KIMBERLY LYNN BOWERS Sixth great granddaughter of progenitor Nicholas Kegg.
LENA PEARL BOWERS (1902 – 1962) daughter of Jefferson and Margaret (Francis) Bowers married Edgar Frederick Stedwill with whom she was mother of (2). **LEROY BOWERS** (1932 – 1936) son of Roy and Ruth (Stevens) Bowers died a result of extensive burns. **LORENZO DOW BOWERS** (1901 – 1938) son of Dow and Bertha (Verity) Bowers married Grace Vita Richardson.
LOU VERITY BOWERS (1900 – 1992) daughter of Dow and Bertha (Verity) Bowers, married Glenn Alexander Allen with whom she was mother of (1). **LOUISE MARY BOWERS** (1910 – 1973) daughter of Allison and Margaret (Keplar) Bowers married Milton Ross Seabrook with whom she was mother of (1). **MARGARET BOWERS** (1904 -?) daughter of Allison and Margaret (Keplar) Bowers.
MARY HELEN BOWERS Fifth great granddaughter of progenitor Nicholas Kegg.
MARY JO BOWERS (1912 – 1940) daughter of Dow and Bertha (Verity) Bowers married Wilfred Stanley Swenson. **MARY MARGARET BOWERS** Fifth great granddaughter of progenitor Nicholas Kegg. **MAX VERITY BOWERS** (1908 – 1933) son of Dow and Bertha (Verity) Bowers.

[2892] p6 Logan Daily News (OH) Jan 3, 1939 [2893] obituary/Find A Grave Memorial #34405585 [2894] Moreland Funeral Home (OH) [2894A] Columbus Dispatch (OH) Nov. 3, 2017, obtained and contributed by D. Sue Dible [2895] p2 Logan Daily News June 24, 1968 Coleman [2896] p B16 - Rockford Morning Star (IL) April 6, 1973

MICHAEL BOWERS Sixth great grandson of progenitor Nicholas Kegg. **MICHAEL D BOWERS** Sixth great grandson of progenitor Nicholas Kegg. **REBEKAH CHRISTINE BOWERS** Sixth great granddaughter of progenitor Nicholas Kegg. **RICHARD BOWERS** Sixth great grandson of progenitor Nicholas Kegg. **ROBERT BOWERS** Fifth great grandson of progenitor Nicholas Kegg. **ROY EUGENE BOWERS** (1901 – 1957) son of Allison and Margaret (Keplar) Bowers married Ruth Naomi Stevens with whom he was father of (9). **SANDRA LOU BOWERS** Fifth great granddaughter of progenitor Nicholas Kegg. **SCOT BOWERS** Sixth great grandson of progenitor Nicholas Kegg. **SCOTT THOMAS BOWERS** [2896A] (1910 – 1997) son of Jefferson and Margaret (Francis) Bowers, married Joan Sposato with whom he was father of (1). He earned his master's and bachelor's degrees from Ohio University and a doctorate in psychology from Case Western Reserve University. In private practice for 30 years, Dr. Bowers was also a consultant to Goodwill Industries and to Dayton Municipal Court's probation department Psychologist He was the court system's first staff psychologist. Scott was also one of the founders of Wright State University's School of Professional Psychology in addition, co-founder of Eastway Corp., which has provided mental health care services to Montgomery County agencies for 40 years, described by former colleagues as warm, supportive and easy to work with, established the Department of Psychology at the former Dayton State Hospital where he served as chief psychologist for 16 years **SONIA LEE BOWERS** Sixth great granddaughter of progenitor Nicholas Kegg. **STELLA M. BOWERS** [2897] (1934 – 2008) daughter of Roy and Ruth (Stevens) Bowers married Charles W. Schulz with whom she was mother of (3). **THOMAS JEFFERSON BOWERS** [2898] (1904 – 1970) aka "Jeff" son of Allison and Margaret (Keplar) Bowers, married Gladys Louise Courts with whom he was father of (1). Jeff was a retired U.S. government employe and a veteran of World War II. **THOMAS JEFFERSON BOWERS** (1940 – 1995) aka "T. J." son of Roy and Ruth (Stevens) Bowers was father of (1). **THOMAS JEFFERSON BOWERS JR.** Sixth great grandson of progenitor Nicholas Kegg. **THOMAS L. BOWERS** Sixth great grandson of progenitor Nicholas Kegg. **THOMAS WILLIAM BOWERS** (1872 – 1955) son of Thomas and Harriet (Cagg) Bowers. **TIMOTHY BOWERS** Fifth great grandson of progenitor Nicholas Kegg. **TOMMY BOWERS** Seventh great grandson of progenitor Nicholas Kegg. **TONIA SUE BOWERS** Sixth great granddaughter of progenitor Nicholas Kegg. **VICTORIA BOWERS** Fifth great granddaughter of progenitor Nicholas Kegg. **WILLIAM CLERMONT BOWERS** (1906 – 1984) aka "Bill" son of Allison and Margaret (Keplar) Bowers married Mabel Bonita Garbe with whom he was father of (5). **WILLIAM M. BOWERS** (1949 – 1995) aka "Bill" son of Roy and Ruth (Stevens) Bowers.

BOWKLEY

MARTHA IRENE BOWKLEY [2898A] (1910 – 1938) daughter of George and Elsie (Harclerode) Bowkley, married Glenn Calvin Horner with whom she was mother of (2). Martha was a member of the Bedford Reformed Church.

BOWLES

BRIAN F. BOWLES Sixth great grandson of progenitor Nicholas Kegg. **EDWARD BOWLES** (1858 – 1916) son of James and Mary Ann (Kegg) Bowles was a wagon maker. He died of chronic Brights disease. **THOMAS E. BOWLES** Sixth great grandson of progenitor Nicholas Kegg.

BOWLSBY

MARK BOWLSBY Sixth great grandson of progenitor Nicholas Kegg.

[2896A] Dayton Daily News (OH) Dec 29, 1997 [2897] Schroedinger-Norris Funeral Home (OH) [2898] p2 Logan Daily News (OH) Feb 9, 1970 [2898A] Bedford County Historical Society (PA), book 120, p. 121 obtained and contributed by D. Sue Dible

BOWLUS

ANA BOWLUS Sixth great granddaughter of progenitor Nicholas Kegg. **ANDREW BOWLUS** Sixth great grandson of progenitor Nicholas Kegg. **ANNE WELLES BOWLUS** Sixth great granddaughter of progenitor Nicholas Kegg. **BETH BOWLUS** Fifth great granddaughter of progenitor Nicholas Kegg. **DANIEL RAY THOMAS BOWLUS** Sixth great grandson of progenitor Nicholas Kegg. **DAVID AUGUST BOWLUS** Fifth great grandson of progenitor Nicholas Kegg.
ELIZABETH ANN BOWLUS [2898B] (1907 – 2008) daughter of Harry and Bertha (Bowser) Bowlus was a veteran of World War II who taught school and managed her brother's medical office. Elizabeth was stationed in Texas, and her familiarity with the Dewey Decimal System earned her the duty of classifying and filing correspondence. She was assigned to the 8th Air Force and arrived in England aboard the Queen Elizabeth on June 6, 1944 - D-Day. She worked in London, post-liberation Paris, and post-war Germany. Miss Bowlus returned to her hometown after the war and lived in the family home. She taught fifth and sixth grades for eight years and cared for her parents until they died. Elizabeth was a detailed person in charge of her brother's medical practice for 25 years. She had been an elder of First United Presbyterian Church in Pemberville and taught Sunday school there. Elizabeth was a trustee of the Pemberville Public Library, also a longtime member of the Mental Culture Club, a women's study group in her hometown, to which her grandmother and mother belonged. **JAMES E. BOWLUS** Fifth great grandson of progenitor Nicholas Kegg. **JAMES EDWARD BOWLUS** Fifth great grandson of progenitor Nicholas Kegg. **JAMES MARCUS BOWLUS** [2899] (1915 – 2005) aka "Coach" son of Harry and Bertha (Bowser) Bowlus, married Mildred Mylott with whom he was father of (2). Coach was a veteran World War II having served as Captain in the U.S. Army Air Forces. **JEANNE BOWLUS** Fifth great granddaughter of progenitor Nicholas Kegg. **JONATHAN PALMER BOWLUS** Fifth great grandson of progenitor Nicholas Kegg. **JOSEPHINE BOWLUS** [2899A] (1909 – 2001) daughter of Harry and Bertha (Bowser) Bowlus, married Melvin Reed with whom she was mother of (3). Josephine was a member of the First Presbyterian Church of Pemberville. **LUIS BOWLUS** Sixth great grandson of progenitor Nicholas Kegg. **MADELYNN BOWLUS** Sixth great granddaughter of progenitor Nicholas Kegg. **MARK S. BOWLUS** Fifth great grandson of progenitor Nicholas Kegg.
PETER MCDONALD BOWLUS Sixth great grandson of progenitor Nicholas Kegg.
REBECCA LYNN BOWLUS aka "Becky" Sixth great granddaughter of progenitor Nicholas Kegg.
SAVANNAH BOWLUS Sixth great granddaughter of progenitor Nicholas Kegg.
STUART WESLEY BOWLUS Sixth great grandson of progenitor Nicholas Kegg.
SUSAN ELIZABETH BOWLUS Fifth great granddaughter of progenitor Nicholas Kegg.
THEODORE BOWLUS [2899B] (1910 – 2006) son of Harry and Bertha (Bowser) Bowlus, married Gertrude Fahning with whom he was father of (3). Ted was a retired longtime manager of the former Hobart-Bowlus Co. department store founded by his grandfather in about 1880. He also was a past president of the board of directors of the former Citizens Savings Bank, Pemberville. Ted was named Pemberville's outstanding citizen for his volunteer work in the community and at the church. During World War II, he was an Army tank commander with the rank of first sergeant in Europe, where he saw action in the Battle of the Bulge. He was in the service from 1942 until his honorable discharge in 1945. **THEODORE BOWLUS** Fifth great grandson of progenitor Nicholas Kegg. **THOMAS BOWLUS** Fifth great grandson of progenitor Nicholas Kegg. **THOMAS BICHAN BOWLUS** Fifth great grandson of progenitor Nicholas Kegg. **TYLER BENJAMIN BOWLUS** Sixth great grandson of progenitor Nicholas Kegg. **THOMAS PALMER BOWLUS** [2899C] (1923 – 2014) son of Harry and Bertha (Bowser) Bowlus, was twice married, first to Madeline Jewel Bichan with whom he was father of (4). Later he married Marilyn Leibius with whom he was father of (3). Tom served in the South Pacific Theater in the 23rd (Americal) Infantry Division as a medic for combat engineers. On returning from the

---

[2898B] The Blade (OH) March 19, 2008 [2899] p.11D - The Columbus Dispatch (OH) March 10, 2005 [2899A] unidentified newspaper library clipping obtained and contributed by D. Sue Dible [2899B] p. A15 - The Blade (OH) April 2, 2006 [2899C] The Blade (OH) July 12, 2014, obtained and contributed by D. Sue Dible

war, he completed his undergraduate degree at Eastern Michigan University and his medical degree at the University of Michigan. He was a kind and gentle doctor who truly enjoyed caring for his patients and he missed them when he retired. He always maintained a large garden and a flock of sheep at his beloved country home. He loved to grow and give away tomato plants to his friends. Tom loved the game of bridge, always seeking to improve his game.   **WILLIAM H. BOWLUS** aka "Bill" Fifth great grandson of progenitor Nicholas Kegg.

BOWMAN

ALYSSA KAYE BOWMAN Seventh great granddaughter of progenitor Nicholas Kegg.
BRODY EDWARD BOWMAN Seventh great grandson of progenitor Nicholas Kegg.
DEBORAH LYNN BOWMAN Seventh great granddaughter of progenitor Nicholas Kegg.
DONALD BOWMAN Fifth great grandson of progenitor Nicholas Kegg.   **GEORGE P. BOWMAN JR** [2899D] (1932 – 2011) son of George and Mabel (Kerr) Bower, married Judith A. Wickline with whom he was father of (4). George served 28 ½ years in the Air Force as a nuclear research engineer stationed in Sacramento, CA; Fairbanks, Alaska; and Washington, DC; and as an instructor of the Institute of Technology, Wright-Patterson Air Force Base in Dayton, OH.   **JAKE BOWMAN** Seventh great grandson of progenitor Nicholas Kegg.   **JENNIFER BOWMAN** Fifth great granddaughter of progenitor Nicholas Kegg.   **KARI REED BOWMAN** Sixth great granddaughter of progenitor Nicholas Kegg. **KENDYL DARCELLE BOWMAN** Eighth great granddaughter of progenitor Nicholas Kegg.   **MARY KATHERINE BOWMAN** Fourth great granddaughter of progenitor Nicholas Kegg. **RICHARD PRICE BOWMAN** [2900] (1962 – 2012) son of George and Judith (Wickline) Bowman married Amy Jeanne Ludwiczak with whom he was father of (2). Richard was a graduate of Fort Hunt High School and Virginia Tech, receiving a B.S. (1984) and M.S. (1986) in Civil Engineering, and became a principal at the firm of Seal Engineering, Inc. in 1990.   **RODNEY LEE BOWMAN** Seventh great grandson of progenitor Nicholas Kegg.   **RUTH BOWMAN** Fifth great granddaughter of progenitor Nicholas Kegg.   **WILLIAM FRANKLIN BOWMAN** Sixth great grandson of progenitor Nicholas Kegg.

BOWSER

APRIL ANNA BOWSER Eighth great granddaughter of progenitor Nicholas Kegg.   **ARI BOWSER** Eighth great grandson of progenitor Nicholas Kegg.   **BERTHA BOWSER** [2900A] (1886 – 1971) daughter of Peter and Annie (Beegle) Bowser, married Harry Marcus Bowlus with whom she was mother of (5). Bertha was a life member of the Eastern Stars, a member of the First United Presbyterian Church and a member of the Mental Culture Club.   **CHARLI DOLAN BOWSER** Eighth great granddaughter of progenitor Nicholas Kegg.   **CHRISTOPHER MICHAEL BOWSER** Seventh great grandson of progenitor Nicholas Kegg.   **CLARENCE EMANUEL BOWSER** (1891 – 1963) son of Peter and Annie (Beegle) Bowser married Pauline M. Warren with whom he was father of (2). Clarence served in the 158 Depot Brigade to Aug 8, 1918; Co C 309 Engineers to Discharge Private, first-class Sept 11, 1918; Corporal Sept 21, 1918. American Expeditionary Forces Sept 9, 1918, to Feb 28, 1919. Honorable discharge March 21, 1919.   **DANIELLE BOWSER** Seventh great granddaughter of progenitor Nicholas Kegg.   **DONALD L. BOWSER** Fifth great grandson of progenitor Nicholas Kegg. **ELIZABETH ANN BOWSER** aka "Betty" Fourth great granddaughter of progenitor Nicholas Kegg. **FLEETIE A. BOWSER** [2900B] (1894 – 1957) daughter of Peter and Annie (Beegle) Bowser, married Peter Everett Kern with whom she was mother of (2). **GERALD SEWELL BOWSER** [2900C] aka "Jerry" (1940 – 2012) son of Gerald and Mary (Grimes) Bower, married Connie McDonald with whom

---

[2899D] Washington Post (DC) July 31, 2011 [2900] The Washington Post (DC) Feb 8, 2012, obtained by D. Sue Dible [2900A] p. 284 - Oberlin alumni magazine, Vol. 3; unidentified newspaper obituary clipping obtained by D. Sue Dible [2900B] Gibsonburg Derrick; News-messenger (OH) no date obtained and contributed by D. Sue Dible [2900C] Dalla Valle Funeral Service (PA)

he was father of (1) After working for Hedstrom Inc. in Bedford, he began working as a truck driver for PennDOT, running snowplow in the winter and transporting supplies throughout the year until retiring. At home he enjoyed watching football, spending time with his family and friends and just enjoyed being at home. **GOLDIE MAY BOWSER** [2901] (1883 – 1952) daughter of Peter and Annie (Beegle) Bowser. Goldie was a high school teacher for 40 years. Her classes were in English, Spanish and History. She was a member of First Methodist Church. **GREGORY R. BOWSER** Fifth great grandson of progenitor Nicholas Kegg. **HARRY MAURICE BOWSER** (1902 – 1991) son of Peter and Annie (Beegle) Bowser was twice married, first to Elma Wilcox. Later, he married Helen Hotchkiss McPherson. **JAMES BOWSER** (1958 – 1958) son of Robert and Patricia (Noll) Bowser. **JASMINE YVONNE BOWSER** Seventh great granddaughter of progenitor Nicholas Kegg. **JASON L. BOWSER** Sixth great grandson of progenitor Nicholas Kegg. **JOHN KERMIT BOWSER** Seventh great grandson of progenitor Nicholas Kegg. **KARSON BOWSER** Eighth great grandson of progenitor Nicholas Kegg. **KATHY BOWSER** Fifth great granddaughter of progenitor Nicholas Kegg. **KENNETH LLOYD BOWSER** [2901A] (1962 – 2015) son of John and Anna (Imler) Bowser, married Robin Lynn Logsdon with whom he was father of (1). Kenny worked as a roofer and other jobs in construction and enjoyed fishing, camping, and spending time with family and friends. **KENNETH L. BOWSER** Eighth great grandson of progenitor Nicholas Kegg. **KIMBERLY S. BOWSER** Sixth great granddaughter of progenitor Nicholas Kegg. **MICHAEL S. BOWSER** Sixth great grandson of progenitor Nicholas Kegg. **MICHAEL SCOTT BOWSER** Sixth great grandson of progenitor Nicholas Kegg. **PATRICK BOWSER** Seventh great grandson of progenitor Nicholas Kegg. **RANDY L. BOWSER** Sixth great grandson of progenitor Nicholas Kegg. **ROBERT W. BOWSER** [2901B] (1922 – 2014) son of Clarence and Pauline (Warren) Bowser, married Patricia Noll with whom he was father of (3) Robert spent many hours in his youth experimenting with electronics and music, both of which would become lifelong vocations. He joined the armed forces as part of the national war effort. Initially slated for pilot training, his electronics experience made him valuable in the growing new field of radar. He spent many missions in the tail of C-47 as a radar operator. Robert spent 3 years in the European theater at Normandy, Northern France, Rhineland and Central Europe. He was honorably discharged in 1946 as a sergeant in the Army. After the war, thru the GI Bill, he attended and graduated from Lawrence Tech with a degree in electrical engineering. The growing field of aircraft radar technology lured him west as a contract engineer in many locations including Rapid City, SD, Ft. Worth, Tx, Tucson, Phoenix, San Diego and Spokane WA. Robert often spoke of his enjoyable time working on the B-36 radar system at Ellsworth AFB in Rapid City. **RODERICK W. BOWSER** Sixth great grandson of progenitor Nicholas Kegg. **RONALD L. BOWSER** Seventh great grandson of progenitor Nicholas Kegg. - **STEVE BOWSER** Fifth great grandson of progenitor Nicholas Kegg. **TERESA LOUISE BOWSER** (1964 – 1964) daughter of John and Anna (Imler) Bowser.

BOYCE

KIERSTEN A. BOYCE (1994 – 2000) daughter of Thomas and Joy (Kesselring) Boyce.

BOYD

CAMILLE BOYD Sixth great granddaughter of progenitor Nicholas Kegg. **CORINNE BOYD** Sixth great granddaughter of progenitor Nicholas Kegg. **STUART BOYD** Sixth great grandson of progenitor Nicholas Kegg.

[2901] p.11-The Canton Repository (OH) Dec 23, 1952 [2901A] Dalla Valle Funeral Service (PA) [2901B] The Arizona Republic (AZ) Sept. 28, 2014

BOYER

AIMEE C. BOYER Seventh great granddaughter of progenitor Nicholas Kegg. **BENJAMIN BOYER** Sixth great grandson of progenitor Nicholas Kegg. **BETH ANN BOYER** [2901C] (1963 – 2011) daughter of John and Marilyn (Wells) Boyer, married David Andrew Grassman with whom she was mother of (3). Beth had been employed with the American Legion for six years and Mansfield Plumbing Products for 13 years and was a member of American Legion Auxiliary as well as Fraternal Order of Eagles, Loudonville. **BRODY BOYER** Seventh great grandson of progenitor Nicholas Kegg. **BROOKLYN BOYER** Seventh great granddaughter of progenitor Nicholas Kegg. **ISABELLE BOYER** Sixth great granddaughter of progenitor Nicholas Kegg. **JOHN R. BOYER** Sixth great grandson of progenitor Nicholas Kegg. **MARY BOYER** Sixth great granddaughter of progenitor Nicholas Kegg. **PEGGY BOYER** Sixth great granddaughter of progenitor Nicholas Kegg. **WILLIAM E. BOYER** [2902] (1957 – 1997) aka "Bill" son of John and Marilyn (Wells) Body married Chris with whom he was father of (1). Bill was employed at Merillat Industries, and he attended Christ Community Evangelical Free Church.

BOYES

BEVERLY JOAN BOYES Fifth great granddaughter of progenitor Nicholas Kegg. **DONALD JOHN BOYES** Sixth great grandson of progenitor Nicholas Kegg. **DORIS ELAINE BOYES** Fifth great granddaughter of progenitor Nicholas Kegg. **LEE CLARENCE BOYES** Fifth great grandson of progenitor Nicholas Kegg.

BOYLES

BRIAN L. BOYLES Sixth great grandson of progenitor Nicholas Kegg. **CHRISTOPHER L. BOYLES** Sixth great grandson of progenitor Nicholas Kegg. **WESLEY BOYLES JR** [2903] (1963 – 1993) son of Wesley and Sally (Sanderson) Boyles. Wesley was a former truck driver for Sturgis Iron and Metal and a former escort driver for Pride Lines, Inc. He had lived most of his life in LaGrange County and he was a member of the Sturgis Toy Run, Inc.

BRABANT

COOPER BRABANT Seventh great grandson of progenitor Nicholas Kegg.
ELYSE BRABANT Seventh great granddaughter of progenitor Nicholas Kegg.

BRABHAM

AMBER L. BRABHAM [2904] (1980 – 2012) daughter of Everett and Sherry (Giesy) Brabham. Amber graduated with a bachelor's degree from University of West Florida. She was a beautiful, gracious daughter, granddaughter, sister, aunt, niece and a very devoted, honest friend to many.

BRABY

ERICA RAE BRABY [2905] (1980 – 1999) daughter of Rick and Charlotte Braby. Erica was killed when her car went off a county road and into a ditch near Ocheyedan. Her car was found by another driver who

---

[2901C] Times Gazette (OH) Sep 18, 2011 [2902] p.8- Mansfield News Journal (OH) Aug 11, 1997, obtained by D. Sue Dible [2903] obituary clipping from Sturgis Daily Journal Contributed by Carole Lynn (Mohney) Carr [2904] Florida Today (FL) Aug 29, 2012 [2905] p.21- The Des Moines Register (IA) Aug 18, 1999

contacted the police.   **RICK WRAY BRABY** Sixth great grandson of progenitor Nicholas Kegg.
TIMOTHY REED BRABY aka "Tim" Sixth great grandson of progenitor Nicholas Kegg.
TRENTON WRAY BRABY Seventh great grandson of progenitor Nicholas Kegg.

BRACELAND

DAVID WARD BRACELAND Seventh great grandson of progenitor Nicholas Kegg.
LAUREN MELISSA BRACELAND Seventh great granddaughter of progenitor Nicholas Kegg.
LINDSAY BRACELAND Seventh great granddaughter of progenitor Nicholas Kegg.
TYLER BRACELAND Eighth great grandson of progenitor Nicholas Kegg.

BRACELIN

BENJAMIN B. BRACELIN Seventh great grandson of progenitor Nicholas Kegg.   **BRADLEY CRAIG BRACELIN** Sixth great grandson of progenitor Nicholas Kegg. **BRENDA KAY BRACELIN** Seventh great granddaughter of progenitor Nicholas Kegg.   **BRENT ALAN BRACELIN** Seventh great grandson of progenitor Nicholas Kegg.   **BRIAN SCOTT BRACELIN** Seventh great grandson of progenitor Nicholas Kegg.   **CONNIE BRACELIN** Sixth great granddaughter of progenitor Nicholas Kegg.   **GARY LEW BRACELIN** Sixth great grandson of progenitor Nicholas Kegg.   **REBECCA JEAN BRACELIN** aka "Becky" Seventh great granddaughter of progenitor Nicholas Kegg. **ROBERT CRAIG BRACELIN,** aka "Bobby" Seventh great grandson of progenitor Nicholas Kegg. **VICTORIA ELAINE BRACELIN,** aka "Vicki" Sixth great granddaughter of progenitor Nicholas Kegg.

BRADISH

CAROLANN BRADISH Sixth great granddaughter of progenitor Nicholas Kegg.
COURTNEY BRADISH Sixth great granddaughter of progenitor Nicholas Kegg.

BRADLEY

ANNA LOUISE BRADLEY [2906] (1885 – 1968) daughter of Orville and Mary (Beis) Bradley married Vincent Charles Turner.   **BARBARA ANNE BRADLEY** Sixth great granddaughter of progenitor Nicholas Kegg.   **BERNE BRADLEY** (1914 – 1916) son of Vitalis and Emma (Studer) Bradley. **BETTY BRADLEY** [2907] (1914 – 2003) daughter of George and Addie (Harter) Bradley married Bernard William Hummel.   **CHARLES WHEELER BRADLEY** (1889 – 1918) aka "Charley" son of Orville and Mary (Beis) Bradley married Gladys Bernice Canfield.   **CHESTER P. BRADLEY** [2908] (1884 – 1903) son of Perry and Cora (Pew) Bradley a Heidelberg freshmen struck by a Pennsylvania passenger train at the East Market Street crossing, one of the most dangerous in that city. A fast passenger train, going to make up lost time, struck the carriage, smashing it to pieces and mangling three of the occupants. Chester Bradley's skull was crushed.   **CHRISTINE LOUISE BRADLEY** Sixth great granddaughter of progenitor Nicholas Kegg.   **EDWARD P. BRADLEY** (1855 – 1926) son of Edward and Ann (Hershiser) Bradley married Mary Ann Barrow with whom he was father of (2).   **EVELYN LUCILLE BRADLEY** [2909] (1917 – 2000) daughter of Harry and Helen (Christman) Bradley married Clebert Eugene Belcher with whom she was mother of (1).   **GAILE M. BRADLEY** (1899 – 1923) daughter of Edward and Mary Ann (Barrow) Bradley.   **GEORGE W. BRADLEY** [2910] (1881 – 1930) son of Orville and Mary (Beis) Bradley married Addie Gertrude Harter with whom he was father of (3). George was employed as assistant trainmaster of the Western division of the Pennsylvania railroad.

[2906] Toledo Blade (OH) Nov 6, 1968 obtained by D. Sue Dible [2907] Dayton Daily News (OH) April 29, 2003 [2908] p 2 Cleveland Plain Dealer (OH) June 2, 1903 [2909] Toledo Blade (OH) May 31, 2000 obtained by D. Sue Dible [2910] Fort Wayne Sentinel (IN) Dec 20, 1916

GERTRUDE ESTHER BRADLEY [2911] (1883 – 1968) daughter of Orville and Mary (Beis) Bradley married Ernest Eugene Hayes with whom she was mother of (2). **GLENN CLAYTON BRADLEY** (1886 – 1943) son of Orville and Mary (Beis) Bradley married Berne Hayes.
HARRY WILLIAM BRADLEY (1888 – 1954) son of Orville and Mary (Beis) Bradley married Helen M. Christman with whom he was father of (2). **HELEN A. BRADLEY** [2912] (1910 – 1994) daughter of Vitalis and Emma (Studer) Bradley married Howard W. Westervelt with whom she was mother of (3).
INFANT BRADLEY (1922 – 1922) son of Harry and Helen (Christman) Bradley.
JOHN JAMES BRADLEY Fifth great grandson of progenitor Nicholas Kegg. **LARK BRADLEY** Eighth great grandson of progenitor Nicholas Kegg. **LOUISE BRADLEY** [2913] (1917 – 2009) daughter of Vitalis and Emma (Studer) Bradley married John Alden Brossart with whom she was mother of (5). Louise was very proud to be the twin sister of Ernest Bradley. Louise attended Purdue University. She was first and foremost a devoted wife and an extraordinary mother, grandmother and friend. Every achievement or interest of her friends and loved ones was celebrated by her. She was known to be a "prayer warrior" and kept a list of people in need of prayer on her refrigerator. Louise counted all children as her children. She was generous with herself and taught Sunday school for years and led boy Scout and Girl Scout troops. At age 45, Louise began taking voice lessons and would sing solos at area churches. After relocating to Detroit, she studied Japanese Silk Embroidery with the Japanese Master. Many of her embroidery and needlepoint pieces hang in her residence. In her later years, she enjoyed watching and feeding the birds and squirrels in her beautiful back yard. **LUCINDA JEAN BRADLEY** Sixth great granddaughter of progenitor Nicholas Kegg. **LUKAS BRADLEY** Eighth great grandson of progenitor Nicholas Kegg. **LYNNE CAROL BRADLEY** Fifth great granddaughter of progenitor Nicholas Kegg.
MABEL BRADLEY (1880 – 1880) daughter of Orville and Mary (Beis) Bradley. **MARION L. BRADLEY** (1889 – 1891) daughter of Perry and Cora (Pew) Bradley. **MARY LEONA BRADLEY** [2914] (1907 – 1989) daughter of Vitalis and Emma (Studer) Bradley married Sumner Aaron Koenigseker with whom she was mother of (2). Mary was one of the last known silent movie house pianists in the Toledo and Whitehouse areas. In addition, she was a title examiner for Louisville Title, Inc., for many years. **NELLIE BRADLEY** (abt 1864 –?) daughter of John and Mary (Hershiser) Bradley.
NELLIE CORNELIA BRADLEY [2915] (1891 – 1980) daughter of Orville and Mary (Beis) Bradley. Nellie was owner of the former Vogue Beauty Shop, Whitehouse, for 15 years, retiring in the 1940's.
ORVILLE WHEELER BRADLEY [2916] (1853 – 1936) son of John and Mary (Hershiser) Bradley married Mary Beis with whom he was father of (9). **PERRY AUGUSTUS BRADLEY** [2917] (1854 – 1929) son of Edward and Ann (Hershiser) Bradley married Cora B. Pew with whom he was father of (3).
RAYMOND PEW BRADLEY (1881 – 1954) son of Perry and Cora (Pew) Bradley married Ruth Evelyn Wehrman. **RHONDA LYNN BRADLEY** Sixth great granddaughter of progenitor Nicholas Kegg. **ROBERT ORVILL BRADLEY** [2918] (1912 – 1995) son of Vitalis and Emma (Studer) Bradley married three times, first to Viola Mary Croft with whom he was father of (1). Later, he married Florine Vilma French Doppler, and then married Dorothea Clara Rose (Hohr) Smith. Robert was an Electrical Engineer and Vice President of Engineering with Toledo Scale for 39 years, retiring in 1975. Robert was a 1935 graduate of Purdue University with a degree in Electrical Engineering. While at the university, Robert became a member of the T.K.E. Fraternity. **VITALIS EBEN BRADLEY** [2919] (1882 – 1964) son of Orville and Mary (Beis) Bradley married Emma Barbara Studer with whom he was father of (6). Vitalis was general superintendent of the Page Dairy Company, Toledo, from 1917-1941. Under his supervision, dairy plants were constructed at Whitehouse, Bluffton, and Findlay, Ohio, and at Weston.
WILLIAM GRANT BRADLEY [2920] (1883 – 1947) son of Edward and Mary Ann (Barrow) Bradley was a retired garage mechanic.

[2911] p17 Toledo Blade (OH) Aug 29, 1968, obtained by D. Sue Dible [2912] Toledo Blade (OH) Feb 9, 1994 [2913] The Times (IN) July 9, 2009 [2914] Toledo Blade (OH) Aug 12, 1989 [2915] Toledo Blade (OH) Sep 22, 1980 obtained by D. Sue Dible [2916] Toledo Blade (OH) July 7, 1936 obtained by D. Sue Dible [2917] Toledo Blade (OH) Jan 4, 1929 obtained by D. Sue Dible [2918] Toledo Blade (OH) June 8. 1995 [2919] Toledo Blade (OH) Oct 6, 1964, obtained by D. Sue Dible [2920] obituary obtained by R. Reed Find A Grave Memorial #93020303

BRADSHER

DANIELE NICOLE BRADSHER Seventh great granddaughter of progenitor Nicholas Kegg.
JAMIE JO BRADSHER Seventh great granddaughter of progenitor Nicholas Kegg.

BRAECKLEIN

HOWARD BRAECKLEIN Fifth great grandson of progenitor Nicholas Kegg.

BRAGG

BONNIE BRAGG [2921] (1890 – 1970) aka "Carrie Minnie", daughter of James and Elenora (Kegg) Bragg married George Frederick Vonslagle with whom she was mother of (2). Bonnie was a member of the First Presbyterian Church, Kendallville, she was active in the Covenant Geneva Circle of the church and active in the Senior Citizens of Kendallville. **MAURICE DELANO BRAGG** (1896 – 1955) son of James and Elenora (Kegg) Bragg married Grace Arline Novinger with whom he was father of (1).

BRALLIER

ELLA BRALLIER Eighth great granddaughter of progenitor Nicholas Kegg. **ERIC BRALLIER** Sixth great grandson of progenitor Nicholas Kegg. **JEFFREY BRALLIER** [2922] (1963 – 2019) son of Clair and Delores (Price) Brallier married Lori Hollar with whom he was father of (3). Jeffrey worked for the Washington, D.C. division of Habitat for Humanity. He found great joy in serving and bettering the community. He was a lifelong Washington Capitals fan. He enjoyed trips to visit his brother, Tim, in Canada for ice fishing. **KENNETH CLAIR BRALLIER** [2923] (1953 – 1954) son of Clair and Delores (Price) Brallier died of pneumonia. **LINDSEY BRALLIER** Sixth great granddaughter of progenitor Nicholas Kegg. **RODNEY BRALLIER** Fifth great grandson of progenitor Nicholas Kegg. **SAMANTHA BRALLIER** Sixth great granddaughter of progenitor Nicholas Kegg. **SAMUEL BRALLIER** Eighth great grandson of progenitor Nicholas Kegg. **TIMOTHY G. BRALLIER** Fifth great grandson of progenitor Nicholas Kegg.

BRAMBLEY

BRENDA MICHELE BRAMBLEY Seventh great granddaughter of progenitor Nicholas Kegg.
LYNNE ANN BRAMBLEY Seventh great granddaughter of progenitor Nicholas Kegg. **MIKA BRUCE BRAMBLEY** Seventh great grandson of progenitor Nicholas Kegg.

BRANDAU

BARBARA ANN BRANDAU Fourth great granddaughter of progenitor Nicholas Kegg. **CHARLES H. BRANDAU** Fourth great grandson of progenitor Nicholas Kegg. **DAVID CONRAD BRANDAU** Fourth great grandson of progenitor Nicholas Kegg.

BRANDEBERRY

HANNAH LEIGH BRANDEBERRY Seventh great granddaughter of progenitor Nicholas Kegg.
HARRISON LEVI BRANDEBERRY Seventh great grandson of progenitor Nicholas Kegg.

[2921] News-Sun, Kendallville (IN) undated obituary obtained by D. Sue Dible [2922] Bedford Gazette (PA) Jan 30, 2019 obtained by Bob Rose [2923] p2 - The Bedford Gazette (PA) Jan. 26,1954

BRANDENBURG

ADA MAY BRANDENBURG (1877 – 1902) daughter of Warren and Emma (Cagg) Brandenburg married twice, first to William Alfred Crance with whom she was mother of (1). Later she married Robert M. Moody.

BRANDYBERRY

ARDIS GAYLE BRANDYBERRY Sixth great granddaughter of progenitor Nicholas Kegg.
BONNIE BRANDYBERRY Sixth great granddaughter of progenitor Nicholas Kegg.
DARLA BRANDYBERRY Sixth great granddaughter of progenitor Nicholas Kegg.
ELAINE PEARL BRANDYBERRY (1911 – 1943) daughter of Walter and Virginia (Knouf) Brandyberry.   **ERIC WALTER BRANDYBERRY** Sixth great grandson of progenitor Nicholas Kegg.
JEANETTE BRANDYBERRY Sixth great granddaughter of progenitor Nicholas Kegg.
LEA ANN BRANDYBERRY Sixth great granddaughter of progenitor Nicholas Kegg.
MELISSA BRANDYBERRY Sixth great granddaughter of progenitor Nicholas Kegg.
NEAL BRANDYBERRY Sixth great granddaughter of progenitor Nicholas Kegg.
PENNY BRANDYBERRY Sixth great granddaughter of progenitor Nicholas Kegg.
TIMOTHY BRANDYBERRY Sixth great grandson of progenitor Nicholas Kegg.
VADA FAY BRANDYBERRY [2925] (1936 – 2003) daughter of Walter and Virginia (Knouf) Brandyberry married Ernest Walter Tallman with whom she was mother of (5). Vada received a bachelor's degree in education from Fort Hays State University. She held various education and child-care positions over the years and also worked for Travenol Laboratories and Development Services of Northwest Kansas, from which she retired. Vada was active in Girl Scouts, Boy Scouts, American Diabetes Association and St. Joseph Catholic Church.   **WESTON ALAN BRANDYBERRY** Sixth great grandson of progenitor Nicholas Kegg.

BRANTNER

ALICE E. BRANTNER Fifth great granddaughter of progenitor Nicholas Kegg.
EARL GEORGE BRANTNER Fifth great grandson of progenitor Nicholas Kegg.
EARL HOWARD BRANTNER [2926] (1920 – 1988) son of George and Alice (Hockenberry) Brantner married Ruby Mastin with whom he was father of (6). Earl retired from Lohman Food in Gorham.
HARRY M. BRANTNER Fifth great grandson of progenitor Nicholas Kegg.   **JOHN G. BRANTNER** Fifth great grandson of progenitor Nicholas Kegg.   **MARILYN A. BRANTNER** Fifth great granddaughter of progenitor Nicholas Kegg.   **PEARL MILDRED BRANTNER** [2927] (1917 – 1979) daughter of George and Alice (Hockenberry) Brantner married John Nelson Warsing with whom she was mother of (11). Pearl was of the Brethren in Christ faith and was employed by the Lion Manufacturing Company in Everett.   **RUTH VANCE BRANTNER** (1922 – 2003) daughter of George and Alice (Hockenberry) Brantner married John S. Porter with whom she was mother of (3).
RUTHANN BRANTNER Fifth great granddaughter of progenitor Nicholas Kegg.

BRATTON

KIRT BRATTON Sixth great grandson of progenitor Nicholas Kegg.

[2925] Hays Daily News (KS) Dec 27, 2003 [2926] Chronicle Express (NY) Nov 9, 1988, obtained by D. Sue Dible [2927] p 3 – Bedford Inquirer (PA) Oct 19, 1979

BRAUN

KIRK ALAN BRAUN Sixth great grandson of progenitor Nicholas Kegg.

BRAY

BRENDA BRAY Fifth great granddaughter of progenitor Nicholas Kegg.
CARL STANLEY H. BRAY [2928] (1891 – 1977) son of Samuel and Nancy (Rice) Bray married Bertha Doll Hall with whom he was father of (3). Carl was a farmer. **DEBRA JEAN BRAY** [2929] (1956 – 1976) daughter of Owen and Dorothy (Thoesen) Bray. Debra graduated from Lawton High School in 1974. **GEORGE SAMUEL BRAY** [2929A] (1920 – 2016) son of Carl and Bertha (Hall) Bray, married Ann Margaret Stephayn with whom he was father of (2). During World War II, he served with the U.S. Naval Intelligence with assignments in Washington D.C. and Aden, Arabia. George was employed by General Adjustment Bureau in Ann Arbor, Michigan, where he worked as a claims adjuster for 35 years, until his retirement. During his retirement, George enjoyed playing golf, crossword puzzles and traveling with his wife. **JOSEPHINE ELIZABETH BRAY** [2930] (1913 – 2006) daughter of Carl and Bertha (Hall) Bray married Willard Clayton Russell with whom she was mother of (2). After earning a rural-education certificate from Western Michigan University, Josephine taught elementary school for 45 years in Van Buren County, Marcellus, Caledonia, Flint and Toledo, Ohio. **KATHY BRAY** Fifth great granddaughter of progenitor Nicholas Kegg. **LINNEA BRAY** Fifth great granddaughter of progenitor Nicholas Kegg. **NANCY BRAY** Fifth great granddaughter of progenitor Nicholas Kegg.
OWEN S. BRAY [2931] (1917 – 1972) son of Carl and Bertha (Hall) Bray married Dorothy Lorraine Thoesen with whom he was father of (3). Owen had been performance supervisor for the Agricultural Stabilization and Conservation Service for 20 years and had been a prominent farmer. He had also served as president of the Lawton School Board of which he was a member for 22 years.

BRAZELL

JESSIE BRAZELL Eighth great granddaughter of progenitor Nicholas Kegg.

BRAZILL

BETHANN BRAZILL Sixth great granddaughter of progenitor Nicholas Kegg. **DOMINIC BRAZILL** Seventh great grandson of progenitor Nicholas Kegg. **JAMES BRAZILL** Sixth great grandson of progenitor Nicholas Kegg.

BRECHTAL

DANIEL BRECHTAL Seventh great grandson of progenitor Nicholas Kegg. **HEATHER BRECHTAL** Seventh great granddaughter of progenitor Nicholas Kegg. **HOLLY BRECHTAL** Seventh great granddaughter of progenitor Nicholas Kegg. **MELANIE BRECHTAL** Seventh great granddaughter of progenitor Nicholas Kegg. **NATHAN BRECHTAL** Seventh great grandson of progenitor Nicholas Kegg. **NICOLE BRECHTAL** Seventh great granddaughter of progenitor Nicholas Kegg. **VIRGINIA BRECHTAL** Seventh great granddaughter of progenitor Nicholas Kegg.

[2928] unidentified publication/library obituary (MI) April 1, 1977 [2929] Kalamazoo Gazette (MI) Aug 13, 1976 [2929A] Langland Family Funeral Homes (MI) [2930] Kalamazoo Gazette (MI) Jun 7, 2006, obtained by D. Sue Dible [2931] Kalamazoo Gazette (MI) Aug 9, 1972

BREHM

ELENI ROSE BREHM Seventh great granddaughter of progenitor Nicholas Kegg. **JACOB BREHM** aka "Jake" Seventh great grandson of progenitor Nicholas Kegg. **MATTHEW E. BREHM** Sixth great grandson of progenitor Nicholas Kegg. **MICHAEL A. BREHM** Sixth great grandson of progenitor Nicholas Kegg.

BREKEL

BROOKS BREKEL Eighth great grandson of progenitor Nicholas Kegg. **LILY BREKEL** Eighth great granddaughter of progenitor Nicholas Kegg. **MASON BREKEL** Eighth great grandson of progenitor Nicholas Kegg.

BRENNAN

MOLLIE BRENNAN Seventh great granddaughter of progenitor Nicholas Kegg.
PATRICK BRENNAN Seventh great grandson of progenitor Nicholas Kegg.

BRENNER

HOWARD W. BRENNER [2932] (1928 – 2005) son of Harry and Mildred (Millin) Brenner. Howard attended McCaskey High School and Stevens Trade School. He was a member of the Church of the Apostles, United Church of Christ. He enjoyed music, painting and reading.

BREUNIG

BRENT W. BREUNIG Sixth great grandson of progenitor Nicholas Kegg. **DANIEL JOSEPH BREUNIG** Sixth great grandson of progenitor Nicholas Kegg. **HUNTER BREUNIG** Seventh great grandson of progenitor Nicholas Kegg. **JASON BREUNIG** Sixth great grandson of progenitor Nicholas Kegg. **JESSICA BREUNIG** Seventh great granddaughter of progenitor Nicholas Kegg.
MIRIAH BREUNIG Seventh great granddaughter of progenitor Nicholas Kegg.
MICHELA BREUNIG Seventh great granddaughter of progenitor Nicholas Kegg.
SCOTT BREUNIG Sixth great grandson of progenitor Nicholas Kegg

BREZOVEC

DEVON MICHAEL BREZOVEC Seventh great grandson of progenitor Nicholas Kegg.
NICOLETTA MARIE BREZOVEC Seventh great granddaughter of progenitor Nicholas Kegg.

BRIDGE

MILDRED MARGUERITE BRIDGE [2933] (1904 – 2000) daughter of Charles and Myrtle (Kegg) Bridge married twice, first to Charles Richard Wright and later to Raymond Keith Straw. Mildred was a bookkeeper in Elkhart for many years.

BRIDGES

ANNA BERYL BRIDGES Fifth great granddaughter of progenitor Nicholas Kegg.

[2932] Lancaster online (PA) [2933] The South Bend Tribune (IN) June 29, 2000

BRIDGEWATER

BAILEY BRIDGEWATER Seventh great grandchild of progenitor Nicholas Kegg.
EMILY TERESA BRIDGEWATER Sixth great granddaughter of progenitor Nicholas Kegg.
JEFFREY JAMES BRIDGEWATER Sixth great grandson of progenitor Nicholas Kegg.

BRIESE

BRYNNA LEA BRIESE Seventh great granddaughter of progenitor Nicholas Kegg. **COURTNEY A. BRIESE** Seventh great granddaughter of progenitor Nicholas Kegg. **DESIREE KAY BRIESE** Seventh great granddaughter of progenitor Nicholas Kegg. **JACOB RYAN BRIESE** aka "Jake" Seventh great grandson of progenitor Nicholas Kegg. **KAELIE R. BRIESE** Seventh great granddaughter of progenitor Nicholas Kegg. **LEIA BRIESE** Eighth great granddaughter of progenitor Nicholas Kegg. **LISA ANN BRIESE** Sixth great granddaughter of progenitor Nicholas Kegg. **SHARON BRIESE** Sixth great granddaughter of progenitor Nicholas Kegg.
SHERA LYNNE BRIESE Seventh great granddaughter of progenitor Nicholas Kegg.

BRIGGS

BRANDI ANN BRIGGS Seventh great granddaughter of progenitor Nicholas Kegg.
CASSIDY JO BRIGGS Seventh great granddaughter of progenitor Nicholas Kegg.

BRIGHT

MARY EVELYN BRIGHT (1910 – 1910) daughter of Harry and Trixie (Arnold) Bright. **SYLVIA BRIGHT** Seventh great granddaughter of progenitor Nicholas Kegg. **WILLIAM BRIGHT** Seventh great grandson of progenitor Nicholas Kegg.

BRILHART

JESSIE BRILHART (1885 – 1891) son of David and Ellen (Stuckey) Brilhart. **RENA M. BRILHART** [2934] (1883 – 1947) daughter of of David and Ellen (Stuckey) Brilhart, married Frank Lester Porter with whom she was mother of (1). Rena had been a faithful attendant of the Christian church. For many years she has been a member of Chapter 8.P.E.O. Rena had a pleasing personality and was held in high esteem by all who knew her.

BRINEGAR

JUDITH LEA BRINEGAR [2935] (1934 – 2021) aka "Judy", daughter of Olin and Ila (Zong) Brinegar married Reuben Arthur Griffith with whom she was mother of (4). Judy was very kind. She always defended the person not present, no matter what. Other family members would consider a difficult situation and say to themselves, "Well, how would Judy handle it?" And from there the better course of action was determined to continue with kindness and grace as Judy always did. Judy was an amazing, steadfast example of these two virtues and a fierce protector of the family. Judy had a very full life raising her children. In the summers when the kids were on vacation, she was very involved in their extracurricular activities from swimming lessons, summer classes, library trips to teaching us life learning activities. Judy and Rueben also had a great sense of and liking for adventure and travel, which led to many wonderful trips to see family in different parts of the country. Some of Judy's loved hobbies were sewing, her rose garden, crafts and reading.

[2934] The Lathrop Optimist (MO) April 24, 1947 [2935] Cochran Mortuary & Crematory (Wichita, KS)

BRININSTOOL

CARL DAVID BRININSTOOL Sixth great grandson of progenitor Nicholas Kegg.
MARGARET ROSE BRININSTOOL Sixth great granddaughter of progenitor Nicholas Kegg.

BRITT

MILDRED A. BRITT Seventh great granddaughter of progenitor Nicholas Kegg.
TANYA LEA BRITT Seventh great granddaughter of progenitor Nicholas Kegg.

BRITTON

ARNOLD B. BRITTON JR. (1935 – 1987) aka "Junior" son of Arnold and Phyllis (Clark) Britton.
ARNOLD CLARK BRITTON Sixth great grandson of progenitor Nicholas Kegg.
DOUGLAS P. BRITTON Sixth great grandson of progenitor Nicholas Kegg.
PHYLLIS MARIE BRITTON [2936] (1945 – 2020) daughter of Arnold and Phyllis (Clark) Britton, married Dennis Jackson Whiteley with whom she was mother of (1). Phyllis proudly dedicated herself to 40 years in a career as a Landperson for Hazelwood production & exploration company. Phyllis was social and active. She was deeply devoted to and involved in her church. She enjoyed dancing, playing bridge, water skiing, playing golf, and spending time with her family. Phyllis was an international globe trotter. Visiting, amongst many other places, the Great Wall of China and the Great Pyramids at Giza. Phyllis is remembered as smart, tough, kind, and generous. Phyllis is an example of life well lived.

BROBERG

TERESA K. BROBERG Sixth great granddaughter of progenitor Nicholas Kegg.

BROCK

KRISTEN BROCK Sixth great granddaughter of progenitor Nicholas Kegg. **LAURA BROCK** Sixth great granddaughter of progenitor Nicholas Kegg. **MELINDA BROCK** Sixth great granddaughter of progenitor Nicholas Kegg. **WESLEY BROCK** Sixth great grandson of progenitor Nicholas Kegg.

BROCKMEYER

ADAM BROCKMEYER Seventh great grandson of progenitor Nicholas Kegg.
LAURA BROCKMEYER Seventh great granddaughter of progenitor Nicholas Kegg.

BRODIE

JOYCE ELAINE BRODIE Fifth great granddaughter of progenitor Nicholas Kegg.
NATALIE BRODIE Fifth great granddaughter of progenitor Nicholas Kegg.

BROOKE

NICHOLAS BROOKE Sixth great grandson of progenitor Nicholas Kegg.
PETER BROOKE Sixth great grandson of progenitor Nicholas Kegg.

[2936] Oklahoman (OK) Sep 18, 2020, obtained by D. Sue Dible

BROOKS

AMBER BROOKS Seventh great granddaughter of progenitor Nicholas Kegg. **CALLY BROOKS** Seventh great granddaughter of progenitor Nicholas Kegg. **CHERYL F. BROOKS** Sixth great granddaughter of progenitor Nicholas Kegg. **GLENN L. BROOKS** Sixth great grandson of progenitor Nicholas Kegg. **JIM A. BROOKS** Sixth great grandson of progenitor Nicholas Kegg. **JOSH A. BROOKS** Sixth great grandson of progenitor Nicholas Kegg. **LISA A. BROOKS** Seventh great granddaughter of progenitor Nicholas Kegg. **MAEGAN BROOKS** Seventh great granddaughter of progenitor Nicholas Kegg. **OLIVIA GLENNON BROOKS** Eighth great granddaughter of progenitor Nicholas Kegg. **ROBERT E. BROOKS** Seventh great grandson of progenitor Nicholas Kegg.

BROPHY

CHARLOTTE BROPHY aka "Charlie" Eighth great granddaughter of progenitor Nicholas Kegg. **JACK BROPHY** Eighth great grandson of progenitor Nicholas Kegg. **MADDIE BROPHY** Eighth great granddaughter of progenitor Nicholas Kegg. **PAIGE BROPHY** Eighth great granddaughter of progenitor Nicholas Kegg.

BROSSART

ANN KATYA BROSSART Sixth great granddaughter of progenitor Nicholas Kegg.
DAVID ERNEST BROSSART [2937] (1946 – 2011) son of John and Louise (Bradley) Brossart married Leslie Bernard Brennan with whom he was father of (2). David was an artist, architect and longtime resident of the area, designing homes for many residents, and doing architectural work for Swarthmore College, churches and health-care facilities. He was a past chair of the Swarthmore Planning Commission. Charity was the centerpiece of David's personal and professional life. He was past president of the Upper Darby- Lansdowne Rotary Club and donated architectural services to Habitat for Humanity of Delaware County and Strath Haven A Better Chance program. A man of wide-ranging and eclectic enthusiasms, he was a passionate fly fisherman, sang bass with Valley Voices of Rose Valley, studied the Russian language, and was a prolific artist, whose paintings have been exhibited in Swarthmore and at the Community Art Center. David taught architecture at Drexel University Nesbitt School of Design and local architectural history and cheesemaking at Wallingford- Swarthmore Community Classes. He graduated from the University of Illinois School of Architecture in 1969. Prior to opening his own firm in Swarthmore 25 years ago, he was associated with the firms of J. Roy Carroll (Swarthmore), Ewing, Cole (Philadelphia), Lou Sauer (Philadelphia) and Warner, Breccha, McPherson of Homewood, IL.
LAURA BROSSART Sixth great granddaughter of progenitor Nicholas Kegg.

BROTHERTON

CORBYN LAYNE BROTHERTON Eighth great grandson of progenitor Nicholas Kegg.
JACKSON BROTHERTON Ninth great grandson of progenitor Nicholas Kegg
JOEY BROTHERTON Eighth great grandson of progenitor Nicholas Kegg.
KELLE R. BROTHERTON Seventh great granddaughter of progenitor Nicholas Kegg.
MICHELE KAY BROTHERTON Seventh great granddaughter of progenitor Nicholas Kegg.
TANYA MARIE BROTHERTON Seventh great granddaughter of progenitor Nicholas Kegg.
TIFFANY LYNNE BROTHERTON Seventh great granddaughter of progenitor Nicholas Kegg.

[2937] The Times (PA) Aug. 14, 2011

BROWN

ALLEN BROWN Seventh great grandson of progenitor Nicholas Kegg. **ANDREW JOSEPH BROWN** Eighth great grandson of progenitor Nicholas Kegg. **ANTIONETTE S. BROWN** aka "Toni" Sixth great granddaughter of progenitor Nicholas Kegg. **ASHLAY MAY BROWN** Seventh great granddaughter of progenitor Nicholas Kegg. **AUSTIN BROWN** Seventh great grandson of progenitor Nicholas Kegg. **AUSTIN BROWN** Eighth great grandson of progenitor Nicholas Kegg. **BABY BROWN** child of Ralph and Mary Jane (Woodard) Brown buried with parents at Fairview Memorial Gardens Rockbridge, Hocking County, Ohio. **BECKY BROWN** Seventh great granddaughter of progenitor Nicholas Kegg. **BETSY DIANE BROWN** [2938] (1943 – 2017) daughter of Emory and Evelyn (Kegg) Brown married Richard Lee O'Brien with whom she was mother of (3). Betsy was a Teacher's Aide for Warren Township at Pleasant Run Elementary School. **BOB BROWN** Sixth great grandson of progenitor Nicholas Kegg. **BRIAN PAUL BROWN** [2939] (1973 – 2021) son of Galen and Mary (Greenawalt) Brown. Brian was a seventh great grandson of progenitor Nicholas Kegg. **CARL ANDREW BROWN JR.** [2940] (1922 – 1943) son of Carl and Clara (Kegg) Brown married Ida May Liskey. Carl was an aviation mechanic in the United States Navy. The patrol plane of which he was a crew member went missing in the North Pacific. **CASSANDRA BROWN** Eighth great granddaughter of progenitor Nicholas Kegg. **CHARLES GERARD BROWN** Fifth great grandson of progenitor Nicholas Kegg. **CHRISTOPHER MICHAEL BROWN** Seventh great grandson of progenitor Nicholas Kegg. **COLE ROBERT BROWN** Sixth great grandson of progenitor Nicholas Kegg. **DANA NOELLE BROWN** Sixth great granddaughter of progenitor Nicholas Kegg. **DAWN LEAH BROWN** Seventh great granddaughter of progenitor Nicholas Kegg. **DEBRA A. BROWN** Sixth great granddaughter of progenitor Nicholas Kegg. **FRANCIS FOLEY BROWN** Fifth great grandson of progenitor Nicholas Kegg. **GAVIN BROWN** Eighth great grandson of progenitor Nicholas Kegg. **GAREN ROBERT BROWN** Sixth great grandson of progenitor Nicholas Kegg. **GREGORY BATES BROWN** Fifth great grandson of progenitor Nicholas Kegg. **HAYDEN JACOB BROWN** Eighth great grandson of progenitor Nicholas Kegg. **HEATHER J. BROWN** Seventh great granddaughter of progenitor Nicholas Kegg. **HOLLY BROWN** Eighth great granddaughter of progenitor Nicholas Kegg. **INFANT BROWN** (1918 – 1918) son of Charles and Bessie (Knouf) Brown. **JACQUELINE ELAINE BROWN** Sixth great granddaughter of progenitor Nicholas Kegg. **JASON ALLEN BROWN** Seventh great grandson of progenitor Nicholas Kegg. **JENNIFER LYNNETTE BROWN** Sixth great granddaughter of progenitor Nicholas Kegg. **JOHN HENRY BROWN** Sixth great grandson of progenitor Nicholas Kegg. **JORDAN BROWN** Seventh great grandson of progenitor Nicholas Kegg. **JUNE LOUISE BROWN** (1912 – 2000) daughter of Andrew and Gretta (Myers) Brown married David Edward Anderson with whom she was mother of (1). **KAREN BROWN** Fifth great granddaughter of progenitor Nicholas Kegg. **KATHLEEN MARIE BROWN** Fifth great granddaughter of progenitor Nicholas Kegg. **KEITH ANDREW BROWN** [2941] (1964 – 2006) son of Edward and Jeanne (Vaughan) Brown. Keith was an alumni of Judson High School class of 1983. **KELLEY AUGUSTIN BROWN** Fifth great grandson of progenitor Nicholas Kegg. **KENNETH ALLEN BROWN** Fifth great grandson of progenitor Nicholas Kegg. **KORY BROWN** Eighth great grandson of progenitor Nicholas Kegg. **LAVON BROWN** Fifth great granddaughter of progenitor Nicholas Kegg. **LEASA BROWN** Seventh great granddaughter of progenitor Nicholas Kegg. **MARILYN BROWN** Fifth great granddaughter of progenitor Nicholas Kegg. **MATTHEW ALLEN BROWN** Seventh great grandson of progenitor Nicholas Kegg. **MELODY ANN BROWN** Seventh great granddaughter of progenitor Nicholas Kegg. **MICHAEL WILLIAM BROWN** Eighth great grandson of progenitor Nicholas Kegg. **MICHELLE BROWN** Sixth great granddaughter of progenitor Nicholas Kegg. **MISSY J. BROWN** Seventh great granddaughter of progenitor Nicholas Kegg

---

[2938] The Indianapolis Star (IN) Feb. 7, 2017 [2939] Bedford Gazette (PA) March 31, 2021 [2940] p7 Sacramento Bee (CA) Sep 2, 1943 [2941] San Antonio Express-News (TX) June 5, 2006

PATRICK TOMAY BROWN Fifth great grandson of progenitor Nicholas Kegg. **PAUL E. BROWN** Sixth great grandson of progenitor Nicholas Kegg. **PAULA BROWN** Seventh great granddaughter of progenitor Nicholas Kegg. **REBECCA DAWN BROWN** Seventh great granddaughter of progenitor Nicholas Kegg. **RICHARD ALLEN BROWN** [2942] (1958 – 1983) aka "Rick", son of Ronald and Margaret (Miller) Brown, married Leticia Montez with whom he was father of (2). **ROBERT BROWN** Seventh great grandson of progenitor Nicholas Kegg. **ROBERT ROY BROWN** Seventh great grandson of progenitor Nicholas Kegg. **ROGER BROWN** Sixth great grandson of progenitor Nicholas Kegg. **RONALD EUGENE BROWN** Sixth great grandson of progenitor Nicholas Kegg. **RONALD E. BROWN** Sixth great grandson of progenitor Nicholas Kegg. **SANDRA BROWN** Seventh great granddaughter of progenitor Nicholas Kegg. **STACY RENEE BROWN** Seventh great granddaughter of progenitor Nicholas Kegg. **STEVEN GLEN BROWN** Sixth great grandson of progenitor Nicholas Kegg. **TERRI LEA BROWN** Sixth great granddaughter of progenitor Nicholas Kegg. **TIMOTHY L. BROWN** Sixth great grandson of progenitor Nicholas Kegg. **TINA BROWN** Sixth great granddaughter of progenitor Nicholas Kegg. **TRAVIS J. BROWN** Sixth great grandson of progenitor Nicholas Kegg. **TRISHA ANN BROWN** Seventh great granddaughter of progenitor Nicholas Kegg. **WILLIAM DALE BROWN** Seventh great grandson of progenitor Nicholas Kegg. **XANDER BROWN** Eighth great grandson of progenitor Nicholas Kegg.

BROWNE

CAMERON SCOTT BROWNE Sixth great grandson of progenitor Nicholas Kegg. **COLTON BROWNE** Seventh great grandson of progenitor Nicholas Kegg. **HARPER BROWNE** Seventh great grandson of progenitor Nicholas Kegg. **TREVOR BROWNE** Sixth great grandson of progenitor Nicholas Kegg.

BROZOVICH

ROBIN L. BROZOVICH Sixth great granddaughter of progenitor Nicholas Kegg.

BRUCE

BONNIE BRUCE Fifth great granddaughter of progenitor Nicholas Kegg. **CLAIRE BRUCE** Fifth great granddaughter of progenitor Nicholas Kegg. **DANAE BRUCE** Seventh great granddaughter of progenitor Nicholas Kegg. **DAVID W. BRUCE** (1967 – 1989) son of David and Janice (Grim) Bruce. **DONALD BRUCE** Seventh great grandson of progenitor Nicholas Kegg. **DONNIE BRUCE** Eighth great grandson of progenitor Nicholas Kegg. **HEATHER BRUCE** Fifth great granddaughter of progenitor Nicholas Kegg. **NICOLE LYNN BRUCE**, aka "Nikki", Eighth great granddaughter of progenitor Nicholas Kegg. **SETH BRUCE** Eighth great grandson of progenitor Nicholas Kegg.

BRUCK

ANTHONY A. BRUCK Sixth great grandson of progenitor Nicholas Kegg. **BETH A. BRUCK** Sixth great granddaughter of progenitor Nicholas Kegg. **PATRICK S. BRUCK** Sixth great grandson of progenitor Nicholas Kegg. **TAMMY S. BRUCK** Sixth great granddaughter of progenitor Nicholas Kegg.

BRUMAGE

LINDA BRUMAGE Fifth great granddaughter of progenitor Nicholas Kegg.
RHEA ANN BRUMAGE (1939 – 1942) daughter of Homer and Mayme (Knouf) Brumage.

[2942] Bellefontaine Examiner (OH) June 25, 1983

BRUMBAUGH

CORTNEY BRUMBAUGH Sixth great granddaughter of progenitor Nicholas Kegg.
DONNA K. BRUMBAUGH Fifth great granddaughter of progenitor Nicholas Kegg.
EILEEN LOUISE BRUMBAUGH Fifth great granddaughter of progenitor Nicholas Kegg.
LAUREN JACOB BRUMBAUGH Fifth great grandson of progenitor Nicholas Kegg.
MASON BRUMBAUGH Seventh great grandson of progenitor Nicholas Kegg.
MEGAN J. BRUMBAUGH Sixth great granddaughter of progenitor Nicholas Kegg.
MELEA BRUMBAUGH Seventh great granddaughter of progenitor Nicholas Kegg.

BRUMLEY

JEFFERY LYNN BRUMLEY [2943] (1947 – 2012) son of Brankley and Helen (Streight) Brumley. Jeff worked as a mechanic in the maintenance department of the Lorain County Metro Parks for 23 years. He enjoyed golfing, bowling, gardening, playing cards, the outdoors, and tinkering. He especially loved cats.
KIMBERLY J. BRUMLEY Seventh great granddaughter of progenitor Nicholas Kegg.
LEANNE ELIZABETH BRUMLEY Seventh great granddaughter of progenitor Nicholas Kegg.
NICOLE MARIE BRUMLEY aka "Nikki" Seventh great granddaughter of progenitor Nicholas Kegg.
PATRICK S. BRUMLEY Seventh great grandson of progenitor Nicholas Kegg.
SEAN LEE BRUMLEY Seventh great grandson of progenitor Nicholas Kegg.
STEVEN PATRICK BRUMLEY (1964 – 1964) son of Francis and Dolores (Corbin) Brumley.

BRUNK

TASHA BRUNK Seventh great granddaughter of progenitor Nicholas Kegg.

BRUNNER

CHRISTOPHER BRUNNER Seventh great grandson of progenitor Nicholas Kegg.
ERIC W. BRUNNER Sixth great grandson of progenitor Nicholas Kegg.
KEVIN BRUNNER Seventh great grandson of progenitor Nicholas Kegg.

BRUSS

ELLA MISHELLE BRUSS Seventh great granddaughter of progenitor Nicholas Kegg.
KEVIN PAUL BRUSS Sixth great grandson of progenitor Nicholas Kegg.
MELISSA ANNE BRUSS Sixth great granddaughter of progenitor Nicholas Kegg.

BRUTTS

CONNER BRUTTS Seventh great grandson of progenitor Nicholas Kegg. **CRYSTAL BRUTTS** Sixth great granddaughter of progenitor Nicholas Kegg. **NICHOLAS HARLAN BRUTTS** [2943A] (1994 – 2014) son of Robert and Holly (Hamm) Brutts was a member of the United Presbyterian Church, Pottsville, where he also volunteered in the soup kitchen. Nick was a 2013 graduate of Nativity High School, Pottsville, where he was very active in several sports. He served in the U.S. Army Reserves, Schuylkill Haven for six months and transferred to the Navy on June 11, 2014, where he had just returned from completing his basic training. Nick enjoyed running marathons, especially for charities. He participated in the Sol Lipton 5K Run and placed in the finish and also did the MS Bike ride from Philadelphia to Ocean City and back. He was a very giving individual and gave the greatest gift of all, his

---

[2943] Dovin Funeral Home (Lorain, Ohio) [2943A] Lord-Bixler Funeral Home, Inc. (PA)

kidney, to his father as a result of his death. **NOELLE K. BRUTTS** Sixth great granddaughter of progenitor Nicholas Kegg. **RYAN BRUTTS** Sixth great grandson of progenitor Nicholas Kegg. **STEVEN BRUTTS** Fifth great grandson of progenitor Nicholas Kegg. **STEVEN R. BRUTTS** Sixth great grandson of progenitor Nicholas Kegg.

BRYANT

DANIELLE L. BRYANT Sixth great granddaughter of progenitor Nicholas Kegg.
JAMIE LYNN BRYANT Sixth great granddaughter of progenitor Nicholas Kegg.
JERRY DALE BRYANT aka "J.D." Sixth great grandson of progenitor Nicholas Kegg.
TAMARA LEE BRYANT aka "Tamy" Sixth great granddaughter of progenitor Nicholas Kegg.

BUCCHIONI

ANTHONY ROBERT BUCCHIONI aka "Tony" Seventh great grandson of progenitor Nicholas Kegg.
TINA MARIE BUCCHIONI Seventh great granddaughter of progenitor Nicholas Kegg.

BUCHANAN

DEBORAH ANN BUCHANAN Sixth great granddaughter of progenitor Nicholas Kegg.
JOHN BARTON BUCHANAN Sixth great grandson of progenitor Nicholas Kegg.
LAURIE LYNN BUCHANAN Sixth great granddaughter of progenitor Nicholas Kegg.
WILLIAM E. BUCHANAN Sixth great grandson of progenitor Nicholas Kegg.

BUCHHEIT

CLAIRE BUCHHEIT Seventh great granddaughter of progenitor Nicholas Kegg.
SAM BUCHHEIT Seventh great grandson of progenitor Nicholas Kegg.

BUFFENMYER

JOHN WILLIAM BUFFENMYER [2943B] (1940 – 2013) son of John and Marian (Burkett) Buffenmyer served in Vietnam with the US Air Force. **MARTHA ELIZABETH BUFFENMYER** Fifth great granddaughter of progenitor Nicholas Kegg.

BUIS

PAMELA JEAN BUIS Sixth great granddaughter of progenitor Nicholas Kegg.
SHARI LIN BUIS Sixth great granddaughter of progenitor Nicholas Kegg.
SUSAN ELIZABETH BUIS Sixth great granddaughter of progenitor Nicholas Kegg.

BULGRIN

BRYNN RENEE BULGRIN Seventh great granddaughter of progenitor Nicholas Kegg.

BUMBAUGH

NICHOLAS BUMBAUGH Seventh great grandson of progenitor Nicholas Kegg. **SCOTT W. BUMBAUGH** Sixth great grandson of progenitor Nicholas Kegg. **VALERIE LYNN BUMBAUGH** Sixth great granddaughter of progenitor Nicholas Kegg. **ZACHARY B. BUMBAUGH** aka "Zach" Seventh great grandson of progenitor Nicholas Kegg.

BUMGARDNER

ANNA VERGENE BUMGARDNER [2944] (1921 – 1996) daughter of Wayne and Jennie (Huddy) Bumgardner, married Paul Edwin Cyrus. **DEBRA BUMGARDNER** Fifth great granddaughter of progenitor Nicholas Kegg. **DIANE E. BUMGARDNER** Fifth great granddaughter of progenitor Nicholas Kegg. **EILEEN AGNES BUMGARDNER** [2945] (1918 – 2009) daughter of Wayne and Jennie (Huddy) Bumgardner, married Dale Vernon Burchfield with whom she was mother of (2). Eileen was a 1936 graduate of Nelsonville High School, a member of the Nelsonville First United Methodist Church and a life member of The Plains VFW Auxiliary. **MARIE HUDDY BUMGARDNER** (1915 – 1989) daughter of Wayne and Jennie (Huddy) Bumgardner married Victor Leroy Dixon with whom she was mother of (3). **MARK BUMGARDNER** Fifth great grandson of progenitor Nicholas Kegg. **MAX CALVIN BUMGARDNER** [2946] (1925 – 2001) son of Wayne and Jennie (Huddy) Bumgardner married twice, first to Doris Jean Hoskins with whom he was father of (5). Later, he married Virgie Thomas. **MICHAEL BUMGARDNER** Fifth great grandson of progenitor Nicholas Kegg. **WILLIAM WAYNE BUMGARDNER** aka "Bill" Fifth great grandson of progenitor Nicholas Kegg.

BUMGARNER

GRAHAM BUMGARNER Sixth great grandson of progenitor Nicholas Kegg. **JANELLE BUMGARNER** Sixth great granddaughter of progenitor Nicholas Kegg. **JEFFREY BUMGARNER** Sixth great grandson of progenitor Nicholas Kegg. **JOSH BUMGARNER** Sixth great grandson of progenitor Nicholas Kegg.

BUNDY

KELLEY MARIE BUNDY Sixth great granddaughter of progenitor Nicholas Kegg.

BUNTING

APRIL MAE BUNTING Eighth great granddaughter of progenitor Nicholas Kegg.
JASON BUNTING Eighth great grandson of progenitor Nicholas Kegg.
KRISTA BUNTING Eighth great granddaughter of progenitor Nicholas Kegg.

BURCHELL

JONATHAN THOMAS BURCHELL Seventh great grandson of progenitor Nicholas Kegg.

BURCHFIELD

LEAH BURCHFIELD Sixth great granddaughter of progenitor Nicholas Kegg. **MATTHEW BURCHFIELD** Sixth great grandson of progenitor Nicholas Kegg. **MAX BURCHFIELD** Fifth great grandson of progenitor Nicholas Kegg. **MOLLY BURCHFIELD** Sixth great granddaughter of progenitor Nicholas Kegg. **STEPHANIE BURCHFIELD** Sixth great granddaughter of progenitor Nicholas Kegg. **TONY BURCHFIELD** Sixth great grandson of progenitor Nicholas Kegg.

[2943B] p14 The Cumberland News (MD) Jan 22, 1960 [2944] Logan Daily News (OH) Feb 6, 1996 [2945] Cardaras Funeral Homes (OH) [2846] Logan Daily News (OH) June 26, 2001

BURD

DONALD BURD [2946A] aka "Jack" (1925 – 2018) son of Frank and Jessie (Heaslip) Burd. Jack joined the military at the age of 17 and served in the U.S. Navy and U.S. Coast Guard. After his retirement from military service, he returned home and became a forklift driver and worked in construction. Jack enjoyed golfing, cooking at the veteran's posts and loved to ride his moped. He was known for playing Santa at many veterans' events.

BURDEN

ALYSSA BURDEN Eighth great granddaughter of progenitor Nicholas Kegg.
ANANBELLE BURDEN Eighth great granddaughter of progenitor Nicholas Kegg.
GUNTER HERBERT BURDEN Seventh great grandson of progenitor Nicholas Kegg.
JONATHAN DONALD BURDEN [2946B] (1974 – 2015) son of Timothy and Pamela (Donner) Burden was father of (3). Jonathan worked as a mail carrier with the US Postal Service and was a member of the Vineyard, Augusta. **KALEB CHRISTYN BURDEN** Eighth great grandson of progenitor Nicholas Kegg. **MATTHEW DAVID BURDEN** (1981 – 1983) son of Timothy and Pamela (Donner) Burden.
NATHANAEL A. BURDEN Seventh great grandson of progenitor Nicholas Kegg.
TRINITY BURDEN Eighth great granddaughter of progenitor Nicholas Kegg.
XIAN BURDEN Eighth great granddaughter of progenitor Nicholas Kegg.

BURELL

JOSHUA BURELL Sixth great grandson of progenitor Nicholas Kegg.

BURGAN

MICHAEL ANDREW BURGAN Sixth great grandson of progenitor Nicholas Kegg.
MICHELE ANN BURGAN Sixth great granddaughter of progenitor Nicholas Kegg.

BURKE

AMANDA BURKE Eighth great granddaughter of progenitor Nicholas Kegg.
RICKY JOSEPH BURKE [2947] (1971 – 2015) son of David and Carol (McWilliams) Burke married Marcy A. McDonald with whom he was father of (2). **TJ BURKE** Eighth great grandson of progenitor Nicholas Kegg.

BURKEN

JOSEPH BURKEN Eighth great grandson of progenitor Nicholas Kegg.

BURKET

CLEO L. BURKET [2948] (1913 – 1972) daughter of Lawrence and Minnie (Hockenberry) Burket. Cleo served as a cook at the Robert P. Smith Elementary School, Yellow Creek.

[2946A] Record Eagle (MI) March 7, 2018 [2946B] Chance & Hydrick Funeral Directors (GA) [2947] Dignity Memorial (IN) Mar 17, 2015 [2948] obituary obtained by Mary Hall Miller Find A Grave Memorial # 60705913

BURKETT

BRANDON BURKETT Eighth great grandson of progenitor Nicholas Kegg. **BRIAN BURKETT** Fifth great grandson of progenitor Nicholas Kegg. **CYNTHIA B. BURKETT** Fifth great granddaughter of progenitor Nicholas Kegg. **DIANA LYNN BURKETT** Fifth great granddaughter of progenitor Nicholas Kegg. **DONALD H. BURKETT** Fourth great grandson of progenitor Nicholas Kegg. **ELIZABETH BURKETT** Sixth great granddaughter of progenitor Nicholas Kegg. **JONATHAN BURKETT** Seventh great grandson of progenitor Nicholas Kegg.
KENNETH ANDREW BURKETT [2948A] son of William and Violet (Hillegass) Burkett was married three times, first to Elma Elizabeth Emerick with whom he was father of (3), then Joan with whom he was father of (2). Lastly, he married Vera Lorraine Bridgewater. In 1979 he opened Ken's Daylight Donut Shop in Glenpool, Oklahoma. He was the kindest and most generous man you would ever want to meet. He never met a stranger and loved everyone. Kenneth had a wonderful sense of humor, an amazing ability to memorize the bible, poems and he loved to bake. Most of all, Kenneth enjoyed spending time with his family whom he loved dearly. He was a long-time member of Beggs Assembly of God Church.
KENNETH BURKETT Fifth great grandson of progenitor Nicholas Kegg.
MARIAN FRANCIS BURKETT (1908 – 1996) daughter of William and Violet (Hillegass) Burkett married Rev. John Hoffer Buffenmyer with whom she was mother of (2). **MARY ANN BURKETT** Fifth great granddaughter of progenitor Nicholas Kegg. **MICHAEL BURKETT**, aka "Mike" Fifth great grandson of progenitorNicholas Kegg. **MAVERICK BURKETT** Ninth great grandson of progenitor Nicholas Kegg. **NATALIE ELISE BURKETT** Seventh great granddaughter of progenitor Nicholas Kegg. **PATRICIA BURKETT** Sixth great granddaughter of progenitor Nicholas Kegg. **PAULETTE BURKETT** Fifth great granddaughter of progenitor Nicholas Kegg.
ROBERT RANDOLPH BURKETT [2948B] son of G. Randolph and Flora Belle (Shoemaker) Randolph, married Evadean Diehl with whom he was father of (2). Robert retired after owning Burkett Motors in Bedford, for more than 45 years. He served in the Army during the Korean War and was stationed in Japan. **RUSSELL ALLAN BURKETT** [2949] (1911 – 1962) aka "Bing" son of William and Violet (Hillegass) Burkett married Sarah Jane Wilson. Russell drowned in the Bergriff River at Tulsa, Oklahoma. **TRAVIS BURKETT** Eighth great grandson of progenitor Nicholas Kegg.

BURKHARDT

KAMI BURKHARDT Seventh great granddaughter of progenitor Nicholas Kegg.
KARA BURKHARDT Seventh great granddaughter of progenitor Nicholas Kegg.

BURKHART

BRAD BURKHART Seventh great grandson of progenitor Nicholas Kegg. **BRYAN BURKHART** Seventh great grandson of progenitor Nicholas Kegg. **CAELAN BURKHART** Eighth great grandson of progenitor Nicholas Kegg. **CORY BURKHART** Eighth great grandson of progenitor Nicholas Kegg. **FARRAH BURKHART** Seventh great granddaughter of progenitor Nicholas Kegg. **GRACELIN BURKHART** Seventh great granddaughter of progenitor Nicholas Kegg. **JAMEY BURKHART** Eighth great grandson of progenitor Nicholas Kegg. **KAIDEN BURKHART** Seventh great grandson of progenitor Nicholas Kegg. **LANDEN BURKHART** Seventh great grandson of progenitor Nicholas Kegg. **LISA ANN BURKHART** Seventh great granddaughter of progenitor Nicholas Kegg. **MICHELLE ANN BURKHART** Seventh great granddaughter of progenitor Nicholas Kegg.

[2948A] Schaudt's Glenpool Funeral Service (OK) [2948B] Bedford Gazette (PA) Jan 13, 2015, obtained and contributed by Bob Rose [2949] Cumberland Evening Times (MD) July 10, 1962

BURMASTER

ANDREW BURMASTER Seventh great grandson of progenitor Nicholas Kegg.
ELI BURMASTER Seventh great grandson of progenitor Nicholas Kegg.
MICAH THOMAS BURMASTER Seventh great grandson of progenitor Nicholas Kegg.

BURMEISTER

CASSIDY SUE BURMEISTER Seventh great granddaughter of progenitor Nicholas Kegg.
DYLAN BURMEISTER Seventh great grandson of progenitor Nicholas Kegg.
JEFF BURMEISTER Sixth great grandson of progenitor Nicholas Kegg.
JEREMY BURMEISTER Sixth great grandson of progenitor Nicholas Kegg.
OWEN BURMEISTER Seventh great grandson of progenitor Nicholas Kegg

BURNHAM

MICHAEL GILLESPIE BURNHAM Sixth great grandson of progenitor Nicholas Kegg.
SARAH BURNHAM Sixth great granddaughter of progenitor Nicholas Kegg.

BURNS

ANNE VICTORINE BURNS [2950] (1927 – 2001) daughter of Stephen and Grace (Daley) Burns married William Paul McKenzie with whom she was mother of (4). Anne was a member of SS. Peter and Paul Catholic Church, and Eucharistic Minister, on the Parish Council and a board director at Friends Aware. **ANTHONY SUTER BURNS** Seventh great grandson of progenitor Nicholas Kegg. **BRITTANY R. BURNS** Seventh great granddaughter of progenitor Nicholas Kegg. **GRACE BURNS** Eighth great granddaughter of progenitor Nicholas Kegg. **JAMES BURNS** Sixth great grandson of progenitor Nicholas Kegg. **JEFF BURNS** Fifth great grandson of progenitor Nicholas Kegg. **JESSICA MARIE BURNS** Seventh great granddaughter of progenitor Nicholas Kegg. **MARGARET RITA BURNS** [2952] (1928 – 1998) daughter of Stephen and Grace (Daley) Burns married Nicholas J. Kozak with whom she was mother of (4). **MARY GRACE BURNS** [2953] (1928 – 2014) daughter of Stephen and Grace (Daley) Burns married William Leo Zaranko with whom she was mother of (2). Mary worked as a teacher's aide for the Avon Lake School System. Mary had a passion for baking and was known for the thousands of Christmas cookies she baked every holiday season. **MIKE BURNS** Fifth great grandson of progenitor Nicholas Kegg. **SHARI A. BURNS** Sixth great granddaughter of progenitor Nicholas Kegg.

BURRITT

DOROTHY VICTORIAN BURRITT (1912 – 1973) daughter of George and Georgia (Lininger) Burritt, married Clyde L. Bireley. Later Dorothy married and divorced Henry Clay Grandstaff and returned to the Bireley surname. **EDNA MARIE BURRITT** (1914 – 1914) daughter of George and Georgia (Lininger) Burritt. **FRANKLIN KENNETH BURRITT** (1910 – 1914) son of George and Georgia (Lininger) Burritt. **LILLIAN BEATRICE BURRITT** (1907 – 1967) daughter of George and Georgia (Lininger) Burritt, married William E. Hoel with whom she was mother of (1).

[2950] Cumberland Times (MD) Nov 8, 2001, obtained by Sheryl Kelso [2952] p6 Plain Dealer (OH) Oct 2, 1998, obtained by D. Sue Dible [2953] Dovin and Reber Jones Funeral & Cremation Center

BURROWS

C. THOMAS BURROWS, aka "Tom" Fifth great grandson of progenitor Nicholas Kegg.
GEORGE M. BURROWS [2954] (1954 – 1992) son of Charles and Georgia (Kegg) Burrows married Patti Holt with whom he was father of (2). George was employed as a security officer at Donald C. Cook Nuclear Plant in Bridgman. He was a member of the Organ Transplant Support Group of St. Joseph.
LINDA BURROWS Fifth great granddaughter of progenitor Nicholas Kegg. **MATTHEW BURROWS** Sixth great grandson of progenitor Nicholas Kegg. **MORGAN BURROWS** Sixth great granddaughter of progenitor Nicholas Kegg. **ROBERT DOUGLAS BURROWS** Fifth great grandson of progenitor Nicholas Kegg. **SUSAN MARIE BURROWS** Fifth great granddaughter of progenitor Nicholas Kegg. **TERRY BURROWS** Fifth great grandson of progenitor Nicholas Kegg.

BURSEY

IVY LILIAN BURSEY Eighth great granddaughter of progenitor Nicholas Kegg.
TYLER BURSEY Seventh great grandson of progenitor Nicholas Kegg.

BURTCH

PAMELA BURTCH Sixth great granddaughter of progenitor Nicholas Kegg.
PAULA BURTCH Sixth great granddaughter of progenitor Nicholas Kegg.
PEGGY BURTCH Sixth great granddaughter of progenitor Nicholas Kegg.

BURTON

EDGAR BURTON Eighth great grandson of progenitor Nicholas Kegg. **FINN DAVID BURTON** Eighth great grandson of progenitor Nicholas Kegg. **JADEN BURTON** Eighth great grandson of progenitor Nicholas Kegg. **JEREMY BURTON** Seventh great grandson of progenitor Nicholas Kegg. **JUSTIN BURTON** Seventh great grandson of progenitor Nicholas Kegg. **MARLEE BURTON** Eighth great granddaughter of progenitor Nicholas Kegg.

BUSHNELL

MARY ELIZABETH BUSHNELL [2954A] daughter of Robert and Marietta (Kegg) Bushnell was married three times, first to Kenneth Wise Horne with whom she was mother of (2). Mary was a commercial artist, and Mel Lamb, who operated the East Hampton Airport at the time, had asked her to design the color combination for the airport's fleet. In lieu of payment, she took flying lessons. Mary owned a Cessna 172 aircraft that was based at the airport. She flew for Montauk Caribbean Airways in the early 1960s Her noteworthy passengers included Richard Nixon and Santa Claus, the latter taking an annual flight to East Hampton in a two-seat Aircoupe, which Mary would then taxi up Main Street, to everyone's delight. She painted sets for productions at Guild Hall and served as a model in Ladies Village Improvement Society fashion shows. Mary was also a dedicated photographer and enjoyed sailing and golf.

BUSSARD

AUSTIN BUSSARD Sixth great grandson of progenitor Nicholas Kegg. **BETTY JANE BUSSARD** [2954B] (1925 – 2013) daughter of Raymond and Anna Belle (Weicht) Bussard, married Rhecy Curtis

---

[2954] obituary newspaper clipping dated June 25, 1992, obtained by D. Sue Dible [2954A] easthamptonstar.com [2954B] Bedford Gazette (PA) Dec 12, 2013, obtained and contributed by Bob Rose

Wigfield. Betty was the mother of (4) During the war she worked for the United States government in Washington D.C. in the war department. She later was employed at Holiday Inn as a waitress and housekeeper for many years. She was a member of the Everett Happy Senior Center, Red Hat Society and loved to travel and read. She enjoyed talking to her friends on the phone. **BLAKE BUSSARD** Seventh great grandson of progenitor Nicholas Kegg. **BONNIE J. BUSSARD** Sixth great granddaughter of progenitor Nicholas Kegg. **BOYD FRANKLIN BUSSARD** [2955] (1931 – 1997) son of Raymond and Anna Belle (Weicht) Bussard married Norma A. Northcraft with whom he was father of (3). Boyd served in the U.S. Army, 1954-56, and was a member of the American Legion William McKinley Post of Artemas. He was a self-employed dairy farmer for 29 years before his retirement.
CARL DEWEY BUSSARD (1928 – 1928) son of Raymond and Anna Belle (Weicht) Bussard.
CARROLL LEE BUSSARD (died 1928) daughter of Lester and Mary (Weicht) Bussard.
CHASE BUSSARD Sixth great grandson of progenitor Nicholas Kegg.
CHERIE JOLENE BUSSARD Sixth great granddaughter of progenitor Nicholas Kegg.
CONNIE S BUSSARD Sixth great granddaughter of progenitor Nicholas Kegg.
CORA REDA BUSSARD [2956] (1891 – 1970) daughter of George and Ocie (Williams) Bussard married Franklin Roy Dibert with whom she was mother of (3). **DAVID BUSSARD** Sixth great grandson of progenitor Nicholas Kegg. **DAVID EUGENE BUSSARD** Sixth great grandson of progenitor Nicholas Kegg. **DENISE LAUREEN BUSSARD** Sixth great granddaughter of progenitor Nicholas Kegg.
DENNIS DUANE BUSSARD (1934 – 1939) son of Raymond and Anna Belle (Weicht) Bussard.
DONALD L. BUSSARD Sixth great grandson of progenitor Nicholas Kegg.
DOROTHY MAY BUSSARD [2957] (1924 – 1968) daughter of Lester and Mary (Weicht) Bussard married Bruce Keller Coleman with whom she was mother of (2). **DOUGLAS STEPHEN BUSSARD** Sixth great grandson of progenitor Nicholas Kegg. **ELDA REBECCA BUSSARD** [2958] (1907 – 1992) daughter of William and Amanda (Redinger) Bussard married Cloyd Rouss Hoffman with whom she was mother of (3). Elda attended Pennsylvania Business College; attended Cavalry Road Church of God; was a member of the Senior Action Center and the East Providence Burial Association; and a former member of the Elderly Day Care Center. **FAYE ARLENE BUSSARD** [2958A] (1929 – 2017) daughter of Raymond and Anna Belle (Weicht) Bussard, married William M. Foster with whom she was mother of (5). Faye enjoyed rocking all her grandchildren and great-grandchildren, playing games and singing songs while swinging on her swing with them. She enjoyed caring for her flowers, feeding and watching birds, reading, yard sales, going out to eat, and visits with her family. She was patient, loving, and kind. She was a blessing in every life she touched. She was a member of Parkview Church of Brethren, where she was a Sunday school teacher for years. In earlier years, Faye enjoyed walking with her friends in the Silver Sneakers program at the YMCA and at Kish Park. **FRANK V. BUSSARD** [2959] (1910 – 1993) son of George and Ocie (Williams) Bussard married Anna M. Ritchey with whom he was father of (5). Frank was a member of the Mt. Union Church of Christ, Menchtown, where he held various church offices over the years. He was a lifelong farmer. **GARY LEE BUSSARD** [2959A] aka "Pete" (1940 – 2019) son of Raymond and Anna Belle (Weicht) Bussard, married Janet Oster with whom he was father of (2). Pete retired from JLG Industries having previously worked at Standard Register as a printing press operator until the plants closing. He enjoyed woodworking, hunting, reloading ammo and attending the coffee group at Marteen's. **GENE F. BUSSARD** 6th great grandson of progenitor Nicholas Kegg.
GEORGE DELMAR BUSSARD (1937 – 1937) son of Raymond and Anna Belle (Weicht) Bussard.
GEORGE WILSON BUSSARD [2959B] (1864 – 1926) son of Simon and Rebecca (Kegg) Bussard, married Ocie Ellen Williams with whom he was father of (11) A schoolteacher, George taught two terms of school in West Providence township. He was a member of the Christian Church.

[2955] Bedford County Genealogical Society obtained by D. Sue Dible [2956] obituary newspaper clipping obtained by Duke Clark [2957] Bedford County Historical Society obtained by D. Sue Dible [2958] p B2 - Patriot-News (Harrisburg, PA) Oct 4, 1992 [2958A] Barr Funeral Home, Inc. and Crematory (PA) [2959] Bedford Inquirer (PA) Aug 20, 1993 obtained by Duke Clark [2959A] Bedford Gazette (PA) April 15, 2018 obtained and contributed by Bob Rose [2959B] Everett Press (PA) June 18, 1926 obtained and contributed by Duke Clark

GERALD L. BUSSARD [2960] (1945 – 1971) son of Frank and Anna (Ritchey) Bussard, married Shirl L. Jones with whom he was father of (1). **GLADYS M. BUSSARD** [2960A] (1932 – 2013) daughter of Lester and Mary (Weicht) Bussard, married Fred W. Pepple with whom she was mother of (1). Gladys worked as a typist for the Department of Public Assistance. She then worked at Better Tires in Bedford as a bookkeeper for 11 years. Later, she worked in the gift shop at Old Bedford Village for several years. Gladys enjoyed collecting drums, working crossword puzzles, and watching sports, especially "her Yankees," her favorite NASCAR driver Jeff Gordon and golfer Tiger Woods. Every spring she loved planting red geraniums around her home and enjoyed listening to music by Danny O'Toole and the Gaithers. **GLENN LESTER BUSSARD** [2960B] (1935 – 1986) son of Lester and Mary (Weicht) Bussard, married Patricia Bookheimer. Glenn was killed in mountainous terrain in Bedford County in a small plane crash. The plane was on its way back from an air show in Oshkosh, Wis. Sunday when it crashed into a mountain while trying to land at Bunn Air Inc. airport about three miles north of Bedford. The plane had been missing for three days because the pilot did not file a flight plan. **GREGORY ALLEN BUSSARD** [2961] (1965 – 1965) son of Boyd and Norma (Northcraft) Bussard. **GREGORY D. BUSSARD** Sixth great grandson of progenitor Nicholas Kegg. **HARLEY EDISON BUSSARD** [2961A] son of Walter and Cora (Andrews) Bussard, married Anna Feryus with whom he was father of (2). A veteran of the U.S. Air Force National Guard, Harley was a Harford County resident for 45 years and worked as a manager of a grocery store, as well as, with Gene's Evergreens in Fallston. He was a member of Calvary Baptist Church, loved gospel music, traveling in his RV with his wife, woodworking and spending time with his grandchildren. **HOLLY ANN BUSSARD** Sixth great granddaughter of progenitor Nicholas Kegg. **IVA ALMEDA BUSSARD** [2962] (1898 – 1940) daughter of William and Amanda (Redinger) Bussard married Curtis Reddecliff with whom she was mother of (3). Iva attended Millersville State Normal School and prepared to teach. She also attended Pennsylvania Business College. She taught in the public schools of East and West Providence Township, Hopewell and Cumberland Valley Townships. **JESSICA BUSSARD** Sixth great granddaughter of progenitor Nicholas Kegg. **JESSIE PEARL BUSSARD** [2962A] (1896 – 1975) daughter of George and Ocie (Williams) Bussard, married John Brumbaugh Smith with whom she was mother of (4). Jessie was a member of the Mt. Union United Church of Christ. **JOHN ROGER BUSSARD** [2962B] (1938 – 2010) son of Raymond and Anna Belle (Weicht) Bussard, married Gloria Jean Foor with whom he was father of (4). John was a truck driver for most of his working years, having worked for B & P Motor Express, Maryland Transportation, Ryder Truck Lines, Munson Transportation, Bedford County Oil, Schneider and retired from R.F. Beyers, Harrisburg. After retirement he continued trucking part time for Beegle's Livestock and Weicht Trucking. He enjoyed hunting, spending time outdoors, woodworking, horses and Farmall tractors. He was a strong supporter of the Bedford County 4-H Horse and Pony Clubs. **JOHNNA R BUSSARD** Sixth great granddaughter of progenitor Nicholas Kegg. **KATHLEEN BUSSARD** Sixth great granddaughter of progenitor Nicholas Kegg. **KENNETH EUGENE BUSSARD** Sixth great grandson of progenitor Nicholas Kegg. **LEE W. BUSSARD** Fifth great grandson of progenitor Nicholas Kegg. **LELA E. BUSSARD** [2963] (1929 – 2011) daughter of Lester and Mary (Weicht) Bussard married Robert Lamont Bailey with whom she was mother of (1). Lela was a graduate of Everett High School, and after graduation, began working as a receptionist and clerk at the Bedford Farm Bureau. Her next position was working as a teller at the First National Bank in Everett for over 30 years, and after retiring from the bank, she worked as an administrative assistant at Everett Cash Mutual, and then as a door greeter at the Bedford Square WalMart. At home, Lela enjoyed watching all sorts of sporting events on television, following political

---

[2955] Bedford County Genealogical Society obtained by D. Sue Dible [2956] obituary newspaper clipping obtained by Duke Clark [2957] Bedford County Historical Society obtained by D. Sue Dible [2958] p B2 - Patriot-News (Harrisburg, PA) Oct 4, 1992 [2958A] Barr Funeral Home, Inc. and Crematory (PA) [2959] Bedford Inquirer (PA) Aug 20, 1993 obtained by Duke Clark [2959A] Bedford Gazette (PA) April 15, 2018 obtained and contributed by Bob Rose [2959B] Everett Press (PA) June 18, 1926 obtained and contributed by Duke Clark [2960, 2961] Duke Clark Obituary Collection [2960A] Bedford Gazette (PA) April 23, 2013 obtained and contributed by Bob Rose [2960B] p.17 - The Indiana Gazette (PA) Aug 6, 1986 [2961A] McComas Funeral Home (MD) [2962] Everett Press (PA) Jan 26, 1940 [2962A] Duke Clark obituary collection p.3918 [2962B] Akers Funeral Home (PA) [2963] Dalla Valle Funeral Home (PA)

news, and was a country music fan that enjoyed traveling with her friends. **LESLIE E. BUSSARD** Fifth great grandson of progenitor Nicholas Kegg. **LESTER VERNON BUSSARD** [2964] (1901 – 1973) son of George and Ocie (Williams) Bussard, married Mary Ethel Weicht with whom he was father of (7). **LILLIE VIOLA BUSSARD** [2964A] (1887 – 1974) daughter of George and Ocie Ellen (Williams) Bussard, married George Oliver Calhoun with whom she was mother of (7). Lillie was a housewife and a member of the Mt. Union United Church of Christ. **LUCINDA ETTA BUSSARD** [2965] (1872 – 1909) aka "Ettie" daughter of Simon and Rebecca (Kegg) Bussard married Watson Emory Barton with whom she was mother of (2). **MADDIE BUSSARD** Seventh great granddaughter of progenitor Nicholas Kegg. **MICHAEL A. BUSSARD** Sixth great grandson of progenitor Nicholas Kegg. **MILDRED MARIE BUSSARD** [2966] (1921 – 2005) daughter of Raymond and Anna Belle (Weicht) Bussard married Clarence Feaster Beegle with whom she was mother of (9). Mildred and her husband bought the Beegle family's centennial dairy farm, which has been owned by the Beegle family since the late 1700s. They owned and operated the farm until retiring in 1988, the property is now known as the Bicentennial Dairy Farm in Ott Town. In years past, Mrs. Beegle was a waitress at the Washington Coffee Shop in Bedford, the Penn Bedford Hotel, and the Holiday Inn in Breezewood. She enjoyed attending and setting up her booth of homemade soap, quilts, hand knotted rugs and other crafts at the annual Fall Foliage Festival in Bedford, as well as traveling to festivals in McConnellsburg, Belleville and other events through-out the area. She was an exceptional cook, especially at cooking from scratch, enjoyed flea markets, gardening and raising flowers at home. **MINNIE ETTA BUSSARD** [2967] (1893 – 1956) daughter of George and Ocie (Williams) Bussard married twice, first to Jacob Clarence Calhoun with whom she was mother of (3). Later she married John E. Mellott. **MOLLIE BUSSARD** Seventh great granddaughter of progenitor Nicholas Kegg. **OLIVE MAY BUSSARD** [2968] (1889 – 1978) daughter of George and Ocie (Williams) Bussard married Russell Mortimer Mellott with whom she was mother of (6). **ORA MARY BUSSARD** [2969] (1905 – 1967) daughter of George and Ocie (Williams) Bussard married Raymond Crawford with whom she was mother of (6). **RAYMOND E BUSSARD** [2969A] (1898 – 1966) son of George and Ocie Ellen (Williams) Bussard, married Anna Belle Weicht with whom he was father of (11). Raymond was a member of the Clear Creek Brethren in Christ Church. **RAYMOND ROBERT BUSSARD** [2970] (1923 – 2001) son of Raymond and Anna Belle (Weicht) Bussard married Evelyn Mae Markle with whom he was father of (5). Raymond was self-employed for many years as a long-haul truck driver, owning his own trucks. He also farmed for a while in Pennsylvania. Later in his career, he drove truck for Bend freight line companies Consolidated, System 99 and Silver Eagle. He was an Army veteran of World War II and was at the Battle of the Bulge. Raymond enjoyed hunting, fishing and camping. He was a member of the Moose, VFW and Eagles, all of Bend. In Pennsylvania he was a member of the American Legion. **RHONDA RENEE BUSSARD** Sixth great granddaughter of progenitor Nicholas Kegg. **RICHARD FRANKLIN BUSSARD** [2971] (1933 – 1997) aka "Dick" son of Frank and Anna (Ritchey) Bussard married twice, first to Shirley Ann Morgart with whom he was father of (2). Later he married Betty Lee Foor. Dick was a tenant dairy farmer for most of his life, working in the Everett and Friends Cove areas and for the Galen Furry farm at New Enterprise RD. He most recently worked in the maintenance department at Morral Bros., Everett. He was a 1950 graduate of the Everett High School, where he played football and was the first captain of the wrestling team. After graduating he was a volunteer wrestling coach in the early 50's. Mr. Bussard was a member of the Everett Church of the brethren, where he had served as a member of the church board and on various commissions and on the Faith and Order Fellowship. He also was the Heritage Fair coordinator, a member of the Chancel Choir and recycling coordinator at the church. In addition, he was a former Sunday school teacher and youth advisor at Friends Cove United Church of Christ, Bedford RD 4, at St. Johns United Church of Christ in Loysburg. **RONALD R. BUSSARD** Sixth great grandson of

---

[2964] Duke Clark Obituary collection pg. 603 [2964A] Bedford Inquirer (PA) Jul 19, 1974 obtained and contributed by Duke Clark [2965] Bedford Gazette Sept 10, 1909 obtained by Bob Rose [2966] Bedford Inquirer (PA) April 1, 2005 obtained by Bob Rose [2967] Everett Press (PA) June 15, 1956 obtained by Duke Clark [2968] Everett Press (PA) April 21, 1978 obtained by Duke Clark [2969] Cumberland Evening Times (MD) Feb 27,1967 [2969A] Duke Clark Obituary collection pg. 604 [2970] The Bulletin (Bend, OR) Oct 10, 2001 [2971] Morrisons Cove Herald (PA) Oct 30, 1997

progenitor Nicholas Kegg. **ROSA ELLEN BUSSARD** [2972] (1869 – 1902) aka "Rosie" daughter of Simon and Rebecca (Kegg) Bussard married John Caleb Streight with whom she was mother of (6).
RUTH D. BUSSARD [2972A] (1926 – 2003) daughter of Lester and Mary (Weicht) Bussard, married Archie Leland Bennett with whom she was mother of (2). Retired from The Bon-Ton, Carlisle, she was a volunteer at Cumberland County Historical Society and a member of Otterbein United Methodist Church.
SARAH BUSSARD Seventh great granddaughter of progenitor Nicholas Kegg.
SCOTT THOMAS BUSSARD Sixth great grandson of progenitor Nicholas Kegg.
SHANA R. BUSSARD Sixth great granddaughter of progenitor Nicholas Kegg.
SHAWN ROBERT BUSSARD Sixth great grandson of progenitor Nicholas Kegg.
TAMMY BUSSARD Sixth great granddaughter of progenitor Nicholas Kegg.
THELMA LOUISE BUSSARD [2972B] aka "Peg" (1927 – 2018) daughter of Raymond and Anna Belle (Weicht) Bussard, married Jacob Andrew Hale with whom she was mother of (2). During WWII she worked for the U.S. War Department in Washington, D.C. After her husband's death she earned her LPN license and worked as a pediatric nurse until retirement. She loved traveling, reading, playing Scrabble and the fellowship of membership in Wesleyville Baptist Church. She was a loving mother, faithful Christian, and genuine representative of the "greatest generation". **THOMAS D. BUSSARD** Fifth great grandson of progenitor Nicholas Kegg. **TRAVIS BUSSARD** Sixth great grandson of progenitor Nicholas Kegg. **TREVIS LEE BUSSARD** Sixth great grandson of progenitor Nicholas Kegg.
TROY A. BUSSARD Sixth great grandson of progenitor Nicholas Kegg.
VERA REBECCA BUSSARD (1923 – 1923) daughter of Lester and Mary (Weicht) Bussard.
VICKI S. BUSSARD Sixth great granddaughter of progenitor Nicholas Kegg.
WALTER GLEN BUSSARD [2973] (1908 – 1984) son of George and Ocie (Williams) Bussard married Cora Arlene Andrews with whom he was father of (2). Walter was a member of the Little River Baptist Church in Baltimore and was retired from the Glenn L. Martin Company.
WILLIAM JAMISON BUSSARD [2974] (1868 – 1957) son of Simon and Rebecca (Kegg) Bussard married Amanda C. Redinger with whom he was father of (2). William had served as a postmaster at Mench for 16 years and had taught in the area elementary schools for eight years. Previous to his retirement he was engaged in farming.

BUSSELL

BRUCE HENRY BUSSELL Fifth great grandson of progenitor Nicholas Kegg.
LINDA RAE BUSSELL Fifth great granddaughter of progenitor Nicholas Kegg.
LOUISE FAYE BUSSELL Fifth great granddaughter of progenitor Nicholas Kegg.
MATTHEW W. BUSSELL Sixth great grandson of progenitor Nicholas Kegg.
STACEY E. BUSSELL Sixth great granddaughter of progenitor Nicholas Kegg.
SHIRLEY ANNE BUSSELL Fifth great granddaughter of progenitor Nicholas Kegg.
STEVEN R. BUSSELL Sixth great grandson of progenitor Nicholas Kegg.

BUSSIERE

AHRIA BUSSIERE Ninth great granddaughter of progenitor Nicholas Kegg. **CHAD BUSSIERE** Eighth great grandson of progenitor Nicholas Kegg. **JULIE E. BUSSIERE** Seventh great granddaughter of progenitor Nicholas Kegg. **KATHY BUSSIERE** Seventh great granddaughter of progenitor Nicholas Kegg. **LUCIUS BUSSIERE** Ninth great grandson of progenitor Nicholas Kegg.
ROBERT JEFFREY BUSSIERE Seventh great grandson of progenitor Nicholas Kegg.
RYAN BUSSIERE Eighth great grandson of progenitor Nicholas Kegg.

[2972] Everett Press (PA) April 22, 1932, obtained by Duke Clark [2972A] p.B7 - The Patriot-News (PA) Jan 22, 2003 [2972B] Akers Funeral Home (PA) [2973, 2974] Bedford County Genealogical Society obtained by D. Sue Dible

BUSTA

JOSALYN FAITH BUSTA Eighth great granddaughter of progenitor Nicholas Kegg.
LORALEI JAYNE BUCCHIONI BUSTA Eighth great granddaughter of progenitor Nicholas Kegg.

BUTCHER

AMANDA MARIE BUTCHER Seventh great granddaughter of progenitor Nicholas Kegg.
ARREN BUTCHER Eighth great granddaughter of progenitor Nicholas Kegg.
BENNETT BUTCHER Seventh great grandson of progenitor Nicholas Kegg. **CHARLIE BUTCHER** Seventh great grandson of progenitor Nicholas Kegg. **DORIS R. BUTCHER**, aka "Dodi" Sixth great granddaughter of progenitor Nicholas Kegg. **FARAH BUTCHER** Eighth great granddaughter of progenitor Nicholas Kegg. **JACE BUTCHER** Seventh great grandson of progenitor Nicholas Kegg. **JAYDEN MARTIN BUTCHER** Seventh great grandson of progenitor Nicholas Kegg. **JILL DIANE BUTCHER** [2974A] (1961 – 2011) daughter of Donald and Patsy (Kutscher) Butcher married Rex Anthony Littleton with whom she was mother of (2). Jill was educated as an LPN and then served in the U.S. Navy for six years. Later, Jill was employed with Windstream as a telecommunications technician. **JOHN D. BUTCHER** Sixth great grandson of progenitor Nicholas Kegg. **JONAH BUTCHER** Sixth great grandson of progenitor Nicholas Kegg. **JUSTIN BUTCHER** Seventh great grandson of progenitor Nicholas Kegg. **LILAH BUTCHER** Seventh great granddaughter of progenitor Nicholas Kegg. **SAMUEL BUTCHER** Sixth great grandson of progenitor Nicholas Kegg.
MICHAEL BUTCHER [2975] son of Donald and Patsy (Kutscher) Butcher, married Tiffany Lee Martin with whom he was father of (2). Michael Served in the U.S. Navy and was employed at BNSF. He never took life for granted, commenting daily how fortunate he was. He was a strong man of faith and always put others needs above his own. **STACI BUTCHER** Seventh great granddaughter of progenitor Nicholas Kegg. **STEPHANIE BUTCHER** Seventh great granddaughter of progenitor Nicholas Kegg. **STEVE BUTCHER** Seventh great grandson of progenitor Nicholas Kegg.

BUTLER

ANTHONY BUTLER aka "Tony" Sixth great grandson of progenitor Nicholas Kegg.
JAMES LELAND BUTLER Sixth great grandson of progenitor Nicholas Kegg. **VICKIE BUTLER** Sixth great granddaughter of progenitor Nicholas Kegg. **JASON BUTLER** Seventh great grandson of progenitor Nicholas Kegg. **ZACARY DAVID BUTLER** Sixth great grandson of progenitor Nicholas Kegg.

BUTSON

ALTON THOMAS BUTSON Sixth great grandson of progenitor Nicholas Kegg. **CHERIE BUTSON** Seventh great granddaughter of progenitor Nicholas Kegg. **DIANA LYNNE BUTSON** Sixth great granddaughter of progenitor Nicholas Kegg. **GEOFFREY P. BUTSON**, aka "Geoff" Seventh great grandson of progenitor Nicholas Kegg. **PAUL ANTON BUTSON** Seventh great grandson of progenitor Nicholas Kegg. **PHILIP DEAN BUTSON** Sixth great grandson of progenitor Nicholas Kegg. **RONALD HARRY BUTSON** Sixth great grandson of progenitor Nicholas Kegg.

[2974A] Zabka Funeral Home Seward (NE) [2975] Lincoln Journal Star (NB) Apr 27, 2016

BYERS

ASHLEY BYERS Sixth great granddaughter of progenitor Nicholas Kegg. **DAVID BYERS** Sixth great grandson of progenitor Nicholas Kegg. **DEBBIE BYERS** Sixth great granddaughter of progenitor Nicholas Kegg. **EMILY JO BYERS** Seventh great granddaughter of progenitor Nicholas Kegg. **ERIC DANIEL BYERS** Seventh great grandson of progenitor Nicholas Kegg. **ERIN RENEE BYERS** Seventh great granddaughter of progenitor Nicholas Kegg. **JAYE DANIEL BYERS** Seventh great grandson of progenitor Nicholas Kegg. **JOSHUA BYERS** Seventh great grandson of progenitor Nicholas Kegg. **MEGAN ANN BYERS** Sixth great granddaughter of progenitor Nicholas Kegg. **MICHAEL LEE BYERS** (1940 – 2003) son of Wilbur and Verlene (Laird) Byers, married LoAnn Lea Jordison with whom he was father of (2). **REBECCA IRENE BYERS** Seventh great granddaughter of progenitor Nicholas Kegg. **TARA BYERS** Seventh great granddaughter of progenitor Nicholas Kegg. **TRAVIS LYNN BYERS** Seventh great grandson of progenitor Nicholas Kegg.

BYRD

ADRIANNE BYRD Fourth great granddaughter of progenitor Nicholas Kegg.

CADWALLADER

JEFFREY B. CADWALLADER [2976] (1949 – 2019) son of Robert and Bette Jane (Bitter) Cadwallader married Mary Flowers with whom he was father of (2). Later he married Diane Turner. Jeff spent his life making everyone laugh. Jeff kept his humor until the very end, even faking his last breath several times, eventually erupting into a weak but genuine laugh saying, "I really had you guys going, didn't I." Jeff enjoyed travel, photography, tennis, golf, sleeping in, eating pie for breakfast, playing pickle ball with Diane, and non-stop banter with his brothers. **KATHERINE CADWALLADER** Sixth great granddaughter of progenitor Nicholas Kegg. **MICHAEL CADWALLADER** Sixth great grandson of progenitor Nicholas Kegg. **ROBERT T. CADWALLADER** Fifth great grandson of progenitor Nicholas Kegg. **STEPHEN C. CADWALLADER** Fifth great grandson of progenitor Nicholas Kegg.

CADY

ANDREA CADY Sixth great granddaughter of progenitor Nicholas Kegg.
DAVID CADY Sixth great grandson of progenitor Nicholas Kegg.
ELLIS CADY Sixth great grandson of progenitor Nicholas Kegg.

CAFFREY

LYDIA CAFFREY Seventh great granddaughter of progenitor Nicholas Kegg.
MAXSON CAFFREY Seventh great grandson of progenitor Nicholas Kegg

CAGG

ABIGAIL CAGG aka "Abby" Seventh great granddaughter of progenitor Nicholas Kegg **AMANDA DAWN CAGG** Sixth great granddaughter of progenitor Nicholas Kegg. **AMANDA SUE CAGG** Sixth great granddaughter of progenitor Nicholas Kegg. **AMY MARIE CAGG** Sixth great granddaughter of progenitor Nicholas Kegg. **ANDREW H. CAGG**, (abt 1850- ?) son of Samuel and Elizabeth (Woods) Cagg. **ANDREW WESLEY CAGG** [2977] (1867 – 1940) son of Samuel and Matilda (Johnson) Cagg, married Minnie J. Johnson with whom he was father of (1). Andrew was

---

[2976] The News and Observer (NC) Jul. 31, 2019, obtained by D. Sue Dible [2977] The Thomas Tribune (OK) March 14, 1940

affiliated with the Baptist church, being a faithful member of the Bear Creek Baptist church at the time of his death. In this church he labored steadfastly for thirteen years as its Sunday School Superintendent. He was also active in the Masonic Lodge. **ANGELA CAGG** aka "Angel", Sixth great granddaughter of progenitor Nicholas Kegg. **ANNA CAGG** (1872 – 1914) daughter of Isaac and Mary Minter (Herton) Cagg, married Sherman Nickels with whom she was mother of (4). **BENJAMIN FRANKLIN CAGG** [2978] (1858 – 1907) aka "Frank", son of Isaac and Sarah (Stanley) Cagg, married Winnifred Ashley with whom he was father of (1). **BERNICE LEONEE CAGG** (1919 – 1985) daughter of Vernon and Lottie (McKee) Cagg. **BERNITA ELLEN CAGG** Fifth great granddaughter of progenitor Nicholas Kegg. **BRETT CAGG** Fifth great grandson of progenitor Nicholas Kegg. **BRIANNA CAGG** Sixth great granddaughter of progenitor Nicholas Kegg. **C. WAYNE CAGG** Sixth great grandson of progenitor Nicholas Kegg. **CARL MILLARD CAGG** (1925 – 1984) son of William and Allie (Britton) Cagg, married Elsie Louise Sweny with whom he was father of (2). Later, he married Laura Viola Overracker with whom he was father of (3). **CARMOLETA ELDORA CAGG** [2979] (1909 – 2003) daughter of Edward and Elizabeth (Gilpin) Cagg, married George Edward Walton with whom she was mother of (3). Carmoleta willed her body to the basic sciences department at Ohio University in Athens. **CASSANDER CAGG**, (1821 – 1901) aka "Cassie", daughter of John and Barbary Cagg, married Campbell Laird with whom she was mother of (9). **CHARLES CAGG** (abt 1857 - ?) son of John and Margaret (Smith) Cagg. **CHARLES ELMER CAGG** [2980] (1822 – 1928) son of Edward and Elizabeth (Gilpin) Cagg died following a three days' illness with scarlet fever. **CHARLEY M. CAGG** (1899 -?) son of Samuel and Leanor (Bush) Cagg. **CHELSEA CAGG** Fifth great granddaughter of progenitor Nicholas Kegg. **CHERYL DARLENE CAGG** Fifth great granddaughter of progenitor Nicholas Kegg. **CHESTER CAGG** [2981] (1890 – 1953) aka "Chiley", son of John and Sarah (Green) Cagg married twice, first to Sarah Bateman with whom he was father of (3). Later, he married Virgie Imes. **CHESTER CAGG** [2982] (1962 – 2013) aka "Dinky", son of Chester and Virginia (Bledsoe) Cagg, married Bev Flaugher Carver with whom he was father of (5). **CHESTER DILLAS CAGG** [2983] (1992 – 1992) son of Chester and Bev (Carver) Cagg. **CHESTER L. CAGG** [2984] (1929 – 1982) son of William and Allie (Britton) Cagg had a relationship with Bonnie M. Whetstone with whom he was father of (1). Later he married Virginia Bledsoe with whom he was father of (4). Last, he married Pamela Neels with whom he was father of (1). Chester was a construction worker. **CHESTER LEE CAGG** [2985] (1933 – 2004) son of Emmett Arthur and Nora (Davis) Cagg, married Wanda Jean Wright with whom he was father of (1). Chester was a 26-year employee of Deed's Dairy and an 11-year employee of Rocky Shoes and Boots. **CHRIS M Cagg** [2986] (1964 – 2017) son of Carl and Laura (Overacker) Cagg. **COURTNEY LYNN CAGG** Seventh great granddaughter of progenitor Nicholas Kegg. **DANIEL EDWARD CAGG** Fifth great grandson of progenitor Nicholas Kegg. **DOROTHY DEBORAH MAY CAGG** (1891 – 1981) daughter of Samuel and Emma (Byers) Cagg married twice, first to Ira Levi Bordner with whom she was mother of (2). Later, she married Stephen Arnold Lacy. **EDWARD JAMES CAGG** (1884 – 1952) son of George and Elizabeth (Brandenburg) Cagg, married Elizabeth Ann Gilpin with whom he was father of (5). **EDWARD NATHAN CAGG** [2987] (1918 – 1995) son of Edward and Elizabeth (Gilpin) Cagg, married Marjorie Virginia Daniel with whom he was father of (2). Edward was a member of Oak Grove Wesleyan Church and Masonic Philodorian Nelsonville Lodge # 175 F&AM. He was a retired iron worker and a member of Local 172 in Columbus. **ELLEN NORA CAGG** (1862 – 1943) daughter of Andrew and Julia (Risley) Henshaw Cagg, married Irvin Patrick Nanna with whom she was mother of (9). **ELMER WARREN CAGG** (1897 – 1918) son of George and Elizabeth (Brandenburg) Cagg. Elmer served as Pvt., 15th Co., 158th Depot Brigade. **EMILY JANE CAGG** aka "Jane", Fifth great granddaughter of progenitor Nicholas Kegg.

[2978] The Hebron Journal (NE) Dec 6, 1907 [2979] Athens County, OH Obit Book obtained by D. Sue Dible [2980] Athens Messenger (OH) Dec 14, 1928 [2981] The Journal Herald (Dayton, OH) June 24, 1953 [2982] Southside Times-Indianapolis June 13, 2013 [2983] p39 The Indianapolis Star (IN) Mar 27, 1992 [2984] The Indianapolis News (IN) Jan 5, 1983 [2985] Lancaster Eagle-Gazette (OH) June 18, 2004 [2986] Arizona Republic (AZ) June 22, 2017 [2987] Athens Messenger (OH) Jan 31, 1995 obtained by D. Sue Dible

ELVIRA CAGG (1842 – 1930) daughter of Samuel and Elizabeth (Woods) Cagg married twice, first to Henry Sharrock with whom she was mother of (1). Later, she married John Henry Dowler with whom she was mother of (1). **EMMA CAGG** Fifth great granddaughter of progenitor Nicholas Kegg. **EMMA JANE CAGG** (1859 – 1947) aka "Em", daughter of Andrew and Julia (Risley) Henshaw Cagg, married Warren T. Brandenburg with whom she was mother of (2). **EMMETT ARTHUR CAGG** [2988] (1911 – 1970) aka "Arthur", son of Edward and Elizabeth (Gilpin) Cagg, married Nora Agnes Davis with whom he was father of (3). Arthur died of a heart attack while grocery shopping at Oak Grove. **EMMETT GEORGE CAGG** [2989] (1893 – 1972) son of George and Elizabeth (Brandenburg) Cagg. Emmett was a World War I veteran and a retired coal miner. **ESTHER FLORENCE CAGG** (1908 – 1987) daughter of Shires and Nellie (Pickett) Cagg married twice, first to Harold Irving Thompson with whom she was mother of (6). Later, she married Carl William Wiegel. Esther enjoyed her housework, flowers and gardening. **FLORENCE MARGARET CAGG** [2990] (1913 – 1995) daughter of Chester and Sarah (Bateman) Cagg, married Paul Edgar Linton with whom she was mother of (4). Florence was a patient relations representative for Doctors Hospital of Nelsonville and had been employed by the hospital for 41 years. In 1994, she was named as the Doctors Hospital Founders Day Honoree.
GARY WAYNE CAGG Fifth great grandson of progenitor Nicholas Kegg. **GAYLA L. CAGG** (1967 – 2004) daughter of Walter and Diana (Williams) Cagg. **GEORGE FRANKLIN CAGG** (1856 – 1913) son of Andrew and Julia (Risley) Henshaw, married Elizabeth Brandenburg with whom he was father of **HARRIET JANE CAGG** (abt 1854 – aft 1882) daughter of John and Margaret (Smith) Cagg, married Thomas Jefferson Bowers with whom she was mother of (5). **HEATHER CAGG** Seventh great granddaughter of progenitor Nicholas Kegg. **HENRY CAGG** (abt 1815 – aft 1851) son of John and Barbary Cagg, married Mary M. Mikes. **IDA CAGG** (1865 – 1884) daughter of Isaac and Sarah (Stanley) Cagg. **IDA JANE CAGG** [2992] (1873 – 1933) daughter of William and Mary (Ross) Cagg, married Charles Pearl Schleich with whom she was a foster mother of (1). **INFANT CAGG** (1862 – 1862) son of Andrew and Julia (Risley) Henshaw Cagg. **INFANT CAGG** (1914 – 1914) son of Edward and Elizabeth (Gilpin) Cagg. **INFANT CAGG** (1917 – 1917) son of Chester and Sarah (Bateman) Cagg. **IRMA ELEANOR CAGG** (1919 – 1974) daughter of Shires and Nellie (Pickett) Cagg married Vernon Calvert Patterson with whom she was mother of (2). **ISAAC M. CAGG** infant son of Isaac and Sarah (Stanley) Cagg lived for 22 days. **ISAAC W. CAGG** (1875 – 1900) son of Isaac and Mary (Minter) Herton Cagg. **ISAAC WESLEY CAGG** (1827 – 1903) son of John and Barbary Cagg married twice, first to Sarah Stanley with whom he was father of (6). Later, he married Mary J. Minter Herton with whom he was father of (4). **IZAIAH F. CAGG** (abt 1837 -?) son of Samuel and Elizabeth (Woods) Cagg. **JAMES H. CAGG** (abt 1868 -?) son of Isaac and Sarah (Stanley) Cagg. **JAMES NATHAN CAGG**, aka "Jim" Fifth great grandson of progenitor Nicholas Kegg. **JAMES WILLIAM CAGG** aka "Jamie" Sixth great grandson of progenitor Nicholas Kegg. **JAMIE LYNN CAGG** Seventh great granddaughter of progenitor Nicholas Kegg. **JASON C. CAGG** Fifth great grandson of progenitor Nicholas Kegg. **JEAN ANNE ELIZABETH CAGG** Sixth great granddaughter of progenitor Nicholas Kegg. **JENNA BROOKE CAGG** Seventh great granddaughter of progenitor Nicholas Kegg. **JENNIFER JEAN CAGG** Sixth great granddaughter of progenitor Nicholas Kegg. **JENNIFER JOHANNA CAGG** Sixth great granddaughter of progenitor Nicholas Kegg. **JENNIFER LYNN CAGG** Sixth great granddaughter of progenitor Nicholas Kegg.
JESSE FRANKLIN CAGG [2993] (1914 – 2002) son of Vernon and Lottie Estella (McKee) Cagg. Jesse retired from Athens Mental Health Center and was a former employee of Southeastern Tuberculosis Hospital in Nelsonville and Athens County Engineers. He also worked on the construction of Poston power plant and was a coal miner and a farmer. Mr. Cagg was an Army veteran of WWII, where he served in the Central European Theater. He was a 1932 graduate of Nelsonville High School, a member

---

[2988] Athens Messenger (OH) June 21, 1970 [2989] p8 Logan Daily News (OH) Nov 11, 1972 [2990] Athens Messenger May 5, 1995, obtained by D. Sue Dible [2991] Logan Daily News (OH) Sep 22, 2008 [2992] Lancaster Eagle-Gazette (OH) Nov 16, 1933 [2993] Athens Messenger (OH) Jan 10, 2002, obtained by D. Sue Dible

of Glenford Dugan Post 229 American Legion of Nelsonville, VFW Post 3467, and a 50-year member of Nelsonville Philodorian Masonic Lodge 157 F&AM and the former York Grange in Nelsonville.
JEWEL DARLENE CAGG Fifth great granddaughter of progenitor Nicholas Kegg.
JOHN EDWARD CAGG (1928 – 1928) son of William and Allie (Britton) Cagg died of malnutrition.
JOHN FRANKLIN CAGG [2994] (1892 – 1942) son of John and Mary Granville Arthur Cagg. John was employed by the Central Ohio Paper Co., He succumbed to a heart attack while driving his auto. The car stopped after it jumped the curb. **JOHN ISAAC CAGG** (1860 – 1921) son of John and Margaret (Smith) Cagg married twice, first to Sarah E. Green with whom he was father of (2). Later, he married Mary Granville Arthur with whom he was father of (3). **JOHN J. CAGG** (born abt.1818) son of John and Barbary Cagg, married Margaret Smith with whom he was father of (8). **JOHN ROBERT CAGG** [2995] (1915 – 1977) son of Chester and Sarah (Bateman) Cagg, married Dorothy Mae Woolever.
JONATHAN BLAINE CAGG Sixth great grandson of progenitor Nicholas Kegg.
JONATHAN EUGENE CAGG Sixth great grandson of progenitor Nicholas Kegg.
JOSEPH WILLIAM CAGG (1919 – 2003) son of William and Allie (Britton) Cagg was married twice, first to Elizabeth Coury, later to Joan Lucille Fite with whom he was father of (1). **JULIA CAGG** (1891 – 1891) daughter of George and Elizabeth (Brandenburg) Cagg. **JULIA E. CAGG** [2996] (1874 – 1933) daughter of William and Mary (Ross) Cagg married twice, first to William Jewett with whom she was mother of (1). Later, she married John Thomas Maneely with whom she was mother of (1). Julia was a member of the Eastern Star lodge, also the Daughters of Veterans. **JULIA M. CAGG** Sixth great granddaughter of progenitor Nicholas Kegg. **JULIUS LEROY CAGG** (1903 – 1903) son of Vernon and Jeannette (Johnson) Cagg. **KAREN SUE CAGG** Fifth great granddaughter of progenitor Nicholas Kegg. **KEVIN CAGG** Fifth great grandson of progenitor Nicholas Kegg. **KRISTA LYNN CAGG** Seventh great granddaughter of progenitor Nicholas Kegg. **LARRY DAVID CAGG** Fifth great grandson of progenitor Nicholas Kegg. **LARRY DAVID CAGG II** Sixth great grandson of progenitor Nicholas Kegg. **LARRY RAY CAGG** Fourth great grandson of progenitor Nicholas Kegg. **LARRY WAYNE CAGG** [2997] (1978 – 2022) son of Robert Louis Cagg was pronounced dead at the scene after being shot. **LAWRENCE E. CAGG** [2998] (1910 – 1962) son of Leroy and Neva (Davis) Cagg married twice, first to Berniece M. Phillips, then to Ethel Vivian Harroun with whom he was father of (4). **LAWRENCE EVERETT CAGG** [2999] (1910 – 1986) son of Shires and Nellie (Pickett) Cagg married twice, first to Dorothy Alberta Dowler with whom he was father of (1). Later, he married Anna Marie (Lawrence) Bunthoff Hartley with whom he was father of (2). Lawrence was a coal miner and was employed by Athens County. He was a World War II Army veteran. **LEROY CAGG** (1910 – 1910) son of Vernon and Lottie Estella (McKee) Cagg. **LEROY GEORGE CAGG** (1881 – 1967) aka "Roy", son of Isaac and Mary Minter Herton Cagg married three times, first to Neva J. Davis with whom he was father of (1), he married Thelma Crabtree and later married Cora Ellen (Byers) Riggs with whom he was father of (4). **LEROY M. CAGG** [3000] (1911 – 1988) aka "Roy", son of Shires and Nellie (Pickett) Cagg, married Arzette Smith with whom he was father of (3). Roy was a retired coal miner and WWII Army veteran. **LEWIS LOREN CAGG** [3001] (1926 – 2017) son of Leroy and Cora Byers Riggs Cagg, married Edith May Gore. **LINDA LEE CAGG** [3002] (1942 – 2001) daughter of Lawrence and Dorothy (Dowler) Cagg, married Arthur Dale Koenig. **LLOYD N. CAGG** Fourth great grandson of progenitor Nicholas Kegg. **LOIS ESTHER CAGG** [3003] (1921 – 2004) daughter of Leroy and Cora Byers Riggs Cagg, married twice, first to George Miller and later to Mr. West. **LUCY JANE CAGG** [3004] (1891 – 1975) daughter of Benjamin Franklin and Winnifred (Ashley) Cagg, married Franklin H. Edgar with whom she was mother of (2). Lucy and her husband operated a prune orchard in Meridian until moving to Loomis in 1919. From Loomis where they owned a fruit and cattle ranch, they moved in 1929 to Chico where they owned a peach orchard on Burnap Avenue off the old Richardson Springs Rd.

[2994] p19 Columbus Dispatch (OH) Dec 17, 1942 [2995] The Logan Daily News (OH) Jan 25, 1977 [2996] p2 Times Recorder (OH) Nov 20, 1933 [2997] Indianapolis Star (IN) July 10, 2022 [2998] St. Joseph News-Press (MO) Jan 26, 1962 [2999] obituary on Find A Grave # 202079731 [3000] Athens Messenger (OH) Apr 7, 1988 obtained by D. Sue Dible [3001] Olinger Crown Hill Mortuary, Cemetery & Arboretum, Wheat Ridge, CO [3002] Logan Daily News (OH) Jan 26, 2001 [3003] Kansas City Star (MO) July 4, 2004 [3004] Family Search.org unidentified publication clipping pencil dated June 30, 1975

LYDIA LOUISE CAGG, Fifth great granddaughter of progenitor Nicholas Kegg. **LYNEL DALE CAGG** Fourth great grandson of progenitor Nicholas Kegg. **MACAYLA RENEA CAGG** Seventh great granddaughter of progenitor Nicholas Kegg. **MADISON RILEY CAGG** Seventh great granddaughter of progenitor Nicholas Kegg. **MAKINZIE CAGG** Seventh great granddaughter of progenitor Nicholas Kegg. **MARLA JEAN CAGG** Fifth great granddaughter of progenitor Nicholas Kegg. **MARTHA ELLEN CAGG** (1868 – 1938) daughter of John and Margaret (Smith) Cagg, married George Washington Goodlive with whom she was mother of (2). **MARTHA ELLEN CAGG** (1885 – 1946) aka "Mattie" daughter of John and Sarah (Green) Cagg, married Orren Bowen Tennihill with whom she was mother of (4). **MARTHA ETHEL CAGG** (1886 - 1970) daughter of Samuel and Leanor (Bush) Cagg married Samuel Jonas Phillips. **MARTHA JANE CAGG** [3005] (1870 – 1963) daughter of Samuel and Matilda (Johnson) Cagg, married John Theodore Braun. Matha lived in Toledo most of her life. She was a member of Collingwood Methodist Church, Eastern Star, Women's Educational Club and the West Toledo Garden Club. **MARY CAGG** (abt 1824 -?) daughter of John and Barbary Cagg. **MARY CAGG** (1850 – 1874) daughter of John and Margaret (Smith) Cagg, married Jarvis Chaney with whom she was mother of (2). **MARY C. CAGG** (1877 -?) aka "Mamie", daughter of William and Mary (Ross) Cagg, married James Thomas Powell with whom she was mother of (4).
MARY EVALENA CAGG (1873 – 1965) daughter of Samuel and Matilda (Johnson) Cagg, married Thomas O'Neill with whom she was mother of (2). **MARY JANE CAGG** (1851 – 1914) daughter of Samuel and Elizabeth (Woods) Cagg, married Civil War Veteran Eber Green Jones with whom she was mother of (1). **MEGAN MARIE CAGG** Sixth great granddaughter of progenitor Nicholas Kegg. **MELISSA LYNN CAGG** [3006] (1986 – 2019) daughter of Chester and Bev (Carver) Cagg married Mr. Philpot with whom she was mother of (1). Melissa was known for her good heart and bright smile. **MICHELE DEE CAGG** Sixth great granddaughter of progenitor Nicholas Kegg.
MILLARD JAMES CAGG (1944 – 2017) son of Carl and Elsie Louise (Sweney) Cagg.
MINERVA ANN CAGG (1845 – 1863) daughter of John and Margaret (Smith) Cagg, married Benjamin H. Six. **NANCY ANN CAGG** Fifth great granddaughter of progenitor Nicholas Kegg.
NATHAN CAGG Fifth great grandson of progenitor Nicholas Kegg. **NORMA JEAN CAGG** Fourth great granddaughter of progenitor Nicholas Kegg. **PARLEY LEO CAGG** (1892 – 1960) son of Samuel and Emma (Byers) Cagg married three times, first to Ruth M. Allis, then to Marie Brown and later, to Hester E. Bosley. **PATRICIA L. CAGG** aka "Trish", Seventh great granddaughter of progenitor Nicholas Kegg. **PATRICIA LYNN CAGG** Sixth great granddaughter of progenitor Nicholas Kegg. **PATRICK DALE CAGG** (1965 – 1999) son of Walter and Diana (Williams) Cagg.
PETER CAGG Fourth great grandson of progenitor Nicholas Kegg. **REBECCA JANE CAGG** [3007] (1840 – 1930) daughter of Andrew C. Cagg, married Capt. James William Combs with whom she was mother of (6). Rebecca was a member of Ballard's last City Council, which was dissolved when its resolution that the community be annexed to Seattle was adopted. She was a member of Eastern Star.
RETHA MAY CAGG (1884 – 1938) daughter of Isaac and Mary Minter Herton Cagg, married Harley A. Myers with whom she was mother of (6). **RHONDA LOUISE CAGG** Fifth great granddaughter of progenitor Nicholas Kegg. **RICHARD CAGG** Fourth great grandson of progenitor Nicholas Kegg. **RICHARD LEE CAGG** (1934 – 1994) son of William and Allie (Britton) Cagg, married Linda Lou Boyd with whom he was father of (3). **RICHARD L CAGG** [3007A] aka "Rick" son of Richard and Linda Lou (Boyd) Cagg married twice, first to Tina Marie Hutchison with whom he was father of (2). Later he married Linda Gail Meadows. Richard was an auto technician who had served his country in the U.S. Navy. Rick enjoyed music, sports, trivia, riding his motorcycle and loved to read.
RICHARD WILLIAM CAGG [3008] (1948 – 2012) aka "Rick", son of Robert and Glenna (Blackburn) Cagg, married Patricia Arlene Method with whom he was father of (2). **ROBERT ALLEN CAGG** Sixth great grandson of progenitor Nicholas Kegg. **ROBERT DAVID CAGG** Sixth great grandson of

---

[3005] p14 The Toledo Blade (OH) Jan 7, 1963 obtained by D. Sue Dible [3006] www.obituare.com/melissa-lynn-philpot-obituary-54611/ [3007] p4 Seattle Daily Times (WA) Jan 5, 1930 [3007A] Daily & Sunday Jeffersonian (OH) Jan 30, 2015 [3008] Dayton Daily News (OH) Sept. 29, 2012

progenitor Nicholas Kegg. **RONALD LEE CAGG** (1948 – 1949) son of Kenneth and Almeda (Masters) Cagg. **ROBERT EARL CAGG** Sixth great grandson of progenitor Nicholas Kegg. **ROBERT LEVI CAGG** (1922 – 1995) son of William and Allie (Britton) Cagg married twice, first to Glenna Ruth Blackburn with whom he was father of (2). Later he married Elsie Mae (Little) Gabbard. **ROBERT LOUIS CAGG** aka "Bobby", Fifth great grandson of progenitor Nicholas Kegg. **ROBERT RAY CAGG** Fifth great grandson of progenitor Nicholas Kegg. **RUTH MARIE CAGG** (1908 – 1908) daughter of Vernon and Clara (Nice) Cagg. **SAMUEL D. CAGG** (1816 – 1907) son of John and Barbary Cagg, married Elizabeth Woods with whom he was father of (5).
SAMUEL ELLSWORTH CAGG [3009] (1863 – 1946) son of Samuel and Matilda (Johnson) Cagg, married Leanor Jane Bush with whom he was father of (3). Samuel moved from the Kansas home to Oklahoma in 1895 and homesteaded thirteen miles southeast of Soiling. In 1906 he moved to Selling where he resided until his death. He united with the Baptist Church at Stuart, Kansas, in 1883, and continued his service here with the Christian Church. **SAMUEL FLETCHER CAGG** (1844 – 1926) son of Samuel and Elizabeth (Woods) Cagg, married Matilda Johnson with whom he was father of (4). **SAMUEL FRANK CAGG** (1866 – 1909) son of John and Margaret (Smith) Cagg, married Emma Byers with whom he was father of (3). **SAMUEL FRANKLIN CAGG** (1896 -?) son of Samuel and Emma (Byers) Cagg. **SARAH ANN CAGG** (1819 – 1889) daughter of John and Barbary Cagg, married Michael Kennedy with whom she was mother of (2). **SARAH J. CAGG** (1861 -?) daughter of Isaac and Sarah (Stanley) Cagg, married Gustave Julius Hahn. **SHARON LEE CAGG** Fifth great granddaughter of progenitor Nicholas Kegg. **SHEILA RAE CAGG** Fourth great granddaughter of progenitor Nicholas Kegg. **SHERRY L. CAGG** Fifth great granddaughter of progenitor Nicholas Kegg. **SHIRES MILBURN CAGG** [3010] (1882 – 1960) son of George and Elizabeth (Brandenburg) Cagg, married Nellie May Pickett with whom he was father of (4), Shires was a retired coalminer. **SHIRLEY CAGG** (1946 – 1946) daughter of Leroy and Arzetta (Smith) Cagg.
SHIRLEY MAY CAGG (1899 – 1989) daughter of Samuel and Leanor (Bush) Cagg, married Lieut. Garland Barber Wale with whom she was mother of (1). Shirley was a schoolteacher.
SHONA LEA CAGG Sixth great granddaughter of progenitor Nicholas Kegg.
STACEY CAGG Seventh great granddaughter of progenitor Nicholas Kegg. **STEVEN LEE CAGG** aka "Steve" Sixth great grandson of progenitor Nicholas Kegg. **SUSAN ELAINE CAGG** Sixth great granddaughter of progenitor Nicholas Kegg. **TABITHA DAWN CAGG** Sixth great granddaughter of progenitor Nicholas Kegg. **THOMAS E. CAGG** (1931 – 1974) son of William and Allie (Britton) Cagg. **TIMOTHY EARL CAGG** (1939 – 1999) son of Walter and Mary (Fitzwalter) Cagg, married Shirley Jean Conkling with whom he was father of (3). **TIMOTHY EARL CAGG** Seventh great grandson of progenitor Nicholas Kegg. **TONYA R. CAGG** Sixth great granddaughter of progenitor Nicholas Kegg. **VERNON LEROY CAGG** [3011] (1880 – 1964) son of George and Elizabeth (Brandenburg) Cagg married three times, first to Jeannette D. Johnson with whom he was father of (1). He married Clara Eldora Nice with whom he was father of (1). Later he married Lottie Estella McKee with whom he was father of (4). Vernon was a retired coal miner and farmer. He was a member of Nelsonville First Methodist Church, York Grange 2136 and the 50-year Miners Club.
VIRGINIA CAGG [3012] (1930 – 1993) daughter of William and Allie (Britton) Cagg, married Charles James Pugh with whom she was mother of (3). **WALTER ALBERT CAGG** [3013] (1938 – 2005) aka "Al", son of Walter and Mary Angeline (Fitzwalter) Cagg married three times, first to Janice Rasdale with whom he was father of (3). He then married Diana Jean Williams with whom he was father of (4). Later he married Clarice Conway. **WALTER WAYNE CAGG** Sixth great grandson of progenitor Nicholas Kegg. **WESLEY ALBERT CAGG** (1972 – 2009) son of Walter and Diana (Williams) Cagg. **WESLEY JOSEPH CAGG** [3014] (1894 – 1951) son of John and Mary Granville Arthur Cagg, married Helen F. Lytle. Wesley was a member of American Legion, Franklin Post No.1. Veteran of World War.
WILLIAM CAGG (1827 -?) son of John and Barbary Cagg, married Sarah A. Johnson.

[3009] p7 Logan Daily News (OH) Apr 25, 1946 [3010] Logan Daily News (OH) April 6, 1960 [3011] p2 Logan Daily News (OH) Aug 12, 1964 [3012] Dayton Daily News (OH) May 3, 1993 [3013] Oklahoman (OK) Jan 1, 2010 [3014] p4 Columbus Dispatch (OH) Jan 17, 1951

WILLIAM HENRY CAGG (born abt.1850) son of John and Margaret (Smith) Cagg, married Mary Ross with whom he was father of (3).   **WILLIAM HENRY CAGG** [3015] (1896 – 1935) aka "Bill", son of John and Mary Granville Arthur Cagg, married Allie Ann Britton with whom he was father of (9).
WILLIAM MICHAEL CAGG Fifth great grandson of progenitor Nicholas Kegg.
WILLIAM KEGG *(spelled)* **CAGG** son of progenitor Nicholas Kegg, married Susannah Koontz with whom he was father of (5).   **ZACH CAGG** Seventh great grandson of progenitor Nicholas Kegg.

CAGLE

BRAIDEN CAGLE Seventh great grandson of progenitor Nicholas Kegg.   **CHRISTIAN CAGLE** Seventh great grandson of progenitor Nicholas Kegg.   **ERIK JON CAGLE** Sixth great grandson of progenitor Nicholas Kegg.   **RYLAN CAGLE** Seventh great grandson of progenitor Nicholas Kegg.

CAHILL

BRENDEN EDWARD CAHILL Eighth great grandson of progenitor Nicholas Kegg.
HAIZE GREGORY LEE HILL Ninth great grandson of progenitor Nicholas Kegg.
KAYLIE CHEYANN CAHILL Eighth great granddaughter of progenitor Nicholas Kegg.
KENNETH JAMES CAHILL Eighth great grandson of progenitor Nicholas Kegg.
NIKKI LOVINA MASHIA CAHILL Eighth great granddaughter of progenitor Nicholas Kegg.

CAIN

BEATRICE ELAINE CAIN Sixth great granddaughter of progenitor Nicholas Kegg.
CAROL ANN CAIN Sixth great granddaughter of progenitor Nicholas Kegg.
CHARLES CARY CAIN aka "Chuck", Sixth great grandson of progenitor Nicholas Kegg.
CHARLES CARY CAIN JR. Seventh great grandson of progenitor Nicholas Kegg.
CHARLES CLEON CAIN [3016] (1917 – 1944) son of Walter and Eula (Hartman) Cain, married Rosemary Crutcher. The military Corporal was struck by a lightning bolt at Drew Field, Tampa, Florida.
CHESTER HARTMAN CAIN (1912 – 1978) son of Walter and Eula Blanche (Hartman) Cain was married twice, He was father of (1) to his first wife, later he married Verna Lee Barnes with whom he was father of (2) a veteran of WWII Chester served in France, Germany, Holland Czechoslovakia, Austria, Ardennes & Battle of the Bulge.   **HERBERT CAREY CAIN** [3016A] (1913 – 1999) son of Walter and Eula Blanche (Hartman) Cain was married three times, first to Cora Beatrice Skaggs with whom he was father of (1) he married Frances Webb and later, married Marilyn Estetle Smith. Herbert had retired as a foreman and engineer with the Kentucky State Highway Department and worked as a manager and engineer with a company developing an artificial snow blowing machine for the Kentucky State Parks. He was made an honorary Kentucky colonel under the administration of Gov. Bert Combs. He was a Master Mason and a member of Grand Lodge 1, Kentucky. He was a member of Lexington Chapter 1 Royal Arch Masons, Washington Council 1 Royal and Select Masters, Webb Commandery 1 Knights Templar, Oleika Shrine Temple, and Henry Clay OES Chapter 398, all of Lexington.
NATHANIEL BARNES CAIN Seventh great grandson of progenitor Nicholas Kegg.   **REE E. CAIN** Fifth great granddaughter of progenitor Nicholas Kegg.   **THOMAS CAIN** (1948 – 1948) son of Chester and Verna (Barnes) Cain.

[3015] p2 Daily Jeffersonian (OH) March 16, 1935, obtained by D. Sue Dible [3016] Paintsville Herald (KY) June 8, 1944 [3016A] St. Petersburg Times (FL) June 3, 1999

CALDWELL

BRANDON MICHAEL CALDWELL (3017) (1982 – 1999) son of James and Kimberly (Creamer) Caldwell was a junior at Southeast High School at the time he was killed in an automobile accident.
CAMERIA ANTWINETTE LICHELLE CALDWELL Eighth great granddaughter of progenitor Nicholas Kegg. **CAMILL ANTHONY JAMES CALDWELL** Eighth great grandson of progenitor Nicholas Kegg. **CODY CALDWELL** Sixth great grandson of progenitor Nicholas Kegg.
KUA SHEAN JAMES CALDWELL Eighth great grandson of progenitor Nicholas Kegg.
JAMES R CALDWELL Sixth great grandson of progenitor Nicholas Kegg.
RICHARD G. CALDWELL Sixth great grandson of progenitor Nicholas Kegg.
SHERMAN JAMES CALDWELL Eighth great grandson of progenitor Nicholas Kegg.

CALHOUN

ADA VIOLA CALHOUN (3018) (1899 – 1951) daughter of Barton and Minnie (Barkman) Calhoun married twice, first to Harold Jones with whom she was mother of (1). Later, she married John Osoling with whom she was mother of (2). **ALBERT F. CALHOUN** (3018A) aka "Abby" (1927 – 2017) son of Theodore and Nellie (Layton) Calhoun, married Ruby Lou Fink with whom he was father of (5). Albert served in the United States Army during the Korean War as an auto mechanic and truck driver. After being discharge from the military he drove milk truck for a few years for his family before starting his forty-year career with New Enterprise Stone and Lime until his retiring. Abby enjoyed spending time with family and friends on holidays and visiting with everyone. He enjoyed racing and was part of the pit crew for #880 Roy Morral Racing Team. **ALBERT J. CALHOUN** Seventh great grandson of progenitor Nicholas Kegg. **ALEXANDER CALHOUN** Eighth great grandson of progenitor Nicholas Kegg.
ALEXIS CALHOUN Eighth great granddaughter of progenitor Nicholas Kegg.
ALICE JEAN CALHOUN (1946 – 2007) daughter of Arnold and Mary (Henry) Calhoun, married Curtis Richard Ashcraft. **ALLEN E. CALHOUN** (3019) (1932 – 2020) son of Simon and Maude (Clark) Calhoun married Joann Truax with whom he was father of (4). Upon graduation Allen worked for a surveying company in Virginia. He was drafted into the U.S. Army from 1952 to 1954, serving during the Korean Conflict. Allen was a school bus contractor for the Everett Area School District for 47 years, also working at Bedford County Oil for 40 years and driving for Bollman's Charter Service for many years. Allen enjoyed his coffee clubs very much at Bedford County Oil as well as the McDonald's gang.
ALLISON CALHOUN Eighth great granddaughter of progenitor Nicholas Kegg.
AMANDA E. CALHOUN (3020) (1869 – 1951) daughter of David and Lucinda (Kegg) Calhoun, married William Francis Biddle. Amanda was a prominent member of the Friends Cove community across a span of 50 years, being active members of the Trinity Reformed church and of the Grange and taking part in all civic affairs of the area. **AMY J. CALHOUN** Seventh great granddaughter of progenitor Nicholas Kegg. **ANDREW J. CALHOUN** (3021) (1861 – 1889) son of David and Lucinda (Kegg) Calhoun, married Mary Amanda McDaniel with whom he was father of (3). **ANGELA CALHOUN** Sixth great granddaughter of progenitor Nicholas Kegg. **ANGELA R. CALHOUN** Fifth great granddaughter of progenitor Nicholas Kegg. **ARLENE R. CALHOUN** Fifth great granddaughter of progenitor Nicholas Kegg. **ARNOLD GAIUS CALHOUN** (3022) (1920 – 1991) son of Walter and Alma (Kegg) Calhoun.
ARNOLD GAIUS CALHOUN Fifth great grandson of progenitor Nicholas Kegg.
AUTUMN REBECCA CALHOUN Seventh great granddaughter of progenitor Nicholas Kegg.
BARBARA CALHOUN Sixth great granddaughter of progenitor Nicholas Kegg.

(3017) GenealogyBuff/Miscellaneous Portage County, Ohio Obituaries (3018) p3 - Bedford Gazette (PA) Apr 24, 1951 (3018A) Akers Funeral Home Inc (PA) (3019) Bedford Gazette (PA) Aug 12, 2020, obtained by Bob Rose (3020) p14 - Huntingdon Daily News (PA) Aug 17, 1951 (3021) Bedford Gazette (PA) Nov 28, 1951 (3022) Arizona Republic (AZ) Jan 22, 1991, obtained by D. Sue Dible

BARTON A. CALHOUN [3023] (1866 – 1937) son of David and Lucinda (Kegg) Calhoun, married Minnie Ray Barkman with whom he was father of (10). **BERNARD PAUL CALHOUN JR** [3024] (1948 – 1967) son of Bernard and Vance (Gordon) Calhoun was dead at the scene of a car accident. **BERNARD PAUL CALHOUN** [3025] (1923 – 1989) son of Jesse and Irene (Sigel) Calhoun, married Vance Ellen Gordon with whom he was father of (4). Bernard had been a farmer. He served in the U.S. Army in World War II in the 303rd Troop Carrier Squadron, 442nd Troop Carrier Group. He was a member of the Breezewood VFW Post 8333, where he had been serving as quartermaster, and the Artemas American Legion. **BETTE MARIE CALHOUN** Fifth great granddaughter of progenitor Nicholas Kegg. **BEVERLY GAIL CALHOUN** [3025A] (1944 – 2014) daughter of Coy and Rebecca (Miller) Calhoun married three times and was the mother of (2). She worked 25 years at Owens Illinois Glass. She always talked about the good times she had on her bowling league with both friends and co-workers. Beverly spent her time listening to country music and watching her shopping networks. Although she did not get out and about often, she loved the latest in fashion, jewelry and skin care. She was an avid reader of mystery romances and a host of magazines. **BEVERLY J. CALHOUN** Sixth great granddaughter of progenitor Nicholas Kegg. **BONITA J. CALHOUN** Sixth great granddaughter of progenitor Nicholas Kegg. **BONNIE SUE CALHOUN** [3026] (1952 -1952) daughter of Guy and Mary (Waltman) Calhoun. **BRADY CALHOUN** Seventh great grandson of progenitor Nicholas Kegg. **BRENDA CALHOUN** Sixth great granddaughter of progenitor Nicholas Kegg. **BRENDA CALHOUN** Sixth great granddaughter of progenitor Nicholas Kegg. **BRYAN CALHOUN** Sixth great grandson of progenitor Nicholas Kegg. **BRYAN CALHOUN** Seventh great grandson of progenitor Nicholas Kegg. **BRYSON MATTHEW CALHOUN** Eighth great grandson of progenitor Nicholas Kegg. **CALIE KAY CALHOUN** Seventh great granddaughter of progenitor Nicholas Kegg. **CARL EUGENE CALHOUN** Sixth great grandson of progenitor Nicholas Kegg. **CAROL CALHOUN** Sixth great granddaughter of progenitor Nicholas Kegg. **CARRIE MELISSA CALHOUN** Seventh great granddaughter of progenitor Nicholas Kegg. **CASEY CALHOUN** Seventh great grandson of progenitor Nicholas Kegg. **CHARLEAN JEANETTE CALHOUN** Seventh great granddaughter of progenitor Nicholas Kegg. **CHARLENE D. CALHOUN** Sixth great granddaughter of progenitor Nicholas Kegg. **CHARLOTTE CALHOUN** Sixth great granddaughter of progenitor Nicholas Kegg. **CHESTER D. CALHOUN** (1885 – 1887) son of Andrew and Mary Amanda (McDaniel) Calhoun. **CHRISTIAN L. CALHOUN** [3026A] (1968 – 2009) son of Clyde and Cheryl (Ickes) Calhoun, married Michelle McGill with whom he was father of (4). He was affiliated with the Messiah Lutheran Church. Christian enjoyed fishing and spending time with his family, and especially his son's sporting events. He was a compassionate and loving person. **CHRISTOPHER CALHOUN** Sixth great grandson of progenitor Nicholas Kegg. **CINDY ANN CALHOUN** [3026B] (1954 – 1972) daughter of Coy and Rebecca (Miller) Calhoun was a senior at Bedford High School and, had been employed part-time at the Dairy Dell when she was fatally injured in an automobile accident. **CINDY K. CALHOUN** Sixth great granddaughter of progenitor Nicholas Kegg. **CLAUDE WILLIS CALHOUN** Fifth great grandson of progenitor Nicholas Kegg. **CLIFFORD ARTHUR CALHOUN** Fifth great grandson of progenitor Nicholas Kegg. **CLYDE DELMAS CALHOUN** [3026C] (1945 – 2007) son of Simon and Maude (Clark) Calhoun, married Cheryl Lynn Ickes with whom he was father of (2). Clyde was a member of the Seventh Day Adventist Church in Everett. He was owner and operator of Clyde's used cars for many years. His passion was restoring cars and motor homes. **CLYDE SHAWN CALHOUN** Sixth great grandson of progenitor Nicholas Kegg. **COREY MATTHEW CALHOUN** Seventh great grandson of progenitor Nicholas Kegg. **COY CALHOUN** Seventh great grandson of progenitor Nicholas Kegg. **COY W. CALHOUN** [3027] (1918 – 1994) son of George and Lillie Viola (Bussard) Calhoun, married

---

[3023] Bedford County Genealogical Society obituary obtained by D. Sue Dible [3024] Bedford Gazette (PA) July 10, 1967 [3025] Bedford County Genealogical Society obituary obtained by D. Sue Dible [3025A] Southern Cremations & Funerals at Chattham Hill [3026] Duke Clark Obituary collection pg. 624 (PA) [3026A] Timothy A. Berkebile Funeral Home (PA) [3026B] p624 Duke Clark Collection [3026C] Timothy A. Berkebile Funeral Home, Inc [3027] Bedford Inquirer (PA) Feb 11, 1994, obtained by Duke Clark

Rebecca Miller with whom he was father of (8). Coy had been employed as a foreman for Roebel Construction of Johnstown. He also was a self-employed carpenter and farmer. He was a member of the Charlesville Grange, Bedford Loyal Order of the Moose and Friends Cove Sportsmen's Club.

CURT CALHOUN Sixth great grandson of progenitor Nicholas Kegg. **DAISY ELLEN CALHOUN** [3029] (1919 – 2003) daughter of Jacob and Minnie Etta (Bussard) Calhoun, married Henry Clair Lee with whom she was mother of (4). Daisy was employed as a seamstress for Lion Manufacturing in Everett, and then worked for Kelly-Springfield in Cumberland. Later, she was a homemaker who enjoyed flower and vegetable gardening, canning, and designing clothing and sewing for her family.

DANA P. CALHOUN Sixth great grandson of progenitor Nicholas Kegg.

DANIEL JOHN CALHOUN (1963 – 1963) son of Darrell and Kaye (Wenglik) Calhoun.

DAVID CALHOUN Eighth great grandson of progenitor Nicholas Kegg. **DAVID CALHOUN** Sixth great grandson of progenitor Nicholas Kegg. **DAVID DARRELL CALHOUN** Seventh great grandson of progenitor Nicholas Kegg. **DAVID EPHRAIM CALHOUN** [3029, 3030] (1885 – 1956) son of Franklin and Permilla Jane (Wilkins) Calhoun, married Myrtle May Hockenberry with whom he was father of (6). The former sheriff and GOP leader served as sealer of weights and measures in Bedford County for a number of years. David was elected sheriff in 1932. Pennsylvania law at that time prohibited a sheriff from serving for two successive terms and Mr. Calhoun, was succeeded in 1936 by Jacob A. Dunkle. He was again elected sheriff in 1949. He also served for two two-year terms as Bedford County Republican chairman, from 1942 to 1946 and during that period also served in a dual capacity as State Republican committeeman. **DEAN E. CALHOUN** Fifth great grandson of progenitor Nicholas Kegg.

DEBORAH A. CALHOUN Sixth great granddaughter of progenitor Nicholas Kegg.

DEBORAH M. CALHOUN [3031] (1962 – 1966) daughter of Harry and Jessie (Lightner) Calhoun.

DEBRA KATHERINE CALHOUN aka "Debi" Sixth great granddaughter of progenitor Nicholas Kegg. **DELORES VIVIAN CALHOUN** [3032] (1933 – 2004) daughter of Jesse and Irene (Sigel) Calhoun, married Leroy D. Leese with whom she was mother of (5). **DESESE LYNNE CALHOUN** Seventh great granddaughter of progenitor Nicholas Kegg. **DENNIS J. CALHOUN** Sixth great grandson of progenitor Nicholas Kegg. **DIANE CALHOUN** Sixth great granddaughter of progenitor Nicholas Kegg. **DICK H. CALHOUN** [3032A] (1928 – 2010) son of Jesse and Irene (Sigel) Calhoun, married Dorothy Pittman with whom he was father of (2). Dick served in the United States Army as a Corporal during the Korean War with the 724th Transportation Battalion Railway Operation as a guard on the trains transporting prisoners. In his youngest years, he began working with his family on their farm, and then worked as a general carpenter for many years on projects such as bridge construction, framing and finishing, the construction of the dam at Shawnee State Park and various projects at Letterkenny Army Depot. He then began working for the Pennsylvania Department of Transportation, where for 15 years, he ran snowplow, and for 13 years operated fuel trucks until his retirement. He was a member of the American Federation of State, County and Municipal Employees, Counsel 13, a member of the Union Memorial Cemetery Association, and was an honorary trustee for the Woodbush Community Center where he was helpful in many phases of the restoration and construction of the building. At home, Dick enjoyed repairing and refinishing antique furniture for his home and for others.

DONALD D. CALHOUN [3033] (1931 – 2010) son of Jesse and Irene (Sigel) Calhoun, married Mary E. Leader with whom he was father of (1). Donald worked at the Harrisburg State Hospital for the Commonwealth of Pennsylvania as a groundskeeper and later in the greenhouse, until retiring. He loved working with flowers and growing vegetables, and one of his main hobbies was building grandfather, grandmother, schoolhouse and steeple clocks. Don built his own home, moving back to Everett, and loved to go hunting with his son. He was an avid groundhog hunter who enjoyed the sport while riding his Gator.

[3028] p3 - Bedford Inquirer, February 7, 2003, obtained by Bob Rose [3029] p6 -The Daily News (Huntingdon, PA) June 5,1956 [3030] A history of the Juniata Valley and its people pg. 618 [3031] p2 - Daily News (Huntingdon, PA) Aug 15, 1966 [3032] Herald Mail (Hagerstown, MD) July 21, 2004 [3032A] p3 - Bedford Inquirer (PA) September 3, 2010, obtained and contributed by Bob Rose [3033] pg. 3 - Bedford Inquirer, November 26, 2010, obtained by Bob Rose

DONALD EUGENE CALHOUN [3033A] (1947 – 2009) son of Randolph and Alma (Spade) Calhoun married Paula Berlin with whom he was father of (4). Donny was called to serve his country in the U.S. Army in 1967 during the Vietnam War. He served one tour of duty in Vietnam and earned several decorations and medals for his service including the Purple Heart. He then spent three more years of service in the Army Reserves. He loved being outdoors and, in the mountains, this is where he was most at peace. He loved fishing, hunting, and horses, these were hobbies he was good at from a very young age. He was a jack of all trades. Throughout his life he worked as a soldier, a farmer, a rancher, an elk feeder at Camp Creek, Gros Ventre and Jewett feed grounds, and as a hunter, and woodsman. **DONNA L. CALHOUN** Fifth great granddaughter of progenitor Nicholas Kegg. **DORIS CALHOUN** Sixth great granddaughter of progenitor Nicholas Kegg. **DOROTHY V. CALHOUN** [3034] (1916 – 2002) aka "Dot", daughter of David and Myrtle (Hockenberry) Calhoun married three times, first to Woodrow Wilson Clapper with whom she was mother of (2). Then married Oscar J. Straub with whom she was mother of (3). Later, she married Conrad Keller Hughes. Admired for always caring and giving of herself. Dot was a stylish, gentle person with a sense of humor who enjoyed being with family and playing bingo and bridge. She was a member of Trinity Lutheran church of Bedford, Chapter No.41, Order of Eastern Star. **DREW T. CALHOUN** Seventh great grandson of progenitor Nicholas Kegg. **EDITH PERMILLA CALHOUN** [3035] (1916 – 1988) daughter of Jacob and Minnie Etta (Bussard) Calhoun, married George A. Smith with whom she was mother of (3). Edith worked at Lion Manufacturing Co. of Everett for eight years and later worked for Botany 500 in Philadelphia.

EDNA GRACE CALHOUN [3036] (1910 – 2000) daughter of George and Lillie (Bussard) Calhoun, married Ralph E. O'Neal with whom she was mother of (6). Edna was a member of the Mt. Union United Church of Christ, where she was the Cradle Roll Superintendent for many years. She was a homemaker and one of the original members of the Lone Girl Scouts. This was the organization through which rural members belonged to the larger association of Girl Scouts and attended meetings by mail and once a year in person. **EDWARD BANTON CALHOUN** [3037] (1925 – 2021) son of William and Ethel (Richards) Calhoun married Vera Idella Gummo. Edward served in the United States Navy as a gunners mate on the Liberty Ships until Dec. 16, 1945, then joined the United States Naval Reserve from 1945-1950 and reenlisted in the United States Air Force on Feb. 1, 1950, as an electronics tech on F-84 aircraft, until being honorably discharged in Jan. 30, 1954. He worked as an electronics technician for the Department of Defense until his retirement. After retirement, Ed worked as a Gettysburg tour guide, driving the tour bus on guides around the Gettysburg area, also working for a motel in the area and doing taxes for folks through Area Agency on Aging. He was a member of the John W. Brown National Maritime Historical Society. Edward enjoyed traveling the world and then living and working on his farm.

EDWARD W. CALHOUN [3038] (1888 – 1978) son of Andrew and Mary (McDaniel) Calhoun, married Carrie Bowen with whom he was father of (3). **ELIZABETH ELLEN CALHOUN** (1942 – 1942) daughter of Arnold and Mary (Henry) Calhoun. **EMILY CALHOUN** Seventh great granddaughter of progenitor Nicholas Kegg. **ERIC CALHOUN** Seventh great grandson of progenitor Nicholas Kegg. **ERICA CALHOUN** Sixth great granddaughter of progenitor Nicholas Kegg.

ETHAN ROBERT CALHOUN Eighth great grandson of progenitor Nicholas Kegg.

ETHEL MAE CALHOUN [3039] (1910 – 1992) daughter of Harry and Blanche (Ford) Calhoun, married Melvin Cleon Price with whom she was mother of (1). Ethel was a seamstress and homemaker. She was a member of Trinity United Methodist Church, Daughters of the Nile, Cedar Chapter Order of Eastern Star, Gethsemane White Shrine, Amber Grotto, El Kahir Shrine Auxiliary and the Cedar Rapids Woman's Club. **FERMAN R. CALHOUN** [3040] (1918 – 2009) son of Jesse and Irene (Sigel) Calhoun, married Hazel Claybaugh with whom he was father of (2). Ferman was a masonry foreman and a retired employee of the Pennsylvania State Hospital, member of Christ Lutheran Church and Adams Lodge 319 F&AM,

---

[3033A] Pinedale Roundup (WY) May 2009 [3034] Timothy A. Berkebile Funeral Home (PA) [3035] Bedford Inquirer (PA) Dec 16, 1988, obtained by Duke Clark [3036] Bedford Inquirer (PA) June 20, 2000, obtained by Bob Rose [3037] Bedford Gazette (PA) Jan 14, 2021 [3038] obituary Duke Obituary Collection pg. 626 [3039] p16 - The Gazette (Cedar Rapids, IA) Feb 2, 1992 [3040] p3 - Bedford Inquirer (PA) July 10, 2009, obtain by Bob Rose

New Bloomfield. He was an Army veteran of World War II and had a passion for collecting and fixing clocks, as well as hunting and fishing.   **FLOYD W. CALHOUN** [3041] (1925 – 1981) son of Solomon and Elda (Hart) Calhoun, married Dorothy Marie Winck with whom he was father of (4). Floyd had served in the U.S. Army during World War II and received numerous decorations and citations, including The American Theatre Ribbon, Army of Occupation Ribbon, Purple Heart, and Purple Heart with Oak Leaf Cluster. He was a member of the First United Church of Christ, Everett, member of American Legion Post No. 8 of Everett, and VFW Post 2088 of Everett.   **FRANK F. CALHOUN** [3042] (1914 – 1989) son of Jesse and Irene (Sigel) Calhoun, married Marjorie J. Harman with whom he was father of (2). Frank had been employed by PennDOT and the Pennsylvania Turnpike Commission, retiring after 25 years of service. He was a member of the Mount Pleasant Lutheran Church and the East Providence Republican Club.   **FRANKLIN JEREMIAH CALHOUN** (1863 – 1927) son of David and Lucina (Kegg) Calhoun, married Permilla Jane Wilkins with whom he was father of (12).   **GARY CALHOUN** Sixth great grandson of progenitor Nicholas Kegg.   **GEORGE WILLIAM CALHOUN** [3043] (1940 – 2022) aka "Bill", son of Coy and Rebecca (Miller) Calhoun married Sharlet Anna Farris with whom he was father of (2). An Army veteran, George worked at Roadway Express/YRC as a systems analysis manager. George enjoyed spending time with his family, bowling, golfing, and his annual fishing trips to New York. Most of all, George could be found anywhere his grandchildren were. Whether watching a sporting event, playing board games, attending school events or any other activity, he was always there. They were his greatest joy.   **GERALD CALHOUN** Sixth great grandson of progenitor Nicholas Kegg.   **GLADYS J. CALHOUN** Sixth great granddaughter of progenitor Nicholas Kegg.
GLEN A. CALHOUN [3043A] (1957 – 1991) son of Albert and Ruby (Fink) Calhoun, married Deanna Taylor with whom he was father of (2). Glen attended the Everett United Methodist Church and was an active staff member of Doc's Run, a local charity in memory of the late Dr. Charles Griffiths. He was also a member of the Loyal Order of the Moose in Bedford. He had been employed as a truck driver for Venezia Transport of Limerick, Pa.   **GLENN DANIEL CALHOUN** [3044,3045] (1914 – 1935) son of David and Myrtle (Hockenberry) Calhoun was acting as a Deputy Sheriff having completed training at the State Highway Patrol School in Harrisburg. An airplane ride, a reward for selling tickets for an air circus, ended in his death when the plane crashed.   **GLENN E. CALHOUN** Sixth great grandson of progenitor Nicholas Kegg.   **GREGORY CALHOUN** Sixth great grandson of progenitor Nicholas Kegg.   **GREGORY GRANT CALHOUN** Sixth great grandson of progenitor Nicholas Kegg.   **GREGORY L. CALHOUN** aka "Greg", Seventh great grandson of progenitor Nicholas Kegg.
GUY M. CALHOUN Seventh great grandson of progenitor Nicholas Kegg.   **GUY M. CALHOUN** Fifth great grandson of progenitor Nicholas Kegg.   **GUY R. CALHOUN** Sixth great grandson of progenitor Nicholas Kegg.   **HAROLD WILSON CALHOUN** [3046] (1916 – 1996) son of George and Lillie (Bussard) Calhoun, married Dorothy Irene Zimmerman with whom he was father of (3). Harold was a member of the Quarter Century Club of New Enterprise Stone & Lime Co. where he worked until his retirement. In addition, he had been employed at the Ashcom Plant and was foreman in the tube mill.
HARRY ANDREW CALHOUN [3047] (1888 – 1970) son of Franklin and Permilla (Wilkins) Calhoun, married Blanche Lillian Ford with whom he was father of (6). Harry was a member of the Everett First United Church of Christ.   **HARRY GRANT CALHOUN** [3047A] (1928 – 2017) son of Harry and Blanche (Ford) Calhoun, married Jessie Lightner with whom he was father of (2). Harry was a self-employed logger and saw mill operator. His passion was working with wood and heavy machinery. Harry served in the United States Army from 1954 to 1956. He was crew chief on a MASH helicopter flying over much of Germany. He was a member of the Everett V.F.W. Post 2088. Harry provided lumber for the President of United States Guest House which is known as the "Blair House" in Washington D.C., the property is used for visiting dignitaries. He was very proud of being selected as the supplier of specialty

---

[3041] obituary from the Duke Clark Obituary collection [3042] Bedford County Genealogical Society obituary obtained by D. Sue Dible [3043] Akron Beacon Journal (OH) Jan 23, 2022, obtained by D. Sue Dible [3043A] Bedford Gazette (PA) July 2, 1991 [3044] The Gettysburg Times (PA) July 22, 1935 [3045] Bedford County Historical Society (PA), book 120, page 16, obtained by D. Sue Dible [3046] Bedford Inquirer (PA) Jan. 13, 1997 obtained by Duke Clark [3047] Duke Clark Obituary collection p.627 [3047A] Bedford Gazette (PA) Jan 26, 2017, obtained and contributed by Bob Rose

wood for the renovations to the property. **HAZEL MARY CALHOUN** [3048] (1917 – 2015) daughter of Walter and Alma (Kegg) Calhoun, married Fred L. Clark with whom she was mother of (4). Hazel was a homemaker and enjoyed reading, crossword puzzles, jigsaw puzzles, playing cards, watching birds and Jeopardy. She loved animals, especially her three dogs, two cats and goose. **HELEN EMMA JEAN CALHOUN** [3049] (1922 – 2001) daughter of Andrew and Blanche (Ford) Calhoun married twice, first to Leonard Warren Martin with whom she was mother of (3). Later, she married John T. Schnorrbusch. **HUNTER CHRISTIAN CALHOUN** [3050] (1998 – 1998) son of Christian and Michelle (McGill) Calhoun. **ILA JANE CALHOUN** [3051] (1932 – 2019) daughter of Theodore and Nellie (Layton) Calhoun, married Robert A. Bollman with whom she was mother of (1). Ila worked as a waitress at the Wildwood Inn at its original location near Breezewood and was a dedicated homemaker who enjoyed all kinds of music, especially music of the 1950's. She also enjoyed reading poems about the "good old days," relaxing on her back porch swing and watching a beautiful sunset. **IRENE CALHOUN** [3051A] (1950 – 2009) daughter of Bernard and Vance (Gordon) Calhoun, married Durban Metzler. Irene was a private practice psychologist in Altoona for 19 years and previously was employed as a psychologist at the Altoona Mental Health facility. She also was a founder of the Central PA Networking Singles. Irene was a 1968 graduate of Everett Area High School and a 1971 graduate of Slippery Rock University, receiving a bachelor's degree in health and physical education. She also received master's and doctorate degrees from Duquesne University, Pittsburgh. She loved Samoyed dogs, the Outer Banks, N.C., and especially loved her work. **IRENE D. CALHOUN** Sixth great granddaughter of progenitor Nicholas Kegg. **JACK M. CALHOUN** [3052] (1929 – 2001) son of Solomon and Elda (Hart) Calhoun married Vera Weicht with whom he was the father of (1). Jack had served in the U.S. Army during the Korean Conflict from 1952 until 1954 serving in Battery A 103rd FA BN 45th Division. He had been a self-employed contractor before his retirement. He was a former member of the American Legion Post 8, Everett and Breezewood VFW which he helped to build. **JACOB CALHOUN** Eighth great grandson of progenitor Nicholas Kegg. **JACOB CLARENCE CALHOUN** [3053] (1891 – 1919) son of Franklin and Permilla (Wilkins) Calhoun, married Minnie Etta Bussard with whom he was father of (3). **JAMES CALHOUN** Seventh great grandson of progenitor Nicholas Kegg. **JAMES AUDELL CALHOUN** [3053A] (1937 – 2015) son of Lloyd and Elda (Williams) Calhoun, married Janet Boore with whom he was father of (3). Jim grew up on the family dairy farm in Everett. He was on the wrestling team at Everett Area High School, from which he graduated in 1956. He attended the University of Pittsburgh before being drafted into the United States Army serving from 1958 to 1960. He worked as an electrician for Bethlehem Steel Corporation in Sparrows Point, Md., for 36 years before retiring in 1999. Jim was inducted into the Bedford County Sports Hall of Fame in 2008 and the District V Hall of Fame in 2011 for his wrestling achievements. He enjoyed spending time with family and friends, hunting, being outdoors, attending auctions, volunteering and helping others. **JAMES C. CALHOUN** [3053B] (1936 – 2008) son of Solomon and Elda (Hart) Calhoun, married Ora Jane Shriner with whom he was father of (3). Jim was an active lifetime member of the Mt. Union Christian Church, where he helped with much of the church's care and preservation. served in the Army National Guard of PA, as a gunner and tank commander, qualifying as a U.S. Carbine, Caliber .30, M1Sharpshotter and Pistol Caliber 45 Marksman, until his Honorable Discharge in 1964. He was then employed as a heavy equipment operator at New Enterprise Stone and Lime Company, J.M. Calhoun Construction Company, PBS Coals of Somerset, Halle Enterprise Construction in Virginia and retired from Valley Quarries of Chambersburg. After retiring, he then worked as a truck driver for Cottle's Asphalt Maintenance of Everett. Jim enjoyed spending time in town with his friends, having breakfast at Kelly's Scenic View Restaurant and spending time at Webster Foor garage and the Mobil Station in Everett. He was a former president and active member of the Everett Area Little League, was an enthusiastic Pittsburgh Steeler football fan, and also

[3048] Leader Times (PA) Nov 19, 2015 [3049] Page: 7B - South Florida Sun-Sentinel (FL) Mar 23, 2001 [3050] Bedford County Historical Society (PA) b 81 p 18 obtained by D. Sue Dible [3051] Bedford Gazette (PA) May 7, 2019, obtained by Bob Rose [3051A] Altoona Mirror (PA) Feb 26, 2009 [3052] Fulton County News (PA) May 31, 2001 [3053] p2 - Bedford Gazette (PA) Dec 17, 1915 [3053A] Bedford Gazette (PA) June 8, 2015, obtained and contributed by Bob Rose [3053B] Bedford County Historical Society (PA); book 99 p.43 obtained and contributed by D. Sue Dible

enjoyed following NASCAR racing. **JEFFREY W. CALHOUN** Sixth great grandson of progenitor Nicholas Kegg. **JENNIFER CALHOUN** Eighth great granddaughter of progenitor Nicholas Kegg. **JENNIFER LEA CALHOUN** Seventh great granddaughter of progenitor Nicholas Kegg. **JESSE CALHOUN** Seventh great grandson of progenitor Nicholas Kegg. **JESSE BART CALHOUN** [3054] (1890 – 1981) son of Franklin and Permilla (Wilkins) Calhoun, married Irene P. Sigel with whom he was father of (11). Jesse was a farmer, a former member of the Breezewood Lions Club, and had been a supervisor for East Providence Township for over 20 years. **JESSICA B. CALHOUN** Seventh great granddaughter of progenitor Nicholas Kegg. **JOANNA L. CALHOUN** Seventh great granddaughter of progenitor Nicholas Kegg. **JOHN CALHOUN** Sixth great grandson of progenitor Nicholas Kegg. **JOHN C. CALHOUN II** Fifth great grandson of progenitor Nicholas Kegg.
JOHN CLAIR CALHOUN [3055] (1909 – 1996) son of Barton and Minnie (Barkman) Calhoun married Nellie Cross, later he married Helen R. Evans with whom he was father of (5).
JOHN HENRY CALHOUN [3055A] (1860 – 1903) son of David and Lucinda (Kegg) Calhoun.
JOHN HENRY CALHOUN [3056] (1926 – 1994) son of Milford and Elsie (Streight) Calhoun, married Esther See with whom he was father of (2). John was a lawn mower technician for J A Williams Co., Pittsburg, from which he retired. An army veteran of WWII, he served in the European Theater with the 5th Armored Division. **JOSEPHINE LUCINDA CALHOUN** [3057] (1902 – 1951) daughter of Franklin and Permilla (Wilkins) Calhoun. **JOSHUA CALHOUN** Eighth great grandson of progenitor Nicholas Kegg. **JOSHUA L. CALHOUN** Seventh great grandson of progenitor Nicholas Kegg.
JOYCE THEORA CALHOUN [3058] (1943 – 2021) daughter of Robert and Mildred (Morse) Calhoun married Donald Eugene Foor with whom she was mother of (3). Joyce had been employed in the Bedford Memorial Hospital snack bar, as a cafeteria worker at Everett Area High School and at OIP, where she felt like the owners treated her like family. She loved and took passion in cooking and talking to her customers and students throughout the years. One of her favorite past times was enjoying a cup of coffee with her friends at local restaurants. **JUDITH ELAIN CALHOUN** Sixth great granddaughter of progenitor Nicholas Kegg. **JULIE A CALHOUN** Sixth great granddaughter of progenitor Nicholas Kegg. **JUNIA AMANDA CALHOUN** [3059] (1899 – 1971) aka "Junie", daughter of Franklin and Permilla (Wilkins) Calhoun, married Charles Franklin Gohn with whom she was mother of (1).
KAREN CALHOUN Sixth great granddaughter of progenitor Nicholas Kegg.
KAREN LEE CALHOUN Sixth great granddaughter of progenitor Nicholas Kegg.
KAREN LOUISE CALHOUN [3060] (1949 – 1967) daughter of Coy and Rebecca (Miller) Calhoun, married Terry Lee Lesh. Karen was a passenger in a car heading south on Route 26, near Manns Choice Friday at 9:45 p.m. The vehicle went out of control, ran off the road and struck an embankment. The car was operated by her husband, Terry Lesh, 19, who was treated at the hospital and released.
KATHY J. CALHOUN Sixth great granddaughter of progenitor Nicholas Kegg.
KEITH W. CALHOUN Sixth great grandson of progenitor Nicholas Kegg.
KELLI ANN CALHOUN Seventh great granddaughter of progenitor Nicholas Kegg.
KELLY CALHOUN Sixth great granddaughter of progenitor Nicholas Kegg.
KERRY C. CALHOUN Sixth great granddaughter of progenitor Nicholas Kegg.
KEVIN CALHOUN Sixth great grandson of progenitor Nicholas Kegg. **KEVIN C. CALHOUN** Sixth great grandson of progenitor Nicholas Kegg. **KRISTEN MARIE CALHOUN** Seventh great granddaughter of progenitor Nicholas Kegg. **LANDON CALHOUN** Seventh great grandson of progenitor Nicholas Kegg. **LARRY L. CALHOUN** 6th great grandson of progenitor Nicholas Kegg.
LAVENIA MAE CALHOUN [3060A] (1930 – 2023) daughter of William and Mary Ethel (Richards) Calhoun married three times, first to Marle R. Miller, then Cletus Maurice Miller with whom she was mother of (1). Later Lavenia married Richard Eugene Tilley. Lavenia grew up on a farm during the Great Depression. She participated in helping to maintain the farm that became more difficult after the death of

---

[3054] Duke Clark PA Obituary collection p. 627 [3055] Everett Press (PA) March 1, 1935 [3055A] Bedford Inquirer (PA) Mar 25, 1994 [3056] Bedford Inquirer (PA) Mar 25, 1994 [3057] p3 - Bedford Gazette (PA) Nov 19, 1951 [3058] Bedford Gazette (PA) Sep 21, 2021 [3059] p2 Somerset Daily American (PA) Mar 17, 1971 [3060] p6 - Cumberland News (MD) May 22, 1967 [3060A] Bedford Gazette (PA) Feb 8, 2023

her father. Lavenia believed in the American Dream and after graduating from H.S., worked for several decades as an accounting clerk. Lavenia was an avid ballroom dancer, an excellent gourmet cook, a stylish dresser, a maker of clothing for husbands, children, and grandchildren, a lover of pets and animals, and a member of the Toastmasters Club. Lavenia had a keen interest in the United States' history and politics, and organized and became the president of the Laurel Women's Republican club. Her immediate and extended family were of utmost importance to her. **LAWRENCE D. CALHOUN** Sixth great grandson of progenitor Nicholas Kegg. **LEIGH CALHOUN** [3061] (1921 – 1985) son of Walter and Alma (Kegg) Calhoun. **LEO W. CALHOUN** Fifth great grandson of progenitor Nicholas Kegg. **LEONA J. CALHOUN** Fifth great granddaughter of progenitor Nicholas Kegg. **LINDA CALHOUN** Sixth great granddaughter of progenitor Nicholas Kegg. **LINDA L CALHOUN** Sixth great granddaughter of progenitor Nicholas Kegg. **LISA CALHOUN** Sixth great granddaughter of progenitor Nicholas Kegg. **LISHA LORRAINE CALHOUN**, aka "Lish", Sixth great granddaughter of progenitor Nicholas Kegg. **LLOYD H. CALHOUN** [3062] (1907 – 1996) son of David and Myrtle (Hockenberry) Calhoun, married Elda Williams with whom he was father of (2). Lloyd was active on the Mt. Union Cemetery Board of Director. **LONALD WARREN CALHOUN** Sixth great grandson of progenitor Nicholas Kegg. **LONDA CALHOUN** aka "Lon", Sixth great granddaughter of progenitor Nicholas Kegg. **LORIE CALHOUN** Sixth great granddaughter of progenitor Nicholas Kegg. **LORRAINE E. CALHOUN** Seventh great granddaughter of progenitor Nicholas Kegg.
LOU ANN CALHOUN Sixth great granddaughter of progenitor Nicholas Kegg.
LOUISE E. CALHOUN [3063] (1929 – 2003) daughter of Simon and Maude (Clark) Calhoun, married Claude W. Imler with whom she was mother of (4). Louise was a member of the Seventh Day Adventist Church and retired after 20 years' service as a cafeteria worker for the Bedford Area School District.
LUCINDA A. CALHOUN Fifth great granddaughter of progenitor Nicholas Kegg.
LUCINDA PEARL CALHOUN [3064] (1897 – 1986) daughter of Barton and Minnie (Barkman) Calhoun, married Americus Enfield Foreman. Lucinda taught school and retired after 30 years.
MABEL LAVERNE CALHOUN [3065] (1904 – 1945) daughter of Barton and Minnie (Barkman) Calhoun, married William Holbert Bridges with whom she was mother of (1).
MARGARET ANN CALHOUN [3066] (1923 – 2020) daughter of William and Ethel (Richards) Calhoun married William Edward Buchanan with whom she was mother of (4). Upon graduating from high school, Margaret moved to Washington, D.C. and worked at the Naval Yard in the Commandant's Office during WW ll. After the war she worked in a patent attorneys' office and later at Standard Homes as a bookkeeper all while attending Benjamin Franklin Business School. In Washington, D.C. she met her beloved husband, SFC William Edward Buchanan, nicknamed "Buck", of Troy, Tennessee. They were wed at Ft. Bragg Chapel #17 on August 19, 1950. As an Army wife, she encouraged her husband to attend Officer Candidate School. She accompanied him, as a new Second Lieutenant, on a three-year tour in West Germany. She took care of their growing family when he was deployed to South Korea and later to the Mekong Delta in Vietnam during the Vietnam War. Their final posting was to Ft. Monroe in 1968. Her husband retired as a Lieutenant Colonel in 1974 and she supported him in his new career in real estate. **MARION F. CALHOUN** [3067] (1907 – 1968) son of George and Lillie (Bussard) Calhoun, married Katherine Price with whom he was father of (3). Marion was a member of the Mt. Union United Church of Christ. **MARJORIE VESTA CALHOUN** [3068] (1918 – 2005) daughter of David and Myrtle (Hockenberry) Calhoun married twice, first to Charles Stauffer Jones with whom she was mother of (3). Later, she married Fred P. Milburn. Marjorie was a longtime salesperson in Bedford for Pennel's Jewelry, Reta's Gift Shop, & Bartons Fashion Shop. She was past secretary for Dr. John Barker, and for Joe Straub at J & S Hearing. Marjorie was a member of the Order of Eastern Star Bedford Springs Chapter. **MARK ALLEN CALHOUN** [3069] (1972 – 2019) son of James and Janet (Boore) Calhoun.

[3061] p14 - Bedford Gazette (PA) Sept 27, 1985 [3062] Bedford County Genealogical Society obituary obtained by D. Sue Dible [3063] p3 - Bedford Inquirer (PA) Jan 17, 2003, obtained by Bob Rose [3064] Bedford County Genealogical Society obituary obtained by D. Sue Dible [3065] p6 Columbus Dispatch (OH) March 7, 1945 [3066] Bedford Gazette (PA) March 26, 2020 obtained by Bob Rose [3067] Bedford County Press and Everett Press (PA) May 23, 1968 obtained by Duke Clark [3068] p3 - Bedford Inquirer (PA) Oct 28, 2005 obtained by Bob Rose [3069] Bedford Gazette (PA) May 10, 2019 obtained by Bob Rose

Mark graduated with a bachelor's degree from Penn State University. He worked in the fields of sales and social work. Mark loved music and playing the guitar and banjo. He performed with his friends in the band, The Coal Mountain Ramblers. Mark also loved rifle and bow hunting. He had a lifelong passion for American history, particularly the Civil War, World War II and local history. He read extensively and enjoyed discussing historical topics. **MARSHA CALHOUN** Sixth great granddaughter of progenitor Nicholas Kegg. **MARTHA REBECCA CALHOUN** [3070] (1876 – 1934) daughter of David and Lucinda (Kegg) Calhoun married twice, first to Philip Americus Wigfield with whom she was mother of (3). Later, she married George Weicht. It can truthfully be said she worked hard and sacrificed much to care for and provide a home for her husband, who was a cripple for fourteen years prior to his death. In early life she connected herself with Mt. Union Christian Church and lived her life in that faith. **MARVIN JUNIOR CALHOUN** [3070A] (1924 – 2017) son of Simon and Maude (Clark) Calhoun, married Marion Kathleen Dodson with whom he was father of (3). Marvin served his country with dedication and courage during World War II as a Staff Sergeant with the Fourth Infantry Division, 22nd Infantry Regiment, Company G, as a bazooka operator in the European Theater. He participated in the Allied invasion of German occupied France landing on Utah Beach in Normandy on D-Day, June 6, 1944. He served in the following battles and campaigns: Normandy, Cherbourg, Ardennes, Rhineland, Northern France, Sainteny France, Hurtgen Forest and Battle of the Bulge. At the conclusion of the war, he was the only surviving member of his original unit. Wounded twice, he received the Purple Heart with one Oak Leaf Cluster, the Good Conduct Medal, American Theater Service Medal, European Theater Service Medal with Four Bronze Stars, Victory Combat Medal and was a lifetime member of the Disabled American Veterans. Like many returning veterans, he preferred not to talk about the horrors he witnessed until pressed later in life. After 27 consecutive months of service to his country, Marvin returned home and worked several years as a heavy equipment operator for local contractors. He worked 15 years as an electrician at Washington Adventist Hospital in Takoma Park, Maryland, and concluded his career working at the Ramada Inn in Breezewood, until he retired to work on his farm near Mattie. Farming was the job he enjoyed most. He always had a picturesque and productive garden. Marvin was a quiet, hard-working man. He enjoyed his family and reached out to help young children who were struggling to find their purpose in life. Over the years, he and his wife cared for 48 foster children, adopting one. **MARY ANNA CALHOUN** [3071] (1893 – 1975) daughter of Franklin and Permilla (Wilkins) Calhoun, married Ross Sylvester Crouse with whom she was mother of (4).

MARY ELENOR CALHOUN [3072] (1871 – 1949) daughter of David and Lucinda (Kegg) Calhoun, married Ezra N. Turner with whom she was mother of (4). Mary was educated at the Poughkeepsie Seminary and was ordained into the ministry in 1898. Three years after ordination she was united in marriage to Rev. Ezrz N. Turner and together they served the Mt. Zion Christian church as well as adjacent churches in that charge. After leaving this community the Turners served at Mill Creek, Clarion and McKean counties and at Prince Albert, Saskatchewan, Canada, finally moving to Vancouver where they both served charges until Rev. Turner's death in 1932. **MARY LUCRETIA CALHOUN** [3073] (1916 – 1988) daughter of Jesse and Irene (Sigel) Calhoun, married Robert H. Weaver. Mary was a retired employee of Jomax Sewering Factory in York. **MASON CALHOUN** Eighth great grandson of progenitor Nicholas Kegg. **MATTHEW CALHOUN** Seventh great grandson of progenitor Nicholas Kegg. **MATTHEW CALHOUN** Sixth great grandson of progenitor Nicholas Kegg.
MATTHEW ROSS CALHOUN Seventh great grandson of progenitor Nicholas Kegg.
MAYE C. CALHOUN [3074] (1915 – 1988) daughter of Milford and Elsie (Streight) Calhoun, married George K. Hart with whom she was mother of (3). Maye was a member of the First Church of Christ, Juanita Gap. **MICAH PAUL CALHOUN** Seventh great grandson of progenitor Nicholas Kegg.
MICHAEL CALHOUN Sixth great grandson of progenitor Nicholas Kegg.
MICHAEL EUGENE CALHOUN Seventh great grandson of progenitor Nicholas Kegg.
MILES E. CALHOUN Fifth great grandson of progenitor Nicholas Kegg.

[3070] Bedford County Historical Society (PA), book 134, p 9 obtained by D. Sue Dible [3070A] Bedford Gazette (PA) April 4, 2017, obtained and contributed by Bob Rose [3071] Duke Clark Obituary collection pg. 954 [3072] p2- Bedford Gazette (PA) Oct 21, 1949 [3073] p3 – Bedford Inquirer (PA) Sep 16, 1988 [3074] Bedford Inquirer (PA) Aug. 5, 1988, obtained by Duke Clark

MINNIE MAE CALHOUN (3075) (1907 – 2001) daughter of Barton and Minnie (Barkman) Calhoun.
MINNIE RAY CALHOUN Fifth great granddaughter of progenitor Nicholas Kegg.
MITCHELL CALHOUN Sixth great grandson of progenitor Nicholas Kegg.
MYRNA Y. CALHOUN Sixth great granddaughter of progenitor Nicholas Kegg.
MYRTLE CALHOUN (3076) (1880 – 1909) daughter of David and Lucinda (Kegg) Calhoun.
NEAL E. CALHOUN aka "Beaver", Sixth great grandson of progenitor Nicholas Kegg.
NELLIE ESTA CALHOUN (3077) (1912 – 1996) daughter of Harry and Blanche (Ford) Calhoun, married Robert Homer Diehl with whom she was mother of (3). Nellie was a member of the former Gospel Hall Assembly of Everett and had been employed 25 years by the former Lion Manufacturing Co. of Everett before retiring. **NILE EDGAR CALHOUN** (3077A) aka "Hot Rod" (1931 – 2012) son of Theodore and Nellie (Layton) Calhoun, married Donna Ruth Leader with whom he was father of (6). Nile was a life member of the Improved Order of Redmen Wambic Tribe Number 507, Everett. Nile was employed at New Enterprise Stone & Lime Company as a heavy equipment operator for more than 36 years until his retirement in 1999. Upon retiring, he could always be seen "tinkering around the house." In his younger days he enjoyed dancing and swimming. He was an avid hunter and enjoyed watching old Westerns. **NORMA CALHOUN** Sixth great granddaughter of progenitor Nicholas Kegg.
OLIVE NELL CALHOUN (3078) (1923 – 1993) daughter of Edward and Carrie (Bowen) Calhoun, married Grover C. Adams with whom she was mother of (1). Olive was a member of the Mt. Union United Church of Christ, Menchtown, and attended Youngsville Free Methodist Church.
ORVILLE EWARD CALHOUN (1909 – 1929) son of Franklin and Permilla (Wilkins) Calhoun.
PALMER S. CALHOUN (3078A) (1929 – 2017) son of Edward and Carrie (Bowen) Calhoun, married Catherine June Simmons with whom he was father of (4). At age 17 Palmer became a Merchant Marine sailor and sailed much of the world. Years later he returned home to Everett where he started his family and began a long career in trucking. He was a member of the Teamsters Local Union No. 453. Palmer enjoyed antiques, classic/antique cars and hunting. **PAMELA JEANNE CALHOUN** Sixth great granddaughter of progenitor Nicholas Kegg. **PAMELA R. CALHOUN** Sixth great granddaughter of progenitor Nicholas Kegg. **PATRICIA A. CALHOUN** Sixth great granddaughter of progenitor Nicholas Kegg. **PATTY LYNN CALHOUN** Sixth great granddaughter of progenitor Nicholas Kegg.
PAUL JACOB CALHOUN (3079) (1924 – 1995) aka "Bud", son of Solomon and Elda (Hart) Calhoun, married Mary Perrin. Paul was retired as a maintenance supervisor from Roadway Express; was a Marine Corps veteran of World War II; a member of the Sixth Marine Division Association, First Provisional Marine Brigade, Marine Corps League, Bedford American Legion Post 113, Mechanicsburg VFW Post 6704, West Shore Elks Lodge 2257 and Marysville Moose Lodge 107; and an honorary member of the Pennsylvania Sheriffs Association. **PAUL MILFORD CALHOUN** (3079A) (1919 – 2017) son of Milford and Elsie (Streight) Calhoun, married Evelyn Mayola Andrews with whom he was father of (3). Paul worked as a self-employed painter, a truck driver for Everett Bottling Works, an inspector for Fairchild Aircraft Corporation from 1943 to 1947 and as an equipment clerk for the Pennsylvania Department of Highways, the forerunner to PennDOT. Paul then worked for New Enterprise Stone and Lime Corporation at the Ashcom plant as a drill operator and dynamiter until retiring after 22 years of service. He was a member of the Teamsters' Union Local 453 of Uniontown, now Cumberland, Md., a founding and former member of the Everett Sportsmen's Association and was an avid hunter who also enjoyed trout fishing. **PAULINE RUTH CALHOUN** (3079B) (1927 – 2014) daughter of Simon and Maude (Clark) Calhoun, married Coy E. Pee with whom she was mother of (4). Pauline was a homemaker and had worked at Everett Lion Manufacturing prior to her marriage. Pauline enjoyed doing puzzles, flower gardening and crocheting and was an amazing cook and talented baker.
PEGGY CALHOUN Sixth great granddaughter of progenitor Nicholas Kegg.

(3075) p 4C - The Columbus Dispatch (OH) Jan 30, 2001 (3076) Bedford Gazette (PA) Mar 26,1909 (3077) Bedford Inquirer (PA) Aug 16, 1996 (3077A) Bedford Gazette (PA) Nov 16, 2012 obtained and contributed by Bob Rose (3078) Bedford Inquirer (PA) Aug 20, 1993 obtained by Duke Clark (3078A) Bedford Gazette (PA) May 27, 2017 obtained and contributed by Bob Rose (3079) Patriot-News (PA) Apr 9, 1995 (3079A) Bedford Gazette (PA) Feb 13, 2017 obtained and contributed by Bob Rose (3079B) Bedford Gazette (PA) April 1, 2014 obtained and contributed by Bob Rose

R. ELLIS CALHOUN [3080] (1914 – 1997) son of George and Lillie (Bussard) Calhoun, married Helen Elizabeth Zimmerman. R. Ellis was a member of the Quarter Century Club of New Enterprise Stone & Lime Co., where he drove a truck until his retirement. **RALPH DAVID CALHOUN** [3080A] aka "Bill" (1911 – 2007) son of David and Myrtle (Hockenberry) Calhoun, married Dorothy Johnston with whom he was father of (2). Bill was the owner of Calhoun's Atlantic and he retired in 1974. He served in the U.S. Army as a Pvt in WW II. He received the European/African/Middle Eastern Campaign Ribbon with four Bronze Stars, the Purple Heart with one Oak Leaf Cluster, Good Conduct Medal, American Theatre Ribbon, and the Combat Infantryman Badge. **RANDOLPH BOWEN CALHOUN** [3081] (1924 – 1997) son of Edward and Carrie (Bowen) Calhoun, married Alma Spade with whom he was father of (4). Primarily, Randolph had been a dairy farmer, but also formerly had been employed by May & Bigley Pin Mill, Bedford; Rockland Manufacturing, Bedford; and by Green Thumb, working at Raystown Ambulance and Everett Little League. He was an avid gardener and fisherman and enjoyed nature most while working in his garden and flower beds. **REBECCA CALHOUN** Sixth great granddaughter of progenitor Nicholas Kegg. **REBEKAH CALHOUN** Seventh great granddaughter of progenitor Nicholas Kegg. **RICHARD R. CALHOUN** [3082] (1941 – 2007) aka "Dick", son of Robert and Mary (Morse) Calhoun, married Emily Jane Dull. Dick was employed as a manager of Howard Johnson's South Midway and Derry Miller's Country Store until his retirement. Richard was a caring man with a cheerful point of view, who would help his family and friends in any manner he could. **RICHARD SAMUEL CALHOUN** [3083] (1915 – 1972) son of Harry and Blanche (Ford) Calhoun, married Helen E. Young with whom he was father of (7). Richard had been employed by the Pennsylvania Masonic Home in Elizabethtown. **RICHARD SAMUEL CALHOUN JR** [3084] (1949 – 1949) son of Richard and Helen (Young) Calhoun. **RICK L. CALHOUN** Sixth great grandson of progenitor Nicholas Kegg. **ROBERT W. CALHOUN** [3084A] (1923 – 2012) son of Simon and Maude (Clark) Calhoun, married Victoria Hoy. Robert served in the United States Army as a Sargent. He worked as an engineer in Washington Adventist Hospital in Takoma, Maryland until his retirement in 1992. He enjoyed working on lawn mowers and lock smiting. Robert like to fish, travel and his constant companion his dog. **RODERICK A. CALHOUN** Sixth great grandson of progenitor Nicholas Kegg. **ROGER CALHOUN** Fifth great grandson of progenitor Nicholas Kegg. **ROGER E. CALHOUN** [3085] (1953 – 1962) son of Guy and Mary (Waltman) Calhoun. Roger was a member of the Assembly of God Village Church and was second grade student at the Bedford North Elementary Grade School. **ROGER RANDOLPH CALHOUN** Sixth great grandson of progenitor Nicholas Kegg. **ROGER RANDOLPH CALHOUN** (1986 – 1986) son of Roger and Nancy (Krautter) Calhoun. **RONALD CALHOUN** aka "Bud", Sixth great grandson of progenitor Nicholas Kegg. **ROSS VERNON CALHOUN** [3085A] (1920 – 1992) son of George and Lillie (Bussard) Calhoun, married Betty Clark with whom he was father of (3). Ross was a charter member of the Everett Sportsmans Club and was very active in the organization and operation of the club, a former member of the board of trustees and the Sr. Rifle Club. He served in the U. S. Army during World War II where he served in the Battle of the Bulge in the 6th Calvary, Troop E. of Patton's 3rd Army, and in the Bahamas, Normandy, and Rhineland Ardennes. During the war he received the Good Conduct Medal, the American Defense Service Medal, American Theater Service Medal, European African Middle Eastern Service Medal with five Bronze Stars. He had been employed as an electrician for the former Service Electric in Everett and retired from the Everett Area School District. He had also been employed on the original construction of the Pennsylvania Turnpike. **ROY CALHOUN** [3085B] a "Sonny" (1934 – 2015) son of Theodore and Nellie (Layton) Calhoun, married Olive Deremer with whom he was father of (3). Sonny served in the United States Army from 1956 to 1958. He was employed for New Enterprise Stone and Lime as a heavy equipment operator for 37 years. He was a life member of the Everett V.F.W. Post No. 2088 and the Quarter Century Club at New Enterprise Stone and Lime. Mr. Calhoun enjoyed tinkering with his tractor

---

[3080] Bedford Inquirer (PA) Apr 18, 1997 obtained by Duke Clark [3080A] Geisel Funeral Home (PA) [3081] Bedford Inquirer (PA) Jan 17, 1997 obtained by Duke Clark [3082] Tribune-Democrat (PA) Apr 27, 2007 [3083] Duke Clark Obituary collection [3084] p2 - Bedford Gazette (PA) Apr. 22, 1949 [3084A] Akers Funeral Home (PA) [3085] Duke Clark Obituary collection [3085A] Bedford Inquirer (PA) Feb 21, 1992 obtained and contributed by Duke Clark [3085B] Bedford Gazette (PA) July 13, 2015 obtained and contributed by Bob Rose

and watching westerns and NASCAR racing. **RUTH MILDRED CALHOUN** [3086] (1919 – 1962) daughter of Solomon and Elda (Hart) Calhoun, married Edgar J. Snyder with whom she was mother of (6). **RYAN CALHOUN** Seventh great grandson of progenitor Nicholas Kegg. **RYAN CALHOUN** Eighth great grandson of progenitor Nicholas Kegg. **SAMUEL CALHOUN** Eighth great grandson of progenitor Nicholas Kegg. **SANDRA L. CALHOUN** Sixth great granddaughter of progenitor Nicholas Kegg. **SANDRA LEE CALHOUN** [3087] (1945 – 1955) daughter of Coy and Rebecca (Miller) Calhoun. Bedford County's most tragic fire accident took the life of Sandra Lee who was burned over more than 80% of her body when her cotton dress touched on a hot burner on an electric stove in the Calhoun kitchen and ignited. **SARAH ADA CALHOUN** [3088] (1882 – 1931) daughter of David and Lucinda (Kegg) Calhoun. Sarah studied nursing at the University of Pennsylvania. She practiced nursing in the community for twenty-five years where she was well known. **SCOTT CALHOUN** Sixth great grandson of progenitor Nicholas Kegg. **SEAN CALHOUN** Eighth great grandson of progenitor Nicholas Kegg. **SETH CALHOUN** Seventh great grandson of progenitor Nicholas Kegg. **SHARON KAY CALHOUN** Sixth great granddaughter of progenitor Nicholas Kegg. **SHAWN BENJAMIN CALHOUN** Sixth great grandson of progenitor Nicholas Kegg. **SHELBY JEAN CALHOUN** Sixth great granddaughter of progenitor Nicholas Kegg. **SHERRY ANN CALHOUN** [3089] (1951 – 1954) daughter of Palmer and Catherine (Simmons) Calhoun. **SHIRLEY F. CALHOUN** Sixth great granddaughter of progenitor Nicholas Kegg. **SHIRLEY I CALHOUN** Sixth great granddaughter of progenitor Nicholas Kegg. **SIMON WILLIAM CALHOUN** [3090] (1895 – 1983) son of Franklin and Permilla (Wilkins) Calhoun, married Maude Erma Clark with whom he was father of (12). Simon farmed and worked as a lumberman in the area all of his life. **SOLOMON FRANKLIN CALHOUN** [3091] (1896 – 1979) son of Franklin and Permilla (Wilkins) Calhoun, married Elda Vennie Hart with whom he was father of (5). Solomon was a member of the Mt. Union United Church of Christ, and a member of the Wambie Tribe No. 507 Improved Order of Redmen of Everett. **STACIE JEAN CALHOUN** Seventh great granddaughter of progenitor Nicholas Kegg. **STACY VAUGHN CALHOUN** 6th great grandson of progenitor Nicholas Kegg. **STELLA C. CALHOUN** [3092] (1887 – 1972) daughter of Andrew and Mary (McDaniel) Calhoun, married Bernard Monroe Williams with whom she was mother of (2). Stella had served as a schoolteacher in West Providence Township as a young woman. She had helped organize the Everett Women's Club, serving two terms as its president, and later served as president of the Bedford County Federation of Women's Clubs. She was a member of the Everett United Methodist Church.
STEPHANIE CALHOUN Eighth great granddaughter of progenitor Nicholas Kegg.
STEPHEN N. CALHOUN Sixth great grandson of progenitor Nicholas Kegg.
STEVEN W. CALHOUN Sixth great grandson of progenitor Nicholas Kegg. **SUSAN CALHOUN** Sixth great granddaughter of progenitor Nicholas Kegg. **SUSAN MARIE CALHOUN** Sixth great granddaughter of progenitor Nicholas Kegg. **TERRY E. CALHOUN** Sixth great grandson of progenitor Nicholas Kegg. **TERRY L. CALHOUN** Fifth great grandson of progenitor Nicholas Kegg. **TERRY L. CALHOUN** Seventh great grandson of progenitor Nicholas Kegg.
THEODORE M. CALHOUN Sixth great grandson of progenitor Nicholas Kegg.
THEODORE MARION CALHOUN [3093] (1907 – 1953) son of Franklin and Permilla (Wilkins) Calhoun, married Nellie Elizabeth Layton with whom he was father of (5). Theodore was killed in a truck accident. **TIM CALHOUN** Sixth great grandson of progenitor Nicholas Kegg. **TIMOTHY CALHOUN** Sixth great grandson of progenitor Nicholas Kegg. **TODD CALHOUN** Seventh great grandson of progenitor Nicholas Kegg. **TRAVIS CALHOUN** Eighth great grandson of progenitor Nicholas Kegg. **TRISTAN L. CALHOUN** Seventh great granddaughter of progenitor Nicholas Kegg. **TYLER K. CALHOUN** Seventh great grandson of progenitor Nicholas Kegg. **VAUGHN LEROY CALHOUN** [3094] (1918 – 1984) son of Harry and Blanche (Ford) Calhoun, married Ruth Virginia Jay with whom he was father of (4). Vaughn was a member of the Logan Country Hunting

---

[3086] Bedford County Genealogical Society obituaries obtained by D. Sue Dible [3087] Bedford Gazette (PA) Jan. 17, 1955 [3088] p4 - The Bedford Gazette (PA) March 27, 1931 [3089] p2 - Bedford Gazette (PA) June 9, 1954 [3090, 3091, 3092] Duke Clark Obituary clipping collection [3093] p3 - Bedford Gazette (PA) March 17, 1953 [3094] The Broadtop Bulletin (PA) May 9, 1984, obtained by Duke Clark

Club and had served in the U. S. Army in World War II, where he had received the Good Conduct medal, the American Theatre Ribbon, European- African- Middle Eastern Theatre Ribbon, Meritorious Unit Award, and a World War II Victory Ribbon. **VELMA ADA VICTORIA CALHOUN** [3095] (1908 – 2000) daughter of David and Myrtle (Hockenberry) Calhoun married twice, first to James William August with whom she was mother of (1). Later she married Coolidge Alexander Karns. Velma was a graduate of Everett High School and Memorial Hospital School of Nursing in Cumberland, Md. She attended Lakemont Starkey Seminary in Watkins Glen, N.Y. She was a member of Bedford Trinity Lutheran Church, Bedford Springs Chapter No. 41 Order of the Eastern Star, member of the Junior Board of Riverside Hospital in Wilmington, Del.; nurses' associations of western Maryland, Virginia and Pennsylvania; and the Delaware Chapter of Emergency Associations. Mrs. Karns was co-writer of the Good Samaritan Act of Delaware. She worked in the nursing field until her retirement.

VERA MAE CALHOUN [3096] (1934 – 2022) daughter of Simon and Maude Erma (Clark) Calhoun married Virgil E. Ramsey with whom she was mother of (7). Vera enjoyed keeping her home clean and tidy and reading her Bible. **VERA MARIE CALHOUN** [3097] (1912 – 1988) daughter of Barton and Minnie (Barkman) Calhoun, married James Madison Wolfe with whom she was mother of (5). **VIRGINIA CALHOUN** Fifth great granddaughter of progenitor Nicholas Kegg.

VIRGINIA ARVILLA CALHOUN [3098] (1902 – 1993) daughter of Barton and Minnie (Barkman) Calhoun married twice, first to William George Longstreth and later to Clyde Elsworth Eisnaugle. Virginia was of the Christian faith and was a lifelong homemaker. **WALTER CHAR CALHOUN** (1913 – 1929) son of Jesse and Irene (Sigel) Calhoun. **WALTER GAIUS CALHOUN** (1893 – 1989) son of Barton and Minnie (Barkman) Calhoun, married Alma Elizabeth Kegg with whom he was father of (4). **WARREN JUSTICE CALHOUN** [3099] (1893 – 1919) son of Barton and Minnie (Barkman) Calhoun, a wagoneer killed during WWI. **WAYNE ROSS CALHOUN** Sixth great grandson of progenitor Nicholas Kegg. **WILLARD N. CALHOUN** Fifth great grandson of progenitor Nicholas Kegg. **WILLIAM BARTON CALHOUN** [3100] (1895 – 1940) son of Barton and Minnie (Barkman) Calhoun, married Ethel Richards with whom he was father of (8). **WILLIAM LYNN CALHOUN** [3100A] (1942 – 2000) son of Ralph and Dorothy (Johnston) Calhoun, married Susan Weak with whom he was father of (1) In his youth he was an avid hunter and fisherman and earned the rank of Eagle Scout. He served in the U.S. Navy in Vietnam in 1969 on the aircraft carrier USS Hancock. He was a member of the Loyal order of Moose, American Legion and Veterans of Foreign Wars.

CALLAHAN

AMY CALLAHAN Seventh great granddaughter of progenitor Nicholas Kegg.
SARAH J. CALLAHAN Seventh great granddaughter of progenitor Nicholas Kegg.

CALLIER

BLAKE ANTHONY CALLIER Seventh great grandson of progenitor Nicholas Kegg. **EARLAMOND MARIE CALLIER** [3101] (1917 – 2004) daughter of Lloyd and Helen (Dean) Callier married Lawrence B. Blanchard with whom she was mother of (2).
EVELYN MARGARET CALLIER [3101A] (1920 – 2004) daughter of Loyd and Helen (Dean) Callier, married Joseph David Konigsmark with whom she was mother of (3) Evelyn was a musician, playing the ukulele, piano and organ and singing. She and her husband performed as a duet at many events, and the entire family sang in the choir at First Baptist Church for many years. She also served as president of the Redlands Investors Club. **LANDRIE CALLIER** Eighth great granddaughter of progenitor Nicholas Kegg. **RYAN JOSEPH CALLIER** Seventh great grandson of progenitor Nicholas Kegg.

[3095] p3 - Bedford Inquirer Mar 24, 2000, obtained by Bob Rose [3096] Bedford Gazette (PA) May 14, 2022 [3097] Bedford Inquirer (PA) Oct 7, 1988 obtained by Duke Clark [3098] Bedford Inquirer (PA) Jun 25, 1995 obtained by Duke Clark [3099] p4 Harrisburg Telegraph (PA) Mar 3, 1919 [3100] Bedford County Historical Society (PA), book 45 p 65 obtained by D. Sue Dible [3100A] Bedford County Historical Society Pioneer Library; book 90, p.55 obtained by D. Sue Dible [3101] The Gazette (IA) April 20, 1941 [3101A] Redlands Daily Facts (CA) Dec 2004

ROBERT LOUIS CALLIER Seventh great grandson of progenitor Nicholas Kegg.
ZYNLIE ANN CALLIER Eighth great granddaughter of progenitor Nicholas Kegg.

CALLIHAN

BRENDA SUE CALLIHAN Seventh great granddaughter of progenitor Nicholas Kegg.
CRAIG STEPHEN CALLIHAN Seventh great grandson of progenitor Nicholas Kegg.
GRAYSEN CALLIHAN Eighth great granddaughter of progenitor Nicholas Kegg.
GRYPHON CALLIHAN Eighth great grandson of progenitor Nicholas Kegg.

CAMACHO

ADRIANNA CAMACHO Sixth great granddaughter of progenitor Nicholas Kegg.
ENRIQUE CAMACHO Sixth great grandson of progenitor Nicholas Kegg.
NINA CAMACHO Sixth great granddaughter of progenitor Nicholas Kegg.

CAMPBELL

ASHLEY CAMPBELL Seventh great granddaughter of progenitor Nicholas Kegg.
CHARLES CAMPBELL aka "Chuck", Fifth great grandson of progenitor Nicholas Kegg.
CINDY L. CAMPBELL Sixth great granddaughter of progenitor Nicholas Kegg.
CONNER CAMPBELL Eighth great grandson of progenitor Nicholas Kegg.
HANNAH MARIE CAMPBELL Seventh great granddaughter of progenitor Nicholas Kegg.
JAMES DENVER CAMPBELL Fifth great grandson of progenitor Nicholas Kegg.
JERRY DON CAMPBELL Fifth great grandson of progenitor Nicholas Kegg.
JULIE LYN CAMPBELL Seventh great granddaughter of progenitor Nicholas Kegg.
KENDALL CAMPBELL Eighth great granddaughter of progenitor Nicholas Kegg.
LISHA K. CAMPBELL Sixth great granddaughter of progenitor Nicholas Kegg.
ROBERT JON CAMPBELL Fifth great grandson of progenitor Nicholas Kegg.
RUDOLPH DOW CAMPBELL Fifth great grandson of progenitor Nicholas Kegg.
THOR D. CAMPBELL Sixth great grandson of progenitor Nicholas Kegg. **TINA M. CAMPBELL** Sixth great granddaughter of progenitor Nicholas Kegg. **VICTORIA MARIE CAMPBELL** aka "Tori" Seventh great granddaughter of progenitor Nicholas Kegg. **ZOETTA GRACE CAMPBELL** [3102] (1928 – 2003) daughter of Charles and Mildred (Huddy) Campbell, married Lester Wayne Lanning with whom she was mother of (1). Zoetta was a graduate of Starr Washington High School.

CANAVARRO

JETT CANAVARRO Seventh great grandson of progenitor Nicholas Kegg.
MARIO PAULO CANAVARRO Seventh great grandson of progenitor Nicholas Kegg.

CANIFORD

GREGORY CANIFORD Sixth great grandson of progenitor Nicholas Kegg.

CANNON

DALTON GAGE CANNON Eighth great grandson of progenitor Nicholas Kegg.
LAURA ELIZABETH CANNON (1925 – 2017) daughter of Lewis and Mildred Jane (Jones) Cannon

---

[3102] GenealogyBuff Athens County, Ohio Obituary Collection

married John Raymond Simms with whom she was mother of (3). **LEWIS RICHARD CANNON JR.** [3103] (1921 – 1965) son of Lewis and Mildred Jane (Jones) Cannon. **MARY ELLA CANNON** (1924 – 1992) daughter of Lewis and Mildred Jane (Jones) Cannon married twice, first to James Walter Sorg with whom she was mother of (1). Later, she married Francis Lester Grubbs. **MILDRED VIRGINIA CANNON** (1919 – 2000) daughter of Lewis and Mildred Jane (Jones) Cannon, married Francis I. Mullin, II with whom she was mother of (2). **NASH TURNER CANNON** Eighth great grandson of progenitor Nicholas Kegg.

CANTARAL

ELLEN KAY CANTARAL Sixth great granddaughter of progenitor Nicholas Kegg.
MICAH CANTARAL Sixth great grandson of progenitor Nicholas Kegg.
NEYLAND CANTARAL [3103A] (1989 – 2015) son of Mark and Deborah (Whetstone) Cantaral. Neyland worked for Goodwill Industries in Falls Creek and was a member of the First United Presbyterian Church in DuBois. He enjoyed vintage video games and was an avid history buff

CANTRELL

BROOKE ANGEL CANTRELL Sixth great granddaughter of progenitor Nicholas Kegg.
TRAVIS DEAN CANTRELL Sixth great grandson of progenitor Nicholas Kegg.

CAPELL

CAROL JEAN CAPELL Fifth great granddaughter of progenitor Nicholas Kegg. **ISAAC CAPELL** Seventh great grandson of progenitor Nicholas Kegg. **ISAIAH CAPELL** Seventh great grandson of progenitor Nicholas Kegg. **JEFFREY SCOTT CAPELL** Sixth great grandson of progenitor Nicholas Kegg. **JOEL ADAM CAPELL** Sixth great grandson of progenitor Nicholas Kegg.
KIMBERLY ANN CAPELL aka "Kim" Sixth great granddaughter of progenitor Nicholas Kegg.
LYLE EDWIN CAPELL Fifth great grandson of progenitor Nicholas Kegg.
NICHOLAS ANDRIEU CAPELL Sixth great grandson of progenitor Nicholas Kegg.
RONALD ARTHUR CAPELL Fifth great grandson of progenitor Nicholas Kegg.
SHANNON R. CAPELL Sixth great granddaughter of progenitor Nicholas Kegg.

CARACCIOLO

ANGELA MARIE CARACCIOLO Seventh great granddaughter of progenitor Nicholas Kegg.
CHRISTOPHER D. CARACCIOLO Seventh great grandson of progenitor Nicholas Kegg.
MICHAEL A. CARACCIOLO Seventh great grandson of progenitor Nicholas Kegg.

CARDINAL

CHRISTOPHER LOUIS CARDINAL Sixth great grandson of progenitor Nicholas Kegg.
JULIA CARDINAL Seventh great granddaughter of progenitor Nicholas Kegg.
MAX CARDINAL Seventh great grandson of progenitor Nicholas Kegg.

CAREY

RICK CAREY Sixth great grandson of progenitor Nicholas Kegg.

[3103] Washington Post, Times Herald (D.C.) 14 Dec 1965 [3103A] Courier Express (PA) July 31, 2015

CARGILL

BRIAN CARGILL Sixth great grandson of progenitor Nicholas Kegg.
DONALD CARGILL Sixth great grandson of progenitor Nicholas Kegg.
EDWARD CARGILL Sixth great grandson of progenitor Nicholas Kegg.

CARL

CAMMIE CARL Seventh great granddaughter of progenitor Nicholas Kegg.
CHRISTIE LYNN CARL Seventh great granddaughter of progenitor Nicholas Kegg.
CONNIE CARL Seventh great granddaughter of progenitor Nicholas Kegg.
CYDNEY CARL Seventh great grandson of progenitor Nicholas Kegg. **MIKE CARL** Seventh great grandson of progenitor Nicholas Kegg. **MIKE CARL JR.** Eighth great grandson of progenitor Nicholas Kegg. **SHELBY CARL** Seventh great granddaughter of progenitor Nicholas Kegg.
TODD CARL Seventh great grandson of progenitor Nicholas Kegg. **TYLER CARL** Eighth great grandson of progenitor Nicholas Kegg.

CARLEY

CHRIS RODNEY CARLEY Fifth great grandson of progenitor Nicholas Kegg.
DANE ALAN CARLEY Sixth great grandson of progenitor Nicholas Kegg.
JEFFREY DEAN CARLEY Sixth great grandson of progenitor Nicholas Kegg.
JOHN DAVID CARLEY [3104] (1945 – 2006) son of Ralph and Marion (Stuckey) Carley, married Shirley Ellyn Smyers with whom he was father of (2). John joined the Navy to see the world and never left California. He was discharged in November 1966. He attended college and graduated from California State College at Long Beach. He worked for Texaco for most of his career. Later, he and Shirley moved to Lake Ida, MN. He loved life by the water with family and friends, sailing, pontoon rides, and relaxing on the deck. **MARY ANN CARLEY** Fifth great granddaughter of progenitor Nicholas Kegg.
MORGAN KRISTINA CARLEY Sixth great granddaughter of progenitor Nicholas Kegg.
NANCY JOAN CARLEY Fifth great granddaughter of progenitor Nicholas Kegg.
STANLEY JOSEPH CARLEY Sixth great grandson of progenitor Nicholas Kegg.
SUSAN JANE CARLEY Fifth great granddaughter of progenitor Nicholas Kegg.
TODD GLOVER CARLEY Sixth great grandson of progenitor Nicholas Kegg.

CARLIN

SHANE CARLIN Sixth great grandson of progenitor Nicholas Kegg.

CARLSON

CHRISTA K. CARLSON Seventh great granddaughter of progenitor Nicholas Kegg.
ERIN R. CARLSON Seventh great granddaughter of progenitor Nicholas Kegg.
LANDON CARLSON Eighth great grandson of progenitor Nicholas Kegg. **LOGAN CARLSON** Eighth great grandson of progenitor Nicholas Kegg. **VIRGINIA ALICE CARLSON** [3105] (1937 – 2005) daughter of John and Wanda (Norman) Carlson was a retired Tool Crib Attendant.

[3104] Orange County Register (CA) Aug 17, 2006 [3105] Wichita Eagle (KS) May 18, 2005

CARLTON

HUNTER CARLTON Eighth great grandson of progenitor Nicholas Kegg.
JONATHON CARLTON Eighth great grandson of progenitor Nicholas Kegg.

CARMAN

DONALD DWAIN CARMAN JR. Sixth great grandson of progenitor Nicholas Kegg.

CARPENTER

SHARON ANN CARPENTER [3106] (1940 – 2005) daughter of Alfred and Martha (Wyckoff) Carpenter, married Thomas Albert Anderson with whom she was mother of (2).

CARRICO

BROCK ALLYN CARRICO Sixth great grandson of progenitor Nicholas Kegg.
ELIZABETH CARRICO, aka "Liz", Fifth great granddaughter of progenitor Nicholas Kegg.
LLOYD RICHARD CARRICO, aka "Dickie", Fifth great grandson of progenitor Nicholas Kegg.
TIMOTHY LLOYD CARRICO [3107] (1959 – 1998) son of George and Annie (McDaniel) Carrico, married Tammy Lynne Kauffman with whom he was father of (1). Timothy was employed with Timbers of Troy, a golf course in Columbia. He had previously worked at Willow Springs Golf Course in Ellicott City. He was an avid fisherman and golfer.

CARRIER

AMY CARRIER Eighth great granddaughter of progenitor Nicholas Kegg. **DENI CARRIER** Seventh great granddaughter of progenitor Nicholas Kegg. **LINDSAY CARRIER** Eighth great granddaughter of progenitor Nicholas Kegg. **SCOTT CARRIER** Seventh great grandson of progenitor Nicholas Kegg.

CARROLL

CHAD ELOITT CARROLL Sixth great grandson of progenitor Nicholas Kegg.
DEBORAH CARROLL Sixth great granddaughter of progenitor Nicholas Kegg.
JENNA CARROLL Sixth great grandson of progenitor Nicholas Kegg. **JOEL LESLIE CARROLL** Sixth great grandson of progenitor Nicholas Kegg. **KELSEY L. CARROLL** Seventh great granddaughter of progenitor Nicholas Kegg. **MARK ASHLEY CARROLL** Sixth great grandson of progenitor Nicholas Kegg. **PAMELA S. CARROLL** Sixth great granddaughter of progenitor Nicholas Kegg. **SHAUNA LYN CARROLL** Sixth great granddaughter of progenitor Nicholas Kegg. **SCOTT CARROLL** Sixth great grandson of progenitor Nicholas Kegg. **T.J. CARROLL** Sixth great grandson of progenitor Nicholas Kegg.

CARSNER

DIANNE ELAINE CARSNER Sixth great granddaughter of progenitor Nicholas Kegg.
HENRY CLEVELAND CARSNER (1909 – 1983) son of Fayette and Jennie (Sharrock) Carsner, married Evelyn Vera Bardsley. **JANICE IRENE CARSNER** Sixth great granddaughter of progenitor Nicholas Kegg. **LINDA RAE CARSNER** Sixth great granddaughter of progenitor Nicholas Kegg.

[3106] Orlando Sentinel (FL) Oct 2, 2005 [3107] Gazette archive 1998 Damascus News 1998

NEIL ALLEN CARSNER Sixth great grandson of progenitor Nicholas Kegg.
VERN FAYETTE CARSNER [3107A] son of Fayette and Jennie (Sharrock) Carsner, married Bertha Irene Blair with whom he was father of (5). Vern served in the Coast Guard. He retired from Corning Glass in Albion He belonged to the IOOF #520 in Litchfield. **VERN STEPHEN CARSNER** Sixth great grandson of progenitor Nicholas Kegg.

CARSON

AMY CARSON Fifth great granddaughter of progenitor Nicholas Kegg. **BEN CARSON** Sixth great grandson of progenitor Nicholas Kegg. **BRENT JAMES CARSON** Fifth great grandson of progenitor Nicholas Kegg. **KATHERINE E. CARSON** aka "Katie" Fifth great granddaughter of progenitor Nicholas Kegg. **LUCAS CARSON** Sixth great grandson of progenitor Nicholas Kegg. **MARGARET GLASGOW CARSON** [3108] (1961 – 1996) aka "Meg", daughter of Norman and Barbara (Bitter) Carson graduated from Duke University with a degree in political science. She worked as the director of international sales for Alantec, and previously for Cisco and NET.
PAULA PENELOPY CARSON Fifth great granddaughter of progenitor Nicholas Kegg
PETER HOWARD CARSON Fifth great grandson of progenitor Nicholas Kegg.

CARSTENS

AUDREY CARSTENS Seventh great granddaughter of progenitor Nicholas Kegg.
LANDON CARSTENS Seventh great grandson of progenitor Nicholas Kegg.

CARTER

CASH CARTER Seventh great grandson of progenitor Nicholas Kegg. **COLT CARTER** Seventh great grandson of progenitor Nicholas Kegg. **JESSE CARTER JR.** Ninth great grandson of progenitor Nicholas Kegg. **LILLIAN CARTER** Ninth great granddaughter of progenitor Nicholas Kegg. **MATTHEW CARTER** Sixth great grandson of progenitor Nicholas Kegg. **PAMELA JO CARTER** (1945 – 1987) daughter of Helen (Fickes) McLallen, married Clarence E. Stephenson with whom she was mother of (4). **WENDY CARTER** Sixth great granddaughter of progenitor Nicholas Kegg.

CASADY

ALBERTA BELL CASADY [3108A] (1925 – 2020) daughter of Henry and Eva Ethel (Laird) Casady married Randall Albert Fowler with whom she was mother of (2). **ANNA BETH CASADY** [3109] (1920 – 2000) daughter of Henry and Eva (Laird) Casady, married Russell Frank Lewis.
EDNA VICTORIA CASADY [3110] (1918 – 2017) daughter of Henry and Eva (Laird) Casady, married Garland D. Murray with whom she was mother of (2). Edna was the most wonderful cook of all times. She prepared three meals a day for her family. She enjoyed gardening in her younger years. Her favorite was meeting up with her neighbor lady, Edith Weller, to go out and pick gooseberries. Once the berries were stemmed, these very delicious gooseberry pies would appear in the kitchen. We couldn't eat them all because some had to be saved and frozen for the Lord's Acre Sale at the church in the fall. She enjoyed her church ladies and helped serve funeral meals. **LOVENIA ETHEL CASADY** [3111] (1916 – 2000) daughter of Henry and Eva (Laird) Casady, married Richard Joseph Horst with whom she was mother of (4).

[3107A] The Index (MI) March 5, 2003 [3108] Paloalto online (NC) Feb 21, 1996 [3108A] Bethany Clipper (MO) May 14, 2020 [3109] Kansas City Star (MO) Dec 17, 2000, ctaz [3110] Roberson Funeral Home (Bethany, MO) [3111] p22 St. Louis Post-Dispatch (MO) Jan 25, 2000

CASELLA

COLE CASELLA Eighth great grandson of progenitor Nicholas Kegg. **DAVID CASELLA** Eighth great grandson of progenitor Nicholas Kegg.

CASEY

BEATRICE CASEY [3112] (1926 – 1926) daughter of Joseph and Vera (Kegg) Casey.
CAROL JEAN CASEY (1930 – 1960) daughter of John and Leah (Huddy) Casey married John Alfred Hunter with whom she was mother of (3). **DANNY CASEY** Fifth great grandson of progenitor Nicholas Kegg. **DEBBIE CASEY** Fifth great granddaughter of progenitor Nicholas Kegg.
INFANT CASEY (1928 – 1928) son of Joseph and Vera (Kegg) Casey. **JENNIFER CASEY** Seventh great granddaughter of progenitor Nicholas Kegg. **JOANNE CASEY** (1936 – 2015) daughter of Joseph and Vera (Kegg) Casey, married Robert Jones Ray. **JO ANN CASEY** (1928 – 1995) daughter of John and Leah (Huddy) Casey, married Philip Eugene Hylbert. **MARJORIE LOU CASEY** [3112A] (1930 – 2004) daughter of Joseph and Vera (Kegg) Casey, married Rodney Stemen with whom she was mother of (4). She was employed by San Bernardino City Schools as a school counselor for 20 years. Marjorie enjoyed Bingo, Lawn Bowling, Reading, watching Jeopardy, traveling, socializing, playing cards and all kinds of music. She never met a stranger and gave generously of her time in volunteer service at Hemet Valley Hospital and St. Bernardines Hospital. **LINDA CAROLL CASEY** (1952 – 1953) daughter of Billy and Beverly (Boissenet) Casey, died a result of 2nd and 3rd degree burns over 80% of her body. **PAMELA KAY CASEY** Fifth great granddaughter of progenitor Nicholas Kegg. **RYAN W. CASEY** Seventh great grandson of progenitor Nicholas Kegg.

CASPER

KENDELL KRISTINE CASPER Seventh great granddaughter of progenitor Nicholas Kegg.

CASPERS

DAVID ALLEN CASPERS Seventh great grandson of progenitor Nicholas Kegg. **DIANE CASPERS** Sixth great granddaughter of progenitor Nicholas Kegg. **JEFF A. CASPERS** Sixth great grandson of progenitor Nicholas Kegg. **RAYMOND LEE CASPERS** Sixth great grandson of progenitor Nicholas Kegg.

CASSIDY

ELEANOR IDA CASSIDY [3113] (1929 – 2007) daughter of Thomas and Gertrude (Mintzer) Cassidy, married James Warren Blough with whom she was mother of (2). Eleanor was a member of St. Benedict's Catholic Church and Geistown Ladies Auxillary.

CASTAGNOLA

CAROLE F. CASTAGNOLA Fourth great granddaughter of progenitor Nicholas Kegg.
VIVIAN AUDREY CASTAGNOLA Fourth great granddaughter of progenitor Nicholas Kegg.

CASTEEL

DAVID L. CASTEEL Sixth great grandson of progenitor Nicholas Kegg.

[3112] Johnstown Tribune (PA) Dec 18, 1926, obtained by D. Sue Dible [3112A] San Bernardino Sun (CA) Mar. 28, 2004 [3113] Tribune Democrat (PA) Sep 14, 2007

EMMA CAROL CASTEEL Fifth great granddaughter of progenitor Nicholas Kegg.
JOSEPH R. CASTEEL Fifth great grandson of progenitor Nicholas Kegg.
LLOYD STAYER CASTEEL [3113A] (1926 – 2014) son of Roy and Mary (Stayer) Casteel, married Gladys Laverne Miller with whom he was father of (2). Lloyd was a lifelong dairy farmer. He enjoyed playing baseball and bowling and loved spending time with his family. Lloyd was a fan of the Pittsburgh Steelers, Pirates and Penguins. **SUSAN L. CASTEEL** Sixth great granddaughter of progenitor Nicholas Kegg.

CASTRANIO

CHELSEA R. CASTRANIO Sixth great granddaughter of progenitor Nicholas Kegg.
CONNIE CASTRANIO Fifth great granddaughter of progenitor Nicholas Kegg.
DAVID R. CASTRANIO Fifth great grandson of progenitor Nicholas Kegg.
ERIN M. CASTRANIO Sixth great granddaughter of progenitor Nicholas Kegg.
JACK MICHAEL CASTRANIO Seventh great grandson of progenitor Nicholas Kegg.
JOHN FRANCIS CASTRANIO Fifth great grandson of progenitor Nicholas Kegg.
JOHN JAMES CASTRANIO II aka "Buddy" Sixth great grandson of progenitor Nicholas Kegg.
MARY ANNE CASTRANIO Fifth great granddaughter of progenitor Nicholas Kegg.

CATANESE

ARETHA CATANESE Sixth great granddaughter of progenitor Nicholas Kegg.
DANIEL CHESTER CATANESE [3114] (1926 – 1980) son of Robert and Violet (Beaver) Catanese married Juanita Smith. Later he married Leah Mae Byrd. Daniel served in the United States Navy. **HOWARD CATANESE** Sixth great grandson of progenitor Nicholas Kegg. **JAMES CATANESE** Sixth great grandson of progenitor Nicholas Kegg. **JAMES LESLIE CATANESE** [3115] (1922 – 1993) aka "Cadillac", son of Robert and Violet (Beaver) Catanese, married Lula Stevens with whom he was father of (7). A former boxer, James was inducted into the Boxer's Hall of Fame on May 23, 1993. He loved all sports. He served in both the U.S. Army and Navy. He was employed for 31 years as a hand grinder at Copperweld Steel Corp. James was a member of the Legion of Leather of Niles, the Has Beens of Cumberland, Md., the American Legion in Columbus, and a charter member of the H.C.B. (Helping Hands) Club. He was a volunteer driver for the American Red Cross. **JEFFREY CATANESE** Sixth great grandson of progenitor Nicholas Kegg. **JERRY CATANESE** Sixth great grandson of progenitor Nicholas Kegg. **JULIE ANN CATANESE** Sixth great granddaughter of progenitor Nicholas Kegg. **KENNETH CATANESE** Sixth great grandson of progenitor Nicholas Kegg. **LOUISE CATANESE** Sixth great granddaughter of progenitor Nicholas Kegg. **MICHAEL CATANESE** Sixth great grandson of progenitor Nicholas Kegg. **PAMELA CATANESE** Sixth great granddaughter of progenitor Nicholas Kegg. **ROBERT CATANESE** [3116] (1932 – 2014) aka "Bob", son of Robert and Violet (Beaver) Catanese, married Wanda Alee Nixon with whom he was father of (5). Bob was a veteran of the Marine Corps in the Korean War. He was a retired financial planner and insurance agent for the Prudential Insurance Company. He enjoyed antiques and collecting. **ROSE MARIE CATANESE** [3116A] (1952 – 2016) daughter of William and Kathleen (Ranels) Catanese married Danny R. Hahn with whom she was mother of (3). Rose loved her family and spending time with her grandchildren and great grandchildren. She enjoyed reading and loved her dog "Spike". **ROSE MARIE CATANESE** [3117] (1936-2011) daughter of Robert and Violet (Beaver) Catanese, married Paul W. Witt with whom she was mother of (4). Rose was a member of St. Paul's Catholic Church, Leesburg. She loved games, especially bowling, bingo and horseshoes. Rose was a giving person, helping others and had a smile for everyone.

[3113A] Bedford Gazette (PA) Nov 26, 2014, obtained and contributed by Bob Rose [3114] The Cumberland News (MD) Nov 28, 1944 [3115] Warren Tribune Chronicle (OH) Oct 3, 1993 [3116] Daily American (Somerset, PA) Jan 25, 2014 [3116A] Bedford Gazette (PA) June 13, 2016 [3117] Cumberland Times News (MD) Dec 24, 2011

TERESA CATANESE Sixth great granddaughter of progenitor Nicholas Kegg. **TINA CATANESE** Sixth great granddaughter of progenitor Nicholas Kegg. **WILLIAM REYNOLDS CATANESE** (1929 – 1994) son of Robert and Violet (Beaver) Catanese, married Kathleen S. Ranels with whom he was father of (1). William served in Korea with the US Marine Corps.

CATES

CLARK EPHRAM CATES Eighth great grandson of progenitor Nicholas Kegg.
HADLEY PARKER CATES Eighth great granddaughter of progenitor Nicholas Kegg.

CATONESE

KATHERINE LEIGH CATONESE Sixth great granddaughter of progenitor Nicholas Kegg.

CAUGHLAN

EMILY CAUGHLAN Seventh great granddaughter of progenitor Nicholas Kegg.
JOSEPH CAUGHLAN aka "Joey", Seventh great grandson of progenitor Nicholas Kegg.

CAUSEY

PRESTON DEE CAUSEY JR. Sixth great grandson of progenitor Nicholas Kegg.

CAVANAUGH

RYAN MICHAEL CAVANAUGH Sixth great grandson of progenitor Nicholas Kegg.
SEAN PATRICK CAVANAUGH Sixth great grandson of progenitor Nicholas Kegg.

CAVELLO

SETH CAVELLO Sixth great grandson of progenitor Nicholas Kegg.

CECIL

AVA LAUREN CECIL Seventh great granddaughter of progenitor Nicholas Kegg.

CEDER

DUSTIN DANIEL CEDER Seventh great grandson of progenitor Nicholas Kegg.

CELLINI

AUSTIN CELLINI aka "Tubb", Sixth great grandson of progenitor Nicholas Kegg.

CENA

BABY CENA Sixth great granddaughter of progenitor Nicholas Kegg.

CERCHIO

GENNARO CERCHIO Sixth great grandson of progenitor Nicholas Kegg.

JACQUELINE CERCHIO Sixth great granddaughter of progenitor Nicholas Kegg.

CESSNA

ADA BELL CESSNA (3118) (1861 – 1953) daughter of Peter and Margaret (Stuckey) Cessna, married Frederick M. Hartsauk with whom she was mother of (1). Ada was highly respected. She was a lifelong member of the Yeager Lutheran church in Rainsburg and was always very generous in her support of her minister and church. **ADAM JACOB CESSNA** Fifth great grandson of progenitor Nicholas Kegg. **ALBERT SIMON CESSNA** (3119) (1852 – 1926) son Peter and Margaret (Stuckey) Cessna, married Anna Rebecca James with hom he was father of (4). Albert was a teacher in his early days. He received his education in the old Rainsburg seminary and taught there from 1876 to 1880. President Garfield appointed him postmaster of Rainsburg which position he held until he was elected Treasurer of Bedford County in 1893. After a term as County Treasurer he went into the mercantile business. In 1917 he was elected associate judge of Bedford County, after which term he was appointed and then elected justice of the peace of Bedford borough. He was very widely known throughout the county, having canvassed it several times for office and having traveled all over it as salesman for Blackburn-Russell company, wholesale grocers. **ALIVIA CESSNA** Sixth great granddaughter of progenitor Nicholas Kegg. **AMANDA CESSNA** Eighth great granddaughter of progenitor Nicholas Kegg.
AMANDA MELIA CESSNA Sixth great granddaughter of progenitor Nicholas Kegg.
AMY G. CESSNA Sixth great granddaughter of progenitor Nicholas Kegg.
ANDREW STEVEN CESSNA, aka "Andy", Sixth great grandson of progenitor Nicholas Kegg.
BARBARA JEAN CESSNA (3119A) (1959 – 2013) daughter of Ronald and Shelvy (Custer) Cessna, An Air Force dependent, she traveled extensively and attended school in various places. She loved travelling, sightseeing, and dining out. Barb was a devoted member of the New Thought Center for Spiritual Living in Lake Oswego, Ore. **BENJAMIN RUSSELL CESSNA** Fifth great grandson of progenitor Nicholas Kegg. **BENNY CHESTER CESSNA** (3120, 3121) (1922 - 1989) son of Chester and Cora (Perdew) Cessna married twice, first to Ruth Louise Hauth with whom he was father of (1). Later, he married Carol M. Schmitt with whom he was father of (2). Benny graduated from the Army Air Force Instruction School at Laredo, Texas. He was in the South Pacific, for 16 months, completed 93 missions. He wore the D. F. C., Air Medal, Silver Star, three Oak Leaf clusters and had a Presidential citation for valor. Benny was an instructor in aerial gunnery. **BETTY JANE CESSNA** (3121A) (1927 – 1996) daughter of Chester and Cora (Perdew) Cessna, had been employed by the Sears Roebuck and Co. store in Bedford for 42 years before retiring in 1990. After her retirement Jane did volunteer work at Old Bedford Village.
BETTY PRISCILLA CESSNA (3121B) (1928 – 2017) daughter of Wilbur and Ethel (O'Neal) Cessna, married William Edward Shriver with whom she was mother of (3). Betty worked at Lions Manor Nursing Home and cleaned homes for private families for over 16 years. She was a member of Flintstone United Methodist Church, where she volunteered tirelessly for the church, donating her well-known baked goods and meals throughout the community. She did a lot of work on the farm, gardening, raising chickens and delivering fresh eggs and vegetables weekly throughout the area.
BRADLEY WADE CESSNA Sixth great grandson of progenitor Nicholas Kegg.
BRENDA KAY CESSNA Fifth great granddaughter of progenitor Nicholas Kegg.
BRIAR ISAIAH CESSNA Sixth great grandson of progenitor Nicholas Kegg.
BRITTANY NICOLE CESSNA Sixth great granddaughter of progenitor Nicholas Kegg.
BRUCE WADE CESSNA Fifth great grandson of progenitor Nicholas Kegg.
BRYAN KEITH CESSNA Seventh great grandson of progenitor Nicholas Kegg.
CANDACE LIANE CESSNA Sixth great granddaughter of progenitor Nicholas Kegg.
CARL FRANKLIN CESSNA (3121C) (1937 – 2007) son of Wilbur and Ethel (O'Neal) Cessna, married

---

(3118) Bedford Gazette (PA) Jan 27, 1953 (3119) Bedford Gazette (PA) May 7, 1926 (3119A) Bedford Gazette (PA) Feb 27, 2013, obtained and contributed by Bob Rose (3120) Bedford County Genealogical Society obituary obtained by D. Sue Dible (3121) p4 - Bedford Gazette (PA) Jan 5, 1946 (3121A) Bedford Pioneer Historical Society obituary obtained and contributed by D. Sue Dible (3121B) Adams Family Funeral Home (MD) (3121C) Bedford Inquirer (PA) Oct 26, 2007 obtained and contributed by Bob Rose

Virginia May Twigg with whom he was father of (4). Carl was a partner in the Cessna Brothers Sawmill in Beans Cove. He was a member of the Prosperity United Methodist Church and the Loyal Order of Moose No. 271, Cumberland, Md. Carl's many interests and hobbies were roller skating, hunting, woodworking, gardening, and going to flea markets. He also had a great interest in the American Revolutionary Era of history. **CAROL LYNN CESSNA** (3121D) (1955 – 2014) daughter of Robert and Helen (Beegle) Cessna was married twice, first to Steve Attig with whom she was mother of (1), later she married Gary Spence with whom she was mother of (1). Carol was employed by Honeywell in the soldering department. She was a beloved "Nana," to her grandchildren whom she adored. She loved crafts, music (especially the Rolling Stones) and gardening. Carol's signature colors were black and gold. **CAROLYN ELIZABETH CESSNA** Eighth great granddaughter of progenitor Nicholas Kegg. **CARRIE CESSNA** Sixth great granddaughter of progenitor Nicholas Kegg. **CATHERINE CESSNA** Sixth great granddaughter of progenitor Nicholas Kegg. **CATHY L. CESSNA** Seventh great granddaughter of progenitor Nicholas Kegg. **CECIL PAUL CESSNA** Fourth great grandson of progenitor Nicholas Kegg. **CHAD GRANT CESSNA** Sixth great grandson of progenitor Nicholas Kegg. **CHANNING CESSNA** Seventh great grandson of progenitor Nicholas Kegg. **CHARLES PAUL CESSNA** (3121E) (1891 – 1958) son of William and Lottie (Filler) Cessna, married Esther Diehl Crouse with whom he was father of (1). Entering the U. S. Army, he served with the hospital corps of the field artillery during World War I, being discharged in 1919. Returning to Gettysburg in that year, he served as assistant professor of physics until 1919 when he accepted a post with the Citizens Trust Co. of Gettysburg. He returned to the college in 1922 to become mathematics teacher and continued in that post until 1937 Charles was assistant to the president of Gettysburg College for public relations and the college historian. He was a charter member of the Gettysburg Lions Club and served as district governor of the Lions in 1934-35. He and Mrs. Cessna operated a gift shop on Chambersburg St. for a period of about 12 years. He was a member of the Phi Sigma Kappa fraternity. **CHELSEA LEANN CESSNA** Sixth great granddaughter of progenitor Nicholas Kegg. **CHELSEA MARIE CESSNA** Eighth great granddaughter of progenitor Nicholas Kegg. **CHERYL LEE CESSNA** Seventh great granddaughter of progenitor Nicholas Kegg. **CHESTER DANIEL CESSNA** (3121F) (1885 – 1965) son of William and Lottie (Filler) Cessna, married Cora Ellen Perdew with whom he was father of (14). Chester was a cattle dealer. **CHRISTINA CESSNA** Sixth great granddaughter of progenitor Nicholas Kegg. **CHRISTOPHER T. CESSNA** Seventh great grandson of progenitor Nicholas Kegg. **CLARISSA ROSE CESSNA** Sixth great granddaughter of progenitor Nicholas Kegg. **CLAYTON MATTHEW CESSNA** Sixth great grandson of progenitor Nicholas Kegg. **CLIFFORD WAYNE CESSNA** (3121G) (1940 – 2013) son of Wilbur and Ethel (O'Neal) Cessna, married Marjorie Miltenberger with whom he was father of (8). Cliff grew up and attended Walnut Grove One Room School House in Beans Cove, and worked at Cessna Brothers Saw Mill. In later years, Cliff attended LaSalle High School for two years and began a life partnership in Cessna Brothers Saw Mill and Farm. He was a very active member of Seven Dolors Catholic Church, where he served as president of the finance committee from 1989 to 2012. Cliff was also a member of the Bedford County Farm Bureau, the NRA, and served on the board of Southern States Cooperative. Cliff was also a member of the Beans Cove Outlaw Hunting Gang and thoroughly enjoyed hunting with all of them. He most enjoyed being out in the field on his tractor or driving his International Harvester combine. **CLINTON CESSNA** Sixth great grandson of progenitor Nicholas Kegg. **CLINTON JOSEPH CESSNA** Fifth great grandson of progenitor Nicholas Kegg. **COLIN DAVID CESSNA** Fifth great grandson of progenitor Nicholas Kegg. **COOPER CESSNA** Sixth great grandson of progenitor Nicholas Kegg. **COOPER PAUL CESSNA** Eighth great grandson of progenitor Nicholas Kegg. **COTY DANIEL CESSNA** Sixth great grandson of progenitor Nicholas Kegg. **CRAIG THOMAS CESSNA** Fifth great grandson of progenitor Nicholas Kegg. **CYNTHIA KAY CESSNA** aka "Cindy", Seventh great granddaughter of progenitor Nicholas Kegg.

(3121D) Bedford Gazette (PA) Jun 19, 2014, obtained and contributed by Bob Rose (3121E) Gettysburg Times (PA) Oct 6, 1958 (3121F) Bedford Gazette (PA) Feb 12, 1965, obtained by Connie Detar shared by Bob Rose (3121G) Bedford Gazette (PA) March 21, 2013, obtained and contributed by Bob Rose

DANIEL SHERMAN CESSNA [3121H] (1955 – 2019) son of Lowell and Mary Louella (Lamb) Cessna married twice, first to Pamela Jane Carrow with whom he was father of (2). Later, he married Carolyn Belcher. **DANIEL SHERMAN CESSNA** Sixth great grandson of progenitor Nicholas Kegg.
DANIEL THEODORE CESSNA [3121I] (1943 – 2020) son of Chester and Cora (Perdew) Cessna married Anna Louise Hite with whom he was father of (2). Daniel was employed by Hedstrom of Bedford, where he held many different positions there, two of them being a welding foreman and floor manager. He was also employed by Lake Raystown Resort as a groundskeeper. Dan served his country as a sergeant in the U.S. Marine Corps and received the Marksman Badge Rifle Good Conduct Medal and the National Defense Service Medal. He was a member of Yeager Lutheran Church. Dan was an avid deer and turkey hunter and enjoyed boating at Raystown Lake with his family. **DANIEL WADE CESSNA** Fifth great grandson of progenitor Nicholas Kegg. **DAVID CESSNA** Sixth great grandson of progenitor Nicholas Kegg. **DAVID CESSNA** [3122] (1942 – 1968) son of Wilbur and Ethel (O'Neal) Cessna, married Shelva Dean Raines with whom he was father of (2). David was engaged in the sawmill business and farming and attended LaSalle High School. He was also a member of Prosperity Methodist Church.
DAVID THEODORE CESSNA Fifth great grandson of progenitor Nicholas Kegg.
DENNIS CESSNA [3122A] (1942 – 2022) aka "Den" son of Wilbur and Ethel (O'Neal) Cessna married Judy Louise Hardman with whom he was father of (6). Den had a lifelong career at the family business, Cessna Brothers Sawmill and Farm. Dennis had many interests and hobbies including woodworking, hammering saws, gardening, and everything to do with construction and sawmill work. He enjoyed being able to help with any project. Den had amazing knowledge of building structures and was always the go to for consulting on a project. **DONALD EDWARD CESSNA** Fourth great grandson of progenitor Nicholas Kegg. **DONALD EDWARD CESSNA JR.** Fifth great grandson of progenitor Nicholas Kegg. **DONALD FRANKLIN CESSNA** [3122B] (1927 – 1999) son of Raymond and Hulda (Shaffer) Cessna, married Margaret Ann Foor with whom he was father of (2). Donald retired as an expeditor for G.O. Carlson, Inc., of Thorndale, where he worked for 30 years. Following retirement, he worked part-time for Hershey Motors of Morgantown and Parksburg, Weis Markets in New Holland and Dart Container of Leola. He was a member of Zeltenreich's United Church of Christ in New Holland, where he served on the consistory and as a deacon. He enjoyed bowling, small game and deer hunting, fishing, including deep sea fishing, and gardening, he served in the US Army's 46th Engineer and Construction Battalion as a medical technician during WWII. **DONALD LURAY CESSNA** Fifth great grandson of progenitor Nicholas Kegg. **DOROTHY FAYE CESSNA** [3123] (1932 – 1988) aka "Dot", daughter of Raymond and Hulda (Shaffer) Cessna, married Jackson Eugene Bussard. Dot had been employed by the former Lion Manufacturing Company for 11 years. Dot was a member of the Everett First United Church of Christ, Eastern Star Chapter #41 of Bedford, Everett Lioness Club, a volunteer at the Church Service Center, Main Street, Everett. **DOROTHY YVONNE CESSNA** Fourth great granddaughter of progenitor Nicholas Kegg. **DOUGLAS CLYDE CESSNA** [3124] (1882 – 1941) son of Albert and Anna (James) Cessna, married Rebecca R. Ritchey with whom he was father of (2). Douglas was employed as a clerk in the local railroad offices. **DOUGLAS CLYDE CESSNA JR.** [3125, 3126] (1913 – 1944) son of Douglas and Rebecca (Ritchey) Cessna was a popular Bedford youth who graduated from Bedford High School in the class of 1931 and entered the service in Oct. 1942. He trained at Camp Atteroury, Indiana and was later transferred to Breckenridge, Ky., Tech Sgt. Douglas went overseas in March 1944. Douglas was a member of Co. L. 331st Infantry. Tech. Sgt. Douglas C. Cessna was killed in action in Normandy at St. Lo, France, July 4. was killed in action in Normandy at St. Lo, France, July 4.
DOUGLAS SCOTT CESSNA Fifth great grandson of progenitor Nicholas Kegg.
DUSTIN EDWARD CESSNA Sixth great grandson of progenitor Nicholas Kegg.
ELIZABETH ANN CESSNA aka "Betsy", Fifth great granddaughter of progenitor Nicholas Kegg.
ELLIOTT CESSNA Seventh great grandson of progenitor Nicholas Kegg.

[3121H] Midland Reporter-Telegram (TX) Nov. 24, 2019 [3121I] Bedford Gazette (PA) Dec 29, 2020 [3122] p25 - Cumberland Times (MD) June 13, 1968 [3122A] Bedford Gazette (PA) Sept 10, 2022 [3122B] Bedford Inquirer (PA) April 23, 1999 [3123] Bedford Inquirer (PA) March 18, 1988 obtained by Duke Clark [3124] Bedford Gazette (PA) April 5, 1992 [3125] https://83rdinfdivdocs.org/documents/331st/331_3rd_Bn_History_June-Aug-1944.pdf [3126] Bedford Gazette (PA) Dec 17, 1948

EMILY JUNE CESSNA Sixth great granddaughter of progenitor Nicholas Kegg. **EMMA CESSNA** Seventh great granddaughter of progenitor Nicholas Kegg. **EMMA RUTH CESSNA** [3126A] (1928 – 2009) daughter of John and Lillie (Sherman) Cessna, married Robert B. Braun. Emma retired after 40 years as an administrative assistant for Liberty Mutual Insurance Company in Boston.
FAITH CESSNA Eighth great granddaughter of progenitor Nicholas Kegg.
FANNIE REBECCA CESSNA [3127] (1874 – 1964) daughter of William and Charlotte (Filler) Cessna, married Rev. John Adam Grose with whom she was mother of (4). **FANNIE REBECCA CESSNA** [3128] (1916 – 1979) aka "Nan", daughter of Raymond and Hulda (Shaffer) Cessna, married Roy Albert Miller. **FLORENCE M. CESSNA** [3129] (1882 – 1973) daughter of Jonathan and Anna Marion (James) Cessna, married Jacob Erhart Malzi. **FRANK B. CESSNA** Sixth great granddaughter of progenitor Nicholas Kegg. **GARY LEE CESSNA** (1939 – 1939) son of Robert and Helen (Beegle) Cessna. **GERALD STEVEN CESSNA** Fifth great grandson of progenitor Nicholas Kegg.
GERALD STEVEN CESSNA JR Sixth great grandson of progenitor Nicholas Kegg.
GERTRUDE MARGARET CESSNA [3130] (1875 – 1943) daughter of William and Charlotte (Filler) Cessna, married Lorenzo Walter Hite with whom she was mother of (8). **GLEN WAYNE CESSNA** Sixth great grandson of progenitor Nicholas Kegg. **GRACE CESSNA** Eighth great granddaughter of progenitor Nicholas Kegg. **GRACE MAY CESSNA** [3130A] aka "Aunt Grace" (1880 – 1975) daughter of Albert and Anna Rebecca (James) Cessna, married John Neil Minnich with whom she was mother of (2). Grace served during World War Two as librarian for the Keystone Naval School held at the Bedford Springs Hotel and was the only librarian to hold that post. Her career as Bedford's Public Librarian had spanned three decades, from 1937 until the early 1960's when the former Bedford Library, located in the Anderson House, was disbanded and merged with the present Bedford County Library. Beginning as assistant to Mrs. John Cessna Smith and Lillian Hall, she assumed the responsibilities as full-time librarian for the old library, continuing capably in that role until she was over 80 years old. She was a member of the Ever Ready Circle of Trinity Lutheran Church, and the Bedford Chapter, Daughters of the American Revolution. She had a memory few could equal. **GRACIE MARIE CESSNA** Sixth great granddaughter of progenitor Nicholas Kegg. **GREGORY JON CESSNA** [3131] (1952 – 2007) son of Donald and Margaret (Foor) Cessna, married Teresa Wolfe with whom he was father of (2). Greg was self-employed and owned Cessna's Painting and Home Repair. He loved to hunt, fly fish, golf, and bowl and was a regular pool shooter for the Everett Legion. He coached little league baseball and elementary basketball. He was also a PIAA Umpire for high school softball. He was a member of the Moose Lodge #480, Down River Golf Course, Everett Legion Post #8 and the Everett Redmen. He lived for his kids and was a generous contributor to children's and veteran's charities. **GREGORY LYNN CESSNA** Fifth great grandson of progenitor Nicholas Kegg. **HAROLD BERTRAM CESSNA** [3132] (1875 – 1946) son of Albert and Anna Rebecca (James) Cessna, married Margaret R. Ritchey with whom he was father of (2). Harold was educated in the public schools and at the old Bedford Academy of Dr. Colfelt. He graduated from Gettysburg College. He took up the practice of law but in 1905 became affiliated with the First National Bank. He had served the First National Bank and Trust Co. as vice president and cashier and later served in the capacity of assistant cashier after its reorganization. He was active in the Lutheran Church and had served continuously as treasurer of both church and Sunday school for almost 40 years. He was a past master of Bedford Lodge No. 321, F. &. A. M. and a life member and Past High Priest of Bedford Chapter, No. 255, R. A. M. and one of the town's leading citizens. **HAROLD B. CESSNA** [3132A] (1913 – 1994) son of H. Bertram and Margaret (Ritchey) Cessna, married Leila Exline with whom he was father of (2). Harold was widely known for the Harold Cessna Orchestra which performed at the Bedford Springs Hotel for 31 years. He also had played music with Bill Reed and together they formed the Reed-Cessna Orchestra in the 30's. Harold was director emeritus of the Bedford Fair Association and

---

[3126A] Timothy A. Berkebile Funeral Home obtained by Glenn Nave shared by Bob Rose [3127] p4 The Post (Frederick, MD) Jan 15, 1964 [3128] Duke Clark obituary clipping [3129] p5 - Bedford Inquirer (PA) Dec 7, 1973 [3130] PA-Roots.org obituary contributed by Kathie Kline [3130A] p.10 - Bedford Gazette (PA) Nov 17, 1975 [3131] Timothy A. Berkebile Funeral Home (PA) [3132] p.11 - Huntingdon Daily News (PA) Apr 5, 1946 [3132A] Bedford Gazette (PA) May 6, 1994, contributed by D. Sue Dible

was a well-known businessman. He retired from the Bedford Gazette after 42 years' service, including being the advertising business manager. He was employed as treasurer for Cessna Communications. A member of Trinity Lutheran Church, Bedford, where he had formerly served on the church council and various other offices. He was past president of the Bedford County Motor Club and Bedford County Library. **HENRY CESSNA** Seventh great grandson of progenitor Nicholas Kegg. **HOWARD LEE CESSNA** Fifth great grandson of progenitor Nicholas Kegg. **INFANT CESSNA** (1930 – 1930) daughter of Wilbur and Ethel (O'Neal) Cessna. **ISABELLA CESSNA** Eighth great granddaughter of progenitor Nicholas Kegg. **ISSAC SCOTT CESSNA** Sixth great grandson of progenitor Nicholas Kegg. **JAMES BUCHANAN CESSNA** [3132B] (1856 – 1946) son of Peter M. and Margaret (Stuckey) Cessna married Henrietta Gump. He was a member of the Bedford IOOF, the POS of A of Charlesville and the Lutheran Church. **JAMES B. CESSNA** Fifth great grandson of progenitor Nicholas Kegg. **JAMES DANIEL CESSNA** Seventh great grandson of progenitor Nicholas Kegg. **JAMES VERNON CESSNA** [3132C] aka "Son" (1930 – 2010) son of Chester Daniel and Cora (Perdew) Cessna, married Marlene Smith with whom he was father of (3). He served in the United States Army during the Korean Conflict from January 1951 and December 1952. James owned and operated Ja-Mar-Cess Dairy Farm, Everett from 1955-1969. He later drove truck for various companies for many years. He was a former co-owner with his brothers at the Cessna Brothers Slaughterhouse in Rainsburg. He worked as a custodian for Everett Area School District at Everett Elementary School until his retirement. James enjoyed hunting, watching wrestling and participating in anything that his grandchildren were involved in. **JANA NICOLE CESSNA** Sixth great granddaughter of progenitor Nicholas Kegg. **JANIE ELLEN CESSNA** (1960 – 1960) daughter of Robert and Helen (Beegle) Cessna. **JASON F. CESSNA** Sixth great grandson of progenitor Nicholas Kegg. **JAY B. CESSNA** Fifth great grandson of progenitor Nicholas Kegg. **JEFFREY THOMAS CESSNA** Sixth great grandson of progenitor Nicholas Kegg. **JEFFREY THOMAS CESSNA** [3133] (1964 – 1998) son of Samuel and Nancy (Williams) Cessna. Jeffrey was employed as a truck driver for Victory Express. He had spent 10 years in the U.S. Air Force, including one year in Korea. He was a member of the National Hot Rod Association and worked on a drag racing pit crew while stationed at Edwards Air Force Base. **JENNIFER LYNN CESSNA** Sixth great granddaughter of progenitor Nicholas Kegg.

JEREMY RICHARD CESSNA Sixth great grandson of progenitor Nicholas Kegg.

JESSICA RENEE CESSNA Sixth great granddaughter of progenitor Nicholas Kegg.

JOHN CESSNA (1928 – 1928) son of John and Lillie (Sherman) Cessna. **JOHN DAVID CESSNA** Seventh great grandson of progenitor Nicholas Kegg. **JOHN H. CESSNA** Fifth great grandson of progenitor Nicholas Kegg. **JOHN P. CESSNA** [3134] (1919 – 1981) aka "Jack", son of Charles and Esther (Crouse) Cessna. Jack taught school in the Gettysburg Area School District for a number of years. He also taught at York High School in York and at the Francis Scott Key High School in Frederick, Md., and, tutored in the Gettysburg area. **JOHN THEODORE CESSNA** [3135] (1936 – 1936) son of Richard and Virginia (Cessna) Cessna. **JOHN THOMAS CESSNA** Sixth great grandson of progenitor Nicholas Kegg. **JOHN THOMAS CESSNA** Fifth great grandson of progenitor Nicholas Kegg. **JOHN W. CESSNA** Sixth great grandson of progenitor Nicholas Kegg. **JOHN WILLIAM CESSNA** [3136] (1901 – 1975) son of Jonathan and Priscilla (Schaeffer) Cessna, married Lillie Victoria Sherman with whom he was father of (8). John cut and hauled timber and had been farming since the early 1920's when he settled in Friends Cove in 1929. He was a school director and a Rural Electric Co-op director. He was known for his excellent memory and knowledge of local history. He served on the Yeager Memorial Lutheran church council and as Sunday school officer and teacher for many years.

JONATHAN GLEN CESSNA Fifth great grandson of progenitor Nicholas Kegg.

JOSEPH LAMONTE CESSNA Fifth great grandson of progenitor Nicholas Kegg.

JOSHUA LEE CESSNA Sixth great grandson of progenitor Nicholas Kegg.

JUNE BEATRICE CESSNA [3137] (1921 – 1992) daughter of Raymond and Hulda (Shaffer) Cessna,

---

[3132B] Johnstown Tribune Democrat (PA) Aug 27, 1946, contributed by D. Sue Dible [3132C] Akers Funeral Home (PA) [3133] p3 - Bedford Inquirer (PA) Jan 23, 1998 [3135] Bedford County, PA newspaper pencil dated obtained by Bob Rose [3136] p.16 - Bedford Gazette (PA) Sept 5, 1975 [3137] p.14 - Bedford Gazette (PA) Feb 6, 1992

married Paul K. Miller with whom she was mother of (2). June was a member of Trinity United Church of Christ, Friends Cove. **KARL EUGENE CESSNA** Fifth great grandson of progenitor Nicholas Kegg. **KATHY CESSNA** Fifth great granddaughter of progenitor Nicholas Kegg.
KRISTA LYNN CESSNA Fifth great granddaughter of progenitor Nicholas Kegg.
KRISTIN MICHELE CESSNA Sixth great granddaughter of progenitor Nicholas Kegg.
KYLE CESSNA Sixth great grandson of progenitor Nicholas Kegg. **LARISSA NICOLE CESSNA** Sixth great granddaughter of progenitor Nicholas Kegg. **LARRY RICHARD CESSNA** Sixth great grandson of progenitor Nicholas Kegg. **LAURA JANE CESSNA** Seventh great granddaughter of progenitor Nicholas Kegg. **LEROY A. CESSNA** Fifth great grandson of progenitor Nicholas Kegg.
LIAM AUSTIN CESSNA Eighth great grandson of progenitor Nicholas Kegg.
LILY GRACE CESSNA Sixth great granddaughter of progenitor Nicholas Kegg.
LISA JUNE CESSNA Fifth great granddaughter of progenitor Nicholas Kegg.
LOGAN ALLEN CESSNA Eighth great grandson of progenitor Nicholas Kegg. **LOIS CESSNA** Fifth great granddaughter of progenitor Nicholas Kegg. **LOIS CESSNA** aka "Susie", Fifth great granddaughter of progenitor Nicholas Kegg. **LOWELL SHERMAN CESSNA** [3137A] (1935 – 2022) son of John and Lillie Victoria (Sherman) Cessna married Mary Louella Lamb with whom he was father of (5). Later he married Carolyn J. Roy. **LUCAS CESSNA** Sixth great grandson of progenitor Nicholas Kegg. **LUKE ANDREW CESSNA** Seventh great grandson of progenitor Nicholas Kegg.
MADISON TYLER CESSNA Eighth great granddaughter of progenitor Nicholas Kegg.
MALLORY CESSNA Eighth great granddaughter of progenitor Nicholas Kegg.
MARGARET CESSNA [3138] (1896 – 1968) aka "Bab", daughter of Jonathan and Priscilla (Schaeffer) Cessna, married Pearl Ake with whom she was mother of (2). **MARGARET ANN CESSNA** [3139] (1937 – 2020) aka "Peggy," daughter of Chester and Cora (Perdew) Cessna married C. Thomas Weaverling with whom she was mother of (3). Peggy worked at the Howard Johnsons Commissary, Hartley Bank, and Susquehanna Bank. Some of her hobbies were spending time with her family, cooking, baking, shopping and working on puzzles. **MARGARET HELEN CESSNA** [3140] (1910 – 1967) aka "Helen", daughter of Raymond and Hulda (Shaffer) Cessna, married Samuel Joseph Diehl with whom she was mother of (3). **MARIA C. CESSNA** Fifth great granddaughter of progenitor Nicholas Kegg.
MARK ALLEN CESSNA Seventh great grandson of progenitor Nicholas Kegg.
MARK WILLIAM CESSNA Seventh great grandson of progenitor Nicholas Kegg.
MARSHALL ALLAN CESSNA Sixth great grandson of progenitor Nicholas Kegg.
MARSHALL N. CESSNA (1879 – 1879) son of William and Charlotte (Filler) Cessna.
MARTHA VIRGINIA CESSNA [3141] (1858 – 1943) aka "Jennie", daughter of Peter and Margaret (Stuckey) Cessna, married Lin Smith with whom she was mother of (1). **MARY A. CESSNA** (1850 – 1851) daughter of Peter and Margaret (Stuckey) Cessna. **MARY EMMA CESSNA** Sixth great granddaughter of progenitor Nicholas Kegg. **MARY RETA CESSNA** [3142] (1883 – 1972) daughter of William and Charlotte (Filler) Cessna. Mary was a schoolteacher in the Bedford area for a number of years. **MARY RUTH CESSNA** [3143] (1918 – 2002) daughter of Douglas and Rebecca (Ritchey) Cessna, married Calvin Henry Wilson with whom she was mother of (1). Mary was a lifetime member of Trinity Lutheran Church, Bedford. **MASON ALEXANDER CESSNA** Sixth great grandson of progenitor Nicholas Kegg. **MATTHEW CESSNA** Fifth great grandson of progenitor Nicholas Kegg.
MATTHEW BRIAN CESSNA Seventh great grandson of progenitor Nicholas Kegg.
MAUDE ESTELLE CESSNA [3144] (1878 – 1967) daughter of Albert and Anna (James) Cessna, married Samuel McCreary Orr. Maude was a member of Trinity Lutheran Church of Bedford.
MAX TIMOTHY CESSNA [3144A] (1958 – 2022) son of Lowell and Mary Louella (Lamb) Cessna married Julie Annette Croker with whom he was father of (2). An enterprising spirit, Max spent his

---

[3137A] Ellis Resthaven Funeral Home and Memorial Park (TX) obtained by D. Sue Dible [3138] p.7 - Bedford Inquirer (PA) Feb 15, 1968 [3139] Bedford Gazette (PA) Dec 26, 2020 [3140] Bedford Gazette (PA) Sep 23, 1967, obtained by Connie Detar contributed by Bob Rose [3141] Bedford County Historical Society obituary obtained by D. Sue Dible [3142] Duke Clark obituary clipping collection [3143] p.3 - Bedford Inquirer (PA) March 1, 2002, obtained by Bob Rose [3144] p8 - Bedford Gazette (PA) June 3, 1967 [3144A] Lewallen-Garcia-Pipkin Funeral Home (TX) obtained by D. Sue Dible

married Julie Annette Croker with whom he was father of (2). An enterprising spirit, Max spent his formative years, and many years thereafter, working in construction and taking pride in his craft as a mason. Max had a heart for the men and women who have served our country and was always promoting the Wounded Warrior Project. Max had a wry smile and loved to laugh, always amused by a good joke. **MAXWELL CESSNA** Sixth great grandson of progenitor Nicholas Kegg. **MEGAN CESSNA** Sixth great granddaughter of progenitor Nicholas Kegg. **MELISSA DAWNE CESSNA** Eighth great granddaughter of progenitor Nicholas Kegg. **MEREDITH B. CESSNA** Sixth great granddaughter of progenitor Nicholas Kegg. **MICHAEL BRIAN CESSNA** Fifth great grandson of progenitor Nicholas Kegg. **MICHELE SUE CESSNA** Eighth great granddaughter of progenitor Nicholas Kegg. **MILES CESSNA** Seventh great grandson of progenitor Nicholas Kegg. **MOLLY CESSNA** Sixth great granddaughter of progenitor Nicholas Kegg. **MOLLY LYNN CESSNA** Sixth great granddaughter of progenitor Nicholas Kegg. **MORGAN COLE CESSNA** Eighth great grandson of progenitor Nicholas Kegg. **NAOMI PEARL CESSNA** [3145] (1894 – 1944) aka "Daisy", daughter of William and Charlotte (Filler) Cessna, married Herbert Ellsworth Snyder with whom she was mother of (2). **NEAL GRANT CESSNA** Fifth great grandson of progenitor Nicholas Kegg.
NELLIE MAY CESSNA [3146] (1877 – 1916) daughter of William and Charlotte (Filler) Cessna, married John Marvin Perdew with whom she was mother of (3). A loving and obedient daughter, a true and loyal sister, a devoted wife, a tender mother, who knew no sacrifice too great, and a bosom friend. Nellie was a member of the M. E. Church, in Rainsburg. **NELLIE MAY CESSNA** Sixth great granddaughter of progenitor Nicholas Kegg. **NICHOLAS CESSNA** Sixth great grandson of progenitor Nicholas Kegg. **OLIVIA SARAH CESSNA** Sixth great granddaughter of progenitor Nicholas Kegg. **OREN DAVID CESSNA** Eighth great grandson of progenitor Nicholas Kegg.
PATRICIA LOUELLE CESSNA Sixth great granddaughter of progenitor Nicholas Kegg. **PATRICK HENRY CESSNA** Fifth great grandson of progenitor Nicholas Kegg.
PAUL ALLEN CESSNA Fifth great grandson of progenitor Nicholas Kegg.
PAUL WILLIAM CESSNA Seventh great grandson of progenitor Nicholas Kegg.
RACHAEL BERRY CESSNA Sixth great granddaughter of progenitor Nicholas Kegg.
RACHEL ANN CESSNA Eighth great granddaughter of progenitor Nicholas Kegg.
RALPH AUSTIN CESSNA [3148] (1880 – 1967) son of William and Charlotte (Filler) Cessna.
RAYMOND FILLER CESSNA [3149] (1888 – 1971) son of William and Charlotte (Filler) Cessna, married Hulda S. Shaffer with whom he was father of (7). **RAYMOND W. CESSNA** Fifth great grandson of progenitor Nicholas Kegg. **REBECCA ANN CESSNA** aka "Becki", Sixth great granddaughter of progenitor Nicholas Kegg. **RENA MARIE CESSNA** Fifth great granddaughter of progenitor Nicholas Kegg. **RICHARD D. CESSNA** Fifth great grandson of progenitor Nicholas Kegg.
RICK LEE CESSNA Seventh great grandson of progenitor Nicholas Kegg.
ROBERT ARCHIE CESSNA [3149A] (1923 – 2007) son of Chester and Cora (Perdew) Cessna, married Marjorie Welsh with whom he was father of (2). Robert retired as a press operator from Hedstrom Corp. He loved to hunt, play horseshoes and spend time with his family. He was a Veteran of World War II and the Korean Conflict; **ROBERT DALE CESSNA JR.** Fifth great grandson of progenitor Nicholas Kegg.
ROBERT DALE CESSNA [3150] (1915 – 1986) son of H. Bertram and Margaret (Ritchey) Cessna, married Edith Marie Rhea with whom he was father of (2). **ROBERT PERRY CESSNA** Fifth great grandson of progenitor Nicholas Kegg. **ROBIN TERRIA CESSNA** Fifth great granddaughter of progenitor Nicholas Kegg. **RONALD LEE CESSNA** Sixth great grandson of progenitor Nicholas Kegg. **RODNEY KEITH CESSNA** Fifth great grandson of progenitor Nicholas Kegg.
ROGER THOMAS CESSNA Sixth great grandson of progenitor Nicholas Kegg.
RONALD LEE CESSNA Seventh great grandson of progenitor Nicholas Kegg.
RUTH CHARLOTTE CESSNA [3151] (1897 – 1967) daughter of William and Charlotte (Filler) Cessna married three times, first to Emory Clayton Nycum with whom she was mother of (3). She married

---

[3145] p2 - Bedford Gazette (PA) March 17, 1944 [3146] Bedford Gazette (PA) May 5, 1916 [3148] Bedford Inquirer (PA) June 2, 1967, obtained by Connie Detar contributed by Bob Rose [3149] Duke Clark obituary clipping collection [3149A] Timothy Berkebile Funeral Home (PA) [3150] p3 – Bedford Inquirer (PA) Dec 12, 1986 [3151] Bedford Gazette (PA) Apr 25, 1967, obtained by Connie Detar contributed by Bob Rose

Wilbur Alvin Hendrickson who died two months later and, married Harold Granville James with whom she was mother of (1).   **RUTH CHARLOTTE CESSNA** [3152] (1921 – 2010) daughter of Chester and Cora (Perdew) Cessna, married William L. Miller with whom she was mother of (4).
SAMUEL ALLEN CESSNA Fifth great grandson of progenitor Nicholas Kegg.
SAMUEL JORDON CESSNA aka "Jordon", Sixth great grandson of progenitor Nicholas Kegg.
SAMUEL RAYMOND CESSNA Fifth great grandson of progenitor Nicholas Kegg.
SARA CESSNA Eighth great granddaughter of progenitor Nicholas Kegg.
SARAH ELIZABETH CESSNA Sixth great granddaughter of progenitor Nicholas Kegg.
SCOTT ALLEN CESSNA (1957 – 1957) son of Robert and Helen (Beegle) Cessna.
SCOTT JERALD CESSNA Sixth great grandson of progenitor Nicholas Kegg.
STAFFORD JAY CESSNA Sixth great grandson of progenitor Nicholas Kegg.
STEPHANIE IRENE CESSNA Sixth great granddaughter of progenitor Nicholas Kegg.
STEPHANIE JEANNE CESSNA Seventh great granddaughter of progenitor Nicholas Kegg.
SUSAN ANN CESSNA Fifth great granddaughter of progenitor Nicholas Kegg.
TAMMY K. CESSNA Fifth great granddaughter of progenitor Nicholas Kegg.
TAMMY MARIE CESSNA Seventh great granddaughter of progenitor Nicholas Kegg.
TERESA ANNETTE CESSNA Seventh great granddaughter of progenitor Nicholas Kegg.
TERRI LOUISE CESSNA Seventh great granddaughter of progenitor Nicholas Kegg.
THOMAS BEEGLE CESSNA Fifth great grandson of progenitor Nicholas Kegg.
THOMAS RALPH CESSNA Sixth great grandson of progenitor Nicholas Kegg.
TINA LOUISE CESSNA Fifth great granddaughter of progenitor Nicholas Kegg.
TODD ALAN CESSNA Seventh great grandson of progenitor Nicholas Kegg.   **TODD LEE CESSNA** Fifth great grandson of progenitor Nicholas Kegg.   **TODD R. CESSNA** Seventh great grandson of progenitor Nicholas Kegg.   **TRAVIS JAY CESSNA** Fifth great grandson of progenitor Nicholas Kegg. **TRENT CESSNA** Sixth great grandson of progenitor Nicholas Kegg.   **TROY ALLAN CESSNA** Fifth great grandson of progenitor Nicholas Kegg.   **TROY DANIEL CESSNA** Seventh great grandson of progenitor Nicholas Kegg.   **TRUDY DIANE CESSNA** Seventh great granddaughter of progenitor Nicholas Kegg.   **TYLER ANDREW CESSNA** Sixth great grandson of progenitor Nicholas Kegg.
VIOLET JOAN CESSNA Fourth great granddaughter of progenitor Nicholas Kegg.
VIRGINIA RUTH CESSNA [3153] (1913 – 1998) daughter of Raymond and Hulda (Shaffer) Cessna, married Richard Samuel Cessna with whom she was mother of (2). Virginia retired from Lion Manufacturing in Everett.   **WAYNE ANDREW CESSNA** aka "Buck" Fifth great grandson of progenitor Nicholas Kegg.   **WENDY LEIGH CESSNA** Sixth great granddaughter of progenitor Nicholas Kegg.   **WILBUR LAMONT CESSNA JR** [3153A] (1927 – 2010) son of Wilbur and Ethel (O'Neal) Cessna, married Emma Jean Twigg with whom he was father of (4). In his earlier years, Wilbur worked for the Cessna Family Sawmill. He was a Veteran of the Merchant Marines during World War II and retired as Plant Manager of Watson Wood Products. Wilbur was a member of the Prosperity United Methodist Church where he held various offices. He was also a member of the Bedford Masonic Lodge No. 360, the Ali Ghan Shrine Club, the Scottish Rite, the Bedford American Legion, the Keystone Mariners of Pennsylvania, the National Rifle Association and the Friends Cove Sportsmen's Club.
WILLIAM AUSTIN CESSNA [3154] (1849 – 1933) son of Peter and Margaret (Stuckey) Cessna, married Charlotte E. Filler with whom he was father of (11).   **WILLIAM AUSTIN CESSNA** [3155] (1933 – 2000) son of Chester and Cora (Perdew) Cessna, married Ruth Genevieve Keller with whom he was father of (3). William had been council member and president at various times since 1958. He was also a Rainsburg Water project member at the time of his death. He was certified as a small water system operator. He was a member of the Woods Church Association and former caretaker of the cemetery. Mr. Cessna also helped to form the Rainsburg-Colerain Recreation Association. He retired from Kennametal after 40 years and worked at the Cessna family butcher shop which was started by his father more than

---

[3152] Timothy A. Berkebile Funeral Home (PA) [3153] Bedford Inquirer (PA) March 27, 1998 [3153A] p3 - Bedford Inquirer (PA) April 23, 2010, obtained and contributed by Bob Rose [3154] BU Data Book; pencil dated 1933 obtained by Dot Duncan in 1985 contributed by Bob Rose [3155] Timothy A. Berkebile Funeral Home (PA)

100 years ago. He was an Army veteran who served during the Korean conflict. **WILLIAM DONALD CESSNA** Sixth great grandson of progenitor Nicholas Kegg. **WILLOW CESSNA** Seventh great granddaughter of progenitor Nicholas Kegg. **WYATT CESSNA** Eighth great grandson of progenitor Nicholas Kegg. **ZACHARY AUSTIN CESSNA** Eighth great grandson of progenitor Nicholas Kegg. **ZACHARY MICHAEL CESSNA** Sixth great grandson of progenitor Nicholas Kegg. **ZANE CESSNA** Sixth great grandson of progenitor Nicholas Kegg.

CEVELA

DARREN LEE CEVELA Seventh great grandson of progenitor Nicholas Kegg.
JAMIE LYNN CEVELA Seventh great granddaughter of progenitor Nicholas Kegg.
MEGAN LEE CEVELA Eighth great granddaughter of progenitor Nicholas Kegg.

CHADSEY

CLARENCE COLLINS CHADSEY (1903 – 1969) son of John and Myrtle (Knouf) Chadsey, married Dorothy Fairchild Islip with whom he was father of (1). **JANIS DOROTHEA CHADSEY** (1931 – 1974) daughter of Clarence and Dorothy (Islip) Chadsey.

CHAFFEE

ELIZABETH MARIE CHAFFEE Fifth great granddaughter of progenitor Nicholas Kegg. **GEORGETTE M. CHAFFEE** Sixth great granddaughter of progenitor Nicholas Kegg. **GRANT CHAFFEE** Sixth great grandson of progenitor Nicholas Kegg. **JOAN CHAFFEE** Fifth great granddaughter of progenitor Nicholas Kegg. **KAREN MAE CHAFFEE** [3155A] (1943 – 2016) daughter of Henry and Melease (Rice) Chaffee married three times, first to Jeffery L. Rumsey. She married Harold Lee Bruce with whom she was mother of (2). Later, she married Richard Leroy Johnson. Karen worked at Mastercraft, Inc. in Shipshewana, IN. **MELODY ROSE CHAFFEE** Seventh great granddaughter of progenitor Nicholas Kegg. **STEVE CHAFFEE** Fifth great grandson of progenitor Nicholas Kegg. **STORM MICHAEL CHAFFEE** Seventh great grandson of progenitor Nicholas Kegg.

CHALFANT

ERIN CHALFANT Seventh great granddaughter of progenitor Nicholas Kegg. **GARY NEWTON CHALFANT** Sixth great grandson of progenitor Nicholas Kegg. **JAMES T. CHALFANT** Seventh great grandson of progenitor Nicholas Kegg. **JOSH CHALFANT** Seventh great grandson of progenitor Nicholas Kegg. **KAREN LYNN CHALFANT** Sixth great granddaughter of progenitor Nicholas Kegg. **NICK CHALFANT** Seventh great grandson of progenitor Nicholas Kegg. **REBECCA ANN CHALFANT** aka "Becky", Seventh great granddaughter of progenitor Nicholas Kegg.

CHALFONT

JOHN R. CHALFONT Seventh great grandson of progenitor Nicholas Kegg. **LISA CHALFONT** Seventh great granddaughter of progenitor Nicholas Kegg.

CHAMBERLAIN

ADAM CHAMBERLAIN Sixth great grandson of progenitor Nicholas Kegg.

[3155A] KPCNews (IN) Aug. 3, 2016, obtained and contributed by D. Sue Dible

EYOBI CHAMBERLAIN Eighth great grandson of progenitor Nicholas Kegg.
JEFFREY CHAMBERLAIN Sixth great grandson of progenitor Nicholas Kegg.
JORDAN CHAMBERLAIN Eighth great grandson of progenitor Nicholas Kegg.
NICK CHAMBERLAIN Seventh great grandson of progenitor Nicholas Kegg.
RYAN CHAMBERLAIN Seventh great grandson of progenitor Nicholas Kegg.

CHAMBERS

JEFFREY K. CHAMBERS Sixth great grandson of progenitor Nicholas Kegg.

CHAMPADA

ALEXIS ANN CHAMPADA Eighth great grandchild of progenitor Nicholas Kegg.

CHAMPLIN

CYNTHIA LYNN CHAMPLIN Sixth great granddaughter of progenitor Nicholas Kegg.
STEPHANIE CHAMPLIN Sixth great granddaughter of progenitor Nicholas Kegg.
STEVEN CURTIS CHAMPLIN Sixth great grandson of progenitor Nicholas Kegg.
SUZANNE CHAMPLIN Sixth great granddaughter of progenitor Nicholas Kegg.

CHANEY

ANDREW D. CHANEY Fifth great grandson of progenitor Nicholas Kegg.
ARMINTA ANN CHANEY (1867 – 1948) aka "Mintie", daughter of Jarvis and Mary (Cagg) Chaney, married Benjamin Franklin Quisenberry. **BOBBIE CHANEY** Sixth great granddaughter of progenitor Nicholas Kegg. **CAMERON ANDREW CHANEY** aka "Beau", Seventh great grandson of progenitor Nicholas Kegg. **CHAD MATHEW CHANEY** Seventh great grandson of progenitor Nicholas Kegg. **CLARK CHRISTOPHER CHANEY** Seventh great grandson of progenitor Nicholas Kegg. **CLAYTON J. CHANEY** Seventh great grandson of progenitor Nicholas Kegg. **DELORES FRANKEE CHANEY** (1913 – 1991) daughter of James and Martha (Kennedy) Chaney married twice **FLOYD JAMES CHANEY** (1892 – 1958) son of James and Martha (Kennedy) Chaney, married Essye Lee (nee Taylor) Cowne. **GODON S. CHANEY** Fifth great grandson of progenitor Nicholas Kegg. **GUY PORTER CHANEY** (1899 – 1921) son of James and Martha (Kennedy) Chaney, married Rhoda May Morrow with whom he was father of (1). Guy accidentally drowns when his car went over an embankment into the water. **HAROLD WESLEY CHANEY** [3156] (1919 – 1969) son of Harry and Rose (Masters) Chaney, married Edith Laura Erne with whom he was father of (1). Harold served with the Army Air Force during World War II. He retired from Pacific Telephone Co. where he was employed as a lineman. **HARRY ELWOOD CHANEY** (1895 – 1967) son of James and Martha (Kennedy) Chaney, married Rose Ellen Masters with whom he was father of (2). **JACK CHANEY** [3157] (1921 – 2003) son of Harry and Rose (Masters) Chaney, married Phyllis Marilee (nee Pillow) Privett with whom he was father of (2). **JACK HAROLD CHANEY** [3157A] (1944 – 2018) son of Harold and Edith (Erne) Chaney, married Olivia Marie Oberti with whom he was father of (4). He served in Vietnam as a Sergeant in the United States Army from 1969 to 1970. He taught school at Washington Union High School from 1968 to 1969, and continued from 1971 to 1985, after finishing his tour. In 1983, he established his business, Chaney Cabinet and Furniture Company, which was known throughout the valley for the gifted quality work that Jack excelled in. Jack was an active member of St. Helen's Catholic Church where he was a Eucharistic Minister and president of the school board. He was grand knight in the Knights of Columbus, and a member of the Easton Lions Club. Jack was very active as a board

---

[3156] The Fresno Bee (CA) March 24, 1969 [3157] Fresno Bee (CA) March 13, 2003 [3157A] Fresno Bee (CA) Jan 7, 2018

member and coach in the Sunnyside Lone Star Little League for 25 years. He loved to golf and was a member of the Sunnyside Country Club. He will be remembered as a lover of history, the Cleveland Indians, the University of Oklahoma Sooners, jazz musicians, Django Reinhardt, and Stephane Grappeli and his three English Springer Spaniels. **JACK LLOYD CHANEY** Sixth great grandson of progenitor Nicholas Kegg. **JAMES DENNIS CHANEY** Sixth great grandson of progenitor Nicholas Kegg. **JAMES ELIAS CHANEY** [3158] (1868 – 1949) son of Jarvis and Mary (Cagg) Chaney, married Martha Irene Kennedy with whom he was father of (7). **JESSAMINE LAVONNE CHANEY** (1907 – 1957) aka "Jessie", daughter of James and Martha (Kennedy) Chaney. **JOSEPH ALEXANDER CHANEY** Seventh great grandson of progenitor Nicholas Kegg. **JUDITH BERNADINE CHANEY** [3158A] (1944 – 2008) daughter of Richard and Delores (Mauler) Chaney, married Delbert Sidney Starr, Jr., with whom she was mother of (3). Judy was a homemaker. Although, a member of Holy Rosary Catholic Church in Hartshorne; Judy was active in several parishes in the Tulsa Diocese. **KAY CHANEY** Sixth great granddaughter of progenitor Nicholas Kegg. **MADGE ELLEN CHANEY** (1902 – 1997) daughter of James and Martha (Kennedy) Chaney, married Sanny Morrow with whom she was mother of (4). **MADISON CHANEY** Eighth great granddaughter of progenitor Nicholas Kegg. **MARGARET IRENE CHANEY** daughter of James and Martha (Kennedy) Chaney, married Arthur Charles Gilbert with whom she was mother of (2). **MCKENZIE CHANEY** Eighth great granddaughter of progenitor Nicholas Kegg. **NATALIE MARIE CHANEY** Seventh great granddaughter of progenitor Nicholas Kegg. **NOELLE MARIE CHANEY** Seventh great granddaughter of progenitor Nicholas Kegg. **PATRICIA SUE CHANEY** [3159] (1951 – 2013) daughter of Richard and Delores (Mauler) Chaney, married Gary D. Hulvey. **PATRICK COLIN CHANEY** Seventh great grandson of progenitor Nicholas Kegg. **RICHARD DONALD CHANEY** [3160] (1921 – 1996) aka "Don", son of Guy and Rhoda (Morrow) Chaney, married Delores Bernadine Mauler with whom he was father of (5). **ROSEANNE CHANEY** Sixth great granddaughter of progenitor Nicholas Kegg. **STUART A. CHANEY** Fifth great grandson of progenitor Nicholas Kegg.

CHAPLIN

LYNN CHAPLIN Sixth great granddaughter of progenitor Nicholas Kegg.
MARK CHAPLIN Sixth great grandson of progenitor Nicholas Kegg.

CHAPMAN

DANIEL CHAPMAN Seventh great grandson of progenitor Nicholas Kegg.
LEILA CHAPMAN Seventh great granddaughter of progenitor Nicholas Kegg.

CHAPPELL

DAVID WILLIAM CHAPPELL Seventh great grandson of progenitor Nicholas Kegg.
ELIZABETH HOPE CHAPPELL [3161] (2002 – 2002) daughter of Ian and Angela (Myers) Chappell.
HAYLEE GRACE CHAPPELL Seventh great granddaughter of progenitor Nicholas Kegg.
IAN V. CHAPPELL Sixth great grandson of progenitor Nicholas Kegg.
MATTHEW ROBERT CHAPPELL Seventh great grandson of progenitor Nicholas Kegg.

CHARNEY

CHRISTOP T. CHARNEY Sixth great grandson of progenitor Nicholas Kegg.
ELISA K. CHARNEY Sixth great granddaughter of progenitor Nicholas Kegg.

[3158] Fresno Bee (CA) Aug 20, 1949 [3158A] Chaney-Harkins Funeral Home (OK) [3159] Tulsa World (OK) Oct 11, 2013 [3160] Tulsa World (OK) Feb 9, 1996 [3161] The Valley News Dispatch (PA) July 8, 2002

CHARRON

ABIGAIL CHARRON Eighth great granddaughter of progenitor Nicholas Kegg.
JESSICA CHARRON Eighth great granddaughter of progenitor Nicholas Kegg.
JOSIAH CHARRON Eighth great grandson of progenitor Nicholas Kegg.

CHAVIS

STEVIE CHAVIS Sixth great grandson of progenitor Nicholas Kegg.

CHEEK

KYLA B. CHEEK Seventh great granddaughter of progenitor Nicholas Kegg.

CHERRY

NAKIYA CHERRY Ninth great granddaughter of progenitor Nicholas Kegg.

CHIDESTER

ALEXIA CHIDESTER aka "Lexi", Seventh great granddaughter of progenitor Nicholas Kegg.
BLAKE CHIDESTER Seventh great grandson of progenitor Nicholas Kegg.

CHIESA

GREG CHIESA Sixth great grandson of progenitor Nicholas Kegg.

CHILDERS

ADELINA MARIE CHILDERS (1931 – 1931) daughter of Jack and Alta (Johnson) Childers.
ARNETTA CHILDERS Sixth great granddaughter of progenitor Nicholas Kegg.
BRENDA CHILDERS Sixth great granddaughter of progenitor Nicholas Kegg.
BRIANNA ELIZABETH CHILDERS Seventh great granddaughter of progenitor Nicholas Kegg.
BRODIE L. CHILDERS Sixth great grandson of progenitor Nicholas Kegg.
CHARLES WILLIAM CHILDERS [3162] (1926 – 2008) aka "Charlie", son of Jack and Alta (Johnson) Childers, married Marlene Jo Kester with whom he was father of (3). Charlie worked as a mechanic for the Hamm Company in Perry, he retired after 32 years of service. He was a U.S. Navy Veteran of WWII, serving from 1943 to 1945, he was a Seaman First Class. He was a member of the Perry American Legion Post #142. **CHARLOTTE L. CHILDERS** Sixth great granddaughter of progenitor Nicholas Kegg.
CHERYL M. CHILDERS Sixth great granddaughter of progenitor Nicholas Kegg.
DAVID CHILDERS Sixth great grandson of progenitor Nicholas Kegg. **DEAN ALLEN CHILDERS** Sixth great grandson of progenitor Nicholas Kegg. **DEBORAH J. CHILDERS** Sixth great granddaughter of progenitor Nicholas Kegg. **DONNA CHILDERS** Sixth great granddaughter of progenitor Nicholas Kegg. **DONNELL L. CHILDERS** Sixth great granddaughter of progenitor Nicholas Kegg. **EUGENE CHILDERS** Fifth great grandson of progenitor Nicholas Kegg.
JACK JO CHILDERS [3162A] aka "Bob" (1923 – 2015) son of Jack and Alta (Johnson) Childers, married Velma Cohrt with whom he was father of (3). He served in the U.S. Army, 101st Airborne, from 1943 to 1945, serving in Ardennes, Rhineland and central Europe. He was in the invasion of Normandy and the Battle of the Bulge in France as a 50-caliber machine gunner and driver. Jack drove army trucks, hauling

---

[3162] Topeka Capital-Journal (KS) May 2, 2008, obtained by D. Sue Dible [3162A] Gazette (Cedar Rapids, IA) June 24, 2015

ammunition, supplies and personnel under enemy gunfire. He also flew gliders during his tour. He received two Purple Hearts, a Bronze Star and a Gold Conduct medal. Jack worked for Concrete Material (Martin Marietta) as a welder and machinist for 45 years. He loved to travel, tinker with mechanics and watch his beloved westerns and grandchildren. **JACKIE SMITH CHILDERS** (1956 – 2012) son of Mernice and Emma (Donham) Childers married twice, first to Carol Ann Owen with whom he was father of (1), later he married Mikki Angelica Whittles. **JACKIE SMITH CHILDERS, JR.** [3162B] (1982 – 2015) son of Jackie and Carol (Owen) Childers, married Tammy Fowler with whom he was father of (1). Jack was a long-time loyal and dedicated employee of Gulf Stream Marine of Corpus Christi. Jack was an amazing man with a bright smile and a wonderful attitude about life, he loved spending time with his son. He was an avid fan of San Francisco 49ers and enjoyed barbecuing, both for his friends and in competitions. He was always there to lend a helping hand or a listening ear.
JAMES EDWARD CHILDERS (1928 – 1994) son of Jack and Alta (Johnson) Childers, married Helen Betty Schultz. **JEAN CHILDERS** Sixth great granddaughter of progenitor Nicholas Kegg. **JENETTA L. CHILDERS** Sixth great granddaughter of progenitor Nicholas Kegg.
JEREMY CHILDERS Seventh great grandson of progenitor Nicholas Kegg.
KARON LYNN CHILDERS Sixth great granddaughter of progenitor Nicholas Kegg.
LINDEN CHILDERS Fifth great grandson of progenitor Nicholas Kegg.
MARGUERITE ALTA CHILDERS Fifth great granddaughter of progenitor Nicholas Kegg.
MARJORIE MARLENE CHILDERS Fifth great granddaughter of progenitor Nicholas Kegg.
MARVIN LEE CHILDERS Sixth great grandson of progenitor Nicholas Kegg.
MARVIN LYNDON CHILDERS (1929 – 2007) son of Jack and Alta (Johnson) Childers.
MERNICE DEAN CHILDERS (1932 – 2003) son of Jack and Alta (Johnson) Childers, married Emma M. Donham with whom he was father of (6). **PAM CHILDERS** Sixth great granddaughter of progenitor Nicholas Kegg. **RALPH LEWIS CHILDERS** [3162C] (1943 – 2018) son of Ronald and Bessie (Funkhouser) Childers, married Margaret Ann Doolittle with whom he was father of (1). Later, he married Catherine Mack. Ralph worked as a Workforce & Planning Coordinator at Iowa Vocational Rehabilitation Service for 35 years. Ralph was a passionate volunteer at LifeServe as well as a 24-gallon blood donor. **REBECCA CHILDERS** aka "Becky", Seventh great granddaughter of progenitor Nicholas Kegg. **RAY ALLEN CHILDERS** Seventh great grandson of progenitor Nicholas Kegg.
REEVON LYNN CHILDERS Sixth great granddaughter of progenitor Nicholas Kegg.
RONALD HAROLD CHILDERS (1921 – 1985) son of Jack and Alta (Johnson) Childers, married Bessie Maxine Funkhouser with whom he was father of (1). Later, he married Opal Rebecca Goodrich. Ronald was a farmer. **RYAN CHILDERS** Eighth great grandson of progenitor Nicholas Kegg. **STEPHEN CHILDERS** Sixth great grandson of progenitor Nicholas Kegg. **TAMMY P. CHILDERS** [3162D] (1968 – 2009) daughter of Terry and Joyce (Price) Childers Tammy was divorced and a mother of (1). **TINA MARIE CHILDERS** [3162E] (1965 – 1997) daughter of Terry and Joyce (Price) Childers, married John Kalfas with whom she was mother of (2). Tina was employed at Green Gardens of Bedford and also the Hurry Sundown bar in Bedford. **TERRY L. CHILDERS** Sixth great grandson of progenitor Nicholas Kegg. **VERLE DEAN CHILDERS** Fifth great grandson of progenitor Nicholas Kegg.

CHILTON

ADAM CHILTON Seventh great grandson of progenitor Nicholas Kegg. **DAVID R. CHILTON** Sixth great grandson of progenitor Nicholas Kegg. **EMILY ODEN CHILTON** Seventh great granddaughter of progenitor Nicholas Kegg. **SARAH CHILTON** Sixth great granddaughter of progenitor Nicholas Kegg.

[3162B] Limbaugh Funeral Home (TX) [3162C] Des Moines Register (IA) Feb. 22, 2018 [3162D] p3 - Bedford Inquirer (PA) May 15, 2009 [3162E] Bedford Inquirer April 25, 1997, contributed by Duke Clark

CHOATE

AIDEN ROBERT CHOATE Seventh great grandson of progenitor Nicholas Kegg.
ANGELA RENAE CHOATE Sixth great granddaughter of progenitor Nicholas Kegg.
LAURIE MORGAN CHOATE Sixth great granddaughter of progenitor Nicholas Kegg.

CHONKO

ANGEL CHONKO Seventh great granddaughter of progenitor Nicholas Kegg.

CHORNAK

ADISON M. CHORNAK Seventh great granddaughter of progenitor Nicholas Kegg.
LILYANA R. CHORNAK Seventh great granddaughter of progenitor Nicholas Kegg.
STELLA J. CHORNAK Seventh great granddaughter of progenitor Nicholas Kegg.

CHRISMAN

BRANDON L. CHRISMAN Sixth great grandson of progenitor Nicholas Kegg.
RAINY LOWELL CHRISMAN Sixth great granddaughter of progenitor Nicholas Kegg.

CHRISTENSEN

CAYDEN CHRISTENSEN Ninth great grandson of progenitor Nicholas Kegg.
JAXEN CHRISTENSEN Ninth great grandson of progenitor Nicholas Kegg.

CHRISTIAN

FREDERICK OLIVER CHRISTIAN [3162F] (1924 – 2009) son of Oscar and Elizabeth (Ditch) Christian was married twice, first to Dorothy Pfund with whom he was father of (2). Later, he married Dianne Louise Zinke. Fred sold life insurance for many years. He also had many income properties. He was a member of the Shrine, the Masons, the York Rite and the Scottish Rite. **GARRETT CHRISTIAN** Sixth great grandson of progenitor Nicholas Kegg. **KAITLYN CHRISTIAN** Sixth great granddaughter of progenitor Nicholas Kegg. **KATHERINE CHRISTIAN** Fifth great granddaughter of progenitor Nicholas Kegg. **LINDA JO CHRISTIAN** Sixth great granddaughter of progenitor Nicholas Kegg. **ROBERT FREDERICK CHRISTIAN** Fifth great grandson of progenitor Nicholas Kegg.

CHRISTIANSEN

DAVID BEEM CHRISTIANSEN (1922 – 1998) son of Ernest and Bessie (Beem) Christiansen, married Mary Jane Simons with whom he was father of (1). **DAVID BEEM CHRISTIANSEN JR.** Sixth great grandson of progenitor Nicholas Kegg.

CHRISTOPHER

AMY DAWN CHRISTOPHER Eighth great granddaughter of progenitor Nicholas Kegg. **ANNA MAE CHRISTOPHER** [3162G] (1941 – 2014) daughter of Thomas and Kathryn (Beegle) Christopher. She was mother of (1). Anna Mae was employed at Post House in Breezewood for several years and after its

---

[3162F] pA6, Wisconsin State Journal (WI) Mar 25, 2009, obtained and contributed by D. Sue Dible [3162G] Bedford Gazette (PA) Oct 27, 2014, obtained and contributed by Bob Rose

closing, she did some private nursing care and house cleaning. Anna Mae enjoyed gardening, cooking, taking her great-grandchildren for walks and spending time with family. **BRIAN L. CHRISTOPHER** Sixth great grandson of progenitor Nicholas Kegg. **BRUCE A. CHRISTOPHER** [3162H] (1961 – 2013) son of Ronald and Jean (College) Christopher. He was father of (1). Bruce was a press operator. He attended college at the University of Phoenix and graduated with a Bachelor of Science degree, human resource management. Bruce loved playing golf and bass fishing and loved God and his family.
COREY A. CHRISTOPHER Sixth great grandson of progenitor Nicholas Kegg.
CORINNA D. CHRISTOPHER Sixth great granddaughter of progenitor Nicholas Kegg.
DYLAN CHRISTOPHER Seventh great grandson of progenitor Nicholas Kegg.
G. TIM CHRISTOPHER Sixth great grandson of progenitor Nicholas Kegg.
GAIL CHRISTOPHER Eighth great granddaughter of progenitor Nicholas Kegg.
GAIL M. CHRISTOPHER Sixth great granddaughter of progenitor Nicholas Kegg.
GEORGE T. CHRISTOPHER [3163] (1941 – 2006) son of Thomas and Kathryn (Beegle) Christopher, married Donna Treece with whom he was father of (4). George was a member of the first graduating class at NBC High School in 1959, formerly attending the Robert P. Smith School. After graduation, he served with the United States Army during the Korean Conflict in the 526th Ordinance Company as auto repairman. Mr. Christopher was a self-employed truck driver and a freelance bus driver for the Everett School District. He was just offered a position as a district school bus driver. He was currently serving as the president of the Everett Lions Club. George was active in the Bloody Run Historical Society and was instrumental in the restoration of the Everett Train Station. He was a passionate outdoorsman, enjoying vegetable and flower gardening, boating, fishing and golf. He was an avid hunter who especially loved deer season. Mr. Christopher was an all-around handyman. He was a remarkable craftsman, working in both wood and stained glass. He loved spending time with his family and took great delight in his granddaughters. **INFANT CHRISTOPHER** daughter of George and Donna (Treece) Christopher.
JACKSON MAVERICK CHRISTOPHER Eighth great grandson of progenitor Nicholas Kegg.
JENNIFER CHRISTOPHER Seventh great granddaughter of progenitor Nicholas Kegg.
KELLIE CHRISTOPHER Sixth great granddaughter of progenitor Nicholas Kegg.
KIERSTEN ALEXIS CHRISTOPHER Eighth great granddaughter of progenitor Nicholas Kegg.
KEVIN E. CHRISTOPHER [3163A] (1985 – 2009) son of Terry and Kay (Breneman) Christopher, married Laura Lee Martin with whom he was father of (1). Kevin enjoyed skateboarding, art, cooking with an interest in culinary school, an avid Dallas Cowboy fan and a Texas Hold'em enthusiast.
LACY JANE CHRISTOPHER Seventh great granddaughter of progenitor Nicholas Kegg.
MARK E. CHRISTOPHER Sixth great grandson of progenitor Nicholas Kegg.
MICHAEL SCOTT CHRISTOPHER Seventh great grandson of progenitor Nicholas Kegg.
NANCY S. CHRISTOPHER Eighth great granddaughter of progenitor Nicholas Kegg.
ALPH S. CHRISTOPHER Fifth great grandson of progenitor Nicholas Kegg. **RANDALL LEE CHRISTOPHER** [3163B] (1963 – 2015) son of Thomas and Janet (Gladhill) Christopher was father of (1). Randy entered the Army National Guard, and eventually the United States Navy. Randy primarily worked as a cook at several restaurants. Cooking and baking brought him…and the recipients of his labor, much pleasure. He was renowned for his carrot cake, chocolate cake with peanut butter icing, macaroni salad, and so many more delicious dishes. His pride in preparing meals for friends and family often required great patience from them because he would not allow any taste testing until the table was set. Randy had many interests, which included karaoke, often at the Mountain Shadow Restaurant in Blue Ridge Summit, PA; traveling; the Washington Redskins; Wrestling; watching Days of Our Lives; The Minions; Storage Wars; old cars; fishing; laughing, and kids. Randy was very patriotic. He adored his 14-year-old cat, Trooper. He loved talking with his family and friends and was a mentor to many. He was a member of the American Legion, Mont Alto Volunteer Fire Company, and Five Forks Brethren in Christ Church, Waynesboro. **RONALD LEE CHRISTOPHER** Fifth great grandson of progenitor Nicholas Kegg.

[3162H] Bedford Gazette (PA) July 19, 2013, obtained and contributed by Bob Rose [3163] p3 - Bedford Inquirer, July 7, 2006, obtained by Bob Rose [3163A] Good Funeral Home & Cremation Centre (PA) [3163B] Bowersox Funeral Home (PA)

RYAN THOMAS CHRISTOPHER Sixth great grandson of progenitor Nicholas Kegg.
SCOTT ALAN CHRISTOPHER Sixth great grandson of progenitor Nicholas Kegg.
SHANNON CHRISTOPHER Seventh great granddaughter of progenitor Nicholas Kegg.
SHIRLEY L. CHRISTOPHER Fifth great granddaughter of progenitor Nicholas Kegg.
STEPHANIE CHRISTOPHER Eighth great granddaughter of progenitor Nicholas Kegg.
STEVEN CHRISTOPHER Sixth great grandson of progenitor Nicholas Kegg.
TERRY RAY CHRISTOPHER JR. Seventh great grandson of progenitor Nicholas Kegg.
TERRY RAY CHRISTOPHER Sixth great grandson of progenitor Nicholas Kegg.
THOMAS H. CHRISTOPHER [3163C] (1937 – 2022) son of Thomas and Kathryn (Beegle) Christopher married Janet M. Gladhill with whom he was father of (6). Tom served his country by enlisting in the United States Air Force. After completing basic training, he was stationed in Amarillo, Texas to become an aircraft mechanic. He was then stationed for four years at Larson Air Force Base in Washington. While he was home on leave, he met the love of his life, Janet. He retired from the James River Corporation after working there for 34 years. Tom enjoyed going to the AMVETs and fishing.
TIMOTHY CHRISTOPHER Seventh great grandson of progenitor Nicholas Kegg.
TIMOTHY CHRISTOPHER Eighth great grandson of progenitor Nicholas Kegg.
TOD A. CHRISTOPHER Sixth great grandson of progenitor Nicholas Kegg.
TRACEY CHRISTOPHER Sixth great granddaughter of progenitor Nicholas Kegg.

CHYNOWETH

EMILY DAWN CHYNOWETH Sixth great granddaughter of progenitor Nicholas Kegg.
MEGHAN MARIE CHYNOWETH Sixth great granddaughter of progenitor Nicholas Kegg.

CICHOCKI

CHRISTOPHER CICHOCKI Eighth great grandson of progenitor Nicholas Kegg.
PAUL CICHOCKI Eighth great grandson of progenitor Nicholas Kegg.

CIKALO

BROOK ASHLEY CIKALO aka "Shorty", Sixth great granddaughter of progenitor Nicholas Kegg.
MIRANDA LEE CIKALO aka "Mandy", Sixth great granddaughter of progenitor Nicholas Kegg.

CIOCCO

GINA CIOCCO Sixth great granddaughter of progenitor Nicholas Kegg.
SAM CIOCCO Sixth great grandson of progenitor Nicholas Kegg.

CIOMEK

NICHOLAS CIOMEK Seventh great grandson of progenitor Nicholas Kegg.

CLAAR

ANNETTE ELAINE CLAAR Sixth great granddaughter of progenitor Nicholas Kegg.
BRANDIN L. CLAAR Seventh great grandson of progenitor Nicholas Kegg.

[3163C] Newcomer Dayton funeral home (OH)

CLAPPER

CHRISTOPHER R. CLAPPER, aka "Chris", Sixth great grandson of progenitor Nicholas Kegg. **EDWARD C. CLAPPER** Fifth great grandson of progenitor Nicholas Kegg. **GARY JAN CLAPPER** [3164] (1934 – 1996) son of Ralph and Mary (Hinish) Clapper, married Mary E. Wilson with whom he was father of (3). Gary retired as a pressman from the Miami Herald, after 29 years of service. He was formerly employed at the Martinsburg and Altoona Shoe companies. He was a graduate of Morrisons Cove High School and was an Army veteran of the Korean conflict. **GREGORY SAMUEL CLAPPER** Sixth great grandson of progenitor Nicholas Kegg. **JAMES CLAPPER** Seventh great grandson of progenitor Nicholas Kegg. **JAMES CARL CLAPPER** (1956 – 1997) aka "Jimmy", son of Gary and Mary (Wilson) Clapper. **JAMES D. CLAPPER** (1941 – 1942) son of Woodrow and Dorothy (Calhoun) Clapper. **JAY SCOTT CLAPPER** Fifth great grandson of progenitor Nicholas Kegg. **JENNA LYNN CLAPPER** Fifth great granddaughter of progenitor Nicholas Kegg. **JOY KAY CLAPPER** [3165] (1975 – 2016) daughter of Gary and Mary (Wilson) Clapper, married Daniel John Fritzie with whom she was mother of (3). Joy was a homemaker and a home schoolteacher to her boys. She loved spending time with her husband and 3 children. They were her world. Joy enjoyed crafts and scrapbooking. She really enjoyed long car rides, being outside in the cooler weather, camping and fishing (especially with her daddy when he was alive). Joy loved fairies, hummingbirds and flowers. She enjoyed watching movies and listening to music. Joy was always there for others to give and help in any way she could. She was a great listener, always willing to lend an ear, give a hug and advice. She had an unwavering faith in God and loved The Lord with everything she had. Joy was the sweetest soul anyone knew. **KAREN CLAPPER** Seventh great granddaughter of progenitor Nicholas Kegg. **KIMBERLY CLAPPER** Seventh great granddaughter of progenitor Nicholas Kegg. **LAURA L. CLAPPER** Fifth great granddaughter of progenitor Nicholas Kegg. **LON ERIC CLAPPER** [3166] (1932 – 2000) son of Ralph and Mary (Hinish) Clapper. Lon retired from the I.F. & T. Railroad, Alexandria, Va., after 10 years of service. Following his retirement, he was a paper bundle carrier for the Altoona Mirror in the Morrison's Cove Area. He attended Morrisons Cove High School, Martinsburg, R.R. 1. He was a Navy veteran of the Korean War and the Vietnam War with 16 years total service, having served on the USS Enterprise. He enjoyed camping, especially at Raystown Lake, and trains. **LUCAS SCOTT CLAPPER** Sixth great grandson of progenitor Nicholas Kegg. **RALPH JOSIAH CLAPPER** [3167] (1913 – 1991) son of Elmer and Elsie (Whetstone) Clapper, married Mary K. Hinish with whom he was father of (3). Ralph retired as an electronics maintenance technician from the Federal Aviation Administration at the Altoona-Blair County Airport, Martinsburg. Prior to that, he was employed as a television repairman at Leidy's Electric, Martinsburg. **RHONDA JANE CLAPPER** Fifth great granddaughter of progenitor Nicholas Kegg. **RUTH MAE CLAPPER** [3168] (1920 – 1998) daughter of Elmer and Elsie (Whetstone) Clapper, married Billy Wayne Byrd with whom she was mother of (1). Ruth graduated from the Flowers Fifth Avenue Hospital School of Nursing in New York. During World War II, she was an Army nurse aboard a hospital ship in the Atlantic and Pacific. After the war, she was a field nurse for the Oklahoma department of health. Later, she moved to the Washington area and began working as a school nurse in Arlington. After retiring, Ruth did volunteer work for Meals on Wheels and the thrift shop at Fort Myer, and she was on the board of EX-POSE, an organization that worked for the rights of former military spouses. **TERRY LANE CLAPPER** [3168A] (1936 – 1997) son of Ralph and Mary (Hinish) Clapper, married Judy Hammel with whom he was father of (3). Terri was a union electrician. He was an Air Force veteran of the Korean War, stationed in Okinawa. Mr. Clapper enjoyed pitching horseshoes, woodworking, computers, reading and furthering his education. He was a member of the D. Merl Tipton Veterans of Foreign Wars Post, Martinsburg, and the International Brotherhood of Electrical Workers Union Local. **TIMOTHY L. CLAPPER** Fifth great grandson of progenitor Nicholas Kegg. **WANDA J. CLAPPER**

[3164] p15 - Altoona Mirror (PA) July 17, 1996 [3165] Find A Grave memorial # 171197806 [3166] pA7 - Altoona Mirror (PA) Oct 23, 2000 [3167] p15 - Altoona Mirror (PA) Dec. 18, 1991 [3168] p.C6 - Washington Post (DC) Dec 12, 1998 [3168A] p15 - Altoona Mirror (PA) July 16, 1997

Fifth great granddaughter of progenitor Nicholas Kegg.   **WOODROW CLAPPER III** Seventh great grandson of progenitor Nicholas Kegg.   **WOODROW W. CLAPPER IV** Eighth great grandson of progenitor Nicholas Kegg.   **WOODROW WILSON CLAPPER JR.** [3169] (1936 – 2018) aka "Woody", son of Woodrow and Dorothy (Calhoun) Clapper married three times, first to Barbara Bender, then to Patricia L (Brallier) Diehl. Later, he married Diane Labuda with whom he was father of (4). Woody was a proud veteran of both the Army and Air Force and was awarded the Purple Heart, during the Korean War. He was an active pilot and enjoyed taking numerous friends flying in the Piper Cub. Woody spent the majority of his career as a truck driver, logging more miles in reverse than most people did forward. He was a collector of many things and through the years owned a corvette, motorcycles, and most recently a scooter. He spent many days hunting the elusive whitetail and black bear on Shaffer Mountain. He was very proud to serve as mayor of Central City, an office he held since 1997. He was a man with many stories and shared them with everyone.

CLARK

ALBERT FRANKLIN CLARK [3170] (1881 – 1966) aka "Bert", son of Lewis and Mary (Rice) Clark, married Mary Adelheid Mess with whom he was father of (7).   **ALBERTA IRENE CLARK** [3171] (1914 – 1996) daughter of Albert and Mary (Mess) Clark married twice; first to Harold W. Rich with whom she was mother of (2). Later, she married Jim Reddy. Alberta retired from the County of Riverside where she worked as dept. supervisor senior clerk.   **ALICIA CLARK** Eighth great granddaughter of progenitor Nicholas Kegg.   **ANITA BELLE CLARK** [3172] (1934 – 2001) daughter of Wylma Elizabeth Clark married twice; first to Richard Albert Drozek with whom she was mother of (6). Later she married Mr. Barkman with whom she was mother of (1).   **ARNOLD EUGENE CLARK** [3173] (1935 – 1944) son of Chalmer and Vesta (Dibert) Clark. The 9-year-old was killed when hit by the milk truck of Oscar Ritchey while crossing the road en route to his school.   **AUBREY R. CLARK** [3174] (1934 – 2021) aka "Hob", Sixth son of Elliot and Hazel (Harclerode) Clark married Donna McDowell with whom he was father of (1). Aubrey worked for Kennametal Inc. for 39 years. Upon retiring, he spent the next 18 ½ years RV'ing and traveling the world. He also had a strong passion for nature, photography and golfing. Aubrey was a member and past master of George A. Holly Masonic Lodge and was a member of the Al Koran Shriner's. Aubrey and his wife were members of Willoughby Eagles 2300, and heavily involved with the Eastlake North Booster Club.   **AVERY CLARK** Seventh great granddaughter of progenitor Nicholas Kegg.   **BARBARA ANN CLARK** Sixth great granddaughter of progenitor Nicholas Kegg.   **BARBARA JEAN CLARK** Fifth great granddaughter of progenitor Nicholas Kegg.   **BERNARD CLARK** Fourth great grandson of progenitor Nicholas Kegg.   **BERNARD L. CLARK** Fifth great grandson of progenitor Nicholas Kegg.   **BRANDON CLARK** Seventh great grandson of progenitor Nicholas Kegg.   **BRIANNA CLARK** Seventh great granddaughter of progenitor Nicholas Kegg.   **CANDICE CLARK** Sixth great granddaughter of progenitor Nicholas Kegg.   **CHANDLER CLARK** Seventh great grandson of progenitor Nicholas Kegg.   **CHARLES B. CLARK** aka "C. B.", Sixth great grandson of progenitor Nicholas Kegg.   **CHARLES RANDOLPH CLARK** (1917 – 1970) son of Bernard and Anna (Stuckey) Clarke, married Meda Susan Carr with whom he was father of (2). **CHELSEA MARIE CLARK** Seventh great granddaughter of progenitor Nicholas Kegg.   **CHRIS CLARK** Seventh great grandchild of progenitor Nicholas Kegg.   **CHRISTOPHER R. CLARK** Sixth great grandson of progenitor Nicholas Kegg.   **CLINTON CLARK** Sixth great grandson of progenitor Nicholas Kegg.   **COLE CLARK** Seventh great grandson of progenitor Nicholas Kegg.   **COREY CLARK** Seventh great grandson of progenitor Nicholas Kegg.   **CORY CLARK** Seventh great grandson of progenitor Nicholas Kegg.   **CRAIG W. CLARK** Seventh great grandson of progenitor Nicholas Kegg.   **DALE S. CLARK** Sixth great grandson of progenitor Nicholas Kegg.   **DARLENE CLARK** Fifth great granddaughter of progenitor Nicholas Kegg.   **DAVID CLARK** son of Fred and

---

[3169] Tribune Democrat (PA) July 11, 2018 [3170] p2 The Tustin News (CA) July 21, 1966 [3171] San Diego Union-Tribune (CA) Jan 8, 1996 [3172] Northwest Herald (IL) Feb 2, 2001 [3173] Bedford Gazette (PA) April 21, 1944 [3174] News-Herald (OH) June 15, 2021

Hazel (Calhoun) Clark. **DAVID CLARK** Sixth great grandson of progenitor Nicholas Kegg. **DENNIS LEE CLARK** (1939 – 1940) son of Harry and Edith (Hebb) Clark. **DIANA CLARK** Sixth great granddaughter of progenitor Nicholas Kegg. **DOLPHUS HENRY CLARK** [3175] (1875 – 1937) aka "Dolphy" son of Lewis and Mary (Rice) Clark, married Orpha Mae Williams with whom he was father of (2). Dolphy attended McPherson College in Kansas and the Grand Island Business College. He was interested in baseball and other sports and as a young man took an active part in them. Dolphy operated a very successful insurance business in Campbell, Nebr. for many years. He had considerable business ability and seemed to be able to succeed in anything he undertook to do. **DONALD CLARK** Sixth great grandson of progenitor Nicholas Kegg. **DORIS JEAN CLARK** Sixth great granddaughter of progenitor Nicholas Kegg. **DOROTHY JANE CLARK** aka "Dottie", Sixth great granddaughter of progenitor Nicholas Kegg. **EARL LANE CLARK** aka "Lane", Sixth great grandson of progenitor Nicholas Kegg. **EARL RICHARD CLARK** [3176] (1937 – 2020) son of Kenneth and Lola (Mischler) Clark, married Rose Marie Harrison with whom he was father of (3). Earl refinished furniture, making the old look brand new. He was an accomplished finish carpenter and taught his children to never cut corners. "If you're going to do a job, do it right the first time!"; He bought Egger's Fix-It Shop and reopened as Country Rose Antiques. Along with Rosie they spent many years traveling to antique shows, making a network of friends and dealers throughout the Northwest. Earl loved stream fishing and fostered in his children and grandchildren a love for the mountains, outdoors and camping. He was a member of the Southwest Carpenters Union and the Weapons Collector's Society of MT. **EDNA MAE CLARK** [3177] (1914 – 2010) daughter of Bernard and Anna (Stuckey) Clarke married twice; first to Andrew Clinton Foster with whom she was mother of (1), later she married Alfred Leroy Bradbury. **EILEEN CLARK** Sixth great granddaughter of progenitor Nicholas Kegg. **ELIZABETH CLARK** Sixth great granddaughter of progenitor Nicholas Kegg. **ELIZABETH M. CLARK** (1895 – 1967) daughter of Lewis and Mary (Rice) Clark, married Albert Noah Fassler with whom she was mother of (5). **ELLEN AUGUSTA CLARK** [3178] (1909 – 1981) daughter of Albert and Mary (Mess) Clark, married Glenn H. Bierwirth with whom she was mother of (5). Ellen was a member of Peoria First Church of the Brethren and taught Sunday school there for 32 years. **ELLIOT EUGENE CLARK** Sixth great grandson of progenitor Nicholas Kegg. **EMERSYN CLARK** Seventh great grandson of progenitor Nicholas Kegg. **ERIN CLARK** Seventh great grandson of progenitor Nicholas Kegg. **FRED L. CLARK** Sixth great grandson of progenitor Nicholas Kegg. **GALE D. CLARK** [3178A] (1938 – 2020) son of Hulbert and Thelma (Diehl) Clark was father of (4). Later, he married Susan Watkins. Gale served in the US Navy. He was employed by the NH State Liquor Outlet. **GAIL L. CLARK** Sixth great granddaughter of progenitor Nicholas Kegg. **GARY RANDOLPH CLARK** (1942 – 1988) son of Charles and Meda (Carr) Clark married Sharon Elizabeth Knotts. **GEORGE EDWARD CLARK** (1910 – 1990) son of Bernard and Anna (Stuckey) Clarke married Pauline Elizabeth Martin with whom he was father of (2). **GLORIA CAROLYN CLARK** Sixth great granddaughter of progenitor Nicholas Kegg. **GRACE RENEE CLARK** Seventh great granddaughter of progenitor Nicholas Kegg. **HAROLD ALAN CLARK** [3178B] aka "Mike" (1936 – 2013) son of George and Pauline (Martin) Clark married Janice Yvonne Mills with whom he was father of (3). He married Carolyn Virginia Garner with whom he was father of (1). Mike was a Construction Manager at BF Saul Co. and JC Penney. He was a member of the Lion's Club, Toastmaster's, and Iron-worker Local 568. **HARRY JAMES CLARK** [3179] (1892 – 1957) son of Lewis and Mary (Rice) Clark, married Edith Mae Hebb with whom he was father of (6). **HULBERT KENNETH CLARK** [3180] (1931 – 2004) son of Hulbert and Irene (Diehl) Clark, married Della R. Nave with whom he was father of (4). Hulbert was a member of St. John's United Church of Christ, Bedford, a graduate of Bedford High School, class of 1950, past member of (USTA (United States Trotters Association) and PHHA (Pa. Harnes Horse Assoc.). **INEZ CLARK** (1872 – 1873) daughter of Lewis and Mary (Rice) Clark. **INFANT CLARK** daughter of Dolphy and Orpha (Williams) Clark. **INFANT CLARK** son of Harry and Edith (Hebb) Clark. **JAMES ALTON CLARK** Fifth great

---

[3175] The Blue Hill Leader (NB) Oct 15, 1937 [3176] Great Falls Tribune (NE) Feb. 2, 2020 [3177] The News (MD) Nov 27, 2010 [3178] p19 Journal Star (Peoria, Illinois) Aug 10, 1981 [3178A] Caledonian Record (NH) Oct 13, 2020 [3178B] The Frederick News-Post (MD) Aug. 19, 2013 [3179] The Blue Hill Leader (NB) Feb 6, 1957 [3180] Bedford Inquirer (PA) Sept 19, 2004, obtained by Bob Rose

grandson of progenitor Nicholas Kegg.   **JAMIE L. CLARK** Seventh great granddaughter of progenitor Nicholas Kegg.   **JENNIFER LYNN CLARK** Seventh great granddaughter of progenitor Nicholas Kegg.   **JEREMIAH CLARK** Seventh great grandson of progenitor Nicholas Kegg.   **JEREMY LYNN CLARK** Seventh great grandson of progenitor Nicholas Kegg.   **JESSE CLARK** Sixth great grandson of progenitor Nicholas Kegg.   **JOANN CLARK** Sixth great granddaughter of progenitor Nicholas Kegg.   **JOHN CLARK** Sixth great grandson of progenitor Nicholas Kegg.
JOHN RICHARD CLARK (1919 – 1980) son of Bernard and Annie (Stuckey) Clarke, married Effie A. Nelson.   **K. RICK CLARK** Sixth great grandson of progenitor Nicholas Kegg.
KAITLYN VICTORIA CLARK Eighth great granddaughter of progenitor Nicholas Kegg.
KEITH CLARK Seventh great grandson of progenitor Nicholas Kegg.   **KENNETH CLARK** Fifth great grandson of progenitor Nicholas Kegg.   **KENNETH RICKEY CLARK** Sixth great grandson of progenitor Nicholas Kegg.   **KENNETH RILEY CLARK** (1907 – 1990) son of Albert and Mary (Mess) Clark, married Lola Fay Mischler with whom he was father of (4).   **KENT CLARK** Seventh great grandson of progenitor Nicholas Kegg.   **KEVIN DALE CLARK** Sixth great grandson of progenitor Nicholas Kegg.   **LACEY RANAE CLARK** Sixth great granddaughter of progenitor Nicholas Kegg.
LAURA E. CLARK Seventh great granddaughter of progenitor Nicholas Kegg.
LAVERNE DEAN CLARK [3181] (1928 – 2001) son of Harry and Edith (Hebb) Clark married Ida Arlene Morris with whom he was father of (2). Laverne was stationed in Korea while serving in the U.S. Navy. A longtime Kearney resident and devoted patron of community arts, Laverne benefits the University of Nebraska Foundation with a $600,000 permanent endowment named the Lavern Clark Memorial Vocal Scholarship Fund to provide annual scholarships for undergraduates studying vocal music.
LESLIE LELAND CLARK (1919 – 2014) son of Albert and Mary (Mess) Clark, married Helen Elizabeth (Schaeffel) Wilson with whom he was father of (4). A WWII veteran, Leslie served in the U.S. Navy.   **LESLIE LELAND CLARK** Fifth great grandson of progenitor Nicholas Kegg.
LEWIS HERMAN CLARK (1916 – 1997) son son of Albert and Mary (Mess) Clark married twice, first to Ella Mae Pledger with whom he was father of (1). Later, he married Pauline Celeste (Sigler) Park.
LINCY RANAE CLARK Sixth great granddaughter of progenitor Nicholas Kegg.
LINDA CLARK Sixth great granddaughter of progenitor Nicholas Kegg.   **LINDA ANN CLARK** (1944 – 1988) daughter of Lewis and Ella (Pledger) Clark.   **LINDSAY YVONNE CLARK** Sixth great granddaughter of progenitor Nicholas Kegg.   **LOAN CLARK** Fifth great granddaughter of progenitor Nicholas Kegg.   **LYNN RAYMOND CLARK** Sixth great grandson of progenitor Nicholas Kegg.
MACKENZIE CLARK Seventh great granddaughter of progenitor Nicholas Kegg.
MADALYNNE CLARK Seventh great granddaughter of progenitor Nicholas Kegg.
MALA LOUISE CLARK Sixth great granddaughter of progenitor Nicholas Kegg.
MARGARET ELEANORA CLARK [3182] (1915 – 2004) daughter of Bernard and Anna (Stuckey) Clarke married three times, first to John Arthur Wilhelm with whom she was mother of (1). She married Harry L. Culp and, Oliver Gladwyn Lewis. Margaret had done electronics assembly work for MD Electronic and Litton Industries, College Park. She was an avid Bingo player, who also enjoyed bowling and Orioles baseball games.   **MARK STEVEN CLARK** (1955 – 1975) son of Marvin and Carlene (Samford) Clark.   **MARLINA MICHELLE CLARK** Sixth great granddaughter of progenitor Nicholas Kegg.   **MARVIN DEAN CLARK** [3183] (1932 – 2005) son of Kenneth and Lola (Mischler) Clark married twice, first to Carlene M. Samford with whom he was father of (3). Later, he married DeLinda Jane Breau. Marvin served our country in the Air Force and as an air traffic controller for the FAA.
MARY MYRTLE CLARK [3184] (1911 – 1985) aka "Myrtle", daughter of Albert and Mary (Mess) Clark, married Carol Dwight Diefenderfer with whom she was mother of (6).   **MELANIE CLARK** Seventh great granddaughter of progenitor Nicholas Kegg.   **MELISSA JO CLARK** Sixth great granddaughter of progenitor Nicholas Kegg.   **MELVIN GRANT CLARK** [3185] (1958 – 1995) son of Melvin and Nancy (Yates) Clark married Gayle Merlene Kline. A graduate of the University of North

---

[3181] Nebraska University Foundation.org [3182] Upchurch Funeral Home (MD) [3183] Prescott Daily Courier (AZ) Dec 11, 2005 [3184] The Folsom Telegraph (CA) Nov 20, 1985 [3185] Roanoke Times (VA) Dec. 12, 1995

Florida, Melvin was employed by the City of Jacksonville as an Engineer. **MICHAEL A. CLARK** Sixth great grandson of progenitor Nicholas Kegg. **MICHAEL D. CLARK** Sixth great grandson of progenitor Nicholas Kegg. **MICHAEL MARVIN CLARK** Sixth great grandson of progenitor Nicholas Kegg. **MILES E. CLARK** Fifth great grandson of progenitor Nicholas Kegg. **MYRTIE CLARK** (1891 – 1891) daughter of Lewis and Mary (Rice) Clark. **NATALIE SUE CLARK** Sixth great granddaughter of progenitor Nicholas Kegg. **NELSON CLARK** Seventh great grandson of progenitor Nicholas Kegg. **OLIVE ELIZABETH CLARK** [3186] (1911 – 1995) daughter of Bernard and Anna (Stuckey) Clarke, married Joseph Stanley Stogdale with whom she was mother of (4). Olive had been a cafeteria manager for the Prince George's County schools. **PAUL A. CLARK** (1903 – 1961) son of Dolphus and Orpha (Williams) Clark. **PHYLLIS MARIE CLARK** [3187] (1914 – 1951) daughter of Forrest and Bernice (Border) Clark, married Judge Arnold Benard Britton with whom she was mother of (3). **RANDY ALLEN CLARK** Sixth great grandson of progenitor Nicholas Kegg. **REBECCA LEE CLARK** Seventh great granddaughter of progenitor Nicholas Kegg. **RICHARD LEE CLARK**, Sixth great grandson of progenitor Nicholas Kegg. **RICHARD P. CLARK** Sixth great grandson of progenitor Nicholas Kegg. **RITA MARILYN CLARK** Fifth great granddaughter of progenitor Nicholas Kegg. **ROBERT CLARK** Sixth great grandson of progenitor Nicholas Kegg. **ROBERT G. CLARK** Sixth great grandson of progenitor Nicholas Kegg. **ROBERT WILBUR CLARK** (1943 – 1990) son of Robert and Edna (Hale) Clark married Sharlene Yvette (Boyd) Gilham. **ROBIN C. CLARK** Sixth great granddaughter of progenitor Nicholas Kegg. **RONALD GERALD CLARK** [3188] (1943 – 2003) son of Gerald and Nellie (Dibert) Clark. Ronald served in the U.S. Navy during the Vietnam War as an electronics technician on the U.S.S. Constellation. A graduate of Everett Southern Joint High School, he also earned his Bachelor of Science in Business Administration from Defiance College in Defiance, Ohio. He was then employed as office manager at Gerald W. Clark Well Drilling and Pumps in Everett, until he and his brother Randy became partners in the business, taking over day to day operations in 1989. Mr. Clark was a member of Everett American Legion, Post #8 and the Breezewood VW Post #8333. **RUTH CLARK** Sixth great granddaughter of progenitor Nicholas Kegg.
SANDRA FAY CLARK Fifth great granddaughter of progenitor Nicholas Kegg.
SEWELL KENNETH CLARK (1930 – 1930) son of Hulbert and Irene (Diehl) Clark.
SHARON LYNNETTE CLARK Sixth great granddaughter of progenitor Nicholas Kegg.
SHELLY ROSE CLARK Sixth great granddaughter of progenitor Nicholas Kegg.
SHIRLEY BERNICE CLARK Fifth great granddaughter of progenitor Nicholas Kegg.
TAYLOR CLARK Eighth great granddaughter of progenitor Nicholas Kegg.
TERRY LYNN CLARK Fifth great grandson of progenitor Nicholas Kegg. **THOMAS CLARK** Sixth great grandson of progenitor Nicholas Kegg. **TIMOTHY M. CLARK** Sixth great grandson of progenitor Nicholas Kegg. **TINA CLARK** Sixth great granddaughter of progenitor Nicholas Kegg. **TOM CLARK** Sixth great grandson of progenitor Nicholas Kegg. **TONYA CLARK** Sixth great granddaughter of progenitor Nicholas Kegg. **TRACIE LYNN CLARK** Sixth great granddaughter of progenitor Nicholas Kegg. **TYLER CLARK** Seventh great grandson of progenitor Nicholas Kegg. **VALERIE CLARK** Fifth great granddaughter of progenitor Nicholas Kegg. **VIRGINIA EILEEN CLARK** [3189] (1934 – 2008) daughter of Kenneth and Lola (Mischler) Clark, married Melvin Lester James with whom she was mother of (1). Virginia retired after 25 years working in the office of the Medford K-Mart. **WENDY CLARK** Sixth great granddaughter of progenitor Nicholas Kegg.
WES CLARK Eighth great grandson of progenitor Nicholas Kegg. **WILLIE LEWIS CLARK** (1886 – 1892) son of Lewis and Mary (Rice) Clark. **WILMA JEAN CLARK** [3190] (1933 – 1933) daughter of Hulbert and Irene (Diehl) Clark. **WYLMA ELIZABETH CLARK** (1912 – 1994) daughter of Albert and Mary (Mess) Clark was mother of (1). She married Frederick N. Pfister.

[3186] pA5 - The News (MD) Dec 28, 1995 [3187] The Oklahoma County Register (OK) May 3, 1951 [3188] pg. 3 - Bedford Inquirer (PA) June 20, 2003, obtained by Bob Rose [3189] Medford Mail Tribune (OR) May 29, 2008 [3190] Bedford County Historical Society (PA), book 134, p 3 obtained by D. Sue Dible

CLARKE

DONA LEE CLARKE Fifth great granddaughter of progenitor Nicholas Kegg. **ELIZABETH CLARKE** (abt 1914 -?) daughter of Harry and Freda (Heffner) Clarke. **HARRY AUSTIN CLARKE** [3191] (1918 – 1966) son of Harry and Freda (Heffner) Clarke, married Verna Irene Brecht. Harry was an employee of Joseph Horne Co. Harry was a member of the Horne's Executive Men's Club, the Geter C. Shidle Masonic Lodge No. 650, and was a former member of the Ancient Accepted Scottish Rite Lodge, Valley of Pittsburgh. **MARSHA LYNN CLARKE** [3192] (1942 – 2021) daughter of Harry and Verna (Brecht) Clarke married Capt. John William Bonnett with whom she was mother of (2). "Be brave, be kind, be strong." Those were the words Marsha Lynn Bonnett lived by up until her passing. Marsha travelled frequently from coast to coast as a Navy spouse and visited many parts of the world. While in Coronado, Marsha worked for the Coronado Unified School District in various roles for 27 years. She loved her job working with children and their families, and she watched generations of Coronadoans attend kindergarten through high school and their children do the same. She made lifelong friends in Coronado -- through her School District work, her involvement as a Navy spouse, and her wonderful outgoing, generous, and compassionate personality. **LESLIE MICHELS CLARKE** Fifth great granddaughter of progenitor Nicholas Kegg.

CLAY

CHERYL CLAY Fifth great granddaughter of progenitor Nicholas Kegg. **EMMA FRANCES CLAY** (1907 – 1989) daughter of John and Catherine (Hillegass) Clay, married Paul Louise Stipp. **HENRY WARD CLAY** [3193] (1902 – 1947) son of John and Catherine (Hillegass) Clay, married Mildred Walker with whom he was father of (4). Henry was killed after falling from a pole, while working as a lineman for the Scranton Electric Company. **JOHN HENRY CLAY** [3194] (1929 – 1992) aka "Jack", son of Henry and Mildred (Walker) Clay, married Jean Marie Robson with whom he was father of (4). Jack was employed as a painter at the John F. Kennedy Medical Center. Prior to that, he was a production manager for Scientific Components, Linden. Jack was a member of the Metuchen Elks and was past exalted ruler of the Colonia Elks. **JOYCE CLAY** Fifth great granddaughter of progenitor Nicholas Kegg. **MADELINE FRANCIS CLAY** Fourth great granddaughter of progenitor Nicholas Kegg. **MADOLYN JENNIE CLAY** (born abt. 1897) daughter of John and Catherine (Hillegass) Clay, married Albert John Kauffman. **MARIE LOUISE CLAY** [3195] (1927 – 1978) daughter of Henry and Mildred (Walker) Clay, married Joseph W. Gillespie with whom she was mother of (3). Marie was employed at Crescent Lodge, Paradise Valley. Prior to that, she worked at Uguccioni's Restaurant, Mountainhome. **MILDRED CLAY** [3196] (1931 – 2009) aka "Millie", daughter of Henry and Mildred (Walker) Clay, married William J. Halligan with whom she was mother of (1). Millie was formerly employed with the Hayne & Co. Department Store in NJ and DiChello Distributors. **PATRICIA ANN CLAY** [3197] (1950 – 2000) daughter of John and Jean (Robson) Clay, married Joseph George Borgquist with whom she was mother of (6). Mr. and Mrs. Borgquist died from injuries suffered in an automobile accident on the Garden State Parkway. **SALLY CLAY** Fifth great granddaughter of progenitor Nicholas Kegg.

CLAYCOMB

CAROLANN CLAYCOMB Sixth great granddaughter of progenitor Nicholas Kegg. **D. SCOTT CLAYCOMB** Sixth great grandson of progenitor Nicholas Kegg. **ERICA CLAYCOMB** Seventh great granddaughter of progenitor Nicholas Kegg. **LUANN CLAYCOMB** Sixth great granddaughter of progenitor Nicholas Kegg. **RACHAEL CLAYCOMB** Sixth great granddaughter of progenitor Nicholas Kegg.

[3191] The Pittsburgh Press (PA) Oct 27, 1966 [3192] Coronado Eagle & Journal (CA) Oct 6, 2021 [3193] The Times-Tribune (Scranton, PA) Dec 4, 1947 [3194] Asbury Park Press (NJ) April 29, 1992 [3195] The Tribune (Scranton, PA) Sep 25, 1978 [3196] p B5 - New Haven Register (CT) Oct 11, 2009 [3197] p39 - Star-Ledger (Newark, NJ) June 15, 2000

CLAYPOOL

JAMES DAVID CLAYPOOL (1963 – 1963) son of Dennis and Verna Merle (Fash) Claypool.
LOGAN MICHAEL CLAYPOOL Eighth great grandson of progenitor Nicholas Kegg.
MELISSA JOANN CLAYPOOL Seventh great granddaughter of progenitor Nicholas Kegg.
MICHAEL DENNIS CLAYPOOL Seventh great grandson of progenitor Nicholas Kegg.
MORGAN RENE CLAYPOOL Eighth great granddaughter of progenitor Nicholas Kegg.
ZACHARY ALLEN CLAYPOOL Eighth great grandson of progenitor Nicholas Kegg.

CLAYTON

DUSTIN J. CLAYTON Seventh great grandson of progenitor Nicholas Kegg. **JILL WINIFRED CLAYTON** Sixth great granddaughter of progenitor Nicholas Kegg. **JULIE CLAYTON** Seventh great granddaughter of progenitor Nicholas Kegg. **KIRK WESLEY CLAYTON** Sixth great grandson of progenitor Nicholas Kegg. **LAUREN CLAYTON** Sixth great granddaughter of progenitor Nicholas Kegg. **LYNETTE SUE CLAYTON**[3198] (1956 – 2012) daughter of William and Shirley (Scritchfield) Clayton, married Paul A. Fitzgerald. A veteran of the Army Reserve, she had been employed by the Military Entrance Processing Station, Pittsburgh. Lynette enjoyed needlepoint and collecting spoons. **SHERRIE CLAYTON** Sixth great granddaughter of progenitor Nicholas Kegg. **WILLA CLAYTON** Seventh great granddaughter of progenitor Nicholas Kegg. **WILLIAM CLAYTON** Sixth great grandson of progenitor Nicholas Kegg.

CLEAR

HEATHER CLEAR Fifth great granddaughter of progenitor Nicholas Kegg. **KASEY CLEAR** Fifth great granddaughter of progenitor Nicholas Kegg. **KATHERINE CLEAR** Fifth great granddaughter of progenitor Nicholas Kegg. **KELLY CLEAR** Fifth great grandson of progenitor Nicholas Kegg. **KELSEY CLEAR** Fifth great granddaughter of progenitor Nicholas Kegg. **KERRY CLEAR** Fifth great grandson of progenitor Nicholas Kegg. **KEVINA CLEAR** Fifth great granddaughter of progenitor Nicholas Kegg. **KIMBERLY CLEAR** Fifth great granddaughter of progenitor Nicholas Kegg. **KRISTEN CLEAR** Fifth great granddaughter of progenitor Nicholas Kegg.

CLEAVENGER

BRETT CLEAVENGER Fifth great grandson of progenitor Nicholas Kegg.

CLEGG

DAN CLEGG Seventh great grandson of progenitor Nicholas Kegg.
NICK CLEGG Seventh great grandson of progenitor Nicholas Kegg.

CLEMENS

SARAH CLEMENS Sixth great granddaughter of progenitor Nicholas Kegg.
SCOTT CLEMENS Sixth great grandson of progenitor Nicholas Kegg.

[3198] Dunmire-Kerr & Rowe Funeral Home, Inc., (PA)

CLEMONS

KAYLEE CLEMONS Sixth great granddaughter of progenitor Nicholas Kegg.
TERRY R. CLEMONS Sixth great grandson of progenitor Nicholas Kegg.

CLEVELAND

MARY LOUISE CLEVELAND Fifth great granddaughter of progenitor Nicholas Kegg.

CLINE

DANIEL CLINE Seventh great grandson of progenitor Nicholas Kegg.
DORIS ELIZABETH CLINE [3198A] (1912 – 2009) daughter of Wesley and Clara (Knouf) Cline, married Clarence Edwin Strickland with whom she was mother of (3). Doris was a wonderful cook and used that talent at her jobs in the Anita School lunch programs for 20 years. She was head cook there for several years, until 1974. She was the lead cook at Colonial Manor when it first opened. Doris will be remembered by her family and friends for her specialization in apple pies and cinnamon rolls. Following a farm accident, Doris took loving care of her husband Clarence for forty years. After she retired, she kept busy with her special interests that included fishing, gardening and her pets. She loved baby animals and raised many of them. She was a past president of the Anita Garden Club.   **FRANKIE B. CLINE** (1867 – 1873) son of Daniel and Harriet (Kegg) Cline/Kline.   **MICHAEL CLINE** Seventh great grandson of progenitor Nicholas Kegg.

CLINGERMAN

JOSHUA L. CLINGERMAN Seventh great grandson of progenitor Nicholas Kegg.
SHAWN CLINGERMAN Seventh great grandson of progenitor Nicholas Kegg.
SHELLY CLINGERMAN Seventh great granddaughter of progenitor Nicholas Kegg.
SLOAN CHARLES CLINGERMAN Seventh great grandson of progenitor Nicholas Kegg.

CLOUD

TYLER ROBERT CLOUD Ninth great grandson of progenitor Nicholas Kegg.

COATES

LARRY ARTHUR COATES (1929 – 1967) son of Gene and Emma (Sanders) Coates married and divorced Hilla (nee unknown).

COBB

AMANDA LYNN COBB Ninth great granddaughter of progenitor Nicholas Kegg.   **IVAN COBB** Ninth great grandson of progenitor Nicholas Kegg.   **SYLVESTER COBB** Ninth great grandson of progenitor Nicholas Kegg.

COCKLIN

JANELLE RANEE COCKLIN Sixth great granddaughter of progenitor Nicholas Kegg.

[3198A] Roland Funeral Service (IA)

CODY

BILLY CODY Eighth great grandson of progenitor Nicholas Kegg. **CHRISTY CODY** Seventh great granddaughter of progenitor Nicholas Kegg. **EMILY CODY** Eighth great granddaughter of progenitor Nicholas Kegg. **JOHN CODY** Seventh great grandson of progenitor Nicholas Kegg. **MATTHEW CODY** Eighth great grandson of progenitor Nicholas Kegg.

COE

TORREY COE Seventh great granddaughter of progenitor Nicholas Kegg.
WYATT COE Seventh great grandson of progenitor Nicholas Kegg.

COEY

CASSANDRA D. COEY Seventh great grandson of progenitor Nicholas Kegg.
COURTNEY MARIE COEY Seventh great granddaughter of progenitor Nicholas Kegg.
FRED STEVEN COEY Sixth great grandson of progenitor Nicholas Kegg.
GARY ALLISON COEY Sixth great grandson of progenitor Nicholas Kegg.
GENE MICHAEL COEY Sixth great grandson of progenitor Nicholas Kegg.
JUSTIN ANDREW COEY Seventh great grandson of progenitor Nicholas Kegg.
ROY WESTLEY COEY [3199] (1952 – 2008) aka "Mike", son of Roy and Gladys (Bowers) Coey. Roy was a member of Fairfield Christian Church and was a former member of the Greenfield Township Fire Department.

COGGER

JESSE COGGER Seventh great grandson of progenitor Nicholas Kegg. **LINETTE COGGER** Seventh great granddaughter of progenitor Nicholas Kegg. **STEPHANIE COGGER** Eighth great granddaughter of progenitor Nicholas Kegg.

COFFIELD

COLIN COFFIELD Sixth great grandson of progenitor Nicholas Kegg. **KENZIE COFFIELD** Sixth great granddaughter of progenitor Nicholas Kegg. **OCTAVIA JADE COFFIELD** Seventh great granddaughter of progenitor Nicholas Kegg.

COFFLAND

KINSLEY BRYN COFFLAND Eighth great granddaughter of progenitor Nicholas Kegg.

COFFMAN

ALLEN BLAINE COFFMAN Fifth great grandson of progenitor Nicholas Kegg. **ANJI COFFMAN** Sixth great granddaughter of progenitor Nicholas Kegg. **BERNARD EARL COFFMAN** Fourth great grandson of progenitor Nicholas Kegg. **BRIAN A. COFFMAN** Fifth great grandson of progenitor Nicholas Kegg. **BRIAN ROY COFFMAN** Sixth great grandson of progenitor Nicholas Kegg. **CALVIN WOODROW COFFMAN** [3200] (1925 – 1992) son of Daniel and Gladys (Westfall) Coffman, married Betty Louise Lamphere with whom he was father of (5). Calvin was a World War II veteran and a salesman for Langendorf Bakery. He was a member of the American Legion Mt. Lassen Post 167 of

---

[3199] Columbus Dispatch (OH) Jan 5, 2008 [3200] Redding Record Searchlight (CA) July 17, 1992

Red Bluff and the International Brotherhood of Teamsters Local 167. **CATHERINE GRACE COFFMAN** Sixth great granddaughter of progenitor Nicholas Kegg. **CHACE COFFMAN** Eighth great grandson of progenitor Nicholas Kegg. **CHARLES COFFMAN** Third great grandson of progenitor Nicholas Kegg. **CHRISTINE ELIZABETH COFFMAN** Sixth great granddaughter of progenitor Nicholas Kegg. **CLEATUS DANIEL COFFMAN** (1920 – 1989) aka "Dan", son of Daniel and Gladys (Westfall) Coffman, married Gladys Pauline Lipsey with whom he was father of (7).
CLEO LUCILE COFFMAN (1918 – 1946) daughter of Daniel and Gladys (Westfall) Coffman.
CLIFFORD LAYTON COFFMAN [3201] (1911 – 1996) son of Roscoe and Emma (Beachler) Coffman, married Florence Esther Yorgason with whom he was father of (4). Clifford was employed as the maintenance man for the utilities division of Fort Ord. **CYNTHIA LOUISE COFFMAN** Sixth great granddaughter of progenitor Nicholas Kegg. **DANIEL COFFMAN** Seventh great grandson of progenitor Nicholas Kegg. **DANIEL SCOTT COFFMAN** Fifth great grandson of progenitor Nicholas Kegg. **DAVID LEE COFFMAN** Sixth great grandson of progenitor Nicholas Kegg.
DEANNA LYNN COFFMAN Fifth great granddaughter of progenitor Nicholas Kegg.
DEBORAH SUSANNE COFFMAN Sixth great granddaughter of progenitor Nicholas Kegg.
DONNA JEAN COFFMAN Sixth great granddaughter of progenitor Nicholas Kegg.
DOROTHY A. COFFMAN (1913 - 2001) daughter of George and Florence (Burns) Coffman, married Mr. Patterson. **EDWARD DANIEL COFFMAN** Fifth great grandson of progenitor Nicholas Kegg.
ELIZABETH COFFMAN [3202] (1918 – 1992) aka "Betty", daughter of George and Florence (Burns) Coffman, married Greydon Pierce Milam with whom she was mother of (3). Betty was a teacher of art at Modesto High School. Reproductions of work done by her students were used in Art In American Schools, a book published by a New York paint company. Her biography appears in The 1938 edition of Who's Who In American Art and, the 1940 edition of Leading Women Of America, published by the Authors International Publishing Company of New York. **ERIC JON COFFMAN** Sixth great grandson of progenitor Nicholas Kegg. **EVA AMELIA COFFMAN** [3203] (1917 – 1999) daughter of Daniel and Gladys (Westfall) Coffman, married Lloyd Clarence Boyes with whom she was mother of (3). Eva graduated from Pierce High School in Arbuckle and attended Healers Business College in Sacramento. She and her husband owned a record store in Colusa and managed a lodge in Grants Pass, Ore. They also built and ran a tarpon fishing lodge in Costa 'Rica for seven years before returning to the Mid-Valley. She was a member and choir member of the Methodist Church in Colusa.
GERALDINE MARIE COFFMAN Fourth great granddaughter of progenitor Nicholas Kegg.
GERTRUDE JEANETTE COFFMAN [3204] (1921 – 2011) daughter of Daniel and Gladys (Westfall) Coffman, married James Henry Bussell with whom she was mother of (4). During her lifetime, she lived in California, Montana, Missouri and North Dakota where her husband's work took them. Having various jobs during her life, she especially loved working as a teacher's aide in local pre-schools. She will be remembered for her kind, compassionate ways, for her diligent work in making so many camping trips to the mountains and beach a great success; for her skills in the kitchen and home; for helping her children graduate from college; for her humor and liveliness in many a spirited conversation; and for her courage, honesty and integrity in so many ways. **HAROLD EUGENE COFFMAN** [3205] (1931 – 1998) son of Daniel and Gladys (Westfall) Coffman was a patrolman for the California Highway Patrol.
JAMES CLIFFORD COFFMAN Fifth great grandson of progenitor Nicholas Kegg.
JAMES MICHAEL COFFMAN Sixth great grandson of progenitor Nicholas Kegg.
JARED COFFMAN Seventh great grandson of progenitor Nicholas Kegg.
JASON RON COFFMAN Sixth great grandson of progenitor Nicholas Kegg. **JAYLIN COFFMAN** Seventh great granddaughter of progenitor Nicholas Kegg. **KEITH CLIFFORD COFFMAN** Sixth great grandson of progenitor Nicholas Kegg. **KYLE CALVIN COFFMAN** Fifth great grandson of progenitor Nicholas Kegg. **KYLE GEOFFRY COFFMAN** Sixth great grandson of progenitor Nicholas Kegg. **LAURA LOUISE COFFMAN** Fifth great granddaughter of progenitor Nicholas Kegg

---

[3201] Sacramento Bee (CA) Apr 25, 1941 [3202] Modesto Bee (CA) May 6, 1940 [3203] Appeal Democrat (CA) Aug 25, 1999 [3204] Sacramento Bee (CA) Jan. 1, 2012 [3205] The Fresno Bee (CA) March 13, 1998

LEANNE COFFMAN Fifth great granddaughter of progenitor Nicholas Kegg. **LORNA FLORENCE COFFMAN** Fifth great granddaughter of progenitor Nicholas Kegg. **LYLEE COFFMAN** Eighth great granddaughter of progenitor Nicholas Kegg. **MARCIA ANN COFFMAN** Sixth great granddaughter of progenitor Nicholas Kegg. **MARK J. COFFMAN** Fifth great grandson of progenitor Nicholas Kegg. **MELISSA KAY COFFMAN** Sixth great granddaughter of progenitor Nicholas Kegg. **MICHAEL ALAN COFFMAN** Fifth great grandson of progenitor Nicholas Kegg. **MICHAEL THOMAS COFFMAN** Sixth great grandson of progenitor Nicholas Kegg. **NORENE MABEL COFFMAN** [3206] (1943 – 2006) daughter of Clifford and Florence (Yorgason) Coffman, married George Harry Siller with whom she was mother of (5). Norene was a social worker for the Sutter County Employment Service office. She was a member The Church of Jesus Christ of Latter-day Saints. **PAULA ANN COFFMAN** Fifth great granddaughter of progenitor Nicholas Kegg. **PEARL MARY COFFMAN** (1884 – 1931) daughter of George and Helen (Cagg) Coffman, married Harvey Jacob Wonderly with whom she was mother of (3). **ROBERT A. COFFMAN** aka "Bob", Fifth great grandson of progenitor Nicholas Kegg. **ROBERT EDWARD COFFMAN** Sixth great grandson of progenitor Nicholas Kegg. **ROBERT NEIL COFFMAN** Fifth great grandson of progenitor Nicholas Kegg. **ROSCOE O. COFFMAN** (1882 – 1996) son of George and Helen (Cagg) Coffman, married Grace Emma Beachler with whom he was father of (1). **RUBY ELSIE COFFMAN** (1887 – 1971) daughter of George and Helen (Cagg) Coffman, married Frank Aten Zong with whom she was mother of (3). **RYKER COFFMAN** Seventh great grandson of progenitor Nicholas Kegg. **SHAWN A. COFFMAN** Sixth great grandson of progenitor Nicholas Kegg. **SHIRLEY JUNE COFFMAN** (1934 – 1934) daughter of Edward and Audrey (Stone) Coffman. **STEVEN DENNIS COFFMAN** Fifth great grandson of progenitor Nicholas Kegg. **STEVEN KENT COFFMAN** Sixth great grandson of progenitor Nicholas Kegg. **THOMAS LEE COFFMAN**, (1880 – 1884) aka "Lee", son of George and Helen (Cagg) Coffman. **VERA PAULINE COFFMAN** [3206A] (1924 – 1989) daughter of James and Lucy (Barbour) Coffman, married Melvin Gilbert Tracy with whom she was mother of (4). Vera was a homemaker. **VICKIE COFFMAN** Fifth great granddaughter of progenitor Nicholas Kegg. **WENDY COFFMAN** Sixth great granddaughter of progenitor Nicholas Kegg. **WILMER WESTFALL COFFMAN** [3207] (1925 – 2022) son of Daniel and Gladys (Westfall) Coffman, married Eleze Butler with whom he was father of (2). Wilmer farmed until he was drafted into the United States Army, he was discharged in 1946, and returned to farming. He loved fishing and enjoyed gardening.

COHEN

SPENCER M. COHEN Sixth great grandson of progenitor Nicholas Kegg.
TYLER M. COHEN Sixth great grandson of progenitor Nicholas Kegg.

COK

ALYCIA L. COK Sixth great granddaughter of progenitor Nicholas Kegg. **BRADLEY JOHN COK** [3207A] (1956 – 2015) son of Arthur and Marilyn (Hershiser) Cok married twice, first to Patti Lavonne Spencer with whom he was father of (1). Later, he married Donna Jean Mahl with whom he was father of (6). Brad drove a truck and worked for CSX Railroad. He enjoyed singing, and sports including the Indians, Cavs, Browns and Ohio State. **CAYTLYN CIERRA COK** Sixth great granddaughter of progenitor Nicholas Kegg. **DAKOTA JEAN COK** Sixth great granddaughter of progenitor Nicholas Kegg. **DEAN A. COK** Fifth great grandson of progenitor Nicholas Kegg. **JACOB BRADLEY COK** aka Jake" Sixth great grandson of progenitor Nicholas Kegg. **KAREN SUE COK** Fifth great grand-daughter of progenitor Nicholas Kegg. **KYLEIGH N. COK** Sixth great granddaughter of progenitor Nicholas Kegg.

[3206] appeal-democrat (CA) Aug 2, 2006 [3206A] Wichita Eagle (KS) Nov10, 1989 [3207] Appeal Democrat (CA) Feb. 2, 2022 [3207A] Lindsey Kocher Funeral Services obtained and contributed by D. Sue Dible

LILY GISELLE COK [3208] (2007 – 2007) daughter of Shane and Daphney (Hall) Cok. **MELISSA COK** Sixth great granddaughter of progenitor Nicholas Kegg. **MIKAELA A. COK** Sixth great granddaughter of progenitor Nicholas Kegg. **RODNEY K. COK**, aka "Rod", Fifth great grandson of progenitor Nicholas Kegg. **SHANE B. COK** Sixth great grandson of progenitor Nicholas Kegg.

COLARIC

BETH ANN COLARIC Seventh great granddaughter of progenitor Nicholas Kegg.
TINA MARIE COLARIC Seventh great granddaughter of progenitor Nicholas Kegg.

COLE

GRIFFYN DRAKE COLE Eighth great grandson of progenitor Nicholas Kegg.
JUSTIN COLE Seventh great grandson of progenitor Nicholas Kegg.

COLEGROVE

ALLISON DANIELLE COLEGROVE Seventh great granddaughter of progenitor Nicholas Kegg.
EDWIN S. COLEGROVE Fifth great grandson of progenitor Nicholas Kegg.
EDWIN WAYNE COLEGROVE aka "Eddie", Seventh great grandson of progenitor Nicholas Kegg.
HEATHER W. COLEGROVE Seventh great granddaughter of progenitor Nicholas Kegg.
WAYNE EDWIN COLEGROVE [3208A] (1956 – 2012) son of Edwin and Helen (Schmoll) Colegrove married twice, first to Regina Gale Adkins with whom he was father of (1). Later, he married Leah Joan Funk with whom he was father of (2). Wayne worked as a painter for St. Gobain in Ravenna.

COLEMAN

AMY MICHELLE COLEMAN Sixth great granddaughter of progenitor Nicholas Kegg.
BONNIE LOU COLEMAN Fifth great granddaughter of progenitor Nicholas Kegg.
DIANNE LOUISE COLEMAN Fifth great granddaughter of progenitor Nicholas Kegg.
DOROTHY LOUISE COLEMAN aka "Dot", Sixth great granddaughter of progenitor Nicholas Kegg.
LINDA JEAN COLEMAN Fifth great granddaughter of progenitor Nicholas Kegg.
MARY ELIZABETH COLEMAN Sixth great granddaughter of progenitor Nicholas Kegg.
SARA BETH COLEMAN Sixth great granddaughter of progenitor Nicholas Kegg.
THOMAS COLEMAN Fifth great grandson of progenitor Nicholas Kegg.

COLLEDGE

ALTON B. COLLEDGE [3209] (1877 – 1896) son of Joseph and Ellen J. College. **AMY J. COLLEDGE** Sixth great granddaughter of progenitor Nicholas Kegg. **ANDREW JACKSON COLLEDGE** [3210] (1847 – 1911) son of Joseph and Sarah (Kegg) College, married Nancy Freidline with whom he was father of (1). **HAROLD FRANKLIN COLLEDGE** (1910 – 2009) son of J. Frank and Edith (Davis) College married twice, first to Judith V. Vanusen. Later he married Eva Josephine Feuerberg. **HELEN VIOLA COLLEDGE** [3210A] (1940 – 2014) daughter of Willard and Hazel (Beegle) Colledge, married Lawrence James Barnes with whom she was mother of (5). Helen retired from York Hospital. She was also a homemaker. She was a longtime member of Red Lion Bible Church. **JESSE C. COLLEDGE** Sixth great grandson of progenitor Nicholas Kegg. **JOSEPH W. COLLEDGE** [3211] (1849 – 1928) aka

---

[3208] Norwalk Reflector (OH) Aug 2007 [3208A] Akron Beacon Journal (OH) July 25, 2012 [3209] p5 Patriot (PA) March 2, 1896 [3210] Ligonier Echo (PA) May 17, 1911 [3210A] York Daily Record & York Dispatch (PA) Dec 12, 2014 [3211] Latrobe Bulletin (PA) Nov 8, 1928

"James", son of Joseph and Sarah (Kegg) College, married Ellen with whom he was father of (7).
MARGUERITE COLLEDGE (1901 – 1989) daughter of J. Frank and Edith (Davis) Colleg.
MARY AGNES COLLEDGE (1893 – 1899) daughter of Joseph and Ellen J. College.
MARY EMMA COLLEDGE [3211A] (1923 – 2008) daughter of Raymond and Lillian (Carnahan) Colledge, married Leslie Logan with whom she was mother of (2). Mary was a registered nurse at Cessna Plant in Hutchinson and later she was a homemaker. **MARY ERMA COLLEDGE** [3211B] (1902 – 1995) daughter of J. Frank and Edith (Davis) Colledge, married Dale P. Lewis with whom she was mother of (1). Irma was employed as a bank teller for many years and a member of First Baptist Church, Altoona.
MILLIE JOSEPHINE COLLEDGE (1876 – 1925) daughter of Andrew and Nancy (Freidline) Colledge, married Samuel M. Robbins with whom she was mother of (1).
NELLIE ROMAINE COLLEDGE (1887 – 1933) daughter of Joseph and Ellen J. Colledge, married twice, first to William Curtis Frayer with whom she was mother of (1). Later, she married Harry Benakis.
PEARL COLLEDGE [3212] (1880 – 1902) daughter of Joseph and Ellen J. College.
RAYMOND DAVIS COLLEDGE [3213] (1898 – 1926) son of J. Frank and Edith (Davis) College, married Lillian F. Carnahan with whom he was father of (1). Raymond killed his wife, Lillian, 21 years old, with a hammer in their home at Cokeville and then committed suicide. Three hours after the woman's body was found on a bed, police located College's body, locked in a cloths press. He had shot himself. Letters found in the house indicated that College was despondent because of illness. He wrote: "Lillian has said she was going to kill me, so I done it." **RICHARD COLLEDGE** Sixth great grandson of progenitor Nicholas Kegg. **SARAH EMMA COLLEDGE** (1884 - ?) aka "Sadie", daughter of Joseph and Ellen J. Colledge.

COLLEGE

J. FRANK COLLEGE [3214] (1873 – 1923) aka "Frank", son of Joseph and Ellen J. Colledge, married Edith L. Davis with whom he was father of (4). Frank held a clerical position in the freight office of the Pennsylvania Railroad Company for a number of years. He was a member of the Blairsville M. E. church.
MARY C. COLLEGE (1851 – 1922) daughter of Joseph and Sarah (Kegg) College married twice, first to John A. Flohr with whom she was mother of (7). Later, she married Archibald Owens.
SARAH MARGARET COLLEGE [3215] (1856 – 1909) daughter of Joseph and Sarah (Kegg) College, married John Finnie with whom she was mother of (1). Later she married William Jahn.

COLLINS

CATHY JEAN COLLINS Sixth great granddaughter of progenitor Nicholas Kegg.
ELIZABETH COLLINS Sixth great granddaughter of progenitor Nicholas Kegg.
JOHN L. COLLINS Sixth great grandson of progenitor Nicholas Kegg.
KIMBERLY KAY COLLINS Sixth great granddaughter of progenitor Nicholas Kegg.
LINDA COLLINS Sixth great granddaughter of progenitor Nicholas Kegg. **RANDAL COLLINS** Sixth great grandson of progenitor Nicholas Kegg. **SHERRY COLLINS** Sixth great granddaughter of progenitor Nicholas Kegg. **TAMARA LYNN COLLINS** "Tami", Sixth great granddaughter of progenitor Nicholas Kegg.

COLOMBO

BRANDY MAE COLOMBO Seventh great granddaughter of progenitor Nicholas Kegg.
JAMES LOUIS COLOMBO Seventh great grandson of progenitor Nicholas Kegg.
JAMIE LEE COLOMBO Seventh great granddaughter of progenitor Nicholas Kegg.

[3211A] The Hutchinson News (KS) - Sept 25, 2008 [3211B] p17 - Altoona Mirror (PA) Nov. 5, 1995 [3212] The Ligonier Echo (PA) Oct 15,1902 [3213] p8 - Indiana Weekly Messenger (PA) Apr 29, 1926 [3214] p4 - Indiana Weekly Messenger (PA) May 24, 1923 [3215] The Ligonier Echo (PA) Oct 20, 1909

LYDIA COLOMBO Seventh great granddaughter of progenitor Nicholas Kegg.
MADELINE COLOMBO Seventh great granddaughter of progenitor Nicholas Kegg.

COLPETZER

BRANDY RENE COLPETZER Sixth great granddaughter of progenitor Nicholas Kegg.
TRACY LYNN COLPETZER Sixth great granddaughter of progenitor Nicholas Kegg.

COLSON

CAROL SUE COLSON Sixth great granddaughter of progenitor Nicholas Kegg. **CHERYL COLSON** Sixth great granddaughter of progenitor Nicholas Kegg. **DAVID COLSON** Sixth great grandson of progenitor Nicholas Kegg. **DENNIS COLSON** Sixth great grandson of progenitor Nicholas Kegg. **JOSEPH E. COLSON** [3216] (1921 – 2007) aka "Joe" son of Joseph and Martha (Ambrosier) Colson, married Lawanda Richardson with whom he was father of (3). Joe was a World War II pilot and flew 35 combat missions as a B-24 aircraft commander and flight control officer in Italy in the 15th Air Force. He was reassigned to Long Beach Army Airfield and flew B-17s and C-54s delivering cargo to Great Falls, Mont. His military decorations include the Distinguished Flying Cross, Air Medal with four oak leaf clusters, two-unit citations and three campaign ribbons. In December 1945 Joe left the military service with the rank of captain. **LISA COLSON** Sixth great granddaughter of progenitor Nicholas Kegg.

COLVIN

CAITLYN COLVIN Seventh great granddaughter of progenitor Nicholas Kegg. **MICHAEL D. COLVIN** Sixth great grandson of progenitor Nicholas Kegg. **SCOTT JAMES COLVIN** Sixth great grandson of progenitor Nicholas Kegg. **TERRENCE COLVIN**, aka "Terry" Sixth great grandson of progenitor Nicholas Kegg.

COMBS

ALLEN CARL COMBS [3217] (1952 – 2010) aka "Big Al", son of Allen and Charlotte (Gardield) Combs. "Big Al" was an avid bowler and loved to shoot pool. He also played football, basketball and was a good pitcher and hitter in baseball. Al was also an excellent woodworker and liked to listen to his music, play pinochle, fish, and loved arts and crafts. He was brought up in church and read the Bible and prayed with his family and friends. He was a medical caregiver, part-time cook, and a member of the Fort Peck Indian Tribe. **AOUDA B. COMBS** (1892 – 1892) daughter of James and Persis (Walker) Combs. **BLANCHE COMBS** (1859 – 1914) daughter of Capt. James and Rebecca (Cagg) Combs. **BLANCHE C. COMBS** (1913 – 1960) daughter of John and Myrtle (Crocker) Combs, married Elmer L. Tuck. **BRIAN EDWARD COMBS** Seventh great grandson of progenitor Nicholas Kegg. **CADENCE COMBS** Eighth great granddaughter of progenitor Nicholas Kegg.
CATHLEEN LOUISE COMBS [3218] (1953 – 2005) daughter of Allen and Charlotte (Gardield) Combs married twice; first to Stanley Walter Cichocki with whom she was mother of (2). Later, she married Richard Lee Squire with whom she was mother of (1). Cathleen was a homemaker who enjoyed bowling, bingo and being with her family. She had served as a director of Indian affairs.
CHRISTIE ERIN COMBS [3218A] daughter of Jeffrey and Linda (Kill) Combs, married Robert J. Ferullo with whom she was mother of (2). She attended Word of Life Bible Institute and Tennessee Temple when she decided she wanted to work in women's ministry. She also took part in the children's ministry at

---

[3216] p.B13 - Fort Worth Star-Telegram Nov 28, 2007 [3217] Kitsap Sun (Bremerton, WA) Aug 27, 2010 [3218] Kitsap Sun (WA) March 8, 2005

Ridge Road Wesleyan Church. She was a collector of Barbie dolls and was considered a beautiful artist. Christie was a peacemaker; she never stopped encouraging people right up to the end. She got to know the people around her. She acknowledged their lives and made a point of letting them know that they were important to her. One could not help but know that the Lord was with her, as she lived her life to serve him. **CHRISTOPHER COMBS** Seventh great grandson of progenitor Nicholas Kegg. **DAVID R. COMBS** Sixth great grandson of progenitor Nicholas Kegg. **DEBBIE COMBS** Sixth great granddaughter of progenitor Nicholas Kegg. **DIANE LINVILLE COMBS** Sixth great granddaughter of progenitor Nicholas Kegg. **DONNA COMBS** Sixth great granddaughter of progenitor Nicholas Kegg. **DOREEN ELIZABETH COMBS** [3219] (1935 – 1998) daughter of Harry and Nelma (Helbig) Combs, married Mr. Cody with whom she was mother of (2). Doreen was employed as a bookkeeper. **DOROTHY R. COMBS** [3220] (1925 – 2005) aka "Dee", daughter of Herbert and Veda (Ragsdale) Combs, married John Wilkins Lohuis with whom she was mother of (3). Dee was widely regarded as one of the sweetest, kindest and most gentle souls one could ever meet. A beautiful woman who, without prejudice, enlightened everyone she met. Her spirit will enrich generations to come. **DWIGHT LAYTON COMBS** Sixth great grandson of progenitor Nicholas Kegg. **ELANA COMBS** Seventh great granddaughter of progenitor Nicholas Kegg. **ETHEL MADIA COMBS** (1893 – 1985) daughter of James and Persis (Walker) Combs, married Dr. Edwin Ruthven Willard with whom she was mother of (1); **GLENNA HULDA COMBS** (1887 – 1960) daughter of William and Elizabeth (Wilson) Combs, married John A. Karterman with whom she was mother of (1); **HARRY JOSEPH COMBS** Seventh great grandson of progenitor Nicholas Kegg; **HARRY WILSON COMBS** [3221] (1885 – 1971) son of William and Elizabeth (Wilson) Combs married twice; first to Zona Winona LeQuatte with whom he was father of (3). Later, he married Mary Eleanor West. **HELEN BLANCHE COMBS** (1882 – 1972) daughter of William and Elizabeth (Wilson) Combs, married Henry Robert Audley with whom she was mother of (2). **HERBERT LEE COMBS** [3222] (1891 – 1970) son of William and Elizabeth (Wilson) Combs, married Veda Mae Ragsdale with whom he was father of (4). **INFANT COMBS** (1896 – 1896) daughter of John and Myrtle (Crocker) Combs. **JAMES BIRD COMBS** [552] (1867 – 1931) aka "Bird", son of Capt. James and Rebecca (Cagg) Combs, married Persis Maola Walker with whom he was father of (3). A retired Seattle capitalist, Bird served for a number of years with the City Health Department and made investments in Seattle real estate. He was a member of Occidental Lodge No. 72, Free and Accepted Masons; past high priest of Ballard chapter No. 26, Royal Arch Masons, and Occidental Chapter No. 28, Order of Eastern Star. **JAMES BRADLEY COMBS** [3223] (1948 – 2011) aka "Brad", son of Herbert and Dorothy (Singer) Combs, married Suzanne Louise Martin. Brad served as a Sergeant with the U. S. Army HHC USA STRATCOM Europe Signal Group Med in Italy and as a Communication Center Specialist in Vietnam, he worked for Boeing as an Aerospace Mechanic and the Water Department. As a boy he was actively involved in the Boy Scouts of America. He was in charge of setting up Boy Scouts for the Trans-Atlantic Jamboree in Tuscany Italy while with the Army. April 2011 Brad retired from King County Department of Parks after 39½ years where he organized the "Turf Team" to build a quality landscape program for King County Parks. Some of his special projects included Seahurst Park's water walk area, Kenmore Park's Rhododendrons and helping renovate Vashon Island's old NE Wing Estate property. Brad will be remembered as an avid outdoorsmen fishing, hiking, camping and hunting. **JEFFREY G. COMBS** [3223A] (1954 – 2011) son of Hugh and Loreen (Woodward) Combs, married Linda Kill with whom he was father of (3). Jeff had been employed over the years at his father's business, Hugh Combs T.V., had his own catering business, and worked videotaping balloon rides at the Adirondack Balloon Festival. Jeff enjoyed camping, fishing and traveling with his family. He had a motorcycle, which he loved going for rides on. Jeff loved any form of electronics; when playing with his electronics, Jeff could be found watching TV. His favorite channel was the Food Network. Jeff loved cooking. Traits described by his

---

[3218A] Post Star (NY) July 9, 2006, obtained and contributed by D. Sue Dible [3219] Las Vegas Sun (NV) Sep 9, 1998 [3220] The Seattle Times (WA) Mar 7, 2005 [3221] p18 Seattle Daily Times (WA) June 23, 1971 [3222] p46 Seattle Daily Times (WA) June 22, 1970 [3223] Seattle Times (WA) Feb. 5, 2012 [3223A] Scott & Barbieri Family Funeral Home (NY)

family include good sense of humor, easy-going, sympathetic of others, good listener, and had a gentle heart. **JEFFREY KEITH COMBS** Seventh great grandson of progenitor Nicholas Kegg.
JOHN WESLEY COMBS (1863 - 1915) son of Capt. James and Rebecca (Cagg) Combs, married Myrtle Anna Crocker with whom he was father of (2). **KENNETH EDWIN COMBS** [3224] (1899 – 1967) son of William and Elizabeth (Wilson) Combs married four times; first to Lydia E. Griffith, then to Alleen Svarz. He married Henrietta Louise Dunbar and Irene Murchison. Kenneth was associated with the National Bank of Commerce 40 years. **KENNETH H. COMBS** Sixth great grandson of progenitor Nicholas Kegg. **KEVIN B. COMBS** Seventh great grandson of progenitor Nicholas Kegg. **KIMBERLY Y. COMBS** [3225] (1957 – 2001) daughter of Allen and Charlotte (Garfield) Combs, married James Dean Bunting with whom she was mother of (3). Kimberly was a homemaker. She enjoyed helping others. She was a member of the Assiniboine-Sioux Tribe and Hillcrest Assembly of God.
LARRY COMBS Sixth great grandson of progenitor Nicholas Kegg. **LAURIE COMBS** Sixth great granddaughter of progenitor Nicholas Kegg. **LOUISE D. COMBS** Seventh great granddaughter of progenitor Nicholas Kegg. **LUKE COMBS** Seventh great granddaughter of progenitor Nicholas Kegg. **MATTHEW COMBS** Seventh great grandson of progenitor Nicholas Kegg. **MICHELLE COMBS** Sixth great granddaughter of progenitor Nicholas Kegg. **PENELOPE COMBS**, aka "Penny", Sixth great granddaughter of progenitor Nicholas Kegg. **RALPH W. COMBS** (1894 – 1962) son of Sherman and Retta (Sperry) Combs, married Angelina B. Steele. **RANI R. COMBS** Seventh great granddaughter of progenitor Nicholas Kegg. **RONALD C. COMBS** [3225A] (1952 – 2012) son of Hugh and Loreen (Woodward) Combs, married Debbie Westerhold with whom he was father of (3). Ron worked with his dad when he was younger, in his TV repair shop, made custom furniture and had a passion for working on cars. He shared his enthusiasm for baseball by devoting countless hours of his time to coaching Little League in South Glens Falls and Luzerne. In his younger years, he raced his car at the South Glens Falls drag strip. Ron enjoyed cooking, fishing with his sons and spending time with his family. **RUTH E. COMBS** (1896 – 1981) daughter of William and Elizabeth (Wilson) Combs married twice; first to Ferdinand S. Hull. Later, she married Henry Joseph Seagroatt. **SABRINA E. COMBS** Seventh great granddaughter of progenitor Nicholas Kegg. **SANDY COMBS** Sixth great granddaughter of progenitor Nicholas Kegg. **SCOTT COMBS** Seventh great grandson of progenitor Nicholas Kegg. **SHERMAN GRANT COMBS** [3226] (1865 – 1925) son of Capt. James and Rebecca (Cagg) Combs, married Retta Jane Sperry with whom he was father of (1). Sherman was a Seattle building contractor. **SKYLER COMBS** Seventh great granddaughter of progenitor Nicholas Kegg.
SONYA RUTH COMBS Seventh great granddaughter of progenitor Nicholas Kegg.
STANLEY LEQUATTE COMBS (1908 – 1973) son of Harry and Zora (LeQuatte) Combs, married Aileen Dallwig with whom he was father of (2). Stanley was a professor of education, having earned his doctorate was well known for his lectures. **TANYA COMBS** Seventh great granddaughter of progenitor Nicholas Kegg. **TIMOTHY PAUL COMBS** Seventh great grandson of progenitor Nicholas Kegg.
VICTORIA COMBS Sixth great granddaughter of progenitor Nicholas Kegg.
VIRGINIA MERLE COMBS [3226A] (1918 – 2008) daughter of Herbert and Veda Mae (Ragsdale) Combs, married Aurlo A. Bonney with whom she was mother of (2). Virginia participated in numerous volunteer projects including Parent-Teacher Association meetings, School Masters' Wives Club, and Lions Club Vision Screening program. She was well known as a door-to-door fund raiser for various charities including the American Heart Association. Virginia was known by many for her love and kindness. She used her gift for service to others and modeled Christ-centered servant-leadership, not expecting recognition for her actions but affecting outcomes for the better, nonetheless.
WILBUR LAFAYETTE COMBS (1896 – 1974) son of William and Elizabeth (Wilson) Combs.

[3224] p86 Seattle Daily Times (WA) Dec 25, 1967 [3225] Kitsap Sun (Bremerton, WA) June 26, 2001 [3225A] Post Star (NY) Sep 9, 2012 [3226] p17 Seattle Daily Times (WA) May 5, 1925 [3226A] West Seattle Herald (WA) June 25, 2008

WILLIAM LAFAYETTE COMBS [3227, 3228] (1856 – 1946) aka "Lafe", son of Capt. James and Rebecca (Cagg) Combs, married Elizabeth Addie Wilson with whom he was father of (8). Lafe was a retired broker. He was a member of Seattle Lodge No. 92, B. P. O.E., and of the I. O. O. F. **ZACHARY COMBS** Seventh great grandson of progenitor Nicholas Kegg.

CONANT

ESTHER MAY CONANT [3229] (1928 – 2018) daughter of Paul and Clara (Knouf) Conant, married Ralph Edward Brown with whom she was mother of (2). Esther was a homemaker and was a member of Cottonwood Baptist Church. **INFANT CONANT** (1921 – 1921) daughter of Paul and Clara (Knouf) Conant.

CONDER

MCKENNA LEIGH CONDER Sixth great granddaughter of progenitor Nicholas Kegg.

CONIS

FOSTER CLAYTON CONIS Seventh great grandson of progenitor Nicholas Kegg.

CONLEY

DALTON CONLEY Seventh great grandson of progenitor Nicholas Kegg.
WALKER CONLEY Seventh great grandson of progenitor Nicholas Kegg.

CONN

HARRIET JOY CONN [3230] (1942 – 2001) daughter of William and Vivian (Edgar) Conn married Ronald Frank Bowles with whom she was mother of (2). She later married Michael J. McFarlane with whom she was mother of (1).

CONNELLY

JOHN CONNELLY Seventh great grandson of progenitor Nicholas Kegg. **JOSEPH CONNELLY** Seventh great grandson of progenitor Nicholas Kegg. **KATHERINE CONNELLY** Seventh great granddaughter of progenitor Nicholas Kegg. **MARY BRIDGET CONNELLY** Seventh great granddaughter of progenitor Nicholas Kegg. **MICHAEL CONNELLY** Seventh great grandson of progenitor Nicholas Kegg. **PATRICK CONNELLY** Seventh great grandson of progenitor Nicholas Kegg. **THOMAS CONNELLY** Seventh great grandson of progenitor Nicholas Kegg.

CONNER

BENTLEE RANDALL CONNER Seventh great grandson of progenitor Nicholas Kegg.
CHRISTINA BETH CONNER Fifth great granddaughter of progenitor Nicholas Kegg.
KATHY SUE CONNER [3230A] (1962 – 2012) daughter of Ronald and Violet (Cessna) Conner married Donald Barton with whom she was mother of (1). **MICHAEL ALLEN CONNER** Sixth great grandson of progenitor Nicholas Kegg. **PATRICK CONNER** Sixth great grandson of progenitor Nicholas Kegg. **RANDALL D. CONNER** [3231] (1963 – 2014) son of Curtis and Rosemary (Kingery) Conner, married Kimberly A. Myers. **RANDALL SCOTT CONNER** Fifth great grandson of

---

[3227] History of Taylor County, p638 published 1881 State Historical Company, (Iowa) [3228] p4 Seattle Daily Times (WA) Oct 26, 1946 [3229] Dyersburg Funeral Home (TN) [3230] The Chico Enterprise-Record (CA) Sep 25, 1962 [3230A] Akers Funeral Home (PA)

progenitor Nicholas Kegg. **RODNEY L. CONNER** Sixth great grandson of progenitor Nicholas Kegg.
RONDA JO CONNER Fifth great granddaughter of progenitor Nicholas Kegg.
TIMOTHY E. CONNER Sixth great grandson of progenitor Nicholas Kegg.
WESTON JOSEPH CONNER Seventh great grandson of progenitor Nicholas Kegg.

CONNOLLY

LYMAN BAIRD CONNOLLY Fifth great grandson of progenitor Nicholas Kegg.

CONRAD

APRIL CONRAD Sixth great granddaughter of progenitor Nicholas Kegg.
EDGAR WALTER CONRAD Fifth great grandson of progenitor Nicholas Kegg.
HAROLD DEAN CONRAD (1943 – 2001) son of Harold and Reba (Dodson) Dean never married. He was a veteran of Vietnam having served in the U.S. Air Force. **JAMES MICHAEL CONRAD** [3231A] aka "Mike" (1951 – 2018) son of Harold and Reba (Dodson) Conrad, married Ellen Claire Manfull. Mike spent 33 months overseas, including Turkey, Taiwan, and Thailand during the ending of the Vietnam War and was discharged as E-4. Mike held many positions, including employment at the Lorain County Airport, Ridge Tool Company, US Steel, retiring after 30 years in building maintenance from the United States Postal Service. **JAMES M. CONRAD** Sixth great grandson of progenitor Nicholas Kegg.
JENNIFER LYNN CONRAD Sixth great granddaughter of progenitor Nicholas Kegg.
MARY E. CONRAD Fifth great granddaughter of progenitor Nicholas Kegg.
ROBERT JOHN CONRAD aka "Bob", Sixth great grandson of progenitor Nicholas Kegg.

CONSTANT

ANGEL CONSTANT Eighth great granddaughter of progenitor Nicholas Kegg.
SARAH CONSTANT Eighth great granddaughter of progenitor Nicholas Kegg.

CONTRILLO

NINA MARIE CONTRILLO Sixth great granddaughter of progenitor Nicholas Kegg.

CONWAY

AMY CONWAY Sixth great granddaughter of progenitor Nicholas Kegg.
RYAN LARRY CONWAY Sixth great grandson of progenitor Nicholas Kegg.

COOK

BRIAN DAVID COOK Sixth great grandson of progenitor Nicholas Kegg. **BRYSON COOK** Seventh great grandson of progenitor Nicholas Kegg. **CATHERINE FAITH COOK** Seventh great granddaughter of progenitor Nicholas Kegg. **CORINNE COOK** Sixth great granddaughter of progenitor Nicholas Kegg. **JB COOK** Seventh great grandson of progenitor Nicholas Kegg.
JESSICA COOK Seventh great granddaughter of progenitor Nicholas Kegg.
JESSICA DAWN COOK Sixth great granddaughter of progenitor Nicholas Kegg. **KAITLIN COOK** Seventh great granddaughter of progenitor Nicholas Kegg. **MITCHEL COOK** Seventh great grandson of progenitor Nicholas Kegg. **MICHELLE COOK** Sixth great granddaughter of progenitor Nicholas Kegg. - **REON J COOK** [3231B] (1938 – 2013) son of Charles and Mary E. (Suder) Cook, married Cora

---

[3231] Kremer Funeral Home (NB) obtained by D. Sue Dible [3231A] The Morning Journal (OH) Mar. 29, 2019 [3231B] Bedford Gazette (PA) Nov 28, 2013, obtained and contributed by Bob Rose

Whitfield with whom he was father of (3). Reon worked for Kelly Springfield Tire for 27 years. He also sold cut firewood for many years. **SANDRA COOK** aka "Sandi" Fifth great granddaughter of progenitor Nicholas Kegg. **SETH COOK** Sixth great grandson of progenitor Nicholas Kegg. **SHANE COOK** Eighth great grandson of progenitor Nicholas Kegg. **SHAWN COOK** Fifth great grandson of progenitor Nicholas Kegg. **SIERRA COOK** Eighth great granddaughter of progenitor Nicholas Kegg. **SUSAN COOK** Fifth great granddaughter of progenitor Nicholas Kegg. **THOMAS LYLE COOK** Fifth great grandson of progenitor Nicholas Kegg. **ZACHERY COOK** Sixth great grandson of progenitor Nicholas Kegg.

COOKE

BONNIE C. COOKE Fourth great granddaughter of progenitor Nicholas Kegg. **CALLY COOKE** Fifth great granddaughter of progenitor Nicholas Kegg. **COVERLY COOKE** Fifth great granddaughter of progenitor Nicholas Kegg. **LIBBY COVERLY COOKE** Fourth great granddaughter of progenitor Nicholas Kegg. **RUSSELL COOKE** Fourth great grandson of progenitor Nicholas Kegg. **YVONNE EDWARDSEN COVERLY COOKE** Fifth great granddaughter of progenitor Nicholas Kegg.

COOLEY

ALYSSA NICOLE COOLEY Seventh great granddaughter of progenitor Nicholas Kegg. **ZACHARY ALAN COOLEY** Seventh great grandson of progenitor Nicholas Kegg.

COOMBS

WALTER ROLAND COOMBS [3232] (1880 – 1953) son of William and Elizabeth (Wilson) Combs, married Genevra E. (nee unknown) Walter was deputy of the Supreme Council of Hawaii, Ancient and Accepted Rite of Freemasonry. He was the senior 33rd Degree Mason in the Pacific Territory.

COON

MARCELLA RENEE COON Sixth great granddaughter of progenitor Nicholas Kegg.
RICHARD CARL COON Fifth great grandson of progenitor Nicholas Kegg.

COONFIELD

CINDY COONFIELD Fifth great granddaughter of progenitor Nicholas Kegg. **LELAND FRANK COONFIELD** Fifth great grandson of progenitor Nicholas Kegg. **RODNEY G. COONFIELD** aka "Skip", Fourth great grandson of progenitor Nicholas Kegg. **SKIP M. COONFIELD** aka "Skipper", Fifth great grandson of progenitor Nicholas Kegg.

COOPER

AARON COOPER Sixth great grandson of progenitor Nicholas Kegg. **AMANDA COOPER** aka "Mandie", Sixth great granddaughter of progenitor Nicholas Kegg. **ASHLIEGH COOPER** Seventh great granddaughter of progenitor Nicholas Kegg. **BENJAMIN EDWARD COOPER** Sixth great grandson of progenitor Nicholas Kegg. **CHAD COOPER** Seventh great grandson of progenitor Nicholas Kegg. **CINDEE LEE COOPER** Sixth great granddaughter of progenitor Nicholas Kegg. **CODY COOPER** Seventh great grandson of progenitor Nicholas Kegg. **CODY ALEXANDER COOPER** Sixth great grandson of progenitor Nicholas Kegg. **DANIEL COOPER** aka "Danny" Sixth

---

[3232] p25 Seattle Daily Times (WA) Feb 3, 1953

great grandson of progenitor Nicholas Kegg. **DANIEL COOPER** Fifth great grandson of progenitor Nicholas Kegg. **DENNIS LEE COOPER** Sixth great grandson of progenitor Nicholas Kegg. **DONALD ROBERT COOPER** Fifth great grandson of progenitor Nicholas Kegg.
EDWARD MICHAEL COOPER Fifth great grandson of progenitor Nicholas Kegg.
ERICA COOPER Sixth great granddaughter of progenitor Nicholas Kegg.
GABRIELLE GRACE COOPER Sixth great granddaughter of progenitor Nicholas Kegg.
JACOB COOPER Seventh great grandson of progenitor Nicholas Kegg. **JOHN W. COOPER** Sixth great grandson of progenitor Nicholas Kegg. **JOSHUA COOPER** Sixth great grandson of progenitor Nicholas Kegg. **KATHERINE ELIZABETH COOPER** Sixth great granddaughter of progenitor Nicholas Kegg. **KATHRYN COOPER** Sixth great granddaughter of progenitor Nicholas Kegg. **KATHY L. COOPER** Fifth great granddaughter of progenitor Nicholas Kegg.
LUCAS CESSNA COOPER Sixth great grandson of progenitor Nicholas Kegg.
MARK COOPER Sixth great grandson of progenitor Nicholas Kegg.
MATTHEW JOSEPH COOPER [3233] (1983 – 2005) son of Michael and Jill (Fagerlund) Cooper.
MICHAEL JOSEPH COOPER Fifth great grandson of progenitor Nicholas Kegg.
MICHAEL S. COOPER Sixth great grandson of progenitor Nicholas Kegg. **NICHOLE COOPER** Seventh great granddaughter of progenitor Nicholas Kegg. **NICOLE COOPER** Sixth great granddaughter of progenitor Nicholas Kegg. **PAMELA JANE COOPER** Fifth great granddaughter of progenitor Nicholas Kegg. **RICHARD VINCENT COOPER** Seventh great grandson of progenitor Nicholas Kegg. **ROBERT KARL COOPER** Sixth great grandson of progenitor Nicholas Kegg.
SHANE AUSTIN COOPER Sixth great grandson of progenitor Nicholas Kegg.
STEPHEN COOPER Fifth great grandson of progenitor Nicholas Kegg.
TARA COOPER Seventh great granddaughter of progenitor Nicholas Kegg.

CORBETT

ALEXIS CORBETT Ninth great granddaughter of progenitor Nicholas Kegg.
ANTHONY JAMES CORBETT Eighth great grandson of progenitor Nicholas Kegg.
CANDACE CORBETT Seventh great granddaughter of progenitor Nicholas Kegg.
JACOB CORBETT Ninth great grandson of progenitor Nicholas Kegg. **JOEL CORBETT** Eighth great grandson of progenitor Nicholas Kegg. **KYLA BETH CORBETT** Eighth great granddaughter of progenitor Nicholas Kegg. **MARC LEWIS CORBETT** Seventh great grandson of progenitor Nicholas Kegg. **MICHAEL LEE CORBETT** [3233A] (1952 – 2014) son of Earl and Francine (Sharrock) Corbett, married Janice M. Hanmi with whom he was father of (1). **MICHAEL CORBETT** Ninth great grandson of progenitor Nicholas Kegg. **SHAYNA CORBETT** Eighth great granddaughter of progenitor Nicholas Kegg. **STEPHANIE KAY CORBETT** Eighth great granddaughter of progenitor Nicholas Kegg.

CORBIN

ELIZABETH A. CORBIN Seventh great granddaughter of progenitor Nicholas Kegg.
MATTHEW SCOTT CORBIN Seventh great grandson of progenitor Nicholas Kegg.

CORLEY

ALYSE CORLEY Seventh great granddaughter of progenitor Nicholas Kegg. **AMARA CORLEY** Eighth great granddaughter of progenitor Nicholas Kegg. **BRIANNA CORLEY** Seventh great granddaughter of progenitor Nicholas Kegg. **DESIREE CORLEY** Seventh great granddaughter of progenitor Nicholas Kegg. **DEVIN CORLEY** Seventh great grandson of progenitor Nicholas Kegg.

[3233] pA4 Daily Journal (Vineland N.J.) Aug 2, 2005 [3233A] Toledo Blade (OH) Jan 14, 2014

DIANA CORLEY Sixth great granddaughter of progenitor Nicholas Kegg. **DONALD CORLEY** Fifth great grandson of progenitor Nicholas Kegg. **GAY CORLEY** Sixth great granddaughter of progenitor Nicholas Kegg. **GLENN E. CORLEY** Sixth great grandson of progenitor Nicholas Kegg. **GLENN HAROLD CORLEY** [3233B] (1936 – 2012) son of Frank and Mabel (Fisher) Corley, married Evelyn Sue Kennell with whom he was father of (5). Glenn's first job was cutting paper wood and then continued on with Eddie Shaffer as a truck driver. He then purchased his own rigging truck and drove as an independent driver starting in 1965 for McQuaide Company. He went on to become an owner/operator of George Transfer Rigging Co. later named Malone Freight Line being awarded 3 million safe driver miles. Glenn served in the U.S. Army on active duty and then the Reserves. **HARLEY CORLEY** Eighth great granddaughter of progenitor Nicholas Kegg. **KYLE CORLEY** Seventh great grandson of progenitor Nicholas Kegg. **LUNA CORLEY** Eighth great granddaughter of progenitor Nicholas Kegg.

CORNELL

BARBARA CORNELL Fourth great granddaughter of progenitor Nicholas Kegg.
CAROL CORNELL Fifth great granddaughter of progenitor Nicholas Kegg.
CATHERINE R CORNELL Fifth great granddaughter of progenitor Nicholas Kegg.
CURTIS CORNELL Sixth great grandson of progenitor Nicholas Kegg. **DAVID D. CORNELL** Fourth great grandson of progenitor Nicholas Kegg. **DONALD I. CORNELL** [3234] (1940 – 2021) son of Blair and Cleva (Ressler) Cornell married Gloria Hite with whom he was father of (1). Don had a long career with Standard Register, working there for more than 25 years. He later worked at JLG and DMP before retiring. Don was devoted to his family and was very proud of his daughter and grandsons. He especially enjoyed spending time with his grandsons, sharing with them his love of the great outdoors, auto racing, and football. He modeled for everyone the important values of working hard and caring for others, and he faced challenges knowing that he could get through anything by living his life "one day at a time." Don enjoyed attending Pennwood Bible Church. **KAREN CORNELL** Sixth great granddaughter of progenitor Nicholas Kegg. **MICHAEL CORNELL** Sixth great grandson of progenitor Nicholas Kegg. **RICHARD F. CORNELL** Fourth great grandson of progenitor Nicholas Kegg. **ROBERT DUANE CORNELL** [3235] (1943 – 1943) son of Blair and Cleva (Ressler) Cornell.
ROGER LEE CORNELL Fifth great grandson of progenitor Nicholas Kegg.
RONALD G. CORNELL Fifth great grandson of progenitor Nicholas Kegg.
SHIRLEY L. CORNELL Fifth great granddaughter of progenitor Nicholas Kegg.
STEPHEN W. CORNELL Fourth great grandson of progenitor Nicholas Kegg.
SUEANN CORNELL Sixth great granddaughter of progenitor Nicholas Kegg.
SUSAN MARGARET CORNELL Fifth great granddaughter of progenitor Nicholas Kegg.

CORRONA

SAMUEL PAUL CORRONA Sixth great grandson of progenitor Nicholas Kegg.
SAVANNAH ELIZABETH CORRONA Sixth great granddaughter of progenitor Nicholas Kegg.
SIMON BENDEL CORRONA Sixth great grandson of progenitor Nicholas Kegg.
SPENCER PHILLIP CORRONA Sixth great grandson of progenitor Nicholas Kegg.

CORTES

JACOB CORTES Seventh great grandson of progenitor Nicholas Kegg.
NICKOLAS CORTES Seventh great grandson of progenitor Nicholas Kegg.

[3233B] Harvey H. Zeigler Funeral Home (MD) [3234] Bedford Gazette (PA) April 17, 2021 [3235] Bedford County Historical Society Pioneer Library, book 31, p 150 obtained by D. Sue Dible

CORTNER

DIXIE ANN CORTNER Fifth great granddaughter of progenitor Nicholas Kegg.
JOSEPH MAX CORTNER Fifth great grandson of progenitor Nicholas Kegg.

CORWIN

DARYL CORWIN Sixth great grandson of progenitor Nicholas Kegg. **DUANE MEADE CORWIN** Fifth great grandson of progenitor Nicholas Kegg. **DUANNA CORWIN** Sixth great granddaughter of progenitor Nicholas Kegg. **GERALD LYNN CORWIN** Sixth great grandson of progenitor Nicholas Kegg. **GLENN CARROL CORWIN** (3236) (1928 – 2009) son of Walter and Leila (Wright) Corwin, married Rosemary Elaine Cornforth with whom he was father of (5). Glenn invested 29 years in the youth and community of the Sanger Unified School District. He was the principal for Fairmont and Jackson Elementary Schools in Sanger, retiring in 1989. He loved the outdoors. He enjoyed hiking, camping, and spending time with family and friends. He sponsored many youth trips hiking in the Sierras, climbing Half Dome & Mt. Whitney, and camping on the beaches of Mexico. He was a member of Fresno Central and Sunnyside Seventh-day Adventist Church. He served as a youth leader and lay elder in several churches. **JAMES D. CORWIN** Sixth great grandson of progenitor Nicholas Kegg. **JOHN W. CORWIN** Sixth great grandson of progenitor Nicholas Kegg. **LONNA CORWIN** Sixth great granddaughter of progenitor Nicholas Kegg. **MICHELLE T. CORWIN** Sixth great granddaughter of progenitor Nicholas Kegg. **MILTON ALFRED CORWIN** (1927 – 1985) son Walter and Leila (Wright) Corwin, married Bernice Elenore Peterson. **SHARON JOAN CORWIN** Sixth great granddaughter of progenitor Nicholas Kegg.

COSTIGAN

WILLIAM MONTE COSTIGAN Seventh great grandson of progenitor Nicholas Kegg.

COTE

SANDY COTE Sixth great granddaughter of progenitor Nicholas Kegg.
SHARON ANN COTE Sixth great granddaughter of progenitor Nicholas Kegg.

COTTER

HENRY VAN TUYL COTTER Fifth great grandson of progenitor Nicholas Kegg.
JEFFREY COTTER Sixth great grandson of progenitor Nicholas Kegg.
LISA COTTER Sixth great granddaughter of progenitor Nicholas Kegg.
MARGARET JENNESS COTTER Fifth great granddaughter of progenitor Nicholas Kegg.

COTTLE

MICHAEL COTTLE Sixth great grandson of progenitor Nicholas Kegg. **RICHARD COTTLE** Sixth great grandson of progenitor Nicholas Kegg. **THERESA COTTLE** Sixth great granddaughter of progenitor Nicholas Kegg.

COTTRELL

JADEN COTTRELL Seventh great grandson of progenitor Nicholas Kegg.

COUCHENOUR

CATHERINE JO COUCHENOUR Fifth great granddaughter of progenitor Nicholas Kegg.
DAVID PAUL COUCHENOUR Fifth great grandson of progenitor Nicholas Kegg.
GARRETT ALEXANDER COUCHENOUR Sixth great grandson of progenitor Nicholas Kegg.
JEFFREY SPENCER COUCHENOUR Fifth great grandson of progenitor Nicholas Kegg.
LAURA ANN COUCHENOUR Fifth great granddaughter of progenitor Nicholas Kegg.
MACIE RAE COUCHENOUR Sixth great granddaughter of progenitor Nicholas Kegg.
MYKAYLA ELIZABETH COUCHENOUR Sixth great granddaughter of progenitor Nicholas Kegg.
STEPHEN MICHAEL COUCHENOUR Fifth great grandson of progenitor Nicholas Kegg.
SUZANNE ELIZABETH COUCHENOUR Fifth great granddaughter of progenitor Nicholas Kegg.

COUGHLIN

CHRISTOPHER N. COUGHLIN Seventh great grandson of progenitor Nicholas Kegg.
TELKA A. COUGHLIN Seventh great granddaughter of progenitor Nicholas Kegg.

COUP

DAVID COUP Seventh great grandson of progenitor Nicholas Kegg.

COURY

LYNN MARIE COURY Sixth great granddaughter of progenitor Nicholas Kegg.
TIM COURY Sixth great grandson of progenitor Nicholas Kegg.

COUZZI

ANDREA NICOLE COUZZI Sixth great granddaughter of progenitor Nicholas Kegg.

COVER

COLTON COVER Seventh great grandson of progenitor Nicholas Kegg.
JAYDEN COVER Seventh great granddaughter of progenitor Nicholas Kegg.

COWELL

HOLLY COWELL Seventh great granddaughter of progenitor Nicholas Kegg.
MELISSA COWELL Sixth great granddaughter of progenitor Nicholas Kegg. **NANCY COWELL** [3237] (1933 – 2022) daughter of Franklin and Hazel (Hanks) Cowell married Dr. William J. McPhee with whom she was mother of (3). Following undergraduate and graduate degrees with honors from SUNY Fredonia, Nancy taught music in the public schools of NY State. Later, as music coordinator for elementary school District #144 in suburban Chicago, she developed and launched the music curriculum. She also initiated and taught courses in education and humanities at Sinclair Community College in Dayton, OH. At various times she directed a recorder consort as well as choirs in IL, NY, SC, and NC. Nancy also sang in the chorus for staged productions of the Dayton and Toledo Opera Companies; as well as with the Dayton Philharmonic and later with Sweet Adelines. Active in community groups, she regularly served as a hospital volunteer in OH and NYS. Along the way, Nancy designed several of the

---

[3236] p. B4 - Fresno Bee (CA) Jan 15, 2009 [3237] Independent Mail (SC) Feb 14, 2022

family's homes, showed Great Danes; and, at obedience shows, the family's retired racing Greyhound. At the same time, she and her horse enjoyed Dressage. Starting at age 55, she swam competitively, ranking consistently in the National Top Ten of U.S. Masters Swimming, celebrating her 70th birthday as silver medalist in the USMS National 3K (ab. 2-mile) Open Water Championship in Lake Hartwell at Clemson. Some of the swimming records she set in both NC and SC still stand. In Anderson she had been active in the choir and handbell groups at First Presbyterian Church, regularly swam laps at the Y, and dabbled in Tai Chi and TRX as health permitted. In 2018 her book Life in Lane 8 (Swimming? More than exercise) was published and is online. **NORMAN COWELL** Sixth great grandson of progenitor Nicholas Kegg. **ROBIN COWELL** Seventh great granddaughter of progenitor Nicholas Kegg. **TERI COWELL** Sixth great granddaughter of progenitor Nicholas Kegg. **WILBUR C. COWELL** [3238] (1923 – 2002) aka "Bill", son of Franklin and Hazel (Hanks) Cowell, married Flossie Mae Adams with whom he was father of (3). Wilbur graduated valedictorian of his high school class in 1941, then began working in the mailroom for Crouse Hinds Co in Syracuse before enlisting in the US Army in 1943. He served as a pilot instructor at Laughlin Army Airfield in Moultree, GA. Upon his discharge in October 1945, he attended Syracuse University where he graduated in 1949 Cum Laude with a degree in Electrical Engineering. He then returned to work with Crouse Hinds as a salesman. He was transferred to Pittsburgh, PA, Cincinnati, OH, Ft Lee, NJ, then back to Syracuse, NY in 1979 when he was promoted to the Vice President of Marketing & Sales. Wilbur represented Florida in the National Senior Olympic games in golf & bowling in Baton Rouge, LA and San Antonio, TX and was the golf club champion for Lake Fairways in 1990 and Pine Lakes in 1992.

COWGER

CHAD LEE COWGER Sixth great grandson of progenitor Nicholas Kegg.
DELANEY GRACE COWGER Seventh great granddaughter of progenitor Nicholas Kegg.
SHANE ALLEN COWGER Sixth great grandson of progenitor Nicholas Kegg.

COX

EDWARD A. COX Fifth great grandson of progenitor Nicholas Kegg. **ELI COX** Seventh great grandson of progenitor Nicholas Kegg. **EZRA COX** Seventh great grandson of progenitor Nicholas Kegg. **ISAAC JOHN COX** [3239] (1995 – 2019) son of John and Amy (Kegg) Cox, attended New Palestine High School. He worked at Jack's Donuts in Greenfield. Isaac enjoyed playing the guitar and listening to music. Playing Dungeon and Dragons was one of his family past times and enjoyed writing and was a fan of J.R.R. Tolkien. **WARREN WILLIAM COX** Fifth great grandson of progenitor Nicholas Kegg.

COZZO

BRITTANY COZZO Seventh great granddaughter of progenitor Nicholas Kegg.
JOEY COZZO Seventh great grandson of progenitor Nicholas Kegg.
KRYSTAL COZZO Seventh great granddaughter of progenitor Nicholas Kegg.

CRABTREE

BRAXTON CRABTREE Eighth great grandson of progenitor Nicholas Kegg.

[3237] Independent Mail (SC) Feb 14, 2022 [3238] The News-Press (FL) March 20, 2002, obtained by D. Sue Dible [3239] Erlewein Mortuary & Crematory in Greenfield (IN)

CRAGER

JAMES ALEX CRAGER Sixth great grandson of progenitor Nicholas Kegg.
PHILIP D. CRAGER Sixth great grandson of progenitor Nicholas Kegg.

CRAIG

ANGELA CRAIG Seventh great granddaughter of progenitor Nicholas Kegg. **MARK CRAIG** Seventh great grandson of progenitor Nicholas Kegg. **MATTHEW CRAIG** Eighth great grandson of progenitor Nicholas Kegg. **MICHAEL E. CRAIG** Seventh great grandson of progenitor Nicholas Kegg. **STUART L. CRAIG** Seventh great grandson of progenitor Nicholas Kegg. **TIMOTHY SHANE CRAIG** (1995 – 1995) son of Stuart and Mia (Pittman) Craig. **ZACHARY CRAIG** Eighth great grandson of progenitor Nicholas Kegg.

CRAIGUE

JACOB CRAIGUE Seventh great grandson of progenitor Nicholas Kegg.
MARIAH CRAIGUE Seventh great granddaughter of progenitor Nicholas Kegg.

CRAMER

FRANK CRAMER (1883 – 1934) son of David and Hattie (Lininger) Cramer was struck by a car and died instantly. **NANNIE BELLE CRAMER** (1889 – 1950) daughter of David and Hattie (Lininger) Cramer married Willard Leroy Repp with whom she was mother of (3). Later Nannie married George J. Goodman and last to Leon Runyon.

CRANE

ANGELA CRANE Sixth great granddaughter of progenitor Nicholas Kegg.
BARBARA GAYLE CRANE (1949 – 1990) daughter OF Walter and Shirley (Locke) Crane, married David T. Irwin with whom she was mother of (1). **BETSY CRANE** Sixth great granddaughter of progenitor Nicholas Kegg. **CHANTELE CRANE** Seventh great granddaughter of progenitor Nicholas Kegg. **CHRISTOPHER T. CRANE** Sixth great grandson of progenitor Nicholas Kegg. **EVERETT LOREN CRANE** [3240] (1896 – 1967) son of William and Ada (Brandenburg) Crane, married Margaret Hubedine Gaspers with whom he was father of (4). Everett was employed as an electrician at the Nelsonville hospital. **GERALD PHILLIP CRANE** Sixth great grandson of progenitor Nicholas Kegg. **JEAN MARIE CRANE** Sixth great granddaughter of progenitor Nicholas Kegg. **JOSEPH CRANE** Sixth great grandson of progenitor Nicholas Kegg. **JUDITH MARY CRANE** Sixth great granddaughter of progenitor Nicholas Kegg. **JULIE CRANE** Sixth great granddaughter of progenitor Nicholas Kegg. **JUSTIN CRANE** Seventh great grandson of progenitor Nicholas Kegg. **LORNA ELIZABETH CRANE** Sixth great granddaughter of progenitor Nicholas Kegg.
MARY MARGARET CRANE (1953 – 1953) daughter of Theodore and Mary (Colburn) Crane.

CRAWFORD

BRANDI RENEE CRAWFORD Seventh great granddaughter of progenitor Nicholas Kegg.
CLAIR E. CRAWFORD [3241] (1934 – 2021) son of Raymond and Ora (Bussard) Crawford began working at age 17 as a clerk in the Department of Labor before enlisting in the U.S. Air Force. He was

---

[3240] p2 Logan Daily News (OH) Jan 26, 1967 [3241] Bedford Gazette (PA) March 23, 2022

stationed at Osan-Ni and Yong Dong Po, Korea. Clair retired from the Department of Commerce and spent his retirement in volunteer work at Goodwill and the Salvation Army. He was a selfless caregiver when family members and friends were in need of help. **DAVID A. CRAWFORD** Sixth great grandson of progenitor Nicholas Kegg. **DEBORAH A. CRAWFORD** Sixth great granddaughter of progenitor Nicholas Kegg. **EVAN CRAWFORD** Seventh great grandson of progenitor Nicholas Kegg. **HOMER L. CRAWFORD** [3242] (1930 – 1975) son of Raymond and Ora (Bussard) Crawford. A veteran of the Korean War, Homer was a member of Mt. Union United Church of Christ.
KAITLIN CRAWFORD Seventh great granddaughter of progenitor Nicholas Kegg.
KAREN CRAWFORD Sixth great granddaughter of progenitor Nicholas Kegg.
KAREN DARLENE CRAWFORD Sixth great granddaughter of progenitor Nicholas Kegg.
KENNETH E. CRAWFORD Sixth great grandson of progenitor Nicholas Kegg.
MARCI CRAWFORD Seventh great granddaughter of progenitor Nicholas Kegg.
NIAL ELWOOD CRAWFORD [3243] (1933 -2022) son of Raymond and Ora Mary (Bussard) Crawford, married Frieda Sartschenko with whom he was father of (3). Nial served in the US Army from April 1953 until April 1963, serving as Chairman of Victim of Hurricanes, medical supplies, food, clothes, and he was honorably discharged in 1963. He received the Defense Service Medal, United Nations Service Medal, Korean Service Medal, Good Conduct Medal, and The Republic of South Korea 50th Anniversary Service Medal. Nial retired from the Commonwealth of Pennsylvania, Department of Health, after 22 years of service. **NIAL ELWOOD CRAWFORD JR.** Sixth great grandson of progenitor Nicholas Kegg. **ROBENA CRAWFORD** [3244] (1941 – 2021) daughter of progenitor Raymond and Ora (Bussard) Crawford married John Fowler with whom she was mother of 2. Robena was employed at the Department of Justice in Washington DC. she finished out her career as a federal employee at USAMRIID. As a military wife, she lived in Turkey, Germany, Guam, Ft. Meade, MD and Pensacola, FL, raising her children along the way. Robena loved to travel and had a passion for exploring the beauty of the world. Robena was an Anglophile who especially enjoyed English mystery novels and WETA UK. She was a lifelong Penn State and Pittsburgh Steelers fan. **ROBERT L. CRAWFORD** Sixth great grandson of progenitor Nicholas Kegg. **SHANE CRAWFORD** Seventh great grandson of progenitor Nicholas Kegg. **STEPHEN CRAWFORD** Seventh great grandson of progenitor Nicholas Kegg.
SUSAN LYNN CRAWFORD Sixth great granddaughter of progenitor Nicholas Kegg.

CREAMER

CHERYL LYNN CREAMER [3245] (1951 – 2021) daughter of Glenn and Joan Issabell (Martin) Creamer married John Gandee with whom she was mother of (3). **EMILY THATCHER CREAMER** Sixth great granddaughter of progenitor Nicholas Kegg. **JEFFREY G. CREAMER** Fifth great grandson of progenitor Nicholas Kegg. **KATHERINE CREAMER** Sixth great granddaughter of progenitor Nicholas Kegg. **MARK HARRIS CREAMER** Fifth great grandson of progenitor Nicholas Kegg.

CREASMAN

DREW CREASMAN Sixth great grandson of progenitor Nicholas Kegg.
IRA CREASMAN Sixth great grandson of progenitor Nicholas Kegg.

CREPS

KELLY MARIE CREPS Sixth great granddaughter of progenitor Nicholas Kegg.
LOUISE C. CREPS [3246] (1927 – 1992) daughter of Roy and Verda (Snyder) Creps, married Theodore

---

[3242] Cumberland Evening Times (MD) July 19, 1975 [3243] Bedford Gazette (PA) June 20, 2022, obtained by Bob Rose [3244] Bedford Gazette (PA) March 23, 2022 [3245] The Review (Alliance, OH) Sep 30, 2021 [3246] Bedford County Genealogical Society obituary obtained by D. Sue Dible

Daniel Snyder with whom she was mother of (2). Louise was a member of the Snake Spring Valley Church of the Brethren and owned and operated Mile Level Pizza and Sub Shop, a 25-year-old family business. **PATRICIA CREPS** Sixth great granddaughter of progenitor Nicholas Kegg.
SHIRLEY JANE CREPS Fifth great granddaughter of progenitor Nicholas Kegg.
TERRY EDWARD CREPS [3247] (1963 – 1984) son of Edward and Mary (Trail) Creps. Terry was a junior at Shippensburg University, majoring in History and Government when he suffered fatal injuries in an automobile accident. Terry was a graduate of Bedford High School, Class of 1981, where he was on the wrestling, football, and track teams.

CREVISON

CHARLES WALTER CREVISON, aka "Chuck", Sixth great grandson of progenitor Nicholas Kegg.
CHARLES WOODARD CREVISON [3248] (1909 – 1959) aka "Sonny", son of Everet and Rosa Belle (Woodward) Crevison married twice; first to Leota Wilhelmina Tapp. Later, he married Florence Marie Piper with whom he was father of (4). Sonny was a building contractor and did much toward the developing of the vacation lands in and around Lake George, NY.
CHARLES WOODARD CREVISON JR. (1932 – 1983) aka "Peter Charles Baish", son of Charles and Constance (Ives) Crevison. Charles was adopted by his mother's 2nd husband Alfred James Baish and changed his name. Peter Charles Baish married Susan L. Gray. Later, he married Linda Kaye (Steffey) Simmons. **EVELYN M. CREVISON** [3249] (1907 – 1970) daughter of Everet and Rosa Belle (Woodward) Crevison, married Glenn Hottman with whom she was mother of (5). Evelyn was associated with the Starr Commonwealth in Van Wert, Ohio, and Albion, MI. She was a member of the First Methodist church and its WSCS. **GENEVA IONE CREVISON** [3250] (1905 – 1934) daughter of Everet and Rosa Belle (Woodward) Crevison, married Edwin Laughlin Hunter with whom she was mother of (1). Geneva was a charter member of the McGrath class and a member of the aid society of the Methodist church. **JAMES CREVISON** Fifth great grandson of progenitor Nicholas Kegg.
JERALD T. CREVISON Fifth great grandson of progenitor Nicholas Kegg.
MARIANA CREVISON Seventh great granddaughter of progenitor Nicholas Kegg.
PAULINE ADELL CREVISON [3251] (1903 – 1964) daughter of Everet and Rosa Belle (Woodward) Crevison, married Willis Wells with whom she was mother of (10).
SETH ADAM CREVISON Seventh great grandson of progenitor Nicholas Kegg.

CRIBBS

LOGAN JAMES CRIBBS Seventh great grandson of progenitor Nicholas Kegg.

CRICK

CHARLES H. CRICK (born abt.1873) aka "Charlie", son of Jacob and Anna (Dean) Crick, married Lottie B. (King) Powell. **DOLLIE CRICK** (born abt. 1871) daughter of Jacob and Anna (Dean) Crick, married Chas Webster Ives.

CRIDER

JOHNATHON RAYMOND CRIDER Eighth great grandson of progenitor Nicholas Kegg.
KENNETH LEONARD CRIDER Eighth great grandson of progenitor Nicholas Kegg.
TAYLOR JOYCELYNN CRIDER Eighth great granddaughter of progenitor Nicholas Kegg.

[3247] Bedford County Historical Society (PA), Book 85, page 40 obtained by D. Sue Dible [3248] p26-Troy Record (Troy, New York) Oct 13, 1959 [3249] p 5 - Kenton Times (OH) Dec 17, 1970, obtained by D. Sue Dible [3250] p22 - The Canton Repository (OH) Oct 19, 1934 [3251] The Plain Dealer (Cleveland, Ohio) Aug. 16, 1964

CRISPEN

CONNER CRISPEN Seventh great grandson of progenitor Nicholas Kegg.
KYLA CRISPEN Seventh great granddaughter of progenitor Nicholas Kegg.

CRISSMAN

ELENORA CRISSMAN aka "Holly", Fourth great granddaughter of progenitor Nicholas Kegg.
MERRY ANN CRISSMAN Fourth great granddaughter of progenitor Nicholas Kegg.

CRIST

ADDILYN GRACE CRIST Eighth great granddaughter of progenitor Nicholas Kegg.
BRADLEY CRIST Seventh great grandson of progenitor Nicholas Kegg. **GARY CRIST** Sixth great grandson of progenitor Nicholas Kegg. **JANAE ELIZABETH CRIST** Seventh great granddaughter of progenitor Nicholas Kegg. **JENNIFER DAWN CRIST** Seventh great granddaughter of progenitor Nicholas Kegg. **KEVIN LEE CRIST** Seventh great grandson of progenitor Nicholas Kegg.
LORRI JO CRIST [3252] (1967 – 1995) daughter of Michael and Barbara (Brallier) Crist, married Mark B. Halwany with whom she was mother of (1). Lorri Jo was a physical therapy assistant for Citrus Memorial Hospital. She was a student at Central Florida Community College, Ocala, and a Protestant.
MARK WAYNE CRIST Seventh great grandson of progenitor Nicholas Kegg. **MATTHEW CRIST** Seventh great grandson of progenitor Nicholas Kegg. **SCOTT L. CRIST** Seventh great grandson of progenitor Nicholas Kegg. **ZAYNE LUKE CRIST** Eighth great grandson of progenitor Nicholas Kegg.

CRITES

DALE CRITES Sixth great grandson of progenitor Nicholas Kegg. **DANIEL EDWIN CRITES** Seventh great grandson of progenitor Nicholas Kegg. **DONNA L. CRITES** Sixth great granddaughter of progenitor Nicholas Kegg. **LARRY EDWIN CRITES** Sixth great grandson of progenitor Nicholas Kegg. **NATALIE CRITES** Seventh great granddaughter of progenitor Nicholas Kegg.
SHANNON CRITES Sixth great grandson of progenitor Nicholas Kegg.
TIARNA LEIGH CRITES Seventh great granddaughter of progenitor Nicholas Kegg.

CRONE

JAMES E. CRONE aka "Jim", Sixth great grandson of progenitor Nicholas Kegg.
JARED RAYMOND CRONE Sixth great grandson of progenitor Nicholas Kegg.
JODY CRONE Sixth great granddaughter of progenitor Nicholas Kegg.

CRONEY

OWEN CRONEY Seventh great grandson of progenitor Nicholas Kegg.

CRONICK

CARRIE ANN CRONICK Sixth great granddaughter of progenitor Nicholas Kegg.
DONALD L. CRONICK Sixth great grandson of progenitor Nicholas Kegg.

[3252] p. 13-St. Petersburg Times (FL) July 23, 1995

CROOKS

DENNIS EDWARD CROOKS Fourth great grandson of progenitor Nicholas Kegg.
JOLENE A. CROOKS Fifth great granddaughter of progenitor Nicholas Kegg.
RICHARD PHILLIP CROOKS Fourth great grandson of progenitor Nicholas Kegg.
ROBERT CROOKS Fifth great grandson of progenitor Nicholas Kegg.
ROGER CROOKS Fourth great grandson of progenitor Nicholas Kegg.

CROSKEY

CHAD E. CROSKEY Sixth great grandson of progenitor Nicholas Kegg. **HEIDI A. CROSKEY** Sixth great granddaughter of progenitor Nicholas Kegg. **LANNY COLE CROSKEY** Seventh great grandson of progenitor Nicholas Kegg.

CROSS

JEFFREY PAUL CROSS Seventh great grandson of progenitor Nicholas Kegg.
JERRAD J. CROSS Seventh great grandson of progenitor Nicholas Kegg. **JORDON ALEX CROSS** Seventh great grandson of progenitor Nicholas Kegg. **MACY MARIE CROSS** Eighth great granddaughter of progenitor Nicholas Kegg.

CROSSER

ABIGAIL M. CROSSER Seventh great granddaughter of progenitor Nicholas Kegg.
CHERYL L. CROSSER Seventh great granddaughter of progenitor Nicholas Kegg.
JENNIFER A. CROSSER Seventh great granddaughter of progenitor Nicholas Kegg.
JOHN ROBERT CROSSER Fifth great grandson of progenitor Nicholas Kegg.
JUDITH KAY CROSSER [3253] (1941 – 1999) daughter of John and Agnes (Shaw) Crosser married twice; first to Paul Dean Smith with whom she was mother of (2). Later she married James C. Tesnow. Judith was a teacher at Chamberlain Hill Elementary School. She formerly worked at Marathon Oil Co. and was the former co-owner and co-founder of Children Corner Preschool. She was a member of Arlington United Methodist Church and a former church organist. **MICHAEL D. CROSSER** aka "Mike", Sixth great grandson of progenitor Nicholas Kegg. **MICHELLE S. CROSSER** Seventh great granddaughter of progenitor Nicholas Kegg. **ROBERT J. CROSSER** Sixth great grandson of progenitor Nicholas Kegg.

CROSSLEY

SCOTT ALAN CROSSLEY Seventh great grandson of progenitor Nicholas Kegg.
TONYA ANN CROSSLEY Seventh great granddaughter of progenitor Nicholas Kegg.
WARREN CROSSLEY, aka "Rex", Seventh great grandson of progenitor Nicholas Kegg.

CROSSON

BRADLEY J. CROSSON Sixth great grandson of progenitor Nicholas Kegg. **CHRISTI CROSSON** Sixth great granddaughter of progenitor Nicholas Kegg. **CRAIG CROSSON** Sixth great grandson of progenitor Nicholas Kegg. **DEBBIE CROSSON** Sixth great granddaughter of progenitor Nicholas [3253] Kegg. **DENISE CROSSON** Sixth great granddaughter of progenitor Nicholas Kegg.

p 5 - The Courier (Findlay, OH) Apr 19, 1999, obtained by D. Sue Dible

DIANE CROSSON Sixth great granddaughter of progenitor Nicholas Kegg. **GLENN RAYMOND CROSSON** Sixth great grandson of progenitor Nicholas Kegg. **JACK D. CROSSON** (1936 – 1973) son of Lysle and Ruby (Richards) Crosson. **JEFFREY LANE CROSSON** Sixth great grandson of progenitor Nicholas Kegg. **LANE LAWRENCE CROSSON** [3254] (1928 – 2009) son of Lysle and Ruby (Richards) Crosson, married Betty Lou Long with whom he was father of (2). Lane worked in various occupations and, for most of his life worked for Forman and Ford Company in Ottumwa as a glazier. Lane was very active all his life. He was a member of the Eddyville Masonic Lodge AF.AM 47 and the Eddyville Lions Club. **LAURIE CROSSON** Sixth great granddaughter of progenitor Nicholas Kegg. **LISA CROSSON** Sixth great granddaughter of progenitor Nicholas Kegg.

PHYLLIS N. CROSSON [3255] (1926 – 2009) daughter of Lysle and Ruby (Richards) Crosson, married Charles William Hale with whom she was mother of (2). **RICHARD CROSSON** (1923 – 1988) aka "Dick", son of Lysle and Ruby (Richards) Crosson. **RICK CROSSON** Sixth great grandson of progenitor Nicholas Kegg.

CROUNAUER

JOHN MARK CROUNAUER Eighth great grandson of progenitor Nicholas Kegg.
LUKE ROBERT CROUNAUER Eighth great grandson of progenitor Nicholas Kegg.
NATHAN MILES CROUNAUER Eighth great grandson of progenitor Nicholas Kegg.

CROUSE

BOBBY CROUSE Seventh great grandson of progenitor Nicholas Kegg. **CHAD CROUSE** Seventh great grandson of progenitor Nicholas Kegg. **CHASE RYAN CROUSE** Eighth great grandson of progenitor Nicholas Kegg. **DAKOTA ROSE CROUSE** Eighth great granddaughter of progenitor Nicholas Kegg. **DOROTHY CATHERINE CROUSE** (born abt. 1915) daughter of Ross and Mary Anna (Calhoun) Crouse married Curtis Edward Hill with whom she was mother of (3). Later, Dorothy married Nelson Watkins with whom she was mother of (2). Last, she married Walter A. Tripp with whom she was mother of (3). **PAULINE ALBERTA CROUSE** [3256] (1921 – 1973) daughter of Ross and Mary Anna (Calhoun) Crouse, married Donald R. Elliott with whom she was mother of (2). Pauline served as city clerk since her appointment in 1967; she was a former secretary of the Hudson schools. Pauline was an active community leader; she was a member of the First United Methodist Church of Hudson, the Hudson American Legion Auxiliary and a former member of the Hudson's Woman's Club and the Order of the Eastern Star. **ROSEANN CROUSE** Sixth great granddaughter of progenitor Nicholas Kegg. **RYAN HENRY CROUSE** Seventh great grandson of progenitor Nicholas Kegg. **THELMA MAE CROUSE** [3257, 3258] (1924 – 2013) daughter of Ross and Mary Anna (Calhoun) Crouse married twice; first to Orville Henry Friemoth with whom she was mother of (4). Later, she married James Morley Zander III. **VERA LOUISE CROUSE** Sixth great granddaughter of progenitor Nicholas Kegg.

CROWERS

KELLY CROWERS Sixth great granddaughter of progenitor Nicholas Kegg.

CROWNOVER

HANNAH RACHELE CROWNOVER Seventh great granddaughter of progenitor Nicholas Kegg.

[3254] Ottumwa Courier (IA) Dec 15, 2009 [3255] p 2B - Wichita Eagle (KS) Jan 20, 2009 [3256] Daily Telegram (MI) 1973 [3257] ottovillehistory.blogspot [3258] Film Number 007616276 The Daily Telegram (MI) Feb 15, 1996

CROWSON

JONATHAN CROWSON Seventh great grandson of progenitor Nicholas Kegg.
MATTHEW RYAN CROWSON Seventh great grandson of progenitor Nicholas Kegg.
MICHAEL CROWSON Seventh great grandson of progenitor Nicholas Kegg.

CROYLE

KEITH E. CROYLE Sixth great grandson of progenitor Nicholas Kegg.   **KEVIN T. CROYLE** Sixth great grandson of progenitor Nicholas Kegg.

CRUM

BRYAN CRUM Eighth great grandson of progenitor Nicholas Kegg.
KRYSTIANA JACLYN CRUM [3258A] (2004 – 2019) daughter of Bryan and Crystal Marie (Shafer) Crum.   **SPENCER CRUM** infant son of Bryan and Crystal Marie (Shafer) Crum.

CRUMP

CAROLYN CRUMP Fifth great granddaughter of progenitor Nicholas Kegg.
DOROTHY JANE CRUMP [3259] (1928 – 1980) daughter of James and Jennie (Durst) Crump, married William Marion McGinnis with whom she was mother of (2).   **JANE ADELIA CRUMP** Fifth great granddaughter of progenitor Nicholas Kegg.   **JUSTIN CRUMP** Sixth great grandson of progenitor Nicholas Kegg.   **MARTHA CRUMP** Fifth great granddaughter of progenitor Nicholas Kegg.
RUSSELL TAYLOR CRUMP Fifth great grandson of progenitor Nicholas Kegg.

CRUMPLER

LILLY CRUMPLER Seventh great granddaughter of progenitor Nicholas Kegg.

CUCHINSKI

DONALD JOHN CUCHINSKI Fifth great grandson of progenitor Nicholas Kegg.
JAMES JOSEPH CUCHINSKI [3260] (1963 – 1963) son of Joseph and June (Kegg) Cuchinski.
MARK CUCHINSKI Sixth great grandson of progenitor Nicholas Kegg.

CUIN

TYNE CUIN Eighth great grandson of progenitor Nicholas Kegg.

CULBERTSON

OWAN CULBERTSON Eighth great grandson of progenitor Nicholas Kegg.
TREVOR CULBERTSON Eighth great grandson of progenitor Nicholas Kegg.

CULLISON

CALEB DONALD CULLISON Ninth great grandson of progenitor Nicholas Kegg.

[3258A] Johnson City Press (TN) April 22, 2019 [3259] p33 Evening Star (DC) May 21, 1980 [3260] p.20 - News-Palladium (MI) May 31, 1963

MARK DEE CULLISON Eighth great grandson of progenitor Nicholas Kegg.

CULP

BRAM CULP Eighth great grandson of progenitor Nicholas Kegg. **DAVID CULP** Seventh great grandson of progenitor Nicholas Kegg. **DEBORAH SUE CULP** Sixth great granddaughter of progenitor Nicholas Kegg. **DUANE ALAN CULP** Fifth great grandson of progenitor Nicholas Kegg. **INFANT CULP** [3261] (1911 – 1911) daughter of John and Nannie (Beaver) Culp. **JEFFORY CLARK CULP** Sixth great grandson of progenitor Nicholas Kegg. **MARALYN ROSE LEONA CULP** Seventh great granddaughter of progenitor Nicholas Kegg.

CUMMINGS

ERIN CUMMINGS Eighth great granddaughter of progenitor Nicholas Kegg. **PEYTON ISABELLA CUMMINS** Seventh great granddaughter of progenitor Nicholas Kegg. **TALON LUCAS CUMMINS** Seventh great grandson of progenitor Nicholas Kegg.

CUNARD

DARCY CUNARD Sixth great granddaughter of progenitor Nicholas Kegg.
RENA BETH CUNARD Sixth great granddaughter of progenitor Nicholas Kegg.

CUNDY

RACHEL CUNDY Eighth great granddaughter of progenitor Nicholas Kegg.

CUNNINGHAM

CHRISTOPHER CUNNINGHAM Sixth great grandson of progenitor Nicholas Kegg.
LEXI CUNNINGHAM Sixth great granddaughter of progenitor Nicholas Kegg.
MITCHELL LYNN CUNNINGHAM Eighth great grandson of progenitor Nicholas Kegg.
PATRICIA ELLEN CUNNINGHAM Fifth great granddaughter of progenitor Nicholas Kegg.
SAVANNAH ANN CUNNINGHAM Eighth great granddaughter of progenitor Nicholas Kegg.

CURRY

AARON LEE CURRY [3262] (1952 – 2016) son of Wilbur and Agnes (Patterson) Curry, married Patricia Faye Hamilton with whom he was father of (3). Aaron served in the U.S. Army during the Vietnam War. He was an engine repairman for Conrail, Norfolk and Western and CS. **ARTHUR M. CURRY** [3263] (1920 – 1976) son of Clem and Mabel (McClellan) Curry married twice; first to Kathleen E. Hardgrove and later to Dorothy Evelyn Ray with whom he was father of (1). Arthur was a member of United Methodist Church at Minerva and its Home Builders Sunday school class, and an Army veteran of World War II, having served in the South Pacific and the Philippines. **CALVIN LEROY CURRY** Sixth great grandson of progenitor Nicholas Kegg. **DANIEL LYNN CURRY** Sixth great grandson of progenitor Nicholas Kegg. **EDNA MAY CURRY** (1919 – 1982) daughter of Clem and Mabel (McClellan) Curry, married Thomas Eugene Mazzaferro with whom she was mother of (3). **LAURA CURRY** Seventh great granddaughter of progenitor Nicholas Kegg. **MARISA CURRY** Seventh great granddaughter of progenitor Nicholas Kegg. **MELANIE CURRY** Fifth great granddaughter of progenitor Nicholas Kegg.

[3261] Bedford Gazette (PA) Jan 20, 1911 [3262] Bartley Funeral Home (OH) [3263] p5 The Daily Reporter (Dover, Ohio) Aug 11, 1976

MICHAEL ALLEN CURRY [3264] (1978 – 2018) son of Aaron and Patricia (Hamilton) Curry married Kerry Ann Jenkins with whom he was father of (2). **PAGE ANDREW CURRY** Sixth great grandson of progenitor Nicholas Kegg. **PAMELA A. CURRY** Fifth great granddaughter of progenitor Nicholas Kegg. **RICKY LYNN CURRY** (1966 – 1988) son of Wilbur and Agnes (Patterson) Curry. **TIMOTHY AARON CURRY** Sixth great grandson of progenitor Nicholas Kegg. **WALTER DENVER CURRY** [3265] (1916 – 2004) son of Clem and Mabel (McClellan) Curry, married Eunice Catherine Frantum with whom he was father of (2). Walter was a US Air Force Veteran of World War II, a member of the Minerva VFW Post #2199, the National AARP and the Wilmont Wilderness Center.

CURTICE

DAVID CLINTON CURTICE Sixth great grandson of progenitor Nicholas Kegg.
MARK EDWARD CURTICE Sixth great grandson of progenitor Nicholas Kegg.
STEPHANIE CURTICE Sixth great granddaughter of progenitor Nicholas Kegg.

CURTIS

DEBRA ANN CURTIS Fifth great granddaughter of progenitor Nicholas Kegg.
JAMES DAVID CURTIS Fifth great grandson of progenitor Nicholas Kegg.
JON ALAN CURTIS Fifth great grandson of progenitor Nicholas Kegg.

CUSTER

COLBY CUSTER Sixth great grandson of progenitor Nicholas Kegg. **HOLLY CUSTER** Sixth great granddaughter of progenitor Nicholas Kegg. **SHELBY CUSTER** Sixth great granddaughter of progenitor Nicholas Kegg.

CUTCHALL

KATIE CUTCHALL Seventh great granddaughter of progenitor Nicholas Kegg.

D'ANNUNZIO

ANTHONY JOSEPH D'ANNUNZIO Fifth great grandson of progenitor Nicholas Kegg.
JULIE CHRISTINE D'ANNUNZIO Fifth great granddaughter of progenitor Nicholas Kegg.
NICOLA FRANKLIN D'ANNUNZIO Fifth great grandson of progenitor Nicholas Kegg.
PATRICIA LOUISE D'ANNUNZIO Fifth great granddaughter of progenitor Nicholas Kegg.

DABNEY

DANA LEE DABNEY Sixth great grandson of progenitor Nicholas Kegg. **DAVID W. DABNEY** Sixth great grandson of progenitor Nicholas Kegg. **DEBORAH DABNEY** Sixth great granddaughter of progenitor Nicholas Kegg.

[3264] The Alliance Review (OH) March 29, 2018, obtained by D. Sue Dible [3265] The Repository (Canton, OH) June 26, 2004

DACY

MARGARET VIVIAN DACY (3266) (1902 – 1960) daughter of James and Jessie (Friend) Dacy, married Glenn Harrison. Margaret was a marker in the laundry for 32 years at the James Whitcomb Riley Hospital for Children.

DAEKE

GUSTAV DAEKE aka "Gus" Seventh great grandson of progenitor Nicholas Kegg.
SAM DAEKE Seventh great grandson of progenitor Nicholas Kegg.

DAHLBERG

JOEL E. DAHLBERG Sixth great grandson of progenitor Nicholas Kegg.
RYAN JAMES DAHLBERG Sixth great grandson of progenitor Nicholas Kegg.

DAKE

DORIS DAKE Fifth great granddaughter of progenitor Nicholas Kegg
LEANNA DAKE Fifth great granddaughter of progenitor Nicholas Kegg.

DALEY

ARAN CHRISTOPHER DALEY Sixth great grandson of progenitor Nicholas Kegg.
ARLINE ANN DALEY Fifth great granddaughter of progenitor Nicholas Kegg.
AUDREY HELEN DALEY aka "Charming", Fifth great granddaughter of progenitor Nicholas Kegg.
BETTY JANE DALEY (3268) (1925 – 2009) daughter of Francis and Laura (Cale) Daley, married Robert E. Miller with whom she was mother of (3). **BRUCE PATRICK DALEY** Fifth great grandson of progenitor Nicholas Kegg. **DANIEL DALEY** Sixth great grandson of progenitor Nicholas Kegg. **DAVID KENNETH DALEY** Sixth great grandson of progenitor Nicholas Kegg. **EMILY DALEY** Sixth great granddaughter of progenitor Nicholas Kegg. **ESSEN G. DALEY** Sixth great grandson of progenitor Nicholas Kegg. **FRANK J. DALEY** Fifth great grandson of progenitor Nicholas Kegg. **FREDA MATILDE DALEY** (3268A) (1926 – 2003) daughter of John and Matilda (Myeskie) Daley, married Charles Joseph Himes with whom she was mother of (3). **GRACE DALEY** (3269) (1894 – 1970) daughter of Joseph and Emma (Beaver) Daley, married Stephen John Burns with whom she was mother of (5). **HARRY PAUL DALEY** Fourth great grandson of progenitor Nicholas Kegg. **INFANT DALEY** (1920 – 1920) daughter of John and Matilda (Myeskie) Daley. **JAMES MICHAEL DALEY** (1956 – 1998) son of Lois Arlene Daley. **JOE DALEY** Sixth great grandson of progenitor Nicholas Kegg. **JOHN DALEY** Sixth great grandson of progenitor Nicholas Kegg. **JOSEPH CHARLES DALEY** (3270) (1921 – 1921) son of John and Matilda (Myeskie) Daley. **KAREN LEE DALEY** Fifth great granddaughter of progenitor Nicholas Kegg. **KATHY DALEY** Fifth great granddaughter of progenitor Nicholas Kegg. **KATIE OSHEA DALEY** Seventh great granddaughter of progenitor Nicholas Kegg. **LAURA DALEY** Fifth great granddaughter of progenitor Nicholas Kegg. **LEO JOSEPH DALEY** Fifth great grandson of progenitor Nicholas Kegg. **LISA DALEY** Fifth great granddaughter of progenitor Nicholas Kegg. **LORI DALEY** Fifth great granddaughter of progenitor Nicholas Kegg.

(3266) The Indianapolis News (IN) Nov 18, 1960 (3267) The Tribune-Democrat (PA) March 16, 2019 (3268) Tribune Democrat (PA) Oct 14, 2009 (3268A) Tribune Democrat (PA) Jan 10, 2003 (3269) CPL Main History Department, obtained by D. Sue Dible (3270) Johnstown Tribune (PA) Sep 2, 1921, obtained by D. Sue Dible

MARY MARGARET DALEY [3271] (1923 – 2006) aka "Peg", daughter of Eugene and Mary (Maier) Daley, married Donald M. Leventry with whom she was mother of (2).   **MICHAEL DALEY** Fifth great grandson of progenitor Nicholas Kegg.   **RACHEL DALEY** Seventh great granddaughter of progenitor Nicholas Kegg.   **RICHARD THOMAS DALEY** Fourth great grandson of progenitor Nicholas Kegg.   **RICKY DALEY** Fifth great grandson of progenitor Nicholas Kegg.

DALTON

IRENE J. DALTON (1921 – 1974) daughter of John and Pearl (Graham) Dalton, married Robert Florain Beedle.   **JAROLD GABRIEL DALTON** Sixth great grandson of progenitor Nicholas Kegg.
JASON GRANT DALTON Sixth great grandson of progenitor Nicholas Kegg.
JEREMIAH GARRETT DALTON Sixth great grandson of progenitor Nicholas Kegg.
JERRY WAYNE DALTON (1943 – 1999) son of Walter and Hilda (Pilcher) Dalton.
JOHN STEVEN DALTON, Fifth great grandson of progenitor Nicholas Kegg.
JOHNNY GRAHAM DALTON [3272] (1928 – 1982) son of John and Pearl (Graham) Dalton, married Shirlee Akers with whom he was father of (1). Johnny was a data processing manager at the St. Joseph Hospital in Parkersburg and previously held this position at Doctors Hospital in Columbus. Johnny was a Veteran of Korean Conflict.   **LELAH PEARL DALTON** [3273] (1919 – 2012) daughter of John and Pearl (Graham) Dalton married twice; first to Charles Willoughby Flynn with whom she was mother of (1). She later married Donald Charles Morton with whom she was mother of (1). Lelah attended business school and studied typing, shorthand, and bookkeeping, which she used in her father's plumbing office. She took sewing and made many of her mothers, sisters and daughters' clothes and in later years beautiful afghans. Lelah enjoyed deep-sea and pier fishing, motor scooters and the beach. She worked at Bayou Manor and The Methodist Home.   **LOUISE CAROLINE DALTON**, Fourth great granddaughter of progenitor Nicholas Kegg.   **LUELLA BERNICE DALTON** [3274] (1924 – 2013) daughter of John and Pearl (Graham) Dalton, married James Lindsey Kelley with whom she was mother of (2). Luella was always a very determined woman. She managed a nursing home and enjoyed people, especially children, and caring for the elderly. She even took care of James for over 10 years until he passed away. Jim was the love of her life. Luella was always active, spiritually and physically. She loved attending church and being with friends and family. She was active and still doing somersaults when she was 82 years old.
ROY DALTON, Fifth great grandson of progenitor Nicholas Kegg.
WALLACE CARLYLE DALTON (1941 – 2012) son of Walter and Hilda (Pilcher) Dalton, married Selma Louise Costello.

DANDREA

PATRICIA L. DANDREA Sixth great granddaughter of progenitor Nicholas Kegg.   **RANDIE LYNN DANDREA** [3275] (1947 – 2008) son of Samuel and Harriet (Ray) Dandrea, married Marsha Sheridan. Randie enjoyed golfing and fishing and loved his German shepherd.   **RENEE LANE DANDREA**, Fifth great granddaughter of progenitor Nicholas Kegg.   **RONA LORRE DANDREA** Fifth great granddaughter of progenitor Nicholas Kegg.   **RUSSELL L. DANDREA**, Sixth great grandson of progenitor Nicholas Kegg.   **RUSSELL LEE DANDREA**, Fifth great grandson of progenitor Nicholas Kegg.

DANFORD

JEFFREY L. DANFORD Sixth great grandson of progenitor Nicholas Kegg.   **JULIE J. DANFORD** Sixth great granddaughter of progenitor Nicholas Kegg.

[3271] Johnstown Tribune Democrat (PA) Jan 2, 2007 [3272] Walnut Grove Cemetery (OH) [3273] p.10 - Times Free Press (TN) April 27, 2012 [3274] Leader (Niles, MI) Sep 26, 2013 [3275] Peninsula Clarion (Kenai, AK) Oct 5, 2008

LORI K. DANFORD Sixth great grand - daughter of progenitor Nicholas Kegg.
STEVEN P. DANFORD Sixth great grandson of progenitor Nicholas Kegg.

DANIEL

CHERYL DANIEL Sixth great granddaughter of progenitor Nicholas Kegg.

DANIELS

BRADY L. DANIELS Seventh great granddaughter of progenitor Nicholas Kegg.
HEATHER MARIE DANIELS Seventh great granddaughter of progenitor Nicholas Kegg.
JAKE ALLEN DANIELS Seventh great grandson of progenitor Nicholas Kegg.
JENNIFER RENEE DANIELS Seventh great granddaughter of progenitor Nicholas Kegg.
JERRY LEE DANIELS [3275A] (1986 – 2010) son of Jerry and Cheryl (Sharrock) Daniels married Arminda McKnight with whom he was father of (2). **JERRY LEE DANIELS** Eighth great grandson of progenitor Nicholas Kegg. **JOSHUA MICHAEL DANIELS** aka "Josh", Seventh great grandson of progenitor Nicholas Kegg. **MATTHEW DANIELS** Eighth great grandson of progenitor Nicholas Kegg. **ZERILDA DANIELS** Seventh great granddaughter of progenitor Nicholas Kegg.

DANKE

WAYNE ALLEN DANKE (born abt.1912) son of William and Mabel (Baer) Danke. Wayne's father died four months before his birth. He was adopted by Arthur A. Armstrong.

DARLING

ADRIAN KAY DARLING Sixth great granddaughter of progenitor Nicholas Kegg. **DELORES MAXINE DARLING** (1938 – 2021) daughter of Everett and Grace Maxine (Beeber) Darling married Ronald Lee Willis with whom she was mother of (3). **EVERETT LEROY DARLING** Fifth great grandson of progenitor Nicholas Kegg. **JANET K. DARLING** Fifth great granddaughter of progenitor Nicholas Kegg. **JASON ALAN DARLING** Sixth great grandson of progenitor Nicholas Kegg. **LINDA DARLENE DARLING** (1943 – 2015) daughter of Everett and Grace Maxine (Beeber) Darling married John L. Collins with whom she was mother of (3). **MARLIN BOYD DARLING** Fifth great grandson of progenitor Nicholas Kegg.

DARLINGTON

FRED GEORGE DARLINGTON [3275B] (1922 – 1933) aka "Freddie", son of Jack and Dora (Kegg) Darlington.

DARNELL

CHRISTINE DARNELL, aka "Chris", Sixth great granddaughter of progenitor Nicholas Kegg.
CONNIE LYNN DARNELL Sixth great granddaughter of progenitor Nicholas Kegg.
MEREDITH DARNELL Seventh great granddaughter of progenitor Nicholas Kegg.

DART

BRANDI LOUISE DART Sixth great granddaughter of progenitor Nicholas Kegg.

[3275A] Littleton & Rue Funeral Home & Crematory (OH) [3275B] p10 Sacramento Bee (CA) Jan 14, 1933

DONNA JEAN DART Sixth great granddaughter of progenitor Nicholas Kegg. **RICHARD W. DART** Sixth great grandson of progenitor Nicholas Kegg.

DASSENKO

PAMELA DASSENKO Fifth great granddaughter of progenitor Nicholas Kegg.
PAUL EDWARD DASSENKO Fifth great grandson of progenitor Nicholas Kegg.

DAUGHTERS

AMY LYNNE DAUGHTERS Sixth great granddaughter of progenitor Nicholas Kegg.

DAVIDSON

BRAD DAVIDSON Fifth great grandson of progenitor Nicholas Kegg.
BEVERLY NICOLE DAVIDSON Eighth great granddaughter of progenitor Nicholas Kegg.
CAROLYN DAVIDSON Fifth great granddaughter of progenitor Nicholas Kegg.
DOLORES DAVIDSON Fifth great granddaughter of progenitor Nicholas Kegg.
HOWARD DAVIDSON Fifth great grandson of progenitor Nicholas Kegg.
JAMES DAVIDSON Fourth great grandson of progenitor Nicholas Kegg.
JESSIE MARGARET DAVIDSON, (1916 -?) daughter of James and Jessie (Williams) Davidson, married Romeo Joseph Doucet. **KARLYN WELLS DAVIDSON** (1958 – 2012) daughter of Charles and Virginia (Holub) Wells, married Edward Louis Schneider with whom she was mother of (2). **KAYLA JANE DAVIDSON** Eighth great granddaughter of progenitor Nicholas Kegg.
KENNETH JAMES DAVIDSON Seventh great grandson of progenitor Nicholas Kegg.
LAURA DAVIDSON (born abt. 1911) daughter of James and Jessie (Williams) Davidson.
LAWRENCE DAVIDSON [3275C] (1915 – 1958) son of James and Jessie (Williams) Davidson, married Esther Ruth Judd with whom he was father of (8). **LEAH DAVIDSON** Seventh great granddaughter of progenitor Nicholas Kegg. **LORNE WILLIAM DAVIDSON** [3275D] (1942 – 1986) son of Lawrence and Esther Ruth (Judd) Davidson. **LUKE DAVIDSON** Seventh great grandson of progenitor Nicholas Kegg. **LYNDA DAVIDSON** Fifth great granddaughter of progenitor Nicholas Kegg.
MARIE DAVIDSON (born abt.1909) daughter of James and Jessie (Williams) Davidson.
PENNY DAVIDSON Fifth great granddaughter of progenitor Nicholas Kegg.
RICHARD DAVIDSON Fifth great grandson of progenitor Nicholas Kegg.
SANDRA JOYCE DAVIDSON [3275E] (1946 – 2001) daughter of Lawrence and Esther Ruth (Judd) Davidson. **SHAWN PATRICK DAVIDSON** Seventh great grandson of progenitor Nicholas Kegg.
THOMAS JEFFREY DAVIDSON Seventh great grandson of progenitor Nicholas Kegg.

DAVIES

STEPHANIE DIANE DAVIES Fifth great granddaughter of progenitor Nicholas Kegg.
TARA IRENE DAVIES Fifth great granddaughter of progenitor Nicholas Kegg.

DAVIS

ABIGAIL DAVIS Eighth great granddaughter of progenitor Nicholas Kegg. **ADAM VINCENT DAVIS** Sixth great grandson of progenitor Nicholas Kegg. **ALICE ANN DAVIS** Sixth great granddaughter of progenitor Nicholas Kegg.

[3275C] The Vancouver Sun (BC) April 16, 1958 [3275D] The Vancouver Sun (BC) March 22, 1986 [3275E] The Vancouver Sun (B.C.) March 27, 2001

ALICE IONA DAVIS [3275F] (1916 – 2010) daughter of Martin and Sylvia (Laird) Davis, married Harold Peck. Alice accepted Christ as her Savior on Oct. 31, 1931, and was baptized by the Rev. Kratzer, pastor of the Christian Church in Kellerton. After finishing school, she spent several years working in department stores as a clerk until 1948 when she started her own store. In 1962 with her husband Alice started farming and raising cattle. Alice taught Sunday school for many years. She also taught at Freedom Bible Camp Alice was gentle, honest, patient and hard working. She was always there when anyone needed anything as long as her health permitted. **ANDREW CARL DAVIS** aka "Drew", Sixth great grandson of progenitor Nicholas Kegg. **ANGELINA DAVIS** aka "Angel", Seventh great granddaughter of progenitor Nicholas Kegg. **BARBARA DAVIS** Sixth great granddaughter of progenitor Nicholas Kegg. **BEATRICE MAE DAVIS** (1915 – 1972) aka "Bea", daughter of Martin and Sylvia (Laird) Davis, married Leslie Austin Fulton with whom she was mother of (8). **BETTY DAVIS** Fifth great granddaughter of progenitor Nicholas Kegg. **BRADLY W DAVIS** [3275G] (1984 – 2006) son of Robert and Deanna (Bennett) Davis married Tiffany Sturtz with whom he was father of (1). Crew supervisor for JIF Fencing, Brad enjoyed hunting, fishing, weightlifting, baseball, and playing on the computer. He also enjoyed riding dirt bikes. **BRANDI DAVIS** Eighth great granddaughter of progenitor Nicholas Kegg. **CHARLES DAVIS** Seventh great grandson of progenitor Nicholas Kegg. **CHARLOTTE LOUISE DAVIS** [3276] (1928 – 2018) daughter of Martin and Sylvia (Laird) Davis, married Charles Granville Overton with whom she was mother of (2). Charlotte enjoyed spending time with family and friends, dancing, a competitive game of cards and collecting Precious Moments. Charlotte was so sweet and greatly loved. **CHERYL DAVIS** Fifth great granddaughter of progenitor Nicholas Kegg. **CHLOE DAVIS** Eighth great granddaughter of progenitor Nicholas Kegg.

DAN DAVIS Fifth great grandson of progenitor Nicholas Kegg. **DEBBIE DAVIS** Fifth great granddaughter of progenitor Nicholas Kegg. **DEBORAH DAVIS** Fifth great granddaughter of progenitor Nicholas Kegg. **DENNIS F. DAVIS** Sixth great grandson of progenitor Nicholas Kegg. **DENNY DAVIS** Fifth great grandson of progenitor Nicholas Kegg. **DONALD JOE DAVIS** Sixth great grandson of progenitor Nicholas Kegg. **DUSTIN MICHAEL DAVIS** Seventh great grandson of progenitor Nicholas Kegg. **DYLLAN C. DAVIS** aka "Dylly", Eighth great grandson of progenitor Nicholas Kegg. **ERIK DAVIS** Sixth great grandson of progenitor Nicholas Kegg. **ETHAN TYLER DAVIS** Seventh great grandson of progenitor Nicholas Kegg. **GARY L. DAVIS** Sixth great grandson of progenitor Nicholas Kegg. **GRANT DAVIS** Sixth great grandson of progenitor Nicholas Kegg. **HANNAH DAVIS** Eighth great granddaughter of progenitor Nicholas Kegg. **HOPE ELIZABETH DAVIS** Sixth great granddaughter of progenitor Nicholas Kegg. **JACKIE CAMEO DAVIS** Eighth great granddaughter of progenitor Nicholas Kegg. **JAMES ANDREW DAVIS** Fifth great grandson of progenitor Nicholas Kegg. **JAMES CARL DAVIS** Seventh great grandson of progenitor Nicholas Kegg. **JEFFREY ALAN DAVIS** aka "Jeff" Fifth great grandson of progenitor Nicholas Kegg. **JEFFREY MACK DAVIS** (1956 – 1975) son of Kenneth and Betty Jeanne (Lawson) Davis, died the result of a stab wound to the neck and chest. **JILL DAVIS** Eighth great granddaughter of progenitor Nicholas Kegg. **JOEY DAVIS** Eighth great grandson of progenitor Nicholas Kegg **JOHN ARTHUR DAVIS** Fifth great grandson of progenitor Nicholas Kegg. **JOSHUA K. DAVIS** Eighth great grandson of progenitor Nicholas Kegg. **JOEY DAVIS** Eighth great grandson of progenitor Nicholas Kegg. **JOHN ARTHUR DAVIS** Fifth great grandson of progenitor Nicholas Kegg. **JOSHUA K. DAVIS** Eighth great grandson of progenitor Nicholas Kegg. **JUDITH ANN DAVIS** Fifth great granddaughter of progenitor Nicholas Kegg. **JUSTIN DAVIS** Eighth great grandson of progenitor Nicholas Kegg. **KAREN DAVIS** aka Kay" Sixth great granddaughter of progenitor Nicholas Kegg. **KATHERINE JEAN DAVIS** Fifth great granddaughter of progenitor Nicholas Kegg. **KEITH DAVIS** Sixth great grandson of progenitor Nicholas Kegg. **KEITH W. DAVIS** Seventh great grandson of progenitor Nicholas Kegg. **KELLY ANN DAVIS** Sixth great granddaughter of progenitor Nicholas Kegg. **KERI DAVIS** Sixth great granddaughter of progenitor Nicholas Kegg.

[3275F] Corydon Times Republican (IA) Sep 13, 2010 [3275G] Daily American (PA) July 5, 2006 [3276] Des Moines Register (IA) Apr. 25, 2018

KRISTIN ANN DAVIS Sixth great granddaughter of progenitor Nicholas Kegg. **LARRY DEAN DAVIS** Sixth great grandson of progenitor Nicholas Kegg. **LAURIE JO DAVIS** Fifth great granddaughter of progenitor Nicholas Kegg. **LINDA R. DAVIS** Sixth great granddaughter of progenitor Nicholas Kegg. **LOGAN DAVIS** Ninth great grandson of progenitor Nicholas Kegg. **LORIE KAY DAVIS** Sixth great granddaughter of progenitor Nicholas Kegg. **LUKE R. DAVIS** Sixth great grandson of progenitor Nicholas Kegg. **LYNN DAVIS** Fourth great grandson of progenitor Nicholas Kegg. **MARVIN RAY DAVIS** [3277] (1922 – 1994) son of Martin and Sylvia (Laird) Davis was father of (1). Marvin retired as a yardman for Consumer Lumber Co. **MARY JANE DAVIS** (1933 – 1933) daughter of Martin and Sylvia (Laird) Davis. **MATTHEW DAVIS** Sixth great grandson of progenitor Nicholas Kegg. **MAX ORVILLE DAVIS** [3278] (1925 – 2000) son of Martin and Sylvia (Laird) Davis married Martha Ann Henson, Max was a veteran of WWII having served in the U.S. Marine Corps. **MEGAN DAVIS** Seventh great granddaughter of progenitor Nicholas Kegg. **MICHALE L. DAVIS** Sixth great grandson of progenitor Nicholas Kegg. **NATHAN DAVIS** aka "Nate", Ninth great grandson of progenitor Nicholas Kegg. **NORMAN DANIEL DAVIS** Fifth great grandson of progenitor Nicholas Kegg. **PAYSEN DAVIS** Ninth great granddaughter of progenitor Nicholas Kegg. **RANDY E. DAVIS** Sixth great grandson of progenitor Nicholas Kegg. **RICHARD DAVIS** Seventh great grandson of progenitor Nicholas Kegg. **RICHARD K. DAVIS** Sixth great grandson of progenitor Nicholas Kegg. **ROBERTA MARIE DAVIS** [3279] (1918 – 2004) daughter of Martin and Sylvia (Laird) Davis married three times; first to Harold Comer, followed by Mr. Kessler and Mr. Russell. **RUSSELL CHALMERS DAVIS** Sixth great grandson of progenitor Nicholas Kegg. **RYLEE JADE DAVIS** Eighth great granddaughter of progenitor Nicholas Kegg. **SCOTT J. DAVIS** [3280] (1982 – 2008) son of Robert and Deanna (Bennett) Davis was father of (1). Scott was employed by Giant Eagle as a butcher. He enjoyed hunting, fishing and video games. Attended Penn Highlands Community College, where he studied computer science. **SKYLAR DAVIS** Eighth great grandson of progenitor Nicholas Kegg. **STEVEN DAVIS** Sixth great grandson of progenitor Nicholas Kegg. **TRENT DAVIS** Seventh great grandson of progenitor Nicholas Kegg. **VERA ELBERTA DAVIS** (1911 – 1980) daughter of Martin and Sylvia (Laird) Davis married three times; first to Ernest Allen Kling with whom she was mother of (2). She later married Lester Alvin Blair and Mr. Cozad. **VESTA ELNORA DAVIS** [3281] (1913 – 1994) daughter of Martin and Sylvia (Laird) Davis, married Francis Eugene Walling with whom she was mother of (1). **WYATT DAVIS** Seventh great grandson of progenitor Nicholas Kegg.

DAVOLI

LAURA ANN DAVOLI Fifth great granddaughter of progenitor Nicholas Kegg.

DAWSON

CRAIG EDMUND DAWSON Fifth great grandson of progenitor Nicholas Kegg.
DARELL DAWSON Fifth great grandson of progenitor Nicholas Kegg. **DAVID T. DAWSON** [3282] (1957 – 2006) son of Loren and Edith (McBride) Dawson a three-time murderer was pronounced dead six minutes after the drugs that killed him began flowing into his veins. The execution took place against a backdrop of debates in courts around the country about the constitutionality of lethal injection. **DENIS KAY DAWSON** Fifth great granddaughter of progenitor Nicholas Kegg. **DORE LEE DAWSON** Fifth great granddaughter of progenitor Nicholas Kegg. **GORDON RAY DAWSON** [3283] (1922 – 2003) son of Delbert and Nellie (Hershiser) Dawson, married Doris Albert Dellevar with whom he was father of (5)

[3277] Des Moines Register (IA) March 18, 1994 [3278] Arizona Republic Feb 3, 2000 [3279] Pueblo Chieftain (CO) April 13, 2004 [3280] Meek Funeral Home (PA) [3281] p 17 Tennessean (Nashville) Jul 30, 1994, Find A Grave memorial # 71924214 Created by: Steven Harrison [3282] USA TODAY Aug 11, 2006 [3283] The Naples Daily News (FL) June 17, 2003

HEIDI DAWSON Sixth great granddaughter of progenitor Nicholas Kegg. **HOWARD MELVIN DAWSON** (1930 – 1930) son of Delbert and Nellie (Hershiser) Dawson. **JEFFREY LYNN DAWSON** Fifth great grandson of progenitor Nicholas Kegg. **JENNIFER DAWSON** Fifth great granddaughter of progenitor Nicholas Kegg. **KAREN J. DAWSON** Sixth great granddaughter of progenitor Nicholas Kegg.

DAY

ARDEN DAY Sixth great granddaughter of progenitor Nicholas Kegg. **CAITLIN DAY** Sixth great granddaughter of progenitor Nicholas Kegg. **CYNTHIA A. DAY** Fifth great granddaughter of progenitor Nicholas Kegg. **DANESSA DAY** Seventh great granddaughter of progenitor Nicholas Kegg. **JOSHUA DAY** Seventh great grandson of progenitor Nicholas Kegg. **KIMBERLE S. DAY** Fifth great granddaughter of progenitor Nicholas Kegg. **LAUREL C. DAY** Fifth great granddaughter of progenitor Nicholas Kegg. **VICTORIA ALICE DAY** [3284] (1872 – 1945) daughter of George and Rebecca (Kegg) Day married, Dr. Joseph D. English; Victoria attended South Side School in 1884-85 when the late Miss Edith Marvin was teacher at that school. She had been a practical nurse for many years.

DE BORTOLI

BRADLEY RYAN DE BORTOLI Fifth great grandson of progenitor Nicholas Kegg. **CAMERON DE BORTOLI** Sixth great grandson of progenitor Nicholas Kegg. **DARIAN DE BORTOLI** Sixth great granddaughter of progenitor Nicholas Kegg. **NATHAN DE BORTOLI** Sixth great grandson of progenitor Nicholas Kegg. **NICHOLAS DE BORTOLI** Sixth great grandson of progenitor Nicholas Kegg. **RANDY JAMES DE BORTOLI** Fifth great grandson of progenitor Nicholas Kegg.

DE LUCCA

JOHN J. DE LUCCA Seventh great grandson of progenitor Nicholas Kegg.
THERESA MARIE DE LUCCA Seventh great granddaughter of progenitor Nicholas Kegg.

DE YOUNG

JEAN ESTHER DE YOUNG [3285] (1915 – 2007) daughter of Dirk and Elta June (Boose) DeYoung, married Frederick Warner Heath with whom she was mother of (4).

DEAL

CAROLYN LOUISE DEAL Fifth great granddaughter of progenitor Nicholas Kegg. **JOYCE MARIE DEAL** Fifth great granddaughter of progenitor Nicholas Kegg. **RODNEY DEAL** Fifth great grandson of progenitor Nicholas Kegg. **SHELLY DEAL** Fifth great granddaughter of progenitor Nicholas Kegg.

DEALAMAN

FREDERIC J. DEALAMAN, aka "Dutch", Fourth great grandson of progenitor Nicholas Kegg. **LAIRD W. DEALAMAN** [3286] (1952 – 2014) aka "Skip", son of Laird and Doris (Wertz) Dealaman.

[3284] Freeport Journal Standard (IL) Aug 22, 1945 [3285] The Central New Jersey Home News (New Brunswick) Dec 19, 1938 [3286] p.47 - Star-Ledger (Newark, NJ) July 9, 2002

Skip graduated from Morristown Beard High School and attended Joans College in Florida. Skip loved animals, and in his free time loved outdoor maintenance work.

DEAN

ANNA MARGARET DEAN (1839 -?) daughter of Daniel and Elizabeth (Knouf) Dean was known to have been married twice; first to Jacob J. Crick with whom she was mother of (2). She later married John Lowe. **BERNARD H. DEAN** (1856 – 1925) aka "Bernie", son of Daniel and Elizabeth (Knouf) Dean married twice; first to Jane (Matthews) Heath and later to Hattie E. (Mark) Lang.
CHARLES O. DEAN (1858 -?) aka "Charley", son of Daniel and Elizabeth (Knouf) Dean, married Ida Fordd Yard with whom he was father of (4). **CLAUDE LESLIE DEAN** [3287] (1888 – 1953) son of Charles and Ida (Yard) Dean, married Ethel A. Davis with whom he was father of (1). Before retiring Claude had been employed for 35 years by John Deere Planter Works. Claude was a member of Moline Eagles and the Gospel Temple. **DANIEL DEAN** (abt 1840 -?) son of Daniel and Elizabeth (Knouf) Dean. **DAISY DALE DEAN** (1891 – 1971) daughter of Henry Clay and Edna Laroy (Owens) Dean married Edwin Arthur Pettit. **DOROTHY MILDRED DEAN** (1911 – 1993) daughter of Henry Clay and Bertha Genette (Miller) Dean married Donald Jackson Martin. **ELMER HUGH DEAN** [3288] (1895 – 1941) son of Johnson and Mary (Voss) Dean, married Helen Marie Dilts with whom he was father of (1). Elmer was an overseas veteran of the World war. He was formerly the second cook and relief chef at the Roosevelt hotel. Elmer was a member of the Maccabees and Hanford post of the American Legion. **ESTHER L. DEAN** (1897 – 1925) daughter of Charles and Ida (Yard) Dean married twice; first to Pearley Horwedel with whom she was mother of (3). Later she married Bert Frye.
FRANK S. DEAN [3289] (1899 – 1935) son of Henry Clay and Bertha Genette (Miller) Dean.
GEORGE DEAN (abt 1866 -?) son of Daniel and Elizabeth (Knouf) Dean. **GEORGE C. DEAN** (abt 1902 -?) son of Charles and Ida (Yard) Dean. **GEORGIA ANN DEAN** (1853 – 1860) daughter of Daniel and Elizabeth (Knouf) Dean. **HELEN MARGARITE DEAN** [3290] (1898 – 1970) daughter of Johnson and Mary (Voss) Dean, married Loyd Leo Callier with whom she was mother of (2). Helen was a member of the Covenant Pres. Church of Long Beach and the Ebell Music Club of Long Beach.
HENRY CLAY DEAN (1871 – 1960) son of Johnson McFadden and Mary (Elliott) Dean married Edna Laroy Owens with whom he was father of (1). Later, he married Bertha Genette Miller with whom he was father of (2). **JOHNSON MCFADDEN DEAN** [3291] (1906 – 1973) aka "Jack," son of Johnson and Mary (Voss) Dean, married Francis Vaverka. A Navy veteran, Jack was a retired electrician for the Santa Fe Railroad. He willed his body to the University of Kansas Medical Center for research.
JOHNSON MCFADDEN DEAN (1849 – 1926) aka "John", son of Daniel and Elizabeth (Knouf) Dean, married Mary Elliott with whom he was father of (3). Later, he married Mary Voss with whom he was father of (3. **LOIS A. DEAN** Fourth great granddaughter of progenitor Nicholas Kegg.
LULA MAY DEAN (1891 – 1977) daughter of Charles and Ida (Yard) Dean, married Lee Allen Moorehouse with whom she was mother of (5). **MARY JANE DEAN** [3292] (1844 – 1933) daughter of Daniel and Elizabeth (Knouf) Dean, married William Alexander Snavely with whom she was mother of (5). **MARY JANE DEAN** [3293] (1891 – 1977) daughter of Johnson McFadden and Mary (Elliott) Dean married William Chauncey Sawyer with whom she was mother of (7). Mary was a member of Royal Neighbors of America and the Melrose American Legion Auxiliary. **MATTIE DEAN** (1863 – 1928) daughter of Daniel and Elizabeth (Knouf) Dean, married James Edward McDermott with whom she was mother of (3). **MILDRED MARIE DEAN** [3294] (1923 – 2002) daughter of Elmer and Helen (Dilts) Dean, married Charles Roy Norberg with whom she was mother of (1); Mildred was a lifelong member of St. John's Episcopal Church, was a life member of St. Luke's Hospital Auxiliary, and was a member of PEO, the EGA and the Creative Book Club. Marie also attended Coe College.

[3287] The Dispatch (Moline, Ill) Mar 19, 1955 [3288] The Gazette (Cedar Rapids, IA) Feb 21, 1941 [3289] The Gazette (Cedar Rapids, IA) Aug 15, 1935 [3290] p.C14 Independent (CA) Dec 28, 1970 [3291] Kansas City Star (MO) Oct 14, 1973 [3292] The Berwyn News (IL) June 16, 1933 [3293] The La Crosse Tribune (WI) April 17, 1977 [3294] The Gazette (Cedar Rapids, IA) April 24, 2002

NETTIE DEAN (1873 – 1948) daughter of Johnson McFadden and Mary (Elliott) Dean married Franklin Hale with whom she was mother of (3). **WILLIAM H. DEAN** (abt 1842 -?) son of Daniel and Elizabeth (Knouf) Dean.

DEANER

DANIEL LYNN DEANER [3295] (1976 – 1988) son of Lynn and Marjorie (Vaughan) Deaner. Daniel was a seventh-grade honor student at Berlin Brothersvalley School. He attended Trinity United Church of Christ, Berlin, where he served as acolyte and was a member of the confirmation class. He was a former Cub Scout and was a second-class scout in Troop 135, Berlin. He was a member of Snyder's Little League Baseball Team and junior high football team. He played saxophone in the junior high band and was an avid pianist. **DOUGLAS LEVI DEANER** Sixth great grandson of progenitor Nicholas Kegg. **MILDRED E. DEANER** [3296] (1908 – 1981) daughter of Howard and Zella (Rose) Deaner, married David Thomas Rees with whom she was mother of (3). Mildred was a former postmaster in Hyndman, a member of Holy Cross Episcopal Church, Cumberland, and a member and past president of The Women's Sport Club.

DEARING

MATTHEW J. H. DEARING Seventh great grandson of progenitor Nicholas Kegg.

DEARMENT

ELISE DEARMENT Seventh great granddaughter of progenitor Nicholas Kegg.

DEASEY

DAVID A. DEASEY Fifth great grandson of progenitor Nicholas Kegg. **GARY DEASEY** Fifth great grandson of progenitor Nicholas Kegg. **PAUL LEE DEASEY** Fifth great grandson of progenitor Nicholas Kegg. **SHARON DEASEY** Fifth great granddaughter of progenitor Nicholas Kegg.

DEASON

ROBERT JOHN SCOTT DEASON Eighth great grandson of progenitor Nicholas Kegg.
SCOTT WAYNE DEASON Seventh great grandson of progenitor Nicholas Kegg.
SHANNON DEASON Seventh great granddaughter of progenitor Nicholas Kegg.

DEBELIUS

BARBARA A. DEBELIUS [3296A] (1928 – 2015) daughter of John and Helen (Bragg) Debelius, married Harold Arthur Davis with whom she was mother of (4). Barb was employed with Duane Axel Insurance in Kendallville for 31 years before retiring. She was an active lifetime member of the First Presbyterian Church in Kendallville. Over many years, she served in various capacities within the church including deacon, elder, clerk of session, president of the Presbyterian Women's Association, and Sunday school teacher. She also belonged to the Mary Martha Circle, helped with countless church bazaars, rummage sales, and many other church activities. Barb was a member of Tri Kappa since high school. She was also actively involved with American Field Service, Kendallville chapter, for many years. She volunteered

---

[3295] Meyersdale Library obtained and contributed by Sally Statler [3296] p.4 Cumberland News (MD) Oct 19, 1981 [3296A] KPCNews (IN) Oct 23, 2015

many hours with the American Red Cross Bloodmobile, Teen-Parent Coop, Meals-On-Wheels, and the Sacred Heart Home. She delivered the Fort Wayne newspaper in the Kendallville area for many years. After she retired, she kept busy by working part time for Anita Hess and her real estate business. Barb was an avid bridge player and member of several bridge clubs. **HELEN ELIZABETH DEBELIUS** aka "Betsy" Fourth great granddaughter of progenitor Nicholas Kegg.

DEBERNARDIS

AVERY DEBERNARDIS Eighth great grandson of progenitor Nicholas Kegg.
COOPER DEBERNARDIS Eighth great grandson of progenitor Nicholas Kegg.
ISABEL DEBERNARDIS Eighth great granddaughter of progenitor Nicholas Kegg.

DEBOCK

CAROLYN ROSE DEBOCK Fifth great granddaughter of progenitor Nicholas Kegg.

DECAMP

CASSIDY DECAMP Seventh great granddaughter of progenitor Nicholas Kegg.
KAYLEE DECAMP Seventh great granddaughter of progenitor Nicholas Kegg.

DECICCO

ASHLEY DECICCO Seventh great granddaughter of progenitor Nicholas Kegg. **DAWN M. DECICCO** Sixth great granddaughter of progenitor Nicholas Kegg. **GABRIELLE DECICCO** Seventh great granddaughter of progenitor Nicholas Kegg. **JAMES A. DECICCO** [3297] (1970 – 2006) son of James and Shirley (Creps) Decicco, married Tracy Mroz with whom he was father of (1). **NICOLE DECICCO** Seventh great granddaughter of progenitor Nicholas Kegg. **PHILLIP DECICCO** Seventh great grandson of progenitor Nicholas Kegg.

DECKER

DOREEN DECKER Sixth great granddaughter of progenitor Nicholas Kegg. **HOLLY DECKER** Sixth great granddaughter of progenitor Nicholas Kegg. **RACHEL DECKER** Sixth great granddaughter of progenitor Nicholas Kegg. **ROBERT DECKER** Sixth great grandson of progenitor Nicholas Kegg. **ROBERT J. DECKER** Fifth great grandson of progenitor Nicholas Kegg. **ROBIN DECKER** Sixth great granddaughter of progenitor Nicholas Kegg. **SHERRY DECKER** Sixth great granddaughter of progenitor Nicholas Kegg. **TIFFANY NICOLE DECKER** Seventh great granddaughter of progenitor Nicholas Kegg.

DEEDS

BRENDA L DEEDS Sixth great granddaughter of progenitor Nicholas Kegg. **BRONSYN JAMES DEEDS** Eighth great grandson of progenitor Nicholas Kegg. **CHARLES DEEDS** Sixth great grandson of progenitor Nicholas Kegg. **DEBORAH A. DEEDS** Sixth great granddaughter of progenitor Nicholas Kegg. **DENNIS R. DEEDS** (1963 – 2012) son of Franklin and Rose (Heinze) Deeds Jr., married Julie Honeywell with whom he was father of (1). Dennis worked for Gleason Construction in

---

[3297] The Record (NJ) Feb. 18, 2006

Holland, Ohio. He enjoyed hunting and fishing and was a member of the National Rifle Association, but playing with his grandson was his greatest joy. **FRANKLIN J. DEEDS** [3298] (1931 – 2006) aka "Wild Bill", son of Franklin and Lucille (Smith) Deeds, married Rose Marie Heinze with whom he was father of (9). Franklin was a retired diesel mechanic. **JUSTIN JAMES DEEDS** Seventh great grandson of progenitor Nicholas Kegg. **LISA MARIE DEEDS** Sixth great granddaughter of progenitor Nicholas Kegg. **ROBERT DEEDS** Sixth great grandson of progenitor Nicholas Kegg. **TIMOTHY F. DEEDS** Sixth great grandson of progenitor Nicholas Kegg. **VICKI LYNN DEEDS** [3299] (1968 – 2019) daughter of Franklin and Rose Marie (Heinze) Deeds married Mark Joseph Murar with whom she was mother of (3). Vickie owned and operated Rejuvenating Affects Tanning and Hair Salon in Lyons. Definitely a "Sun Goddess," she loved being outdoors soaking up the sun every chance she had. She also enjoyed riding Harley motorcycles and working puzzles. Vickie also had a passion for flower gardening. She was known for her large and meticulously maintained flowerbeds outside her home. People would come from all around to admire them and take photos. **WALTER RONALD DEEDS** Sixth great grandson of progenitor Nicholas Kegg.

DEEL

ERICA DEEL Sixth great granddaughter of progenitor Nicholas Kegg. **MICHELLE DEEL** Sixth great granddaughter of progenitor Nicholas Kegg.

DEEMER

MATTHEW E. DEEMER Seventh great grandson of progenitor Nicholas Kegg.
SCOTT MICHAEL DEEMER Seventh great grandson of progenitor Nicholas Kegg.

DEFEBIO

CARL DEFEBIO (1952 – 1973) son of Frank and Theo (Thomas) Defebio.
DOMINICK NICHOLAS DEFEBIO Fifth great grandson of progenitor Nicholas Kegg.
THEODORE THOMAS DEFEBIO aka "Teddy", Fifth great grandson of progenitor Nicholas Kegg.

DEFIBAUGH

AMY DEFIBAUGH Seventh great granddaughter of progenitor Nicholas Kegg.
COURTNEY DEFIBAUGH Seventh great granddaughter of progenitor Nicholas Kegg.
ERIN DEFIBAUGH Seventh great granddaughter of progenitor Nicholas Kegg.
KAREN L. DEFIBAUGH [3299A] (1958 – 2015) daughter of Willard and Velma (Crawford) Defibaugh, married David Eugene Burns with whom she was mother of (3). Karen was part of a military family and traveled the world. Her most treasured memories were of life at Lajes Air Force Base on Terceira Island, Azores. At Frederick Community College, she worked in the admissions office, then in publications and marketing for over 30 years. Karen was a creative talent and a treasured colleague and mentor.
HANNAH GRACE DEFIBAUGH Seventh great granddaughter of progenitor Nicholas Kegg.
JOSHUA G. DEFIBAUGH, aka "Josh", Seventh great grandson of progenitor Nicholas Kegg.
MARY CATHERINE DEFIBAUGH Seventh great granddaughter of progenitor Nicholas Kegg.
ROGER L. DEFIBAUGH Sixth great grandson of progenitor Nicholas Kegg. **SHIRLEY RENEE DEFIBAUGH** Sixth great granddaughter of progenitor Nicholas Kegg.

[3298] Toledo Blade (OH) Feb 26, 2006, obtained by D. Sue Dible [3299] The Blade (OH) Dec. 2, 2019 [3299A] Bedford Gazette (PA) July 30, 2015, obtained by Bob Rose

DEFRUSCIO

THOMAS E. DEFRUSCIO Eighth great grandson of progenitor Nicholas Kegg.

DEIBERT

ADAM JACOB DEIBERT Sixth great grandson of progenitor Nicholas Kegg.
ALICIA MARIE DEIBERT Sixth great granddaughter of progenitor Nicholas Kegg.
ANDREW T. DEIBERT Sixth great grandson of progenitor Nicholas Kegg.

DELAET

BRIAN DELAET Sixth great grandson of progenitor Nicholas Kegg. **DOUGLAS DELAET** Sixth great grandson of progenitor Nicholas Kegg. **GREGORY DELAET** Sixth great grandson of progenitor Nicholas Kegg.

DELAHUNTY

BRIAN CARL DELAHUNTY Fourth great grandson of progenitor Nicholas Kegg.
CARL THOMAS DELAHUNTY [3300] (1928 – 2019) son of Thomas and Minnie (Kegg) Delahunty, married Martha Ella Zess with whom he was father of (8). Carl was employed as a linotype operator at the Warren Tribune Chronicle and was Supervisor and Vice President of Crook's Bottled Gas Company in Cortland. He was a lover of anything with wheels from bicycles to cars. Carl was an avid vegetable gardener and traveler with his wife after retirement. He loved to tinker with and repair anything that was in need of a good fix. Carl was a longtime member of St. Elizabeth Ann Seton Parish-St. James Catholic Church in Warren and was a member of the Knights of Columbus St. James Council and the Outspoken Wheelmen of Youngstown. **CARLA JO DELAHUNTY** Fourth great granddaughter of progenitor Nicholas Kegg. **DIANE MARIE DELAHUNTY** Fourth great granddaughter of progenitor Nicholas Kegg. **EDWARD CARL DELAHUNTY** Fourth great grandson of progenitor Nicholas Kegg. **LAVERN MARY ELIZABETH DELAHUNTY** [3301] (1916 – 2001) daughter of Thomas and Minnie (Kegg) Delahunty, married Karl Fred Crooks with whom she was mother of (3). Laverne was a member of the Blessed Sacrament Church in Warren and was a volunteer for Hospice, Mobile Meals and St. Vincent DePaul and was a Pastoral volunteer at Trumbull Memorial Hospital. She was chairman of the board and owner of Crooks Bottled Gas Co. **LAVERNE MARIE DELAHUNTY** Fourth great granddaughter of progenitor Nicholas Kegg. **LINDA J DELAHUNTY** Fourth great granddaughter of progenitor Nicholas Kegg. **MARY SUSAN DELAHUNTY** Fourth great granddaughter of progenitor Nicholas Kegg. **THOMAS ANDREW DELAHUNTY** Fourth great grandson of progenitor Nicholas Kegg.

DELASKO

NATHAN DELASKO Sixth great grandson of progenitor Nicholas Kegg. **ROBERT DELASKO** Fifth great grandson of progenitor Nicholas Kegg. **SALLY ANN DELASKO** Fifth great granddaughter of progenitor Nicholas Kegg. **WANDA JEAN DELASKO** Fifth great granddaughter of progenitor Nicholas Kegg.

DELP

CALEB DELP Seventh great grandson of progenitor Nicholas Kegg. **DAVID EDWARD DELP** Sixth

---

[3300] Staton-Borowski Funeral Home (OH) [3301] p. B4 - The Vindicator (OH) Oct. 6, 2001

great grandson of progenitor Nicholas Kegg. **KYLIE DELP** Seventh great granddaughter of progenitor Nicholas Kegg. **LISA ANN DELP** Sixth great granddaughter of progenitor Nicholas Kegg.

DELUCIA

ANGELA DELUCIA Sixth great granddaughter of progenitor Nicholas Kegg.

DELVALLE

AIVEN DELVALLE Eighth great grandson of progenitor Nicholas Kegg.

DEMKO

CORY J. DEMKO Seventh great grandson of progenitor Nicholas Kegg.
MEGAN DEMKO Seventh great granddaughter of progenitor Nicholas Kegg.

DEMSKI

IAN FREDERICK DEMSKI Fifth great grandson of progenitor Nicholas Kegg.
ZACHARY ADAM DEMSKI Fifth great grandson of progenitor Nicholas Kegg.

DENNIS

SONDRA LOU DENNIS Fifth great granddaughter of progenitor Nicholas Kegg.

DENNISON

CATHERINE DENNISON Seventh great granddaughter of progenitor Nicholas Kegg.

DEPUTY

DOMINICK DEPUTY Eighth great grandson of progenitor Nicholas Kegg. **JOSHUA DEPUTY** aka "Josh", Seventh great grandson of progenitor Nicholas Kegg. **KOHYN DEPUTY** Eighth great grandson of progenitor Nicholas Kegg. **KOOPER DEPUTY** Eighth great grandson of progenitor Nicholas Kegg. **MATTHEW DEPUTY** Seventh great grandson of progenitor Nicholas Kegg.

DERBY

COURTNEY DANIELLE DERBY Eighth great granddaughter of progenitor Nicholas Kegg. **DANEEN EVANA DERBY** Seventh great granddaughter of progenitor Nicholas Kegg. **KAITLYN DERBY** Eighth great granddaughter of progenitor Nicholas Kegg. **KENDRA J. DERBY** Seventh great granddaughter of progenitor Nicholas Kegg. **SARA NICOLE DERBY** Eighth great granddaughter of progenitor Nicholas Kegg. **WILLIAM DERBY** Seventh great grandson of progenitor Nicholas Kegg. **WILLIAM STEPHEN DERBY** aka "Lil Will", Eighth great grandson of progenitor Nicholas Kegg.

DERRICKSON

ANDREA DERRICKSON [3302] (1954 – 1985) daughter of Vernon and Patricia (Reed) Derrickson, married Lex Joseph Burkett with whom she was mother of (2). An elementary school teacher, Andrea had

---

[3302] Sunday News Journal (Wilmington, Del.) June 23, 1985

taught at the Broadmeadows School in Middle-town and at the Ursuline Academy. She was an active member of Westminster Presbyterian Church in Wilmington and the Junior League of Delaware.
NANCY BLADES DERRICKSON Fifth great granddaughter of progenitor Nicholas Kegg.
PATRICIA REED DERRICKSON aka "Trish", Fifth great granddaughter of progenitor Nicholas Kegg.

DESHONG

ALAN B. DESHONG Fourth great grandson of progenitor Nicholas Kegg. **ALICIA DESHONG** Fifth great granddaughter of progenitor Nicholas Kegg. **BENJAMIN LEWIS DESHONG** Fifth great grandson of progenitor Nicholas Kegg. **BRENNA DESHONG** Fifth great granddaughter of progenitor Nicholas Kegg. **JESSICA DESHONG** Fifth great granddaughter of progenitor Nicholas Kegg.
KEITH ALAN DESHONG Fifth great grandson of progenitor Nicholas Kegg.
NOAH BENJAMIN DESHONG [3303] (2008 – 2008) son of Benjamin and Jenna (Gruber) Deshong.
PAUL RICHARD DESHONG Fourth great grandson of progenitor Nicholas Kegg.
SAMANTHA L. DESHONG Fifth great granddaughter of progenitor Nicholas Kegg.
THOMAS H. DESHONG Fourth great grandson of progenitor Nicholas Kegg.
WILLARD F. DESHONG Fourth great grandson of progenitor Nicholas Kegg.

DETWEILER

EMILY DETWEILER Sixth great granddaughter of progenitor Nicholas Kegg.
SARAH DETWEILER Sixth great granddaughter of progenitor Nicholas Kegg.

DEVER

HANNAH DEVER Seventh great granddaughter of progenitor Nicholas Kegg.
SARAH ELIZABETH DEVER Seventh great granddaughter of progenitor Nicholas Kegg.

DEVERS

GERALDINE IRIS DEVERS, aka "Dina", Sixth great granddaughter of progenitor Nicholas Kegg.
WILLIAM F. DEVERS Sixth great grandson of progenitor Nicholas Kegg.

DEVINE

IDA CATHERINE DEVINE [3304] (1937 – 2000) daughter of James and Gladys (McDaniel) Devine, married Alfred Charles Lee with whom she was mother of (3). **JAMES CLYDE DEVINE** (1934 – 1990) son of James and Gladys (McDaniel) Devine, married Carol Homyak.
NATALIE ANN DEVINE Fifth great granddaughter of progenitor Nicholas Kegg.
SCOTT M. DEVINE Sixth great grandson of progenitor Nicholas Kegg. **SHAWN R. DEVINE** Sixth great grandson of progenitor Nicholas Kegg. **STACI LEE DEVINE** Sixth great granddaughter of progenitor Nicholas Kegg. **STEPHEN ROBERT DEVINE JR.** Sixth great grandson of progenitor Nicholas Kegg.

DEVRIES

KENDALL DEVRIES Seventh great grandson of progenitor Nicholas Kegg. **KILEY DEVRIES** Seventh great granddaughter of progenitor Nicholas Kegg.

[3303] Lebanon Daily News (PA) Mar 11, 2008, obtained by D. Sue Dible [3304] Tribune Democrat Newspaper Archives p.31

DEWAARD

MARSHALL DEWAARD Eighth great grandson of progenitor Nicholas Kegg.

DEWITT

BRIAN PATRICK DEWITT Fifth great grandson of progenitor Nicholas Kegg.

DE YOUNG

RUTH EVELYN DE YOUNG [3304A] daughter of Dirk and Elta June (Boose) De Young, married Frederick Hubert Heiss with whom she was mother of (4). Ruth was registered nurse.

DI LULLO

ELLA MARIA DI LULLO Eighth great granddaughter of progenitor Nicholas Kegg.
GIANNA ROSE DI LULLO Eighth great granddaughter of progenitor Nicholas Kegg.

DIALS

DAMIEN DIALS Seventh great grandson of progenitor Nicholas Kegg. **ERIC DIALS** Sixth great grandson of progenitor Nicholas Kegg. **MADELYNN DIALS** Seventh great granddaughter of progenitor Nicholas Kegg.

DIAZ

ARTHUR DIAZ [3305] (2006 – 2006) son of Arthur and Cassandra (Middleton) Diaz. **CHRISTINA MARIE DIAZ** Sixth great granddaughter of progenitor Nicholas Kegg. **CORINNA JO DIAZ** Seventh great granddaughter of progenitor Nicholas Kegg. **KEVIN ROY DIAZ** Seventh great grandson of progenitor Nicholas Kegg. **XAVIER DIAZ** [3306] (2008 – 2008) son of Arthur and Cassandra (Middleton) Diaz.

DIBERT

ANNALEIS DIBERT Sixth great granddaughter of progenitor Nicholas Kegg. **BECKY DIBERT** Sixth great granddaughter of progenitor Nicholas Kegg. **CHASE DIBERT** Seventh great grandson of progenitor Nicholas Kegg. **JENNIE M. DIBERT** Fifth great granddaughter of progenitor Nicholas Kegg. **JOHN C. DIBERT** Fifth great grandson of progenitor Nicholas Kegg. **JOSEPH E. DIBERT** Fifth great grandson of progenitor Nicholas Kegg. **JOSH DIBERT** Sixth great grandson of progenitor Nicholas Kegg. **LUKE DIBERT** Sixth great grandson of progenitor Nicholas Kegg. **MARIE VIOLA DIBERT** [3307] (1915 – 2001) daughter of Franklin Roy and Cora Reda (Bussard) Dibert, married Kenneth D. Mellott with whom she was mother of (1). Marie attended the Clear Creek Brethren in Christ Church, where she was a former treasurer and Sunday school teacher. **MICAH DIBERT** Sixth great grandson of progenitor Nicholas Kegg. **NELLIE V. DIBERT** [3308] (1917 – 1989) daughter of Franklin Roy and Cora Reda (Bussard) Dibert, married Gerald Wilson Clark with whom she was mother of (2). Nellie owned and operated Gerald W. Clark Well Drilling in Everett. She was a charter member of the Ladies Auxiliary of the Raystown Ambulance. She had served as president and had been serving as treasurer of the auxiliary and was a member of the ambulance service's board of directors. Nellie had also

---

[3304A] Orange County Register (CA) Dec 17, 2004 [3305] Daily Chief Union (OH) Oct 21, 2006 [3306] Daily Chief Union (OH) Apr 4, 2008 [3307] p.3 - Bedford Inquirer (PA) Jan 4, 2002, obtained by Bob Rose [3308] Bedford Inquirer (PA) Aug 1, 1989, obtained by Duke Clark

been a Sunday School teacher at the Clear Creek Brethren in Christ Church. **PAUL H. DIBERT** [3309] (1975 – 1997) son of John and Freda (Hall) Dibert. Paul was a 1993 graduate of Berlin-Brothersvalley High School and was employed at North View Farms of Berlin. He was a member of Heritage Baptist Church in Friedens. **RYAN DIBERT** Sixth great grandson of progenitor Nicholas Kegg. **SAMUEL DIBERT** Fifth great grandson of progenitor Nicholas Kegg. **SANDRA L. DIBERT** Fifth great granddaughter of progenitor Nicholas Kegg. **VESTA MAY DIBERT** [3310] (1912 – 1999) daughter of Franklin Roy and Cora Reda (Bussard) Dibert, married Chalmer Clayton Clark with whom she was mother of (4). Vesta was a homemaker on the farm she owned with her husband. She was a member of the Clear Ridge Independent Fellowship, a former secretary for the Cherry Lane Cemetery Association and was a church organist for Rock Hill United Church of Christ.

DICK

CHRISTOPHER DICK Sixth great grandson of progenitor Nicholas Kegg. **KELSEY DICK** Sixth great granddaughter of progenitor Nicholas Kegg. **KYLIE DICK** Sixth great granddaughter of progenitor Nicholas Kegg.

DICKENSON

RONALD W. DICKENSON Fifth great grandson of progenitor Nicholas Kegg.

DICKERHOFF

ANDREW DICKERHOFF aka "A.J.", Seventh great grandson of progenitor Nicholas Kegg.
BLAKE DAVID DICKERHOFF Seventh great grandson of progenitor Nicholas Kegg.
DAVID G. DICKERHOFF Sixth great grandson of progenitor Nicholas Kegg.
JANE LYNN DICKERHOFF Sixth great granddaughter of progenitor Nicholas Kegg.
JOHN L. DICKERHOFF Sixth great grandson of progenitor Nicholas Kegg.
JOHN LOYD DICKERHOFF Seventh great grandson of progenitor Nicholas Kegg.
REESE DICKERHOFF Seventh great grandson of progenitor Nicholas Kegg.
ROBERT L. DICKERHOFF aka "Robbie", Seventh great grandson of progenitor Nicholas Kegg.

DICKERSON

DALTON WALKER DICKERSON Seventh great grandson of progenitor Nicholas Kegg.

DICKINSON

DAVID ROBERT DICKINSON Sixth great grandson of progenitor Nicholas Kegg.
HEATHER MARIE DICKINSON Seventh great granddaughter of progenitor Nicholas Kegg.
JOHN CHARLES DICKINSON Sixth great grandson of progenitor Nicholas Kegg.
MARTHA LYN DICKINSON Sixth great granddaughter of progenitor Nicholas Kegg.
SALLY LOUISE DICKINSON Sixth great granddaughter of progenitor Nicholas Kegg.

DICKSON

HEATHER NICOLE DICKSON Sixth great granddaughter of progenitor Nicholas Kegg.
JENNIFER DICKSON Seventh great granddaughter of progenitor Nicholas Kegg.

[3309] p.8 – Bedford Gazette (PA) June 5, 1997 [3310] Bedford Inquirer (PA) Aug 27, 1999, obtained by Duke Clark

JIMMY DICKSON Seventh great grandson of progenitor Nicholas Kegg.
JOSHUA PAUL DICKSON Sixth great grandson of progenitor Nicholas Kegg.

DIEFENDERFER

CAROLYN DIEFENDERFER Fifth great granddaughter of progenitor Nicholas Kegg.
DAN DIEFENDERFER Sixth great grandson of progenitor Nicholas Kegg.
DAWN DIEFENDERFER Sixth great granddaughter of progenitor Nicholas Kegg.
EDITH LUCILLE DIEFENDERER (1941 – 2010) daughter of Carol and Myrtle (Clark) Diefenderfer, married David Norman Deubner. **JEFF DIEFENDERFER** Sixth great grandson of progenitor Nicholas Kegg. **JOHN E. DIEFENDERFER** Sixth great grandson of progenitor Nicholas Kegg. **MARK R. DIEFENDERFER** Sixth great grandson of progenitor Nicholas Kegg. **MICHAEL K. DIEFENDERFER** Sixth great grandson of progenitor Nicholas Kegg. **STACY DIEFENDERFER** Sixth great granddaughter of progenitor Nicholas Kegg. **TERI DIEFENDERFER** Sixth great granddaughter of progenitor Nicholas Kegg.

DIEHL

ALAN DIEHL Fifth great grandson of progenitor Nicholas Kegg. **ALLAN DIEHL** Sixth great grandson of progenitor Nicholas Kegg. **ANNA ELIZABETH DIEHL** [3311] (1910 – 1974) daughter of Harry and Ada (Bingham) Diehl, married Sherman Edgar Barnes with whom she was mother of (10). Anna was a member of the Seventh Day Adventist Church and an active member of the Dorcas Society. **ANNA KATHRYN DIEHL** [3312] (1916 – 2006) aka "Kay", daughter of Clyde and Claribel (Minnich) Diehl, married Dean Hamilton Reynolds with whom she was mother of (3). Primarily a homemaker, Kay had formerly been an active antique dealer and enthusiast. She enjoyed the outdoors, gardening, cooking and spending time with her family. Kay was a member of the Huntingdon Presbyterian Church. She was a former member of the Huntingdon Music Club. **ARLENE HATTIE DIEHL**, aka "Peg", Fifth great granddaughter of progenitor Nicholas Kegg. **BARBARA JEAN DIEHL** Sixth great granddaughter of progenitor Nicholas Kegg. **BARBARA R. DIEHL** Sixth great granddaughter of progenitor Nicholas Kegg. **BEATRICE K. DIEHL** [3313] (1905 – 1986) daughter of Sewell and Bertha (Milburn) Diehl, married Harry Clay Way with whom she was mother of (2). Beatrice was a member of the Friends Meeting at Fishertown **BEATRICE R. DIEHL** (1916 – 1990) daughter of Fred and Gladys (Himmelwright) Diehl, married Norris C. Prinkey. **BENJAMIN FRANKLIN DIEHL** [3314] (1835 – 1900) son of Isaac and Catherine (Kegg) Diehl, married Eve Ann Diehl with whom he was father of (7). Everyone knew him as a generous, upright, Christian man, always willing to lend a helping hand to the distressed. Benjamin was an active member of the Reformed church. He was superintendent of the Sunday school for a long time and served as a deacon and elder in his church for many years. **BERNARD DIEHL** [3315] (1924 – 2002) son of Oscar and Ethel (Wilson) Diehl. Bernard was a salesman, employed by Sears Roebuck Co. of Greensburg for over 25 years. He was a member of St. Paul's United Methodist Church of Youngwood. He was also a life member of the Youngwood Volunteer Fire Department. Bernard served in World War II in the U.S. Army. **BERNICE DIEHL** [3316] (1907 – 1997) daughter of Oscar and Ethel (Wilson) Diehl, married Clarence William Beck with whom she was mother of (2). **BETTY E. DIEHL** Fourth great granddaughter of progenitor Nicholas Kegg. **BLANCHE ALICE DIEHL** [3317] (1878 – 1941) daughter of William and Sophia (Diehl) Diehl, married William S. Snyder with whom she was mother of (3). **BRENDA DIEHL** Fifth great granddaughter of progenitor Nicholas Kegg. **CAROL DIEHL** Fifth great granddaughter of progenitor Nicholas Kegg.

[3311] Bedford County Genealogical Society obituary obtained by D. Sue Dible [3312] p. 2A - Huntingdon Daily News (PA) Aug 10, 2006 [3313] Bedford County Genealogical Society obituary obtained by D. Sue Dible [3314] Bedford Gazette (PA) Dec 28, 1900 [3315] Daily Courier (Connellsville, PA) [3316] Pittsburgh Post-Gazette (PA) Apr 8, 1997 [3317] Bedford County Historical Society Pioneer Library (PA); book 52, p S-113, obtained by D. Sue Dible (

CARRIE CATHERINE DIEHL [3319] (1881 – 1968) daughter of William and Sophia (Diehl) Diehl, married Charles Ellis Diehl with whom she was mother of (3).   **CHARLES ELLIS DIEHL** [3320] (1919 – 2000) son of Charles and Carrie (Diehl) Diehl, married Carolyn Evelyn Miller with whom he was father of (5). Charles retired as an engineer from Conrail in 1980 with 39 years of service. He was a graduate of Woodbury High School and had attended Penn State, Altoona for one year. Mr Diehl enjoyed vegetable gardening and hunting. He was a member of Railroaders Local Brotherhood of Fireman and Engineers and the National Rifle Association.   **CHARLES MARSHALL RUEBEN DIEHL** (1900 – 1951) son of Rueben and Mary Jane (Kegg) Diehl, married Marie E. Herold with whom he was father of (3). **CHARLES MICHAEL DIEHL** Sixth great grandson of progenitor Nicholas Kegg.
CHARLES ROY DIEHL [3321] (1903 – 1993) son of Joseph and Nellie (Shoemaker) Diehl, married Fern Amanda Shaffer with whom he was father of (2). C. Roy was a dairy farmer in Friends Cove for 37 years and was formerly employed as a school bus and milk truck driver. C. Roy was a member of Friends Cove United Church of Christ, where he was a former Consistory member and Sunday school teacher. He was also a member of Charlesville POS of A, Charlesville Grange, Bedford County Grange, 7th Degree, and the former Charlesville Band and was Dreviously a director of the Friends Cove Mutual Insurance Co. from 1943 to 1991, and director and secretary of the Friends Cove Cemetery Association. C. Roy was a 1921 graduate of Rainsburg Normal School, where he earned a teaching certificate.
CHARLES WILSON DIEHL (1858 – 1862) son of Benjamin and Eva (Diehl) Diehl.
CHERYL DIEHL Fifth great granddaughter of progenitor Nicholas Kegg.   **CHERYL SUSAN DIEHL** Sixth great granddaughter of progenitor Nicholas Kegg.   **CHRISTEN K. DIEHL** Sixth great granddaughter of progenitor Nicholas Kegg.   **CLARK TALMADGE DIEHL** [3322] (1890 – 1970) son of Michael and Elizabeth (Diehl) Diehl, married Nellie G. Overholt with whom he was father of (3). Clark retired from Coventry Cereamics.   **CLYDE HOMER DIEHL** [3323] (1886 – 1955) son of Judge William and Laura (Shoemaker) Diehl, married Claribel Minnich with whom he was father of (2). **DALE DIEHL** Sixth great grandson of progenitor Nicholas Kegg.   **DARLEEN DIEHL** Sixth great granddaughter of progenitor Nicholas Kegg.   **DARLENE DIEHL** Fourth great granddaughter of progenitor Nicholas Kegg.   **DEBBIE DIEHL** Fifth great granddaughter of progenitor Nicholas Kegg. **DEBRA MICHELLE DIEHL** Sixth great granddaughter of progenitor Nicholas Kegg.
DEBRA RAE DIEHL Seventh great granddaughter of progenitor Nicholas Kegg.
DENNIS W. DIEHL Sixth great grandson of progenitor Nicholas Kegg.   **DIANNE DIEHL** Fifth great granddaughter of progenitor Nicholas Kegg.   **DIANNE RUTH DIEHL** Sixth great granddaughter of progenitor Nicholas Kegg.   **DONALD RICHARD DIEHL** [3324] (1927 – 2004) son of Charles and Marie (Herold) Diehl, married Kathryn Virginia Trenton with whom he was father of (4).
DONALD W. DIEHL Fifth great grandson of progenitor Nicholas Kegg.   **DONNA J. DIEHL** Fifth great granddaughter of progenitor Nicholas Kegg.   **EARL JOHN NICKOLAS DIEHL** [3325] (1917 – 1983) son of Elias and Nettie (Kegg) Diehl, married Evelyn M. Price with whom he was father of (3). Earl retired from the Pennsylvania Railroad after 32 years. He was a veteran of the army having served as a private first class in the Army Air Corps.   **EARNEST DIEHL** Fourth great grandson of progenitor Nicholas Kegg.   **EDITH VIRGINIA DIEHL** [3326] (1913 – 2004) daughter of Sewell and Bertha (Milburn) Diehl, married Earl E. Adams with whom she was mother of (1). Edith was a homemaker, who will be remembered as a very loving mother, grandmother, great-grandmother and friend.
EFFIE CATHERINE DIEHL [3327] (1893 – 1966) daughter of Michael and Elizabeth (Diehl) Diehl married twice; first to John Carl Duvall with whom she was mother of (3). Later, she married Charles Lewis Cochran.   **ELIZABETH JOANNE DIEHL** [3328] (1975 – 2003) daughter of Thomas and Jean (Fish) Diehl, married Ralph D. Heaton with whom she was mother of (1). Elizabeth obtained a Bachelor of Arts degree in biology from Bucknell University, and a master's degree in public policy from the University of Oklahoma. She was a homemaker and volunteer for a number of military agencies.

[3319] Tyrone Daily Herald (PA) April 5, 1968 [3320] Altoona Mirror (PA) Jan 19, 2000 [3321] p.B3 - Altoona Mirror (PA) Aug 8, 1993 [3322] The Akron Beacon Journal (OH) Sep 29, 1970 [3323] p.2 - Bedford Gazette (PA) Sep 7, 1955 [3324] The Baltimore Sun (MD) Aug 26, 1987 [3325] p.2 - The Daily News (PA) Jul 12, 1983 [3326] Kepple-Graft Funeral Home, Inc.,(TX) Apr 7, 2004 [3327] The Sacramento Bee (CA) Nov 15, 1966 [3328] Herald Mail (MD) July 14, 2003

ELLEN J. DIEHL Fourth great granddaughter of progenitor Nicholas Kegg. **ELWOOD D. DIEHL** Fifth great grandson of progenitor Nicholas Kegg. **ELWOOD JOHN DIEHL** [3329] (1914 – 1984) son of Henry and Jennie (Clites) Diehl, married Ruby Mae Dunnegan Froelick. **EVA ANNA DIEHL** [3330] (1848 – 1918) daughter of Isaac and Catherine (Kegg) Diehl, married Henry H. Bingham with whom she was mother of (5). Eva was a member of the reformed church since childhood and died in that faith. **EYVONNE A. DIEHL** Fifth great granddaughter of progenitor Nicholas Kegg. **FAYE DIEHL** Fifth great granddaughter of progenitor Nicholas Kegg. **FERN ISABEL DIEHL** [3331] (1908 – 1956) daughter of Charles and Carrie (Diehl) Diehl, married Harry Lincoln Karns. **FRED GILBERT DIEHL** [3332] (1893 – 1963) son of Judge William and Laura (Shoemaker) Diehl, married Gladys Amelia Himmelwright with whom he was father of (1). **GARVIN SCOTT DIEHL** Sixth great grandson of progenitor Nicholas Kegg. **GARY DIEHL** Fifth great grandson of progenitor Nicholas Kegg. **GEORGE ALTON DIEHL** [3333] (1923 – 2004) son of Elias and Nettie (Kegg) Diehl, married Ruby Everetts with whom he was father of (1). George began working for REA Express making deliveries in Huntingdon and the Mount Union area. Later, he was employed at Boyle Ice Plant, Huntingdon, followed by Juniata Locomotive Shops, retiring from Consolidated Rail Corporation after 42 years of service. George was an avid hunter and gentleman farmer. **GLENN EMANUEL DIEHL** [3334] (1901 – 1975) son of Emanuel and Maryann (Diehl) Diehl. Glenn was never married. He was employed by the state for a number of years. **GREGORY D. DIEHL** Fifth great grandson of progenitor Nicholas Kegg. **GROVER CLEVELAND DIEHL** [3335] (1886 – 1966) son of William and Sophia (Diehl) Diehl, married Lena M. James. Grover was a member of the Bedford Elks and the Bedford Moose. **HAROLD DAVID DIEHL** [3336] (1912 – 2000) aka "Skinny", son of Henry and Jennie (Clites) Diehl, married Rhea C. Fleegle with whom he was father of (4). Harold retired from PennDOT. He also was a sawmiller and worked in construction. He was an avid hunter. He was a member of Trinity United Church of Christ on Dry Ridge but was a longtime attendee with his wife of the Manns Choice Church of God. He was a member of the Schellsburg Lions Club. **HAROLD VERNON DIEHL** [3337] (1921 – 1998) son of Elias and Nettie (Kegg) Diehl, married Esther Belle Isenberg with whom he was father of (3). Harold had served in the U.S. Army from 1942-46 as a sergeant and drill instructor in Northern France and Rhineland Germany during World War II. He was also a member of the veterans of Foreign Wars, Blazing Hook and Ladder Volunteer Fire Company, Tyrone, and the Warriors Mark-Franklin Volunteer Fire Company. He retired from Conrail after 35 years of service. **HARVEY HERMAN DIEHL** (1894 – 1979) son of Michael and Elizabeth (Diehl) Diehl, married Gladys Grace Stanley. Harvey was a veteran of WWI. **HARVEY R. DIEHL** [3338, 3339] (1918 – 1978) son of Russell and Mary (Lehman) Diehl, married Ramona Mae Dyche with whom he was father of (1). Harvey served in the Army in Europe during WWII and was employed for more than 30 years as a disability claims examiner for the Social Security Administration. **HENRY FRANK DIEHL** [3340] (1889 – 1960) son of Rueben and Mary (Kegg) Diehl, married Jennie Myrtle Clites with whom he was father of (5). **HILDA VIOLA DIEHL** [3341] (1925 – 2013) daughter of Elias and Nettie (Kegg) Diehl, married Richard Cunningham McMahon with whom she was mother of (7). **IDA M. DIEHL** [3342] (1884 – 1924) daughter of William and Sophia (Diehl) Diehl, married David Reiley Pepple with whom she was mother of (2). **IONE DIEHL** [3343] (1919 – 2005) daughter of Sewell and Bertha (Milburn) Diehl, married Blair Lewis Foor with whom she was mother of (3). Ione worked as a cook at Snyder's Gateway in Breezewood and was also a homemaker who enjoyed making quilts and caring for her family.

[3329] Bedford County Historical Society Nov 1984, obtained by D. Sue Dible [3330] Bedford Gazette (Bedford County, PA.) Jan. 24, 1919 [3331] The Everett Press (PA) Sep 21, 1956 [3332] p.13 - The Daily Courier (PA) April 2, 1963 [3333] USGenWeb Project obituary contributed by Sharon Culp [3334, 3335] Bedford County Genealogical Society obituary obtained by D. Sue Dible [3336] p.3 - Bedford Inquirer (PA) Aug 11, 2000, obtained by Bob Rose [3337] p.2 - Daily News (PA) May 27, 1998 [3338] p.12 - Cumberland Times (MD) Apr. 5, 1953 [3339] The Evening Sun (Baltimore, MD) Aug 4, 1978 [3340] p.20 - Cumberland Times (MD) June 26, 1960 [3341] Daily News (Huntingdon, PA) Jul 23, 2013 [3342] The Bedford Gazette (PA) Apr 18, 1924 [3343] Bedford Inquirer (PA) March 11, 2005 obtained by Bob Rose

IRA WILLIAM DIEHL [3344] (1889 – 1931) son of Judge William and Laura (Shoemaker) Diehl, married Peggy Weekly with whom he was father of (1). **IRENE THELMA DIEHL** [3344A] (1907 – 1986) daughter of Sewell and Bertha (Milburn) Diehl, married Hulbert Kenneth Clark with whom she was mother of (4). Irene worked as a seamstress at Deis Cleaners in Bedford for many years. **JACOB DIEHL** Eighth great grandson of progenitor Nicholas Kegg. **JAMES A. DIEHL** Sixth great grandson of progenitor Nicholas Kegg. **JASON DARYL DIEHL** Sixth great grandson of progenitor Nicholas Kegg. **JENNY L. DIEHL** Fifth great granddaughter of progenitor Nicholas Kegg. **JERRY DAVID DIEHL** (1952 – 1952) son of Earl and Evelyn (Price) Diehl. **JOAN DIEHL** Fifth great granddaughter of progenitor Nicholas Kegg. **JOHN ALVIN DIEHL** Fourth great grandson of progenitor Nicholas Kegg. **JOHN WILLIAM DIEHL** [3345] (1906 – 1975) son of Charles and Hattie (Beegle) Diehl married twice; first to Alberta Ruth Bowman with whom he was father of (3). Later, he married Maudie Lee Boswell. **JOYCE A. DIEHL** Fifth great granddaughter of progenitor Nicholas Kegg. **KATHRYN MARIE DIEHL** Sixth great granddaughter of progenitor Nicholas Kegg. **KENNETH DIEHL** Fifth great grandson of progenitor Nicholas Kegg. **KIMBERLY L. DIEHL** Seventh great granddaughter of progenitor Nicholas Kegg. **LISA DIEHL** Sixth great granddaughter of progenitor Nicholas Kegg. **KIYA LEIGH DIEHL** Sixth great granddaughter of progenitor Nicholas Kegg. **LARRY EDWIN DIEHL** Fifth great grandson of progenitor Nicholas Kegg. **LARRY THOMAS DIEHL** Sixth great grandson of progenitor Nicholas Kegg. **LAURA LEE DIEHL** Seventh great granddaughter of progenitor Nicholas Kegg. **LENA IRENE DIEHL** (1896 – 1973) daughter of Michael and Elizabeth (Diehl) Diehl, married Clarence Charles Gross with whom she was mother of (2). **LEONARD DIEHL** Fourth great grandson of progenitor Nicholas Kegg. **LILLIAN MARGARET DIEHL** aka "Peg", Sixth great granddaughter of progenitor Nicholas Kegg. **LINDA DIEHL** Fifth great granddaughter of progenitor Nicholas Kegg. **LINDA DIEHL** Fifth great granddaughter of progenitor Nicholas Kegg. **LINDA ANN DIEHL** Sixth great granddaughter of progenitor Nicholas Kegg. **LINETTE F. DIEHL** Fourth great granddaughter of progenitor Nicholas Kegg. **LISA J. DIEHL** Fifth great granddaughter of progenitor Nicholas Kegg. **LLOYD RAYMOND DIEHL** Fifth great grandson of progenitor Nicholas Kegg. **LOGAN DIEHL** Eighth great grandson of progenitor Nicholas Kegg. **LORENE ELIZABETH DIEHL** Seventh great granddaughter of progenitor Nicholas Kegg. **LORETTA DIEHL** Fifth great granddaughter of progenitor Nicholas Kegg. **LORETTA WILEY DIEHL** [3346] (1905 – 1956) daughter of Michael and Elizabeth (Diehl) Diehl, married James S. Higgins. **LUKE M. DIEHL** Sixth great grandson of progenitor Nicholas Kegg. **MARGARET CATHERINE DIEHL** [652] (1906 – 1989) daughter of Michael and Florence (Shoemaker) Diehl, married Lamont Cessna Stunkard with whom she was mother of (2). **MARGARET VIOLA DIEHL** Fourth great granddaughter of progenitor Nicholas Kegg. **MARK PHILLIP DIEHL** Sixth great grandson of progenitor Nicholas Kegg. **MARY ELAINE DIEHL** (1965 – 1966) daughter of Leonard and Margaret (Hankinson) Diehl. **MARY ELIZABETH DIEHL** [653] (1898 – 1988) daughter of Michael and Elizabeth (Diehl) Diehl, married Cecil Ashford Grimes with whom she was mother of (1). **MARY ELIZABETH DIEHL** [3347] (1913 – 2014) daughter of Elias and Nettie (Kegg) Diehl, married Melvin Austin Rose with whom she was mother of (3). **MARY IRENE DIEHL** [3348] (1915 – 2004) daughter of Harry and Ada (Bingham) Diehl married twice; first to Conda Melvin Johnson with whom she was mother of (1). Later, she married John Blankley with whom she was mother of (2). Mary was a member of the Black Valley Federated Church of the Brethren and Christian, where she also served with the Ladies Aid of the Church. She was a homemaker, and with her husband, owned and operated their Monroe Township dairy farm throughout their lifetime. She was a member of the Chaneysville Senior Citizens, and especially enjoyed flower gardening.

[3344] Greensburg Daily Tribune (PA) March 28, 1931, Find A Grave Memorial # 93708514 Added by: Jill [3344A] Bedford County Historical Society (PA), book68, p. 76 obtained by D. Sue Dible [3345] p.40 Richmond Times Dispatch (VA) July 13, 1975 [3346] pg. 34 - Cleveland Plain Dealer (OH) July 23, 1956 [3347] The Daily News (Huntingdon, PA) Dec 29, 2014 [3348] Bedford Inquirer (PA) Dec 31, 2004, obtained by Bob Rose

MARYANN CATHERINE DIEHL (3349) (1868 – 1944) daughter of Benjamin (Diehl) Diehl, married Emanuel Peter Diehl with whom she was mother of (2). Maryann was a member of the Church of God.
MATTHEW DIEHL Sixth great grandson of progenitor Nicholas Kegg.
MAUDE E. DIEHL (3350) (1906 – 1997) daughter of Judge William and Laura (Shoemaker) Diehl, married Clyde W. Miner with whom she was mother of (1). **MICHAEL DIEHL** Sixth great grandson of progenitor Nicholas Kegg. **MICHAEL ENOS DIEHL** (1860 – 1932) son of Benjamin and Eve (Diehl) Diehl, married Elizabeth Lincoln Diehl with whom he was father of (10).
MICHAEL W. DIEHL Sixth great grandson of progenitor Nicholas Kegg.
MILDRED MANON DIEHL (3351) (1906 – 1997) daughter of Charles and Carrie (Diehl) Diehl, married Ralph Edward Jones. **NANCY LOUISE DIEHL** Fourth great granddaughter of progenitor Nicholas Kegg. **NELLIE MAE DIEHL** Sixth great granddaughter of progenitor Nicholas Kegg.
NELSON EMERSON DIEHL (3352) (1925 – 2005) son of Charles and Marie (Herold) Diehl, married Norma Passey with whom he was father of (3). Nelson was an auto mechanic for 40 years. He was a member of International Association of Machinists and Aerospace Workers Lodge 1414, Turlock Horseshoe Club and American Legion Post 74. He was a Navy veteran of World War II.
NORMA JANE DIEHL Fifth great granddaughter of progenitor Nicholas Kegg.
OSCAR MILTON DIEHL (3353) (1883 – 1969) son of Judge William and Laura (Shoemaker) Diehl, married Ethel May Wilson with whom he was father of (2). Oscar was a retired engineer for the Pennsylvania Railroad. He was a member of St. Paul's United Methodist Church, Youngwood and the Brotherhood of Locomotive Engineers of Youngwood. **PAUL WRIGHT DIEHL** (3354) (1902 – 1921) son of Selby and Ida (Diehl) Diehl. **PAULINE LAURITE DIEHL** (1897 – 1986) daughter of Judge William and Laura (Shoemaker) Diehl, married Patrick Moriarty with whom she was mother of (3).
PEARL KATHLEEN DIEHL (3355) (1911 – 1985) daughter of Elias and Nettie (Kegg) Diehl, married George Fritz. **PENNY DIEHL** Fifth great granddaughter of progenitor Nicholas Kegg.
RALPH BURNETTE DIEHL (1888 – 1896) son of Michael and Elizabeth (Diehl) Diehl.
RANDALL DIEHL Sixth great grandson of progenitor Nicholas Kegg. **RANDALL F. DIEHL**, aka "Randy", Fourth great grandson of progenitor Nicholas Kegg. **RANDY DIEHL** Seventh great grandson of progenitor Nicholas Kegg. **RAYMOND HOWARD DIEHL** (3356) (1913 – 1922) son of Charles and Hattie (Beegle) Diehl. **REBECCA DIEHL** (1850 – 1916) daughter of Isaac and Catherine (Kegg) Diehl, married George Henry Beegle with whom she was mother of (7). **REBECCA MARGARET DIEHL** (1863 – 1895) daughter of Benjamin and Eve (Diehl) Diehl, married John Philip Harclerode with whom she was mother of (9). **RENEE EILEEN DIEHL** Sixth great granddaughter of progenitor Nicholas Kegg. **RHONDA KAY DIEHL** (3356A) (1958 – 2016) daughter of Russell and Esther (Stroll) Diehl married twice, first to Timothy Michael Haag with whom she was mother of (2). She later married Barry L. McBurney. **RICHARD DIEHL** Fifth great grandson of progenitor Nicholas Kegg.
RICKY DIEHL Sixth great grandson of progenitor Nicholas Kegg. **ROBBIN LEE DIEHL** Sixth great granddaughter of progenitor Nicholas Kegg. **ROBERT DIEHL** (3357) (1919 – 1979) son of Russell and Mary (Lehman) Diehl married Catherine Geraline Parker with whom he was father of (3). Robert was a retired carpenter. **ROBERT ELIAS DIEHL** (3358) (1919 – 1986) aka "Doc", son of Elias and Nettie (Kegg) Diehl, married Dorothy Jane McMahon with whom he was father of (2). Robert had worked as a farmer in Logan Township. He attended the Bedford public schools and was a member of the Bedford High School Class of 1937. **ROBERT WILLIAM DIEHL** (1951 – 2005) son of William and Mavis (Hobson) Diehl, married Dorotea Agero with whom he was father of (2). **RONALD CLARK DIEHL** Sixth great grandson of progenitor Nicholas Kegg. **RONALD CLARK DIEHL** Seventh great grandson of progenitor Nicholas Kegg. **RUSSELL CONWELL DIEHL** (3359) (1891 – 1969) aka

---

(3349) The Bedford Gazette (PA) November 10, 1944 (3350) p.6 - The Valley Independent (PA) April 24, 1973 (3351) Bedford County Historical Society Pioneer Library obituary (PA) obtained by D. Sue Dible (3352) p.B4 - The Modesto Bee (CA) Feb 24, 2005 (3353) p.13 - Daily Courier (PA) Oct 4,1969 (3354) The Bedford Gazette (PA) July 8,1921 (3355) p.2 - The Daily News (PA) Dec 27,1985 (3356) Bedford County Historical Society Pioneer Library obituary (PA) obtained by D. Sue Dible (3356A) Akron Beacon Journal (OH) Jan. 10, 2016, obtained by D. Sue Dible (3357) The Evening Sun (Hanover, PA) Oct 15, 1979 (3358) p.2 - The Daily News (PA) Aug 23,1986 (3359) p.11 - The Cumberland News (MD) Fri., Aug. 22, 1969

"Mike" son of Michael and Elizabeth (Diehl) Diehl married twice; first to Mary Elsie Lehman with whom he was father of (2). Later, he married Ada (Nelson) Wagner. Mike was a retired manager of the local office of the C & P Telephone Company and a member of the Western Council Telephone Pioneers of Maryland. He was a former player and manager of the Cumberland Colts and managed the Frostburg Demons. **RUSSELL CONWELL DIEHL** [3360] (1950 – 1968) aka "Mike" son of Robert and Catherine (Parker) Diehl was a senior at Beall High School. **RUSSELL HERMAN DIEHL** [3360A] (1919 – 2007) son of Clark and Nellie (Overholt) Diehl married four times, first to Grace Belle Sears with whom he was father of (1). He married Mildred Clark, later married Esther Mae Stroll with whom he was father of (8), last he married Kitty Mae Lykins with whom he was father of (1). Russell spent thirty years in the trucking industry and nineteen years as a school crossing guard. He served his country during World War II in the Army receiving the Purple Heart. **RUSSELL HERMAN DIEHL** Sixth great grandson of progenitor Nicholas Kegg. **RUSSELL JOSEPH DIEHL** Seventh great grandson of progenitor Nicholas Kegg. **SANDRA MARIE DIEHL** [3361] (1948 – 1999) daughter of Stanley and Mary (Davidson) Diehl, married Michael Joseph Ray with whom she was mother of (4). Sandra worked at Reed's Havre de Grace Middle School, Havre de Grace High School, The Record and Cello. **SANDRA DIEHL** Fifth great granddaughter of progenitor Nicholas Kegg. **SARAH DIEHL** (abt 1842 -?) daughter of Isaac and Catherine (Kegg) Diehl. **SARAH EVA DIEHL** (1904 – 1968) daughter of Selby and Ida (Diehl) Diehl, married John Roy Batzel with whom she was mother of (2). **SELBY MYERS DIEHL** [3362] (1865 – 1929) son of Benjamin and Eve (Diehl) Diehl, married Ida Mary Diehl with whom he was father of (3). Selby lived all his life in Friends Cove except for a few years when he bought and moved to Monroe Township where he worked ardently to build the Reformed church at Clearville. Selby was a member of the Fellowship of The Cross Mission of Bedford and the P.O.S. of No. 412 of Charlesville. **SEWELL WRIGHT DIEHL** [3363] (1881 – 1953) son of Benjamin and Eve (Diehl) Diehl, married Bertha Viola Milburn with whom he was faher of (5). Sewell was a retired Colerain township farmer. He was a member of Trinity Reformed church of Friends Cove. **STANLEY EDWIN DIEHL** [3364] (1922 – 2011) son of Charles and Marie (Herold) Diehl married twice; first to Mary Edith Davidson with whom he was father of (2). Later, he married Inez Irene Puschell with whom he was father of (2). Stan was a Christ follower, devoted husband and father. He served as a music and Sunday school leader at First Baptist Church of Northeast, Maryland, was a member of College Road Baptist Church, Ocala, and served with Gideon's International and Campers on Mission. Stan was an avid water sportsman, volunteer Aquatic Director for the YMCA and a diver with Tri-County Dive and Rescue Club. Mr. Diehl served in the Navy during WWII. He was stationed at Ocracoke Island, NC, to protect the coastline from German saboteurs, later becoming trained in submarine warfare as a Soundman 3rd class. He retired from Aberdeen Proving Ground as a materials tester and owned his own business as a master watchmaker. **STEPHEN R. DIEHL** Fourth great grandson of progenitor Nicholas Kegg. **SUSAN ELIZATH DIEHL** Sixth great granddaughter of progenitor Nicholas Kegg. **SUZANNE K. DIEHL** Fourth great granddaughter of progenitor Nicholas Kegg. **TENNA ALMA DIEHL** [3365] (1875 – 1950) daughter of Benjamin and Ave (Diehl) Diehl, married Emanuel Ranson Koontz with whom she was mother of (6). **TENA CATHERINE DIEHL** (born abt.1898) daughter of Emanuel and Maryann (Diehl) Diehl. **THOMAS EDWARD DIEHL** Fifth great grandson of progenitor Nicholas Kegg. **THOMAS ROBERT DIEHL** Sixth great grandson of progenitor Nicholas Kegg. **TRAVIS DIEHL** Seventh great grandson of progenitor Nicholas Kegg. **VICKI L. DIEHL** Fifth great granddaughter of progenitor Nicholas Kegg. **VICKIE DIEHL** Fifth great granddaughter of progenitor Nicholas Kegg. **VIRGINIA A. DIEHL** Fifth great granddaughter of progenitor Nicholas Kegg. **VIRGINIA RUTH DIEHL** [3366] (1899 – 1983) daughter of Michael and Elizabeth (Diehl) Diehl, married Robert W. Knight with whom she was mother of (1).

[3360] Cumberland News (MD) Jan 18, 1968 [3360A] Akron Beacon Journal (OH) June 15, 2007 [3361] The Aegis (Havre de Grave, MD) March 26, 1999, obtained by D. Sue Dible [3362] p.4 The Bedford Gazette (PA) Aug. 16, 1929 [3363] p.2 - Bedford Gazette (PA) July 6, 1953 [3364] Ocala Star-Banner (FL) Oct 23, 2011 [3365] p.5 - The Bedford Gazette (PA) November 8, 1950 [3366] Find A Grave Memorial # 44140067 Cumberland Times obituary Obtained and Contributed by Lila Baier

WENDY S. DIEHL Seventh great granddaughter of progenitor Nicholas Kegg. **WILLIAM A. DIEHL** [3367] (1919 – 2004) son of Clyde and Claribel (Minnich) Diehl married twice; first to Rhonda Horne who divorced the WWII Sergeant during the war. A year later, William married Mavis Isabel Hobson, an Austrain girl in Melborne. The Huntingdon County residents extended a cordial welcome when she arrived. Which was documented in a story on page 8, written By Anna Mae Geissinger, a reporter for the Huntingdon Daily News June 24, 1946, transcribed as follows; The other day this reporter had a most enjoyable interview with an Australian girl, wife of William Diehl of 1300 Mifflin Street, Huntingdon. Mrs. Diehl and her husband, who spent two and a half years in Australia, gave us such a wonderful description of that country that we almost imagined that we, too, had been there. The young Australian bride arrived in Huntingdon on Friday to make her home with her husband at the home of his parents, Mr. and Mrs. C. H. Diehl of the above address. On August 4, 1945, Mavis Isibel Hobson, daughter of Jonathan Hobson of Melbourne, Victoria Australia, and Staff Sergeant William Diehl were united in marriage in the Wesley Methodist Church at Melbourne. Immediately after the wedding they moved to Sydney, Australia, where they spent three and a half months. Then at Brisbane, Australia, on December 8, 1945, they were parted when Sergeant Diehl returned to the States. After her husband's return to America, Mrs. Diehl again returned to Melbourne where she was employed as a process worker in a war factory. Then on May 17 she received her travel orders to come to this country and on her birthday, May 27, she set sail from her Sydney for her husband's native country aboard the SS Monterey. There were about 760 wives and 250 children aboard the ship, all of them coming from New Zealand or Australia. When speaking of her birthday Mrs. Diehl stated that getting to sail to America on that day was the nicest present she ever expected to receive. However, upon her arrival here she was presented with a beautiful watch by her husband, and needless to say, she was very much pleased with it. She told us that she never saw as pretty a watch as this one in Melbourne. Mavis has two sisters and two brothers, and her father was born in Lancashire, England. However, he has lived in Australia for the past thirty years and it was there that he met and married his Australian wife. When we asked Mavis how she happened to meet the Huntingdon soldier she informed us that it was in her mother's restaurant in Melbourne. Then William spoke up and told us that a buddy of his wanted to take him to a restaurant where the food was really good. So, it was there, in August 1942, that the young couple met. Three years later they were married. She is of small stature, being just five feet tall. She has auburn hair and has a slightly dark complexion. She has lived all her life in Melbourne, a city similar in size to Philadelphia. It was one o'clock on Sunday morning, June 9, when the SS Monterey neared the Golden Gate at San Francisco, California, and this war bride told us that the decks of the ship were jammed with its many passengers, eager to get a glimpse of the famous entrance, to San Francisco Bay. It was about eight o'clock that same morning that the ship dropped anchor. The transport stopped at Honolulu for seven hours and there the shiploads of passengers were graciously entertained and welcomed by a U.S. Army band. Mrs. Diehl was enthusiastic about her journey across the ocean. The accommodations aboard the ship greatly surprised her and the other wives as there were so many modern appliances on the ship that just don't exist in her native country. Red Cross Workers were aboard the big ship to aid the war brides and the children. "The Red Cross workers and the Army doctors and nurses were really wonderful to us girls," said Mrs. Diehl. "The Red Cross workers not only accompanied us on the ship but traveled across the country on the trains with us, being relieved in the big cities. They taught handicraft to any of us who desired to learn, had dances, showed us movies and then led us in worship while we were crossing the ocean. Our meals were really marvelous, and I had my first taste of cream in years while aboard the ship. I have found that their hospitality is being extended by others here in your country as the people seem to be so friendly." A girl whom Mavis went to school with also made the journey to America at that time. This friend has joined her husband in Hamburg, New Jersey. It was autumn in Australia when Mavis left, and she is anxious to have winter come for she has never seen snow. She has experienced much rainy weather in Melbourne, so she is quite accustomed to the wet season we are now having. We were told that Melbourne is a beautiful city, having wide streets, many shade trees and parks. This was easily proved by showing us some lovely pictures of the parks and

[3367] p.10 - Huntingdon Daily News (PA) July 17, 1942

countryside surrounding Melbourne. The picture which most appealed to us was the Shrine of Remembrance, located near Melbourne. At the top of this shrine there is a cross and before the shrine a grave, representing the tomb of all unknown soldiers of Australia. We were told that at the eleventh hour of the eleventh day of the eleventh month, in every year the sun shines directly on the center of this grave. This is the only time of the whole year that the sun casts its rays directly on the center of the grave; William Diehl entered the service in 1939 and left Huntingdon with the National Guard unit on February 17, 1941. He went to Australia on June 4, 1942. He also served at Manila, Okinawa, Leyte, Saipan and many other places in the Pacific area. His entire service while overseas was with the Engineers and he sailed for home with the 1538th Engineer Battalion of the 13rd Division. The former staff sergeant landed in the 8tates on January 6, 1946 and was discharged on January 11 at Fort George G. Meade, Maryland. Mrs. Diehl the first Australian war bride in Huntingdon, thinks that the borough is a pretty place and feels certain that she will like it here. Her parents, and perhaps a brother-in-law and sister, hope to come to Huntingdon to visit the Diehl family whenever transportation is available. Mavis hopes that their plans need not be in vain because she desires that her family may have the great privilege of visiting our land and to see for themselves just what her life is like in America. William and Mavis were the parents of (2). **WILLIAM DALE DIEHL** [3367A] (1930 – 2005) son of Samuel and Margaret (Cessna) Diehl, married Freda Pauline Whetstone with whom he was father of 5, William was a retired mail carrier for the US Postal service, and a dairy farmer. He was a member of Friends Cove United Church of Christ. He was an avid hunter and enjoyed bowling and reading the bible. **WILLIAM HENRY DIEHL** [3368, 3369] (1848 – 1917) son of Isaac and Catherine (Kegg) Diehl married twice; first to Sophia Alice Diehl who died in childbirth delivering the couples 5th child. Later, he married Lavanda Irene Ott who raised all five children. William was an enterprising farmer and stock raiser of Colerain. **WILLIAM H. DIEHL** Fourth great grandson of progenitor Nicholas Kegg. **WILLIAM JACKSON DIEHL** [3370] (1911 – 1998) son of Ira and Peggy (Weekley) Diehl, married Martha Myrtilla Llewelyn. William was a banker, retiring from Port Charlotte Bank & Trust Co. as senior vice president. He was a member of the Port Charlotte United Methodist Church and a former member of Charlotte Harbor Yacht Club, Port Charlotte Golf Club and the Kingsway Country Club. **WILLIAM LAWRENCE DIEHL** [3371] (1932 – 1953) son of John and Alberta (Bowman) Diehl, married Janet Moyer with whom he was father of (1). William was employed as a tractor truck driver. **WILLIAM RAYMOND DIEHL** [3372A] (1936 – 2006) son of Russell and Grace (Sears) Diehl married three times, first to Barbara Marie Mayer with whom he was father of (4), 2nd he married Juanita Rebecca Critchfield, last he married Marjory Allene Friedline with whom he was father of (1). William had been a criminal bailiff in Summit County Domestic Relations Court and had been a Summit County Special Deputy retiring after 33 years. He had previously worked for Mohawk Rubber and had his own security business for 25 years. William was Past Master of Adoniram-Joppa Lodge 517, was a 32nd Degree Mason, and a member of F.O.P. 123 and the Akron Crime Clinic. He had a passion for fishing and loved basketball. **WILLIAM RAYMOND DIEHL** Seventh great grandson of progenitor Nicholas Kegg. **WILMA A. DIEHL** Fifth great granddaughter of progenitor Nicholas Kegg.

DIER

JOSEPH DAVID DIER Seventh great grandson of progenitor Nicholas Kegg.
NICOLE LYNNE DIER Seventh great granddaughter of progenitor Nicholas Kegg.

DIETRICH

ISAIAH DIETRICH Eighth great grandson of progenitor Nicholas Kegg.
OLIVIA DIETRICH Eighth great granddaughter of progenitor Nicholas Kegg.

[3367A] Bedford Inquirer (PA) Oct 28, 2005, obtained by Bob Rose [3368] p. 328 & 329. Biographical Review, 1899, Bedford, PA [3369] Bedford Gazette (PA) Aug 17, 1917 [3370] p.8B - Sarasota Herald-Tribune (FL) June 10, 1998 [3371] Bedford Gazette (PA) Sept 15,1953 [3372] Brattleboro Reformer (VT) May 22, 2002 [3372A] Akron Beacon Journal (OH) Feb 17, 2006

DIETZ

CHRISTOPHER LEE DIETZ Sixth great grandson of progenitor Nicholas Kegg. **JIM DIETZ** Sixth great grandson of progenitor Nicholas Kegg. **JOHN DIETZ** Sixth great grandson of progenitor Nicholas Kegg. **KAREN ANN DIETZ** Sixth great granddaughter of progenitor Nicholas Kegg. **PATRICK ALAN DIETZ** Sixth great grandson of progenitor Nicholas Kegg.

DIGGINS

DORIS JEANNE DIGGINS [3372] (1932 – 2002) daughter of Harry and Ione (Freer) Diggins, married Lawrence S. Toms with whom she was mother of (3). Doris became an active member of the First Congregational Church and had served as a past Deaconess and also served as wedding hostess for the church. She was also a volunteer for the American Cancer Society. Through her service to the society, she was awarded the Order of the Sword in 1994. Doris was also a member of the P.E.O., Chapter P, in Wolfeboro. She loved to play bridge and was a member of the Hospital Bridge Club.
HARRY D. DIGGINS [3373] (1909 – 1981) son of Vernon and Ada (Claar) Diggins married twice; first to Ione Freer with whom he was father of (1). Later, he married Evelyn C. Hensle.
MARY ADA DIGGINS Fifth great granddaughter of progenitor Nicholas Kegg.
MERRIL D. DIGGINS [3374] (1913 – 1981) son of Vernon and Ada (Claar) Diggins, married Nellie Greenawalt. Merril enlisted in the Army Air Corps., where he studied glider piloting.
PATRICIA JEAN DIGGINS [3375] (1933 – 2017) daughter of Vernon and Dorothea (Wiseman) Diggins married twice; first to Kenneth Hancuff with whom she was mother of (5). Later, she married Edward B. Roessler with whom she was mother of (1). **VERNON L. DIGGINS** Sixth great grandson of progenitor Nicholas Kegg. **VERNON L. DIGGINS** Fifth great grandson of progenitor Nicholas Kegg.
VERNON LEON DIGGINS [3376] (1911 – 1986) son of Vernon and Ada (Claar) Diggins, married Dorothea Wiseman with whom he was father of (3). Vernon retired as a carman from the Pennsylvania Railroad reclamation plant, Hollidaysburg. He was a member of the National Rifle Association, Blair County Game, Fish and Forestry Association and Transportation Workers Union.
VERNON RITNER DIGGINS [3377] (1891 – 1972) aka "Bill", son of Emanuel and Ida (Ditch) Diggins married three times; first to Ada Ella Claar with whom he was father of (3). Later he married Edna Grace Shatzer and Margaret I. Shoup. Bill retired after more than 44 years of service as a machinist in the PRR Juanita shops. He was a member of the Frohsinn Singing Society and a life member of the Elks.

DIGGS

DIANA DEVONNA DIGGS Sixth great granddaughter of progenitor Nicholas Kegg.

DILLARD

JENNIFER LEE DILLARD Sixth great granddaughter of progenitor Nicholas Kegg.
MICHAEL D. DILLARD Sixth great grandson of progenitor Nicholas Kegg.

DILLEY

ERIC DAVID DILLEY Sixth great grandson of progenitor Nicholas Kegg.

[3373] Washington Post (D.C.) Jan 25, 1981 [3374] p.2 Altoona Tribune (PA) Nov 22, 1944 [3375] Altoona Mirror (PA) Apr 10, 2017 [3376] p.11 - Altoona Mirror (PA) June 2, 1986 [3377] p.30 – Altoona Mirror (PA) May 24, 1972

DILLING

CAROL ANNE DILLING Fifth great granddaughter of progenitor Nicholas Kegg.
NANCY LEE DILLING [3378] (1935 – 2014) daughter of Elmer and Olive (Koontz) Dilling, married Earl George Beach with whom she was mother of (2). Nancy retired as a secretary from North Woodbury Township in 1996, and before that was employed at Montgomery Ward, Martinsburg, and as a teller at Mid-State Bank, Martinsburg, for many years. She was a member of Clover Creek Church of the Brethren, rural Martinsburg. Nancy enjoyed reading, crafting, bowling, card playing and especially loved wintering in Tarpon Springs, Fla.

DIMOND

CLAIRE DIMOND Sixth great granddaughter of progenitor Nicholas Kegg. **ELISA DIMOND** Sixth great granddaughter of progenitor Nicholas Kegg. **ERIN DIMOND** Sixth great granddaughter of progenitor Nicholas Kegg. **RYAN J. DIMOND** Sixth great grandson of progenitor Nicholas Kegg.

DINIUS

DAVID ALLEN DINIUS Fifth great grandson of progenitor Nicholas Kegg.
GARLAND ROBERT DINIUS [3379] (1918 – 1982) son of David and Mary (Steele) Dinius, married Nelta Nedine Johnson with whom he was father of (3). **JAMIE ANN DINIUS** Sixth great granddaughter of progenitor Nicholas Kegg. **MARY JOAN DINIUS** aka "Joanie" Fifth great granddaughter of progenitor Nicholas Kegg. **VIOLA ANN DINIUS** aka "Viann" Fifth great granddaughter of progenitor Nicholas Kegg.

DIRR

ASPEN DIRR Eighth great granddaughter of progenitor Nicholas Kegg. **BROOKE DIRR** Eighth great granddaughter of progenitor Nicholas Kegg. **CHRISTOPHER DIRR** Eighth great grandson of progenitor Nicholas Kegg.

DISHONG

EVAN DISHONG Seventh great grandson of progenitor Nicholas Kegg. **JOSHUA DISHONG** Seventh great grandson of progenitor Nicholas Kegg. **LINDA JEAN DISHONG** Sixth great granddaughter of progenitor Nicholas Kegg. **NATHAN DISHONG** Seventh great grandson of progenitor Nicholas Kegg.

DISMUKE

MAISON DISMUKE Ninth great granddaughter of progenitor Nicholas Kegg.

DITCH

CAROLINE MAY DITCH [3380] (1874 – 1928) aka "Carrie", daughter of William and Mary Amanda (Stuckey) Ditch, married Edward David Lafferty with whom she was mother of (8).
CHARLES DITCH (born abt. 1867) son William and Mary Amanda (Stuckey) Ditch.

[3378] Altoona Mirror (PA) June 10, 2017 [3379] Fort Wayne Newspapers (IN) Jun. 18, 2007 [3380] p.12 Altoona Tribune (PA) Feb 14, 1928

ELIZABETH KATHRYN DITCH [3381] (1905 – 1989) aka "Betty", daughter of Simon and Rose (Schneider) Ditch married twice; first to Oscar W. Christian with whom she was mother of (1). Later, she married Carl Crawford Cox.   **FRED W. DITCH** [3382] (1902 – 1980) son of Simon and Rose (Schneider) Ditch, married Claire Z. Suttmiller. Fred was a member of the Stubenville Pigeon Racing Club.   **IDA M DITCH** [3383] (1871 – 1953) daughter of William and Mary Amanda (Stuckey) Ditch married four times; first to Emanuel Bailey, then to William H. Knott, she married Emanuel Diggins with whom she was mother of (1). Later, she married Samuel Detwiler.   **MARGARET DITCH** (born abt. 1868) daughter of William and Mary Amanda (Stuckey) Ditch.   **MAUDE M. V. DITCH** [3384] (1880 – 1962) daughter of William and Mary Amanda (Stuckey) Ditch married twice; first to Howard Gray McClellan with whom she was mother of (9). Later, she married Ira Sylvester Freet.   **SARAH DITCH** (1869 – 1894) aka "Sallie", daughter of William and Mary Amanda (Stuckey) Ditch, married Lewis Mathias Smith with whom she was mother of (4).   **SIMON SAMUEL DITCH** [3385] (1875 – 1918) son of William and Mary Amanda (Stuckey) Ditch, married Rose Ann Schneider with whom he was father of (2).   **VIRGINIA C. DITCH** [3386] (1872 – 1950) aka "Jennie", daughter of William and Mary Amanda (Stuckey) Ditch, married Harry Tyler Daugherty.

DITZ

BRIAN JAMES DITZ Fifth great grandson of progenitor Nicholas Kegg.
CHRISTOPHER JOSEF DITZ Fifth great grandson of progenitor Nicholas Kegg.   **GAVIN DITZ** Sixth great grandson of progenitor Nicholas Kegg.   **LILLIAN DITZ** Sixth great granddaughter of progenitor Nicholas Kegg.   **SHANA KRISTINE DITZ** Fifth great granddaughter of progenitor Nicholas Kegg.

DIVELY

CAROL ELIZABETH DIVELY [3386A] (1938 – 2009) daughter of Paul and Dorothy (Kegg) Dively, married Roger Thomas Kidneigh with whom she was mother of (3). **DALE ALBERT DIVELY** [3386B] (1935 – 2010) son of Paul and Dorothy (Kegg) Dively, married Sylvia Lee Howell with whom he was father of (3). Dale was a retired truck driver and U.S. Army veteran, was a charitable contributor to the Friends Cove United Church of Christ in his hometown of Bedford, Pa.   **DALE DIVELY** [3387] (1958 – 1993) son of Dale and Sylvia (Howell) Dively. Dale was a graduate of Timken High School and had attended Stark Technical College. He had owned and operated the All Rite Body Shop in Canton. **KRIS DIVELY** Fifth great granddaughter of progenitor Nicholas Kegg.   **RENEE DIVELY** Fifth great granddaughter of progenitor Nicholas Kegg.   **RICHARD L. DIVELY** [3388] (1932 – 2019) son of Paul and Dorothy (Kegg) Dively.

DIVENCENZO

DANIELLE GWEN DIVENCENZO Seventh great granddaughter of progenitor Nicholas Kegg.

DIVINE

JARED L. DIVINE Sixth great grandson of progenitor Nicholas Kegg.   **PAUL DIVINE** Sixth great grandson of progenitor Nicholas Kegg.

[3381] Akron-Summit County Public Library obituary obtained by D. Sue Dible [3382] Herald Star (OH) Dec 6, 1980, obtained by D. Sue Dible [3383] p.2 Bedford Gazette (PA) Oct 1, 1953 [3384] The Sacramento Bee (CA) Nov 21, 1962 [3385] p.10 - Altoona Mirror (PA) Nov 5, 1918 [3386] p.2 Bedford Gazette (PA) Oct 13, 1950 [3386A] Las Vegas Review-Journal (NV) Nov24, 2009 [3386B] p.E2 - Repository (OH) Feb 14, 2010 [3387] p.D7 – Canton Repository (OH) July 7, 1993 obtained by D. Sue Dible [3388] Bedford Gazette (PA) March 9, 2019

DIVIS

COLEEN A. DIVIS Fifth great granddaughter of progenitor Nicholas Kegg. **RANDOLPH DIVIS** Fifth great grandson of progenitor Nicholas Kegg.

DIXON

AMY JO DIXON Sixth great granddaughter of progenitor Nicholas Kegg. **BARBARA A. DIXON** [3389] (1937 – 2007) daughter of Victor and Marie (Bumgardner) Dixon married George Max Sufronko Jr. with whom she was mother of (3). Later, she married William H. Wilson. Barbara was a member of Thea Chapter #192; member of the order of Eastern Star, for 25 years; member of the First United Methodist Church in Nelsonville; and member of the Moose in Logan. **CHERISH J. DIXON** Eighth great granddaughter of progenitor Nicholas Kegg. **CORISSA L. DIXON** Eighth great granddaughter of progenitor Nicholas Kegg. **DEREK VICTOR DIXON** Sixth great grandson of progenitor Nicholas Kegg. **EDDIE DEAN DIXON** Eighth great grandson of progenitor Nicholas Kegg. **JANET MARIE DIXON** Fifth great granddaughter of progenitor Nicholas Kegg. **JEFFREY WAYNE DIXON** Sixth great grandson of progenitor Nicholas Kegg. **RICHARD SHAWN DIXON** Eighth great grandson of progenitor Nicholas Kegg. **VICTOR WAYNE DIXON** [3390] (1939 – 2013) son of Victor and Marie (Bumgardner) Dixon married Mildred Marie Malone with whom he was father of (3). Victor retired from AEP after nearly 40 years of service; member of the Nelsonville Elks #543, VFW, and Logan Moose; played basketball, football, and track and field at Nelsonville High School and Miami University; lifelong dedication to farming; and many years of service on the York Twp. Board of Trustees.

DODDS

LAWRENCE E. DODDS Fifth great grandson of progenitor Nicholas Kegg.
ROBERT JAY DODDS Fifth great grandson of progenitor Nicholas Kegg.

DODSON

ALLEN L. DODSON Sixth great grandson of progenitor Nicholas Kegg. **ALVIN E. DODSON** Sixth great grandson of progenitor Nicholas Kegg. **ALVIN EARL DODSON** [3391] (1937 – 2002) aka "Gabby", son of Alvin and Catherine (Benton) Dodson, married Eunice McGarvey with whom he was father of (6). **ALVIN SHERATON DODSON** [3392] (1915 – 1984) son of Elmer and Minnie (Lafferty) Dodson, married Catherine Ellen Benton with whom he was father of (4). Alvin retired after 30 years of service as a welder from Youngstown Sheet and Tube Co. He was an Army veteran of World War II, where he was the recipient of the Purple Heart. He was a member of the Youngstown VFW Post. **DARLA ELAYNE DODSON** Seventh great granddaughter of progenitor Nicholas Kegg.
DONNA MAY DODSON Fifth great granddaughter of progenitor Nicholas Kegg.
E. MARIA DODSON Fifth great granddaughter of progenitor Nicholas Kegg. **EARL A. DODSON** Sixth great grandson of progenitor Nicholas Kegg. **EILEEN DODSON** Seventh great granddaughter of progenitor Nicholas Kegg. **ELAINE DODSON** aka "Cat", Fifth great granddaughter of progenitor Nicholas Kegg. **ELMER DAVID DODSON** [3393] (1918 – 1988) son of Elmer and Minnie (Lafferty) Dodson, married Elizabeth Pentz with whom he was father of (2). **ERIC DAVID DODSON** [3394] (1980 – 1980) son of Eunice E. Dodson and Edward McConahy. **EUNICE E. DODSON** Sixth great granddaughter of progenitor Nicholas Kegg. **HANNAH DODSON** Sixth great granddaughter of progenitor Nicholas Kegg. **JACQUELINE RACHELLE DODSON** Seventh great granddaughter of progenitor Nicholas Kegg. **JEFFREY D. DODSON** Sixth great grandson of progenitor Nicholas Kegg.

[3389] Athens Messenger (OH) Dec 1, 2007 [3390] The Athens Messenger (OH) Jan 7, 2013 [3391] p.A11 – Altoona Mirror (PA) Dec 26, 2002 [3392] p.B3 - Altoona Mirror (PA) Jul 23, 1984 [3393] p.40 Newark Star-Ledger (NJ) June 1, 1988 [3394] p.4 – Altoona Mirror (PA) Feb 11, 1980

JENNIFER LESA DODSON [3395] (1960 – 1960) daughter of Darrell and Elaine (Whited) Dodson.
KAREN A. DODSON Fifth great granddaughter of progenitor Nicholas Kegg.
MILDRED L. DODSON [3396] (1916 – 2003) aka "Morie", daughter of Elmer and Minnie (Lafferty) Dodson, married Albert Joseph Lestochi with whom she was mother of (2). Morie had been employed at Warnaco Sportswear and the Juniata Silk Mill. She enjoyed bingo and the Pennsylvania lottery.
REBA ELIZABETH DODSON Fourth great granddaughter of progenitor Nicholas Kegg.
SCOTT DODSON Sixth great grandson of progenitor Nicholas Kegg. **SHIRLEY J. DODSON** Sixth great granddaughter of progenitor Nicholas Kegg. **THELMA DODSON** [3396A] aka "Girlie" (1919 – 2011) daughter of Elmer and Minnie (Lafferty) Dodson, married Paul Tomasetti with whom she was mother of (5). Thelma previously had worked at Faith Vending and Puritan Sportswear. She was a member of Sacred Heart Catholic Church, where she was a past member of Christian Mothers. She was a homemaker who enjoyed baking and cooking a variety of ethnic foods. Thelma also enjoyed bingo, going to DelGrosso's Amusement Park and spending time with her family and many good friends.
TIMOTHY DODSON Sixth great grandson of progenitor Nicholas Kegg. **WILLIAM C. DODSON** [3397] (1942 – 1998) son of Alvin and Catherine (Benton) Dodson was father of (2). William retired as an engineer from Tripp Manufacturing Co., Chicago. He was a graduate of Williamson Trade School, Lancaster, and attended Penn State University. Mr. Dodson served with the Air Force in Grande Forks, N.D., attaining the rank of airman third class. He was noted for mathematical research and physics at Penn State University.

DOEBEL

LEO DOEBEL Fifth great grandson of progenitor Nicholas Kegg.

DOHNER

ALAN CHARLES DOHNER Fifth great grandson of progenitor Nicholas Kegg.
CAROL J. DOHNER [3398] (1912 – 2006) son of Alvin and Nora (Fisher) Dohner, married Carolyn Ruth Metcalf with whom he was father of (2). Carol was an avid ham radio operator for 70 years (W2FHY), and longtime member Salem County Archeological Society. He was employed as a lab technician for the DuPont Chambers Works where he retired after more than 30 years' service.
FREDERICK JAY DOHNER Fifth great grandson of progenitor Nicholas Kegg.
LACY KAITLYN DOHNER Sixth great granddaughter of progenitor Nicholas Kegg.

DOLER

ALEX DOLER Sixth great grandson of progenitor Nicholas Kegg. **AMY DOLER** Sixth great granddaughter of progenitor Nicholas Kegg. **BELINDA GAY DOLER** Fifth great granddaughter of progenitor Nicholas Kegg. **BONNIE SUZANNA DOLER** (1951 – 2004) daughter of Earl and Ardith (Snell) Doler married teice, first to Dale Rasmussen, later to Mr. Sitz. **BRIAN FORD DOLER** [3399] (1963 – 1999) son of Earl and Ardith (Snell) Doler. Brian was a professional house painter for many years in Lincoln County. He enjoyed fishing, camping, bike riding and snow skiing. He was attending classes at Oregon Coast Community College. **DARCY DOLER** Sixth great granddaughter of progenitor Nicholas Kegg. **JENNIFER DOLER** Sixth great granddaughter of progenitor Nicholas Kegg. **JORDANN DOLER** Sixth great grandson of progenitor Nicholas Kegg.
REBECCA A. DOLER Fifth great granddaughter of progenitor Nicholas Kegg.
ROBERT EARL DOLER [3399A] aka "Bob" (1947 – 2012) son of Earl and Ardith (Snell) Doler, married Marian Hopkins with whom he was father of (6). Over the years Robert had an illustrious career as a

---

[3395] Bedford Gazette (PA); Bedford County Historical Society, book 4, p. 1346 obtained by D. Sue Dible [3396] p.A9 – Altoona Mirror (PA) Mar 4, 2003 [3396A] Altoona Mirror (PA) Feb 5, 2011 [3397] p. A11 – Altoona Mirror Mar 18, 1998 [3398] Today's Sunbeam (Salem, NJ) Sept 2, 2006 [3399] GenLookups.com/Oregon Obituary and Death Notice Archive - Page 80 [3399A] Spokesman-Review (ID) Aug 15, 2012

certified professional geologist, working at places such as Hecla Mining Co., Placer Dome, Strata Inc., Sunshine Mine, the U.S. Bureau of Land Management and North Idaho College, where he taught geology. Bob enjoyed music, collecting rocks, hunting, fishing and the outdoors, but his biggest passion in life was his family. He loved encouraging others and making everyone feel good about themselves. He touched the lives of all who knew him. **TRALEN DOLER** Sixth great grandson of progenitor Nicholas Kegg. **WILLIAM L. DOLER** aka "Bill", Fifth great grandson of progenitor Nicholas Kegg.

DOLL

HAILEY DOLL Eighth great granddaughter of progenitor Nicholas Kegg.

DONALDSON

CHARLES S. DONALDSON (1916 – 1936) son of Charles and Jennie (Thompson) Donaldson.
ETHAN ASHOR DONALDSON Sixth great grandson of progenitor Nicholas Kegg.
JAMES DONALDSON Seventh great grandson of progenitor Nicholas Kegg.
JORDAN DONALDSON Seventh great grandson of progenitor Nicholas Kegg.

DONNER

PAMELA DAWN DONNER Sixth great granddaughter of progenitor Nicholas Kegg.

DORAN

DARYL J. DORAN aka "Duke", Sixth great grandson of progenitor Nicholas Kegg.

DOREY

SHIRLEY ANN DOREY [3400] (1931 – 2005) daughter of Lewis and Jessie (Kennedy) Dorey, married Gene Titus. Shirley was a homemaker most of her life, Shirley also was a foster parent. She volunteered at Hospice and worked at SRS as a home healthcare provider. Shirley was a former teacher's aide in the Newton school district. She was a member of Trinity Heights United Methodist Church and a member of the M.E.O. Club of Newton. Her favorite pastimes were spending quality time with her grandchildren and family, and she also enjoyed painting.

DORMAN

ASHLEY N. DORMAN Seventh great granddaughter of progenitor Nicholas Kegg.

DORNIC

ELYSSA DORNIC Eighth great granddaughter of progenitor Nicholas Kegg. **JEVIN DORNIC** Eighth great grandson of progenitor Nicholas Kegg. **MATTHEW DORNIC** Eighth great grandson of progenitor Nicholas Kegg.

DORR

MICAH E. DORR Seventh great granddaughter of progenitor Nicholas Kegg.

[3400] Newton Kansan (KS) Oct 12, 2005

DORRELL

ELAINE ANN DORRELL Fourth great granddaughter of progenitor Nicholas Kegg.
JANICE GAIL DORRELL Fourth great granddaughter of progenitor Nicholas Kegg.
LYNN GERTRUDE DORRELL Fourth great granddaughter of progenitor Nicholas Kegg.

DOTY

CHRISTOPHER ROBIN DOTY Sixth great grandson of progenitor Nicholas Kegg.
CYNTHIA DANEEN DOTY Sixth great granddaughter of progenitor Nicholas Kegg.
SCOTT ALAN DOTY Sixth great grandson of progenitor Nicholas Kegg.

DOUGHTY

AARON DOUGHTY Sixth great grandson of progenitor Nicholas Kegg. **MARY BETH DOUGHTY** Sixth great granddaughter of progenitor Nicholas Kegg. **MEGHAN DOUGHTY** Sixth great granddaughter of progenitor Nicholas Kegg.

DOWD

CARTER DOWD Eighth great grandson of progenitor Nicholas Kegg. **LAUREN DOWD** Eighth great granddaughter of progenitor Nicholas Kegg.

DOWLER

DYLVIN GRANT DOWLER, (1898 – 1900) son of Percival and Etta (Ferguson) Dowler.
PERCIVAL GRANT DOWLER, (1867 – 1936) aka "Percy", son of John and Elvira (Cagg) Dowler, married Etta F. Ferguson with whom he was father of (1).

DOWNEN

DYLAN DOWNEN Eighth great grandson of progenitor Nicholas Kegg.

DOWNING

IVER J. DOWNING Seventh great grandson of progenitor Nicholas Kegg.

DRAG

BARBARA J. DRAG Fifth great granddaughter of progenitor Nicholas Kegg.
ROBYN DRAG Fifth great granddaughter of progenitor Nicholas Kegg.

DRAGERT

AMANDA DRAGERT Seventh great granddaughter of progenitor Nicholas Kegg.
JOSHUA DRAGERT Seventh great grandson of progenitor Nicholas Kegg.

DRAIME

BARBARA JEAN DRAIME Fifth great granddaughter of progenitor Nicholas Kegg.
BEVERLY SUE DRAIME Fifth great granddaughter of progenitor Nicholas Kegg.

BRENT NORWOOD DRAIME Fifth great grandson of progenitor Nicholas Kegg.
DERRICK C. DRAIME Sixth great grandson of progenitor Nicholas Kegg.
TRAVIS N. DRAIME Sixth great grandson of progenitor Nicholas Kegg.

DREES

JENNIFER MARIE DREES Sixth great granddaughter of progenitor Nicholas Kegg.

DREWRY

JAMES M. DREWRY, III. Aka "Chip", Fifth great grandson of progenitor Nicholas Kegg.
JULIE DREWRY Fifth great granddaughter of progenitor Nicholas Kegg. **LYNNE DREWRY** Fifth great granddaughter of progenitor Nicholas Kegg.

DRINNEN

CLINTON LEE DRINNEN Seventh great grandson of progenitor Nicholas Kegg. **CYNTHIA DIANE DRINNEN** Seventh great granddaughter of progenitor Nicholas Kegg. **DONAVAN DEAN DRINNEN** Seventh great grandson of progenitor Nicholas Kegg. **KALENE DRINNEN** Seventh great granddaughter of progenitor Nicholas Kegg. **KYLE LINN DRINNEN** Seventh great grandson of progenitor Nicholas Kegg.

DROSJACK

DEBRA LYNN DROSJACK Sixth great granddaughter of progenitor Nicholas Kegg.
ROBERT DROSJACK Sixth great grandson of progenitor Nicholas Kegg.

DROZEK

CYNTHIA DROZEK Sixth great granddaughter of progenitor Nicholas Kegg. **KATHLEEN DROZEK** Sixth great granddaughter of progenitor Nicholas Kegg. **LAURA DROZEK** Sixth great granddaughter of progenitor Nicholas Kegg. **MARK ALLEN DROZEK** Sixth great grandson of progenitor Nicholas Kegg. **RICHARD DROZEK** Sixth great grandson of progenitor Nicholas Kegg. **VIRGINIA DROZEK** Sixth great granddaughter of progenitor Nicholas Kegg.

DUCHENE

ELIZABETH ANN DUCHENE Seventh great granddaughter of progenitor Nicholas Kegg.
EMILY CHRISTINE DUCHENE Seventh great granddaughter of progenitor Nicholas Kegg.
MARGARET GRACE DUCHENE aka "Maggie", Seventh great granddaughter of progenitor Nicholas Kegg. **MARY ELIZABETH BELT DUCHENE** [3401] (1996 – 1996) daughter of Todd and Jennifer (Belt) Duchene.

DUCKWORTH

ANTHONY L. DUCKWORTH aka "Tony", Sixth great grandson of progenitor Nicholas Kegg.
BENJAMIN DUCKWORTH Seventh great grandson of progenitor Nicholas Kegg.
BRITTAIN DUCKWORTH Seventh great granddaughter of progenitor Nicholas Kegg.
DANA RENEE DUCKWORTH Sixth great granddaughter of progenitor Nicholas Kegg.

[3401] Lima News (OH) Dec 14, 1996

DAWN DUCKWORTH Sixth great granddaughter of progenitor Nicholas Kegg.
DUSTIN WAYNE DUCKWORTH Sixth great grandson of progenitor Nicholas Kegg.
ELIZABETH E. DUCKWORTH Sixth great granddaughter of progenitor Nicholas Kegg.
GARRETT MICHAEL DUCKWORTH Seventh great grandson of progenitor Nicholas Kegg.
GREGORY ALLEN DUCKWORTH Sixth great grandson of progenitor Nicholas Kegg.
JOSEPH DUCKWORTH aka "Scott", Sixth great grandson of progenitor Nicholas Kegg.
MYLA MAY DUCKWORTH Seventh great granddaughter of progenitor Nicholas Kegg.
SARAH E. DUCKWORTH Seventh great granddaughter of progenitor Nicholas Kegg.
SARAH M. DUCKWORTH Seventh great granddaughter of progenitor Nicholas Kegg.
TRACY LYNN DUCKWORTH Sixth great granddaughter of progenitor Nicholas Kegg.

DUELING

CARMEN DUELING [3402] (1968 – 2017) daughter of James and Harold (Weems) Dueling, married Don Allen and later married Michael Villa. **JAMES HAROLD DUELING** [3403] (1943 – 2003) aka "Jim", son of Harold and Rose (Wyckoff) Dueling, married Donna Weems with whom he was father of (2). Jim was in the United States Marines from 1963 to 1966 in which he served two tours of duty in Vietnam. He was a truck driver for Reames Foods for 29 years. **JOY DUELING** [3404] (1937 – 2018) daughter of Harold and Rose (Wyckoff) Dueling, married Jerry Kinney with whom she was mother of (3). Joy was employed as a media specialist with the Area Education Agency 6. She was a secretary at the E-Free Church in Iowa Falls and participated in the Church Women's United group in Iowa Falls. Joy's most important things in her life were her faith in God, her large family, her love of music, and fishing. **SHANNON KYLE DUELING** Sixth great grandson of progenitor Nicholas Kegg.

DUERRING

AMANDA DUERRING Sixth great granddaughter of progenitor Nicholas Kegg.
ASHLEY DUERRING Sixth great granddaughter of progenitor Nicholas Kegg.
JESSICA DUERRING Sixth great granddaughter of progenitor Nicholas Kegg.

DUGAN

ALEX DUGAN Seventh great grandson of progenitor Nicholas Kegg. **JAMES BLAKE DUGAN** Eighth great grandson of progenitor Nicholas Kegg. **JODIE DUGAN** Seventh great granddaughter of progenitor Nicholas Kegg. **MEGAN DUGAN** Seventh great granddaughter of progenitor Nicholas Kegg. **WESTON DUGAN** Seventh great grandson of progenitor Nicholas Kegg.

DUKE

JOHN CHARLES HARRIS DUKE [3405] (1926 – 1981) aka "Jack", son of Lawrence and Wilma (Harris) Duke married Virginia LeCompte with whom he was father of (3). Jack was the assistant supervisor of the New Jersey State Game Farm. He was a life member and past chief of the Whitesville, NJ, Volunteer Fire Co. and a Navy veteran of WWII. **JOHN H. DUKE** Sixth great grandson of progenitor Nicholas Kegg. **KAREN M DUKE** (1948 – 1965) daughter of John and Virginia (LeCompte) Duke. **SHARON LEE DUKE** Sixth great granddaughter of progenitor Nicholas Kegg.

[3402] Find A Grave memorial# 190363906 [3403] iagenweb.orgWinterset Madisonian (IA) July 23, 2003Posted By: Treva Patterson [3404] Linn's Funeral Home(IA) [3405] p7c-Fort Wayne Journal Gazette (IN) Aug 5, 1981, obtained by D. Sue Dible

DUKERY

TARA L. DUKERY Sixth great granddaughter of progenitor Nicholas Kegg.

DUKES

ROGER E. DUKES [3406] (1920 – 1942) son of Merritt and Mildred (Wells) Dukes.

DUMMELDINGER

DAVID WALTER DUMMELDINGER Fifth great grandson of progenitor Nicholas Kegg.
FAITH DUMMELDINGER Fifth great granddaughter of progenitor Nicholas Kegg.
MARK DUMMELDINGER Fifth great grandson of progenitor Nicholas Kegg.

DUNCAN

ALISHA LYNN DUNCAN Seventh great granddaughter of progenitor Nicholas Kegg.
BRICE ANDREW DUNCAN Seventh great grandson of progenitor Nicholas Kegg.
EASTON ANDREW DUNCAN [3407] (2014 – 2014) son of Brice and Abigail (Marsch) Duncan.
JAYDEN DUNCAN Eighth great grandson of progenitor Nicholas Kegg. **SUMMER DAY DUNCAN** Sixth great granddaughter of progenitor Nicholas Kegg.

DUNFORD

CLARK EDWARD DUNFORD [3408] (1954 – 2009) son of Joseph and Betty (Diehl) Dunford married three times; first to Vicki Lee Thomas Ware with whom he was father of (2). He married Robin Lutzweiller with whom he was father of (1). Later he married Michelle Dawn Barr.
DAVID W. DUNFORD Sixth great grandson of progenitor Nicholas Kegg.
JOSEPH LANE DUNFORD [3409] (1947 – 1976) son of Joseph and Betty (Diehl) Dunford, married Patricia Ann Gween. **JOSEPH ROBERT DUNFORD** Seventh great grandson of progenitor Nicholas Kegg. **JOSHUA NICHOLAS DUNFORD** Seventh great grandson of progenitor Nicholas Kegg.
KAREN L. DUNFORD Sixth great granddaughter of progenitor Nicholas Kegg.
THERESA LEE DUNFORD Seventh great granddaughter of progenitor Nicholas Kegg.

DUNHAM

KAYLIN DUNHAM Eighth great granddaughter of progenitor Nicholas Kegg.
MARK ANDREW DUNHAM Seventh great grandson of progenitor Nicholas Kegg.
RUSSELL LEE DUNHAM Seventh great grandson of progenitor Nicholas Kegg.
RUSSELL ALLEN DUNHAM Eighth great grandson of progenitor Nicholas Kegg.

DUNKLE

SAMUEL M. DUNKLE Sixth great grandson of progenitor Nicholas Kegg.

DUNLAP

ALLEN P. DUNLAP Sixth great grandson of progenitor Nicholas Kegg.
SANDRA LOUISE DUNLAP Sixth great granddaughter of progenitor Nicholas Kegg.

[3406] Findlay Courier (OH) [3407] Gibson & Son Funeral Home, Hawesville, KY, obtained by D. Sue Dible [3408] Record Pub (OH) March 22, 2009 [3409] pC13 Akron Beacon Journal (OH) Apr 8, 1976, obtained by D. Sue Dible

DUNN

AIDEN DUNN Seventh great grandson of progenitor Nicholas Kegg. **BETH DUNN** Fifth great granddaughter of progenitor Nicholas Kegg. **JILLIAN DUNN** Seventh great granddaughter of progenitor Nicholas Kegg. **KAYLA DUNN** Sixth great granddaughter of progenitor Nicholas Kegg. **LORELEI DUNN** Seventh great granddaughter of progenitor Nicholas Kegg. **PATRICIA JO DUNN** Sixth great granddaughter of progenitor Nicholas Kegg. **REBECCA DUNN** Fifth great granddaughter of progenitor Nicholas Kegg. **SHANE DUNN** Sixth great grandson of progenitor Nicholas Kegg.

DUPERRON

VELTA ANN DUPERRON Seventh great granddaughter of progenitor Nicholas Kegg.

DURST

BARBARA ELMIRA DURST [3410] (1893 – 1941) daughter of Norman and Annie (Turner) Durst, married Harrison Ellis Lemmert. **DOROTHY LOUISE DURST** Fifth great granddaughter of progenitor Nicholas Kegg. **ICA M. DURST** [3411] (1891 – 1950) daughter of Norman and Annie (Turner) Durst, married Harry Edwin Poleman. **JANICE M. DURST** Fifth great granddaughter of progenitor Nicholas Kegg. **JENNIE MYRTLE DURST** [3412] (1888 – 1953) daughter of Norman and Annie (Turner) Durst, married James Taylor Crump with whom she was mother of (3). Jennie was a member of the First Methodist Church and a life member of Mountain Chapter 15, Order of Eastern Star. **MAMIE BLANCHE DURST** [3413] (1896 – 1923) daughter of Norman and Annie (Turner) Durst, married William Lewis Hetz with whom she was mother of (2).

DUTTON

CHARLES DUTTON aka "Chuck", Sixth great grandson of progenitor Nicholas Kegg. **DEANNE DUTTON** Seventh great granddaughter of progenitor Nicholas Kegg. **DENISE DUTTON** aka "Nisy" Seventh great granddaughter of progenitor Nicholas Kegg. **DOROTHY ARLENE DUTTON** Sixth great granddaughter of progenitor Nicholas Kegg. **MARK K. DUTTON** Sixth great grandson of progenitor Nicholas Kegg. **WALTER DUTTON** Sixth great grandson of progenitor Nicholas Kegg.

DUVALL

DUANE CHARLES DUVALL Sixth great grandson of progenitor Nicholas Kegg. **JANET ANN DUVALL** Sixth great granddaughter of progenitor Nicholas Kegg. **KATHERINE MAY DUVALL** [3414] (1910 – 1989) daughter of John and Effie (Diehl) Duvall married four times, first to Homer P. Jenkins with whom she was mother of (1). She married Edward Darst Stonebraker, Frank Beach and lastly Duane Arthur Bever. **RICHARD CARL DUVALL** [3415] (1912 – 1946) son of John and Effie (Diehl) Duvall. **ROBERT DALE DUVALL** Sixth great grandson of progenitor Nicholas Kegg. **UPTON EUGENE DUVALL** (1924 – 2011) son of John and Effie (Diehl) Duvall married three times. First to Betty Jane Dickinson, Later, he married Janet S. Eick with whom he was father of (3). He married Anita Frances Callahan.

[3410] p.11- Cumberland Evening Times (MD) Jan 22, 1941 [3411] Cumberland Evening Times (MD) May 22, 1950 [3412] p.5 - Cumberland Evening Times (MD) Feb 2, 1953 [3413] p.15 - Cumberland Evening Times (MD) Mar 1, 1923 [3414] Tyler Morning Telegraph (TX) Dec 30, 1989 [3415] The Pittsburgh Press (PA) March 19, 1946

DWIGANS

ARTHUR REXFORD DWIGANS, [3416] (1896 – 1961) aka "Rex", son of William and Hattie (Knouf) Dwigans married Addie Laura Flood with whom he was father of (1). Rex was a member of Western Riders Club and active in Alberta Light Horse Assn.   **BERNICE E. DWIGANS** [3417] (1893 – 1987) daughter of William and Hattie (Knouf) Dwigans, married George W. Porter with whom she was mother of (1). Bernice was a schoolteacher in Adair County. She took a very active part in any and all Jefferson Center United Methodist Church functions. Her door was always open, and her family was first and foremost in her life.   **BESSIE UNA DWIGANS** [3418] (1886 – 1941) daughter of William and Hattie (Knouf) Dwigans, married Clarence Elmer Hulbert with whom she was mother of (3).
DONA BELLE DWIGANS [3419] (1931 – 1971) daughter of Arthur and Addie (Flood) Dwigans married Gerald Roy Evans with whom she was mother of (3).   **EDWARD JAMES DWIGANS** (1910 – 1911) son of Winfield and Alice (Cunningham) Dwigans.   **HAZEL ALBERTA DWIGANS** [3420] (1891 – 1962) daughter of William and Hattie (Knouf) Dwigans, married Francis Eli Messinger with whom she was mother of (8). Hazel was a member of the Methodist church at Waite Park, Minn. and the VFW auxiliary of Glenwood.   **HELEN LUCILLE DWIGANS** [3421] (1920 – 2010) daughter of Winfield and Alice (Cunningham) Dwigans, married Phillip M. Toner with whom she was mother of (1).
LELA AGNES DWIGANS (1914 – 2003) daughter of Winfield and Alice (Cunningham) Dwigans, married Charles Arthur Holaday with whom she was mother of (3).   **NAOMI ISAL DWIGANS** [3422] (1898 – 1961) daughter of William and Hattie (Knouf) Dwigans married twice; first to Edward Levi Richards with whom she was mother of (3). Later she married Carl Fred Richmann.
WINFIELD E. DWIGANS [3423] (1887 – 1970) son of William and Hattie (Knouf) Dwigans, married Alice Loretta Cunningham with whom he was father of (3). Winfield had been engaged in agricultural pursuits all his adult life.

DWORZYNSKI

JEROD MILTON DWORZYNSKI Sixth great grandson of progenitor Nicholas Kegg.
TRAVIS LAWRENCE DWORZYNSKI Sixth great grandson of progenitor Nicholas Kegg.

DWYER

DANIEL P. DWYER Seventh great grandson of progenitor Nicholas Kegg.   **DOUGLAS M. DWYER** Seventh great grandson of progenitor Nicholas Kegg.   **ERIC DWYER** Sixth great grandson of progenitor Nicholas Kegg.   **TERRENCE DWYER**, aka "Terry", Sixth great grandson of progenitor Nicholas Kegg.   **WILLIAM F. DWYER** Sixth great grandson of progenitor Nicholas Kegg.

DZBYNSKI

SARAH N. DZBYNSKI Seventh great granddaughter of progenitor Nicholas Kegg.

EADS

CHARLES C. EADS [3424] (1916 – 1974) aka "Doc", son of Claude and Mary (Powell) Eads. An artist, who once drew cartoons on the television program "Casper." Doc was a member of Our Lady of Mt. Carmel Catholic Church. Buckeye Lake.

[3416] Calgary Herald (Alberta, Canada) April 11, 1961 [3417] Stuart Herald (IA) Dec 24, 1987, obtained by D. Sue Dible [3418] p.9 Daily Nonpareil (Council Bluffs, IA) Nov 5, 1941 [3419] Calgary Herald (Alberta, Canada) Nov 25, 1971 [3420] St. Cloud Times (MN) Nov 29, 1962 [3421] p.13 Des Moines Register (IA) July 26, 1940 [3422] unidentified obituary library clipping obtained by D. Sue Dible [3423] Greenfield News (IA) April 8, 1970, obtained by D. Sue Dible [3424] p.16 Lancaster Eagle-Gazette (OH) March 23, 1974

EARL

MICHAEL EARL Eighth great grandson of progenitor Nicholas Kegg   **MICHELLE EARL** Eighth great granddaughter of progenitor Nicholas Kegg.

EARMAN

DAVID ERIC EARMAN Sixth great grandson of progenitor Nicholas Kegg.

EASH

HAZEL EASH Sixth great granddaughter of progenitor Nicholas Kegg.   **JOANNA EASH** Fifth great granddaughter of progenitor Nicholas Kegg.   **JOHN KENTON EASH** Fifth great grandson of progenitor Nicholas Kegg.   **TAMMY JO EASH** Sixth great granddaughter of progenitor Nicholas Kegg.   **THOMAS LEE EASH** Sixth great grandson of progenitor Nicholas Kegg.

EAST

PAISLEY GRACE EAST Seventh great granddaughter of progenitor Nicholas Kegg.

EASTEP

COLTON EASTEP Seventh great grandson of progenitor Nicholas Kegg.   **LAKE EASTEP** Seventh great grandson of progenitor Nicholas Kegg.

EASTON

ADRIANNA EASTON Sixth great granddaughter of progenitor Nicholas Kegg.
ANGEL RENAE EASTON Sixth great granddaughter of progenitor Nicholas Kegg.
BETSY DIANE EASTON Fifth great granddaughter of progenitor Nicholas Kegg.
BRENTEN EASTON Sixth great grandson of progenitor Nicholas Kegg.   **CONNIE SUE EASTON** Fifth great granddaughter of progenitor Nicholas Kegg.   **JOHN E. EASTON** Seventh great grandson of progenitor Nicholas Kegg.   **JOHN EMMETT EASTON** aka "Madman", Fifth great grandson of progenitor Nicholas Kegg.   **JOHN EMMETT EASTON** Sixth great grandson of progenitor Nicholas Kegg.   **KATHY LOU EASTON** Fifth great granddaughter of progenitor Nicholas Kegg.
KEITH EUGENE EASTON Fifth great grandson of progenitor Nicholas Kegg.
KEITH THOMAS EASTON Sixth great grandson of progenitor Nicholas Kegg.
LINDA C. EASTON Fifth great granddaughter of progenitor Nicholas Kegg.   **MARISSA EASTON** Sixth great granddaughter of progenitor Nicholas Kegg.   **MICHAEL DAVID EASTON** Sixth great grandson of progenitor Nicholas Kegg.   **MICHAEL LYNN EASTON** Fifth great grandson of progenitor Nicholas Kegg.   **NANCY JO EASTON** Fifth great granddaughter of progenitor Nicholas Kegg.   **NATALIE EASTON** Seventh great granddaughter of progenitor Nicholas Kegg.
NICOLE EASTON Sixth great granddaughter of progenitor Nicholas Kegg.
ROBERT ALLEN EASTON Fifth great grandson of progenitor Nicholas Kegg.
TAMARA ANN EASTON Sixth great granddaughter of progenitor Nicholas Kegg.

EASTWOOD

KRISTILYNN EASTWOOD Sixth great granddaughter of progenitor Nicholas Kegg.

EATON

RAYMONA LOU EATON [3425] (1948 – 2006) daughter of James and Thelma (Fickes) Eaton, married Douglas L. Brunk with whom she was mother of (1). Raymona was employed as a convenience store manager. **SUSAN EATON** aka "Sue", Sixth great granddaughter of progenitor Nicholas Kegg.

EBBERTS

JULIA EBBERTS Eighth great granddaughter of progenitor Nicholas Kegg. **MADELYN EBBERTS** Eighth great granddaughter of progenitor Nicholas Kegg.

EBERHART

ELICIA MARIE EBERHART Seventh great granddaughter of progenitor Nicholas Kegg. **HEATHER ROSE EBERHART** Seventh great granddaughter of progenitor Nicholas Kegg.

EBERSOLE

MICHAEL L. EBERSOLE aka "Mike", Fifth great grandson of progenitor Nicholas Kegg. **SPENCER EBERSOLE** Sixth great grandson of progenitor Nicholas Kegg. **SYMON EBERSOLE** Sixth great grandson of progenitor Nicholas Kegg.

EBERT

ALLYSON EBERT Sixth great granddaughter of progenitor Nicholas Kegg. **JARRYD JAMES EBERT** Sixth great grandson of progenitor Nicholas Kegg. **JEREMY JEFFREY EBERT** Sixth great grandson of progenitor Nicholas Kegg. **JORDYN ELAINE EBERT** Sixth great granddaughter of progenitor Nicholas Kegg.

EBY

MORGAN EBY Sixth great granddaughter of progenitor Nicholas Kegg.

EDGAR

EUGENE HOLTON EDGAR [3426] (1921 – 1980) son of Franklin and Lucy (Cagg) Edgar married Rilla Joy Tyler with whom he was father of (2). Eugene was a veteran of World War II and a retired supervisor for Campbell Soup Co. **JILL DIANE EDGAR** Fifth great granddaughter of progenitor Nicholas Kegg. **PATRICIA LEE EDGAR** Fifth great granddaughter of progenitor Nicholas Kegg. **VIVIAN RUTH EDGAR** [3427] (1912 – 2012) daughter of Franklin and Lucy (Cagg) Edgar married William Conn with whom she was mother of (1). Vivian was a homemaker and nurse.

EDWARDS

ADAM EDWARDS Sixth great grandson of progenitor Nicholas Kegg. **AXLE EDWARDS** Seventh great grandson of progenitor Nicholas Kegg. **BRODY EDWARDS** Seventh great grandson of progenitor Nicholas Kegg. **CAMERON EDWARDS** Seventh great grandson of progenitor Nicholas Kegg. **JAMES ROBERT EDWARDS** [3428] (1945 – 2019) son of Hiram Pearl and Mary Mildred

---

[3425] The Review (Alliance, OH) March 12, 2006 [3426] The Chico Enterprise-Record (CA) Feb 20, 1980 [3427] Oroville Mercury-Register (CA) Aug 15, 2012 [3428] Red Bluff Daily News (CA) Jan 15, 2020

(Veeder) Edwards, married Huyen Thi with whom he was father of (2). James was a proud patriot, US Navy and Army veteran, raconteur, and comedian. He is remembered for his strong work ethic, legendary attention to detail and recordkeeping, his love for ketchup and all things science fiction. James was a veteran of the Vietnam War, and throughout his military career earned the Silver Star, Bronze Star, and several Letters of Commendation. He became passionate about restoring cars which included a 1969 Mustang and spent countless hours on his 1949 Military Jeep Willys. **JOHN H. EDWARDS** Fifth great grandson of progenitor Nicholas Kegg. **JUDITH ANN EDWARDS** Fifth great granddaughter of progenitor Nicholas Kegg. **REBECCA EDWARDS** aka "Becca", Sixth great granddaughter of progenitor Nicholas Kegg. **ROBERT EDWARDS** Sixth great grandson of progenitor Nicholas Kegg. **NANCY EDWARDS** Sixth great granddaughter of progenitor Nicholas Kegg. **SOFIA AMELIA EDWARDS** Seventh great granddaughter of progenitor Nicholas Kegg.

EDWINS

ASHLEE EDWINS Sixth great granddaughter of progenitor Nicholas Kegg.

EETEN

RODNEY EETEN Sixth great grandson of progenitor Nicholas Kegg. **ROSEMARY EETEN** Sixth great granddaughter of progenitor Nicholas Kegg.

EGGERT

CHRISTOPHER KYLE EGGERT Seventh great grandson of progenitor Nicholas Kegg.
JENNIFER L. EGGERT Seventh great granddaughter of progenitor Nicholas Kegg.

EHKO

DUANE EHKO Sixth great grandson of progenitor Nicholas Kegg.

EHLEN

BEVERLY EHLEN Fifth great granddaughter of progenitor Nicholas Kegg. **GRANT EHLEN** Fifth great grandson of progenitor Nicholas Kegg. **JANET EHLEN** Fifth great granddaughter of progenitor Nicholas Kegg. **KAROL EHLEN** Fifth great granddaughter of progenitor Nicholas Kegg.
LINDA EHLEN Fifth great granddaughter of progenitor Nicholas Kegg.

EHRET

FORREST EHRET Seventh great grandson of progenitor Nicholas Kegg.

EHRLICH

JAXON EHRLICH Eighth great grandson of progenitor Nicholas Kegg.

EHRMAN

BRYANT EHRMAN Eighth great grandson of progenitor Nicholas Kegg.
JONATHAN DAVID EHRMAN Eighth great grandson of progenitor Nicholas Kegg.
KYLE EHRMAN Ninth great grandson of progenitor Nicholas Kegg. **LUKE EHRMAN** Ninth great grandson of progenitor Nicholas Kegg.

EIDE

ALEICIA EIDE Seventh great granddaughter of progenitor Nicholas Kegg. **AMY DELORES EIDE** Fifth great granddaughter of progenitor Nicholas Kegg. **BARBARA JO EIDE** Fifth great granddaughter of progenitor Nicholas Kegg. **CINDY RAE EIDE** Sixth great granddaughter of progenitor Nicholas Kegg. **CONNIE FAY EIDE** Fifth great granddaughter of progenitor Nicholas Kegg. **CORY ALAN EIDE** Sixth great grandson of progenitor Nicholas Kegg. **DEAN PERRY EIDE** Fifth great grandson of progenitor Nicholas Kegg. **DERRICK BRADLEY EIDE** Sixth great grandson of progenitor Nicholas Kegg. **GRETCHEN CHRISTINE EIDE** [3429] (1964 – 2021) daughter of Peter and Mary Lucinda (Souders) Eide married Mr. Lewellen with whom she was mother of (1). Later she married Joseph Romelli with whom she was mother of (1). Gretchen was a dynamo, a remarkably kind person who also did not put up with any nonsense, someone you wanted by your side as you faced challenges or navigated day-to-day life, a true Valkyrie. Gretchen was brilliant, stylish, well-traveled, and creative in every endeavor she undertook. Her cakes and cookies were works of art, her meals were heavenly, and she brought her amazing food to friends and family in any crisis or celebration. She embodied the Scandinavian concept of hygge, "providing comfort." She was a fierce and loyal friend who was also so much fun—witty, beautiful, full of wonder and wonderful—and she never stopped trying to make the world around her a better place. She was there before you even knew you needed her, super supportive and willing to do anything for a friend. Gretchen was incredibly protective of her children as well, and she was deeply involved in providing the best life for them. She co-founded Autistic Endeavors, a non-profit that worked to raise funds and awareness of the educational and socialization needs of children with autism. She worked tirelessly for this cause. Gretchen was a professor of sociology who taught at Cincinnati State, IvyTech, and Mount St. Joseph University. She was also employed by Mercy Health Jewish Hospital in Kenwood. Her life was centered on doing what she could for others in so many ways, and so many who benefited from knowing her are far better people for having had her in their lives. **JAKOB ALLEN EIDE** Seventh great grandson of progenitor Nicholas Kegg. **JEAN ARLYSS EIDE** Fifth great granddaughter of progenitor Nicholas Kegg. **KIRK PATRICK EIDE** Sixth great grandson of progenitor Nicholas Kegg. **LEIF ERIC EIDE** [3430] (1968 – 2017) son of Peter and Mary Lucinda (Souders) Eide married Michele L. Wanek with whom he was father of (1). After joining the Army Leif served in Desert Storm. He was later employed in the roofing industry. He displayed some of the strongest work ethics and dedication around; no job was ever too big. Leif's smile, laugh and humor were contagious-a true friend to all. He enjoyed playing flag football and coaching pee-wee football. An avid motorcyclist, Leif spent his weekends on the road with his friends. **LEO MAX EIDE** [3431] (1947 – 2012) son of Elmer and Mildred (Kirkpatrick) Eide, married Mary Janet Kelly with whom he was father of (1). Leo is remembered for his uncompromising character, quiet intelligence and unique artistic talents. **MARTY DEAN EIDE** Sixth great grandson of progenitor Nicholas Kegg. **MOLLY KRISTEN EIDE** Sixth great granddaughter of progenitor Nicholas Kegg. **OLAF KAISTIN EIDE** Sixth great grandson of progenitor Nicholas Kegg. **OLAF RAYMOND EIDE** Seventh great grandson of progenitor Nicholas Kegg. **PETER DALE EIDE** Fifth great grandson of progenitor Nicholas Kegg.

EIKENBARY

LATHAN ALAN EIKENBARY Seventh great grandson of progenitor Nicholas Kegg.

EISENHOUR

ALAN EISENHOUR Fourth great grandson of progenitor Nicholas Kegg.
KAMERON EISENHOUR Fifth great grandson of progenitor Nicholas Kegg.
KYANNE EISENHOUR Fifth great granddaughter of progenitor Nicholas Kegg.

[3429, 3430] Ralph Meyer & Deters Funeral Home, Inc. (OH)obtained by D. Sue Dible [3431] p. 6B- Star Tribune (MN) Jan 26, 2012

MARTIN J. EISENHOUR aka "Marty", Fourth great grandson of progenitor Nicholas Kegg.

EISNAUGLE

ANNA EISNAUGLE Fifth great granddaughter of progenitor Nicholas Kegg.

EITNIEAR

STACY LYNN EITNIEAR Seventh great granddaughter of progenitor Nicholas Kegg.

ELAM

JANE ELLEN Sixth great granddaughter of progenitor Nicholas Kegg. **JILL ELAM** Sixth great granddaughter of progenitor Nicholas Kegg. **JULIE ELAM** Sixth great granddaughter of progenitor Nicholas Kegg.

ELBELL

SHELLY ELBELL Sixth great granddaughter of progenitor Nicholas Kegg. **TIM ELBELL** Sixth great grandson of progenitor Nicholas Kegg.

ELDER

ADAM ELDER Eighth great grandson of progenitor Nicholas Kegg. **ANDREW DOUGLAS ELDER** Seventh great grandson of progenitor Nicholas Kegg. **ANTHONY DEAN ELDER** Seventh great grandson of progenitor Nicholas Kegg. **ASHLEY DANIEL ELDER** Seventh great grandson of progenitor Nicholas Kegg. **BERTHA A. ELDER** [3434] (1884 – 1938) daughter of Robert and Emma (Martin) Elder, married Reuben Davis Parvin. **BETH ELDER** Seventh great granddaughter of progenitor Nicholas Kegg. **BRIAN ELDER** Eighth great grandson of progenitor Nicholas Kegg.
CAMMY J. ELDER Seventh great granddaughter of progenitor Nicholas Kegg.
DAVID MICHAEL ELDER (1961 – 1966) son of Robert and Mary Jane (King) Elder.
ELESHA ELDER Eighth great granddaughter of progenitor Nicholas Kegg. **INA GAY ELDER** (1887 – 1888) daughter of Robert and Emma (Martin) Elder. **JAMES CHRISTOPHER ELDER** Eighth great grandson of progenitor Nicholas Kegg. **JENNIFER MARIE ELDER** Eighth great granddaughter of progenitor Nicholas Kegg. **JESSICA N. ELDER** Eighth great granddaughter of progenitor Nicholas Kegg **JORDAN ELDER** Seventh great grandson of progenitor Nicholas Kegg.
LEILLA MAY ELDER [3435] (1885 – 1969) daughter of Robert and Emma (Martin) Elder, married Don Andrew Cotner. **LORI ELDER** Seventh great granddaughter of progenitor Nicholas Kegg.
LOU ANN ELDER [3436] (1953 – 1959) daughter of Everett and Martha (Altman) Elder.
LUKE ELDER Ninth great grandson of progenitor Nicholas Kegg. **MARTHA A. ELDER** died July 5, 1930, daughter of Harley and Georgia (Lease) Elder. **MARTIN A. ELDER** aka "Chip" Seventh great grandson of progenitor Nicholas Kegg. **MARTIN EDWARD ELDER** Eighth great grandson of progenitor Nicholas Kegg. **MARY L. ELDER** [3437] (1923 – 2007) daughter of Wilbur and Goldie (Brown) Elder, married William Thomas Gregory with whom she was mother of (2). Mary was employed as an administrative assistant for Dumbaugh Insurance for over 28 years, was a member of the American Legion Auxiliary for 59 years and was a member of the First Christian Church Disciples of Christ.
MICHAEL DAVID ELDER Seventh great grandson of progenitor Nicholas Kegg.
RICHARD HOMER ELDER Sixth great grandson of progenitor Nicholas Kegg.

[3434] Lima News (OH) Aug. 21, 1938 [3435] p.32 - News Journal (OH) July 24, 1969 [3436] p.3 - The Courier (OH) Aug 24, 1959, obtained by D. Sue Dible [3437] Mount Vernon News (OH) Dec. 25, 2007, obtained by D. Sue Dible

RUTH ELLA ELDER [3438] (1925 – 1926) daughter of Harley and Georgia (Lease) Elder.
SAMANTHA ELDER Eighth great granddaughter of progenitor Nicholas Kegg.
STEPHANIE ELDER Seventh great granddaughter of progenitor Nicholas Kegg. **STEVE ELDER** Eighth great grandson of progenitor Nicholas Kegg. **STEVEN K. ELDER** Sixth great grandson of progenitor Nicholas Kegg. **WENDELL E. ELDER** Seventh great grandson of progenitor Nicholas Kegg.

ELDRED

ANGELA MILLER ELDRED Sixth great granddaughter of progenitor Nicholas Kegg.

ELDREDGE

JAKE ELDREDGE Sixth great grandson of progenitor Nicholas Kegg.
MICHAEL ELDREDGE aka "Mike", Sixth great grandson of progenitor Nicholas Kegg.

ELEK

ROBERT STEVEN ELEK Eighth great grandson of progenitor Nicholas Kegg.

ELIJAH

XAVIER ELIJAH Seventh great grandson of progenitor Nicholas Kegg.

ELL

JASON A. ELL Seventh great grandson of progenitor Nicholas Kegg. **RICHARD ELL** Sixth great grandson of progenitor Nicholas Kegg.

ELLERBROOK

CAROLYN MARIE ELLERBROOK Sixth great granddaughter of progenitor Nicholas Kegg.

ELLIOTT

CARSON ELLIOTT Seventh great grandson of progenitor Nicholas Kegg. **JAMA ELLIOTT** Sixth great grandson of progenitor Nicholas Kegg. **JAMES ELLIOTT** Sixth great grandson of progenitor Nicholas Kegg. **JEANEL ELLIOTT** Sixth great granddaughter of progenitor Nicholas Kegg. **PARKER EVERETT ELLIOTT** Seventh great grandson of progenitor Nicholas Kegg. **ROBERT ALAN ELLIOTT** Sixth great grandson of progenitor Nicholas Kegg. **WILLIAM ELLIOTT** Sixth great grandson of progenitor Nicholas Kegg.

ELLIS

CHARLES R. ELLIS aka Charlie", Fifth great grandson of progenitor Nicholas Kegg.
JAMES BURDINE ELLIS (1902 – 1978) son of Robert and Kathryn (Myers) Ellis, married Elsie Lorraine Berkey with whom he was father of (2). **LYDIA KATHRYN ELLIS** Fifth great granddaughter of progenitor Nicholas Kegg.

[3438] p.3 Morning Rep (OH) May 13, 1926, obtained by D. Sue Dible

ELLYSON

JESSICA LYNN ELLYSON Seventh great granddaughter of progenitor Nicholas Kegg.
JUSTIN ELLYSON Seventh great grandson of progenitor Nicholas Kegg.
PRESTON JEAN ELLYSON [3438A] (1941 – 2017) son of Clarence and Thelma (Graham) Ellyson married Jayne Riedel with whom he was father of (2). Preston was an over the road truck driver.
RICHARD ARTHUR ELLYSON Sixth great grandson of progenitor Nicholas Kegg.
ROXANNA LIN ELLYSON Sixth great granddaughter of progenitor Nicholas Kegg.

ELMER

KAREN ELMER Seventh great granddaughter of progenitor Nicholas Kegg. **NANCY ELMER** Seventh great granddaughter of progenitor Nicholas Kegg. **SUZI ELMER** Seventh great granddaughter of progenitor Nicholas Kegg.

ELMORE

RONALD ELMORE Seventh great grandson of progenitor Nicholas Kegg.

EMBREE

BRENTON EMBREE Sixth great grandson of progenitor Nicholas Kegg. **DEBBIE EMBREE** Fifth great granddaughter of progenitor Nicholas Kegg. **DEVON LEIGH EMBREE** Sixth great granddaughter of progenitor Nicholas Kegg. **GAVON EMBREE** Seventh great grandson of progenitor Nicholas Kegg. **THOMAS JOHN EMBREE** Sixth great grandson of progenitor Nicholas Kegg.

EMBREY

TAYLOR E. EMBREY Seventh great granddaughter of progenitor Nicholas Kegg.

EMERT

ADAM D. EMERT Seventh great grandson of progenitor Nicholas Kegg. **ALLEN EMERT** Seventh great grandson of progenitor Nicholas Kegg. **AME EMERT** Sixth great granddaughter of progenitor Nicholas Kegg. **AME EMERT** Seventh great granddaughter of progenitor Nicholas Kegg. **AUSTIN EMERT** Seventh great grandson of progenitor Nicholas Kegg. **CHERYL EMERT** Sixth great granddaughter of progenitor Nicholas Kegg. **CHRIS EMERT** Sixth great grandson of progenitor Nicholas Kegg. **DALTON EMERT** Seventh great grandson of progenitor Nicholas Kegg. **DAVID E. EMERT** Sixth great grandson of progenitor Nicholas Kegg. **ROBERT EMERT** Sixth great grandson of progenitor Nicholas Kegg. **SCOTT EMERT** Sixth great grandson of progenitor Nicholas Kegg. **WILLIAM EMERT** Seventh great grandson of progenitor Nicholas Kegg.

EMIG

ANDREW EMIG Seventh great grandson of progenitor Nicholas Kegg. **DAVID M. EMIG** [3439] son of Joseph and Judy (Baughman) Emig, married twice, first to Pamela Lynn Twiest with whom he was father of (2). David was working as an independent contractor and realtor and previously worked for First Energy for over 25 years. He was a member of the Chapel in North Canton. Dave was a member of the Stark County Realtor's Association and was an avid Pittsburgh Steelers Fan, loved the outdoors, hunting

---

[3438A] Hoffen Funeral Home (IL) [3439] Arnold Funeral Home (OH)

and especially loved family and friends.   **JOHN GREGORY EMIG** Sixth great grandson of progenitor Nicholas Kegg.   **PATTY EMIG** Sixth great granddaughter of progenitor Nicholas Kegg.
PAUL EMIG Seventh great grandson of progenitor Nicholas Kegg.

EMMENDORFER

DERRICK R. EMMENDORFER Sixth great grandson of progenitor Nicholas Kegg.
KEVIN L. EMMENDORFER Sixth great grandson of progenitor Nicholas Kegg.

EMRICK

DAYLEE SAWYER EMRICK Eighth great granddaughter of progenitor Nicholas Kegg.

ENCE

CHERYL ANN ENCE Sixth great granddaughter of progenitor Nicholas Kegg.

ENEGREN

JACK ENEGREN Sixth great grandson of progenitor Nicholas Kegg.   **LEVI ENEGREN** Sixth great grandson of progenitor Nicholas Kegg.   **T.J. ENEGREN** Sixth great grandson of progenitor Nicholas Kegg.

ENGLAND

DANIEL BERNARD ENGLAND Fifth great grandson of progenitor Nicholas Kegg.
DAVID SAMUEL CLYDE ENGLAND (1913 – 1996) son of Harvey and Grace (Shaffer) England, married Esther Verdine Yutzy.   **GAYLE R. ENGLAND** Sixth great granddaughter of progenitor Nicholas Kegg.   **JEFFREY ROBERT ENGLAND** Sixth great grandson of progenitor Nicholas Kegg.
JOHN HARVEY ENGLAND (1916 – 2005) son of Harvey and Grace (Shaffer) England, married Carrie LaVerne Kniseley with whom he was father of (2).   **JOHN RONALD ENGLAND** Fifth great grandson of progenitor Nicholas Kegg.   **JOSHUA ENGLAND** Sixth great grandson of progenitor Nicholas Kegg.   **JOSHUA DAVID ENGLAND** Seventh great grandson of progenitor Nicholas Kegg.
LISA ROSEMARY ENGLAND [3940] (1965 – 2021) aka "Rosemary", daughter of S. Bernard and Sara (Hershberger) England married James Clapper with whom she was mother of (1).   Rosemary was an animal lover and was active with 4-H and FFA; she was also crowned the Bedford County Lamb and Wool Queen. She was a member of Snake Spring Valley Church of the Brethren, in her earlier years she taught Sunday School. Lisa was hardworking and a person you could always count on.

ENGLISH

EDMUND ENGLISH Seventh great grandson of progenitor Nicholas Kegg.

ENZ

GRETCHEN ENZ Sixth great granddaughter of progenitor Nicholas Kegg.   **HANNA ENZ** Sixth great granddaughter of progenitor Nicholas Kegg.   **HEIDI ENZ** Sixth great granddaughter of progenitor Nicholas Kegg.   **MICHAEL ENZ** Sixth great grandson of progenitor Nicholas Kegg.

[3440] Bedford Gazette (PA) Dec 29, 2021

EPLEY

JACQUELINE EPLEY Sixth great granddaughter of progenitor Nicholas Kegg.
THOMAS EPLEY Sixth great grandson of progenitor Nicholas Kegg.

EPPS

HOMER LOREN EPPS (1940 – 1940) son of Harry and Lois (Johnson) Epps.
MARILYN JOAN EPPS [3441] (1935 – 1981) daughter of Harry and Lois (Johnson) Epps, married twice; first to Wesley Freeman Stringfield with whom she was mother of (1). Later, she married Richard L. Culp with whom she was mother of (3) known children.

ERB

ELENA ERB Seventh great granddaughter of progenitor Nicholas Kegg.   **JONATHAN ROSS ERB** Sixth great grandson of progenitor Nicholas Kegg.   **RACHEL LEAH ERB** Sixth great granddaughter of progenitor Nicholas Kegg.

ERDMAN

KALIANA ROSE ERDMAN Eighth great granddaughter of progenitor Nicholas Kegg.
MADDOX BROCK ERDMAN Eighth great grandson of progenitor Nicholas Kegg.

ESHELMAN

ANNEMARIE ESHELMAN Fifth great granddaughter of progenitor Nicholas Kegg.
BENJAMIN ESHELMAN Fifth great grandson of progenitor Nicholas Kegg.
BEVERLY JOANN ESHELMAN [3442] (1948 – 2002) aka "Bev", daughter of Joseph and Vada (Schokey) Eshelman married (3) times and was mother of (4); Bev married Randolph B. Barnes with whom she was mother of (3). She married Charles Edward Smith. Later, she married Samuel Thomas Vick.   **BRAD W. ESHELMAN** Sixth great grandson of progenitor Nicholas Kegg.
CHRISTIAN ESHELMAN Seventh great grandson of progenitor Nicholas Kegg.
DENNY ESHELMAN Sixth great grandson of progenitor Nicholas Kegg.
DONIA LEE ESHELMAN Sixth great granddaughter of progenitor Nicholas Kegg.
EUGENE ALLEN ESHELMAN [3443] (1949 – 1949) aka "Butchy", son of Roy and Edith (Deck) Eshelman.   **EVAN ESHELMAN** Seventh great grandson of progenitor Nicholas Kegg.
FRANCIS ESHELMAN Fifth great grandson of progenitor Nicholas Kegg.   **GLADYS ESHELMAN** [3444] (1922 – 1976) daughter of Benjamin and Mary (Biddle) Eshelman married twice; first to John N. Metz with whom she was mother of (2). Later, she married Leroy F. Seifert with whom she was mother of (1). Gladys was a member of Transit Motors and Whetstone Insurance Bowling Leagues; a member of the WIBC; and a member of the auxiliary of the VFW.   **JARET ESHELMAN** Seventh great grandson of progenitor Nicholas Kegg.   **JENNIFER LEE ESHELMAN** Sixth great granddaughter of progenitor Nicholas Kegg.   **JOSEPH ESHELMAN** (1953 – 2014) son of Joseph and Margaret (Carmody) Eshelman married Billy Lee Richards with whom he was father of (3).
JOSHEPH FRANKLIN ESHELMAN [3445] (1926 – 1997) son of Benjamin and Mary (Biddle) Eshelman married three times; first to Vada Nadine Schokey with whom he was father of (1). He married Margaret T. Carmody with whom he was father of (2). Later he married Doris Hall with whom he was father of (2). Joseph had been employed as a mechanic for the former Eastern Express, Inc. of Bedford. He was a decorated Air Force veteran who served during World War II. He received the World War II

[3441] Austin American-Statesman (PA) Jan 3, 1981 [3442] Progress-Index (VA) June 13, 2002 [3443] p.4 - Morning Herald (PA) Dec 1, 1949 [3444] Bedford County Historical Society Obituary obtained by D. Sue Dible [3445] p.2 - Bedford Gazette (PA) June 16, 1997

Victory Medal, Army of Occupation (German) EAME Camp Medal and the National Defense Medal. His most significant duty assignment was the 1401st MTRVEHRON (MATS). He was a member of the American Legion Post 2088 in Everett and the Bedford VFW Post. **JULIE E. ESHELMAN** Sixth great granddaughter of progenitor Nicholas Kegg. **KAREN JO ESHELMAN** Sixth great granddaughter of progenitor Nicholas Kegg. **KAREN L. ESHELMAN** Fifth great granddaughter of progenitor Nicholas Kegg. **LAUREN ESHELMAN** Seventh great granddaughter of progenitor Nicholas Kegg. **LAURETTA MARY JANE ESHELMAN** [3446] (1914 – 2000) daughter of Benjamin and Mary (Biddle) Eshelman, married Melvin R. Ritchy. Lauretta was the mother of three foster children. **MEAH ESHELMAN** Seventh great granddaughter of progenitor Nicholas Kegg. **MELVIN DOUGLAS ESHELMAN** (1952 – 1952) son of Raymond and Janet (Miller) Eshelman. **ROBERT ESHELMAN** [3447] (1916 – 1962) son of Benjamin and Mary (Biddle) Eshelman married twice; first to Betty Ruth Lilley with whom he was father of (1). Later, he married Juliette Cordelia Foreman with whom he was father of (1). Robert was a trucker and killed when the tractor-trailer he was operating went out of control and crashed in Weirton, W. Va. The Rig went out of control on icy U.S. 22 and knocked down two utility poles on the outskirts of Weirton. **ROBERT M. ESHELMAN** Sixth great grandson of progenitor Nicholas Kegg. **RYAN ESHELMAN** Seventh great grandson of progenitor Nicholas Kegg. **SAMANTHA ANN ESHELMAN** Sixth great granddaughter of progenitor Nicholas Kegg. **SCOTT ESHELMAN** Sixth great grandson of progenitor Nicholas Kegg. **SHARON ESHELMAN** Fifth great granddaughter of progenitor Nicholas Kegg. **SHELLY LYNN ESHELMAN** [3448] (1971 – 2014) daughter of Joseph and Billy (Richards) Eshelman. Shelly was mother of (3). She married David Duane Garmoe. **SUSAN A. ESHELMAN**, aka "Sue", Fifth great granddaughter of progenitor Nicholas Kegg. **VAUGHN MICHAEL ESHELMAN** [3449] (1969 – 2018) son of Larry and Janet Eshelman, married Julie Menard with whom he was father of (2). Vaughn pitched for Blinn College and the University of Houston and then in the Major Leagues with the Boston Red Sox. He had a successful 11-year professional baseball career, making many lifelong friends. Rather than taking opportunities to coach at the professional level he chose to stay at home in the Spring area with his family, looking forward to the challenges of the business world. He worked for Stanley, Black and Decker Tools and Fasteners as an area sales manager, enjoyed his job and the people he met and had great success. Vaughn enjoyed fishing very much and spent many hours on his pontoon boat, mainly on Lake Conroe. He also enjoyed working with his sons and their various teams coaching at the Little League through High School levels. He coached the summer league teams for the high school for 8 years, He was always positive with the players and many continued to seek his advice after they had grown. He loved kids and they loved him for his honesty as well as ability to help them. He also enjoyed golf and played it very well when he had the chance. **ZACKERY JOSEPH ESHELMAN** Seventh great grandson of progenitor Nicholas Kegg.

ESHNAUR

JOHN ESHNAUR Fifth great grandson of progenitor Nicholas Kegg. **SHERYL ESHNAUR** Fifth great granddaughter of progenitor Nicholas Kegg.

ESPORITE

BENJAMIN RILEY ESPORITE Seventh great grandson of progenitor Nicholas Kegg.
KAITLYN JOLIE ESPORITE Seventh great granddaughter of progenitor Nicholas Kegg.

[3446] Morning Herald (PA) March 23, 2000 [3447] p.10 - Evening Times (MD) Mar 10, 1962 [3448] Commercial Appeal (TN) June 14, 2014 [3449] Klein Funeral Home (TX)

ESSEN

JENNIFER ESSEN Seventh great granddaughter of progenitor Nicholas Kegg.

ESTEL

DIANA LYNN HUDDY ESTEL Sixth great granddaughter of progenitor Nicholas Kegg.

ESTEP

ANNA LOUISE ESTEP [3450] (1910 – 1981) daughter of Professor Thomas and Kathryne (Beaver) Estep, married Lester Guy Stewart with whom she was mother of (1).

ESTERBERG

CHLOE ESTERBERG Eighth great granddaughter of progenitor Nicholas Kegg.
COLBY ESTERBERG Eighth great grandson of progenitor Nicholas Kegg.
COLLEEN M. ESTERBERG Seventh great granddaughter of progenitor Nicholas Kegg.
LORI ESTERBERG Seventh great granddaughter of progenitor Nicholas Kegg.
DAVID HARTIN ESTERBURG [3451] (1918 – 1996) son of Clyde and Susie (Kegg) Esterburg married twice; first to Catherine Dudish with whom he was father of (2). Later, he married Althea Sylvia Kincaid Robison. **GREGORY ALAN ESTERBURG** Seventh great grandson of progenitor Nicholas Kegg.
INFANT ESTERBURG (1914 – 1914) son of Clyde and Susie (Kegg) Esterburg.
JACKSON ESTERBURG Eighth great grandson of progenitor Nicholas Kegg.
JEFFREY ESTERBURG Sixth great grandson of progenitor Nicholas Kegg.
KEVIN PATRICK ESTERBURG Seventh great grandson of progenitor Nicholas Kegg.
MERWIN C. ESTERBURG [3452] (1922 – 1982) aka "Boots", son of Clyde and Susie (Kegg) Esterburg, married Helen Shupink with whom he was father of (1). **ROBERT J. ESTERBURG** [3453] (1947 – 1972) son of David and Catherine (Dudish) Esterburg, married Mildred Masley with whom he was father of (2). **TODD JEFFREY ESTERBURG** Seventh great grandson of progenitor Nicholas Kegg.

ESTES

ANDREW A. ESTES Sixth great grandson of progenitor Nicholas Kegg. **CONSTANCE N. ESTES** Sixth great granddaughter of progenitor Nicholas Kegg. **VERONICA M. ESTES** Sixth great granddaughter of progenitor Nicholas Kegg.

ESTRADA

JAIME FLOREZ ESTRADA Sixth great grandson of progenitor Nicholas Kegg.
KRISTA FLOREZ ESTRADA Sixth great granddaughter of progenitor Nicholas Kegg.

ETOLL

DENNIS ETOLL Seventh great grandson of progenitor Nicholas Kegg.

[3450] p.2 Huntingdon Daily News (PA) Apr 3, 1981 [3251] p.B-11, Pittsburgh Post-Gazette (PA) April 26, 1996 [3252] p.39 Pittsburgh Press (PA) Jan 2, 1983 [3453] p.25 Pittsburgh Press (PA) Nov 28, 1972

EURITT

DONALD EVERETT EURITT (1931 – 1947) son of Everett and Bernice (Laird) Euritt.
MARION EURITT (1916 – 1996) son of Everett and Bernice (Laird) Euritt. **EVELYN EURITT** [3453A] (1921 – 2004) daughter of Everett and Bernice (Laird) Euritt married twice, first to Paul Pratt with whom she was mother of (2). Later she married Paul Llewellyn Carson with whom she was mother of (2). Evelyn was an excellent student and talented high school debater, being recognized at the State level. She attended Northwest Missouri Teacher's College in Marysville, Missouri. In 1939 she started teaching in one room, eight-grade level county schools in Southern Iowa, and later in Lebanon, Oregon. Evelyn was a member of the Brookings Hospital Auxiliary, the South Dakota State College AAUW, the Crafts Group and the Saturday Literary Club. She enjoyed the many happy times she spent at neighborhood coffee parties, bridge playing, antiquing, crocheting, cooking, fishing, entertaining, and gardening. **MARGARET EURITT** [3454] (1918 – 2016) daughter of Everett and Bernice (Laird) Euritt, married Ira John Campbell with whom she was mother of (2).Margaret was a school teacher and High School guidance counselor for more than 30 years. In her retirement years she and Ira did a lot of traveling. She especially enjoyed watching her grandkids and great- grandkids growing up. Family and Church were very important to her.

EVANS

ANDRA EVANS Sixth great granddaughter of progenitor Nicholas Kegg. **ANGELA RANAI EVANS** Sixth great granddaughter of progenitor Nicholas Kegg. **BONNIE GAYLE EVANS** Fifth great granddaughter of progenitor Nicholas Kegg. **BRITTANY SUZAN EVANS** Seventh great granddaughter of progenitor Nicholas Kegg. **BROOKE ELIZABETH EVANS** Seventh great granddaughter of progenitor Nicholas Kegg. **CAMERON EVANS** Seventh great grandson of progenitor Nicholas Kegg. **CAROLYN EVANS** aka "Keri" Seventh great granddaughter of progenitor Nicholas Kegg. **CHRISTINE MARIE EVANS** Seventh great granddaughter of progenitor Nicholas Kegg. **CHRISTOPHER JON EVANS** Sixth great grandson of progenitor Nicholas Kegg.
CONSTANCE EVANS Sixth great granddaughter of progenitor Nicholas Kegg. **DALE EVANS** Fifth great grandson of progenitor Nicholas Kegg. **DENNIS EVANS** Fifth great grandson of progenitor Nicholas Kegg. **DREW EVANS** Seventh great grandson of progenitor Nicholas Kegg.
ELIZABETH EVANS aka "Liz", Seventh great granddaughter of progenitor Nicholas Kegg. **ELIZABETH ANN EVANS** Sixth great granddaughter of progenitor Nicholas Kegg.
GILLIAN EVANS Fifth great grandson of progenitor Nicholas Kegg.
GRAHAM CHRISTOPHER EVANS Seventh great grandson of progenitor Nicholas Kegg.
GREGORY WILLIAM EVANS (1944 – 1946) son of John and Joann (Peters) Evans.
HEATHER EVANS Fifth great granddaughter of progenitor Nicholas Kegg. **INFANT EVANS** (1946 – 1946) son of John and June (Bingham) Evans died the result of a premature birth. **JENNY EVANS** Seventh great granddaughter of progenitor Nicholas Kegg. **JOHN GREGORY EVANS** Sixth great grandson of progenitor Nicholas Kegg. **JOSHUA EVANS** Seventh great grandson of progenitor Nicholas Kegg. **JOY EVANS** Fifth great granddaughter of progenitor Nicholas Kegg.
KATHERINE EVANS Seventh great granddaughter of progenitor Nicholas Kegg.
MARGERY EVANS Sixth great granddaughter of progenitor Nicholas Kegg. **MARK EVANS** Fifth great grandson of progenitor Nicholas Kegg. **MARK D. EVANS** Sixth great grandson of progenitor Nicholas Kegg. **MCKENNA EVANS** Seventh great granddaughter of progenitor Nicholas Kegg. **MICHAEL EVANS** Fifth great grandson of progenitor Nicholas Kegg. **PARKER EVANS** Seventh great grandson of progenitor Nicholas Kegg. **REXFORD JOHN EVANS** [3456] (1964 – 1968) son of Gerald and Dona Belle (Dwigans) Evans. **ROBERT MICHAEL EVANS** Sixth great grandson of progenitor Nicholas Kegg. **SABRINA EVANS** Sixth great granddaughter of progenitor Nicholas Kegg.

[3453A] Eidsness Funeral Home (SD) [3454] Watson-Armstrong Funeral Home (IA) [3456] Calgary Herald (Alberta, Canada) April 3, 1968

SONYA EVANS Sixth great granddaughter of progenitor Nicholas Kegg. **SPENCER EVANS** Seventh great grandson of progenitor Nicholas Kegg. **THEODORE VINCENT EVANS** Sixth great grandson of progenitor Nicholas Kegg. **TOMMY EVANS** Seventh great grandson of progenitor Nicholas Kegg. **WELDON LAWSON EVANS** Sixth great grandson of progenitor Nicholas Kegg.

EVENSON

MICHAEL A. EVENSON Sixth great grandson of progenitor Nicholas Kegg.
ROGER DALE EVENSON Sixth great grandson of progenitor Nicholas Kegg.
SPENCER EVENSON Fourth great grandson of progenitor Nicholas Kegg.

EVERETTS

LUCRETIA MARIE EVERETTS Fifth great granddaughter of progenitor Nicholas Kegg.
VIRGINIA ALICE EVERETTS Fifth great granddaughter of progenitor Nicholas Kegg.

EVERHART

JOSEPH EVERHART Ninth great grandson of progenitor Nicholas Kegg.

EVEY

JOEL EVEY Sixth great grandson of progenitor Nicholas Kegg. **JONATHAN CHARLES EVEY** Sixth great grandson of progenitor Nicholas Kegg. **KRISTEN LORENE EVEY** Sixth great granddaughter of progenitor Nicholas Kegg. **MATTHEW ALAN EVEY** Sixth great grandson of progenitor Nicholas Kegg. **PATRICIA JOY EVEY** Sixth great granddaughter of progenitor Nicholas Kegg. **REBECCA EVEY** Sixth great granddaughter of progenitor Nicholas Kegg.

EWART

BILLY EWART Sixth great grandson of progenitor Nicholas Kegg. **DANIEL J. EWART** aka "Danny", Sixth great grandson of progenitor Nicholas Kegg. **MIKE T. EWART** Seventh great grandson of progenitor Nicholas Kegg. **RICKY L EWART** Sixth great grandson of progenitor Nicholas Kegg.

FACCHINEI

RHIANNON NOELLE FACCHINEI Seventh great granddaughter of progenitor Nicholas Kegg.

FAGANS

BRODY R. FAGANS Seventh great grandson of progenitor Nicholas Kegg.
HANNAH E. FAGANS Seventh great granddaughter of progenitor Nicholas Kegg.

FAHRENBACH

ERIC DANIEL FAHRENBACH Seventh great grandson of progenitor Nicholas Kegg.
MICHAEL E. FAHRENBACH aka "Mike", Seventh great grandson of progenitor Nicholas Kegg.

FAIR

LARRY LEE FAIR Fifth great grandson of progenitor Nicholas Kegg. **VICKI LYNN FAIR** Fifth great granddaughter of progenitor Nicholas Kegg.

FAIRCHILD

JOSEPH DUANE FAIRCHILD (3457) (1910 – 1927) son of William and Hope (Shrock) Fairchild. **VIRGIL WILLARD FAIRCHILD** (3458) (1909 – 1927) son of William and Hope (Shrock) Fairchild. The deaths of these two brothers resulted from a collision between an auto and a train at Holly.

FANCHER

JON THOMAS FANCHER Sixth great grandson of progenitor Nicholas Kegg.

FARRAND

ASHLIE FARRAND Seventh great granddaughter of progenitor Nicholas Kegg. **BABY FARRAND** (1948 – 1948) son of progenitor Nicholas Kegg. **BABY FARRAND** (1948 – 1948) daughter of progenitor Nicholas Kegg. **BRADLEY FARRAND** aka "Brad", Seventh great grandson of progenitor Nicholas Kegg. **BRE FARRAND** Eighth great granddaughter of progenitor Nicholas Kegg. **BRIAN FARRAND** Seventh great grandson of progenitor Nicholas Kegg. **CADEN FARRAND** Eighth great grandson of progenitor Nicholas Kegg. **CASSANDRA FARRAND** Seventh great granddaughter of progenitor Nicholas Kegg. **CRAIG FARRAND** Seventh great grandson of progenitor Nicholas Kegg. **DANA FARRAND** Seventh great granddaughter of progenitor Nicholas Kegg. **DAVID FARRAND** Seventh great grandson of progenitor Nicholas Kegg. **EMALYNE STAY FARRAND** Eighth great granddaughter of progenitor Nicholas Kegg. **JERRY FARRAND** aka "Bubba", Sixth great grandson of progenitor Nicholas Kegg. **MELISSA FARRAND** Seventh great granddaughter of progenitor Nicholas Kegg. **MICHAEL FARRAND** Seventh great grandson of progenitor Nicholas Kegg. **MICHAEL FARRAND** aka "Micky", Sixth great grandson of progenitor Nicholas Kegg. **NICHOLAS FARRAND** Seventh great grandson of progenitor Nicholas Kegg. **SHANE FARRAND** Eighth great grandson of progenitor Nicholas Kegg. **SHERYL L. FARRAND** Sixth great granddaughter of progenitor Nicholas Kegg. **TAYLOR FARRAND** Eighth great granddaughter of progenitor Nicholas Kegg.

FARRELL

ANDREW THOMAS SUTER FARRELL Sixth great grandson of progenitor Nicholas Kegg. **JENNIFER ASHLEY FARRELL** Sixth great granddaughter of progenitor Nicholas Kegg. **TIMOTHY JOHN PATRICK FARRELL** Sixth great grandson of progenitor Nicholas Kegg.

FARRINGTON

KATHLEEN KAY FARRINGTON (3458A) (1946 – 2011) daughter of Robert and Irene (Muncy) Farrington, married Jack Murray with whom she was mother of (2). Kay enjoyed quilting, gardening and, most importantly, shopping. She worked for Putnam Investments.

(3457, 3458) p.21 Detroit Times (MI) May 1, 1927 (3458A) The Country Gazette (MA) May 10, 2011

FASH

DAVID EMERY FASH (3459) (1940 – 1963) son of Jesse and Doris (Kegg) Fash. David suffered fatal injuries when his auto crashed into the rear of a slow-moving truck on icy roads west of Terre Haute. **DAVID EMERY FASH** (3460) (1966 – 1967) son of James and Pat (Cline) Fash. **EVAN FASH** Eighth great grandson of progenitor Nicholas Kegg. **JAMES NOBLE FASH** Sixth great grandson of progenitor Nicholas Kegg. **JOEY FASH** Eighth great grandson of progenitor Nicholas Kegg. **JOHN RICHARD FASH** (3461) (1965 – 2021) son of James and Patricia (Cline) Fash married Tori Campbell with whom he was father of (3). John was a farmer and loved the outdoors. **JOHN FASH** Seventh great grandson of progenitor Nicholas Kegg. **KAREN JOANNE FASH** Seventh great granddaughter of progenitor Nicholas Kegg. **MATTHEW FASH** Eighth great grandson of progenitor Nicholas Kegg.

FASSLER

CRYSTAL DAWN FASSLER (3462) (1977 – 1999) daughter of Richard and Debra (Anderson) Fassler graduated from Poudre High School in Ft. Collins. She then worked at the Holiday Inn in Ft. Collins and later the Ft. Collins Sonic Drive-In. She attended Hastings College. She worked at Grandview Manor Nursing Home in Campbell until returning to Ft. Collins to work. **DALE ALBERT FASSLER** (3463) (1924 – 1995) son of Albert and Elizabeth (Clark) Fassler, married Evelyn (Todd) Fassler with whom he was father of (3). Dale served in the army during World War II in Japan. He was employed by Pet Milk and retired after 30 years. Dale enjoyed camping, fishing, working with his hands and macrame lawn chairs. **DARLENE FASSLER** (3463A) (1928 – 2019) daughter of Albert and Elizabeth (Clark) Fassler, married Stanley Frank Pavelka with whom she was mother of (4). Darlene was a dedicated "Farm Wife" sharing in field work, raising livestock and the myriad of other duties that come with living on a farm. Her greatest joy was her family and cooking for them all. Many meals were served at her table including her family's favorite…. the dressing cooked with the turkey at holiday time. Her delicious homemade Kolaches always brought smiles. **ELAINE M. FASSLER** (3464) (1920 – 1992) daughter of Albert and Elizabeth (Clark) Fassler, married Ray Meissner with whom she was mother of (3). **HAROLD CLAYTON FASSLER** (3465) (1914 – 1999) son of Albert and Elizabeth (Clark) Fassler, married June Elaine Favinger with whom he was father of (5). Harold was a retired farmer. He was an Army veteran having served during WWII. **JEREMY FASSLER** Sixth great grandson of progenitor Nicholas Kegg. **LACI FASSLER** Sixth great granddaughter of progenitor Nicholas Kegg. **LINDA FASSLER** Fifth great granddaughter of progenitor Nicholas Kegg. **LORI LYNN FASSLER** Fifth great granddaughter of progenitor Nicholas Kegg. **MARGARET FASSLER** Fifth great granddaughter of progenitor Nicholas Kegg. **MICHAEL DEAN FASSLER** Fifth great grandson of progenitor Nicholas Kegg. **NANCY K. FASSLER** Fifth great granddaughter of progenitor Nicholas Kegg. **RICHARD H. FASSLER** Fifth great grandson of progenitor Nicholas Kegg. **ROGER W. FASSLER** Fifth great grandson of progenitor Nicholas Kegg. **VERNA M. FASSLER** (3466) (1916 – 2013) daughter of Albert and Elizabeth (Clark) Fassler, married Raymond Roy Reigle.

FAULKNER

DAMIAN EDWARD FAULKNER Eighth great grandson of progenitor Nicholas Kegg.
EDDIE JOE SPARKS FAULKNER Seventh great grandson of progenitor Nicholas Kegg.
JAMES A. FAULKNER III Eighth great grandson of progenitor Nicholas Kegg.
JAMES ARNOLD FAULKNER JR. aka "J.J.", Seventh great grandson of progenitor Nicholas Kegg.

(3459) Logansport Press (IN) Jan 22, 1963 (3460) p.2 - Terre Haute Tribune (IN) Apr. 25, 1967 (3461) Pearce Funeral Home (IL) Oct 6, 2021 (3462) Genlookups.com obtained by D. Sue Dible (3463) Buhl Herald (ID) July 26, 1996, obtained by D. Sue Dible (3463A) Hastings Tribune (NE) April 3, 2019 (3464) p.2 South Idaho Press (Burley, Idaho) Dec 20, 1992 (3465) p.4 - Lincoln Journal Star (NE) Oct 12, 1999 (3466) Times-News (Twin Falls, ID) Dec 5, 2013

SUSAN MICHELLE FAULKNER Eighth great granddaughter of progenitor Nicholas Kegg.
WENDY MICHELLE FAULKNER Seventh great granddaughter of progenitor Nicholas Kegg.

FAVARA

ASHLEY FAVARA Sixth great granddaughter of progenitor Nicholas Kegg.
JORDAN TYLER FAVARA Sixth great grandson of progenitor Nicholas Kegg.

FEATHER

BARBARA JO FEATHER 7th great granddaughter of progenitor Nicholas Kegg.
BONNIE FEATHER Fourth great granddaughter of progenitor Nicholas Kegg.
BRIAN R. FEATHER Seventh great grandson of progenitor Nicholas Kegg.   **DAVID J. FEATHER** Seventh great grandson of progenitor Nicholas Kegg.   **DEVON N. FEATHER** Seventh great grandson of progenitor Nicholas Kegg.   **GLORIA ANN FEATHER** Seventh great granddaughter of progenitor Nicholas Kegg.   **HAROLD FEATHER** Sixth great grandson of progenitor Nicholas Kegg.
HAROLD ELWYN FEATHER Fifth great grandson of progenitor Nicholas Kegg.
JOHN WARREN FEATHER 7th great grandson of progenitor Nicholas Kegg.
JUDITH LYNN FEATHER [3467] (1941 – 1971) daughter of Harold and Helen Christine (Slagle) Feather, married Mr. Gibbons. She died of Tuberculosis at the Municipal TB Sanitarium, Chicago.
LARRY MILTON FEATHER Fourth great grandson of progenitor Nicholas Kegg.

FEBUS

BRIDGET LEE FEBUS Seventh great granddaughter of progenitor Nicholas Kegg.
MARTIN SHANE FEBUS Seventh great grandson of progenitor Nicholas Kegg.

FEDALEI

CHRISTOPHER ALBERT FEDALEI Sixth great grandson of progenitor Nicholas Kegg.
ELIZABETH ANN FEDALEI Sixth great granddaughter of progenitor Nicholas Kegg.

FEIGHT

ANDREW FEIGHT Sixth great grandson of progenitor Nicholas Kegg.
DUSTIN FEIGHT Sixth great grandson of progenitor Nicholas Kegg.

FEIST

LAURA FEIST Fifth great granddaughter of progenitor Nicholas Kegg.
RAYMOND SCOTT FEIST Fifth great grandson of progenitor Nicholas Kegg.

FELIX

PAMELA CAROLANN FELIX Seventh great granddaughter of progenitor Nicholas Kegg.
TIMOTHY WILLIAM FELIX Seventh great grandson of progenitor Nicholas Kegg.

[3467] Noble County Library obituary

FELTEN

E. VERYL FELTEN Fifth great grandson of progenitor Nicholas Kegg. **JESSIE LUTHER FELTEN** [3468] (1918 – 1987) son of Jesse and Marian (Nycum) Felten, married Bertha M. Fischer with whom he was father of (1). Jesse had been employed as a truck driver by the former Transcon, Inc., in Everett. **MARJORIE L. FELTEN** [3469] (1921 – 2006) aka "Peggy", daughter of Jesse and Marian (Nycum) Felten, married Kenneth M. Morris with whom she was mother of (4). Peggy retired from the Corporate Tax Office of the Department of State after twenty-one years of service as a secretary. Peggy was also a member of Emmanuel Baptist Church, Mechanicsburg. Peggy's greatest joys were her grandchildren and flowers. **NATASHA FELTEN** Sixth great granddaughter of progenitor Nicholas Kegg. **SHANE FELTEN** Sixth great grandson of progenitor Nicholas Kegg. **SHARON FELTEN** Sixth great granddaughter of progenitor Nicholas Kegg. **SHAWN FELTEN** Sixth great grandson of progenitor Nicholas Kegg.

FELTON

ADAM FELTON Seventh great grandson of progenitor Nicholas Kegg. **BONITA A. FELTON** aka "Bonnie" Fifth great granddaughter of progenitor Nicholas Kegg. **CAROL FELTON** Fifth great granddaughter of progenitor Nicholas Kegg. **DANIEL LYNN FELTON** aka "Danny", Fifth great grandson of progenitor Nicholas Kegg. **DAVID FELTON** Seventh great grandson of progenitor Nicholas Kegg. **DONALD WILSON FELTON** [3469A] aka "Don" (1924 – 2019) son of Frank and Mildred (Nycum) Felton, married Helen Mae Hoy with whom he was father of (4). Don worked at Snyder Gateway Inn and did custom farming. Then went into Motel business with his two Brothers, building the Quality Inn Breeze Manor Motel in 1952. He was a member of the Everett Lodge No. 524 of Free and Accepted Masons, a member of the Valley of Harrisburg Consistory, as well as a member of the Scottish Rite of Jaffa, Altoona. Donald served on the board of the Breezewood Branch of the Everett Bank. He also served on the East Providence Municipal Authority. He was President of the Crystal Spring Camp Association and served on the board for a number of years. Don was one of the original members of Breezewood Lions Clubs. He was past president of the Breezewood and Bedford County Tourist Association. Mr. Felton served on the board of Quality Inns for regions four and five. Don was an avid hunter, local and in the West as well as British Columbia. He also enjoyed skiing in the West and Canada. **JAMES H. FELTON** Fifth great grandson of progenitor Nicholas Kegg. **JEFFREY W. FELTON** [3469B] (1959 – 2014) son of Donald and Helen (Hoy) Felton. Jeff was a member of the Breezewood United Methodist Church. He owned and operated ProOne Contractors in Severn, Md. Jeff was an outdoorsman who loved hunting, snow skiing, being on the water and riding his Harleys.
JERRY LEE FELTON [3470] (1953 – 1953) son of Donald and Helen (Hoy) Felton.
JOHN ROBERT FELTON [3471] (1917 – 1978) son of Frank and Mildred Nycum Felton, married Catherine Elizabeth Whetstone. Together with his two brothers, J. Robert owned and operated the Breeze Manor Quality Inn Motel in Breezewood for 25 years. He was a veteran of Navy service, serving in World War II, a member of Everett Pose 8 American Legion: Everett Lodge No. 524 F & AM; Harrisburg Consistory; Jaffa Shrine; Bedford County Shrine Club; Shawnee Forest No. 167 Tall Cedars of Lebanon; Bedford Lodge No. 1707 BPOE: and the Breezewood Volunteer Fire Company.
JUDY MAE FELTON Sixth great granddaughter of progenitor Nicholas Kegg.
LOIS JANE FELTON Fourth great granddaughter of progenitor Nicholas Kegg. **MARK D. FELTON** Sixth great grandson of progenitor Nicholas Kegg. **SALLY FELTON** Sixth great granddaughter of progenitor Nicholas Kegg. **SARA JANE FELTON** Sixth great granddaughter of progenitor Nicholas Kegg. **WILLIAM G. FELTON** [3472] (1925 – 1989) aka "Bill", son of Jesse and Marian (Nycum) Felten, married Gladys Arlene Jay with whom he was father of (2). Bill was a retired truck driver who

---

[3468] p.14 - Bedford Gazette (PA) Aug 27, 1987 [3469] Patriot-News (PA) June 23, 2006 [3469A] Bedford Gazette (PA) March 16, 2019, contributed by Bob Rose [3469B] Bedford Gazette (PA) Aug 27, 2014, contributed by Bob Rose [3470] p.6 - Bedford Gazette (PA) Aug. 3, 1953 [3471] Duke Clark obituary clipping collection [3472] Bedford Inquirer (PA) Oct. 20, 1989

was employed for many years with Maryland Transportation, Horizon Trucking and Smith Trucking. He was also a member of the Wesley Chapel United Methodist Church, the Everett Lions Club, the Breezewood VFW Post, and the Everett American Legion Post No. 8.

FERENCZ

CHERYL FERENCZ Fifth great granddaughter of progenitor Nicholas Kegg.
KAREN JEAN FERENCZ Fifth great granddaughter of progenitor Nicholas Kegg.

FERGUSON

CARL JOSEPH FERGUSON [3473] (1947 – 1988) son of Joseph and Ethel Pearl (Kegg) Ferguson, married Ada C. Smith. Carl was a 17-year employee of the Bedford office of the Bureau of Employment Security, where he was an unemployment claims examiner. He was an Army veteran during the Vietnam War era, having served in Europe; was a 1964 graduate of Chestnut Ridge High School, and was a member of the BPOE of Bedford. **GARY W. FERGUSON** Fifth great grandson of progenitor Nicholas Kegg. **RONALD L. FERGUSON** Fifth great grandson of progenitor Nicholas Kegg.

FERIA

ALEXIS FERIA Sixth great granddaughter of progenitor Nicholas Kegg.

FERLATTE

DAVE FERLATTE Seventh great grandson of progenitor Nicholas Kegg. **WILL FERLATTE** Seventh great grandson of progenitor Nicholas Kegg.

FERNANDEZ

DAVID W. FERNANDEZ Sixth great grandson of progenitor Nicholas Kegg.
DIEGO FERNANDEZ Sixth great grandson of progenitor Nicholas Kegg. **F. LARRY FERNANDEZ** Sixth great grandson of progenitor Nicholas Kegg. **FREDERICK A. FERNANDEZ** Fifth great grandson of progenitor Nicholas Kegg. **FREDERICK A. FERNANDEZ** Sixth great grandson of progenitor Nicholas Kegg. **JOHN M. FERNANDEZ** Sixth great grandson of progenitor Nicholas Kegg. **LUIS MIGUEL FERNANDEZ** Sixth great grandson of progenitor Nicholas Kegg.
RALPH L. FERNANDEZ Sixth great grandson of progenitor Nicholas Kegg.
WILLIAM W. FERNANDEZ Fifth great grandson of progenitor Nicholas Kegg.

FERRARA

ANNA MAE FERRARA Sixth great granddaughter of progenitor Nicholas Kegg.
JOSEPH LUCUS FERRARA Seventh great grandson of progenitor Nicholas Kegg.
JOSEPH P. FERRARA Sixth great grandson of progenitor Nicholas Kegg.

FERRELL

BETTY L. FERRELL [3474] (1921 – 1990) daughter of William and Carolyn (Drews) Ferrell, married Joseph Edward Pleban with whom she was mother of (1). **CAREN PATRICIA FERRELL** Fourth great granddaughter of progenitor Nicholas Kegg.

[3473] p.15 - Bedford Gazette (PA) Sep 17, 1988 [3474] Herald Standard (PA) Jan 2, 1991, obtained by D. Sue Dible

CHARLES EDWARD FERRELL [3475] (1902 – 1964) son of Robert and Jennie (Kegg) Ferrell, married Zana Wilkins. **DOLORES ANN FERRELL,** [3476] (1938 – 2000) daughter of Robert and Theresa (Stasco) Ferrell, married Kenneth W. Low with whom she was mother of (3).
EDITH ELIZABETH FERRELL (1919 – 1960) daughter of Harry and Helen (Bundy) Ferrell, married Harry Frederick West with whom she was mother of (4). **HARRY T. FERRELL** [3477] (1899 – 1964) son of Robert and Jennie (Kegg) Ferrell married twice; first to Helen Bundy with whom he was father of (2). Later, he married Irene Lillian Mercer. Harry was known in Fayette County as a baseball player and bowler. He retired in 1961 after a long career with the engineering corps of U.S. Steel Corp. He was a member of Central Christian Church. **INFANT FERRELL** (1911 – 1911) son of Robert and Jennie (Kegg) Ferrell. **JAMES LEROY FERRELL** [3478] (1893 – 1967) son of Robert and Jennie (Kegg) Ferrell, married Anna Druck. James had been a conductor for the Pennsylvania Railroad; a veteran of World War I. **KAREN FERRELL** Fifth great granddaughter of progenitor Nicholas Kegg. **KATHRYN FERRELL** [3479] (1930 – 2017) aka "Kay", daughter of Robert and Theresa (Stasco) Ferrell, married Herbert F. Hamilton with whom she was mother of (3). **KATHRYN IRENE FERRELL** [3480] (1914 – 1999) daughter of Robert and Jennie (Kegg) Ferrell, married Paul Jesko with whom she was mother of (9). **KENNETH FERRELL** [3481] (1907 – 1960) aka "Whitey", son of Robert and Jennie (Kegg) Ferrell. Ken was a surveyor of the Civil Engineering Firm of E.R. DeForest. He was a veteran of World War II and prisoner of war in Germany for thirty months. He was a member of the VFW post 47, Uniontown and Hutchinson's Sportsmen's Club. **MABLE ELIZABETH FERRELL** [3482] (1895 – 1957) daughter of Robert and Jennie (Kegg) Ferrell, married Frank Malosky with whom she was mother of (8). Mable was a member of the Central Christian Church and G.A.R.
MARGARET ELLEN FERRELL Fourth great granddaughter of progenitor Nicholas Kegg. **MARGARET LORAINE FERRELL** [3483] (1933 – 1933) daughter of Robert and Theresa (Stasco) Ferrell. **MARY ALICE FERRELL** [3484] (1925 – 2003) daughter of William and Carolyn (Drews) Ferrell, married Charles Eugene Rice with whom she was mother of (1).
RICHARD EUGENE FERRELL Fifth great grandson of progenitor Nicholas Kegg.
RICHARD EUGENE FERRELL [3485] (1932 – 2001) aka "Lucky", son of Robert and Theresa (Stasco) Ferrell, married Dorothy E. Garrison with whom he was father of (3). Lucky was a US Army Veteran of the Korean Conflict, having served in Alaska. He was employed at the former Owens-Illinois Glass Company in Bridgeton for over thirty years. He retired from the maintenance department in 1985 when the plant closed. Mr. Ferrell was a member of the Fifth Ward Athletic Association in Bridgeton and a former member of the Italian American Civic Club. In addition, he was an avid hunter and member of the National Rifle Association. He also enjoyed fishing and owned the "Lucky D" which he kept in Fortescue. He was also a member of the Shoemaker Post #95 American Legion of Bridgeton and was a longtime supporter of the Disabled American Veterans. **ROBERT MORRIS FERRELL** [3486] (1905 – 1955) son of Robert and Jennie (Kegg) Ferrell, married Theresa Stasco with whom he was father of (6). Robert was a member of the Central Christian Church, Uniontown and UMWA local 6330, Chartiers.
SHIRLEY FERRELL Fifth great granddaughter of progenitor Nicholas Kegg.
WILLIAM WADSWORTH FERRELL [3487] (1897 – 1957) son of Robert and Jennie (Kegg) Ferrell, married Carolyn Lena Drews with whom he was father of (3). William was a machinist and had been employed by the U.S. Steel Co., at Robena Mine for seventeen years. He was a veteran of World War I; a member of the Central Christian Church and UMWA, Robena local 6321 and Hutchinson Sportsman's Club.

[3475] p17 - Evening Standard (PA) July 6, 1964 [3476] Press of Atlantic City (NJ) Dec 8, 2000 [3477] p.31 - Daily Courier (PA) Nov. 19, 1964 [3478] p.27 - The Evening Standard (PA) Dec. 6, 1967 [3479] South Jersey Times (NJ) May 27, 2017 [3480] Savanna Now (GA) June 22, 1999 [3481] p.17 - The Evening Standard (PA) Nov. 7, 1960 [3482] p.6 - The Evening Standard (PA) Jan 7, 1957 [3483] p.3 - Morning Herald (PA) Nov. 22, 1933 [3484] Pittsburgh Post Gazette (PA) Oct 16, 1947 [3485] Freitag Funeral Home (NJ) obtained by D. Sue Dible [3486] p.2 - The Morning Herald (PA) Dec 31, 1955 [3487] p.4 - Evening Standard (PA) Dec. 5, 1957

FERULLO

ETHAN DANIEL FERULLO Eighth great grandson of progenitor Nicholas Kegg.
ISAAC GABRIEL FERULLO Eighth great grandson of progenitor Nicholas Kegg.

FETHEROLF

ANN MARIE FETHEROLF Seventh great granddaughter of progenitor Nicholas Kegg.
CASEY FETHEROLF Sixth great grandson of progenitor Nicholas Kegg. **DAKODA FETHEROLF** Eighth great granddaughter of progenitor Nicholas Kegg. **DANIEL LEE FETHEROLF** [3488] (1950 – 2007) son of Russell and Kathleen (White) Fetherolf. Daniel was an avid fan of softball both as a player and coach. **DENNIS EUGENE FETHEROLF** [3488A] (1949 – 2020) son of Russell and Ruth (White) Fetherolf married Geraldine Lantz with whom he was father of (4). **EDWARD LEE FETHEROLF** [3488B] (1966 – 2018) son of Thomas and Gail Fetherolf married twice, first to Paula Beasley and later to Sandra McGee with whom he was father of (4). Edward served his country in the U.S. Army and worked as a paramedic. - **IRMA MARIE FETHEROLF** Sixth great granddaughter of progenitor Nicholas Kegg. **KAILYN FETHEROLF** Eighth great granddaughter of progenitor Nicholas Kegg.
KEVIN WAYNE FETHEROLF Seventh great grandson of progenitor Nicholas Kegg.
LANCE EUGENE FETHEROLF Seventh great grandson of progenitor Nicholas Kegg.
LARRY FETHEROLF Sixth great grandson of progenitor Nicholas Kegg.
LEVI CHARLES FETHEROLF Seventh great grandson of progenitor Nicholas Kegg.
LORI FETHEROLF Seventh great granddaughter of progenitor Nicholas Kegg.
MARY JO FETHEROLF Sixth great granddaughter of progenitor Nicholas Kegg.
MELINDA LYNN FETHEROLF aka "Mendy" Seventh great granddaughter of progenitor Nicholas Kegg. **MELISSA LYNN FETHEROLF** [3488C] (1975 – 2021) daughter of Dennis and Geraline (Lantz) Fetherolf married Shane D. Kees with whom she was mother of (2). Melissa was a twin who was practically inseparable from her other half. **NICHOLAS FETHEROLF** Eighth great grandson of progenitor Nicholas Kegg. **PAUL LEE FETHEROLF** Seventh great grandson of progenitor Nicholas Kegg. **PENNY SUE FETHEROLF** Sixth great granddaughter of progenitor Nicholas Kegg.
RUSSELL J. FETHEROLF aka "Rusty", Sixth great grandson of progenitor Nicholas Kegg.
TAMI FETHEROLF Seventh great granddaughter of progenitor Nicholas Kegg.
TARA FETHEROLF Eighth great granddaughter of progenitor Nicholas Kegg.
THOMAS LEE FETHEROLF Sixth great grandson of progenitor Nicholas Kegg.
TIMOTHY LEE FETHEROLF (1952 – 1952) son of Russell and Kathleen (White) Fetherolf.
TOMMY FETHEROLF Seventh great grandson of progenitor Nicholas Kegg.
VERONICA JEAN FETHEROLF [3489] (1946 – 2011) aka "Vonnie", daughter of Russell and Kathleen (White) Fetherolf, married Warren Rex Crossley with whom she was mother of (3). Vonnie was a Browns fan, liked bowling and softball, but above all she was a loving and devoted mother and grandmother.

FICKES

ANGEL FICKES Sixth great granddaughter of progenitor Nicholas Kegg.
ANNA REBECCA FICKES [3490] (1874 – 1942) daughter of Winfield and Sarah (Beegle) Fickes, married Walter Arthur Foor with whom she was mother of (3). **BARBARA FICKES** [3491] (1945 – 2013) daughter of Edwin and Irene (Corbin) Fickes married twice; first to Richard Wigfield with whom she was mother of (3). Later, she married Franklin D. Hall. **BERNARD H. FICKES** [3492] (1909 – 1991) son of John and Daisy (Diehl) Fickes, married Dora Kissel with whom he was father of (3).

[3488] Columbus Dispatch (OH) June 13, 2007 [3488A] This Week Community Newspapers (OH) Jan. 8, 2020 [3488B] Athens Messenger (OH) April 7, 2018, contributed by D. Sue Dible [3488C] O.R. Woodyard Co., Funeral and Cremation Services (OH) [3489] Cook & Son-Palley Funeral Home (OH) [3490] p.10 - Daily News (PA) June 22, 1942 [3491] York Daily Record & York Dispatch (PA) Jan. 29, 2013 [3492] Bedford Gazette (PA) March 8, 1991, obtained by Carol Eddleman

Bernard retired as a turnpike employee after 25 years of service. **CHARLES CLYDE FICKES** [3493] (1908 – 1987) son of Emanuel and Amanda (Smith) Fickes married twice; first to Melva Irene Dodds with whom he was father of (1). Later, he married Marian Walker. C. Clyde was a surveyor for AT&T, was a supervisor for the Harris-Boyer Bread Co., and was well known in the Bedford area as the Sealtest Milk man. Prior to his retirement he had been Bedford Borough Tax Collector for eight years and a part time farmer for many years. **CRAIG D. FICKES** Sixth great grandson of progenitor Nicholas Kegg. **DALE FRANKLIN FICKES** (1940 – 1993) son of Edwin and Irene (Corbin) Fickes, married Catherine Elizabeth Russell. **DANIEL R. FICKES** Sixth great grandson of progenitor Nicholas Kegg. **DARLENE FICKES** Fifth great granddaughter of progenitor Nicholas Kegg. **DAVID W. FICKES** Sixth great grandson of progenitor Nicholas Kegg. **DIANA FICKES** Fifth great granddaughter of progenitor Nicholas Kegg. **DONALD WARREN FICKES** (1928 – 1983) son of Warren and Louise (Turner) Fickes married twice; first to Thelma J. Jackson with whom he was father of (4). Later he married Deborah Denise (Williams) Jordan. **DONALDA FICKES** Fifth great granddaughter of progenitor Nicholas Kegg. **DOROTHY LOUISE FICKES** [3494] (1907 – 2002) daughter of John and Daisy (Diehl) Fickes, married George Percy Batzel with whom she was mother of (3). Dorothy was employed by Lion Manufacturing in Everett for many years until her retirement. She was also a homemaker who enjoyed gardening and canning, sewing and caring for her family.
EDWIN PARK FICKES [3495] (1904 – 1957) son of John and Daisy (Diehl) Fickes married twice; first to Irene Mabel Corbin with whom he was father of (7). Later, he married Mela Leydig Albright. **EMANUEL BEEGLE FICKES** [3496] (1882 – 1965) son of Winfield and Sarah (Beegle) Fickes, married Amanda Viola Smith with whom he was father of (6). **EMMA ELLEN FICKES** [3496A] (1878 – 1950) daughter of Winfield and Sarah (Beegle) Fickes, married Edward Ross Stayer with whom she was mother of (5). **FREDA E. FICKES** [3497] (1912 – 2010) daughter of John and Daisy (Diehl) Fickes, married Glenn Henry Koontz with whom she was mother of (2). Freda was a member of the Everett Church of the Brethren, where she previously served as a deaconess, was a Sunday school teacher, a delegate to the Annual Conference of the Church of the Brethren, and was active in many other church activities. In her early years, she worked as a clerk at the Everett Supply Store and at Wigfield's Shoe Store in Everett, and in 1958, she and her husband Glenn purchased Everett Marble and Granite Works, where they owned and operated the business. **GENE ALTON FICKES** (1930 – 1980) son of Edwin and Irene (Corbin) Fickes. **GERALD W. FICKES** Sixth great grandson of progenitor Nicholas Kegg.
GLENN BEEGLE FICKES [3498] (1914 – 1985) son of Emanuel and Amanda (Smith) Fickes, married Mildred Lucille Weimer with whom he was father of (3). Glenn retired from Burkett Motor Sales. He was a member of St. Mark's Lutheran Church, an Army veteran of World War II, member of the American Legion, and Bedford County Sportsmen's Club. **JACK R. FICKES** [3499] (1930 – 1997) son of Bernard and Dora (Kissel) Fickes, married Carolyn R. Keys with whom he was father of (2). Jack retired from the Highway Transportation Department in Tampa, Fla., as a civil engineer and designer. He was a United States Air Force veteran of the Korean Conflict. He was a member of the Lakeside Golf and Country Club. **JANET FICKES** (1935 – 1984) daughter of Warren and Louise (Turner) Ficks, married James M. Bondoni with whom she was mother of (5). **JESSICA MARTINA FICKES** Seventh great granddaughter of progenitor Nicholas Kegg. **JOANNE FICKES** [3500] (1932 – 2000) daughter of Edwin and Irene (Corbin) Fickes, married John W. May with whom she was mother of (2). Joanne had worked as a nurse's aide at Bedford Hospital. **JOHN EDWIN FICKES** (1926 – 1990) son of Edwin and Irene (Corbin) Fickes, married Mary Catherine McGinnis. **JOHN WILLIAM FICKES** [3501] (1876 – 1953) son of Winfield and Sarah (Beegle) Fickes, married Daisy Mae Diehl with whom he was father of (6). **KASSANDRA KAE FICKES** Seventh great granddaughter of progenitor Nicholas Kegg. **LINDA FICKES** Fifth great granddaughter of progenitor Nicholas Kegg.

[3493] Bedford County Genealogical Society obituary obtained by D. Sue Dible [3494] p.12 - Bedford Gazette (PA) Nov 29, 2002 [3495] p.12 - Cumberland Evening Times (MD) Dec 10, 1957 [3496] p.4 - The Cumberland News (MD) Dec. 27, 1965 [3496A] p3 - Bedford Gazette (PA) Nov 10, 1950 [3497] p.8 - Bedford Inquirer (PA) Jan 8, 2010, obtained by Bob Rose [3498] Bedford County Genealogical Society obituary obtained by D. Sue Dible [3499] p.3 - Bedford Inquirer (PA) Sep 26, 1997 [3500] p.3 - Bedford Inquirer (PA) Sept 24, 2000 obtained by Bob Rose [3501] The Bedford Gazette (PA) May 18, 1953

MABEL FERN FICKES [3502] (1901 – 1989) daughter of John and Daisy (Diehl) Fickes, married Lewis Carl Manspeaker with whom she was mother of (4). Mabel attended Juanita College and taught grades one through eight at the former Blue Spruce School. She was a lifetime member of the Zion Lutheran Church, Everett. She was also a member of the Lutheran Christian Women and the board of Allegheny Lutheran Homes. **MARGARET JANE FICKES** (1925 – 1998) daughter of Edwin and Irene (Corbin) Fickes, married Samuel McClellen Ruby with whom she was mother of (1).
MICHAEL GLENN FICKES Fifth great grandson of progenitor Nicholas Kegg.
PAMMIE SARAH FICKES [3503] (1875 – 1907) daughter of Winfield and Sarah (Beegle) Fickes, married Nicholas Edward Koontz with whom she was mother of (5). **ROGER PAUL FICKES** Fifth great grandson of progenitor Nicholas Kegg. **SAMUEL HENRY FICKES** [3504] (1883 – 1937) son of Winfield and Sarah (Beegle) Fickes, married Rosalia Elizabeth Wolfhope. **SAMUEL S. FICKES** [3505] (1918 – 1985) son of Emanuel and Amanda (Smith) Fickes, married Vera Risbon with whom he was father of (3). Samuel was a self-employed farmer, an Army veteran of World War II. He was the former owner of Penn West Hotel, member of Bedford Elks #1707, Improved Order of Redmen of Cumberland, VFW of Bedford and Cumberland, and American Legion Post # 113 of Bedford.
SARAH MARGAURITE FICKES [3506] (1910 – 2004) daughter of Emanuel and Amanda (Smith) Fickes, married Blair Gregory Fisher with whom she was mother of (1). Sarah was a woman of great character, who never focused on the 'things' of life. Her top priority was her family and her relationship with her Creator. Her ever-strong example for living a Christian life that touched everyone she met along her journey. **TERESA J. FICKES** Fifth great granddaughter of progenitor Nicholas Kegg.
TERRY FICKES Sixth great grandson of progenitor Nicholas Kegg. **THELMA LOUISE FICKES** (1926 – 1986) daughter of Warren and Louise (Turner) Fickes, married James Howard Eaton with whom she was mother of (2). **VALERENE DAY FICKES** [3507] (1956 – 1988) daughter of Donald and Thelma (Jackson) Fickes married twice; first to Gary Thomas Nunnery. Later, she married Bobby Maximo Pagaling with whom she was mother of (3). Valerene was a member of the TEMOAK Indian Tribe of Elko, Nev., and the Assembly of God Church. **WARREN A. FICKES** [3508] (1902 – 1950) son of John and Daisy (Diehl) Fickes, married Louise C. Turner with whom he was father of (4). Warren was a painting contractor and interior decorator, operating his own business for 25 years.
WILLIAM WINFIELD FICKES [3509] (1905 – 1908) son of Emanuel and Amanda (Smith) Fickes. Little William was unusually bright for one of such tender years. He was of a kind, amiable disposition and consequently endeared himself to all who knew him, both old and young.

FIEDLER

BRANDON FIEDLER Fifth great grandson of progenitor Nicholas Kegg. **JAMES FIEDLER** Fifth great grandson of progenitor Nicholas Kegg. **RENEE FIEDLER** Fifth great granddaughter of progenitor Nicholas Kegg.

FIEGER

ROBERT L. FIEGER Fifth great grandson of progenitor Nicholas Kegg.

FIELD

ARTHUR FIELD JR. Sixth great grandson of progenitor Nicholas Kegg.

[3502] The Daily News (Huntingdon, PA) Apr 22, 1989 [3503] Bedford Gazette (PA) June 21, 1907 [3504] Akron Beacon Journal (OH) May 1937 obtained by D. Sue Dible [3505] Bedford County Genealogical Society obituary obtained by D. Sue Dible [3506] Bedford Inquirer (PA) Aug 6, 2004, obtained by Bob Rose [3507] Miner Newspaper (Newport, WA) Find A Grave Memorial# 38979997 [3508] Bedford County Genealogical Society obituary obtained by D. Sue Dible [3509] Bedford Gazette (PA) Sept 4, 1908

FIELDING

EVELYN VIOLETTE FIELDING (1911 – 1995) daughter of Daniel and Mayme (Kegg) Fielding. Evelyn was employed as a Physical Education Teacher.

FIELDS

JOSH FIELDS Sixth great grandson of progenitor Nicholas Kegg. **NICK FIELDS** Sixth great grandson of progenitor Nicholas Kegg.

FIGARD

HELENE E. FIGARD [3510] (1916 – 2005) daughter of George and Helene (Gump) Figard, married William B. Monahan with whom she was mother of (2). Helene loved teaching and taught for five years at Riddlesburg in Bedford County and for more than 25 years in elementary schools in New Britain Twp. for the Central Bucks School District. Helene was also a poet. She was a member of Six Mile Run Church of God in Bedford County and Silverdale Brethren in Christ Church in Silverdale. **SANDY D. FIGARD** Sixth great granddaughter of progenitor Nicholas Kegg. **STANLEY CALVIN FIGARD** (1950 – 1950) son of William and Mary (Batzel) Figard. **WILLIAM LOUIS FIGARD** [3511] (1953 – 1958) son of William and Mary (Batzel) Figard. William had been ill since birth.

FILER

DAMIAN WILLIAM FILER Seventh great grandson of progenitor Nicholas Kegg.
HANS WILLIAM ALEXANDER FILER Eighth great grandson of progenitor Nicholas Kegg.
KIRSTEN LYNN FILER Seventh great granddaughter of progenitor Nicholas Kegg.

FILIP

DAWN MARIE FILIP Fifth great granddaughter of progenitor Nicholas Kegg.
KIMBERLI A. FILIP Fifth great granddaughter of progenitor Nicholas Kegg.

FILLER

MATTHEW FILLER Sixth great grandson of progenitor Nicholas Kegg. **NATHANIEL C. FILLER** aka "Nate", Seventh great grandson of progenitor Nicholas Kegg. **SCOTT A. FILLER** Sixth great grandson of progenitor Nicholas Kegg. **WANDA LEE FILLER** Fifth great granddaughter of progenitor Nicholas Kegg. **WILLIAM ARTHUR FILLER** Sixth great grandson of progenitor Nicholas Kegg. **WILLIAM CLYDE FILLER** [3511A] aka "Big Willy" (1933 – 2021) son of Franklin and Mary Emma (Kidd) Filler married Nancy Gutshall with whom he was father of (3). Bill was a US Army Veteran of the Korean War as a member of the 7th Cavalry Division under the First Division. He handled the lanyard on the 155 Howitzer. Bill worked at the Nabisco plant in Altoona for 2 years after returning from military service. He was a lifelong fan of the Pittsburgh Pirates and Baltimore/Indianapolis Colts. He was an Assistant Coach with Automotive of the Altoona Little League and later coached Brunswick Billiards in the George B. Kelly Federation in addition he assisted Bud Wertz on the Sheetz AAABA baseball team. Bill was a member of several bowling teams throughout his life. He was proficient in carpentry and helped to build homes and to do odd jobs throughout his career. More than anything else he loved spending time with his family and loved ones. In his younger years he enjoyed playing guitar and performed with Robert Cummings singing and picking at the old Musselman's Grove

---

[3510] The Reporter (Lansdale, PA) Aug 9, 2005 [3511] p.5 - Huntingdon Daily News (PA) Dec 13, 1958 [3511A] Altoona Mirror (PA) Dec 6, 2021

stage in Claysburg. He also enjoyed deer hunting with his sons. Bill was a member and past president of the United Steel Workers of America Local 7853 and also a member of the Bavarian Aid Society. Bill was a lifelong member of Bethany Lutheran Church in Altoona, where he was on the church council and played softball in the church league for many years.

FINDO

MARCELLA FINDO Seventh great granddaughter of progenitor Nicholas Kegg.

FINDLEY

HAILEY FINDLEY Eighth great granddaughter of progenitor Nicholas Kegg.
JOHN FINDLEY Seventh great grandson of progenitor Nicholas Kegg.

FINE

KRISTINA E. FINE Seventh great granddaughter of progenitor Nicholas Kegg. **ROB FINE** Seventh great grandson of progenitor Nicholas Kegg. **SEAN FINE** Seventh great grandson of progenitor Nicholas Kegg.

FINK

AMY FINK Sixth great granddaughter of progenitor Nicholas Kegg. **ERICA FINK** Seventh great granddaughter of progenitor Nicholas Kegg. **JAYCE FINK** Eighth great grandson of progenitor Nicholas Kegg. **SCOTT FINK** Sixth great grandson of progenitor Nicholas Kegg.

FINLEY

KARSON FINLEY Eighth great grandson of progenitor Nicholas Kegg.

FINNERLY

ALICE ANN FINNERLY Sixth great granddaughter of progenitor Nicholas Kegg. **BRIDGETT PORTER FINNERLY** Sixth great granddaughter of progenitor Nicholas Kegg. **EILEEN FINNERLY** Sixth great granddaughter of progenitor Nicholas Kegg. **JOSEPH G. FINNERLY** Sixth great grandson of progenitor Nicholas Kegg. **KATHLEEN FINNERLY** Sixth great granddaughter of progenitor Nicholas Kegg. **SARA ELIZABETH FINNERLY** Sixth great granddaughter of progenitor Nicholas Kegg. **THOMAS PATRICK FINNERLY** Sixth great grandson of progenitor Nicholas Kegg.

FINNERTY

AARON FINNERTY Sixth great grandson of progenitor Nicholas Kegg.
AMY KATHERINE FINNERTY Sixth great granddaughter of progenitor Nicholas Kegg.
ANGELA KAY FINNERTY Sixth great granddaughter of progenitor Nicholas Kegg.
HEATHER MAE FINNERTY Sixth great granddaughter of progenitor Nicholas Kegg.
JOHN PATRICK FINNERTY Sixth great grandson of progenitor Nicholas Kegg.
JOSEPH GREGORY FINNERTY [3512] (1937 – 2013) son of Joseph and Sara (Porter) Finnerty married twice. Joseph was father of (6). Later, he married Deborah Barrett with whom he was father of (1).
KELLY CHARLES FINNERTY Fifth great grandson of progenitor Nicholas Kegg.

[3512] Baltimore Sun (MD) Sept. 7, 2013

KEVIN SHAWN FINNERTY Fifth great grandson of progenitor Nicholas Kegg.
RACHELLE ANN FINNERTY Sixth great granddaughter of progenitor Nicholas Kegg.
REBECCA KATHLEEN FINNERTY Sixth great granddaughter of progenitor Nicholas Kegg.
RONALD CRAGG FINNERTY Fifth great grandson of progenitor Nicholas Kegg.
SHARON L. FINNERTY Fifth great granddaughter of progenitor Nicholas Kegg.
THOMAS FINNERTY (1939 – 1939) son of Joseph and Sara (Porter) Finnerty.

FINNEY

CHEYENE FINNEY Sixth great granddaughter of progenitor Nicholas Kegg;

FINNIE

MORNIE J. FINNIE [3513] (1876 – 1911) daughter of John and Sarah Margaret (College) Finnie married Edward J. Keys with whom she was mother of (1).

FIRMAN

DOROTHY FIRMAN Fifth great granddaughter of progenitor Nicholas Kegg. **FRANCES FIRMAN** Fifth great granddaughter of progenitor Nicholas Kegg. **JODY FIRMAN** Fifth great granddaughter of progenitor Nicholas Kegg. **JOSEPH HOLFERTY FIRMAN** (1918 – 1990) son of Royal and Lillian (Holferty) Firman married Catherine King with whom he was father of (4). **MELANIE A. FIRMAN** Fifth great granddaughter of progenitor Nicholas Kegg. **NANCY FIRMAN** Fifth great granddaughter of progenitor Nicholas Kegg. **NIKOLE FIRMAN** Sixth great granddaughter of progenitor Nicholas Kegg. **RENE FIRMAN** Sixth great granddaughter of progenitor Nicholas Kegg.
THOMAS FIRMAN Fifth great grandson of progenitor Nicholas Kegg. **VICTOR V. FIRMAN** [3513A] (1992 – 2015) son of William and Georgia (Poulopoulos) Firman. Victor was a graduate of Weston High School and was completing his studies in clinical psychology at the University of Pittsburgh. While in high school, Victor spent his summers working at Peter's Market in Weston and the Weston Department of Public Works. In college, Victor completed internships in youth addiction rehabilitation at various clinics and hospitals and more recently at the University of Pittsburgh's Medical Center.
WILLIAM WILLARD FIRMAN [3514] (1921 – 1976) son of Royal and Lillian (Holferty) Firman married twice; first to Daphne Brock with whom he was father of (2). Later, he married Helen Gough Carey. William was vice president of marketing for the American Broadcasting Company television division. He began his career with the Columbia Broadcasting System radio network in Chicago in 1951. In 1961 he was promoted to general sales manager. He joined ABC in 1963 as director of news and special sales and was elected vice president in 1967. In 1969 he was named vice president of marketing, responsible for bringing numerous advertisers into television for the first time. A graduate of the University of Michigan, Mr. Firman served with the OSS in Europe during World War II as a lieutenant in the Army. **WILLIAM WILLARD FIRMAN JR.** aka "Bill", Fifth great grandson of progenitor Nicholas Kegg.

FISHBURN

ERIN MARIE FISHBURN Seventh great granddaughter of progenitor Nicholas Kegg.

[3513] The Ligonier Echo (PA) Jan 11, 1911 [3513A] Weston Forum (CT) Aug 26, 2015 [3514] p.6 Daily Advocate (Stamford, CT) Feb 5, 1976

FISCHER

BRIANNA FISCHER Eighth great granddaughter of progenitor Nicholas Kegg. **EARL JOSEPH FISCHER** Sixth great grandson of progenitor Nicholas Kegg. **LYNN ERRYN FISCHER** Sixth great granddaughter of progenitor Nicholas Kegg. **MARK JAMES FISCHER** Sixth great grandson of progenitor Nicholas Kegg. **RICHELLE FISCHER** Eighth great granddaughter of progenitor Nicholas Kegg. **SETH M. FISCHER** Seventh great grandson of progenitor Nicholas Kegg.

FISHER

ANDREW ALLEN FISHER [3515] (1887 – 1966) aka "Pat", son of Winfield and Sarah (Stuckey) Fisher, married Anna Mann with whom he was father of (2). Pat was a graduate of McConnellsburg High School, class of 1906. He taught school for one year in Little Cove and from there went with the Pullman Company of the Seaboard Air Line Railroad out of New York City. He was with the Pullman Company 45 years before retiring. **ANGELA FISHER** Seventh great granddaughter of progenitor Nicholas Kegg. **BENJAMIN WOLLETT FISHER** [3516] (1890 – 1946) son of Winfield and Sarah (Stuckey) Fisher, married Ferne May Flanders with whom he was father of (6). A World War I veteran, Ben was a member of Victory Post No. 25 of the Selinsgrove American Legion. **BONNIE FISHER** Fifth great granddaughter of progenitor Nicholas Kegg. **BRADLEY RAY FISHER** Fifth great grandson of progenitor Nicholas Kegg. **BRETT M. FISHER** Sixth great grandson of progenitor Nicholas Kegg. **BURR D. FISHER** Fifth great grandson of progenitor Nicholas Kegg. **CANDACE FISHER** Fifth great granddaughter of progenitor Nicholas Kegg. **CHARLES ALBERT FISHER** [3517] (1920 – 1964) son of Irvin and Buelah (Suder) Fisher. **COLE EDWARD FISHER** [1168] (2001 – 2007) son of Ronald and Tanya (Elliott) Fisher. Cole was in first grade and an avid St. Louis Cardinal fan. **CODY FISHER** Seventh great grandson of progenitor Nicholas Kegg. **DAMON FISHER** Tenth great grandson of progenitor Nicholas Kegg. **DAYNA D. FISHER** Fifth great granddaughter of progenitor Nicholas Kegg. **DEREK LYNN FISHER** Sixth great grandson of progenitor Nicholas Kegg.
DORIS FISHER Fifth great granddaughter of progenitor Nicholas Kegg.
DOROTHY ARLENE FISHER (1931 -?) daughter of Frederick and Hope (Raker) Fisher.
ELLE FISHER Seventh great granddaughter of progenitor Nicholas Kegg.
FREDERICK STUCKEY FISHER [3518] (1897 – 1981) aka "Mut", son of Winfield and Sarah (Stuckey) Fisher, married Hope Audrey Raker with whom he was father of (6). A veteran of World War I, he was a member of the American Legion Post, McConnellsburg, for 61 years, and a member of the Pennsylvania Sheriff's Association, the McConnellsburg Volunteer Fire Company, and the Veterans of World War I, USA. Mut served as sheriff from 1960 to 1968 and as game protector in Fulton, Union and Susquehanna counties for 18 years. **GEORGE MARK FISHER** Fifth great grandson of progenitor Nicholas Kegg.
GLENNA JEANNE FISHER Fifth great granddaughter of progenitor Nicholas Kegg.
JACOB FISHER Tenth great grandson of progenitor Nicholas Kegg. **JAMES FISHER** Tenth great grandson of progenitor Nicholas Kegg. **JAN F. FISHER** Fifth great grandson of progenitor Nicholas Kegg. **JEANBELLE FISHER** [3518A] (1920 – 2011) daughter of Benjamin and Ferne (Flanders) Fisher, married David Harold Bodtke with whom she was mother of (3). Jeanbelle was always tanned, healthy and up for whatever, especially golf and swimming. Remembered as a captivating beauty with snowy white hair and sparkling blue eyes, a charming and generous person, joking, comforting, and displaying her signature sign of two thumbs up. She was a communicant at St. Paul's Methodist Church in Largo, a senior advisory board member at the Largo Community Center, a regular volunteer at the Largo Cultural Center and a gala member of the Largo Chapter of the Red Hat Society. **JERRY WINFIELD FISHER** [3519] (1912 – 2004) son of Benjamin and Ferne (Flanders) Fisher was a veteran, serving in the Army during World War II. He was in the European Theatre and received several Good Conduct Medals and

---

[3515] Fulton County Historical Society Library obtained by D. Sue Dible [3516] The Sunbury Daily Item (PA) obtained by Jacquelyn Rubin [3517] The Daily American (Somerset, PA) Sep 10, 1964 [3517A] St. Louis Post-Dispatch (MO) Sept 30, 2007 [3518] Public Opinion (Chambersburg, PA) March 17, 1981 [3518A] The Daily Item (Sunbury, PA) Dec 28, 2011 [3519] The Daily Item (Sunbury, PA) April 26, 2004

Bronze Stars. Jerry was employed as a truck driver and retired from L. B. Water Service Inc. of Selinsgrove. He maintained life memberships with Selinsgrove Moose Lodge 1173; Veterans of Foreign Wars Post 6631, Selinsgrove; American Legion Post 25 of Selinsgrove; and the Dauntless Hook & Ladder Company of Selinsgrove. Jerry enjoyed hunting and boating and the activities of the Susquehanna River. **JO ADRIENNE FISHER** Fifth great granddaughter of progenitor Nicholas Kegg. **JOHN HAYES FISHER** Fifth great grandson of progenitor Nicholas Kegg. **JULIE ROSE FISHER** Fifth great granddaughter of progenitor Nicholas Kegg. **KAREN JANE FISHER** Fifth great granddaughter of progenitor Nicholas Kegg. **KATHERINE LEA FISHER** aka "Kathy", Fifth great granddaughter of progenitor Nicholas Kegg. **KEENE CURTIS FISHER** Fifth great grandson of progenitor Nicholas Kegg. **KERRI FISHER** Sixth great granddaughter of progenitor Nicholas Kegg. **LANA GAY FISHER** Fifth great granddaughter of progenitor Nicholas Kegg. **LATICIA M. FISHER** aka "Trish", Sixth great granddaughter of progenitor Nicholas Kegg. **LAURA E. FISHER** [3520] (1916 – 1974) daughter of Irvin and Beulah (Suder) Fisher, married Harold J. Wyant with whom she was mother of (5). **LAURA HAYES FISHER** Sixth great granddaughter of progenitor Nicholas Kegg. **LAUREN R. FISHER** Seventh great granddaughter of progenitor Nicholas Kegg. **LOGAN P.W. FISHER** Seventh great grandson of progenitor Nicholas Kegg. **LUCINDA A. FISHER** Fifth great granddaughter of progenitor Nicholas Kegg. **MABEL SOPHIA FISHER** [3521] (1914 – 2000) daughter of Irvin and Beulah (Suder) Fisher married twice; first to Frank Albert W. Corley with whom she was mother of (2). Later, she married Elwood Ray Smith with whom she was mother of (6). Mabel was a homemaker. **MARION ELIZABETH FISHER** [3521A] (1916 – 2011) daughter of Andrew and Anna (Mann) Fisher, married Clarence Fiveash with whom she was mother of (5). Marion was an independent woman with impeccable manners who loved her daily crossword puzzle, dark chocolate, and shortbread cookies. She enjoyed reading and watching golf on television. She was a veteran of the USNR-WAVES and faithfully served her country during WWII. **MARY LOUELLA FISHER** [3522] (1917 – 2003) daughter of Irvin and Beulah (Suder) Fisher, married Wilbur Chess Hill with whom she was mother of (4). Mary Lou graduated from Selinsgrove High School, Selinsgrove, Pa., and Jefferson School of Nursing in Pennsylvania. A lieutenant in the U.S. Navy during World War II, she was a registered nurse. She worked at Cabarrus Memorial Hospital, now NorthEast Medical Center, and Five Oaks Nursing Center. She later volunteered at Blowing Rock Hospital. She was a member of First Presbyterian Church, the adult Sunday school class and was den mother of Pack 33 for many years. Also, she was a member of Kannapolis County Club and Blowing Rock Country Club. **MARY MARGARET FISHER** [3523] (1901 – 1990) daughter of Winfield and Sarah (Stuckey) Fisher married twice; first to Peter Morton with whom she was mother of (4). Later, she married Russell Blaine Akers. Mary was the first cafeteria manager for McConnellsburg schools. A charter member of McConnellsburg American Legion Auxiliary, she was a life member of Fulton County Historical Society. **MELISSA FISHER** Sixth great granddaughter of progenitor Nicholas Kegg. **MICHELLE LYNN FISHER** Sixth great granddaughter of progenitor Nicholas Kegg. **NANCY JANE FISHER** Fifth great granddaughter of progenitor Nicholas Kegg. **NORA JACQUELINE FISHER** aka Jackie", Fourth great granddaughter of progenitor Nicholas Kegg. **NORA O'NEIL FISHER** [3524] (1882 - 1962) daughter of Winfield and Sarah (Stuckey) Fisher, married Alvin Jacob Dohner with whom she was mother of (1). A graduate of Shippensburg State Normal school, Nora taught for two years in the primary grades in McConnellsburg. She was an active member of St. Paul's Methodist church of Penns Grove, N.J. having taught the ladies Bible class for 27 years, also a member of the Women's Society for Christian Service. **PATRICIA RAE FISHER** [3524A] (1929 – 2008) daughter of Blair and Sarah (Fickes) Fisher, married Frank Thomas Jones with whom she was mother of (3). One of the delights of her life was the abundant love of her two grandchildren. Patricia attended the Phoenix First Assembly of God Church. **QUINN ANGELA FISHER** Fifth great granddaughter of progenitor Nicholas Kegg.

[3520] Meyersdale Republican (PA) Feb 21, 1974, obtained by Sally Statler [3521] Tribune Review (PA) Jul 17, 2000 [3521A] Tulsa World (OK) Nov 23, 2011 [3522] Salisbury Post (NC) Jan 30, 2003 [3523] Fulton County Historical Society Library obituary obtained by D. Sue Dible [3524] The Fulton Democrat (McConnellsburg, PA) June 14, 1962 [3524A] Timothy A. Berkible Funeral Home Inc (PA)

RAYNA FISHER Sixth great granddaughter of progenitor Nicholas Kegg. **ROGER ALLEN FISHER** (1934 – 1985) son of Frederick and Hope (Raker) Fisher was employed by the Forestry Department in Fulton County. **RONALD CLYDE FISHER** [3524B] (1948 – 2010) son of Clyde and Blanche (Bollman) Fisher married twice, first to Nina Webb with whom he was father of (2). The United States Army veteran proudly served his country during the Vietnam War. Ron enjoyed his years of being a mechanic. He was a member of the Town and Country Gun Club and was an avid deer hunter enthusiast and enjoyed his days tending to his yard. **RONALD CLYDE FISHER** Sixth great grandson of progenitor Nicholas Kegg. **ROSE E. FISHER** [3525] (1893 – 1985) daughter of Winfield and Sarah (Stuckey) Fisher, married Robert Brigham. Rose was a housewife. Prior to her marriage, she was a legal secretary in Philadelphia. **SARAH JANE FISHER,** [3526] (1919 – 1987) aka "Sally", daughter of Andrew and Anna (Mann) Fisher, married Frederick Ross Hamil with whom she was mother of (2). Sally was employed at the American Legion and JLG Industries, McConnellsburg. **SETH T. FISHER** Fifth great grandson of progenitor Nicholas Kegg. **SHANE FISHER** Tenth great grandson of progenitor Nicholas Kegg. **STEPHANIE FISHER** Fifth great granddaughter of progenitor Nicholas Kegg. **SIDNEY R. FISHER** [3526A] (1931 – 2011) son of Frederick and Hope (Raker) Fisher, married Shirley Truax with whom he was father of (3). Sidney was a mechanic for Dauphin Oil, Carlisle, for most of his working life. He really enjoyed the outdoors, especially hunting, fishing and metal detecting. He was a music lover who played guitar for the Keystoners. He proudly served his country in the U.S. Marine Corps during the Korean Conflict. He was a member of American Legion # 101, Carlisle.
TONI A. FISHER Fifth great granddaughter of progenitor Nicholas Kegg. **THOMAS F. FISHER** Fifth great grandson of progenitor Nicholas Kegg. **TONI A. FISHER** Fifth great granddaughter of progenitor Nicholas Kegg. **TRAVIS P.W. FISHER** Sixth great grandson of progenitor Nicholas Kegg. **TREAD WINFIELD FISHER** Fifth great grandson of progenitor Nicholas Kegg. **TRUDY S. FISHER** Fifth great granddaughter of progenitor Nicholas Kegg. **VINCENT FISHER** Fifth great grandson of progenitor Nicholas Kegg. **WENDY FISHER** Fifth great granddaughter of progenitor Nicholas Kegg. **WILLIAM S. FISHER** aka "Bill", Fifth great grandson of progenitor Nicholas Kegg. **ZACKARY FISHER** Tenth great grandson of progenitor Nicholas Kegg.

FITCH

BRITT FITCH Seventh great granddaughter of progenitor Nicholas Kegg.
NICOLE FITCH Seventh great granddaughter of progenitor Nicholas Kegg.

FITES

KAREEN FITES Sixth great granddaughter of progenitor Nicholas Kegg.
ROBERT EDWIN FITES (1946 – 2020) son of Robert and Dorothelle Maola (Willard) Fites.

FITTING

BOBBIE JOE FITTING Sixth great grandson of progenitor Nicholas Kegg.
JENNIFER LYNN FITTING Sixth great granddaughter of progenitor Nicholas Kegg.
MARY REBECCA FITTING Sixth great granddaughter of progenitor Nicholas Kegg.

FITZGERALD

ELIZABETH ANN FITZGERALD Fifth great granddaughter of progenitor Nicholas Kegg.
ERIN FITZGERALD Sixth great granddaughter of progenitor Nicholas Kegg.

[3524B] Granite City News (IL) Nov 1, 2010 [3525] Public Opinion (PA) Feb 21, 1985, obtained by D. Sue Dible [3526] Public Opinion (Chambersburg, PA) Jan 21, 1987 [3526A] Fulton County News (PA) July 28, 2011

JOHN GARY FITZGERALD Fifth great grandson of progenitor Nicholas Kegg. **LEANNE FITZGERALD** Fifth great granddaughter of progenitor Nicholas Kegg. **MEGAN FITZGERALD** Sixth great granddaughter of progenitor Nicholas Kegg. **REGINA G. FITZGERALD** Sixth great granddaughter of progenitor Nicholas Kegg. **RICHARD R. FITZGERALD** Sixth great grandson of progenitor Nicholas Kegg.

FITZPATRICK

BRITTNEY FITZPATRICK Eighth great granddaughter of progenitor Nicholas Kegg. **HANNAH FITZPATRICK** Seventh great granddaughter of progenitor Nicholas Kegg. **KAYLA FITZPATRICK** Eighth great granddaughter of progenitor Nicholas Kegg. **LIAM PRESTON FITZPATRICK** Seventh great grandson of progenitor Nicholas Kegg.

FITZWATER

JOHANA LEE FITZWATER Sixth great granddaughter of progenitor Nicholas Kegg
REAGAN EARL FITZWATER Sixth great grandson of progenitor Nicholas Kegg.

FIVEASH

ADAM E. FIVEASH Sixth great grandson of progenitor Nicholas Kegg. **DAVID EARL FIVEASH** Fifth great grandson of progenitor Nicholas Kegg. **DIANE FIVEASH** Fifth great granddaughter of progenitor Nicholas Kegg. **LUKE ROBERT FIVEASH** Sixth great grandson of progenitor Nicholas Kegg. **NANCY FIVEASH** Fifth great granddaughter of progenitor Nicholas Kegg.

FLATHERS

CHRISTOPHER FLATHERS Sixth great grandson of progenitor Nicholas Kegg.
DEAN FLATHERS Sixth great grandson of progenitor Nicholas Kegg.
KIMBERLY FLATHERS Sixth great granddaughter of progenitor Nicholas Kegg.

FLATNESS

CASSIDY FLATNESS Seventh great granddaughter of progenitor Nicholas Kegg.
HANNA FLATNESS Seventh great granddaughter of progenitor Nicholas Kegg.

FLECK

GABRIEL ANTHONY FLECK Seventh great grandson of progenitor Nicholas Kegg.
JONAH RYAN FLECK Seventh great grandson of progenitor Nicholas Kegg. **LUKE FLECK** Seventh great grandson of progenitor Nicholas Kegg. **MICHAEL P. FLECK** Sixth great grandson of progenitor Nicholas Kegg. **OLIVIA FLECK** Seventh great granddaughter of progenitor Nicholas Kegg. **RYAN P. FLECK** Sixth great grandson of progenitor Nicholas Kegg. **SOPHIA FLECK** Seventh great granddaughter of progenitor Nicholas Kegg.

FLEECE

CHASE FLEECE Eighth great grandson of progenitor Nicholas Kegg. **CRAIG W. FLEECE** Seventh great grandson of progenitor Nicholas Kegg. **EVELYN FLEECE** Eighth great granddaughter of progenitor Nicholas Kegg.

FLEMING

CHRISTOPHER MICHAEL FLEMING Sixth great grandson of progenitor Nicholas Kegg.
EUGENE KENNETH FLEMING (1934 – 2015) son of Kenneth and Edith (Mess) Fleming, married Betty Joan Gross. **JEFFREY PAUL FLEMING** Sixth great grandson of progenitor Nicholas Kegg. **LILLIAN JEAN FLEMING** [3256B] daughter of Kenneth and Edith (Mess) Fleming, married William D. Olmstead with whom she was mother of (2). Lillian worked in laundry at the Hilton Hotel, and later at Holiday Inn.

FLESHER

BRAYDEN PHILIP FLESHER Seventh great grandson of progenitor Nicholas Kegg.
MACI JEAN FLESHER Seventh great granddaughter of progenitor Nicholas Kegg.

FLESZAR

LAUREL FLESZAR Sixth great granddaughter of progenitor Nicholas Kegg.

FLETCHALL

NATHAN FLETCHALL aka "Max", Seventh great grandson of progenitor Nicholas Kegg.

FLOHR

EDNA VIOLET FLOHR [3527] (1883 – 1946) daughter of John and Mary (College) Flohr, married Benjamin Lawrence Griffith with whom she was mother of (1). **INFANT FLOHR** (1881 – 1881) daughter of John and Mary (College) Flohr. **JOSIE P. FLOHR** (1877 – 1880) daughter of John and Mary (College) Flohr. **RAYDON P. FLOHR** [3528] (1886 – 1903) son of John and Mary (College) Flohr. **RAYMOND C. FLOHR** (1876 – 1877) son of John and Mary (College) Flohr.

FLOWERS

KATHRYN FLOWERS Seventh great granddaughter of progenitor Nicholas Kegg.
MITCHELL FLOWERS Seventh great grandson of progenitor Nicholas Kegg.

FLOYD

ANDY FLOYD Sixth great grandson of progenitor Nicholas Kegg. **CANDICE FLOYD** Sixth great granddaughter of progenitor Nicholas Kegg. **JENNIFER FLOYD** Sixth great granddaughter of progenitor Nicholas Kegg.

FLUKE

EBAN FLUKE Sixth great grandson of progenitor Nicholas Kegg. **MENDY ANN FLUKE** Seventh great granddaughter of progenitor Nicholas Kegg. **RUSTY FLUKE** Seventh great grandson of progenitor Nicholas Kegg. **WAYLON FLUKE** Seventh great grandson of progenitor Nicholas Kegg.

[3526B] Lincoln Journal Star (NE) Feb 22, 2002 [3527] The News Journal (DE) Aug 30, 1946 [3528] Pittsburg Press (PA) May 24, 1903

FOCHTMAN

STEVEN JOHN FOCHTMAN (1972 – 1974) son of Douglas and Nancy (Bartholow) Fochtman.
SUSAN FOCHTMAN Sixth great granddaughter of progenitor Nicholas Kegg.

FOGLE

MEGAN RENEE FOGLE Sixth great granddaughter of progenitor Nicholas Kegg.
RACHEL LYNN FOGLE Sixth great granddaughter of progenitor Nicholas Kegg.

FOLEY

MEAGAN FOLEY Eighth great granddaughter of progenitor Nicholas Kegg.

FOLKENS

BRADLEY DEAN FOLKENS Sixth great grandson of progenitor Nicholas Kegg.
KELLIE JEAN FOLKENS Sixth great granddaughter of progenitor Nicholas Kegg.

FOOR

ALEXANDER XERXES FOOR Seventh great grandson of progenitor Nicholas Kegg.
AMANDA J. FOOR aka "Mandy", Sixth great granddaughter of progenitor Nicholas Kegg.
AMANDA KLOY FOOR Seventh great granddaughter of progenitor Nicholas Kegg.
ANNETTE DIANE FOOR Sixth great granddaughter of progenitor Nicholas Kegg.
ASHLEY NICOLE FOOR Seventh great granddaughter of progenitor Nicholas Kegg.
BARBARA LEE FOOR Fifth great granddaughter of progenitor Nicholas Kegg.
BOBBY DEAN FOOR [3529] (1960 – 2001) son of Norman and Jacqueline (Stine) Foor, married Orchid Elias with whom he was father of (2). Bobby enjoyed fishing and target shooting. **BRANDON FOOR** Seventh great grandson of progenitor Nicholas Kegg. **BRENDA JEAN FOOR** Sixth great granddaughter of progenitor Nicholas Kegg. **BRITTANY L. FOOR** Seventh great granddaughter of progenitor Nicholas Kegg. **CARRIE L. FOOR** Sixth great granddaughter of progenitor Nicholas Kegg. **CHRISTINA ROSE FOOR** Seventh great granddaughter of progenitor Nicholas Kegg.
DALTON FOOR [3529A] (1995 – 2023) son of Randy and Lisa (Jay) Foor married Rachel Miller with whom he was father of (1). Dalton had a fondness for driving which led him to pursue his dream of being a truck driver for Central States Manufacturing. He was a fantastic father, taking pride in the many milestones achieved by his toddler. Dalton found hunting to be a rewarding skill in precisely hitting a target. His competitive nature inspired his satisfaction in playing video games while he possessed a sense of accomplishment after putting a puzzle together. **DARL E. FOOR** Sixth great grandson of progenitor Nicholas Kegg. **DARL EUGENE FOOR** [3530] (1946 – 1971) son of Ellis and Helen Margaret (Smith) Foor, married Cathy Collins with whom he was father of (1). Darl was employed at the U.S. Post Office in La Puente. He served four years in the U.S. Navy. **DEBRA ANN FOOR** aka "Debbie", Sixth great granddaughter of progenitor Nicholas Kegg. **DIANA DENISE FOOR** Sixth great granddaughter of progenitor Nicholas Kegg. **DOLORES MARIE FOOR** aka "Debbie'" [3531] (1941 – 2022) daughter of Ellis and Margaret (Smith) Foor married William Roy Sleek. Later, she married Richard Wayne Mardis with whom she was mother of (2). Dolores enjoyed baking, cooking and adored her grandchildren and great grandchildren. **ELIAS FOOR** Seventh great grandson of progenitor Nicholas Kegg.
ELIZABETH MARIE FOOR Seventh great granddaughter of progenitor Nicholas Kegg.

[3529] The Tribune (San Luis Obispo, CA) July 12, 2001 [3529A] Bedford Gazette (PA) Apr 9, 2023, obtained by Bob Rose [3530] http://www.foorgenealogy.com/d0000/g0000063.html#I1168 [3531] Akers Funeral Home (PA)

ELLIS MICHAEL FOOR Sixth great grandson of progenitor Nicholas Kegg. **EMMA FOOR** [3532] (1912 – 1977) daughter of Walter and Anna (Fickes) Foor, married Holmes Edmund Pick with whom she was mother of (2). Emma belonged to Juniata Valley Court, Order of the Amaranth and the United Commercial Travelers Auxiliary. Mrs. Pick worked for 20 years as a nurse at J.C. Blair Memorial with most of her employment there being in the maternity ward. **FLEETA CATHERINE FOOR** [3533] (1906 – 1998) daughter of Walter and Anna (Fickes) Foor, married Walter L. Layton with whom she was mother of (1). Fleeta was an active member of the Stone Church of the Brethren, Huntingdon, its Delta Alpha Sunday School Class and the Women's Fellowship. She was also a member of the J.C. Blair Memorial Hospital School of Nursing Alumnae Association. An alumna of Broad Top City High School, Fleeta also graduated from the J.C. Blair Memorial Hospital School of Nursing. She was first employed as a registered nurse at the former State Hospital for Crippled Children in Elizabethtown. Later, in addition to being a homemaker, she returned to work at J.C. Blair Memorial Hospital, Huntingdon, from which she retired from the nursing staff. She also did some private duty nursing through the years. **GILBERT PETER FOOR** Sixth great grandson of progenitor Nicholas Kegg. **JAMIE LEE FOOR** Sixth great grandson of progenitor Nicholas Kegg. **JANE L. FOOR** Fifth great granddaughter of progenitor Nicholas Kegg. **JUSTIN PHILIP FOOR** Sixth great grandson of progenitor Nicholas Kegg. **KARL FOOR** Seventh great grandson of progenitor Nicholas Kegg. **KENTON CHARLES FOOR** Seventh great grandson of progenitor Nicholas Kegg. **KIM LEE FOOR** Sixth great granddaughter of progenitor Nicholas Kegg. **LORIE ANN FOOR** Sixth great granddaughter of progenitor Nicholas Kegg. **MARGARET JANE FOOR** aka "Peggy", Fifth great granddaughter of progenitor Nicholas Kegg. **MICHAEL LYNN FOOR** Sixth great grandson of progenitor Nicholas Kegg. **MILES NELSON FOOR** (1948 – 2002) son of Ellis and Helen Margaret (Smith) Foor, married Linda S. Laverd. **MAYA LYNN FOOR** Eighth great granddaughter of progenitor Nicholas Kegg. **NATALIE FOOR** Seventh great granddaughter of progenitor Nicholas Kegg. **PATRICIA LYNN FOOR** Sixth great granddaughter of progenitor Nicholas Kegg. **PAUL E. FOOR** [3534] (1938 – 1995) aka "Smokey", son of Blair and Ione (Diehl) Foor, married Betty V. Bennett with whom he was father of (1). Paul was formerly employed by Kelly-Spring Tire Co., Cumberland, Md., for 21 years and was a driver for Arkansas Best Freight of Carlisle. He served in the U.S. Army National Guard, was a member of the Loyal Order of the Moose, Bedford. **RANDOLPH FOOR** Seventh great grandson of progenitor Nicholas Kegg. **RANDY L. FOOR** Sixth great grandson of progenitor Nicholas Kegg. **RANDY LYNN FOOR** Seventh great grandson of progenitor Nicholas Kegg. **REBECCA FOOR** Seventh great granddaughter of progenitor Nicholas Kegg. **RENEE LYNN FOOR** Spouse of fifth great grandson of progenitor Nicholas Kegg. **RICK LAMONT FOOR** Sixth great grandson of progenitor Nicholas Kegg. **RICKY LYNN FOOR** Seventh great granddaughter of progenitor Nicholas Kegg. **RUTH ELLEN FOOR** Fifth great granddaughter of progenitor Nicholas Kegg. **SHAWN FOOR** Sixth great grandson of progenitor Nicholas Kegg. **SHIRAH FOOR** Seventh great granddaughter of progenitor Nicholas Kegg. **TAMMI LYNORE FOOR** Sixth great granddaughter of progenitor Nicholas Kegg. **TERRI LYN FOOR** (1958 – 2006) daughter of Charles and Charlotte (Green) Foor. **TERRY FOOR** Seventh great grandson of progenitor Nicholas Kegg. **TYLER FOOR** Seventh great grandchild of progenitor Nicholas Kegg. **VICKI ANN FOOR** Fifth great granddaughter of progenitor Nicholas Kegg.

FOORE

ARVILLA EVELYN FOORE (1918 – 1997) daughter of Marshall and Bertha (Stayer) Foore, married Malcolm O. Whited with whom she was mother of (3). **DALE EUGENE FOORE** [3535] (1924 – 2007) son of Marshall and Bertha (Stayer) Foore, married Mary Gene Sheterom with whom he was father of (2). Dale dropped out of high school at the start of World War II, to enlist in the Navy. Following his basic

---

[3532] Daily News, (PA) Nov 11, 1977, obtained by Niki Moore [3533] p.2 – Huntingdon Daily News (PA) Apr 28, 1998 [3534] p.8 – Bedford Gazette (PA) Feb 2, 1995 [3535] Tulsa World (OK) April 12, 2007

training, completed at the Chicago Shipping Yard, he spent the rest of the war flying PBM airplanes, searching for German submarines in the Atlantic. He often kidded about the irony that a Pennsylvania coal miner's son spent the war stationed on various Caribbean islands, flying over beautiful blue water. Dale completed his high school credits at the University of Tulsa, which had created a school for returning veterans, and later finished his aeronautical mechanics training at the Spartan School of Aeronautics. Dale retired from American Airlines, after almost 37 years of employment, as a Mechanic, Crew Chief, and Foreman, having served in numerous shops. Dale was a life member of Delta Masonic Lodge, as well as being a 32nd life member of the Tulsa Scottish Rite, where he was a longtime member of the Supernumerary Club, and a member of the American Legion. **ELIZABETH ANN FOORE** Sixth great granddaughter of progenitor Nicholas Kegg. **JOHN BARRY FOORE** Seventh great grandson of progenitor Nicholas Kegg. **JOSEPH ROSS FOORE** [3536] (1919 – 1993) son of Marshall and Bertha (Stayer) Foore married twice; first to Ardath Mae Mort with whom he was father of (1). Later, he married Cleoma Swope with whom he was father of (2). Joseph was a coal miner and farmer for several years. He was a veteran of World War II and served in the U.S. Army, 4th infantry division. He was also a member of the Disabled War Veterans. **JUSTIN BARRY FOORE** Eighth great grandson of progenitor Nicholas Kegg. **MARISSA ELIZABETH FOORE** Seventh great granddaughter of progenitor Nicholas Kegg. **MARSHALL BRADLEY FOORE** Sixth great grandson of progenitor Nicholas Kegg. **SHARON FOORE** Seventh great granddaughter of progenitor Nicholas Kegg. **TAYLOR YVETTE FOORE** Eighth great granddaughter of progenitor Nicholas Kegg.

FORCZEK

KAREN JENNIFER FORCZEK Sixth great granddaughter of progenitor Nicholas Kegg.
KELLY A. FORCZEK Sixth great granddaughter of progenitor Nicholas Kegg.
LOREEN KATHERINE FORCZEK Sixth great granddaughter of progenitor Nicholas Kegg.

FORD

AMY LYNN FORD Seventh great granddaughter of progenitor Nicholas Kegg. **CHRISTIAN FORD** Sixth great grandson of progenitor Nicholas Kegg. **DANA FORD** Sixth great grandson of progenitor Nicholas Kegg. **DANIEL FORD** Fifth great grandson of progenitor Nicholas Kegg. **GLENDA FORD** Sixth great granddaughter of progenitor Nicholas Kegg. **JOHNNY DEWAYNE FORD** Sixth great grandson of progenitor Nicholas Kegg. **JULIE LEE FORD** Seventh great granddaughter of progenitor Nicholas Kegg. **KAREN FORD** Sixth great granddaughter of progenitor Nicholas Kegg. **STACY ANN FORD** Fifth great granddaughter of progenitor Nicholas Kegg. **TREVOR FORD** Seventh great grandson of progenitor Nicholas Kegg. **TYLER BLAKE FORD** Seventh great grandson of progenitor Nicholas Kegg. **WILLIAM DEAN FORD JR.** Fifth great grandson of progenitor Nicholas Kegg.

FORE

BRANDI LYN FORE Seventh great granddaughter of progenitor Nicholas Kegg.
CONNIE KAY FORE Sixth great granddaughter of progenitor Nicholas Kegg.

FOREMAN

MATTHEW PAUL FOREMAN Sixth great grandson of progenitor Nicholas Kegg.

[3536] Bedford County Genealogical Society obituary obtained by D. Sue Dible

FORKEY

RONALD FORKEY Sixth great grandson of progenitor Nicholas Kegg. **TARA FORKEY** Sixth great granddaughter of progenitor Nicholas Kegg.

FORRESTER

AUBREY FORRESTER Ninth great granddaughter of progenitor Nicholas Kegg. **BEN FORRESTER** Eighth great grandson of progenitor Nicholas Kegg. **DYLAN FORRESTER** Eighth great grandson of progenitor Nicholas Kegg. **MASON FORRESTER** Ninth great grandson of progenitor Nicholas Kegg.

FOSTER

CAROLYNN E. FOSTER Sixth great granddaughter of progenitor Nicholas Kegg. **DONNA SUSAN FOSTER** Sixth great granddaughter of progenitor Nicholas Kegg. **WANDA ELAINE FOSTER** Sixth great granddaughter of progenitor Nicholas Kegg. **WILLIAM CLINTON FOSTER** [3536A] aka "Bill" (1932 – 2015) son of Andrew and Edna Mae (Clark) Foster married Peggy with whom he was father of (1). Bill was known for his kind manner and sense of humor. He loved the water, boating, camping at the beach - especially Turtle Beach in Sarasota. **WILLIAM LEE FOSTER** Sixth great grandson of progenitor Nicholas Kegg. **LINDA FOSTER** Sixth great granddaughter of progenitor Nicholas Kegg. **LISA MARIE FOSTER** Seventh great granddaughter of progenitor Nicholas Kegg. **MARSHA FOSTER** Sixth great granddaughter of progenitor Nicholas Kegg. **PAUL ANDERSON FOSTER** Seventh great grandson of progenitor Nicholas Kegg.

FOUNTAIN

CHERYL L. FOUNTAIN Sixth great granddaughter of progenitor Nicholas Kegg. **JEFFREY C. FOUNTAIN** Sixth great grandson of progenitor Nicholas Kegg. **KENNETH G. FOUNTAIN** Sixth great grandson of progenitor Nicholas Kegg. **LORIE FOUNTAIN** Sixth great granddaughter of progenitor Nicholas Kegg.

FOWLER

AMBER NATASHA FOWLER (1973 – 1981) daughter of Harold Irving and Ruth Ann (Moorehouse) Fowler. **DAVID EVAN FOWLER** Sixth great grandson of progenitor Nicholas Kegg. **LORA FOWLER** Sixth great granddaughter of progenitor Nicholas Kegg. **MARK FOWLER** Sixth great grandson of progenitor Nicholas Kegg. **MEGAN FOWLER** Sixth great granddaughter of progenitor Nicholas Kegg. **MIKE FOWLER** Fifth great grandson of progenitor Nicholas Kegg. **ROSS FOWLER** Sixth great grandson of progenitor Nicholas Kegg. **TOM FOWLER** Fifth great grandson of progenitor Nicholas Kegg.

FOX

JAMES FOX Seventh great grandson of progenitor Nicholas Kegg.
MICHELLE FOX Sixth great granddaughter of progenitor Nicholas Kegg.

[3536A] Beall Funeral Home (MD)

FOY

DEBORAH FOY aka Debbie", Fifth great granddaughter of progenitor Nicholas Kegg. **PATRICK J. FOY** Fifth great grandson of progenitor Nicholas Kegg. **PAUL FOY** Fifth great grandson of progenitor Nicholas Kegg. **RICHARD FOY** Fifth great grandson of progenitor Nicholas Kegg.

FRALEY

DONALD S. FRALEY Sixth great grandson of progenitor Nicholas Kegg.

FRANCO

HEATHER FRANCO Seventh great granddaughter of progenitor Nicholas Kegg.
SCOTT FRANCO Seventh great grandson of progenitor Nicholas Kegg.

FRANK

DENNIS A. FRANK Fifth great grandson of progenitor Nicholas Kegg. **DIETER FRANK** Sixth great grandson of progenitor Nicholas Kegg. **HANA FRANK** Sixth great grandchild of progenitor Nicholas Kegg. **JEFFREY ALLEN FRANK** Sixth great grandson of progenitor Nicholas Kegg. **LEE MICHAEL FRANK JR.** Sixth great grandson of progenitor Nicholas Kegg. **LORI A FRANK** Sixth great granddaughter of progenitor Nicholas Kegg. **MATTHEW B. FRANK** Sixth great grandson of progenitor Nicholas Kegg. **REINHARDT FRANK** Sixth great grandson of progenitor Nicholas Kegg.

FRANKLIN

AUSTIN ALLEN FRANKLIN Eighth great grandson of progenitor Nicholas Kegg.
DUSTIN DON FRANKLIN Eighth great grandson of progenitor Nicholas Kegg.

FRANKS

JASON A. FRANKS Sixth great grandson of progenitor Nicholas Kegg.
NATHAN DAVID FRANKS Sixth great grandson of progenitor Nicholas Kegg.

FRASURE

JEFFREY FRASURE Seventh great grandson of progenitor Nicholas Kegg.

FRATELLO

JAMIN FRATELLO Seventh great grandson of progenitor Nicholas Kegg.
KELSEY HANNAH FRATELLO Seventh great granddaughter of progenitor Nicholas Kegg.
NOAH FRATELLO Seventh great grandson of progenitor Nicholas Kegg.

FRAYER

JAMES LEWIS FRAYER [3536B] aka "Jim" (1929 – 2011) son of Mildred Alline Frayer married three times, first to Paula Arlene Decker with whom he was father of (4). Jim served in the National Guard. He worked for Dave Walsh Company and was a warehouse manager for Calpine Containers in Oxnard

[3536B] Ted Mayr Funeral Home (CA)

providing packaging solutions to the surrounding agricultural community until his retirement. Jim loved to fly and was a long-time member of the local Civil Air Patrol. He spent hundreds of hours searching with his CAP buddies for down aircraft and missing persons throughout California. Also of great enjoyment, Jim was a model railroader specializing in N-gauge. Along with his model railroading gang, they built a complete model layout of mountains, lakes, cities, mining towns, forests, and tunnels with shops, cars and people. They ran trains by the hour sometimes with precise timetables of train pick-ups and delivery. **JAMES LEWIS FRAYER** Sixth great grandson of progenitor Nicholas Kegg. **KATHILEEN JOAN FRAYER** aka "Kathi", 6th great granddaughter of progenitor Nicholas Kegg. **MILDRED ALLINE FRAYER** (1909 – 1960) daughter of William and Nellie (Colledge) Frayer was mother of (1). She married Edward Frank Froelich. **NANCY GAYLE FRAYER** Sixth great granddaughter of progenitor Nicholas Kegg. **SUSAN ALENE FRAYER** Sixth great granddaughter of progenitor Nicholas Kegg.

FRAZIER

EMMA FRAZIER Seventh great granddaughter of progenitor Nicholas Kegg. **JOE FRAZIER** Seventh great grandson of progenitor Nicholas Kegg. **LENNA FRAZIER** Seventh great granddaughter of progenitor Nicholas Kegg. **MIA KATE FRAZIER** Seventh great granddaughter of progenitor Nicholas Kegg. **MIKEY LYNN FRAZIER** Sixth great granddaughter of progenitor Nicholas Kegg. **TERRY LEE FRAZIER** Sixth great grandson of progenitor Nicholas Kegg. **TIMOTHY LYLE FRAZIER** Sixth great grandson of progenitor Nicholas Kegg.

FREEMAN

LEAH DIANE FREEMAN Seventh great granddaughter of progenitor Nicholas Kegg.
RYAN ALLEN FREEMAN Seventh great grandson of progenitor Nicholas Kegg.

FREDERICK

CARTER FREDERICK Seventh great grandson of progenitor Nicholas Kegg.
CHERLY PATRICIA FREDERICK Fifth great granddaughter of progenitor Nicholas Kegg.
DEVIN ROLLAND FREDERICK Ninth great grandson of progenitor Nicholas Kegg.
ELIZABETH FREDERICK Sixth great granddaughter of progenitor Nicholas Kegg.
EVELYN ROSE FREDERICK (1920 – 2015) daughter of Carl and Mavie (Nelson) Frederick married Joe Frank Hauf with whom she was mother of (2). **HANNAH FREDERICK** Sixth great granddaughter of progenitor Nicholas Kegg. **HERMAN GILMORE FREDERICK** [3537] (1930 – 2020) son of Carl and Mavie (Nelson) Frederick married Helen Leonard. Herman a had a long career in the U.S. Armed Forces, serving in the Army, Navy, and the Air Force. After retirement, he then became a commercial fisherman out of Bowers Beach. **JERRY WALTER FREDERICK** Fifth great grandson of progenitor Nicholas Kegg. **JONATHAN FREDERICK** Sixth great grandson of progenitor Nicholas Kegg. **LYDIA FREDERICK** Seventh great granddaughter of progenitor Nicholas Kegg.
MILDRED LUCILLE FREDERICK [3538] (1924 – 2012) daughter of Carl and Mavie (Nelson) Frederick married Perry Leslie Guthrie with whom she was mother of (1). **PEGGY ANN FREDRICK** Fourth great granddaughter of progenitor Nicholas Kegg.

FREED

KATHY LEE FREED Fifth great granddaughter of progenitor Nicholas Kegg.
SETH MICHAEL FREED Sixth great grandson of progenitor Nicholas Kegg.

[3537] Solanco Chronicle (CA) May 22, 2020 [3538] Blackwell Daily Journal (OK) June 4, 1940

FREEMAN

DAVID A. FREEMAN Sixth great grandson of progenitor Nicholas Kegg.
JACQUELI R. FREEMAN Sixth great granddaughter of progenitor Nicholas Kegg.
ROBERT A. FREEMAN Sixth great grandson of progenitor Nicholas Kegg.

FRENCH

AUSTIN FRENCH Seventh great grandson of progenitor Nicholas Kegg.
BETHANY BROOKE FRENCH (1985 – 1985) daughter of Mark and Kimmy Jo (McBride) French.
CHASE FRENCH Seventh great grandson of progenitor Nicholas Kegg. **ISAAC KYLE FRENCH**, aka "Patchy", Seventh great grandson of progenitor Nicholas Kegg. **LASHAY FRENCH** Seventh great granddaughter of progenitor Nicholas Kegg. **NOAH FRENCH** Seventh great grandson of progenitor Nicholas Kegg. **TAVI FRENCH** Seventh great granddaughter of progenitor Nicholas Kegg.

FRESH

WINIFRED RAE FRESH Fifth great granddaughter of progenitor Nicholas Kegg.

FREY

SAMANTHA FREY Seventh great granddaughter of progenitor Nicholas Kegg.
VICTORIA FREY Seventh great granddaughter of progenitor Nicholas Kegg.

FRICK

LESA FRICK Sixth great granddaughter of progenitor Nicholas Kegg. **STEPHANIE FRICK** Sixth great granddaughter of progenitor Nicholas Kegg.

FRIEMOTH

BEVERLY ANN FRIEMOTH (1948 – 1948) daughter of Orville and Thelma (Crouse) Friemoth.
BRENDA SUE FRIEMOTH Sixth great granddaughter of progenitor Nicholas Kegg.
PAULLETTE KAY FRIEMOTH [3539] (1943 – 1996) aka "Pam" daughter of Orville and Thelma (Crouse) Friemoth, married Thomas Rondo with whom she was mother of (2). Later she married James Lawrence Isabel. Paulette had been a volunteer at Kalkaska Memorial Center. She attended the New Hope Tabernacle and enjoyed snowmobile and boating. **PRUDENCE ANN FRIEMOTH** (1950 – 1950) daughter of Orville and Thelma (Crouse) Friemoth.

FRIEND

JESSIE FRIEND [3540] (1886 – 1956) daughter of Daniel and Eva (Lininger) Friend, married James Edward Dacy with whom she was mother of (1). She married Peter J. Mayer with whom she was mother of (2). Later, she married John Francis Morrow and Clarence Elmer Gard.

FRIESZELL

KARAUNA FRIESZELL Eighth great granddaughter of progenitor Nicholas Kegg.

[3539] The Daily Telegram (MI) May 14, 1996 [3540] The Indianapolis Star (IN) Aug 31, 1956

FRISBY

DIANE E. FRISBY Sixth great granddaughter of progenitor Nicholas Kegg.   **JERRY P. FRISBY** Sixth great grandson of progenitor Nicholas Kegg.   **JOHN MICHAEL FRISBY** Sixth great grandson of progenitor Nicholas Kegg.

FRISCH

CHARLES JOSEPH FRISCH [3541] (1949 – 1953) son of Charles and Francis Josephine (Davis) Frisch. Little Charles Joseph Frisch, 4, was fatally injured when he was struck by a car in front of his parents' home. The little boy and his mother were walking across the road to get the mail when the accident occurred. His mother had stopped at the roadside until it was cleared of traffic while she held her little boy by the hand. The Mailbox is on the opposite side of the road from the home. Suddenly the boy broke from his mother's grasp and started running across the road directly in front of a car.
CYNTHIA MARIE FRISCH aka "Cindy", Sixth great granddaughter of progenitor Nicholas Kegg.
JOHN ROBERT FRISCH [3542] (1951 – 1951) son of Charles and Francis Josephine (Davis) Frisch.
PATRICIA ANN FRISCH aka "Pat", Sixth great granddaughter of progenitor Nicholas Kegg.

FRITSCH

BRAYDEN FRITSCH Eighth great grandson of progenitor Nicholas Kegg.   **JULIE FRITSCH** Seventh great granddaughter of progenitor Nicholas Kegg.   **MICHAEL FRITSCH** Seventh great grandson of progenitor Nicholas Kegg.

FRITZ

DEVIN MICHAEL FRITZ Seventh great grandson of progenitor Nicholas Kegg.
JAMES WILLIAM FRITZ aka "Jim", Fifth great grandson of progenitor Nicholas Kegg.
RALPH W. FRITZ [3543] (1920 – 1994) son of Clarence and Edna (Hershiser) Fritz, married Mildred L. Crile with whom he was father of (1). Ralph had operated a furnace and air conditioning service for 10 years and retired from Standard Oil. He was a member of the Kingdom Hall of Jehovah's Witnesses of Wooster.   **TREY WILLIAM FRITZ** Seventh great grandson of progenitor Nicholas Kegg.
TROY DEAN FRITZ Sixth great grandson of progenitor Nicholas Kegg.

FRITZIE

HAILEY FRITZIE Sixth great granddaughter of progenitor Nicholas Kegg.   **JACOB FRITZIE** Sixth great grandson of progenitor Nicholas Kegg.   **RYAN FRITZIE** Sixth great grandson of progenitor Nicholas Kegg.

FROHM

MATT FROHM Sixth great grandson of progenitor Nicholas Kegg.

FRY

ROBERT FRY Fifth great grandson of progenitor Nicholas Kegg.

[3541] Daily Chief Union (OH) Aug 17, 1953, obtained by D. Sue Dible [3542] Daily Chief Union (OH) Apr 30, 1951, obtained by D. Sue Dible
[3543] p.C11 he Daily Record (OH) Sep 19, 1994, obtained by D. Sue Dible

FRYE

DAYLON FRYE Seventh great grandson of progenitor Nicholas Kegg. **DONNA FRYE** Sixth great granddaughter of progenitor Nicholas Kegg. **FREDERICK FRYE** Sixth great grandson of progenitor Nicholas Kegg. **ROBERT K. FRYE** Sixth great grandson of progenitor Nicholas Kegg.

FUENTES

NOUR LOVISA FUENTES Seventh great granddaughter of progenitor Nicholas Kegg.

FUGATE

ALEXA FUGATE Ninth great granddaughter of progenitor Nicholas Kegg.
BARBARA SUE FUGATE Sixth great granddaughter of progenitor Nicholas Kegg. **DALE FUGATE** Seventh great grandson of progenitor Nicholas Kegg. **DEWAINE FUGATE** Seventh great grandson of progenitor Nicholas Kegg. **HALDON FUGATE** Eighth great grandson of progenitor Nicholas Kegg. **JAMES FRANCIS FUGATE** Sixth great grandson of progenitor Nicholas Kegg. **JOSHUA FUGATE** Eighth great grandson of progenitor Nicholas Kegg. **KEVIN FUGATE** Seventh great grandson of progenitor Nicholas Kegg. **KIM FUGATE** Seventh great granddaughter of progenitor Nicholas Kegg. **MEGAN FUGATE** Eighth great granddaughter of progenitor Nicholas Kegg.

FULLER

ALEX FULLER Seventh great grandson of progenitor Nicholas Kegg. **BETHANY LEA FULLER** Seventh great granddaughter of progenitor Nicholas Kegg. **GABRIEL FULLER** Seventh great granddaughter of progenitor Nicholas Kegg. **JOSEPH CARL FULLER** Seventh great grandson of progenitor Nicholas Kegg. **STEFFEN FULLER** Seventh great grandson of progenitor Nicholas Kegg.

FULTON

BOB FULTON Sixth great grandson of progenitor Nicholas Kegg. **CALVIN FULTON** Eighth great grandson of progenitor Nicholas Kegg. **CHRISTOPHER JAMES FULTON** Eighth great grandson of progenitor Nicholas Kegg. **JANICE FULTON** Sixth great granddaughter of progenitor Nicholas Kegg. **JEFF FULTON** Sixth great grandson of progenitor Nicholas Kegg. **JULIE FULTON** Sixth great granddaughter of progenitor Nicholas Kegg. **KAREN MAUREE FULTON** Seventh great granddaughter of progenitor Nicholas Kegg. **LEROY DEAN FULTON** Sixth great grandson of progenitor Nicholas Kegg. **NATALIE FULTON** Eighth great granddaughter of progenitor Nicholas Kegg. **RONALD A. FULTON** Sixth great grandson of progenitor Nicholas Kegg.
S. JOYCE FULTON Sixth great granddaughter of progenitor Nicholas Kegg.
SCOTT ALAN FULTON Seventh great grandson of progenitor Nicholas Kegg.
SHELLE RAE FULTON Seventh great granddaughter of progenitor Nicholas Kegg.

FUNK

ROBERT TYLER FUNK Sixth great grandson of progenitor Nicholas Kegg.

FUNOVITS

MICHAEL FUNOVITS Seventh great grandson of progenitor Nicholas Kegg.
RICHARD FUNOVITS Seventh great grandson of progenitor Nicholas Kegg.

FYOCK

BRIAN WINGARD FYOCK Fifth great grandson of progenitor Nicholas Kegg.

GABEL

LAUREL L. GABEL Fifth great granddaughter of progenitor Nicholas Kegg.
ROBERT M. GABEL Fifth great grandson of progenitor Nicholas Kegg.

GABRIEL

ANTHONY GABRIEL Seventh great grandson of progenitor Nicholas Kegg.
JENNIFER GABRIEL aka "Jenny", Seventh great granddaughter of progenitor Nicholas Kegg.
MARI ELIZABETH GABRIEL Seventh great granddaughter of progenitor Nicholas Kegg.

GAIETTO

NATHAN PAUL GAIETTO Eighth great grandson of progenitor Nicholas Kegg.

GALARSA

MISCHELL GALARSA Sixth great granddaughter of progenitor Nicholas Kegg.
TRISHA L. GALARSA Sixth great granddaughter of progenitor Nicholas Kegg.

GALINAT

DANIEL VERMONT GALINAT Fifth great grandson of progenitor Nicholas Kegg.

GALISZEWSKI

RICHARD GALISZEWSKI aka "Ian", Seventh great grandson of progenitor Nicholas Kegg.
RICHARD MICHAEL GALISZEWSKI Sixth great grandson of progenitor Nicholas Kegg.

GALLEY

JOHN R. GALLEY Fourth great grandson of progenitor Nicholas Kegg.

GALLIA

AVA GALLIA Seventh great granddaughter of progenitor Nicholas Kegg.   **LOUIS GALLIA** Seventh great grandson of progenitor Nicholas Kegg.   **SAMANTHA GALLIA** Seventh great granddaughter of progenitor Nicholas Kegg.

GALLUCCI

BENJAMIN GALLUCCI Seventh great grandson of progenitor Nicholas Kegg.
WILLIAM GALLUCCI Seventh great grandson of progenitor Nicholas Kegg.

GALVIN

BESSIE REA GALVIN (1889 - 1982) daughter of John and Naomi Evaline (Curtis) Galvin, married

James Anthony Watson with whom she was mother of (2). **GEORGE GALVIN** (1868 -?) son of Michael and Mary Jane (Hill) Galvin. **HENRY JAMES GALVIN**, (1866 -?) son of Michael and Mary Jane (Hill) Galvin. **JOHN WILLIAM GALVIN** [3544] (1864 - 1950) son of Michael and Mary Jane (Hill) Galvin, married Evaline (Curtis) Galvin with whom he was father of (2). At an early age John obtained employment in the Katy railroad foundry, where he worked for 40 years before his retirement. Since then, he had occupied his time by looking after his property interests. He was a charter member of Aerie 411, Fraternal Order of Eagles. **ROY HENRY GALVIN** [3545] (1892 – 1951) of John and Naomi Evaline (Curtis) Galvin, married Virginia Belle Coomes with whom he was father of (1). Roy was a well-known Parsons painter who was active in politics, he served a period as a state hotel inspector. He was a member of the painters and musicians' union and was active in Masonic work, holding memberships in all of the Parsons bodies and in Mirza Shrine at Pittsburgh.

GANDEE

ANGELA MARIE GANDEE Sixth great granddaughter of progenitor Nicholas Kegg. **BAILEY GANDEE** Seventh great granddaughter of progenitor Nicholas Kegg. **ELIZABETH GANDEE** Seventh great granddaughter of progenitor Nicholas Kegg. **HALIE GANDEE** Seventh great granddaughter of progenitor Nicholas Kegg. **JOHN GANDEE** Sixth great grandson of progenitor Nicholas Kegg. **JUSTIN GANDEE** Seventh great granddaughter of progenitor Nicholas Kegg. **MARY JANE LOUISE GANDEE** Sixth great granddaughter of progenitor Nicholas Kegg.

GANGER

JOSEPH WAYNE GANGER (1916 – 1916) son of Ralph and Hazelle (Sholl) Ganger.
JOYCE GANGER aka "Joy", Sixth great granddaughter of progenitor Nicholas Kegg.
TAMILA GANGER Sixth great granddaughter of progenitor Nicholas Kegg.

GANGONE

ALYSSA E. GANGONE Fifth great granddaughter of progenitor Nicholas Kegg. **ANDREW GANGONE** Fifth great grandson of progenitor Nicholas Kegg. **ELIZABETH GANGONE** Fifth great granddaughter of progenitor Nicholas Kegg. **MARISSA GANGONE** Fifth great granddaughter of progenitor Nicholas Kegg. **MICHELLE GANGONE** Fifth great granddaughter of progenitor Nicholas Kegg. **STEPHEN E. GANGONE** (1951 – 2002) son of Alexander and Ruth (Kegg) Gangone.

GANNAN

CARISSA JANINE GANNAN Sixth great granddaughter of progenitor Nicholas Kegg.
FRANCHESCA RENEE GANNAN Sixth great granddaughter of progenitor Nicholas Kegg.
KATLYN JOANNE GANNAN Sixth great granddaughter of progenitor Nicholas Kegg.
NORMA LOU GANNAN Fifth great granddaughter of progenitor Nicholas Kegg.
ROBIN ELIZABETH GANNAN Sixth great granddaughter of progenitor Nicholas Kegg.

GARCIA

ISABELLA GARCIA Seventh great granddaughter of progenitor Nicholas Kegg.
MIA GARCIA Seventh great granddaughter of progenitor Nicholas Kegg.

[3544] The Parsons Sun (Parsons, Kansas) Feb 8, 1950 [3545] The Parsons Sun (KS) Dec 15, 1951

GARDNER

AMY N. GARDNER Seventh great granddaughter of progenitor Nicholas Kegg.
BRAELYN ROSE GARDNER Eighth great granddaughter of progenitor Nicholas Kegg.
DANIEL GLENN GARDNER Sixth great grandson of progenitor Nicholas Kegg.
ELLIE GARDNER Eighth great granddaughter of progenitor Nicholas Kegg.
GARRETT DANIEL GARDNER Seventh great grandson of progenitor Nicholas Kegg.
GLENN DANIEL GARDNER Seventh great grandson of progenitor Nicholas Kegg.
JUSTINE P. GARDNER Fifth great granddaughter of progenitor Nicholas Kegg.
KAREN GAIL GARDNER Sixth great granddaughter of progenitor Nicholas Kegg.
KIRK R. GARDNER Sixth great grandson of progenitor Nicholas Kegg.
KYLE THOMAS GARDNER Seventh great grandson of progenitor Nicholas Kegg.
LARRY L. GARDNER Sixth great grandson of progenitor Nicholas Kegg. **LINDA GARDNER** Sixth great granddaughter of progenitor Nicholas Kegg. **LORI ANNE GARDNER** Sixth great granddaughter of progenitor Nicholas Kegg. **MARGARET EVELYN GARDNER** aka "Peggy", Fifth great granddaughter of progenitor Nicholas Kegg. **MICHAEL N. GARDNER** Sixth great grandson of progenitor Nicholas Kegg. **NANCY JO GARDNER** Sixth great granddaughter of progenitor Nicholas Kegg. **VANCIL GARDNER** Fifth great grandson of progenitor Nicholas Kegg.
ZACHARY JAMES GARDNER Seventh great grandson of progenitor Nicholas Kegg.

GARGULINSKI

ALEXANDRA GRACE GARGULINSKI Sixth great granddaughter of progenitor Nicholas Kegg.
BENEDICT RICHARD GARGULINSKI Sixth great grandson of progenitor Nicholas Kegg.
MARGARET ISABEL GARGULINSKI Sixth great granddaughter of progenitor Nicholas Kegg.

GARLITZ

DANIEL GARLITZ Sixth great grandson of progenitor Nicholas Kegg. **FABIAN GARLITZ** Seventh great grandson of progenitor Nicholas Kegg. **GERALD LYNN GARLITZ** Fifth great grandson of progenitor Nicholas Kegg. **LINDA ANN GARLITZ** Fifth great granddaughter of progenitor Nicholas Kegg. **LINDSEY GARLITZ** Sixth great granddaughter of progenitor Nicholas Kegg. **RICHARD GARLITZ** Fifth great grandson of progenitor Nicholas Kegg. **RONALD FRANCIS GARLITZ** [3546] (1945 – 2007) son of Ronald and Ethel (Durst) Garlitz. Ronald had served in the Army Reserve. He had been an accountant for 37 years with the Defense Contract Audit Agency. He was an avid golfer.

GARNER

PAUL DANIEL GARNER Sixth great grandson of progenitor Nicholas Kegg.
PHILIP SPENCER GARNER Sixth great grandson of progenitor Nicholas Kegg.

GARRAND

KADE GARRAND Seventh great grandson of progenitor Nicholas Kegg.
KELSI ARIELLE GARRAND Seventh great granddaughter of progenitor Nicholas Kegg.

[3546] The Baltimore Sun (MD) Nov 25, 2007

GARRETT

AIDEN GARRETT Eighth great grandson of progenitor Nicholas Kegg. **JUSTIN GARRETT** Sixth great grandson of progenitor Nicholas Kegg. **KATHRYN GARRETT** Eighth great granddaughter of progenitor Nicholas Kegg. **LUCAS GARRETT** Seventh great grandson of progenitor Nicholas Kegg. **LYNN R. GARRETT** Fifth great granddaughter of progenitor Nicholas Kegg. **LOGAN GARRETT** Eighth great grandson of progenitor Nicholas Kegg. **PAUL RENE GARRETT** [3547] (1927 – 2007) son of Paul and Ruth (Knouf) Garrett married twice; first to Eva Doyne Rippee with whom he was father of (1). Later, he married again and was father of (4). Paul had worked as a diesel mechanic and welder. **PAULA R. GARRETT** [3548] (1950 – 2009) daughter of Paul and Eva (Rippee) Garrett was mother of (2). **RAVEN KAYE GARRETT** Fifth great granddaughter of progenitor Nicholas Kegg. **REBECCA MARY GARRETT** Fifth great granddaughter of progenitor Nicholas Kegg. **ROBIN GARRETT** Fifth great granddaughter of progenitor Nicholas Kegg. **STANLEY GARRETT** Fifth great grandson of progenitor Nicholas Kegg. **STANLEY EUGENE GARRETT** [3549] (1923 – 2005) son of Paul and Ruth (Knouf) Garrett married twice; first to Barbara Battey with whom he was father of (3). Later, he married Helen Wilson. Stanley was an orchardist and had also worked for the city of Omak Parks Department. **SUSAN GARRETT** Fifth great granddaughter of progenitor Nicholas Kegg. **VINCENT GARRETT** Eighth great grandson of progenitor Nicholas Kegg.

GARRISON

CHRISTOPHER RYAN GARRISON [3550] (1972 – 2018) aka "Viper", son of Gaylord and Barbara (Hubbard) Garrison, married Branda Hoover with whom he was father of (2). Christopher was a singer-songwriter and multi-instrumentalist who began playing the guitar as a child. He went on to influence an entire generation of musicians in the St. Joseph area. Ryan dedicated his life to his family and traveled extensively throughout the United States. **COY CHARLES GARRISON** Seventh great grandson of progenitor Nicholas Kegg. **GAYLORD ROBERT GARRISON** Sixth great grandson of progenitor Nicholas Kegg. **GEOFFREY GARRISON** Seventh great grandson of progenitor Nicholas Kegg. **GRANT GARRISON** Seventh great grandson of progenitor Nicholas Kegg. **GRANT ORION GARRISON** Seventh great grandson of progenitor Nicholas Kegg. **HANNAH GARRISON** Seventh great granddaughter of progenitor Nicholas Kegg. **ISAAC DIEHL GARRISON** Seventh great grandson of progenitor Nicholas Kegg. **MELISSA JOAN GARRISON** Seventh great granddaughter of progenitor Nicholas Kegg. **TORMIE GARRISON** Seventh great granddaughter of progenitor Nicholas Kegg.

GARTIN

CASSANDRA MCLAUGHLIN GARTIN Sixth great granddaughter of progenitor Nicholas Kegg. **DANIEL CARROLL GARTIN** Fifth great grandson of progenitor Nicholas Kegg. **DONALD LEE GARTIN** Fifth great grandson of progenitor Nicholas Kegg. **JERRY MICHAEL GARTIN** Fifth great grandson of progenitor Nicholas Kegg. **JIM GARTIN** Fifth great grandson of progenitor Nicholas Kegg. **LAWRENCE LEE GARTIN** Fifth great grandson of progenitor Nicholas Kegg. **MARTIN EUGENE GARTIN** Fifth great grandson of progenitor Nicholas Kegg. **PATRICK RAYMOND GARTIN** Fifth great grandson of progenitor Nicholas Kegg. **RAYMOND KEITH GARTIN** [3551] (1923 – 2001) son of Luther and Barbara (Laird) Gartin married Gretchen Wardrip with whom he was father of (1). He married Katherine May Roberts with whom he was father of (1) and last, he married Helen Lenore Cutler with whom he was father of (1). Keith was a retired magazine editor for Donnellelley Marketing in Nevada and an Army veteran of World War II. He enjoyed

---

[3547] p.4A - Wenatchee World (WA) Nov 23, 2007 [3548] Wenatchee World (WA) Dec 2, 2009 [3549] Wenatchee World (WA) Feb 24, 2005 [3550] Meierhoffer Funeral Home (MO) [3551] The Des Moines Register (IA) March 10, 2001

woodworking. **RICHARD LAURENCE GARTIN** [3551A] aka "Dick", son of Luther and Barbara (Laird) Gartin, married Jean Francis Menter with whom he was father of (2). Dick was a teacher at DMACC until his retirement. **SANDY KAE GARTIN** Fifth great granddaughter of progenitor Nicholas Kegg.

GARVER

BELLE PARENT GARVER [3552] (1895 – 1983) daughter of Alfred and Kittie (Parent) Garver, married Lloyd Milan Wire with whom she was mother of (4). **CHARLES BYRON GARVER** [3553] (1897 – 1966) son of Alfred and Kittie (Parent) Garver married three times; first to Ellen Josephine Wahls with whom he was father of (1). He married Winifred Valentine Deutschman. Later, he married Marvel Blodgett Seabold with whom he was father of (3). Charles was employed as chief engineer for the J.I. Case Co. in Churubusco. **JEAN JOAN GARVER** [3554] (1930 – 2016) aka "Jeanne", daughter of Charles and Marvel (Blodgett) Garver married three times; first to John Henry Thompson with whom she was mother of (6). Later, she married Clarence Everette Bell and Robert Albion Volker.
MICHAEL BYRON GARVER Fifth great grandson of progenitor Nicholas Kegg.
VERONIKA ELLEN GARVER Sixth great granddaughter of progenitor Nicholas Kegg.
VIRGINIA GARVER [3555] (1922 – 2014) daughter of Alfred and Kathryn (Vogel) Garver married and divorced Ray Albert Beberstein. Later she married Mr. Lea.

GARVIN

DIANA LYNN GARVIN Sixth great granddaughter of progenitor Nicholas Kegg.

GASKIN

ELISE CHRISTY GASKIN Eighth great granddaughter of progenitor Nicholas Kegg.
ELLIOTT RAY GASKIN Eighth great grandson of progenitor Nicholas Kegg.
ETHAN GASKIN Eighth great grandson of progenitor Nicholas Kegg.

GASPER

JASON A. GASPER Seventh great grandson of progenitor Nicholas Kegg.

GASTON

AUSTIN GASTON Seventh great grandson of progenitor Nicholas Kegg.

GATES

MIKAYLA GATES Seventh great granddaughter of progenitor Nicholas Kegg. **MONTANA GATES** Seventh great grandchild of progenitor Nicholas Kegg. **SHAYLEA GATES** Seventh great granddaughter of progenitor Nicholas Kegg. **TIA GATES** Seventh great granddaughter of progenitor Nicholas Kegg.

GATEWOOD

CHRISTOPHER GATEWOOD Seventh great grandson of progenitor Nicholas Kegg.
KIM GATEWOOD Seventh great granddaughter of progenitor Nicholas Kegg.

[3551A] p.22 Des Moines Register (IA) Jan 1, 2008 [3552] Fort Wayne Journal Gazette (IN) Feb 12, 1983, obtained by D. Sue Dible [3553] The Indianapolis News (IN) Nov 26, 1966 [3554] Fort Wayne Newspapers (IN) Dec 24, 2016 [3555] Fort Wayne Newspapers (IN) May 30, 2014

VALERIE GATEWOOD Seventh great granddaughter of progenitor Nicholas Kegg.

GAULE

ANDREA MAUREEN GAULE Fifth great granddaughter of progenitor Nicholas Kegg.
DALE GAULE [3555A] (1967 – 2007) son of Raymond and Ginger (Reynolds) Gaule married Michelle Baughman. Dale worked in restaurant management throughout his career. He enjoyed family, friends and was an avid sports fan. **JANET SUE GAULE** Fifth great granddaughter of progenitor Nicholas Kegg. **RAYMOND EUGENE GAULE** [3555B] (1937 – 2017) son of Melvin and Nina Estelle (Wyckoff) Gaule married Virginia "Ginger" (Reynolds) with whom he was father of (4). Raymond proudly served his country in the United States Air Force. The most important thing to Raymond was his family. He retired from Northwestern Bell (Quest) where he worked as a Switching Control Tech. Ray enjoyed being outside and gardening. One of his favorite pastimes was reading, especially about WWII, and he had a special place in his heart for Iowa Folks. **RONALD LEE GAULE** Fifth great grandson of progenitor Nicholas Kegg. **DOUGLAS GAULE** Sixth great grandson of progenitor Nicholas Kegg. **DOUGLAS GAULE JR.** Seventh great grandson of progenitor Nicholas Kegg. **LISA GAULE** Sixth great granddaughter of progenitor Nicholas Kegg. **TERESA GAULE** aka "Terri" Sixth great granddaughter of progenitor Nicholas Kegg. **TWYLA ARLENE GAULE** Fifth great granddaughter of progenitor Nicholas Kegg.

GAULT

JEFFREY THOMAS GAULT Eighth great grandson of progenitor Nicholas Kegg.

GAUTHIER

TODD JAMES GAUTHIER Sixth great grandson of progenitor Nicholas Kegg.

GAYNOR

MEGAN LYNN GAYNOR Seventh great granddaughter of progenitor Nicholas Kegg.
MOLLY BROOKE GAYNOR Seventh great granddaughter of progenitor Nicholas Kegg.
WADE RANDALL GAYNOR Seventh great grandson of progenitor Nicholas Kegg.

GEARY

PATRICIA GEARY Sixth great granddaughter of progenitor Nicholas Kegg. **WILLIAM GEARY** aka "Bill", Sixth great grandson of progenitor Nicholas Kegg.

GEBHARDT

COREY GEBHARDT Sixth great grandson of progenitor Nicholas Kegg. **MATTHEW GEBHARDT** Sixth great grandson of progenitor Nicholas Kegg.

[3555A] Westover Funeral Home (IA) [3555B] The Des Moines Register (IA) Aug 27, 2017

GEDDES

CORY O. GEDDES Sixth great grandson of progenitor Nicholas Kegg. **MAYA GEDDES** Seventh great granddaughter of progenitor Nicholas Kegg. **MEADOW LEE GEDDES** Sixth great granddaughter of progenitor Nicholas Kegg.

GEILING

KIMBERLY ANN GEILING aka "Kimmy", Fifth great granddaughter of progenitor Nicholas Kegg. **WILLIAM GEILING** Fifth great grandson of progenitor Nicholas Kegg.

GEISE

ADAM GEISE Sixth great grandson of progenitor Nicholas Kegg. **CHRISTA GEISE** Sixth great granddaughter of progenitor Nicholas Kegg. **ERIN GEISE** Sixth great granddaughter of progenitor Nicholas Kegg. **JACQUELYN GEISE** Sixth great granddaughter of progenitor Nicholas Kegg. **LAWRENCE D. GEISE** Fifth great grandson of progenitor Nicholas Kegg.

GEIST

BRODY FORREST GEIST Sixth great grandson of progenitor Nicholas Kegg.
LOGAN ANTHONY GEIST Sixth great grandson of progenitor Nicholas Kegg.

GELENSER

SUSAN E. GELENSER Sixth great granddaughter of progenitor Nicholas Kegg.

GELLER

CONNIE GELLER Fifth great granddaughter of progenitor Nicholas Kegg. **CORTNEY P. GELLER** Sixth great grandson of progenitor Nicholas Kegg. **GARY GELLER** Fifth great grandson of progenitor Nicholas Kegg. **JACKLYN GELLER** Fifth great granddaughter of progenitor Nicholas Kegg. **JANET GELLER** [3556] (1947 – 2021) daughter of John and Dorothy (Diehl) Geller married Mr. Hershberger with whom she was mother of (1). Janet cleaned for several local businesses and organizations including SVVFC, the Post Office, VFW and Geisel Funeral Home. She was a member of the Ladies Auxiliary, VFW and SVVF Company. Janet was also a member of Christ Victory Church, New Buena Vista. Janet was an amazing and kindhearted person that was loved by all who knew her. **JOHN J. GELLER** [3557] (1920 – 1984) son of George and Essie (Kerr) Geller, married Dorothy M. Diehl with whom he was father of (7). John was a retired employee of the Pennsylvania Turnpike Commission, a U.S. Army veteran of World War II, member of VFW Post #4440 of Schellsburg, and St. Mark's United Church of Christ at New Buena Vista. **MARY JANE GELLER** Fifth great granddaughter of progenitor Nicholas Kegg. **PAUL KERR GELLER** [3558] (1925 – 1972) son of George and Essie (Kerr) Geller, was a carpenter and a member of St. Marks United Church of Christ, New Buena Vista. He was a veteran of World War Two, a member of VFW Post 4440 in Schellsburg, and a member of the New Baltimore Sportsmen's Club. **ROBERT JOHN GELLER** [3558A] (1951 – 2001) son of Jacob and Dorothy (Diehl) Geller married Nancy Mellott with whom he was father of (1). Robert was a business coordinator for Seagate in Pittsburgh. **SARA R. GELLER** [3559] (1923 – 2020) daughter of George and Essie (Kerr) Geller married William E. Oyler with whom she was mother of (4). Sara was

---

[3556] Bedford Gazette (PA) Nov 30, 2021 [3557, 3558] Bedford County Historical Society obituary obtained by D. Sue Dible [3858A] Bedford Inquirer (PA) May 11, 2001, obtained by Bob Rose [3559] Bedford Gazette (PA) April 16, 2020, obtained by Bob Rose

a cook in the school cafeteria for Bedford Area School District. She was a member of Bedford United Methodist Church. **SHAWN R. GELLER** Sixth great grandson of progenitor Nicholas Kegg. **VESTA A. GELLER** Fifth great granddaughter of progenitor Nicholas Kegg. **VESTA P. GELLER** [3560] (1914 – 1980) daughter of George and Essie (Kerr) Geller, married Ernest John Renchy with whom she was mother of (1). Vesta was a member of Bethel Chapter 71, Order of Eastern Star.

GELVIN

NIKOLE GELVIN Seventh great granddaughter of progenitor Nicholas Kegg.

GENESER

KATHRYN LYNN GENESER aka "KitKat", Fifth great granddaughter of progenitor Nicholas Kegg. **RANDALL GENESER** aka "Randy", Fifth great grandson of progenitor Nicholas Kegg.

GENGER

ANN GENGER Seventh great granddaughter of progenitor Nicholas Kegg. **CECE GENGER** Eighth great granddaughter of progenitor Nicholas Kegg. **CLARA GENGER** Eighth great granddaughter of progenitor Nicholas Kegg. **DRU GENGER** Seventh great grandson of progenitor Nicholas Kegg. **JAKE EZRA GENGER** Eighth great grandson of progenitor Nicholas Kegg. **JAMES MATTHEW GENGER** Eighth great grandson of progenitor Nicholas Kegg. **NOAH MICHAEL GENGER** Seventh great grandson of progenitor Nicholas Kegg.

GEORGESON

CHRISTINE GEORGESON Sixth great granddaughter of progenitor Nicholas Kegg.
DAVID GEORGESON Sixth great grandson of progenitor Nicholas Kegg.
GAIL E. GEORGESON Sixth great granddaughter of progenitor Nicholas Kegg.
RICHARD GEORGESON aka Rick" Sixth great grandson of progenitor Nicholas Kegg.

GERBASI

CYNTHIA JENEE GERBASI Fifth great granddaughter of progenitor Nicholas Kegg.
MARTIN G. GERBASI Fifth great grandson of progenitor Nicholas Kegg.

GERBER

DAVID GERBER aka "Scott" Sixth great grandson of progenitor Nicholas Kegg. **DIANE J. GERBER** Sixth great granddaughter of progenitor Nicholas Kegg. **KYLE J. GERBER** Seventh great grandson of progenitor Nicholas Kegg. **LAUREN MICHELLE GERBER** Seventh great granddaughter of progenitor Nicholas Kegg.

GERVAIS

CHRISTIAN GERVAIS Seventh great grandson of progenitor Nicholas Kegg.
NOAH GERVAIS Seventh great grandson of progenitor Nicholas Kegg.

[3560] Bedford County Historical Society obituary obtained by D. Sue Dible

GIARTH

LYRIC GIARTH [3560A] (2013 – 2015) daughter of Michael and Jessabelle (Barnes) Giarth passed through the Heavenly Gates after a tragic fire at their home.

GIBBENS

ARDELL HARLAN GIBBENS [3560B] (1933 – 2013) daughter of Harlan and Louise (Stuckey) Gibbens married twice, first to Rex Leibert with whom she was mother of (4). Later she married William Weiman with whom she was mother of (1). **BONNIE GIBBENS** Sixth great granddaughter of progenitor Nicholas Kegg. **GARY STUART GIBBENS** Sixth great grandson of progenitor Nicholas Kegg. **PEGGY LOUISE GIBBENS** (1938 – 2012) daughter of Harlan and Louise (Stuckey) Gibbens married Lester Honts with whom she was mother of (3). Later, she married Ronald Edward Barnes. **MICHAEL HARLEN GIBBENS** Sixth great grandson of progenitor Nicholas Kegg. **RICHARD WILLIAM GIBBENS** (1935 – 2016) son of Harlan and Louise (Stuckey) Gibbens married Mernalee May Harms with whom he was father of (4). He later married Roberta Kay Jardin. **RICHARD WILLIAM GIBBENS JR.** Sixth great grandson of progenitor Nicholas Kegg.

GIBBONEY

DOROTHY ELIZABETH GIBBONEY [3561] (1915 – 1988) daughter of Oliver and Mary Alice (Gump) Gibboney.

GIBSON

ALISON GIBSON Sixth great granddaughter of progenitor Nicholas Kegg. **DEE ANN GIBSON** Fourth great granddaughter of progenitor Nicholas Kegg. **JERALD R. GIBSON** [3561A] (1948 – 2018) aka "Jerry" son of Roland and Doris (Rice) Gibson married and was father of (2). Jerry was an engineer at Pfizer. **JIM GIBSON** Sixth great grandson of progenitor Nicholas Kegg. **JO ANN GIBSON** [3561B] (1938 – 2016) daughter of Roland and Doris (Rice) Gibson, married Wendell Jerry McCormick with whom she was mother of (6). Jo Ann worked briefly at TRW in Ogallala before going to work at Golden Ours Convalescent Home in Grant. It was at Golden Ours that she came to realize her passion and life's calling, to live a life in the service of others. Jo Ann found great meaning in the scripture Matthew 25:40: "The King will answer, 'Truly I say to you, as you have done it for one of the least of these brothers of Mine, you have done it for Me.'" Jo Ann started as a Care Staff Member and played an integral role in the formation of the Activity Department, eventually working her way into the director position. She had been involved with the activity department for nearly 30 years at the time of her retirement. Jo Ann was the proud recipient of the Perkins County Good Neighbor Award. **JUDITH ELLEN GIBSON** [3561C] (1942 – 2016) aka "Judy" daughter of Roland and Doris (Rice) Gibson married John Sharp with whom she was mother of (2).

GIERSDORF

LYNNE JANETTE GIERSDORF Fifth great granddaughter of progenitor Nicholas Kegg.

GIESY

CARLENE RENEA GIESY Seventh great granddaughter of progenitor Nicholas Kegg.
CAROLYN ELAINE GIESY aka "Mickey", Sixth great granddaughter of progenitor Nicholas Kegg.

[3560A] Bedford Gazette (PA) Jan 22, 2015, contributed by Bob Rose [3560B] Anderson Bethany Funeral Home (NM) [3561] Bedford County Historical Society obituary clipping obtained by D. Sue Dible [3561A] Lincoln Journal Star (NE) Feb 5, 2018 [3561B] Bullock-Long Funeral Home (CO) [3561C] Schrader Funeral Home and Crematory (MO)

CHELSEA E. GIESY Eighth great granddaughter of progenitor Nicholas Kegg. **DAWN GIESY** Seventh great granddaughter of progenitor Nicholas Kegg. **HOWARD MORRIS GIESY** [3562] (1914 – 1961) son of William and Leota (Kegg) Giesy, married Dolores Elaine Rose with whom he was father of (4). Howard was four years of age when his mother died. His father followed in death five years later. Howard was raised by neighbors George and Mathilda Clary. **HOWARD SCOTT GIESY** [3563] (1944 – 2022) son of Howard Morris and Dolores Elaine (Rose) Giesy married Regina Klein with whom he was father of (1). Later, he married Helen Hottenfeller with whom he was father of (3). Howard was a proud veteran of the United States Army serving in the Vietnam War. **KATHLEEN JEANNINE GIESY** aka "Kathy", Seventh great grandson of progenitor Nicholas Kegg. **LIAM SCOTT GIESY** Ninth great grandson of progenitor Nicholas Kegg. **LORI ANN GIESY** Seventh great granddaughter of progenitor Nicholas Kegg. **LYNN LORRIS GIESY** [3564] (1934 – 2017) aka "Skip", son of Howard and Dolores (Rose) Giesy married twice, first to Ruby Frances James and Later to Joan Patricia McGrail. Lynn had been employed as a Master Captain of large river boats with Consol Energy. **SHERRY JEAN GIESY** Seventh great granddaughter of progenitor Nicholas Kegg. **SIERRA GIESY** Eighth great granddaughter of progenitor Nicholas Kegg. **TAMARA MARIE GIESY** aka "Tamra", Eighth great granddaughter of progenitor Nicholas Kegg. **TANYR GIESY** Eighth great granddaughter of progenitor Nicholas Kegg. **TATUM GIESY** Eighth great granddaughter of progenitor Nicholas Kegg. **THOMAS H. GIESY** Eighth great grandson of progenitor Nicholas Kegg. **THOMAS HOWARD GIESY** Seventh great grandson of progenitor Nicholas Kegg. **TIFFANI GIESY** Eighth great granddaughter of progenitor Nicholas Kegg. **TRACI LYNN GIESY** Seventh great granddaughter of progenitor Nicholas Kegg. **WILLIAM ALTON GIESY** Sixth great grandson of progenitor Nicholas Kegg. **WILLIAM EUGENE GIESY** Seventh great grandson of progenitor Nicholas Kegg.

GIFFIN

ALEXIS ELAINE GIFFIN Seventh great granddaughter of progenitor Nicholas Kegg.
ASHLEY MARIE GIFFIN Eighth great granddaughter of progenitor Nicholas Kegg.
BENJAMIN ISAAC GIFFIN Seventh great grandson of progenitor Nicholas Kegg.
BENJAMIN M. GIFFIN aka "Ben", Seventh great grandson of progenitor Nicholas Kegg.
BETSY JO GIFFIN Sixth great granddaughter of progenitor Nicholas Kegg.
BRADLEY JOE GIFFIN Sixth great grandson of progenitor Nicholas Kegg. **BRADY GIFFIN** Seventh great grandson of progenitor Nicholas Kegg. **BRITON GIFFIN** Seventh great grandson of progenitor Nicholas Kegg. **CALVIN J. J. GIFFIN** [3564A] (1929 – 1975) son of Carl and Bessie (Kreis) Giffin, married Mary Lou Heil with whom he was father of (4). A former general supervisor of curriculum and instruction in the Bellaire School System, he had also been general supervisor of elementary and secondary education with the Martins Ferry School System. Serving the Bellaire High School football team as assistant coach for 18 years and assistant basketball coach for six years, he had also been the school track coach, and was director of the Bellaire Relays, an event that through his endevors had developed into one of the finest meets statewide. **CALVIN JEFFREY GIFFIN** Sixth great grandson of progenitor Nicholas Kegg. **CARL ALEXANDER GIFFIN** [3565] (1898 – 1979) son of James and Emma (Wise) Giffin, married Bessie M. Kreis with whom he was father of (2). Carl was a retired cost analyst for the Wheeling-Pittsburgh Steel, Benton Division, and was a member of Rock Hill Presbyterian Church and the Rock Hill Grange. **CAROL GIFFIN** Fifth great granddaughter of progenitor Nicholas Kegg. **CHESTER RUSSELL GIFFIN** [3565A] (1943 – 2018) son of Paul and Beatrice (Althar) Giffin married Linda J. (Leonard) with whom he was father of (3). Chester was a member of the Rock Hill Presbyterian Church, was a retired Iron worker of Local 549 and was a veteran of the United States Army. **CHESTER R. GIFFIN** Sixth great grandson of progenitor Nicholas Kegg.

[3562] p.40 Pittsburgh Press (PA) Jul 26, 1961 [3563] W. F. Conroy Funeral Home (PA) [3564] Herald Standard (PA) Sep 24, 2017 [3564A] Times Leader (OH) Oct 27, 1975 [3565] Wooster Daily Record (OH) Sep 13, 1979, obtained by D. Sue Dible [3565A] Wilson Funeral Home (OH)

COLTON GIFFIN Eighth great grandson of progenitor Nicholas Kegg. **ELLEN J. GIFFIN** Sixth great granddaughter of progenitor Nicholas Kegg. **EWING ALEXANDER GIFFIN** Fifth great grandson of progenitor Nicholas Kegg. **GLEN GIFFIN** Fifth great grandson of progenitor Nicholas Kegg. **ISABELL GIFFIN** Seventh great granddaughter of progenitor Nicholas Kegg. **JACOB PAUL GIFFIN** Seventh great grandson of progenitor Nicholas Kegg. **JESSE MARSHALL GIFFIN** Seventh great grandson of progenitor Nicholas Kegg. **JILLIAN ELIZABETH GIFFIN** Seventh great granddaughter of progenitor Nicholas Kegg. **JOAN ELIZABETH GIFFIN** [3565B] (1928 – 2016) aka "Jo" daughter of Russell and Helen (Kreis) Giffin, married James Clifford Belt with whom she was mother of (4). Jo became an art teacher and continued her love of art for her entire life. She loved painting, ceramics and jewelry making as well as doing crafts with her children and grandchildren. Jo was instrumental in the re-establishment of the Delphos Historical Society. In 1968, she was named the Tri-County Woman of the Year. **JONAS PAUL GIFFIN** Seventh great grandson of progenitor Nicholas Kegg. **KIMBERLY J. GIFFIN** [3565C] (1967 – 2015) daughter of Chester R. and Linda (Leonard) Giffin married Emile "Todd" Medicus with whom she was mother of (2). Kimberly was a member of the Labor's Union #1149 Wheeling, and a member of the Rock Hill Presbyterian Church Bellaire. **KRISTIE GIFFIN** Sixth great granddaughter of progenitor Nicholas Kegg. **LANDON GIFFIN** Eighth great grandson of progenitor Nicholas Kegg. **LOGAN GIFFIN** Seventh great grandson of progenitor Nicholas Kegg. **LOU ANN GIFFIN** Sixth great granddaughter of progenitor Nicholas Kegg. **MIRIAM GIFFIN** [3565D] (1937 – 2015) daughter of Robert and Laura (Alther) Giffin, married H. Ralph Kinney with whom she was mother of (7). Miriam was a retired dietary supervisor at Barnesville Hospital and also worked for several years at the Belmont County ASC office. Miriam will always be remembered for her devotion to her family, her love of cooking, and her dedication to her community. **NOAH GIFFIN** Seventh great grandson of progenitor Nicholas Kegg. **PAUL EDWARD GIFFIN** Sixth great grandson of progenitor Nicholas Kegg. **R. PAUL GIFFIN** Fifth great grandson of progenitor Nicholas Kegg. **ROBERT PAUL GIFFIN** [3566] (1906 – 1979) son of James and Emma (Wise) Giffin, married Laura Beatrice Alther with whom he was father of (5). Robert was a retired employee of Krob Dairy, Bridgeport, and a member and trustee of the Rock Hill Presbyterian Church, and a member of the Rock Hill Grange. **RUSSELL E. GIFFIN** [3567] (1901 – 1981) son of James and Emma (Wise) Giffin, married Helen E. Kreis with whom he was father of (1). Russell was employed by the Farm Bureau for 40 years and was a retired insurance agent for Grange Mutual Insurance Co. **RYLEIGH NICOLE GIFFIN** Eighth great granddaughter of progenitor Nicholas Kegg. **SARAH GIFFIN** Seventh great granddaughter of progenitor Nicholas Kegg. **STEPHEN GIFFIN** Sixth great grandson of progenitor Nicholas Kegg. **VALERIE SUE GIFFIN** Sixth great granddaughter of progenitor Nicholas Kegg.

GIGLIOTTI

EMELIA GIGLIOTTI Seventh great granddaughter of progenitor Nicholas Kegg. **JANET E. GIGLIOTTI** Sixth great granddaughter of progenitor Nicholas Kegg. **MATILDA GIGLIOTTI** Sixth great granddaughter of progenitor Nicholas Kegg. **NICOLE GIGLIOTTI** Seventh great granddaughter of progenitor Nicholas Kegg. **PETER GIGLIOTTI** Sixth great grandson of progenitor Nicholas Kegg. **RALPH A. GIGLIOTTI** Sixth great grandson of progenitor Nicholas Kegg.

GILBERT

ANNA GILBERT Seventh great granddaughter of progenitor Nicholas Kegg.
JACK ARTHUR GILBERT [3568] (1929 – 1999) son of Arthur and Margaret (Chaney) Gilbert, was a

---

[3565B] Lima News (OH) Feb 3, 2016 [3565C] Wilson Funeral Homes – Bridgeport [3565D] Harper Funeral Home (OH) contributed by D. Sue Dible [3566] library obituary clipping obtained by D. Sue Dible [3567] Lima News (OH) Dec 23, 1981, obtained by D. Sue Dible [3568] Tulsa World (OK) Jan 26, 1999

retired salesman. **JUSTIN GILBERT** Seventh great grandson of progenitor Nicholas Kegg. **KENDRA GILBERT** Fifth great granddaughter of progenitor Nicholas Kegg. **LYDIA J. GILBERT** Sixth great granddaughter of progenitor Nicholas Kegg. **NATHAN GILBERT** Seventh great grandson of progenitor Nicholas Kegg. **ROBERT E. GILBERT** Sixth great grandson of progenitor Nicholas Kegg. **ROBERT LEON GILBERT** (1918 – 1984) aka "Bobbie", son of Arthur and Margaret (Chaney) Gilbert, married Rosa K. Bean. **SHANE MICHAEL GILBERT** Ninth great grandson of progenitor Nicholas Kegg. **SHANNON GILBERT** Fifth great granddaughter of progenitor Nicholas Kegg. **WILLIAM LYNN GILBERT** Sixth great grandson of progenitor Nicholas Kegg.

GILDERSLEEVE

FERN RUTH GILDERSLEEVE Sixth great granddaughter of progenitor Nicholas Kegg.

GILE

ALISSA HOPE GILE Eighth great granddaughter of progenitor Nicholas Kegg. **CHLOE GILE** Eighth great granddaughter of progenitor Nicholas Kegg. **JAMES ALLEN GILE**, aka "Jimmie", Seventh great grandson of progenitor Nicholas Kegg. **JILLISSA GILE** Eighth great granddaughter of progenitor Nicholas Kegg. **JOHN GILE** Seventh great grandson of progenitor Nicholas Kegg. **JOSHUA ALLEN GILE** Eighth great grandson of progenitor Nicholas Kegg. **KENNEDY GILE** Eighth great granddaughter of progenitor Nicholas Kegg. **MELISSA ELLEN GILE** [3568A] (1968 – 1994) daughter of Wilbur and Constance (Macauley) Gile. Melissa was employed by Burke Marketing Co. in Nevada. She was an Air Force veteran.

GILLASPIE

BROOKLYNN ROSE GILLASPIE Eighth great granddaughter of progenitor Nicholas Kegg. **DONOVAN EUGENE GILLASPIE** Eighth great grandson of progenitor Nicholas Kegg.

GILLESPIE

JOHN W. GILLESPIE aka "Jack" Fifth great grandson of progenitor Nicholas Kegg.
JOSEPH W. GILLESPIE Fifth great grandson of progenitor Nicholas Kegg.
MAUREEN GILLESPIE [3568B] (1951 – 2009) daughter of Joseph and Marie (Clay) Gillespie, married Kevin S. Koch with whom she was mother of (1). Maureen graduated from St. Agnes Hospital School of Nursing, Philadelphia as an RN, and worked in Orthopedics/Med- Surgical and Nursing Administration for 22 years. **SCOTT HANKS GILLESPIE** (1908 – 1908) son of Zenas and Charlotte (Hanks) Gillespie.

GILLETT

ERIC ALLEN GILLETT Fifth great grandson of progenitor Nicholas Kegg.

GILLETTE

CHRISTOPHER GILLETTE Seventh great grandson of progenitor Nicholas Kegg.
HAYLEY ANN GILLETTE Seventh great granddaughter of progenitor Nicholas Kegg.

[3568A] p.5 Des Moines Register (IA) Jan 3, 1995   [3568B] Richmond Times-Dispatch (VA) Sept 6, 2009

GILLIAM

JERRY GILLIAM Sixth great grandson of progenitor Nicholas Kegg. **LORENE GILLIAM** aka "Lori", Sixth great granddaughter of progenitor Nicholas Kegg. **YVONNE GILLIAM** Sixth great granddaughter of progenitor Nicholas Kegg.

GILLIAN

JESSIE M. GILLIAN [3569] (1885 – 1957) daughter of John and Catherine (Knouf) Gillian.
NETA JEAN GILLIAN, (1891 –?)) daughter of John and Catherine (Knouf) Gillian.
PEARL GILLIAN [3570] (1881 – 1950) daughter of John and Catherine (Knouf) Gillian, married Miles Richards with whom she was mother of (2).

GILLILAN

DAREL J. GILLILAN [3570A] (1919 – 1979) son of Delaney and Frances (Williams) Gillilan, married Madeleine Elva Peberty with whom he was father of (2). Darel served in the U.S. Army during World War II. Darel was involved in a variety of businesses including the service station business, the automobile business and the insurance and finance business. He was an avid supporter of numerous community and athletic activities while in Rawlins. Darel was a member of the Rawlins I.O.O.F Lodge, the Rawlins Elks, the American Legion the VFW and the Cowboy Joe Club. **DELANEY J. GILLILAN** [3571] (1896 – 1968) aka "Dee", son of John and Catherine (Knouf) Gillian, married Frances Williams with whom he was father of (2). Dee operated the Fort Steele filling station before moving to Rawlins in 1960 when he took his retirement. **GRACIE VIRGINIA GILLILAN** [3571A] (1922 – 2013) daughter of Richard and Vernice Gillian, married Herbert Price with whom she was mother of (5). 1942, Gracie went to work as a civilian clerk/typist at the U.S. Naval Training Station at Farragut. After several years as a homemaker, Gracie worked 15 years as an assembler, machine operator, and keyboard line lead for the Post Falls' manufacturing company known as Clare Pendar, C.P Clare, and eventually General Instrument Corporation. **FERN LOLA GILLILAN** [3572] (1915 – 1993) daughter of Delaney and Frances (Williams) Gillilan, married John Joseph McIntyre with whom she was mother of (4).
NETIA JEAN GILLILAN [3573] (1891 – 1945) daughter of John and Cassie (Knouf) Gillilan married Harvey Christopher Schrengohst with whom she was mother of (4). **RICHARD J. GILLILAN** Fifth great grandson of progenitor Nicholas Kegg. **RICHARD NIXON GILLILAN** [3574] (1893 – 1956) aka "Dick", son of John and Catherine (Knouf) Gillian married Vernice with whom he was father of (2). Dick was a Great Northern railway worker. **VERNON LEROY GILLILAN** [3575] (1920 – 2009) son of Richard and Vernice Gillilan, married Anna Lewis. Vern attended elementary school in Sandpoint, Idaho but suffered from polio and did not finish school. He was inducted into the United States Army in 1942 and served with the 274th Infantry Regiment in a Rhineland Central European campaign. He was a pistol marksman, and his military occupational specialty was meatcutter. He was honorably discharged at the grade of Corporal on December 15, 1946. Following Vern's military service, he moved to Spokane, Washington, where the Gillilan family had relocated. For several years Vern was employed by McKesson & Robbins Inc. **WILLIAM JOSEPH GILLILAN** [3575A] (1955 – 2003) son of Darl and Madeleine (Peberdy) Gillilan. William had been employed as an insurance agent.

[3569] Ainsworth Star Journal (NE) June 27, 1957 [3570] Eddyville Tribune (IA) Apr 13,1950, obtained by D. Sue Dible [3570A] Carbon County Library obituary contributed by D. Sue Dible [3571] p. 23 - Rawlins Daily Times (WY) April 30, 1968, obtained by D. Sue Dible [3571A] Bonner County Daily Bee (ID) Feb 5, 2013 [3572] Arizona Republic (AZ) July 3, 1993, obtained by D. Sue Dible [3573] Reno Gazette-Journal (NV) April 23, 1945 [3574] Spokane Chronicle (WA) April 21, 1956 [3575] Spokesman-Review (WA) Nov13, 2009 [3575A] Las Vegas Sun (NV) Feb 20, 2003 contributed by D. Sue Dible

GIMSON

IAN BOYD GIMSON Eighth great grandson of progenitor Nicholas Kegg.
KAI LILIAN GIMSON Eighth great granddaughter of progenitor Nicholas Kegg.

GINGERICK

ADAIR JEAN GINGERICK Sixth great granddaughter of progenitor Nicholas Kegg.
AUDREY L. GINGERICK Sixth great granddaughter of progenitor Nicholas Kegg.
ERIN MARIE GINGERICK Sixth great granddaughter of progenitor Nicholas Kegg.

GIVENS

KRYSTLE GIVENS Eighth great granddaughter of progenitor Nicholas Kegg.
MEGAN GIVENS Eighth great granddaughter of progenitor Nicholas Kegg.

GLADWELL

EMMA GLADWELL Eighth great granddaughter of progenitor Nicholas Kegg.
JOHN ANDREW GLADWELL aka "Drew", Seventh great grandson of progenitor Nicholas Kegg.
NICHOL SUZANNE GLADWELL aka "Nikki", Seventh great granddaughter of progenitor Nicholas Kegg.

GLEE

BETTY LOU GLEE [3576] (1931 – 2016) daughter of William and Genevieve (Clark) Glee, married Warren E. Scherbarth with whom she was mother of (6). Betty was a schoolteacher, in addition she worked hard raising a garden, sewing and cooking for her family. She was a lifelong member of the Lutheran Church. Sundays were spent going to church and having company for dinner. She enjoyed many Ladies Aide meetings with her friends at church. She also loved to listen to the Sunday school children singing. **CHARLES D. GLEE** Fifth great grandson of progenitor Nicholas Kegg.
ROBERT C. GLEE [3577] (1933 – 1933) infant son of William and Genevieve (Clark) Glee.
WAYNE WILLIAM GLEE [3578] (1934 – 1952) son of William and Genevieve (Clark) Glee. Wayne was enrolled in a three-year pastor's preparatory course at Moody Bible Institute when he contracted bulbar polio that took his life.

GLENNEY

ABBY GLENNEY Seventh great granddaughter of progenitor Nicholas Kegg. **JACK GLENNEY** Seventh great grandson of progenitor Nicholas Kegg. **LILY GLENNEY** Seventh great granddaughter of progenitor Nicholas Kegg.

GLESSNER

ANDREA LYNN GLESSNER Sixth great granddaughter of progenitor Nicholas Kegg. **PHILIP NEAL GLESSNER** [3579] (1984 – 2006) son of Thomas and Karen (Hay) Glessner. Philip was employed by Somerset Barn Equipment.

[3576] Sheridan County Journal Star (NE) June 27, 2016 [3577] Morrill Mail (NB) Sep 21, 1933 [3578] p.7 Lincoln Star (NB) Sep 17, 1952 [3579] The Daily American (PA) May 17, 2006

GLOSSER

CHRISTOPHER J. GLOSSER Seventh great grandson of progenitor Nicholas Kegg.
CORI MARIE GLOSSER Seventh great granddaughter of progenitor Nicholas Kegg.
NOAH GLOSSER Seventh great grandson of progenitor Nicholas Kegg.

GLOTFELTY

ALISSA GLOTFELTY Sixth great granddaughter of progenitor Nicholas Kegg.
JOSHUA GLOTFELTY Sixth great grandson of progenitor Nicholas Kegg.

GLOVER

ABIGAIL GLOVER Eighth great granddaughter of progenitor Nicholas Kegg.
DIANA MAE GLOVER [3579A] (1940 – 2013) daughter of Henry and Evelyn (Thompson) Glover married twice. Diana married Ray Douglas Burtch with whom she was mother of (3). Later, she married David Ray Wedel. Diana was a member of the Confederated Salish and Kootenai Tribes and started her professional career working for them. She also was a legal secretary for several law firms and newspapers. Her Latin classes sparked a lifelong interest in wordsmithing that evolved into her love for Scrabble. She was the Scrabble queen and there is only a short list that could best her. She had an amazing ability for recalling names and family connections. Diana crocheted beautiful afghans and every new addition to the family received one of her creations. She loved watching college basketball and was an avid Zags fan. Diana also had a passion for gardening; her flower beds bloomed from early spring to late fall. **ELEANOR GLOVER** Eighth great granddaughter of progenitor Nicholas Kegg.
JEANETTE GLOVER Fifth great granddaughter of progenitor Nicholas Kegg.
PAMELA L. GLOVER aka "Pam" Fifth great granddaughter of progenitor Nicholas Kegg.
SHERYL GLOVER aka "Duzzie" Fifth great granddaughter of progenitor Nicholas Kegg.

GLUNT

DAVID VAUGHAN GLUNT Seventh great grandson of progenitor Nicholas Kegg.
GERALD PAUL GLUNT Sixth great grandson of progenitor Nicholas Kegg. **MAGGIE GLUNT** Sixth great granddaughter of progenitor Nicholas Kegg. **MARY GLADYS GLUNT** Fifth great granddaughter of progenitor Nicholas Kegg. **SAMUEL DAVID GLUNT** Sixth great grandson of progenitor Nicholas Kegg. **SAMUEL JOSEPH GLUNT** [3579B] (1944 – 2011) son of Samuel B. and Mary Ellen (Hahn) Glunt married twice, first to Phyllis Lane Joy with whom he was father of (3). Later, he married Linda (Mrus) Hansel. Samuel was a US Army Veteran of the Vietnam War. He also worked and retired from American Welding after 30 plus years of service. Samuel was a member of the Lordstown Christian Church and the Newton Falls VFW Post #3332. He loved Disney World, horseshoes, and NASCAR-Dale Earnheart.

GNAGEY

ELIZABETH K. GNAGEY Fifth great granddaughter of progenitor Nicholas Kegg.
ERIN L. GNAGEY Sixth great granddaughter of progenitor Nicholas Kegg. **GLENDA GNAGEY** Fifth great granddaughter of progenitor Nicholas Kegg. **GRETCHEN GNAGEY** Sixth great granddaughter of progenitor Nicholas Kegg. **MARGIE G. GNAGEY** Fifth great granddaughter of progenitor Nicholas Kegg. - **PRESTON KEITH GNAGEY** [3579C] (1935 – 2015) son of Homer and

---

[3579A] Lake County Leader & Advertiser (Polson, MT) April 26, 2013 [3579B] Carl W Hall Funeral Service (OH) [3579C] Vistoso Funeral Home, Oro Valley, Arizona contributed by D. Sue Dible

Tolva (Hillegas) Gnagey, married Fay Rhodes with whom he was father of (2). Preston spent many years in the accounting field in the DC area, Maryland, Virginia and Ohio. After retirement, he became an excellent chef and connoisseur of wines. He was an avid golfer, playing several times a week. Preston was a friendly man with a positive spirit.

GOCHNOUR

LINDA M. GOCHNOUR Sixth great granddaughter of progenitor Nicholas Kegg.

GODARD

J. RICHARD GODARD Sixth great grandson of progenitor Nicholas Kegg.

GODBEY

JAMIE GODBEY Fifth great granddaughter of progenitor Nicholas Kegg. **JEFF GODBEY** Fifth great grandson of progenitor Nicholas Kegg. **KELLY GODBEY** Fifth great granddaughter of progenitor Nicholas Kegg.

GODDEN

ANGELA KAY GODDEN Seventh great granddaughter of progenitor Nicholas Kegg.
AUSTIN GODDEN Seventh great grandson of progenitor Nicholas Kegg. **ERIC GODDEN** Seventh great grandson of progenitor Nicholas Kegg. **JUSTINA GODDEN** Seventh great granddaughter of progenitor Nicholas Kegg. **MATTHEW GODDEN** Seventh great grandson of progenitor Nicholas Kegg. **MICHELLE GODDEN** Seventh great granddaughter of progenitor Nicholas Kegg. **PHILLINA GODDEN** Seventh great granddaughter of progenitor Nicholas Kegg.
RAYMOND LEROY GODDEN [3579D] (1947 – 2016) son of Glen and Viola (Laird) Godden married twice, first to Connie Munyon with whom he was father of (4). Later, he married Donna Jo Ernst with whom he was father of (2). Raymond began driving a rock truck for Charlie Gorman. He would eventually drive a milk route picking up the raw milk in the Kellerton area. He had a bread truck route delivering bread to southern Iowa and northern Missouri; and he would eventually move to over-the-road truck driving delivering a variety of products cross country. Raymond's other passion and love was for his Lord. **WILLIAM LEROY GODDEN** aka "Willie", Seventh great grandson of progenitor Nicholas Kegg.

GODSEY

JAMES LEE GODSEY Sixth great grandson of progenitor Nicholas Kegg.
SHERRI LYNNE GODSEY Sixth great granddaughter of progenitor Nicholas Kegg.

GODWIN

ASHLEY GODWIN Seventh great granddaughter of progenitor Nicholas Kegg.
BRIANNA GODWIN Seventh great granddaughter of progenitor Nicholas Kegg.
JILLIAN GODWIN Sixth great granddaughter of progenitor Nicholas Kegg.

[3579D] Mount Ayr Record News (IA) May 4, 2016

GOETZ

LINDA GOETZ Sixth great granddaughter of progenitor Nicholas Kegg. **MICHAEL GOETZ** Sixth great grandson of progenitor Nicholas Kegg. **SHIRLEY GOETZ** Sixth great granddaughter of progenitor Nicholas Kegg.

GOFF

JAYCEE LYNN GOFF Seventh great granddaughter of progenitor Nicholas Kegg.
TYLER GOFF Seventh great grandson of progenitor Nicholas Kegg.

GOLDIZEN

BRENDEN LEE GOLDIZEN Seventh great grandson of progenitor Nicholas Kegg.
CANDANCE ANNETTE GOLDIZEN Sixth great granddaughter of progenitor Nicholas Kegg.

GOLDMAN

GLENN S. GOLDMAN Sixth great grandson of progenitor Nicholas Kegg.

GOLDSTEIN

HARRIS GOLDSTEIN Eighth great grandson of progenitor Nicholas Kegg.

GOMOCHAK

STEPHEN T. GOMOCHAK [3580] (1964 – 1996) son of John and Vicki (Oster) Gomochak. Stephen was a maitre d' for various restaurants.

GOMPF

ADEANA GOMPF Sixth great granddaughter of progenitor Nicholas Kegg. **JUDITH A. GOMPF** Sixth great granddaughter of progenitor Nicholas Kegg. **LLOYD CHRIS GOMPF** Sixth great grandson of progenitor Nicholas Kegg. **ROBERT DEAN GOMPF** Fifth great grandson of progenitor Nicholas Kegg. **VICKIE GOMPF** Sixth great granddaughter of progenitor Nicholas Kegg.

GONSMAN

JAMIE GONSMAN Seventh great granddaughter of progenitor Nicholas Kegg.

GONZALEZ

ELI GONZALEZ Ninth great grandson of progenitor Nicholas Kegg.

GOOD

MARGARET GOOD [3581] (1922 – 1990) daughter of Jerome and Jennie (Boose) Good. Margaret had been employed as a medical secretary and X-ray technician for many years. Miss Good was a member of the A.A.R.P. of Forked River.

[3580] p.B4 - Vindicator (OH) July 29, 1996, obtained by D. Sue Dible [3581] Daily American (PA) June 7, 1990, Myersdale Library transcribed by Jessica Orr

GOODLIN

ALLISON GOODLIN Seventh great granddaughter of progenitor Nicholas Kegg.
ALYSHA GOODLIN Seventh great granddaughter of progenitor Nicholas Kegg.
ASHLEY GOODLIN Seventh great granddaughter of progenitor Nicholas Kegg.
CIARRA GOODLIN Seventh great granddaughter of progenitor Nicholas Kegg.
DONALD E. GOODLIN Fifth great grandson of progenitor Nicholas Kegg. **DONALD E. GOODLIN** Sixth great grandson of progenitor Nicholas Kegg. **ERIC GOODLIN** Seventh great grandson of progenitor Nicholas Kegg. **KEVIN LARRY GOODLIN** Sixth great grandson of progenitor Nicholas Kegg. **LARRY RUDELL GOODLIN** aka "Doug", Fifth great grandson of progenitor Nicholas Kegg. **LELAND R. GOODLIN** Sixth great grandson of progenitor Nicholas Kegg.
LELAND RUSSELL GOODLIN aka "Skip", Fifth great grandson of progenitor Nicholas Kegg.
LINDSEY GOODLIN Seventh great granddaughter of progenitor Nicholas Kegg.
LOIS HAZEL GOODLIN [3582] (1940 – 1997) daughter of Rudell and Edith (Calhoun) Goodlin. Lois was a member of the former Redeemer Lutheran Church in Cookport. She was employed by Westinghouse in Blairsville and the FMC in Homer City. **RODNEY ALLAM GOODLIN** Sixth great grandson of progenitor Nicholas Kegg. **SANDRA KAY GOODLIN** Fifth great granddaughter of progenitor Nicholas Kegg. **SETH GOODLIN** Seventh great grandson of progenitor Nicholas Kegg. **SONYA K GOODLIN** Sixth great granddaughter of progenitor Nicholas Kegg. **VAUGHN BRIAN GOODLIN** Sixth great grandson of progenitor Nicholas Kegg. **WANDA L. GOODLIN** Fifth great granddaughter of progenitor Nicholas Kegg.

GOODLIVE

LOETA MAE GOODLIVE [3583] (1887 – 1972) daughter of George and Martha (Cagg) Goodlive, married Abraham Graffis McVeigh with whom she was mother of (1).
MARGARET ELEANOR GOODLIVE [3584] (1889 – 1957) daughter of George and Martha (Cagg) Goodlive, married Chris Henry Gompf with whom she was mother of (4). Margaret assisted her husband for many years in operating the Gompf Greenhouse on S. Mulberry St.

GOODMAN

GREGORY GOODMAN Fifth great grandson of progenitor Nicholas Kegg.
JACQUELINE GOODMAN Fifth great granddaughter of progenitor Nicholas Kegg.

GOON

TOD GOON Seventh great grandson of progenitor Nicholas Kegg.

GOODWIN

ENZO GOODWIN Ninth great grandson of progenitor Nicholas Kegg. **KATIE GOODWIN** Eighth great granddaughter of progenitor Nicholas Kegg. **KYLE GOODWIN** Eighth great grandson of progenitor Nicholas Kegg.

GORDON

ARIANA GORDON Seventh great granddaughter of progenitor Nicholas Kegg.

[3582] p. 18 - Indiana Gazette (PA) June 13, 1997 [3583] p.2 The Logan Daily News (OH) Jan 21, 1972 [3584] p.2 The Logan Daily News (OH) Feb 18, 1957

CHRISTIE GORDON Seventh great granddaughter of progenitor Nicholas Kegg.
HELEN M. GORDON [3585] (1919 – 2000) daughter of Thomas and Grace (Kegg) Gordon married twice; first to Charles Krist with whom she was mother of (1). Later, she married William C. Walus. Helen retired from the Coventry School System in 1974 after 30 years of teaching. She was a member of the Delta Kappa Gamma, the Portage Lakes OES, and was an active member of the Green Valley United Methodist Church.   **MARIJEAN ROSE GORDON** [3586] (1937 – 2009) daughter of Theodore and Mildred (Richmond) Gordon married twice; first to Jesse Joseph Ayala with whom she was mother of (10). Later, she married James Louis May.   **MARY JANE GORDON** [3587] (1916 – 1995) daughter of Thomas and Grace (Kegg) Gordon, married Robert Warren Lythgoe with whom she was mother of (1). Mary Jane was employed as a schoolteacher, retiring after 43 years. She was a member of West Des Moines United Methodist Church, Delta Kappa Gamma, and Sigma Kappa.
PENNY LYNN GORDON Seventh great granddaughter of progenitor Nicholas Kegg.

GORE

JOHN DANIEL GORE Sixth great grandson of progenitor Nicholas Kegg.
MOLLY JEAN GORE Sixth great granddaughter of progenitor Nicholas Kegg.

GORSUCH

LANE THOMAS GORSUCH Seventh great grandson of progenitor Nicholas Kegg.

GOTTSHALL

CORY GOTTSHALL Sixth great grandson of progenitor Nicholas Kegg.
JACOB GOTTSHALL Sixth great grandson of progenitor Nicholas Kegg.

GOULD

KELSEY RENEE GOULD Seventh great granddaughter of progenitor Nicholas Kegg.
ROBERT TYLER GOULD Seventh great grandson of progenitor Nicholas Kegg.
RONALD GOULD Seventh great grandson of progenitor Nicholas Kegg.

GOURLEY

ANN BOOSE GOURLEY Fifth great granddaughter of progenitor Nicholas Kegg.

GOVER

CHARLES HALE GOVER Fifth great grandson of progenitor Nicholas Kegg.

GRABILL

ALEXIS GRABILL Seventh great granddaughter of progenitor Nicholas Kegg.

[3585] p.B5 - Akron Beacon Journal (OH) May 1, 2000 [3586] Denver Post, The (CO) June 3, 2009 [3587] p.D13 - Akron Beacon Journal (OH) Dec15, 1995

GRABLE

JUSTIN GRABLE Seventh great grandson of progenitor Nicholas Kegg.
REBECCA GRABLE Seventh great granddaughter of progenitor Nicholas Kegg.

GRADY

BRANDON PATRICK GRADY Seventh great grandson of progenitor Nicholas Kegg. **CATHERINE ANN GRADY** Sixth great granddaughter of progenitor Nicholas Kegg. **MARY BETH GRADY** Sixth great granddaughter of progenitor Nicholas Kegg. **STEPHANIA MARIE GRADY** Seventh great granddaughter of progenitor Nicholas Kegg. **STEPHEN PATRICK GRADY** Sixth great grandson of progenitor Nicholas Kegg. **SUSAN MAE GRADY** [3588] (1898 – 1974) daughter of Hiram and Anna (Kegg) Grady. Susan was a schoolteacher, having taught in the Shade Township, Conemaugh Township and Shanksville-Stoneycreek Township School Districts.

GRAF

DAVID LEE GRAF Seventh great grandson of progenitor Nicholas Kegg.
PRESTON EUGENE GRAF Seventh great grandson of progenitor Nicholas Kegg.

GRAFFIOUS

BONITA GRAFFIOUS Sixth great granddaughter of progenitor Nicholas Kegg.
DENNIS GRAFFIOUS Sixth great grandson of progenitor Nicholas Kegg.
HEATHER GRAFFIOUS Seventh great granddaughter of progenitor Nicholas Kegg.
JANET GRAFFIOUS Sixth great granddaughter of progenitor Nicholas Kegg.
LINDA GRAFFIOUS Sixth great granddaughter of progenitor Nicholas Kegg.
PHILIP LAWRENCE GRAFFIOUS Sixth great grandson of progenitor Nicholas Kegg.
PATRICIA GRAFFIOUS Sixth great granddaughter of progenitor Nicholas Kegg.
SAMANTHA GRAFFIOUS Seventh great granddaughter of progenitor Nicholas Kegg.
SAMUEL LEROY GRAFFIOUS [3588A] aka "Sam" (1951 – 2018) son of Samuel and Betty (Batzel) Graffious married Donna Jean Allen with whom he was father of (3). Sam was the owner of S & S Janitorial Service which he founded in 1978. He was a bit of a workaholic, but he did enjoy crabbing, fishing, and trips to Pennsylvania to see family. **SAMUEL LEROY GRAFFIOUS III** Seventh great grandson of progenitor Nicholas Kegg. **SUSAN GRAFFIOUS** Sixth great granddaughter of progenitor Nicholas Kegg.

GRAHAM

ALAN GRAHAM Sixth great grandson of progenitor Nicholas Kegg. **ALMEDA GRAHAM** (1925 – 1925) daughter of Earl and Esther (Mikkelsen) Graham. **ALVAN LEON GRAHAM** Fifth great grandson of progenitor Nicholas Kegg. **ANITA KAY GRAHAM** Sixth great granddaughter of progenitor Nicholas Kegg. **BERTHA LUELLA GRAHAM** [3589] (1890 – 1992) daughter of John and Eva (Mead) Graham, married Robert Leander Underwood with whom she was mother of (1). Bertha was a retired music teacher for the Georgia Cumberland Conference of the Seventh-day Adventist Church. **CAROL NETA GRAHAM** (1917 – 1999) daughter of Earl and Esther (Mikkelsen) Graham, married Wildred Daniel Nevis with whom she was mother of (2). **CHARLES/CHUCK CASPER GRAHAM**, (1940 – 1976) aka "Buddy" son of Irving and Mildred (Mize) Graham married four times; first to

---

[3588] Daily American (PA) Feb 21, 1974, Myersdale Library transcribed by Sally Statler/Jesse Davis [3588A] Gonce Funeral Service, P.A. [3589] Chattanooga Historical Society obituary clipping obtained by D. Sue Dible

Sandra Lee Richardson with whom he was father of (1). He married Geraldine Rebecca McRee with whom he was father of (1). He married Edna M. Kleckner. Later, he married Terry (nee unknown) with whom he was father of (1). **CHARLES CASPER GRAHAM** Sixth great grandson of progenitor Nicholas Kegg. **CHARLES JASPER GRAHAM** [3590] (1879 – 1961) son of Jacob and Ella (Costteter) Graham married three times; first to Mary E. Lamper, then to Ethel E. Barry later to Beatrice (nee unknown) **CHARRAN DOWNING GRAHAM** [3591] (1910 – 1977) son of Elzie and Amanda (Schuster) Graham, married Mary Evelyn Lewis Lyle. **CHARRAN GLENDENNING GRAHAM** Fifth great grandson of progenitor Nicholas Kegg. **CHESTER F. GRAHAM** Fifth great grandson of progenitor Nicholas Kegg. **CHLOE EMELINE GRAHAM** [3591A] (1930 – 2012) daughter of Elzie and Amanda (Schuster) Graham, married Fred E. Acuff with whom she was mother of (3). Chloe was a teacher's aide at Oak Hill Elementary School, and a former employee of Broughton Hospital. She was a very active member of Table Rock Seventh-Day Adventist Church, where she served in many official capacities and offices. Chloe will always be remembered for her encouragement and helpfulness to others. **CINDY GRAHAM** Fifth great granddaughter of progenitor Nicholas Kegg. **CODY JO GRAHAM** Sixth great grandson of progenitor Nicholas Kegg. **DARLENE MARIE GRAHAM** Fifth great granddaughter of progenitor Nicholas Kegg. **DARRELL JAMES GRAHAM** Fifth great grandson of progenitor Nicholas Kegg. **DORA VIOLA GRAHAM** (1888 – 1909) daughter of John and Eva (Mead) Graham. **EARL MEADE GRAHAM** (1891 – 1966) son of John and Eva (Mead) Graham, married Esther Mikkelsen with whom he was father of (5). **EARNEST EARL GRAHAM** Fourth great grandson of progenitor Nicholas Kegg. **EDITH BER GRAHAM** (1897 – 1985) daughter of John and Eva (Mead) Graham, married Wayland M. Hamren. **ELAINE EMILIA GRAHAM** Sixth great granddaughter of progenitor Nicholas Kegg. **ELEANOR SUE GRAHAM** Fifth great granddaughter of progenitor Nicholas Kegg. **ELLA NETTIE PEARL GRAHAM** (1896 – 1995) aka "Pearl", daughter of John and Eva (Mead) Graham married three times; first to Mr. Hile, later to John Dalton with whom she was mother of (6). Lastly, she married Mr. Fingerle. **ERICA REBECCA GRAHAM** Seventh great granddaughter of progenitor Nicholas Kegg. **ERMA EMELINE GRAHAM** Fifth great granddaughter of progenitor Nicholas Kegg. **FLORABELLE KATHLEEN GRAHAM** (1949 – 2023) daughter of Alvan and Lucille (Peterson) Graham married John Wayne Wear with whom she was mother of (6). **FLORENCE ELVA GRAHAM**, (1886 – 1976) daughter of John and Eva (Mead) Graham married five times; first to Albert S. Wright with whom she was mother of (2). Later, she married William Howard Mills, Mr. Van Kirk and Alfred Eugene Christe. **FLOY O. GRAHAM** Fourth great grandson of progenitor Nicholas Kegg. **FRANK J. GRAHAM** (1882 – 1908) son of John and Eva (Mead) Graham. **GLORIA B. GRAHAM** [3592] (1877 – 1943) daughter of Jacob and Ella (Costteter) Graham married Edward R. Walsh. **GRACE DAY GRAHAM** (1887 – 1982) aka "Gracie", daughter of Jacob and Ella (Costteter) Graham, married Theodore Davenport Thomas with whom she was mother of (2). **HAZEL SERENA GRAHAM** [3593] (1894 – 1972) daughter of John and Eva (Mead) Graham married twice; first to Archie Lafayette Underwood with whom she was mother of (2). Later, she married Ernest W. Schroeder. **IRVING LAVERNE GRAHAM** [3594] (1918 – 2004) son of Elzie and Amanda (Schuster) Graham, married Mildred Francis Mize with whom he was father of (6). **JACOB LOUIS GRAHAM** [3595, 3596] (1855 – 1912) aka "Jake", son of James and Mary Ann (Kegg) Graham, married Ella Costteter with whom he was father of (7). Jake was a hard worker all his life, starting in business without a dollar, in the manufacture of buggies, he built up a large business, which required the employment of a large force of mechanics, with one of the largest factories in Ligonier to accommodate the industry. **JAMES LEVI GRAHAM** [3597] (1891 – 1964) son of Jacob and Ella (Costteter) Graham married twice, first to Frances Blanche Batz and later, to Esther Lorine Johnson. **JEFFREY MICHAEL GRAHAM** Sixth great grandson of progenitor Nicholas Kegg.

[3590] p.25 - San Diego Union (CA) June 10, 1961 [3591] p38 Evening Star (DC) March 31, 1977 [3591A] p.A2 - News Herald (NC) Oct14, 2012 [3592] Chicago Tribune (IL) Jan 22, 1943 [3593] The San Bernardino County Sun (CA) March 1, 1972 [3594] p.3 - Idaho Statesman (Boise, ID) Aug 26, 2004 [3595] p.6 - Goshen Weekly News (IN) June 7, 1912 [3596] Alvord's History of Noble County F. Bowen, Publisher 1902 [3597] p.50 - San Diego Union (CA) May 21, 1964

JIMMY GRAHAM Sixth great grandson of progenitor Nicholas Kegg. **KAREN GRAHAM** Fifth great granddaughter of progenitor Nicholas Kegg. **KATHRYN ANN GRAHAM** Fifth great granddaughter of progenitor Nicholas Kegg. **KATIE HELEN GRAHAM** (1929 – 1986) daughter of William and Helena (Houseman) Graham, married twice; first to James Albert Baehler with whom she was mother of (4). Later she married Clayton Grant Lawrence. **LARRY W. GRAHAM** [3598] (2002 – 2022) son of Harry and Rhonda (Cagg) Graham loved fishing, mudding, and riding in the truck with his dad. Larry loved to eat. **LAURIE KAY GRAHAM** Sixth great granddaughter of progenitor Nicholas Kegg. **LAVERNE GRAHAM** aka "Lonnie", Fifth great grandson of progenitor Nicholas Kegg. **LESTER MEADE GRAHAM** [3599] (1925 – 2005) son of Earl and Esther Mikkelsen. Lester was employed as a truck driver. He was a veteran of WWII. **LILITH ANNABEL GRAHAM**, aka "Lily", Sixth great granddaughter of progenitor Nicholas Kegg. **LOTTIE MAE GRAHAM** [3600] (1927 – 2020) daughter of William and Helena (Houseman) Graham married Watson D. Ledbetter with whom she was mother of (5). Lottie worked in a sewing factory before World War II. She was working as a waitress when she met and married her husband, Watson Ledbetter Jr. They raised their family in Southern California before moving to New Mexico when they purchased their first restaurant. A few years later they moved to Houston where they owned and operated several restaurants, their last restaurant was Ledbetter's Steak and Bar-b-q. Lottie took great enjoyment coming up with specials for the restaurants as well as cooking for her family and friends. Through the years she was quite a seamstress for her girls, always making outfits to match each other. Lottie was a very social lady and was a member of a quilting group, "The Cut-Ups". She was an active member of the Church of Jesus Christ of Latter-Day Saints. **LUCAS ELZIE GRAHAM** Sixth great grandson of progenitor Nicholas Kegg. **LUKE GRAHAM** Seventh great grandson of progenitor Nicholas Kegg. **MABEL B. GRAHAM** [3601] (1883 – 1945) daughter of Jacob and Ella (Costteter) Graham, married Hugh Frederick Hutchison with whom she was mother of (2). **MALEA ANNE GRAHAM** Sixth great granddaughter of progenitor Nicholas Kegg. **MARIE ANNA GRAHAM** [3602] (1890 -?) daughter of Jacob and Ella (Costteter) Graham, married Willard Milburn Pearson. **MARK GRAHAM** Sixth great grandson of progenitor Nicholas Kegg. **MAYNA D. GRAHAM** [3603] (1885 – 1964) daughter of Charles and Catherine (Rex) Graham married twice; first to Claude Emmet Elder and later to Charles Anthony Coda. **MIA GRAHAM** Sixth great granddaughter of progenitor Nicholas Kegg. **MICHAEL THOMAS GRAHAM** Seventh great grandson of progenitor Nicholas Kegg. **MICHELLE GRAHAM** Sixth great granddaughter of progenitor Nicholas Kegg. **MILDRED MARIE GRAHAM** Fifth great granddaughter of progenitor Nicholas Kegg. **MITCHELL GRAHAM** Sixth great grandson of progenitor Nicholas Kegg. **NATHAN GRAHAM** Seventh great grandson of progenitor Nicholas Kegg. **PAULINE MARGARETE GRAHAM** [3604] (1895 – 1983) daughter of Jacob and Ella (Costteter) Graham, married Gordon Serrell Nathans with whom she was mother of (1). **PHILLIP GRAHAM** Sixth great grandson of progenitor Nicholas Kegg. **RALPH ELWARD GRAHAM** Fifth great grandson of progenitor Nicholas Kegg. **RANDY GRAHAM** Fifth great grandson of progenitor Nicholas Kegg. **ROMAN GRAHAM** Eighth great grandson of progenitor Nicholas Kegg. **RONAL DOWNING GRAHAM** Fifth great grandson of progenitor Nicholas Kegg. **RUTH ANN GRAHAM** Fifth great granddaughter of progenitor Nicholas Kegg. **SANDY GRAHAM** (1941 – 1941) son of Earnest and Francis (Johnson) Graham. **SETH GRAHAM** Seventh great grandson of progenitor Nicholas Kegg. **STEPHANIE LYNEE GRAHAM** Sixth great granddaughter of progenitor Nicholas Kegg. **STEVEN JAMES GRAHAM** aka "Charles" Fifth great grandson of progenitor Nicholas Kegg. **THELMA BELLE GRAHAM** [3605] (1915 – 1998) daughter of Elzie and Amanda Schuster) Graham, married Clarence Richard Ellyson with whom she was mother of (1). Thelma was a member of Table Rock Seventh Day Adventist Church. **TRACY DENISE GRAHAM** [3606] (1970 – 2009) daughter of Charles and Geraldine (McRee) Graham was mother of (2).

[3598] Black-Epperson Funeral Home (OH) [3599] The Fresno Bee (CA) Nov 20, 2005 [3600] Bluebonnet News (TX) Dec 4, 2020 [3601] Ligonier Leader (IN) Dec 6, 1945, obtained by D. Sue Dible [3602] Fort Wayne News Sentinel (IN) June 7, 1919 [3603] Ligonier Leader (IN) Jul 1964, obtained by D. Sue Dible [3604] Chicago Tribune (IL) Dec 4, 1983 [3605] News Herald (NC) March 1998, obtained by D. Sue Dible [3606] Athens Banner-Herald (GA) June 4, 2009, obtained by D. Sue Dible

VICTORIA LYNN GRAHAM aka "Vicki", Fifth great granddaughter of progenitor Nicholas Kegg.
WAYNE HUBERT GRAHAM [3607] (1923 – 2014) son of Earl and Esther (Mikkelsen) Graham married Nicolene Marie Cheney with whom he was father of (3). **WILLIAM EARNEST GRAHAM** [3608] (1879 – 1963) aka "Willie", son of John and Eva (Mead) Graham married twice; first to Flora A. Murdock. Later, he married Helena Vanada Houseman with whom he was father of (4).
WILMONT CHARRAN GRAHAM Sixth great grandson of progenitor Nicholas Kegg.
ZOE ELIZABETH GRAHAM Seventh great granddaughter of progenitor Nicholas Kegg.

GRAMA

AMBER GRAMA Sixth great granddaughter of progenitor Nicholas Kegg.
HEATHER MICHELLE GRAMA Sixth great granddaughter of progenitor Nicholas Kegg.
MELISSA ANN GRAMA Sixth great granddaughter of progenitor Nicholas Kegg.

GRANDA

KIMBERLY ANN GRANDA (1969 – 1969) Fifth great granddaughter of progenitor Nicholas Kegg.

GRANT

ELLIE GRANT Seventh great granddaughter of progenitor Nicholas Kegg. **JACK GRANT** Seventh great grandson of progenitor Nicholas Kegg. **ROSALEE GRANT** Seventh great granddaughter of progenitor Nicholas Kegg. **ZELDA GRANT** Seventh great granddaughter of progenitor Nicholas Kegg.

GRAPES

ANGELINE RACHELLE GRAPES Sixth great granddaughter of progenitor Nicholas Kegg.
ESTHER MARIE GRAPES Sixth great granddaughter of progenitor Nicholas Kegg.
HANNAH FAITH GRAPES Seventh great granddaughter of progenitor Nicholas Kegg.
JAMES ANDREW GRAPES aka "Jimmy", Seventh great grandson of progenitor Nicholas Kegg.
JAMES ANDREW GRAPES Sixth great grandson of progenitor Nicholas Kegg.
KATRINA GRAPES Seventh great granddaughter of progenitor Nicholas Kegg.
LEAH ROSE GRAPES Sixth great granddaughter of progenitor Nicholas Kegg.
MARK JAMES GRAPES Sixth great grandson of progenitor Nicholas Kegg.
MICHELLE LYNNE GRAPES Sixth great granddaughter of progenitor Nicholas Kegg.
NATHAN D. GRAPES Sixth great grandson of progenitor Nicholas Kegg. **PRISCILLA GRAPES** Seventh great granddaughter of progenitor Nicholas Kegg. **SAWYER GRAPES** Eighth great grandson of progenitor Nicholas Kegg.

GRASSI

DOROTHY ANN GRASSI aka "Dottie", Fifth great granddaughter of progenitor Nicholas Kegg.
MARY LOUISE GRASSI Fifth great granddaughter of progenitor Nicholas Kegg.

GRASSMAN

JAIME GRASSMAN Seventh great granddaughter of progenitor Nicholas Kegg.
JESSICA GRASSMAN Seventh great granddaughter of progenitor Nicholas Kegg.

[3607] Chino Valley Funeral Home (AZ) June 21, 2014 [3608] p.17 The San Bernardino County Sun (CA) Sep 27, 1963

JOSHUA ANDREW GRASSMAN aka "Josh", Seventh great grandson of progenitor Nicholas Kegg.

GRAY

BILLIE DEAN GRAY [3609] (1924 – 2015) son of John and Florence (Laird) Gray, married Nancy Bandy with whom he was father of (4). Billie proudly served our country in the U.S. Navy. He earned a BS degree in Electrical Engineering. Billie worked in civil service for over 30 years. **ETHAN THOMAS GRAY** Seventh great grandson of progenitor Nicholas Kegg. **JIMMY LLOYD GRAY** Fifth great grandson of progenitor Nicholas Kegg. **LOREN GRAY** Fifth great grandson of progenitor Nicholas Kegg. **NANCY GRAY** [3610] (1891 – 1957) aka "Nannie", daughter of Richard and Sarah (Riley) Knouf, married Hugh Gray with whom she was mother of (2). Nannie was united with the Greenfield Methodist church, and for many years taught a class of small children in the Primary Department of the Sunday school. **RANDY GRAY** Sixth great grandson of progenitor Nicholas Kegg. **RUSSELL GRAY** Sixth great grandson of progenitor Nicholas Kegg. **SARAH AGNES GRAY** (1889 – 1973) daughter of Hugh and Nancy (Knouf) Gray, married John Elmer Abbott with whom she was mother of (9). **TERRY GRAY** Sixth great grandson of progenitor Nicholas Kegg. **TOM GRAY** Sixth great grandson of progenitor Nicholas Kegg.

GREEN

EMMA JEAN GREEN [3611] (1858 – 1934) daughter of Jacob and Eleanor (Kegg) Greene married twice; first to Abraham E. Stutzman and later to Dr. Jesse Hutchinson Hall. **ETTA M. GREEN** (1860 – 1956) daughter of Jacob and Eleanor (Kegg) Greene married twice; first to Rev. Frank D. Allen with whom she was mother of (1). Later, she married Joel Yeager. **JOHNNIE GRAHAM GREEN** Sixth great grandson of progenitor Nicholas Kegg. **JOSEPH R. GREEN** Sixth great grandson of progenitor Nicholas Kegg. **KANE ALLEN GREEN** Seventh great grandson of progenitor Nicholas Kegg. **KELLY MAXINE GREEN** Sixth great granddaughter of progenitor Nicholas Kegg. **RICHARD J. GREEN** Sixth great grandson of progenitor Nicholas Kegg.

GREENAWALT

ALISA GREENAWALT Seventh great granddaughter of progenitor Nicholas Kegg.
JOANN GREENAWALT Sixth great granddaughter of progenitor Nicholas Kegg.
JUDY L. GREENAWALT Fifth great granddaughter of progenitor Nicholas Kegg.
MARK K. GREENAWALT Sixth great granddaughter of progenitor Nicholas Kegg.
PEGGY J. GREENAWALT Fifth great granddaughter of progenitor Nicholas Kegg.
SCOTTY GREENAWALT Seventh great grandson of progenitor Nicholas Kegg.
THOMAS C. GREENAWALT Seventh great grandson of progenitor Nicholas Kegg.
THOMAS C. GREENAWALT Sixth great grandson of progenitor Nicholas Kegg.
TODD GREENAWALT Seventh great grandson of progenitor Nicholas Kegg.
TROY GREENAWALT Seventh great grandson of progenitor Nicholas Kegg.
WALTER LEE GREENAWALT Sixth great grandson of progenitor Nicholas Kegg.

GREENE

CHARLES FREDERICK GREENE [3612] (1924 – 1987) aka "Chuck", son of Henry and Margaret (Owens) Green married Rosalie J. McInnis with whom he was father of (4). Chuck owned and operated Greene's Diner in Woburn for 35 years. Chuck was a U.S. Navy veteran of World War II. He was a

---

[3609] Watson-Hunt Funeral Home Perry, Georgia [3610] Library obituary clipping obtained by D. Sue Dible [3611] p.2 - Elyria Chronicle Telegram (OH) Dec 12, 1934 [3612] St. Lucie News Tribune (FL) Sep 22, 1987

member of the Knights of Columbus of Stuart, BPO Elks of Woburn and Stuart, and a past president of the Kiwanis of Woburn. **CHARLES FREDERICK GREENE II** Fifth great grandson of progenitor Nicholas Kegg. **CHARLES FREDERICK GREEN III** Sixth great grandson of progenitor Nicholas Kegg. **CHARLIE GREENE** Seventh great grandson of progenitor Nicholas Kegg.
ELIZABETH LOUISE GREEN/E [3613] (1921 – 2006) aka "Betty", daughter of Henry and Margaret (Owens) Green married Emery Robert Vlasaty with whom she was mother of (5). Later, she married George Richard Jones. Betty was president of Texas School Food Services in Arlington, Texas. She received her bachelor's degree from North Texas University. **EVA A. GREENE** [3614] (1856 – 1943) daughter of Jacob and Eleanor (Kegg) Greene married twice; first to Jesse Minier with whom she was mother of (2). Later she married Civil War veteran James A. Steece. Eva was a member of the Seventh Day Adventist church. **INFANT GREENE** (1927 – 1927) son of Henry and Margaret (Owens) Green. **INFANT GREENE** (1930 – 1930) son of Henry and Margaret (Owens) Green. **ISABELLE GREENE** Seventh great granddaughter of progenitor Nicholas Kegg. **JACQUELINE GREENE** Sixth great granddaughter of progenitor Nicholas Kegg. **JENNIFER ARLENE GREENE** Sixth great granddaughter of progenitor Nicholas Kegg. **KEVIN GREENE** Sixth great grandson of progenitor Nicholas Kegg. **MISHKA ROSE GREENE** Eighth great granddaughter of progenitor Nicholas Kegg. **PAUL HENRY GREENE** aka "Duke", Fifth great grandson of progenitor Nicholas Kegg.
RICHARD ALLAN GREENE Fifth great grandson of progenitor Nicholas Kegg.
RICHARD ALLAN GREENE II Sixth great grandson of progenitor Nicholas Kegg.
RICHARD GREENE Fourth great grandson of progenitor Nicholas Kegg.
RYAN EDWARD GREENE Sixth great grandson of progenitor Nicholas Kegg.
THERESE MARIE GREENE Fifth great granddaughter of progenitor Nicholas Kegg.

GREENFIELD

MONICA MICHELE GREENFIELD Sixth great granddaughter of progenitor Nicholas Kegg.

GREENLEAF

ANDREW T. GREENLEAF Fifth great grandson of progenitor Nicholas Kegg.
MATTHEW J. GREENLEAF Fifth great grandson of progenitor Nicholas Kegg.
REBECCA L. GREENLEAF aka "Becky", Fifth great granddaughter of progenitor Nicholas Kegg.
THOMAS A. GREENLEAF Fifth great grandson of progenitor Nicholas Kegg.

GREGG

ROMAN OSIRIS GREGG Ninth great grandson of progenitor Nicholas Kegg.

GREGORY

WILLIAM MICHAEL GREGORY Sixth great grandson of progenitor Nicholas Kegg.

GREVEY

COLT GREVEY Ninth great grandson of progenitor Nicholas Kegg.

GRICE

BRYAN CHRISTOPHER GRICE Seventh great grandson of progenitor Nicholas Kegg.

[3613] St. Lucie News Tribune (FL) Oct 25, 2006 [3614] Journal and Courier (Lafayette, Indiana) April 9, 1943

GRIDER

JOELLE SUZETTE GRIDER Fifth great granddaughter of progenitor Nicholas Kegg.
BILL GRIDER Fifth great grandson of progenitor Nicholas Kegg.

GRIFFIE

EVERETT DALE GRIFFIE Fifth great grandson of progenitor Nicholas Kegg.
HELEN LOUISE GRIFFIE Fifth great granddaughter of progenitor Nicholas Kegg.
RICHARD ALLEN GRIFFIE Fifth great grandson of progenitor Nicholas Kegg.
TAMMY LYNN GRIFFIE Fifth great granddaughter of progenitor Nicholas Kegg.

GRIFFIN

BRANDON GRIFFIN Fifth great grandson of progenitor Nicholas Kegg. **COLTON P. GRIFFIN** Fifth great grandson of progenitor Nicholas Kegg. **DEVIN GRIFFIN** Sixth great grandson of progenitor Nicholas Kegg. **GARY D. GRIFFIN** Sixth great grandson of progenitor Nicholas Kegg. **LINDA GRIFFIN** Sixth great granddaughter of progenitor Nicholas Kegg.

GRIFFITH

ARTHUR GRIFFITH Sixth great grandson of progenitor Nicholas Kegg.
EDGAR Z. GRIFFITH [3615] (1915 – 1989) son of Benjamin and Edna (Flohr) Griffith. Edgar was a farmer. **NANCY RUTH GRIFFITH** Sixth great granddaughter of progenitor Nicholas Kegg.
TWILA JENE GRIFFITH Sixth great granddaughter of progenitor Nicholas Kegg.
WILLIAM ARTHUR GRIFFITH Sixth great grandson of progenitor Nicholas Kegg.

GRIFFITHS

ALEX GRIFFITHS Eighth great grandson of progenitor Nicholas Kegg. **EMMA GRIFFITHS** Eighth great granddaughter of progenitor Nicholas Kegg. **JULIANA GRIFFITHS** Seventh great granddaughter of progenitor Nicholas Kegg. **XANDER GRIFFITHS** Seventh great grandson of progenitor Nicholas Kegg.

GRIGG

GERTRUDE DEE GRIGG [3616] (1923 – 1925) daughter of George and Cleo (Laird) Grigg aged one year, ten months and twenty-two days. Her mother preceded her in death just eleven days. The life of the darling baby was short and sweet. It appeared she had been sent to earth to take her mother home, but God in His mercy spared her a few days longer that her presence might somewhat comfort the sorrowing dear ones. She seemed too pure for earth. Everything she encountered was either nice or pretty, and to every request made to her she invariably responded, "All right." While the home had been deeply overshadowed with gloom, for over two years, owing to the great suffering of her dear mother, her sweet smile, gentle ways and loving heart often dispelled the gloom. Never having been tainted with sin or evil of this world, her passing has been merely a transfer from earth to God's garden.

GRIMES

CECIL ASHLAND GRIMES JR. [3617] (1924 – 1998) son of Cecil and Mary (Diehl) Grimes, married

---

[3615] The News Journal (DE) Oct 19, 1989 [3616] Mount Ayr Record-News, 1925/IAGENWEB transcribed by Sharon R. Becker [3617] p.7 Cumberland Times News (MD) Aug 1, 1998

Angela Grahame. Cecil was the retired owner and operator of Cecil's Corner Cafe on Park Street, and he was a retired employee of C&P Telephone Company. He was a member of the Maryland Fraternal Order of Police, a life member of the Cumberland Outdoor Club, Veterans of Foreign Wars Henry Hart Post #1411, F.O.E. #245 Eagles, V.F.W. Distinguished Supporter, member of several bowling leagues, and was a former coach in Little League. He was a veteran of the U.S. Army in World War II.

DANIEL SNYDER GRIMES [3618] (1912 – 1987) aka "Bush", son of Daniel and Amelia (Smith) Grimes, married C. Elizabeth Avey with whom he was father of (1). Bush was of the Protestant faith, a member of Everett Fire Company #1 since 1944 where he had served as a driver, was on the investigating committee for one year, served as auditor for one year, trustee for two years, served on several carnival committees, was assistant chief for three years, and served as chief from 1962 - 1965, then again from 1967 - 1976. He retired from Exxon Corp. after 35 years of service, was a member of the Exxon Retirement Club, and had been assistant manager at Bedford Midway, North and Cove Valley. He and his wife owned and operated the Everett Flower Shop. **DIANE GRIMES** Seventh great granddaughter of progenitor Nicholas Kegg. **DONNA GRIMES** Seventh great granddaughter of progenitor Nicholas Kegg. **HOLLY C. GRIMES** Sixth great granddaughter of progenitor Nicholas Kegg. **JASON M. GRIMES** Sixth great grandson of progenitor Nicholas Kegg. **LAUREN GRIMES** Sixth great granddaughter of progenitor Nicholas Kegg. **MARY ELIZABETH GRIMES** [3619] (1917 – 2005) daughter of Daniel and Amelia (Smith) Grimes, married Gerald Homer Bowser with whom she was mother of (2). Mary was a homemaker who enjoyed her family and church. **ROBERT W. GRIMES** Sixth great grandson of progenitor Nicholas Kegg. **TORI ARLENE GRIMES** Sixth great granddaughter of progenitor Nicholas Kegg.

GRIMM

AUSTIN GRIMM Eighth great grandson of progenitor Nicholas Kegg. **EMMA GRIMM** Eighth great granddaughter of progenitor Nicholas Kegg. **HAZEL GRIMM** Eighth great granddaughter of progenitor Nicholas Kegg. **WESLEY GRIMM** Eighth great grandson of progenitor Nicholas Kegg.

GRINDLE

SUSAN GRINDLE Fifth great granddaughter of progenitor Nicholas Kegg. **WILLIAM GRINDLE** aka "Bill", Fifth great grandson of progenitor Nicholas Kegg.

GRISSINGER

LYNN D. GRISSINGER Sixth great granddaughter of progenitor Nicholas Kegg **SAMANTHA GRISSINGER** Seventh great granddaughter of progenitor Nicholas Kegg. **SCOTT R. GRISSINGER** Sixth great grandson of progenitor Nicholas Kegg. **TYLER GRISSINGER** Seventh great grandson of progenitor Nicholas Kegg.

GROSE

MARGARET C. GROSE [3620] (1918 – 2010) daughter of Rev. John and Fannie (Cessna) Grose, married Louis Earl Armiger with whom she was mother of (2). Margaret was a 1939 graduate of Sibley Hospital, Washington, D.C., and was a registered nurse. She was a member of St. Paul's United Methodist Church in Kensington.

[3618] pg. 12 - Bedford Gazette (PA) July 24, 1987 [3619] p.3 - Bedford Inquirer (PA) Feb 4, 2005, obtained by Bob Rose [3620] Gazette.Net (MD) March 3, 2010

GROSS

ALLISON L. GROSS Seventh great granddaughter of progenitor Nicholas Kegg.
CLARENCE CHARLES GROSS [3621] (1919 – 1980) son of Clarence and Lena (Diehl) Gross, married Helen J. Heller. **JOHN A. GROSS** Sixth great grandson of progenitor Nicholas Kegg.
JOHN A. GROSS Seventh great grandson of progenitor Nicholas Kegg. **JOHN ARTHUR GROSS** [3622] (1926 – 2004) aka "Jack", son of Clarence and Lena (Diehl) Gross, married Lois with whom he was father of (2). **JOYCE GROSS** Sixth great granddaughter of progenitor Nicholas Kegg.

GROSSMAN

LIZZIE GROSSMAN Eighth great granddaughter of progenitor Nicholas Kegg.
MICAH GROSSMAN Eighth great grandson of progenitor Nicholas Kegg.
NOAH GROSSMAN Eighth great grandson of progenitor Nicholas Kegg.
REGGIE GROSSMAN Eighth great grandson of progenitor Nicholas Kegg.

GROUP

BAILEY LYNN GROUP Eighth great granddaughter of progenitor Nicholas Kegg.

GROVE

ALEX GROVE Seventh great grandson of progenitor Nicholas Kegg.
HANNA GROVE Seventh great granddaughter of progenitor Nicholas Kegg.

GROWDEN

AMBER GROWDEN Fifth great granddaughter of progenitor Nicholas Kegg.
DEETTA IRENE GROWDEN Fourth great granddaughter of progenitor Nicholas Kegg.
ERIC LEE GROWDEN [3623] (1974 – 2014) son of Thomas and Althea (Kegg) Growden. Eric worked as a Property Maintenance Manager for Brajo Inc., for 7 years, and Walmart D.C. for 14 years. He was a member of Kennell's Mill Sportsman Club, Barrelville Sportsman Club, Pleasantville VFW Post #9219, Schellsburg VFW Post 4419, and Sons of the American Legion Post #113. He was an avid hunter and fisherman, loved the outdoors, four-wheeling, and riding his motorcycle. He had a strong faith, was conscientious, and proud of his work. **GERALD WALTER GROWDEN** Fourth great grandson of progenitor Nicholas Kegg. **GINA JEAN GROWDEN** Fifth great granddaughter of progenitor Nicholas Kegg. **HEATHER ANN GROWDEN** Fifth great granddaughter of progenitor Nicholas Kegg.
JACOB WALTER GROWDEN Fifth great grandson of progenitor Nicholas Kegg.

GRUBB

BARBARA GRUBB Fifth great granddaughter of progenitor Nicholas Kegg.
BONNIE JEAN GRUBB Fifth great granddaughter of progenitor Nicholas Kegg.
CODY ALLEN GRUBB Sixth great grandson of progenitor Nicholas Kegg.
DARIN ALLEN GRUBB Sixth great grandson of progenitor Nicholas Kegg. **DAWN GRUBB** Sixth great granddaughter of progenitor Nicholas Kegg. **TERI GRUBB** Sixth great granddaughter of progenitor Nicholas Kegg.

[3621] p.24 Pittsburgh Post Gazette (PA) July 31, 1980 [3622] Pittsburgh Post-Gazette (PA) Aug 4, 2004 [3623] Berkebile Funeral Home (PA) contributed by Bob Rose

GRUBE

MICHELLE ANN GRUBE Seventh great granddaughter of progenitor Nicholas Kegg.

GUDAKUNST

DOUGLAS GUDAKUNST Seventh great grandson of progenitor Nicholas Kegg.
RILEY GUDAKUNST Seventh great grandson of progenitor Nicholas Kegg.

GUERRA

ARYELLA ROSE GUERRA Ninth great granddaughter of progenitor Nicholas Kegg.
ROICE REY GUERRA Ninth great grandson of progenitor Nicholas Kegg.

GUESS

JENNA MARIE GUESS Sixth great granddaughter of progenitor Nicholas Kegg.
JUSTIN MIKHAEL GUESS Sixth great grandson of progenitor Nicholas Kegg.

GUINTER

JANICE GUINTER Fifth great granddaughter of progenitor Nicholas Kegg.
NANCY LYNN GUINTER Fifth great granddaughter of progenitor Nicholas Kegg.

GUIRRERI

CHRISTIAN WILLIAM GUIRRERI Sixth great grandson of progenitor Nicholas Kegg. **GAIL DEE GUIRRERI** Sixth great granddaughter of progenitor Nicholas Kegg. **JOSEPH LEE GUIRRERI** Sixth great grandson of progenitor Nicholas Kegg. **MARCY DELL GUIRRERI** Sixth great granddaughter of progenitor Nicholas Kegg.

GULA

JAKE GULA Seventh great grandson of progenitor Nicholas Kegg.
JESTEN GULA Seventh great grandson of progenitor Nicholas Kegg.

GUMMO

DYLAN GUMMO Sixth great grandson of progenitor Nicholas Kegg.
EMILY CHRISTINE GUMMO Sixth great granddaughter of progenitor Nicholas Kegg.
QUINTON JAMES GUMMO Sixth great grandson of progenitor Nicholas Kegg.

GUMP

ANN MARIE GUMP Fifth great granddaughter of progenitor Nicholas Kegg. **ANNA MARGARET GUMP** [3624] (1848 – 1938) aka "Maggie", daughter of John and Elizabeth (Stuckey) Gump, married John Quincy Adams Nycum with whom she was mother of (7). **BARBARA GUMP** Fourth great granddaughter of progenitor Nicholas Kegg. **BETTY JANE GUMP** [3625] (1920 – 2002) daughter of William and Georgia (Zembower) Gump, married Edward William Cox with whom she was mother of

---

[3624] Johnstown Tribune Democrat (PA) Aug 15, 1938, obtained by D. Sue Dible [3625] p.2 - Daily News (PA) Nov 7, 2002

(2). Betty was a member of Grace United Methodist Church, Somerset. She was a member of FOE Aerie 1801 Auxiliary. She was a 1938 graduate of Huntingdon High School. Reading, knitting and gardening were some of the pastimes she enjoyed. **CHARLES EDWARD GUMP** (1862 – 1890) son of John and Elizabeth (Stuckey) Gump, married Clara Belle Barnes with whom he was father of (4).
CHARLES HANKS GUMP [3626] (1884 – 1938) son of Charles and Clara (Barnes) Gump married twice; first to Elizabeth May Horner with whom he was father of (2). Later, he married Ruth E. (Suloff) Hart.
CHARLES RONALD GUMP [3626A] (1932 – 1983) son of Charles and Dorothy (McGraw) Gump, married Patricia Peterchuck with whom he was father of (6). **CHARLES W. GUMP** [3627] (1908 – 1989) son of Dr. Charles and Elizabeth (Horner) Gump, married Dorothy McGraw with whom he was father of (1). **CLARA BELLE GUMP** Fourth great granddaughter of progenitor Nicholas Kegg.
CLARENCE BARNDOLLAR GUMP [3628] (1878 – 1924) son of Henry and Elizabeth (Barndollar) Gump, married Arlene E. Frantz with whom he was father of (3).
CLARENCE BARNDOLLAR GUMP (1907 – 1989) son of Clarence and Arlene (Frantz) Gump, married Olene Ferguson with whom he was father of (1). **CONSTANCE GUMP** aka "Connie", Fourth great granddaughter of progenitor Nicholas Kegg. **CYNTHIA LEE GUMP** Sixth great granddaughter of progenitor Nicholas Kegg. **DARLIS GUMP** Fifth great granddaughter of progenitor Nicholas Kegg.
DAVID P. GUMP Sixth great grandson of progenitor Nicholas Kegg. **DAVID ROY GUMP** [3629] (1881 – 1953) son of Erastus and Marie (Black) Gump, married Maude Schulte. David was a Spanish War veteran. **DEBORAH KAREN GUMP** Fifth great granddaughter of progenitor Nicholas Kegg.
DEBORAH LOUISE GUMP aka "Debbie", Sixth great granddaughter of progenitor Nicholas Kegg.
DIANNE L GUMP [3630] (1952 – 2017) daughter of Robert and Alice (Tighe) Gump. Dianne was a talented woman with a passion for life and adventure. She loved and rode Harley Davidson motorcycles. She rode and showed horses that her family raised on their Barrett Road Farm. Her favorite show horse was names Chad Hanna. She also had a modeling career and restored panel trucks that were manufactured in the 1950's. Dianne was an excellent chef and owned & operated a catering business in Berea, Culinary Capers for many years. She had the distinction of catering for the Cleveland Browns along with Parker Hannifin & Figgie Gulfstream jets out of Cleveland Hopkins Airport. **DOROTHY GUMP** [3630A] (1923 – 2012) daughter of William and Georgia (Zembower) Gump, married Harry Hanks with whom she was mother of (1). Dorothy worked at Shaffer's Store and General Finance in Huntingdon. After moving to Everett, she was a seamstress at Barndollar Men's Shop and Beck's Men's Shop for over 23 years until retiring. A dedicated homemaker, Dorothy was a great cook who enjoyed caring for her home and family. She was a collector of Hummel figurines and was thoughtful of many different pets and animals, making her own donations to our local humane societies throughout the years. **DOROTHY HELEN GUMP** [3631] (1910 – 2008) daughter of Henry and Ethel (Young) Gump, married John Frederick Jackson. Dorothy was a member of Spanish Fort Presbyterian Church. She had co-written a Gump family genealogy book and had a deep appreciation of nature and enjoyed teaching sign language to her co-residents. She retired from the US Dept. of Health, Education and Welfare. **EDWARD GUMP** son of Charles and Clara (Barnes) Gump. **EDWARD GUMP** [3632] (1907 – 1969) aka "Andy", son of William and Georgia (Zembower) Gump. **ELIZABETH GUMP** [3633] (1909 – 1995) daughter of Samuel and Alice (Grove) Gump, married Jesse Wilson Snapp with whom she was mother of (1). Elizabeth was a retired Army Corps of Engineers secretary. **ELWOOD THEODORE GUMP** (1917 – 2010) son of William and Georgia (Zembower) Gump, married Gladys Carper.
ERASTUS JEREMIAH GUMP [3634] (1845 – 1923) son of John and Elizabeth (Stuckey) Gump, married Marie Zeigler Black with whom he was father of (2). Erastus was a leather goods merchant and a veteran of the 194th Regiment, Pennsylvania Infantry. **EVELYN GUMP** (1906 – 1906) daughter of William and Georgia (Zembower) Gump. **FREDERICK BLACK GUMP** [3635] (1874 – 1956) son of Erastus

---

[3626] p.2 - The Daily News (PA) Feb14,1938 [3626A] p7 E, The Plain Dealer (OH) Sep 8, 1983 contributed by D. Sue Dible [3627] p.63 Plain Dealer (Cleveland, Ohio) July 11, 1989 [3628] Bedford Gazette (PA) Jul 25, 1924, obtained by Bob Rose [3629] Independent (Long Beach, CA) Feb 26, 1953 [3630] The Plain Dealer (OH) June 4, 2017 [3630A] Bedford Gazette (PA) June 29, 2012, contributed by Bob Rose [3631] Hughes Cremation and Funeral Service in Daphne, AL [3632] p.2 -The Daily News (PA) Oct 10,1969 [3633] Bedford Inquirer (PA) Jan 27, 1995 [3634] p.9 - Evening Outlook (CA) Oct 31, 1923, obtained by D. Sue Dible [3635] The Kansas City Times (MO) Oct 5, 1956

and Marie (Black) Gump, married Lucy Mabel Settle with whom he was father of (2). Fred graduated from the University of Kansas, where he excelled as a boxer. He owned the old E.J. Gump Trunk company at Ninth and Main streets and operated a leather goods factory on Holmes Street before he moved to Los Angeles. **FREDERICK MICHAEL GUMP** (1940 – 1987) son of Frederick and Margaret (Bremyer) Gump, married Rita Jane Pitcher. **GEORGE MARTIN GUMP** Fourth great grandson of progenitor Nicholas Kegg. **GEORGE MARTIN GUMP** Fifth great grandson of progenitor Nicholas Kegg. **GERALD BOWEN GUMP** Fifth great grandson of progenitor Nicholas Kegg. **GERALD SAWYER GUMP JR.** Fourth great grandson of progenitor Nicholas Kegg. **GERALD SAWYER GUMP** [3636] (1887 – 1935) son of George and Mabel (Sawyer) Gump, married Lois J. Bowen with whom he was father of (2). Gerald had been a faithful and efficient employe of the Huntingdon and Broad Top Railroad in the office at South Huntingdon. He was taken to Devitt's Camp, a tuberculosis sanitarium and officials of the institution held hope that his condition would improve. However, meningitis developed, which was the immediate cause of his death. Gerald was a faithful member of the Abbey church, was active in the Kappa Chi Sunday School class and was also a member of the official board. Fraternally, he was a member of the Royal Arcanum.
HARRIET ARVILLA GUMP [3637] (1907 – 1996) daughter of William and Georgia (Zembower) Gump, married Patrick Rohm with whom she was mother of (1). Harriett was a member of St. John's United Church of Christ and was an honorary member of the Bedford Fire Department. She was a retired cafeteria worker at Bedford High School. **HELEN GUMP** [3638] (1918 – 1969) daughter of William and Georgia (Zembower) Gump, married Walter Anthony Tuchalski. Helen was formerly employed in the Meat Department of the A. & P. Store of Stubenville. She was a member of the First Christian Church and Order of the Eastern Star. **HELENE GUMP** [3639] (1893 – 1916) daughter of George and Mabel Sawyer Gump, married George Lloyd Figard with whom she was mother of (1). Helene was a member of Trinity Reformed church and of the choir. **HENRY FRANKLIN GUMP** [3640] (1882 – 1941) son of Henry and Elizabeth (Barndollar) Gump, married Ethel McEwen Young with whom he was father of (4). Henry had been one of Everett's leading citizens, conducting a general hardware and furniture business on Main Street. Henry was a member of the Masonic fraternity, a director of the First National Bank of Everett, the Everett Cemetery Association, the Pittsburgh Silica Sand Company, an active member of the Boosters' Association and an officer in the Barndollar Methodist church.
HENRY FRANKLIN GUMP [3641] (1912 – 1975) son of Henry and Ethel (Young) Gump, married Betty Jean Whetstone with whom he was father of (5). During World War II, Henry was employed by the United States Steel Company. Later, he joined TWA, serving as the airline's overseas relations manager. For a time, he was associated with the Campbell Soup Company in an administrative position, and in later years, he established his own business as a management consultant. **HENRY FRANKLIN GUMP IV** Fifth great grandson of progenitor Nicholas Kegg. **HERBERT J. GUMP** Fourth great grandson of progenitor Nicholas Kegg. **IDA GUMP** (1864 – 1864) daughter of John and Elizabeth (Stuckey) Gump. **JAMES ALLEN GUMP** [3642] (1917 – 2001) son of Walter and Margaret (Irwin) Gump, married Dorothy Speece with whom he was father of (4). James retired as a brakeman from the former Reading Railroad. **JANET GUMP** Fifth great granddaughter of progenitor Nicholas Kegg.
JANET ELIZABETH GUMP (1894 – 1989) daughter of Samuel and Mary (Pettigrew) Gum.
JEAN ETHEL GUMP (1908 – 1919) daughter of Henry and Ethel (Young) Gump.
JEAN MERRILL GUMP Fifth great granddaughter of progenitor Nicholas Kegg. **JOANNE GUMP** (1960 – 2009) daughter of John and Ann (Grimmer) Gump. **JOHN A. GUMP** (1885 – 1951) son of Erastus and Marie (Black) Gump was father of (1). **JOHN ALEXANDER GUMP** [3643] (1907 – 1975) son of Dr. Samuel and Alice (Grove) Gump, married Miriam Jacob with whom he was father of (2).
JOHN ERASTUS GUMP [3644] (1887 – 1968) son of Charles and Clara (Barnes) Gump married twice. first to Ethel Youngblood. Later, he married Ruth Romaine Cannon with whom he was father of (1).

[3636] p.10 -The Daily News (PA) June 1,1935 [3637] Everett Public Library obituary clipping obtained by D. Sue Dible [3638] p.2 -Weirton Daily Times (W.VA) Sept 9,1969 [3639] The Bedford Gazette (PA) Feb 18, 1916 [3640] p.5 - The Daily News (PA) July 28,1941 [3641] Bedford County Genealogical Society obituary clipping obtained by D. Sue Dible [3642] p.B3 - Patriot-News (Harrisburg, PA) Aug 12, 2001 [3643] Bedford County Genealogical Society obituary clipping obtained by D. Sue Dible [3644] p.33 Pittsburgh Press (PA) Jan 11, 1968

JOHN H.W. GUMP [3645] (1925 – 2022) son of John and Ethel (Jones) Gump married Ann Evelyn Grimmer with whom he was father of (4). **JOHN HAROLD GUMP** [3646] (1879 – 1941) son of Simon and Mary (Chamberlain) Gump, married Ethel Winder Jones with whom he was father of (5). John was employed as a salesman for a Dental Supply Co. **JOHN RANDOLPH GUMP** (1850 – 1852) son of John and Elizabeth (Stuckey) Gump. **JOHN RICHARD GUMP** Fifth great grandson of progenitor Nicholas Kegg. **JUDITH BLESSING GUMP** [3647] (1919 – 2007) daughter of Henry and Ethel (Young) Gump, married Clarence Arthur McLaughlin with whom she was mother of (1). Judith was a member of Spanish Fort Presbyterian Church and an avid golfer and bridge player **JULIE GUMP** Fifth great granddaughter of progenitor Nicholas Kegg. **KARLI JORDAN GUMP** Sixth great granddaughter of progenitor Nicholas Kegg. **KATHERINE FRANTZ GUMP** (1904 – 1981) daughter of Clarence and Arlene (Frantz) Gump married Louie Stow Neese and later married Cornelius V. Cryan. **KATHLEEN ANN GUMP** aka "Kathy" Sixth great granddaughter of progenitor Nicholas Kegg. **KATHY GUMP** Fifth great granddaughter of progenitor Nicholas Kegg. **LAURA J. GUMP** [3648] (1865 – 1950) daughter of John and Elizabeth (Stuckey) Gump, married William H. Howard with whom she was mother of (2). Laura was a member of the Trinity and Evangelical Reformed Church in Everett. **LAUREN E. GUMP** Sixth great granddaughter of progenitor Nicholas Kegg.
LOIS REBECCA GUMP [3650] (1918 – 2008) daughter of William and Georgia (Zembower) Gump married twice; first to Jasper Hare. Later, she married George Stefl with whom she was mother of (2). **LOUISE GUMP** (1911 -?) daughter of Frederick and Lucy (Settle) Gump married twice; first to William H. Gambill and later to Jagjit Singh Rosha. **MARGARET ANNE GUMP** 5th great granddaughter of progenitor Nicholas Kegg. **MARGARET ELEANOR GUMP** [3651] (1951 – 2012) aka "Maggie", daughter of Walter and Naomi (Bell) Gump married three times including to John Leonard Plasker with whom she was mother of (2). Maggie had a love for animals, cooking, crafts, music, trivia and making new friends. She was a fun, humorous, and inviting person to be around. Maggie was most known for her dedication to the less fortunate. She provided meals and shelter to those in need for over 25 years. **MARJORIE GUMP** [3652] (1904 – 1988) daughter of Samuel and Alice (Grove) Gump married twice; first to John Lloyd Jackson. Later, she married Samuel Albert McKinney. Marjorie was of the Dutch Reform faith. **MARY ALICE GUMP** [3653] (1884 – 1963) daughter of Simon and Mary (Chamberlain) Gump, married Oliver Lawrence Gibboney with whom she was mother of (1). Mary had worked for several years on the Everett Republican newspaper. **MARY ANN GUMP** Fifth great granddaughter of progenitor Nicholas Kegg. **MARY DOROTHY GUMP** (1895 – 1896) daughter of Samuel and Mary (Pettigrew) Gump. **MARY ELIZABETH GUMP** Fifth great granddaughter of progenitor Nicholas Kegg. **MARY E. GUMP** (1843 – 1862) daughter of John and Elizabeth (Stuckey) Gump. **MAUREEN E. GUMP** Sixth great granddaughter of progenitor Nicholas Kegg.
MELINDA M. GUMP Sixth great granddaughter of progenitor Nicholas Kegg. **MELISSA B. GUMP** Sixth great granddaughter of progenitor Nicholas Kegg. **MICHELE GUMP** Sixth great granddaughter of progenitor Nicholas Kegg. **MYRA ELIZABETH GUMP** [3654] (1883 – 1951) daughter of Henry and Elizabeth (Barndollar) Gump. **NANCY GUMP** Fifth great granddaughter of progenitor Nicholas Kegg. **PATRICIA GUMP** Fifth great granddaughter of progenitor Nicholas Kegg. **PETER GUMP** Fourth great grandson of progenitor Nicholas Kegg. **PETER DUDLEY GUMP** Fifth great grandson of progenitor Nicholas Kegg. **RICHARD E. GUMP** aka "Rich", Fifth great grandson of progenitor Nicholas Kegg. **RICHARD EDGAR GUMP** [3655] (1919 – 1995) son of John and Ethel (Jones) Gump, married Doris Bull with whom he was father of (2). A graduate of the former Eckel's Embalming School, Philadelphia, Richard was a licensed funeral director for the former Wetzel & Son Funeral Home, Philadelphia. He also worked for the former Arthur W. Treffinger Funeral Home, Quakertown, 1963-78. Richard was a custodian at the Upper Bucks Vo-Tech School, from 1978 until retiring in 1982. After

---

[3645] https://www.echovita.com/us/obituaries/pa/warminster/john-h-gump-14959399 [3646] Everett Press (PA) Oct 10, 1941 [3647] Hughes Cremation and Funeral Service in Daphne, Ala [3648] p.2 - Bedford Gazette (PA) Dec 28, 1950 [3650] Bedford Inquirer (PA) Dec 26, 2008, obtained by Bob Rose [3651] Tillamook Headlight Herald (OR) March 27, 2012 [3652] St. Petersburg Times (FL) Nov 22, 1988 [3653] p.5 - Bedford Gazette (PA) Sept 7, 1963 [3654] p.3 The Bedford Gazette (PA) June 13, 1951 [3655] p.B10 - Morning Call, The (PA) Nov 15, 1995

retiring, he was a supervisor and maintenance man for Gilliand's Wonderland Pier, Ocean City, N.J., for over five years, and the pier's Santa. Richard was a Navy veteran of World War. **ROBERT M. GUMP** aka "Bobby", Sixth great grandson of progenitor Nicholas Kegg. **ROBERT MERRILL GUMP** [3656] (1902 – 1975) son of Clarence and Arlene (Frantz) Gump, married Dorothy Eloise Watkins with whom he was father of (3). Robert was the owner of Door Operators Inc., He was a charter member of the Society for the Preservation and Encouragement of Barber Shop Quartet Singing in America in Tulsa, Okla., where he lived as a youth. Robert was a member of the Lakewood Masonic Lodge.
ROBIN EILEEN GUMP Fifth great granddaughter of progenitor Nicholas Kegg.
ROBIN LYNN GUMP Fifth great granddaughter of progenitor Nicholas Kegg.
SAMUEL HOWARD GUMP [3657] (1906 – 1989) son of Samuel and Alice (Grove) Gump, married Martha Jackson with whom he was father of (2). Samuel retired from the Gump Insurance Agency, Everett, which he started in 1941 as a Nationwide agent. Before that he was employed by the Exxon Corp. He was a member of F&AM Lodge 524, Everett, for over 50 years. He was a member of the Ancient Accepted Scottish Rites, Valley of Harrisburg; Jaffa Temple of Altoona; and the Bedford County Shrine Club and had been an active member of the circus committee for many years. He was an active member of the Everett Fire Co. for 54 years and a former member of the Everett Rotary Club.
SAMUEL HOWARD GUMP (1927 – 2001) son of Samuel and Martha (Jackson) Gump, married Jane Perdew. Sam was a retired owner/operator of a truck stop. He was a member of the Free and Accepted Masons No. 524. He was a U.S. Army veteran of Korea. **SARAH ELIZABETH GUMP** [3658] (1853 – 1924) daughter of John and Elizabeth (Stuckey) Gump, married George W. Mellott. Sarah had been a resident of Everett all her life and was highly respected. **SHARON ELIZABETH GUMP** Fifth great granddaughter of progenitor Nicholas Kegg. **SHERRI GUMP** Fifth great granddaughter of progenitor Nicholas Kegg. **SIM A. GUMP** [3659] (1890 – 1964) son of George and Mabel (Sawyer) Gump, married Flora McCall with whom he was father of (5). Sim was employed by the Huntingdon Bank Book Company, retiring in 1957. He was raised in Everett but went to Hesston in 1926, where he spent the rest of his life. **SIMON ALBERT GUMP** (1854 – 1890) son of John and Elizabeth (Stuckey) Gump, married Mary Alice Chamberlain with whom he was father of (3). **SUSAN ELIZABETH GUMP** Fifth great granddaughter of progenitor Nicholas Kegg. **TERENCE P. GUMP**, aka "Terry", Sixth great grandson of progenitor Nicholas Kegg. **TIMOTHY SCOTT GUMP** Sixth great grandson of progenitor Nicholas Kegg. **TODD CHRISTOPHER GUMP** Sixth great grandson of progenitor Nicholas Kegg. **TYLER FRANKLIN GUMP** Sixth great grandson of progenitor Nicholas Kegg. **TYLER WESLEY GUMP** Sixth great grandson of progenitor Nicholas Kegg. **VICKI LEE GUMP** Fifth great granddaughter of progenitor Nicholas Kegg. **VIRGINIA GUMP** [3660] (1912 – 1999) daughter of William and Georgia (Zembower) Gump married twice; first to Arthur Decker with whom she was mother of (1). Later, she married Robert Varner. Virginia retired from the National Institute of Health in Bethesda, Md., where she served as travel consultant for the medical staff. Following her retirement, she was employed by the Seventh Day Adventist Hospital in Tacoma Park, Md., for four years as an employee benefits specialist. Virginia enjoyed working with flowers. Virginia was of the Protestant faith. She was a life member of the auxiliary to the Frank P. Hommon Post No. 24, American Legion; the Standing Stone Post No. 1754, VFW auxiliary; and the Women of the Moose Lodge. No. 220, all of Huntingdon. **WILLIAM GUMP** (1856 – 1860) son of John and Elizabeth (Stuckey) Gump.
WILLIAM ARCHIBALD GUMP [3661] (1886 – 1972) son of Charles and Clara (Barnes) Gump, married Georgia Zembower with whom he was father of (10). During World War II, William was an ordinance inspector and prior to his retirement he held the same capacity in Springfield, Ohio. He was a member of the Marion Chapter of 62 Royal Arch Masons of Marion, Ohio, Marion Commandry of Knights Templar, Marion Council 22 of Royal and Select Masters. The Home Association of Frank T. Hommon and the American Legion Post 24 of Huntingdon. **WILLIAM ARCHIBALD GUMP JR.** [3662] (1910 – 1991) aka "Archie", son of William and Georgia (Zembower) Gump. William retired after a 30-year career as a

---

[3656] p.12A -The Plain Dealer (OH) July 25, 1975 [3657] Bedford County Genealogical Society obituary clipping obtained by D. Sue Dible [3658] Bedford Gazette (PA) Jul 25, 1924, obtained by D. Sue Dible [3659] p.2 - Daily News (Huntingdon, PA) Oct. 22, 1964 [3660] p.2 - Daily News (PA) Oct 21, 1999 [3661] p.10 - Bedford Gazette (PA) July 6, 1972 [3662] p.2 - The Daily News (PA) Nov 6, 1991

driver for Eastern Express. He was a veteran of World War II, having served with the 138th Quartermaster Corps, 55th Battalion, in which he attained the rank of corporal. William was a member of the First United Methodist Church, Huntingdon. He was also a life member of Benevolent and Protective Order of the Elks Lodge 976, Frank P. Hommon Post 24, American Legion, and Standing Stone Post 1754, Veterans of Foreign Wars, all in Huntingdon, and a charter member of the Huntingdon County Humane Society.

GUNNARSON

BLAYDE GUNNARSON Eighth great grandson of progenitor Nicholas Kegg.
CYNTHIA DANETTE GUNNARSON Sixth great granddaughter of progenitor Nicholas Kegg.
JAMES MICHAEL CODY GUNNARSON Seventh great grandson of progenitor Nicholas Kegg.
LHONDA MICHELLE GUNNARSON Sixth great granddaughter of progenitor Nicholas Kegg.
RYLEE GUNNARSON Eighth great granddaughter of progenitor Nicholas Kegg.

GUTHLAND

AARON ANDREW GUTHLAND Seventh great grandson of progenitor Nicholas Kegg.
CHRISTINE GUTHLAND Sixth great granddaughter of progenitor Nicholas Kegg.
DAVID EDWARD GUTHLAND [3663] (1952 – 1984) son of Lt. Col. Robert and Lillian (Sickels) Guthland, married Donna Joyce McFarland with whom he was father of (2); David obtained his Bachelor of Science degree from Northwest Missouri State University, and a nation honor fellowship at Rice University, Houston, Texas. David had been a systems engineer at Phillips Petroleum Co for six years.
HANNAH ELIZABETH GUTHLAND Seventh great granddaughter of progenitor Nicholas Kegg.
REX GUTHLAND Sixth great grandson of progenitor Nicholas Kegg.
SCOTT GUTHLAND Sixth great grandson of progenitor Nicholas Kegg.

GUTHRIE

BAMBI N. GUTHRIE Sixth great granddaughter of progenitor Nicholas Kegg. **BRYAN GUTHRIE** Sixth great grandson of progenitor Nicholas Kegg. **CASSIE GUTHRIE** Sixth great granddaughter of progenitor Nicholas Kegg. **ERIC D. GUTHRIE** Fifth great grandson of progenitor Nicholas Kegg. **FRANCES MARILYN GUTHRIE** Fifth great granddaughter of progenitor Nicholas Kegg.
KARI GUTHRIE Sixth great granddaughter of progenitor Nicholas Kegg.
ROBERT STEVEN GUTHRIE Fifth great grandson of progenitor Nicholas Kegg.

GUYER

JASON GUYER Sixth great grandson of progenitor Nicholas Kegg. **JOY GUYER** Sixth great granddaughter of progenitor Nicholas Kegg. **JUSTIN GUYER** Sixth great grandson of progenitor Nicholas Kegg.

GUZMAN

BENJAMIN ISAAC GUZMAN Eighth great grandson of progenitor Nicholas Kegg.

GWIN

BEN GWIN Seventh great grandson of progenitor Nicholas Kegg. **BRADLEY GWIN** Seventh great grandson of progenitor Nicholas Kegg. **BROOKE GWIN** Seventh great granddaughter of progenitor Nicholas Kegg. **BRUCE GWIN** Sixth great grandson of progenitor Nicholas Kegg.

ELIZABETH GWIN Seventh great granddaughter of progenitor Nicholas Kegg. **JEAN GWIN** Sixth great granddaughter of progenitor Nicholas Kegg. **RACHEL GWIN** Seventh great granddaughter of progenitor Nicholas Kegg. **RICHARD CRAIG GWIN** Sixth great grandson of progenitor Nicholas Kegg.

HAAG

AMBER MICHELE HAAG Seventh great granddaughter of progenitor Nicholas Kegg.
JAMES RUSSELL HAAG Seventh great grandson of progenitor Nicholas Kegg.

HAAS

ANNA MAE HAAS aka "Danny", Seventh great granddaughter of progenitor Nicholas Kegg. **NATHAN DANIEL HAAS** [3664] (1983 – 2008) son of Delvin and Marjorie (Jones) Haas. Nathan graduated from Southeast High School, and attended Manatee Technical Institute, working for Best Buy. **RACHEL HAAS** Seventh great granddaughter of progenitor Nicholas Kegg.

HAASE

FINN LIAM HAASE Seventh great grandson of progenitor Nicholas Kegg.

HABERMAN

ABIGAIL JANE HABERMAN Eighth great granddaughter of progenitor Nicholas Kegg.
CHRISTIAN HABERMAN Eighth great grandson of progenitor Nicholas Kegg.

HACKER

ADDISON HACKER Ninth great granddaughter of progenitor Nicholas Kegg.
ANNABELLE HACKER Ninth great granddaughter of progenitor Nicholas Kegg.
SHANE M. HACKER Eighth great grandson of progenitor Nicholas Kegg.

HACKETT

PRISCILLA A. HACKETT Sixth great granddaughter of progenitor Nicholas Kegg.
RUTH R. HACKETT Sixth great granddaughter of progenitor Nicholas Kegg.

HADADORN

BRIONA LYN HADADORN Eighth great granddaughter of progenitor Nicholas Kegg.
DAVID MICHAEL HADADORN Eighth great grandson of progenitor Nicholas Kegg.
SHAWN EDWARD HADADORN Eighth great grandson of progenitor Nicholas Kegg.

HADIX

GAIL ANN HADIX Fifth great granddaughter of progenitor Nicholas Kegg.

HAEB

KYLIE HAEB Seventh great granddaughter of progenitor Nicholas Kegg.

HAEGELE

CARTER GRAHAM HAEGELE Seventh great grandson of progenitor Nicholas Kegg.
CHARLES PRESTON HAEGELE Seventh great grandson of progenitor Nicholas Kegg.

HAESSIG

LAY HAESSIG Sixth great grandson of progenitor Nicholas Kegg. **RHIO REID HAESSIG** Sixth great grandson of progenitor Nicholas Kegg. **SEAN REID HAESSIG** Seventh great grandson of progenitor Nicholas Kegg.

HAFER

AVERY MARIE HAFER Eighth great granddaughter of progenitor Nicholas Kegg. **BORDOR WILLIAM HAFER** Eighth great grandson of progenitor Nicholas Kegg. **JAMES V. HAFER** Eighth great grandson of progenitor Nicholas Kegg. **JAMES V. HAFER**, aka "Jim", Seventh great grandson of progenitor Nicholas Kegg. **JOHN STEVEN HAFER** Seventh great grandson of progenitor Nicholas Kegg.

HAGADORN

ANDRA HAGADORN Sixth great granddaughter of progenitor Nicholas Kegg. **COLIN K. HAGADORN** Sixth great grandson of progenitor Nicholas Kegg. **DERRY L. HAGADORN** Sixth great granddaughter of progenitor Nicholas Kegg. **TAWN HAGADORN** Sixth great granddaughter of progenitor Nicholas Kegg.

HAGERICH

JENNIFER MICHELE HAGERICH Eighth great granddaughter of progenitor Nicholas Kegg.
KENNA SUZANNE HAGERICH Eighth great granddaughter of progenitor Nicholas Kegg.

HAGERUD

HAYLEY J. HAGERUD Sixth great granddaughter of progenitor Nicholas Kegg.
LORELEI EVE HAGERUD Sixth great granddaughter of progenitor Nicholas Kegg.

HAHN

CARRIE HAHN Seventh great granddaughter of progenitor Nicholas Kegg.
HAZEL VIRGINIA MAE HAHN (1909 – 1978) daughter of Nelson and Estella (Troutman) Hann, married Mr. Brooks. **JOSEPH HOWARD HAHN** [3665] (1916 – 1927) son of Nelson and Estella (Troutman) Hann. **MARY ELLEN HAHN** (1919 – 1992) daughter of Nelson and Estella (Troutman) Hann married twice; first to Samuel Benjamin Glunt with whom she was mother of (2). Later, she married Paul E. Dourm. **NORA HAHN** Seventh great granddaughter of progenitor Nicholas Kegg. **RUTH NAOMI HAHN** Fourth great granddaughter of progenitor Nicholas Kegg. **STILLBORN HAHN** (1925 – 1925) son of Nelson and Estella (Troutman) Hann. **TARA HAHN** Seventh great granddaughter of progenitor Nicholas Kegg. **WILLA PEARL HAHN** Seventh great granddaughter of progenitor Nicholas Kegg.

[3663] IAGENWEB.org obituary transcriber by Sharon R. Becker [3664] The Bradenton Herald (FL) May 14, 2008 [3665] Altoona Mirror (PA) March 1, 1927, Find A Grave Memorial# 33145467 Created by: Sky

HAINES

ANDREW H. HAINES Sixth great grandson of progenitor Nicholas Kegg. **DAVID KRIS HAINES** Fifth great grandson of progenitor Nicholas Kegg. **DEBRA L. HAINES** Fifth great granddaughter of progenitor Nicholas Kegg. **DOUGLAS ARTHUR HAINES** Fifth great grandson of progenitor Nicholas Kegg. **LUKE A. HAINES** Sixth great grandson of progenitor Nicholas Kegg. **MYLA HAINES** Seventh great granddaughter of progenitor Nicholas Kegg.

HAKALA

LINDA MARIE HAKALA Sixth great granddaughter of progenitor Nicholas Kegg.
LYNETTE NANCY HAKALA Sixth great granddaughter of progenitor Nicholas Kegg.

HALE

ALEXANDRA HALE Seventh great granddaughter of progenitor Nicholas Kegg.
ALVIN FRANK HALE [3666] (1930 – 1969) son of Glen and Ruth (Lutz) Hale, married Eunice Marlene Morningstar with whom he was father of (6). Alvin was a supervisor for the Eastern Express Trucking Company of Palmyra, NJ and a former employee of the Eastern Express Trucking Company, Bedford. He was a veteran of WWII. **ALVIN FRANK HALE** Sixth great grandson of progenitor Nicholas Kegg. **BETTY ANN HALE** Sixth great granddaughter of progenitor Nicholas Kegg. **BETTY RUTH HALE** [3666A] (1923 – 1979) daughter of Glen and Ruth (Lutz) Hale, married Donald G. Seifert with whom she was mother of (3). Betty was employed as a waitress at the Roll Arena Restaurant. **BILL HALE** Sixth great grandson of progenitor Nicholas Kegg. **BRAD HALE** Sixth great grandson of progenitor Nicholas Kegg. **BRYAN EDWARD HALE** Sixth great grandson of progenitor Nicholas Kegg. **DEAN HALE** Sixth great grandson of progenitor Nicholas Kegg. **DEAN LEONARD HALE** [3667] (1900 – 1962) son of Franklin and Nettie (Dean) Hale married Katherine Harriet Fry. Dean was a member of the First Church of Christ Scientist and the Brotherhood of Railway Clerks. **DEAN T. HALE** Sixth great grandson of progenitor Nicholas Kegg. **DOROTHY LOUISE HALE** [3667A] (1924 – 1979) daughter of Glen and Ruth (Lutz) Hale, married Lloyd Henry Imler with whom she was mother of (4). Dorothy was a former employee of the Lions Manufacturing Company in Everett. **EDNA MAE HALE** (1921 – 1981) daughter of Glen and Ruth (Lutz) Hale married twice; first to Robert William Clark with whom she was mother of (2). Later, she married August Lucito with whom she was mother of (2). **EMILY HALE** Seventh great granddaughter of progenitor Nicholas Kegg. **FRANK HALE** Sixth great grandson of progenitor Nicholas Kegg. **GARY HALE** Sixth great grandson of progenitor Nicholas Kegg. **GLADYS RITA HALE** [3667B] (1927 – 2003) daughter of Glen and Ruth (Lutz) Hale, married John Frank Williams with whom she was mother of (6). **GLENN ROY HALE** Sixth great grandson of progenitor Nicholas Kegg. **HELEN CATHERINE HALE** [3668] (1931 – 2005) daughter of Glen and Ruth (Lutz) Hale married twice; first to Mr. Weyant with whom she was mother of (3). Later, she married N. J. Bankes. **JACOB HALE** aka "Jake", Seventh great grandson of progenitor Nicholas Kegg. **JEFFREY HALE** Seventh great grandson of progenitor Nicholas Kegg.
KENNETH C. HALE Seventh great grandson of progenitor Nicholas Kegg.
KENNETH CARL HALE [3669] (1962 – 2016) son of Alvin and Eunice (Morningstar) Hale, married Marilyn Whalin with whom he was father of (3). Ken retired from Willingboro M.U.A., where he enjoyed a long career as a Water Treatment Operator. Ken was a man of many diverse talents and interests. He was an avid animal lover, cook, gardener, carpenter, plumber, electrician, mechanic, and history buff.
LAURA FRANCES HALE [3669A] (1928 – 1964) daughter of Glen and Ruth (Lutz) Hale,

---

[3666] Bedford County Historical Society (PA), book 6, p. 1974 obtained by D. Sue Dible [3666A] Bedford County Historical Society, bk 10, p 3842 contributed by D. Sue Dible [3667] The Gazette (Cedar Rapids, IA) Feb 20, 1962 [3667A] p.3 Bedford Inquirer (PA) Mar 23, 1979 [3667B] The Citizen (GA) Feb 14, 2003 [3668] p25 Des Moines Register (IA) Jan 30, 2005 [3669] Burlington County Times (NJ) Feb 14, 2006, obtained by D. Sue Dible [3669A] Bedford County Genealogical Society contributed by D. Sue Dible

married William E. Poole with whom she was mother of (1). Laura was an employee of the Cancer Research Department of the M.D. Anderson Hospital of Houston. **LINDA JEAN HALE** Sixth great granddaughter of progenitor Nicholas Kegg. **NATHLENE HALE** Sixth great granddaughter of progenitor Nicholas Kegg. **NELSON A. HALE** [3670] (1902 – 1954) son of Franklin and Nettie (Dean) Hale married Myra Decima Janes with whom he was father of (1). **NELSON A. HALE JR.** [3671] (1923 – 1982) son of Nelson and Myra Decima (Janes) Hale married Fay Inez Howell with whom he was father of (5). **NINA IRENE HALE** (1894 – 1919) daughter of Franklin and Nettie (Dean) Hale never married and was employed as a bank clerk. **RANDALL C. HALE** Sixth great grandson of progenitor Nicholas Kegg. **RUTH ELLEN HALE** Sixth great granddaughter of progenitor Nicholas Kegg. **TONY HALE** Sixth great grandson of progenitor Nicholas Kegg. **WAYNE ANDREW HALE** Sixth great grandson of progenitor Nicholas Kegg.

HALES

BRYAN HALES Sixth great grandson of progenitor Nicholas Kegg. **LINDA HALES** Fifth great granddaughter of progenitor Nicholas Kegg. **RONALD GENE HALES** aka "Ronnie" Fifth great grandson of progenitor Nicholas Kegg.

HALL

ALEXANDER M. HALL Seventh great grandson of progenitor Nicholas Kegg.
BARBARA ANN HALL Fourth great granddaughter of progenitor Nicholas Kegg. **BETH K. HALL** Sixth great granddaughter of progenitor Nicholas Kegg. **BLAKE HALL** Eighth great grandson of progenitor Nicholas Kegg. **BONNIE RUTH HALL** Fourth great granddaughter of progenitor Nicholas Kegg. **BRANDI M. HALL** Seventh great granddaughter of progenitor Nicholas Kegg. **CHARLOTTE JEAN HALL** Fourth great granddaughter of progenitor Nicholas Kegg. **CYNTHIA LYNN HALL** aka "Cindy", Sixth great granddaughter of progenitor Nicholas Kegg. **DANIELLE RENAE HALL** Seventh great granddaughter of progenitor Nicholas Kegg. **DANIELLE N. HALL** Seventh great granddaughter of progenitor Nicholas Kegg. **DENNIS HALL** Fifth great grandson of progenitor Nicholas Kegg. **DENNIS EUGENE HALL** [3672] (1951 – 2001) son of George and Edna Romaine (Whetstone) Hall, married Shirley with whom he was father of (2); Dennis was employed by the U.S. Department of Agriculture in Washington, D.C. He was a veteran of the Vietnam War, serving in the U.S. Army. He was a member of Jefferson United Methodist Church in Jefferson, Md. He was a member of VFW Post 10421 of Brunswick. **FREDA LOUISE HALL** Fourth great granddaughter of progenitor Nicholas Kegg. **GARY EDWARD HALL** Fourth great grandson of progenitor Nicholas Kegg. **GEORGE WAYNE HALL** Fourth great grandson of progenitor Nicholas Kegg. **JAMES ALLEN HALL** Sixth great grandson of progenitor Nicholas Kegg.
JULIANA DAWN HALL Sixth great granddaughter of progenitor Nicholas Kegg.
MARY ELENA HALL Sixth great granddaughter of progenitor Nicholas Kegg.
MICHAEL LEE HALL Seventh great grandson of progenitor Nicholas Kegg.
PATRICIA ANN HALL aka "Patti", Sixth great granddaughter of progenitor Nicholas Kegg.
SAMUEL BARRY HALL Fourth great grandson of progenitor Nicholas Kegg.
SANDRA DIANE HALL Sixth great granddaughter of progenitor Nicholas Kegg.
STEPHANIE HALL Seventh great granddaughter of progenitor Nicholas Kegg.
STEPHEN SCOTT HALL Seventh great grandson of progenitor Nicholas Kegg.
TERRANCE WAYNE HALL aka "Terry", Sixth great grandson of progenitor Nicholas Kegg.
THOMAS A. HALL Fifth great grandson of progenitor Nicholas Kegg. **THOMAS A. HALL** [3673] (1946 – 1972) son of George and Edna Romaine (Whetstone) Hall, married Bonnie J. Bingenheimer with

---

[3670] The Atlanta Constitution (GA) Dec 18, 1954 [3671] The Atlanta Constitution (GA) Sep 20, 1982 [3672] Herald-Mail (Hagerstown, MD) Apr 13, 2001 [3673] p.4 – Bedford Inquirer (PA) June 16, 1972

whom he was father of (2). Thomas was employed by the Peter Gordon Water Proofing Company in Washington. He died of injuries suffered in a fall from a four-foot scaffold onto a cement sidewalk. **TIFFANY HALL** Seventh great granddaughter of progenitor Nicholas Kegg. **VALERIE DAWN HALL** Fifth great granddaughter of progenitor Nicholas Kegg.

HALLENBERG

JONATHAN EDWARD HALLENBERG Sixth great grandson of progenitor Nicholas Kegg. **ROBERT LEWIS HALLENBERG** Sixth great grandson of progenitor Nicholas Kegg.

HALLIGAN

BARBARA HALLIGAN Fifth great granddaughter of progenitor Nicholas Kegg.

HALLMAN

PENNIE ANN HALLMAN [3673A] (1950 – 2017) daughter of Richard and Donna (Clarke) Hallman, married Cameron Carl with whom she was mother of (3). Pennie was a teacher in Blue Springs and taught first grade, second grade, and special education. While starting a family, she became a stay-at-home mother. Pennie was the Beauty Queen in Warrensburg, MO in 1969 and was also in the Miss Kansas City Pageant in 1971. She was known for her colorful stories and willingness for any adventure. She was a long time Girl Scout and Girl Scout leader and received her 42-year Girl Scout pin. Pennie was a jack of all trades ranging from a Beauty Queen to working on vehicles, softball coach, artist and home room mother. **RICHARD HALLMAN** Seventh great grandson of progenitor Nicholas Kegg. **RICK DEAN HALLMAN** Sixth great grandson of progenitor Nicholas Kegg.

HALLOWELL

DICK EASTIN HALLOWELL Sixth great grandson of progenitor Nicholas Kegg. **ELISA LENORA HALLOWELL** Sixth great granddaughter of progenitor Nicholas Kegg.

HALWANY

HALEY MARKEY HALWANY Eighth great granddaughter of progenitor Nicholas Kegg.

HAMANN

JAXON HAMANN aka "Jax", Seventh great grandson of progenitor Nicholas Kegg.

HAMIL

ANDREW HAMIL aka "Andy", Sixth great grandson of progenitor Nicholas Kegg. **FREDERICK R. HAMIL** [3674] (1943 -2020) aka "Buck", son of Frederick and Sarah Jane (Fisher) Hamil married Susan Steedle with whom he was father of (2). Buck was commissioned to Second Lieutenant in the Marine Corps and served in the Vietnam War. He enjoyed a successful career as a salesman for Master Builders and BASF. Buck was his happiest with his family and enjoyed golf. **JUDITH MARIE HAMIL** [3675] (1942 – 1994) daughter of Frederick and Sarah (Fisher) Hamil, married Robert John Crowers with whom she was mother of (1). Judith had been employed at the Philadelphia Quartz Co., as a private secretary. **KATIE HAMIL** Sixth great granddaughter of progenitor Nicholas Kegg.

[3673A] Meyers Funeral Chapel (MO) [3674] Richmond Times (VA) May 17, 2020 [3675] p.14 News Journal (Wilmington, Delaware) May 10, 1994

HAMILTON

CAROL ANN HAMILTON Fifth great granddaughter of progenitor Nicholas Kegg.
CHARLES H. HAMILTON aka "Skip", Sixth great grandson of progenitor Nicholas Kegg.
CHERYL HAMILTON Fifth great granddaughter of progenitor Nicholas Kegg.
COLTON HAMILTON Eighth great grandson of progenitor Nicholas Kegg.
CORALIE ALICE HAMILTON Eighth great granddaughter of progenitor Nicholas Kegg.
JAMES LOVE HAMILTON JR [3675A] (1928 – 1959) son of James and Florence (Barkell) Hamilton, married Eileen Silman with whom he was father of (1). Following service with the U.S. Army, James began his professional career with a heavy construction firm at Pittsburgh. Later, he joined the Mead-Morrison Division of the McKiernan-Terry Corp. where he was employed as division sales manager.
JAMES LOVE HAMILTON III Sixth great grandson of progenitor Nicholas Kegg.
JESSICA KAY HAMILTON [3675B] (1987 – 2019) daughter of Sharon Kay Hamilton was mother of (3). Jessica was a fiery and determined spirit. **KAILA HAMILTON** Seventh great granddaughter of progenitor Nicholas Kegg. **LAURA HAMILTON** Sixth great granddaughter of progenitor Nicholas Kegg. **LINDA K. HAMILTON** Fifth great granddaughter of progenitor Nicholas Kegg.
LUKE HAMILTON Seventh great grandson of progenitor Nicholas Kegg.
NANCY LEE HAMILTON Fifth great granddaughter of progenitor Nicholas Kegg.
ROSS HAMILTON Sixth great grandson of progenitor Nicholas Kegg. **RYLEE HAMILTON** Seventh great granddaughter of progenitor Nicholas Kegg. **SHARON KAY HAMILTON** Sixth great granddaughter of progenitor Nicholas Kegg. **SYLVIE HAMILTON** Eighth great granddaughter of progenitor Nicholas Kegg. **TREATON HAMILTON** Eighth great grandson of progenitor Nicholas Kegg.

HAMLET

ERIC WADE HAMLET Sixth great grandson of progenitor Nicholas Kegg.
YVONNE LOUISE HAMLET Sixth great granddaughter of progenitor Nicholas Kegg.

HAMMON

ANNIKA MARIE HAMMON Fifth great granddaughter of progenitor Nicholas Kegg.
KARENA ANN HAMMON Fifth great granddaughter of progenitor Nicholas Kegg.

HAMMOND

JENNIFER HAMMOND Seventh great granddaughter of progenitor Nicholas Kegg.
JESSICA HAMMOND Seventh great granddaughter of progenitor Nicholas Kegg.
TRAVIS WAYNE HAMMOND [3676] (1985 – 2006) son of Allen and Lois (White) Hammond, was a painter for Quality Custom Coating of Bradenton.

HAMPTON

ALEX HAMPTON Sixth great grandson of progenitor Nicholas Kegg. **BRITTANY HAMPTON** Seventh great granddaughter of progenitor Nicholas Kegg. **ELI HAMPTON** Seventh great grandson of progenitor Nicholas Kegg. **INFANT HAMPTON** (1962 – 1962) son of Don and Karen (Pratt) Hampton. **JON HAMPTON** Sixth great grandson of progenitor Nicholas Kegg.

[3675A] p.14-The Evening Standard (Uniontown, PA) Aug 29, 1959 [3675B] Roger W Davis Funeral Home (OH) [3676] Herald Tribune (FL) Jan. 21, 2006

KELSEY HAMPTON Seventh great granddaughter of progenitor Nicholas Kegg.
SYDNEY HAMPTON Seventh great granddaughter of progenitor Nicholas Kegg.
TONI RENE HAMPTON Sixth great granddaughter of progenitor Nicholas Kegg.

HANCOCK

EZRA HANCOCK Eighth great grandson of progenitor Nicholas Kegg.
JJ HANCOCK Eighth great grandson of progenitor Nicholas Kegg.

HANCUFF

DEBRA K. HANCUFF Sixth great granddaughter of progenitor Nicholas Kegg.
DOROTHEA L. HANCUFF Sixth great granddaughter of progenitor Nicholas Kegg.
JEAN ANN HANCUFF Sixth great granddaughter of progenitor Nicholas Kegg. **LINDA HANCUFF** Sixth great granddaughter of progenitor Nicholas Kegg. **PATTY D. HANCUFF** aka "Doll", Sixth great granddaughter of progenitor Nicholas Kegg.

HANDLEY

DAWN AMBER HANDLEY Seventh great granddaughter of progenitor Nicholas Kegg.
DUSTIN EDWARD LEW HANDLEY Seventh great grandson of progenitor Nicholas Kegg.

HANEY

DESTINY CHANIELLE HANEY Seventh great granddaughter of progenitor Nicholas Kegg.
JAZZY HANEY Seventh great granddaughter of progenitor Nicholas Kegg.

HANK

CHARLOTTE HANK Seventh great granddaughter of progenitor Nicholas Kegg.
TABOR HANK Seventh great grandson of progenitor Nicholas Kegg.

HANKS

BRIAN HANKS Sixth great grandson of progenitor Nicholas Kegg.
CHARLOTTE ELIZABETH HANKS [3677] (1882 – 1923) aka "Lizzie", daughter of Dr. Coriolanus and Hannah (Gump) Hanks married twice; first to Zenas Chittenden Gillespie with whom she was mother of (1). Later, she married Chester Arthur Rote. **CHESTER GUMP HANKS** (1878 – 1907) son of Dr. Coriolanus and Hannah (Gump) Hanks, married Elsie Keto Ayers with whom he was father of (2). **DAVID HANKS** Sixth great grandson of progenitor Nicholas Kegg. **DOROTHY ELIZABETH HANKS** [3678] (1901 – 1993) daughter of Chester and Elsie (Ayers) Hanks, married William H. Lunn with whom she was mother of (3). Dorothy graduated in 1920 from Oneonta Normal School, a teaching college. After being diagnosed with multiple sclerosis she was active with the Indoor Sports Club, a club for the physically disabled, and the Pima County Republican Women's Club. When her cat died, she wanted to get another pet, but the city of Tucson had taken over the apartment complex and denied her request. Her grandson, Greg Lunn, a former Pima County supervisor and Tucson legislator, got a law passed in the mid-1980's in the Arizona Legislator allowing elderly residents in federal subsidized housing to have pets.

[3677] Hudson Evening Register (NY) Jan 30, 1914 [3678] p.14 Arizona Daily Star (Tucson, AZ) Oct 20, 1993

HAZEL MILLARD HANKS [3679] (1905 – 1997) daughter of Chester and Elsie (Ayers) Hanks, married Franklin Benjamin Cowell with whom she was mother of (3). Hazel was formerly employed with General Electric Co. for 10 years. After moving to Florida, she did volunteer work with Lee Memorial Hospital for 22 years.   **STANLEY B. HANKS** (1877 – 1878) son of Dr. Coriolanus and Hannah (Gump) Hanks. **THOMAS L. HANKS** Fifth great grandson of progenitor Nicholas Kegg.

HANLEY

DANA ARTHUR HANLEY Fifth great grandson of progenitor Nicholas Kegg.
DAVID GRATTAN HANLEY (1916 – 1992) son of Thomas and Grace (Turner) Hanley married Alva Jean Baldwin with whom he was father of (4).   **DAVIDA JEAN HANLEY** Fifth great granddaughter of progenitor Nicholas Kegg.   **DOUGLAS ALAN HANLEY** Fifth great grandson of progenitor Nicholas Kegg. **JOHN THOMAS HANLEY** [3680] (1946 – 1993) son of George and Mary (Brilman) Hanley, married Gertrude Elizabeth Bayus with whom he was father of (3). John was employed as a Sheetrock applicator.   **JONATHAN THOMAS HANLEY** Sixth great granddaughter of progenitor Nicholas Kegg.   **MONICA HANLEY** Sixth great granddaughter of progenitor Nicholas Kegg. **TABITHA JANE HANLEY** Sixth great granddaughter of progenitor Nicholas Kegg.
THELISA T. HANLEY Sixth great granddaughter of progenitor Nicholas Kegg.
THOMAS ALVA HANLEY Fifth great grandson of progenitor Nicholas Kegg.

HANN

CHARLES WILLIAM FREDERIC HANN [3681] (1911 – 1996) son of Nelson and Estella (Troutman) Hann, married Pauline Esther Folk with whom he was father of (1); Charles was a truck driver for Ricketts Bag Company. He was a member of the Church of the Brethren.
PATRICIA LOUISE HANN Fifth great granddaughter of progenitor Nicholas Kegg.

HANNAH

MARY BETH HANNAH Fifth great adopted granddaughter.

HANNAHS

JACK FREDRICK HANNAHS Fifth great grandson of progenitor Nicholas Kegg.
JAMES HANNAHS aka "Jim", Fifth great grandson of progenitor Nicholas Kegg.
JANE HANNAHS Fifth great granddaughter of progenitor Nicholas Kegg.

HANSEN

CARRIE MICHELLE HANSEN aka "Mikki", Fifth great granddaughter of progenitor Nicholas Kegg. **ERICKA JUNE HANSEN** aka "Ricki", Fifth great granddaughter of progenitor Nicholas Kegg. **ZAYBREON J. REED HANSEN** Seventh great grandson of progenitor Nicholas Kegg.

HANSON

ALEXIS HANSON Ninth great granddaughter of progenitor Nicholas Kegg.
BRAYLEE HANSON Seventh great granddaughter of progenitor Nicholas Kegg.

[3679] p.B4 - Syracuse Post Standard (NY) July 10, 1997 [3680] p.C14 - Fresno Bee, The (CA) Nov 23, 1993 [3681] St. Petersburg Times (FL) June 8, 1996

HANSSEN

HARRY HOLBROOK HANSSEN (3682) (1947 – 2013) son of Robert and Barbara (McFall) Hanssen. Harry perished trying to save his mother from a house fire. **ROBERT JAMES HANSSEN** Sixth great grandson of progenitor Nicholas Kegg.

HARALDSON

BERNITA KAY HARALDSON Fifth great granddaughter of progenitor Nicholas Kegg. **DAVID R. HARALDSON** Fifth great grandson of progenitor Nicholas Kegg. **KACIE HARALDSON** Sixth great granddaughter of progenitor Nicholas Kegg. **SEAN HARALDSON** Sixth great grandson of progenitor Nicholas Kegg. **TYLER HARALDSON** Sixth great grandson of progenitor Nicholas Kegg.

HARBIN

HOLLY MARIE HARBIN Sixth great granddaughter of progenitor Nicholas Kegg.

HARCLERODE

ANDREW COOLEDGE HARCLERODE (1887 – 1887) son of John and Rebecca (Diehl) Harclerode. **ANN HARCLERODE** Fourth great granddaughter of progenitor Nicholas Kegg. **ANNA GRACE HARCLERODE**, (1890 – 1890) daughter of John and Rebecca (Diehl) Harclerode. **ANNA JANET HARCLERODE** (3682A) aka "Skip" (1933 – 2019) daughter of John and Janet (Morgart) Harclerode married Cecil P. Cessna with whom she was mother of (5). Janet taught children's choir at St. Thomas Lutheran. In addition to her love for music and her church, she loved spending time with family, was fond of horses and a passionate gardener. She started her nursing career at Bedford Memorial Hospital and retired as a nursing supervisor from Chambersburg Hospital. **ANNA M. HARCLERODE** (3682B) aka "Betty" (1924 – 2014) daughter of Walter and Anna (Campbell) Harclerode, married Richard David Greenawalt with whom she was mother of (3). Betty was employed at Howard Johnsons, Bedford, and later at UPMC Bedford Memorial Hospital as a dietician until her retirement. She enjoyed her flower gardens, sewing and especially going to Kelly's for lunch with her family and friends. Betty loved the Lord; she served as a deaconess of Bethel Church of the Brethren. In later years, she couldn't get around well but was always willing to help people, support missions, church and veterans. **BABY HARCLERODE** (1939 – 1939) daughter of Elmer and Catherine (Anders) Harclerode. **BENJAMIN THATCHER HARCLERODE** (1907 – 1997) son of Walter and Anna Blanche (Campbell) Harclerode, married Ada Pearl Beaver with whom he was father of (2). **BENJAMIN THATCHER HARCLERODE JR.** (1929 – 1930) son of Benjamin and Ada (Beaver) Harclerode. **CAROL L. HARCLERODE** Fifth great granddaughter of progenitor Nicholas Kegg. **CHARLES GEARY HARCLERODE** (3683) (1895 – 1972) son of John and Rebecca (Diehl) Harclerode, married Rebecca Hershberger with whom he was father of (4). Charles had worked for over 42 years for the Reading Railroad. **CLARENCE LEO HARCLERODE** (3684) (1912 – 1997) son of Walter and Anna Blanche (Campbell) Harclerode. Clarence was of the Protestant faith. He had been employed as a waiter in New York City for many years. **CONSTANCE HARCLERODE** Sixth great granddaughter of progenitor Nicholas Kegg. **DAVID ALAN HARCLERODE** Fourth great grandson of progenitor Nicholas Kegg. **DEBRA EILEEN HARCLERODE** Fifth great granddaughter of progenitor Nicholas Kegg. **DESSA L. HARCLERODE** (3685) (1885 – 1926) daughter of Isaac and Martha Anna (Whetstone) Harclerode. Dessa had been employed as an inspector by the General Electric Company. **DOROTHY LOUISA HARCLERODE** Sixth great grandson of progenitor Nicholas Kegg.

(3682) thepinetree.net obituary posted by John Hamilton (3682A) Bedford Gazette (PA) Dec 31, 2019 (3682B) Bedford Gazette (PA) May 9, 2014, contributed by Bob Rose (3683) Bedford Inquirer (PA) Aug. 11, 1972 (3684) Bedford County (PA) Genealogical Society obituary clipping obtained by D. Sue Dible (3685) Bedford Gazette (PA) May 7, 1926

EDGAR MELVIN HARCLERODE (3686) (1891 – 1978) son of Isaac and Martha Anna (Whetstone) Harclerode married twice; first to Mary Mabel Walizer and later, to Olive Douglas Chirdon. Edgar retired from the former PA Railroad. He was a Veteran of WWI, member of Barracks 1035, WWI Veterans; Scottish Rite bodies, Williamsport; and Summit Lodge F & A M Ebensburg.
ELMER GIBSON HARCLERODE (1909 – 1949) son of John and Marjorie (Booth) Harclerode, married Catherine Andres with whom he was father of (1). Elmer retired from the Army.
FRED JERVIS HARCLERODE (3687) (1922 – 2002) son of John and Marjorie (Booth) Harclerode, married Betty Ann Batcheller with whom he was father of (2). Fred was a U.S. Navy veteran of World War II, serving in the South Pacific. Mr. Harclerode was a custodian at the University of New Hampshire for 13 years and then worked in the Newmarket School system for many years before retiring in 1985. The 1985 School Yearbook was dedicated to him. He drove the bus for athletic games and for special needs students and was a truant officer for many years. He was a life member of the Newmarket Fire Department and was co-founder of the Tiger No. 1, Newmarket Handtub Association in 1954 and helped restore the Handtub for pumping competition. He was a past president and was foreman from 1965 to 1967. He has remained a very active member of the association, serving in many offices and was vice president at the time of his death. He helped to coordinate many Handtub Musters in Newmarket. He was a life member of the New England States Veterans Fireman's League and served as president in 1985. He had served on the Muster Committee and was a paper judge. Over the years he had piped many handtubs. He traveled throughout New England, New York and as far as Nebraska to attend Handtub Musters. He collected handtub memorabilia for many years and attended almost all the league-sponsored musters. He was a member of the North American Class C Handtub Association. He was a 55-year member of the Robert G. Durgin American Legion Post 67 in Newmarket. **HAZEL DELRAY HARCLERODE** (3688) (1909 – 1996) daughter of Walter and Anna Blanche (Campbell) Harclerode married twice, first to Elliot Malin Clark with whom she was mother of (3). Later, she married Theodore C. Greenawalt with whom she was mother of (1). Hazel was a member of the Tatesville United Methodist Church.
HESTER ELLA HARCLERODE (3689) (1882 – 1945) aka "Hattie", daughter of Isaac and Martha Anna (Whetstone) Harclerode, married Daniel Webster Wolf with whom she was mother of (2).
JACK E. HARCLERODE Fourth great grandson of progenitor Nicholas Kegg.
JAMES FRANKLIN HARCLERODE (3690) (1938 – 2021) aka "Jim", son of John and Mary Janet (Morgart) Harclerode married Bonnie Rae Foor with whom he was father of (2). Jim was an Army veteran. He worked for Bedford Valley Petroleum for over 38 years and in his spare time he worked with his dad at J. F. Harclerode Sales and Service and eventually took over the business and relocated it to his home. He was committed to his customers and made many friends over the years. In his younger days, he enjoyed playing ISL Softball and hit the first home run at the Schellsburg ball fields under their new lights. He also enjoyed following his sons in the sports they played while growing up. After retirement, he enjoyed his daily coffee time with his friends at the Landmark Restaurant.
JENNIFER L. HARCLERODE Fifth great granddaughter of progenitor Nicholas Kegg.
JANET ELIZABETH HARCLERODE Sixth great granddaughter of progenitor Nicholas Kegg.
JEREMY J. HARCLERODE Fifth great grandson of progenitor Nicholas Kegg.
JOHN ELMER HARCLERODE (3691) (1879 – 1948) son of Isaac and Martha Anna (Whetstone) Harclerode, married Marjorie Ann Booth with whom he was father of (4). John was employed by the Penna. Railroad for 51 years and was a member of the I.O.O. F. Lodge Knights of Pythias, Railroad Brotherhood and the Ebensburg Congregational Church. **JOHN THOMAS HARCLERODE** (1914 – 1944) aka "Jack", son of John and Marjorie (Booth) Harclerode, married Florence Marie Leary. John served with the U.S. Coastguard during WWII. **JULIE LYNNE HARCLERODE** Seventh great granddaughter of progenitor Nicholas Kegg. **KAY HARCLERODE** (3692) (1954 – 2015) daughter of Paul and Florence (Courtot) Harclerode, married Michael A. Simmons. Kay enjoyed quilting and loved her dogs, Rudy and Oliver.

(3686) Johnstown Tribune-Democrat (PA) May 17, 1978, obtained by D. Sue Dible (3687) Seacoast Media (NH) April 02, 2002 (3688) Bedford County (PA) Genealogical Society obituary clipping obtained by D. Sue Dible (3689) p.2 Altoona Tribune (PA) Nov 1, 1945 (3690) Bedford Gazette (PA) April 14, 2021 (3691) Bedford Gazette (PA) April 29, 1948 (3692) Times Herald (PA) Mar 15, 2015

LOUISE P. HARCLERODE (3692A) (1919 – 2016) daughter of Charles and Rebecca (Hershberger) Harclerode, married Richard W. Newswanger with whom she was mother of (3). Louise was a homemaker, longtime member of St. Matthews Lutheran Church in Lancaster, Conestoga Country Club and the Towne Club. Louise loved to play bridge, enjoyed the beach, sewing and traveling with her sister Miriam to Elderhostel. During the 1940's Louise was an executive secretary with Armstrong World Industries. She enjoyed spending time with her family and friends. **LUCY JANE HARCLERODE** (3692B) (1915 – 2007) daughter of Walter and Anna (Campbell) Harclerode. Lucy was a waitress at the Landmark Restaurant in Everett and Saylor's Restaurant. She enjoyed gardening, and quilting and was a dedicated sister and daughter who made a home for her mother in her later years.
MIRIAM HARCLERODE (3692C) (1921 – 2016) daughter of Charles and Rebecca (Hershberger) Harclerode, married Richard Darlington Kepner with whom she was mother of (3). Miriam graduated from Shippensburg University, 1942, BA., University of Missouri, MA. 1970 commissioned into the USNR, May 1943 - 1946, as a Lt. **MITCHELL HARCLERODE** Fifth great grandson of progenitor Nicholas Kegg. **PAUL ISAAC HARCLERODE** (1917 – 1993) son of John and Marjorie (Booth) Harclerode, married Florence Courtot with whom he was father of (5). Paul was an Aviation Cadet who attended American Air Force technical training command school at Yale University.
PAUL J. HARCLERODE Fourth great grandson of progenitor Nicholas Kegg.
PAULINE E. HARCLERODE (3693) (1925 – 1994) daughter of Robert and Virginia (Finch) Harclerode, married Robert Lester Brown with whom she was mother of (4). Pauline had been employed at John Deere Insurance and was a bookkeeper at Royal Neighbors of America.
PETER FRED HARCLERODE Fifth great grandson of progenitor Nicholas Kegg.
RAYMOND HARCLERODE (1927 - 1927) son of Robert and Virginia (Finch) Harclerode.
REBECCA HARCLERODE Sixth great granddaughter of progenitor Nicholas Kegg.
RICHARD D. HARCLERODE Fourth great grandson of progenitor Nicholas Kegg.
RICHARD DEAN HARCLERODE (1931 – 1939) son of Benjamin and Ada (Beaver) Harclerode.
ROBERT HARCLERODE (1927 – 1927) son of Robert and Virginia (Finch) Harclerode.
ROBERT FRANKLIN HARCLERODE Seventh great grandson of progenitor Nicholas Kegg.
ROBERT GUY HARCLERODE (3694) (1902 – 1973) son of Walter and Anna Blanche (Campbell) Harclerode, married Virginia Finch with whom he was father of (1). Robert was employed as an engineer with the Operating Engineers of Rock Island and was a member of the international union of Operating Engineers. **ROBERT JOHN HARCLERODE** (3694A) (1947 – 2019) son of John and Mary Janet (Morgart) Harclerode married Connie Leister with whom he was father of (2). Bob served his military duty as a SPC 5 in the Army Signal Corp. He was stationed at Fort Ritchey, MD during the Vietnam conflict. Part of his duty included military police assignments. His work career started at the Sunoco gas stations at the Bedford and Breezewood interchanges. Following his military duty, he started working for Blackburn and Russell for nine years while venturing into his own business in 1972. C&C Cycle Sales and Service started out as a motorcycle sales and repair shop that developed into an outdoor power equipment business. He enjoyed his customers and the challenges of working on their equipment. He was a lifetime NRA patron member and lifetime member of the American Motorcycle Association - AMA and the Bedford County Motorcycle Club where he served as referee at the Black Valley Hill Climbs. Bob participated in district 5 motorcycle events including motocross, hare scrambles and hill climbs. He enjoyed participating in the Bedford Band Boosters while his daughters were in band. He served on the Bedford Area Ambulance Association Board of Directors for over 30 years serving in many capacities including President. He enjoyed being with his family and friends, especially his grandsons and loved his pets. He loved golfing, Nascar racing, hunting, fishing, camping, and riding and racing motorcycles. He was also involved in racing his own cars and also building and tuning engines for local stock car drivers like Jack Pencil and Eric Zembower in their early days at the local racetracks.

(3692A) Charles F. Snyder Funeral Home (Lancaster, PA) (3692B) p.3 - Bedford Inquirer (PA) March 30, 2007, contributed by Bob Rose (3692C) Arizona Daily Star (Tucson) Apr. 17, 2016 (3693) Dispatch-Argus (IL) Apr 14, 1994 (3694) Muscatine Journal (IA) Dec 31, 1973/FindAGrave memorial# 91294847 added by Lois Bopp Retherford (3694A) Bedford Gazette (PA) Nov 18, 2019, contributed by Bob Rose

ROYDEN FRANKLIN HARCLERODE [3695] (1883 – 1943) son of John and Rebecca (Diehl) Harclerode, married Ethel May Nycum with whom he was father of (2). Royden was employed as a moulder at the steel plant in Johnstown. **RUBY C. HARCLERODE** [3696] (1891 – 1918) daughter of John and Rebecca (Diehl) Harclerode, married Richard Bruce Morgart with whom she was mother of (3). Ruby was a member of Trinty Reformed church, Friend's Cove.
SALLY MARGARET HARCLERODE [3696A] (1893 – 1971) daughter of John and Rebecca (Diehl) Harclerode, married Ross Albert Reed with whom she was mother of (4). Sally was a member of Trinity United Church of Christ of Friend's Cove. **SARA C. HARCLERODE** Fifth great granddaughter of progenitor Nicholas Kegg. **SELBY PHILLIP HARCLERODE** [3696B] aka "Happy" (1888 – 1949) son of John and Rebecca (Diehl) Harclerode. Happy was a farmer by occupation and was never married. **SUSAN HARCLERODE** Fourth great granddaughter of progenitor Nicholas Kegg.
SUZANNE MARIE HARCLERODE (1975 – 1997) daughter of Robert and Connie (Liester) Harclerode. **TIMOTHY JAMES HARCLERODE** Seventh great grandson of progenitor Nicholas Kegg. **WALTER HENRY HARCLERODE** [3697] (1881 – 1958) son of John and Rebecca (Diehl) Harclerode, married Anna Blanche Campbell with whom he was father of (7).

HARDACRE

AMY KATHLEEN HARDACRE Fifth great granddaughter of progenitor Nicholas Kegg. **BLAINE HARDACRE** Fourth great grandson of progenitor Nicholas Kegg. **BRYAN SCOTT HARDACRE** Fifth great grandson of progenitor Nicholas Kegg. **CALEB MARK HARDACRE** Sixth great grandson of progenitor Nicholas Kegg. **EMILY SUE HARDACRE** Sixth great granddaughter of progenitor Nicholas Kegg. **FAITH REBEKAH HARDACRE** Sixth great granddaughter of progenitor Nicholas Kegg. **JEFFREY BLAINE HARDACRE** Fifth great grandson of progenitor Nicholas Kegg
JOSHUA SCOTT HARDACRE Sixth great grandson of progenitor Nicholas Kegg.
JUSTIN BLAINE HARDACRE Sixth great grandson of progenitor Nicholas Kegg.
KATHERINE JEAN HARDACRE Sixth great granddaughter of progenitor Nicholas Kegg.
SYDNEY ELIZABETH HARDACRE Sixth great granddaughter of progenitor Nicholas Kegg.

HARDEN

BONNIE HARDEN Fourth great granddaughter of progenitor Nicholas Kegg. **BRADY E. HARDEN** Seventh great grandson of progenitor Nicholas Kegg. **BRADLEY L. HARDEN** (1970 – 1970) son of Neil and Judith (Crawford) Harden. **CARRIE RAE HARDEN** Fifth great granddaughter of progenitor Nicholas Kegg. **CHRISTINE M. HARDEN** Fifth great granddaughter of progenitor Nicholas Kegg. **DALE EUGENE HARDEN** [3698] (1940 – 2017) son of Lawrence and Madeline (Myers) Harden, married Carol Deanna Duzan with whom he was father of (3). Later, he married Sharon Lynn Dunn. Dale retired from the Kroger Co as transportation manager after 27 years of service. He also retired from Meijer after 10 years in management. From 1987 to 1996 he and his wife owned and operated The Harden House Restaurant. For more than 15 years he volunteered at Wheeler Mission, Shepherd Community and Neighborhood Fellowship. The Sunday school kids at His Place will always remember him for his quote "Guess what?" Unselfish man that he was, he donated his body to IU School of Medicine to further help people. Dale loved spending time with his family, helping/working at his church, volunteering, fishing and watching the Colts. **DALE EUGENE HARDEN II** Fifth great grandson of progenitor Nicholas Kegg. **DIANNE MADELINE HARDEN** Fourth great granddaughter of progenitor Nicholas Kegg.

[3695] Bedford County (PA) Genealogical Society obituary clipping obtained by D. Sue Dible [3696] Bedford Inquirer (PA) Jan 10, 1919 [3696A] Bedford County Historical Society (PA), book 10, p. 3572 contributed by D. Sue Dible [3696B] p.3 - The Bedford Gazette (PA) Dec. 23, 1949 [3697] Bedford County Press and Everett Press (PA) July 18, 1958 [3698] The Indianapolis Star (IN) Oct 17, 2017

DON LAWRENCE HARDEN [3699] (1938 – 1987) son of Lawrence and Madeline (Myers) Harden, married Lorna Theo Grant.   **EUGENE ROBERT HARDEN** aka "Gene", Sixth great grandson of progenitor Nicholas Kegg.   **FAYE EUGENE HARDEN** Fifth great grandson of progenitor Nicholas Kegg.   **LESLIE CAMILLE HARDEN** Fifth great granddaughter of progenitor Nicholas Kegg.
LINDA MAE HARDEN Fourth great granddaughter of progenitor Nicholas Kegg.
LOGAN G. HARDEN Seventh great grandson of progenitor Nicholas Kegg.
MAGEN JANE HARDEN [3700] (1966 – 1973) daughter of Neil and Judith (Crawford) Harden.
MICHAEL J. HARDEN, aka "Mike", Sixth great grandson of progenitor Nicholas Kegg.
MICHELE KAY HARDEN Fifth great granddaughter of progenitor Nicholas Kegg.
SHELLEY B. HARDEN Fifth great granddaughter of progenitor Nicholas Kegg.

HARDESTY

JACEY HARDESTY Seventh great granddaughter of progenitor Nicholas Kegg.
JULIA LEE HARDESTY Seventh great granddaughter of progenitor Nicholas Kegg.

HARDING

MICHAEL HARDING Fifth great grandson of progenitor Nicholas Kegg.
MICHAEL L. HARDING Sixth great grandson of progenitor Nicholas Kegg.
MITCHELL E. HARDING Sixth great grandson of progenitor Nicholas Kegg.
PHYLLIS HARDING Fifth great granddaughter of progenitor Nicholas Kegg.

HARDS

ALEXANDER MILO HARDS Seventh great grandson of progenitor Nicholas Kegg.
EILEEN NICOLE HARDS Seventh great granddaughter of progenitor Nicholas Kegg.
LUELLA FLORENCE HARDS Fifth great granddaughter of progenitor Nicholas Kegg.
ROBERT HARDS aka "Bobby", Sixth great grandson of progenitor Nicholas Kegg.
ROBERT MILO HARDS (1917 – 1987) son of Milo and Goldie (Thompson) Hards, married Beverly Madge Raynolds with whom he was father of (1).

HARDWICK

KATLIN ABIGAILE HARDWICK Sixth great granddaughter of progenitor Nicholas Kegg.
RICHARD DELBERT HARDWICK, aka "Rick", Sixth great grandson of progenitor Nicholas Kegg.

HARDY

LAUREN HARDY Sixth great granddaughter of progenitor Nicholas Kegg.

HARE

ASHLEY NICOLE HARE Seventh great granddaughter of progenitor Nicholas Kegg.
KAYLA RENAE HARE Seventh great granddaughter of progenitor Nicholas Kegg.
SHAYNA CHERI HARE Seventh great granddaughter of progenitor Nicholas Kegg.

[3699] The Sacramento Bee (CA) Jan 6, 1987   [3700] The Press-Tribune (Roseville, CA) Aug 9, 1973

HARGROVE

DEREK MATTHEW HARGROVE Seventh great grandson of progenitor Nicholas Kegg.
SEAN MICHAEL HARGROVE Seventh great grandson of progenitor Nicholas Kegg.

HARLAN

ELSIE HARLAN Eighth great granddaughter of progenitor Nicholas Kegg. **RHEA HARLAN** Eighth great granddaughter of progenitor Nicholas Kegg. **SIMONE HARLAN** Eighth great granddaughter of progenitor Nicholas Kegg.

HARLOW

CONNER HARLOW Eighth great grandson of progenitor Nicholas Kegg.
GARRETT HARLOW Eighth great grandson of progenitor Nicholas Kegg.

HARMON

H. DAVID HARMON Fifth great grandson of progenitor Nicholas Kegg. **JUDY ANN HARMON** [3701] (1957 – 2002) daughter of Howard and Bethlin (Judd) Harmon. Judy was a high school business and computer teacher at Molalla High School for 18 years and later at Milwaukie High School.
STEVE HARMON Fifth great grandson of progenitor Nicholas Kegg.

HARMS

BARBARA JEAN HARMS Sixth great granddaughter of progenitor Nicholas Kegg.

HARPER

CLARA A. HARPER [3702] (1881 – 1937) daughter of Jackson and Lucretia (May) Harper married twice; first to Samuel Newcomer Kelley. Later she married William Stafford. **CLAUDE J. HARPER** (1874 – 1897) son of Jackson and Lucretia (May) Harper. **JESSICA LESLIE HARPER** Sixth great granddaughter of progenitor Nicholas Kegg. **JESSIE HARPER** [3703] (1884 – 1955) aka "Jess", daughter of Jackson and Lucretia (May) Harper. Jess studied nursing at St. Luke's hospital, NY and served as a nurse there until she retired. **MAE ELIZABETH HARPER** [3704] (1875 – 1937) daughter of Jackson and Lucretia (May) Harper, married Harry Rohrback Snyder with whom she was mother of (1). Mae was organist at St. Paul's Church, Hagerstown, Maryland. **MILES AUSTIN HARPER** Sixth great grandson of progenitor Nicholas Kegg. **RUSSELL SPENCER HARPER** [3705] (1882 – 1945) son of Jackson and Lucretia (May) Harper, married Lorena Ketchum Henninger.
STACIE MICHELLE HARPER Seventh great granddaughter of progenitor Nicholas Kegg.
SYDNEY CAMILLE HARPER Sixth great granddaughter of progenitor Nicholas Kegg.

HARRINGTON

ELIZABETH HARRINGTON Fifth great granddaughter of progenitor Nicholas Kegg.
JOHN ROBERT HARRINGTON Fifth great grandson of progenitor Nicholas Kegg.
JOSHUA W HARRINGTON Sixth great grandson of progenitor Nicholas Kegg.
KATHLEEN HARRINGTON Fifth great granddaughter of progenitor Nicholas Kegg.
LEVI HARRINGTON Eighth great grandson of progenitor Nicholas Kegg.

[3701] Oregonian (OR) Nov 22, 2002 [3702] Morning Herald (MD) Jan 12, 1937 [3703] Daily Mail (Hagerstown, MD) Oct 11, 1955, FindAGrave Memorial# 142200299 Created by: Sanebee [3704] p.12 - Daily Mail (MD) July 20, 1937 [3705] p.12 - Morning Herald (MD) Sept 10, 1945

MEGAN HARRINGTON Sixth great granddaughter of progenitor Nicholas Kegg.
MEREDITH ROSE HARRINGTON Fifth great granddaughter of progenitor Nicholas Kegg.

HARRIS

BROOK HARRIS Seventh great granddaughter of progenitor Nicholas Kegg.
CAROL LYNN HARRIS [3706] (1948 – 2008) daughter of John and Ruth (Euritt) Harris, married Douglas L. Siperly with whom she was mother of (2). **CHARLES ELWOOD HARRIS** [3707] (1905 – 1978) aka "Charlie", son of Charles and Emma (Smith) Harris, married Clara Rosella Hensch with whom he was father of (2). Charlie was a former member of the Merchant Marine. He was self-employed throughout most of his working life. **CHRYS HARRIS** Sixth great granddaughter of progenitor Nicholas Kegg. **COLE HARRIS** Seventh great grandson of progenitor Nicholas Kegg. **DARLENE HARRIS** Sixth great granddaughter of progenitor Nicholas Kegg. **ERIKA HARRIS** Sixth great granddaughter of progenitor Nicholas Kegg. **JAMES F. HARRIS** [3708] (1929 – 1987) son of Charles and Clara (Hensch) Harris. James retired from work as an expeditor at International Harvester. He was a WWII Army veteran. **JOAN ELLEN HARRIS** [3709] (1927 – 2019) daughter of Charles and Clara (Hensch) Harrismarried twice; first to Merle Lewis Rigby and later to Irvin William Whiteman. **JOHN HARRIS** Fifth great grandson of progenitor Nicholas Kegg. **KATHY SUE HARRIS** Fifth great granddaughter of progenitor Nicholas Kegg. **KEITH HARRIS** Sixth great grandson of progenitor Nicholas Kegg. **LAURA HARRIS** Sixth great granddaughter of progenitor Nicholas Kegg. **SCOTT HARRIS** Sixth great grandson of progenitor Nicholas Kegg. **TRISHA HARRIS** Seventh great granddaughter of progenitor Nicholas Kegg. **WILMA B. VIOLET HARRIS** [3710] (1903 – 1967) daughter of Charles and Emma (Smith) Harris, married Lawrence Clifford Duke with whom she was mother of (1). Wilma was a 24-year employee of the Wayne Pump Co. before retiring and was a member of the Auxiliary of the Spanish-American War Veterans.

HARRISON

ISABELLA HARRISON Sixth great granddaughter of progenitor Nicholas Kegg.
PARKER HARRISON Sixth great grandson of progenitor Nicholas Kegg.

HART

ALEX HART Eighth great grandson of progenitor Nicholas Kegg. **ALEXANDER JOHN HART** aka "Alex", Seventh great grandson of progenitor Nicholas Kegg. **ANDREW HART** Eighth great grandson of progenitor Nicholas Kegg. **BENJAMIN HART** Seventh great grandson of progenitor Nicholas Kegg. **BENJAMIN MICHAEL HART** Seventh great grandson of progenitor Nicholas Kegg. **CARRIE L. HART** Sixth great granddaughter of progenitor Nicholas Kegg.
CHASE ALEXANDER HART [3711] (1989 – 2000) son of Kenneth and Colette (West) Hart was a very beautiful and loving child to all of those around him. He had an infectious giggle and loved to run.
CHRISTOPHER HARRISON HART Sixth great grandson of progenitor Nicholas Kegg.
DANIEL HART Seventh great grandson of progenitor Nicholas Kegg. **DAVID G. HART** Sixth great grandson of progenitor Nicholas Kegg. **DEVIN HART** Seventh great grandson of progenitor Nicholas Kegg. **JOHN MICHAEL HART** Sixth great grandson of progenitor Nicholas Kegg.
KAMDEN HART Eighth great grandson of progenitor Nicholas Kegg. **LINDSAY RAE HART** Seventh great granddaughter of progenitor Nicholas Kegg. **MATTHEW HART** Seventh great grandson of progenitor Nicholas Kegg. **MITCHELL HART** Eighth great grandson of progenitor Nicholas Kegg. **NICHOLAS G. HART** Seventh great grandson of progenitor Nicholas Kegg.

[3706] Orange County Register (CA) June 11, 2008 [3707] p.3A Ft. Wayne Journal Gazette (IN) June 22, 1978, obtained by D. Sue Dible [3708] p.4C Fort Wayne Journal Gazette (IN) Nov 18, 1987, obtained by D. Sue Dible [3709] Fort Wayne Newspapers (IN) May 12, 2019 [3710] p.2A Ft. Wayne Journal Gazette (IN) Mar 21, 1967, obtained by D. Sue Dible [3711] Virginian-Pilot (Norfolk, VA) Oct 11, 2000

PATRICK JASON HART Sixth great grandson of progenitor Nicholas Kegg. **SARAH E. HART** Sixth great granddaughter of progenitor Nicholas Kegg. **VICTOR BRANT HART** Sixth great grandson of progenitor Nicholas Kegg.

HARTMAN

AMY HARTMAN Seventh great granddaughter of progenitor Nicholas Kegg.
ANTHONY RYAN HARTMAN [3711A] (1985 – 2008) son of Kenneth and Joyce (Johnson) Hartman was an avid Pittsburgh Steelers fan and also a fan of the Boston Celtics. He enjoyed listening to music, from Oldies to Rap to Rock and Roll. He also enjoyed playing video games and being online with his friends. Anthony's wit, charm and sarcasm will be missed by all who knew him. He overcame many personal hurdles in his life, learning how to cope with his disability; he never let it hold him back.
CARRIE HARTMAN Seventh great granddaughter of progenitor Nicholas Kegg.
CHARLE HARTMAN Seventh great grandson of progenitor Nicholas Kegg. **E. LYNN HARTMAN** Sixth great grandson of progenitor Nicholas Kegg. **EULA BLANCHE HARTMAN** [3712, 3713] (1892 – 1985) daughter of Robert and Mary (Keggs) Hartman married three times; first to Walter Lee Cain with whom she was mother of (3). She married Kevin Gilmore and later, married Thomas Joseph Ready.
KELLY HARTMAN Seventh great granddaughter of progenitor Nicholas Kegg.
KIMBERLY A. HARTMAN Sixth great granddaughter of progenitor Nicholas Kegg.
MAKAYLA HARTMAN Seventh great granddaughter of progenitor Nicholas Kegg.
MARY LEE HARTMAN Seventh great granddaughter of progenitor Nicholas Kegg. **MONTGOMERY SHAWN HARTMAN** [3713A] aka "Monty" (1970 – 2019) son of Darwin and Mary Ann (Herrington) Hartman, married Angie A. Young with whom he was father of (2). Monty enlisted in the United States Army and was stationed in Germany. He enjoyed watching football, wrestling and doing activities with his two daughters. **PHEBE E. HARTMAN** [3714] (1896 – 1966) daughter of Robert and Mary (Keggs) Hartman, married Charles Painter Shannon with whom she was mother of (1). Phebe was a member of the Methodist Church and the Louise Chapter of the Order of Eastern Star.
SHANNON HARTMAN Seventh great granddaughter of progenitor Nicholas Kegg.
TREY HARTMAN Seventh great grandson of progenitor Nicholas Kegg.

HARTSAUK

CORA LYNN HARTSAUK [3715] (1878 – 1944) daughter of Frederick and Ada Bell (Cessna) Hartsauk married twice; first to Ward C. Mauk with whom she was mother of (1). Later, she married Sanford Alston Shearer.

HARTUNG

EMILY KRISTINE HARTUNG Eighth great granddaughter of progenitor Nicholas Kegg.

HARTZ

GRACE E. HARTZ Seventh great granddaughter of progenitor Nicholas Kegg.

HARTZELL

DUSTIN W. HARTZELL [3716] (1983 – 2006) son of Steven and Allison (Swikoski) Hartzell. Dustin was a graduate of Kalkaska High School who was killed suddenly of an automobile accident.

[3711A] Daily News (CA) May 30, 2008 [3712] Big Sandy News (KY) Aug 25, 1922 [3713] Miami Herald (FL) Jan 5, 1985 [3713A] Earthman Baytown Funeral Home (TX) obtained by D. Sue Dible [3714] Big Sandy News (KY) Dec 22, 1966 [3715] p.2 Bedford Gazette (PA) June 23, 1944 [3716] Gladwin County Record & Clarion (MI) May 2, 2006

LACEE J. HARTZELL Seventh great granddaughter of progenitor Nicholas Kegg.

HARVEY

ADALYNN HARVEY Seventh great granddaughter of progenitor Nicholas Kegg.
ALICIA SUZANNE HARVEY Sixth great granddaughter of progenitor Nicholas Kegg.
BRANDEN KEITH HARVEY [3716A] (2006 – 2007) son of Jamie and Misty (Marrs) Harvey was always happy, enjoying Dumbo, Monsters and The Jungle Book. **BROOK ELIZABETH HARVEY** Eighth great granddaughter of progenitor Nicholas Kegg. **DRAKE DONOVAN HARVEY** Sixth great grandson of progenitor Nicholas Kegg. **GABRIEL HARVEY** Seventh great grandson of progenitor Nicholas Kegg. **JAMIE KEITH HARVEY** [3716B] (1975 – 2019) son of Keith and Betty Jane (Davis) Harvey married Misty Marrs with whom he was father of (2). Jamie was employed by Wolverine World Wide for 18 years until his health declined due to cancer. Jamie enjoyed music, playing his guitar and singing. He collected Star Wars memorabilia, played video games, and he looked forward to riding his recumbent bicycle. **THERESA HARVEY** Sixth great granddaughter of progenitor Nicholas Kegg. **LYNN ELIZABETH HARVEY** Sixth great granddaughter of progenitor Nicholas Kegg.
WILLIE LEE HARVEY Sixth great grandson of progenitor Nicholas Kegg.

HASENFRATZ

HOLLEY ROSE HASENFRATZ Seventh great granddaughter of progenitor Nicholas Kegg.

HATHAWAY

ALLI HATHAWAY Sixth great granddaughter of progenitor Nicholas Kegg.
AMY ELIZABETH HATHAWAY Sixth great granddaughter of progenitor Nicholas Kegg.
ANDREW SCOT HATHAWAY Sixth great grandson of progenitor Nicholas Kegg.
CAITIE HATHAWAY Sixth great granddaughter of progenitor Nicholas Kegg.

HATLEY

VINCENT HATLEY Seventh great grandson of progenitor Nicholas Kegg.

HAUCH

ALYSSA HAUCH Seventh great granddaughter of progenitor Nicholas Kegg. **CHASE HAUCH** Seventh great grandson of progenitor Nicholas Kegg. **DANIELLE HAUCH** Seventh great granddaughter of progenitor Nicholas Kegg. **EMILY HAUCH** Seventh great granddaughter of progenitor Nicholas Kegg. **TREY HAUCH** Seventh great grandson of progenitor Nicholas Kegg.

HAUF

HELEN HAUF Fifth great granddaughter of progenitor Nicholas Kegg.
PHYLLIS HAUF Fifth great granddaughter of progenitor Nicholas Kegg.

HAUGEN

JOHANNA L. HAUGEN Fifth great granddaughter of progenitor Nicholas Kegg.
MARY KATHRYN HAUGEN aka "Katie", Fifth great granddaughter of progenitor Nicholas Kegg.

[3716A, 3716B] Daggett-Gilbert Funeral Home (MI)

HAUGH

JANE HAUGH Fifth great granddaughter of progenitor Nicholas Kegg. **JOLENE HAUGH** Fifth great granddaughter of progenitor Nicholas Kegg. **ROBERT M. HAUGH** [3717] (1914 – 1994) aka "Bob", son of Harry and Laura (Turner) Haugh, married Lorraine Dingman with whom he was father of (2).

HAUSE

KELLY HAUSE Seventh great grandson of progenitor Nicholas Kegg.
STACY LYNN HAUSE Seventh great granddaughter of progenitor Nicholas Kegg.

HAUSEN

ROBERT D. HAUSEN Sixth great grandson of progenitor Nicholas Kegg.
STACI MICHELLE HAUSEN Sixth great granddaughter of progenitor Nicholas Kegg.
TAREN DANIELLE HAUSEN Sixth great granddaughter of progenitor Nicholas Kegg.

HAUSER

RICK HAUSER Seventh great grandson of progenitor Nicholas Kegg.

HAVENS

KATIE MARIE HAVENS Seventh great granddaughter of progenitor Nicholas Kegg.
RILEY HAVENS Seventh great granddaughter of progenitor Nicholas Kegg.

HAVERFIELD

BETTY JEANNE HAVERFIELD [3717A] (1927 – 2004) daughter of Carl and Blanche (Wertz) Haverfield, married James Wallace Holloman with whom she was mother of (1). Betty retired from Uforma, after thirty-seven years of service. She had attended the first Baptist Church. Betty enjoyed crocheting and making baby blankets which she donated to charity. **CHARLENE HAVERFIELD** Fifth great granddaughter of progenitor Nicholas Kegg. **CHARLES EDWIN HAVERFIELD** [3717B] (1922 – 1998) son of Carl and Blanche (Wertz) Haverfield, married Bertadean Ola Cole with whom he was father of (3). Charles was a retired self-employed painter/contractor. He was a member of the Park Avenue Baptist Church and in the past had served on several committees within the church. Charles was a veteran of the U.S. Marines serving in WWII in the Marshall Islands. **EVELYN IRENE HAVERFIELD** [3717C] (1918 – 2005) daughter of Carl and Blanche (Wertz) Haverfield, married James Lee O'Hearn. Evelyn retired from Uforma Shelby Business Forms. She was a member of the Ontario United Methodist Church, Ontario Senior Citizens and AARP. **JAMES CHARLES HAVERFIELD** aka "Jim", Fifth great grandson of progenitor Nicholas Kegg. **JAN HAVERFIELD** Fifth great granddaughter of progenitor Nicholas Kegg. **JEFF HAVERFIELD** Sixth great grandson of progenitor Nicholas Kegg. **KEVIN HAVERFIELD** Sixth great grandson of progenitor Nicholas Kegg.
MILDRED MARIE HAVERFIELD [3718] (1920 – 2003) daughter of Carl and Blanche (Wertz) Haverfield, married Woodrow Carter Roberts with whom she was mother of (3). Mildred retired from Shelby City Schools where she had been a secretary for many years. She was a member of the First Christian Church. **STEVEN HAVERFIELD** Fifth great grandson of progenitor Nicholas Kegg.

[3717] p.14 Register Star (Rockford, IL) Sep 11, 1994 [3717A] News Journal (Mansfield, Ohio) Nov 30, 2004 [3717B] p.8 - News Journal (OH) Jan 29, 1998, contributed by D. Sue Dible [3717C] Coshocton Tribune (OH) Jan 7, 2005 [3718] Turner Funeral Home (Shelby, OH)

HAW

MAKAYLA GAYLE HAW Seventh great granddaughter of progenitor Nicholas Kegg.

HAY

CARL A. HAY Fifth great grandson of progenitor Nicholas Kegg. **CARLA HAY** Sixth great granddaughter of progenitor Nicholas Kegg. **DWAYNE A. HAY** Sixth great grandson of progenitor Nicholas Kegg. **KAREN HAY** Fifth great granddaughter of progenitor Nicholas Kegg.

HAYES

HARRIET HAYES [3718A] (1919 – 2011) daughter of Ernest and Gertrude (Bradley) Hayes, married William S. Fisher with whom she was mother of (3). Becoming a fashion designer was nothing she had planned on. A graduate of the University of Toledo who had won a scholarship to Parsons, she was interested in display and advertising art. A Milwaukee firm had offered an opportunity to her sister who wasn't interested. Harriet answered the letter, got the job and began designing sportswear in a career that lasted six decades. Beginning her career with Petti, she also worked as a designer creating sportswear lines for Junior House, Jack Winter and later Imperial Knit, where her clients included Pendleton, Bogner and others. She won many awards, including The Fashion Academy Award. While designing for Jack Winter she traveled frequently to Europe and met with Salvador Dali to collaborate on a swimsuit. A young championship tennis player in Toledo, Harriet brought her love of tennis to Milwaukee, playing in Whitefish Bay and at the Town Club. She also loved art and remained an active artist in pastels, drawing and clay. Harriet was an avid cross-country skier and horsewoman throughout her life.
MARY LUEETTA HAYES [3719] (1917 – 1984) daughter of Ernest and Gertrude (Bradley) Hayes, married Frederic Baker Smead with whom she was mother of (1). Mary was a fashion coordinator for many years with the Lasalle's department store.

HAYTER

APRIL J. HAYTER Sixth great granddaughter of progenitor Nicholas Kegg. **AUTUMN L. HAYTER** Sixth great granddaughter of progenitor Nicholas Kegg. **HALEY MCKENZIE HAYTER** Seventh great granddaughter of progenitor Nicholas Kegg. **LORELEI ANN HAYTER** Sixth great granddaughter of progenitor Nicholas Kegg. **MELODY J. HAYTER** Sixth great granddaughter of progenitor Nicholas Kegg.

HAZELRIGG

ANDREW HAZELRIGG Sixth great grandson of progenitor Nicholas Kegg.
JESSICA HAZELRIGG Sixth great granddaughter of progenitor Nicholas Kegg.

HEAD

COLLEEN AGATHA HEAD Seventh great granddaughter of progenitor Nicholas Kegg.
ROBERT VINCENT HEAD JR. Seventh great grandson of progenitor Nicholas Kegg.

HEARD

GARRETT HEARD Seventh great grandson of progenitor Nicholas Kegg.

[3718A] Milwaukee Journal Sentinel (WI) Nov 15, 2011 [3719] Toledo Blade (OH) Nov 25, 1984

GARY DEE HEARD Sixth great grandson of progenitor Nicholas Kegg.

HEASTON

SUSAN KAY HEASTON Sixth great granddaughter of progenitor Nicholas Kegg.

HEATH

AUGIE HEATH Sixth great grandson of progenitor Nicholas Kegg.
FREDERICK LOWRY HEATH Fifth great grandson of progenitor Nicholas Kegg.
FREDERICK WARNER HEATH [3720] (1947 – 2002) son of Fred and Jean (De Young) Heath, was father of (1). Colonel Heath served in the United States Army for 27 years including a tour in Vietnam. His final duty was President of the Disability Board at Walter Reed Army Hospital. During his service he received numerous medals to include: the Silver Star, Legion of Merit, Bronze Star for Valor, Purple Heart, 4 awards of the Meritorious Service Medal, Army Commendation Medal, and the Vietnam Service Medal, among many others. **INFANT HEATH**, (1943 – 1943) son of Fred and Jean (De Young) Heath. **INFANT HEATH** (1944 – 1944) daughter of Fred and Jean (De Young) Heath. **JESSICA HEATH** Seventh great granddaughter of progenitor Nicholas Kegg. **KIRK HEATH III** Eighth great grandson of progenitor Nicholas Kegg. **KIRK B. HEATH II** Seventh great grandson of progenitor Nicholas Kegg. **SMITH HEATH** Sixth great grandson of progenitor Nicholas Kegg.
SOPHIA MARIE HEATH [3720A] (2014 – 2014) daughter of Kirk and Grace (Byrd) Heath.
SUSAN DE YOUNG HEATH Fourth great granddaughter of progenitor Nicholas Kegg.

HEATON

WILLIAM D. HEATON Seventh great grandson of progenitor Nicholas Kegg.

HEDRICK

LORNA ANN HEDRICK Sixth great granddaughter of progenitor Nicholas Kegg.
LEANN RAE HEDRICK Sixth great granddaughter of progenitor Nicholas Kegg.

HEETER

GERALDINE E. HEETER [3721] (1921 – 2002) aka "Geri", daughter of Elmer and Flora (Smith) Heeter, married Arthur S. Amick with whom she was mother of (2). Geri served in the Army Medical Corps as a dental laboratory technician. She was a member of the Beaver Memorial United Methodist Church, Lewisburg, and had taught Sunday School. She was also a member of the American Legion, Kratzer-Dull American Post 182, Lewisburg, the Crimson Rebekah Lodge 312, Lewisburg, a former Girl Scout leader, Mother Advisor of the Rainbow Girls and a member of the Turbot Hills Golf Course, Milton, where in July 1988, she made a hole-in-one on the 16th green. She enjoyed golfing, traveling and gardening and was an avid reader.

HEFFELBOWER

BRELYN HEFFELBOWER Sixth great grandson of progenitor Nicholas Kegg.
DARL JAY HEFFELBOWER Fifth great grandson of progenitor Nicholas Kegg.
GAIL MARIE HEFFELBOWER Fifth great granddaughter of progenitor Nicholas Kegg.
KAMRON DORY HEFFELBOWER Sixth great granddaughter of progenitor Nicholas Kegg.

[3720] arlingtoncemetery.net [3720A] Bedford Gazette (PA) July 14, 2014, contributed by Bob Rose [3721] GenealogyBuff/Sun Gazette (Williamsport, Lycoming Co., PA)

KENDRA C. HEFFELBOWER Sixth great granddaughter of progenitor Nicholas Kegg.
KENT LEWIS HEFFELBOWER Fifth great grandson of progenitor Nicholas Kegg.

HEFFNER

ARLENE AMELIA HEFFNER [3722] (1927 – 2000) daughter of Benjamin and Mabel (Hilty) Heffner married twice; first to William David Kern with whom she was mother of (1). Later, she married William Feher. Arlene was an employee of Clark Candy Co. **BENJAMIN F. HEFFNER** [3723] (1890 – 1940) son of Benjamin and Nora (May) Heffner, married Mabel Eugenia Hilty with whom he was father of (4). **DALE FRANKLIN HEFFNER** [3724] (1934 – 2012) son of Benjamin and Mabel (Hilty) Heffner married twice; first to Brenda Faye Bowser. Later, he married Delores Janet Johnson with whom he was father of (2). Dale was a retired Master Sergeant with the U.S. Marine Corps serving his country in the Korean and Vietnam Wars. He retired after more than 20 years of active service after which he worked at Simplimatic Engineering Company which was later renamed Crown Simplimatic for 23 years before retiring in 2000. While on active duty with the Marine Corps, he served at one time or another with the 1st, 2nd and 3rd Marine Divisions: the 1st, 2nd and 3rd Marine Air Wings as well as other posts and duty stations throughout the world. Dale was a member of Fairview Christian Church and was a long-time member of the Christian Workers Sunday School Class. **DONALD WALTER HEFFNER** Fifth great grandson of progenitor Nicholas Kegg. **DUWANE HILTY HEFFNER JR.** Fifth great grandson of progenitor Nicholas Kegg. **ETHEL M. HEFFNER** [3725] (1895 – 1932) daughter of Benjamin and Nora (May) Heffner, married Joseph F. Roberts. **EUGENE G. HEFFNER** [3726] (1925 – 1944) son of Benjamin and Mabel (Hilty) Heffner. **EUGENIA A. HEFFNER** aka "Gina", Fifth great granddaughter of progenitor Nicholas Kegg. **EVELYN LAURA HEFFNER** [3727] (1904 – 1949) daughter of Benjamin and Nora (May) Heffner, married Henry Halstead. **FREDA H. HEFFNER** (1897 – 1983) daughter of Benjamin and Nora (May) Heffner married three times; first to Harry Clarke with whom she was mother of (2). Later she married John Leroy Davis and John George Brecht. **GALEN HEFFNER** Fifth great grandson of progenitor Nicholas Kegg. **HELEN HARPER HEFFNER** [3728] (1888 – 1976) daughter of Benjamin and Nora (May) Heffner, married Charles Frederick Smith with whom she was mother of (8). Helen was a Gold Star Mother; a member of the American Legion Auxiliary; The VFW Auxiliary; a member of the Good Cheer Class Sunday School of the Presbyterian church and the WCTU. **JAMES A. HEFFNER** Fifth great grandson of progenitor Nicholas Kegg. **JANET S. HEFFNER** Fifth great granddaughter of progenitor Nicholas Kegg. **LEAH H. HEFFNER** Fifth great granddaughter of progenitor Nicholas Kegg. **PAUL ANDREW HEFFNER** Fifth great grandson of progenitor Nicholas Kegg. **PAUL JOSEPH HEFFNER** Fourth great grandson of progenitor Nicholas Kegg. **SHERI LYNN HEFFNER** Fifth great granddaughter of progenitor Nicholas Kegg. **WILLIAM HENRY HEFFNER** [3729] (1892 – 1971) son of Benjamin and Nora (May) Heffner, married Ida Blanche Kilbrige Matheny. William was a retired steel worker with A.M. Byers Co., a member of Clearview United Methodist Church, St. Petersburg and a life member of the Elks Club, Ambridge, Pa.

HEID

HEATHER HEID Sixth great granddaughter of progenitor Nicholas Kegg.
JOHN HEID Sixth great grandson of progenitor Nicholas Kegg.

HEIDORN

ANGELMARIE HEIDORN Ninth great granddaughter of progenitor Nicholas Kegg.

[3722] p.32 Pittsburgh Post Gazette (PA) July 15, 2000 [3723] p.22 Pittsburgh Post Gazette (PA) June 25, 1940 [3724] Heritage Funeral Service and Crematory (VA) [3725] Pittsburgh Daily Post (PA) Aug 2, 1914 [3726] p.18 Pittsburgh Post Gazette (PA) Jan 21, 1944 [3727] p.18 Pittsburgh Post Gazette (PA) Jan 21, 1944 [3728] Bedford County Historical Society (PA), book 11 page 4065 obtained by D. Sue Dible [3729] Tampa Bay Times (FL) June 26, 1971

HEIMAN

BLAKE HEIMAN Seventh great grandson of progenitor Nicholas Kegg. **LUKE HEIMAN** Seventh great grandson of progenitor Nicholas Kegg. **ROSS HEIMAN** Seventh great grandson of progenitor Nicholas Kegg.

HEISS

ALI K. HEISS Fifth great granddaughter of progenitor Nicholas Kegg.
BONNIE KATHLEEN HEISS Fourth great granddaughter of progenitor Nicholas Kegg.
BRIDGETTE JOKAY MARIE HEISS Fifth great granddaughter of progenitor Nicholas Kegg.
CLAIRE DEYOUNG HEISS Fourth great granddaughter of progenitor Nicholas Kegg.
DANIEL TUPOU HEISS Fifth great grandson of progenitor Nicholas Kegg
DIRK F. HEISS Fourth great grandson of progenitor Nicholas Kegg.

HEIT

SHADIE HEIT Seventh great granddaughter of progenitor Nicholas Kegg.

HELBIG

CORY JAMES HELBIG Sixth great grandson of progenitor Nicholas Kegg.
JOSEPH EUGENE HELBIG Fifth great grandson of progenitor Nicholas Kegg.
JUSTIN EUGENE HELBIG Sixth great grandson of progenitor Nicholas Kegg.
TERRY R. HELBIG Fifth great grandson of progenitor Nicholas Kegg.

HELFERT

MARK HELFERT Sixth great grandson of progenitor Nicholas Kegg.

HELFRICH

CHRISTOPHER ALLEN HELFRICH (1973 – 1975) son of Claude and Barbara (Smith) Helfrich was accidentally killed when run over by an automobile wheel.

HELIE

ERIC A. HELIE Seventh great grandson of progenitor Nicholas Kegg. **JESSICA L. HELIE** Seventh great granddaughter of progenitor Nicholas Kegg.

HELMS

EMILY P. HELMS Sixth great granddaughter of progenitor Nicholas Kegg.
REBECCA R. HELMS [3730] (1993 – 1993) daughter of Rev. Timothy and Lisa (Diehl) Helms.

HEMENWAY

HOLY EILEEN HEMENWAY (1996 – 1996) daughter of Todd and Jill (Hollenbeck) Hemenway.
KATHRYN HEMENWAY aka "Katie", Seventh great granddaughter of progenitor Nicholas Kegg.
PATRICK HEMENWAY Seventh great grandson of progenitor Nicholas Kegg.

[3730] Morning Call (PA) Oct 25, 1993

HEMSLEY

CHRISTINA LYNN HEMSLEY Sixth great granddaughter of progenitor Nicholas Kegg.

HENDEN

ASHER HENDEN Seventh great grandson of progenitor Nicholas Kegg.
RYKER DONALD HENDEN Seventh great grandson of progenitor Nicholas Kegg.

HENDERSON

AUSTIN HENDERSON Seventh great grandson of progenitor Nicholas Kegg. **AMANDA HENDERSON** Seventh great granddaughter of progenitor Nicholas Kegg. **JEFFERY HENDERSON** Sixth great grandson of progenitor Nicholas Kegg. **KEIRSTYN HENDERSON** Seventh great granddaughter of progenitor Nicholas Kegg. **MATTHEW HENDERSON** Seventh great grandson of progenitor Nicholas Kegg. **REBECCA HENDERSON** Sixth great granddaughter of progenitor Nicholas Kegg. **ZACHARY HENDERSON** Seventh great grandson of progenitor Nicholas Kegg.

HENDRICKS

BARBARA HENDRICKS Seventh great granddaughter of progenitor Nicholas Kegg.
JENNIFER L. HENDRICKS aka "Jenn", Seventh great granddaughter of progenitor Nicholas Kegg.
KATHRYN M. HENDRICKS Seventh great granddaughter of progenitor Nicholas Kegg.
RODGER PAUL HENDRICKS Sixth great grandson of progenitor Nicholas Kegg.

HENDRICKSON

JOSEPH ROBERT HENDRICKSON Sixth great grandson of progenitor Nicholas Kegg.
KYLE HENDRICKSON Seventh great grandson of progenitor Nicholas Kegg.

HENDRIX

ELLEN HENDRIX Sixth great granddaughter of progenitor Nicholas Kegg. **JONATHAN MICHAEL HENDRIX** Fifth great grandson of progenitor Nicholas Kegg. **JULIA HENDRIX** Sixth great granddaughter of progenitor Nicholas Kegg. **LORIAN KAY HENDRIX** Fifth great granddaughter of progenitor Nicholas Kegg. **SUSAN ELAINE HENDRIX** Fifth great granddaughter of progenitor Nicholas Kegg.

HENGSTELER

ELIZABETH HENGSTELER Eighth great granddaughter of progenitor Nicholas Kegg.
MICHAEL STEVEN HARLOW HENGSTELER Seventh great grandson of progenitor Nicholas Kegg. **SAMANTHA HENGSTELER** Eighth great granddaughter of progenitor Nicholas Kegg.
STEVEN HENGSTELER Eighth great grandson of progenitor Nicholas Kegg.
TIA HENGSTELER Eighth great granddaughter of progenitor Nicholas Kegg.

HENNESSE

DENISE HENNESSE Eighth great granddaughter of progenitor Nicholas Kegg.
ZACHARY HENNESSE Eighth great grandson of progenitor Nicholas Kegg.

HENRY

AARON ROBERT HENRY Seventh great grandson of progenitor Nicholas Kegg.   **KERRI LYNN HENRY** Seventh great granddaughter of progenitor Nicholas Kegg.   **LAURA HENRY** Sixth great granddaughter of progenitor Nicholas Kegg.   **MATTHEW IAN HENRY** Seventh great grandson of progenitor Nicholas Kegg.   **SARAH MARIE HENRY** Seventh great granddaughter of progenitor Nicholas Kegg.

HENSCHEN

KATHLEEN A. HENSCHEN aka Katie", Sixth great granddaughter of progenitor Nicholas Kegg.

HENSLEY

HALEY JO HENSLEY Sixth great granddaughter of progenitor Nicholas Kegg.
KATELYN ELIZABETH HENSLEY Sixth great granddaughter of progenitor Nicholas Kegg.
RYLEE GRACE HENSLEY Sixth great granddaughter of progenitor Nicholas Kegg.
STEVEN HENSLEY Seventh great grandson of progenitor Nicholas Kegg.

HENSON

JOHN RYAN HENSON Sixth great grandson of progenitor Nicholas Kegg.

HEPHNER

DIANA COLLETTE HEPHNER [3731] (1946 – 1984) daughter of John and Dorothy (Coffman) Hephner married twice; first to Donald Dean Drinnen with whom she was mother of (2). Later, she married Jerry Morgan. Diana was a homemaker.   **ROXANNA JEANNE HEPHNER** Sixth great granddaughter of progenitor Nicholas Kegg.

HERDT

AMBER HERDT Seventh great granddaughter of progenitor Nicholas Kegg.   **CHRISTIAN HERDT** Seventh great grandson of progenitor Nicholas Kegg.

HERLOFSKY

BEAU BRINKLEY HERLOFSKY Seventh great granddaughter of progenitor Nicholas Kegg.

HERMAN

CAREN LYNN HERMAN Sixth great granddaughter of progenitor Nicholas Kegg.
CARRIE ELIZABETH HERMAN Sixth great granddaughter of progenitor Nicholas Kegg.
COLLEEN HERMAN Sixth great granddaughter of progenitor Nicholas Kegg.
DALE JEFFREY HERMAN Sixth great grandson of progenitor Nicholas Kegg.
LYNDA JANETTE HERMAN Sixth great granddaughter of progenitor Nicholas Kegg.
TIM ALLEN HERMAN Sixth great grandson of progenitor Nicholas Kegg.

[3731] p.8 Wichita Eagle (KS) March 14, 1984

HERNANDEZ

GABRIEL LOREN HERNANDEZ Seventh great grandson of progenitor Nicholas Kegg.
OLIVIA HERNANDEZ Seventh great granddaughter of progenitor Nicholas Kegg.

HERNDON

CHRISTOPHER HEATH HERNDON (3731A) (1970 -2010) son of Clifford ana Lila (Minear) Herndon. Christopher was a security guard and father of a son. **JERRID LARENCE HERNDON** Seventh great grandson of progenitor Nicholas Kegg.

HERR

JASON HERR Sixth great grandson of progenitor Nicholas Kegg.

HERRELL

FRANKIE DEE CREACH HERRELL (1949 – 1994) son of Floyd and Zelma (Shirley) Creach was married twice, first to Sally Ann Graffis and later to Vickie Ann Day. **WANDA JEAN HERRELL** aka "Dodi", Fifth great granddaughter of progenitor Nicholas Kegg.

HERRING

GRACE O. HERRING (3731B) (1917 – 1995) daughter of William and Golda (Boissenet) Herring, married Forrest Paul Knepper with whom she was mother of (4). Grace formerly owned Little Turtle Child Care Center 10 years, was a member of Trinity Episcopal Church and was an Allen County 4-H leader.

HERRINGTON

CONNIE JEAN HERRINGTON (3732) (1953 – 2018) daughter of James and Norma (Bowen) Herrington was with the graduating class of 1973 at the Iowa Braille and Sight Saving School. At the age of 19, after spending a month of examinations and tests, at the University of Iowa Hospital, in Iowa City, about 50 specialists from all over the world tried to determine why Connie had become deaf and blind. She was diagnosed with spinal cerebellar ataxia; they estimated that Connie would not survive past the age of 30. Her neurologist calls her the miracle lady and said they would have to name this ataxia after her as hers was so unique. Connie went on to work at Options of Linn County doing a variety of jobs. She has attended Camp Courageous and in 1988 she attended the American Association of the Deaf Blind National Conference, in Baton Rouge, Louisiana. **DAVID LEROY HERRINGTON** (1937 – 1990) son of Marion and Ruth (Jacobs) Herrington, married Teresa. **DOLORES JEAN HERRINGTON** (3733) (1929 – 2004) aka "Dee", daughter of Marion and Ruth (Jacobs) Herrington, married Leland Merle Butler with whom she was mother of (3). During her life Dee worked as a waitress, sold Avon, worked as a sizer at the cap factories in Grant City, Misouri and Mount Ayr, Iowa and as a clerk at McNeily and Mitchell Drug Stores in Mount Ayr. She was an excellent seamstress, evidence by ensembles she made for the county fair and the school dresses she made for her daughter, as well as the dozens of costumed rabbits and handkerchief and pillow slip dolls gracing the homes of many friends and relatives. In her younger days, Dee was a meticulous wallpaper-hanger, earning her a fine reputation for her craftsmanship

---

(3731A) The Graham Leader (TX) Apr 9, 2010 (3731B) Fort Wayne News Sentinel (IN) Oct 16, 1995 (3732) Pauley Jones Funeral Homes, LLC (IA) obtained by D. Sue Dible (3733) Mount Ayr Record-News (IA) Sep 23, 2004, IAGENWEB/transcribed by Sharon R. Becker

and extra money to contribute to the household. Dee was an outgoing person with a wonderful sense of humor, a great laugh and a big smile. **JAMES EDWIN HERRINGTON** [3733A] aka "Jim" (1932 – 2012) son of Marion and Ruth (Jacobs) Herrington married twice, first to Norma Jean Bowen with whom he was father of (2). Jim enlisted in the U.S. Army during the Korean War and, received his basic training at Camp Roberts in California and later, was stationed at Baumholder, Germany with the Army Corp of Engineers. From this unit he and one other were selected to go to Kaiserschlautern, Germany for Morse Code training to be translators. After his honorable discharge as a corporal, Jim worked in heavy equipment until 1960. Jim was employed by Collins Radio and retired from Rockwell Collins as an industrial engineer in the telecommunications division. He had a great sense of humor, and one could expect to chuckle at some quip and one liner that would just pop out of his mouth.
MARY ANN HERRINGTON Fifth great granddaughter of progenitor Nicholas Kegg.
MAX E. HERRINGTON [3733B] (1930 – 2016) son of Marion and Ruth (Jacobs) Herrington, married Helen Ruth Turnball with whom he was father of (2). Max was the manager at Warin Oil Company, south of Atlantic on Highway 6. In years to follow, he managed the Warin Truckstop at The Valley when the Interstate first came through Cass County in 1967 and later, Hoegh Tire and Oil. Max retired as First Whitney Bank's custodian after 13 years. He took every opportunity, often with family at his side, to throw his line in the water. Max especially loved catfishing on the Nishnabotna; one trip ending with a 10-pound catch. He loved to feed the birds and squirrels every day. Max was one of those guys that would do anything for others and not expect a single thing in return. He and Helen often sent care packages home with family filled with household necessities. The couple treasured time with family.
PAMELA KIM HERRINGTON Sixth great granddaughter of progenitor Nicholas Kegg.
RANDY HERRINGTON Sixth great grandson of progenitor Nicholas Kegg.
STEVE HERRINGTON Sixth great grandson of progenitor Nicholas Kegg.

HERRON

JACOB DANIEL HERRON Seventh great grandson of progenitor Nicholas Kegg.

HERSHBERGER

AARON JOSEPH HERSHBERGER Sixth great grandson of progenitor Nicholas Kegg.
ALECIA N. HERSHBERGER Eighth great granddaughter of progenitor Nicholas Kegg.
ALISON KAY HERSHBERGER Sixth great granddaughter of progenitor Nicholas Kegg.
ANDREA HERSHBERGER Sixth great granddaughter of progenitor Nicholas Kegg.
CHARLES GALEN HERSHBERGER (1916 – 1919) son of James and Mary (Kegg) Hershberger.
DANA LEROY HERSHBERGER Sixth great grandson of progenitor Nicholas Kegg.
EMILY BERNICE HERSHBERGER [3733C] (1920 – 2017) daughter of James and Mary (Kegg) Hershberger, married Glen Otis Pepple with whom she was Mother of (5). Emily enjoyed gardening, sewing, quilting and was a 4-H leader for many years. **ERIN LAYLA HERSHBERGER** Seventh great granddaughter of progenitor Nicholas Kegg. **FLORENCE H. HERSHBERGER** [3733D] (1935 – 2014) daughter of Francis and Romaine (Kegg) Hershberger, married Bernard I Jaffe with whom she was mother of (2). **GALEN J. HERSHBERGER** Fifth great grandson of progenitor Nicholas Kegg.
GAYLENE S. HERSHBERGER Fifth great granddaughter of progenitor Nicholas Kegg.
JAMES S. HERSHBERGER [3734] (1929 – 2003) son of James and Mary (Kegg) Hershberger, married Barbara D. King with whom he was father of (3). James was a farmer and retired from Lion Manufacturing in Everett after 20 years of service. **JOHN HERSHBERGER** Sixth great grandson of progenitor Nicholas Kegg. **JOSEPH BIXLER HERSHBERGER**, aka "Joe", Fifth great grandson of progenitor Nicholas Kegg. **KATHRYN HERSHBERGER** Fifth great granddaughter of progenitor

---

[3733A] Mount Ayr Record News (IA) Oct 24, 2012 [3733B] Mount Ayr Record News (IA) Aug 3, 2016, contributed by D. Sue Dible [3733C] Bedford Gazette (PA) Jan 30, 2017, obtained by Bob Rose [3733D] Bedford Gazette (PA) Jan 4, 2014, contributed by Bob Rose [3734] p.3 Bedford Inquirer (PA) Aug 29, 2003, obtained by Bob Rose

Nicholas Kegg. **KERRY N. HERSHBERGER** Sixth great grandson of progenitor Nicholas Kegg. **MARY LOUISE HERSHBERGER** Fourth great granddaughter of progenitor Nicholas Kegg. **NANCY ELIZABETH HERSHBERGER** [3735] (1956 – 2020) daughter of Thomas and Janet (Spinos Hershberger married Mr. Cocklin with whom she was mother of (2). Later, she married Walter Darl Brendlinger. Nancy was employed as a nurse's aide at Brookdale Senior Living. She enjoyed Calligraphy and spending time with her family. **REBECCA MAE HERSHBERGER** [3735A] (1922 – 2014) daughter of James and Mary (Kegg) Hershberger, married Leroy O'Neal with whom she was mother of (1). Rebecca was employed at Lion Manufacturing, Everett, for many years until its closing. She was a meticulous housekeeper and enjoyed crafting and sewing. She along with her husband designed and created many beautiful quilts. **SARA E. HERSHBERGER** [3736] (1926 – 2003) daughter of James and Mary (Kegg) Hershberger, married S. Bernard England with whom she was mother of (2). Sara was a member of the Snake Spring Valley Church of the Brethren, where she served as a deacon. She was a member of the National Holstein Association and was employed by the Lion Manufacturing Company of Everett for over 14 years. Sara was a farm wife who enjoyed her family, grandson and friends. She loved cooking, baking and helping on the farm, driving tractor and making hay.
TARA SUE HERSHBERGER Sixth great granddaughter of progenitor Nicholas Kegg.
TESSA HERSHBERGER Eighth great granddaughter of progenitor Nicholas Kegg.
THOMAS F. HERSHBERGER [3737] (1934 – 2022) aka "Tom" son of Francis and Romaine (Kegg) Hershberger married Janet Spinos with whom he was father of (2). Later, he married Darlene Shoemaker Rice. Tom served in the Army National Guard and retired from New Enterprise Stone & Lime. He was an avid hunter and woodworker making numerous furniture pieces. Tom also enjoyed working in his yard, gardening, and landscaping. **TROY A. HERSHBERGER** Fifth great grandson of progenitor Nicholas Kegg.

HERSHEY

CHARMAR YVONNE HERSHEY Fifth great granddaughter of progenitor Nicholas Kegg.
COLIN HARRY HERSHEY Fifth great grandson of progenitor Nicholas Kegg.
WILLIAM NYCUM HERSHEY Fifth great grandson of progenitor Nicholas Kegg.

HERSHISER

ADDIE HERSHISER (1852 – 1854) daughter of Peter and Catherine (Person) Hershiser.
ALEDA HERSHISER [3738] (1911 – 2001) daughter of William and Vesta Pearl (Fast) Hershiser, married Floyd Peter Peck. Aleda taught and was a guidance counselor for the Attica schools for 36 years; was a member of the Attica United Methodist Church where she served as various officers including church secretary for 30 years and lay delegate to annual conference; was 4-H adviser in the 1940s, a former member of chapter of the OES serving as secretary and past worthy matron and state representative; OES 189 Tiffin Chapter, past mother advisor of Willard Rainbow Girls, Knights Templer Ladies Club of Tiffin, Dendarah 10 of Toledo, Daughters of the American Revolution and the Delta Cappa Gamma Society International; **ALICE FAY HERSHISER** Fifth great granddaughter of progenitor Nicholas Kegg. **ALICE MARIE HERSHISER** [3739] (1933 – 1933) daughter of Almon and June (Hart) Hershiser. **ALLISON GRACE HERSHISER** aka "Allie", Sixth great granddaughter of progenitor Nicholas Kegg. **ALMON WILLARD HERSHISER** [3740] (1903 – 1973) son of Lawrence and Sarah (Fink) Hershiser, married June Elizabeth Hart with whom he was father of (9). Almon was a B&O Railroad engineer, retiring in 1969 after 46 years of service. He was a member of the First United Methodist Church, Eagles Lodge and the Brotherhood of Railroad Engineers.

[3735] Matthew X. Merlin Funeral Home (PA) [3735A] Bedford Gazette (PA) Sept 29, 2014, contributed by Bob Rose [3736] p.3 - Bedford Inquirer (PA) Oct 24, 2003, obtained by Bob Rose [3737] Bedford Gazette (PA) July 29, 2022 [3738] Genlookups.comOhio Obituary and Death Notice Archive - p1729 Advertiser Tribune (OH) [3739] p.10 The Mansfield News (OH) May 3,1933 [3740] p.3 Mansfield News Journal (OH) Aug 25, 1973

ALMON WILLARD HERSHISER [3741] (1926 – 2009) aka "Willie", son of Almon and June (Hart) Hershiser married twice; first to Lafyrnn E. Cross with whom he was father of (1). Later, he married Gwendolyn Carnock. Almon was a truck driver and farmer. He served in the U.S. Marines during WWII and was a member of the Plymouth American Legion. **ANN ELIZABETH HERSHISER**, (abt 1829 – bef 1860) daughter of Henry and Barbara (Kegg) Hershiser, married Edward P. Bradley with whom she was mother of (2). **ANNIE HERSHISER** Sixth great granddaughter of progenitor Nicholas Kegg. **ANTHONY HERSHISER** aka "Tony", Sixth great grandson of progenitor Nicholas Kegg. **AUGUSTUS W. HERSHISER** (1877 – 1903) son of David and Mary (Garner) Hershiser, married Mattie Astelle Eswine with whom he was father of (1). **BRADEN HERSHISER** Sixth great grandson of progenitor Nicholas Kegg. **BRIAN SCOTT HERSHISER** Sixth great grandson of progenitor Nicholas Kegg. **CALEB WILLIAM HERSHISER** [3741A] (2002 – 2017) son of Robert and Anna (Cummings) Hershiser. Caleb was an eighth grader who enjoyed camping, swimming, fishing and being outside, but most of all enjoyed spending time with his family and friends. Caleb was always smiling and would do whatever he could to help others. **CHARLES HENRY HERSHISER** (1870 – 1926) son of David and Mary (Garner) Hershiser. Charles had worked as a bookkeeper, a wholesale lumber dealer and was a retired realtor. **CHESTER PERRY HERSHISER** [3742] (1887 – 1966) son of Franklin and Mary Belle (Miller) Hershiser, married Estella Faye Hutchison with whom he was father of (2). Chester was a farmer and a member of the Richmond EUB Church, Farm Bureau Council and was a former member of the Richmond Township School Board. He had served several terms as a township trustee.
CHRISTA ANN HERSHISER Fifth great granddaughter of progenitor Nicholas Kegg.
CODY HERSHISER Sixth great grandson of progenitor Nicholas Kegg.
COLTEN ADAM HERSHISER (2005 – 2005) son of John and Heather (Fife) Hershiser.
DANIEL ALLEN HERSHISER Fifth great grandson of progenitor Nicholas Kegg.
DARIN HERSHISER Fifth great grandson of progenitor Nicholas Kegg.
DARYL DAVID HERSHISER [3743] (1945 – 2011) son of Augustus and Frances (Landis) Hershiser.
DAVID F. HERSHISER (1836 – 1900) son of Henry and Barbara (Kegg) Hershiser married twice; first to Catherine Jane Keesey with whom he was father of (2). Later, he married Mary J. Garner with whom he was father of (2). David was a veteran of Company C, 164th Infantry Regiment, Ohio. He was employed as the foreman of a lumber yard. **DAWN RAE HERSHISER** Fifth great granddaughter of progenitor Nicholas Kegg. **DEAN KEITH HERSHISER** Fifth great grandson of progenitor Nicholas Kegg. **DEREK SEAN HERSHISER** [3743A] aka "The Bear" (1979 – 2011) son of Darrell and Linda (Ganzhorn) Hershiser, married Robin Lynn Schrader with whom he was father of (1). Derek worked at Snyders-Lance in Ashland, Ohio. He loved his dog, Kayla. He enjoyed football, fishing and camping; especially lighting a bonfire when the sun went down. One of his many hobbies was helping his friends and family with their home improvement projects. **DIANE HERSHISER** Fifth great granddaughter of progenitor Nicholas Kegg. **DONNA MARIE HERSHISER** Sixth great granddaughter of progenitor Nicholas Kegg. **DUANE ROGER HERSHISER** Fifth great grandson of progenitor Nicholas Kegg.
DUANE SHERMAN HERSHISER Fourth great grandson of progenitor Nicholas Kegg.
EDNA ARDELL HERSHISER [3744] (1918 – 2000) daughter of William and Vesta Pearl (Fast) Hershiser, married Henry Arthur Capell with whom she was mother of (3). Edna was a homemaker and worked for many years at the Village Pastry in Willard. She was a member of the Richmond United Methodist Church, the Missionary Society of the church and the Huron County Farm Bureau.
EDNA CORA HERSHISER [3745] (1880 – 1962) daughter of Franklin and Mary Belle (Miller) Hershiser married twice; first to William Henry Crabaugh. Later, she married Clarence Brosia Fritz with whom she was mother of (1). **EMILY HERSHISER** Sixth great granddaughter of progenitor Nicholas Kegg.
FRANKLIN C. HERSHISER [3746] (1854 – 1919) aka "Frank", son of Peter and Catherine (Person) Hershiser, married Mary Belle Miller with whom he was father of (5). Frank was prominent in

---

[3741] Lindsey-Kocher Funeral Service (Willard, OH) [3741A] Sandusky Register (OH) Apr 8, 2017 [3742] Library obituary clipping obtained by D. Sue Dible [3743] p3B Columbus Dispatch (OH) - March 20, 2011 [3743A] News Journal (OH) Oct 21, 2011 [3744] Bloomfield Gazette (OH) Jan 2000 [3745] p2 Norwalk Reflector Herald (OH) July 31, 1962, obtained by D. Sue Dible [3746] Sandusky Daily Register (OH) Dec 15, 1919, obtained by D. Sue Dible

Republican political affairs and was held in high esteem in his community. **HAROLD EDSON HERSHISER** [3747] (1899 – 1960) son of Lawrence and Sarah (Fink) Hershiser, married Mildred E. Stephenson with whom he was father of (3). Harold was employed as superintendent of the Huron County Highway Department, and prior to employment with the highway department was a construction worker with Richards Construction Co. Mr. Hershiser was a member of the EUS Church, and a member and past president of the Willard Conservation League. **HENRY KEGG HERSHISER** [3748, 3749] (1831 – 1901) son of Henry and Barbara (Kegg) Hershiser, married Susan D. Myers with whom he was father of (1). Dr. Hershiser read medicine in the office of Dr. J. P. Kinnaman and graduated from the Columbus Medical School. He served in the Civil war as a surgeon and was assistant surgeon of the 147th O.V.J., when he quit the service. After the close of the war, he engaged in the drug business in Tiffin and continued in it for nine years. Henry was a member of the Masonic fraternity having attained the degree of Knight Templar. He was one of the pioneer physicians of this county and a highly esteemed man. He also belonged to the G.A.R. **IDA BARBARA HERSHISER** (1862 – 1917) daughter of David and Catherine (Keesy) Hershiser, married Emery Allen Keesy with whom she was mother of (1). **IDA L. HERSHISER** [3750] (1898 – 1984) daughter of Lawrence and Sarah (Fink) Hershiser, married Charles Bryan Kochel with whom she was mother of (5). Ida was a member of the Union Pisgah United Methodist Church of Attica. **INFANT HERSHISER** (1850 – 1850) child of Peter and Catherine (Person) Hershiser. **INFANT HERSHISER** (1856 – 1856) child of Peter and Catherine (Person) Hershiser. **INFANT HERSHISER** (1925 – 1925) son of Almon and June (Hart) Hershiser. **INFANT HERSHISER** (1930 – 1930) daughter of Almon and June (Hart) Hershiser.
JACOB HERSHISER Sixth great grandson of progenitor Nicholas Kegg. **JANET HERSHISER** Fifth great granddaughter of progenitor Nicholas Kegg. **JASON CRAIG HERSHISER** Sixth great grandson of progenitor Nicholas Kegg. **JASON LEE HERSHISER** Sixth great grandson of progenitor Nicholas Kegg. **JEANA K. HERSHISER** Sixth great granddaughter of progenitor Nicholas Kegg.
JEFFREY HERSHISER Fifth great grandson of progenitor Nicholas Kegg.
JEFFREY RAY HERSHISER Fifth great grandson of progenitor Nicholas Kegg.
JEFFREY TODD HERSHISER Sixth great grandson of progenitor Nicholas Kegg.
JOAN ELAINE HERSHISER aka "Joanie" Fifth great granddaughter of progenitor Nicholas Kegg.
JOHN ADAM HERSHISER Fifth great grandson of progenitor Nicholas Kegg.
JOHN FRANKLIN HERSHISER [3751] (1902 – 1968) son of Lawrence and Sarah (Fink) Hershiser, married Edna Mae Martin with whom he was father of (3). John retired from Willard Police Department where he had been a patrolman for 20 years. He was a lifelong resident of Willard and he belonged to the Evangelical United Brethren Church, the Willard Conservation League, and the Fraternal Order of Police in Mansfield. **JOSHUA HERSHISER** Sixth great grandson of progenitor Nicholas Kegg.
KARL GLENN HERSHISER Fifth great grandson of progenitor Nicholas Kegg.
KATHLEEN ANN HERSHISER Fifth great granddaughter of progenitor Nicholas Kegg.
KELLY ANNETTE HERSHISER Fifth great granddaughter of progenitor Nicholas Kegg.
KENDALANN GRACE HERSHISER Sixth great granddaughter of progenitor Nicholas Kegg.
KENSLEY P. HERSHISER Seventh great granddaughter of progenitor Nicholas Kegg.
KYLE MARK HERSHISER Seventh great grandson of progenitor Nicholas Kegg.
LAWRENCE DAVID HERSHISER [3752] (1864 – 1958) son of David and Catherine (Keesy) Hershiser, married Sarah Elizabeth Fink with whom he was father of (9). Lawrence retired from B&O where he was employed as a stationary engineer. **LEON CLYDE HERSHISER** [3753] (1892 – 1946) son of Lawrence and Sarah (Fink) Hershiser, married Gazle Bell Slinker with whom he was father of (3). Leon was employed as a brakeman for the railroad. **LIBBY MAE HERSHISER** Seventh great granddaughter of progenitor Nicholas Kegg **LINDA HERSHISER** Fifth great granddaughter of progenitor Nicholas Kegg. **LISA JEAN HERSHISER** Fifth great granddaughter of progenitor

---

[3747] p.19 Sandusky Register (OH) Aug 17, 1960 [3748] p.783 Biographical Sketches Clinton Township and Tiffin City [3749] p4 col 4 Tiffin Daily Tribune (OH) Oct 8, 1901, obtained by D. Sue Dible [3750] p.6 Norwalk Reflector (OH) Aug 18, 1984, obtained by D. Sue Dible [3751] p.2 Norwalk Relector (OH) April 20, 1968, obtained by D. Sue Dible [3752] Library obituary clipping obtained by D. Sue Dible [3753] p.10 Mansfield News Journal (OH) Oct 21, 1946

Nicholas Kegg. **MADISON ELISA HERSHISER** Sixth great granddaughter of progenitor Nicholas Kegg. **MARDELL HERSHISER** [3754] (1908 – 1979) daughter of Lawrence and Sarah (Fink) Hershiser, married John Lewis Wilkinson with whom she was mother of (2). Mardell was a member of the Attica United Methodist Church, its Rachelle Ann Circle, and the Order of Eastern Star. **MARGARET HERSHISER** [3755] (1923 – 2009) daughter of Leon and Gazle (Slinker) Hershiser married twice; first to Carl Jacob Pfleiderer with whom she was mother of (2). Later, she married Wilbur J. Scott. Margaret was past auxiliary commander in the D.A.V. of Ottawa County, member of Norwalk Eagles Aerie 711 auxiliary, and enjoyed playing bingo. **MARILYN SUE HERSHISER** [3756] (1936 – 2021) daughter of John and Edna (Martin) Hershiser, married Arthur Paul Cok with whom she was mother of (4). Marilyn was formerly employed at Celeryville Greenhouse, Mad Rags, Industrial Savings & Loan and the Carraige House Florist. **MARK ALAN HERSHISER** Sixth great grandson of progenitor Nicholas Kegg. **MARY ELEANOR HERSHISER** Fifth great granddaughter of progenitor Nicholas Kegg. **MARY ESTER HERSHISER** (1833 – 1922) daughter of Henry and Barbara (Kegg) Hershiser, married John Wesley Bradley with whom she was mother of (2). **NANCY HERSHISER** Fifth great granddaughter of progenitor Nicholas Kegg. **NATHAN ALAN HERSHISER** Sixth great grandson of progenitor Nicholas Kegg. **NATHAN SCOTT HERSHISER** Seventh great grandson of progenitor Nicholas Kegg. **NELLIE RUTH HERSHISER** [3757] (1896 – 1962) daughter of Lawrence and Sarah (Fink) Hershiser, married Delbert George Dawson with whom she was mother of (4). Nellie was a member of Richmond EUB church, Daughters of Union Veterans Lodge and of the 3-A Farm Bureau council. **PAULA JEAN HERSHISER** Fifth great granddaughter of progenitor Nicholas Kegg. **RALPH CYRELL HERSHISER** [3758] (1894 – 1940) son of Franklin and Mary Belle (Miller) Hershiser married twice; first to Genevieve Himler. Later, he married Odessa Marie Spitler with whom he was father of (1). Ralph was employed as an automobile salesman. **RAYMOND CARLTON HERSHISER** [3759] (1905 – 1980) son of Lawrence and Sarah (Fink) Hershiser, married Dorothy Mardell Dorf with whom he was father of (1). Raymond was retired and had been superintendent of Willard's electricity, water and street departments. He was a member of First United Methodist Church of Willard and was a veteran of WWII. **ROBERT WILLIAM HERSHISER** Fifth great grandson of progenitor Nicholas Kegg. **RUTH E. HERSHISER** Fourth great granddaughter of progenitor Nicholas Kegg. **RYAN CLARK HERSHISER** Sixth great grandson of progenitor Nicholas Kegg. **SAMUEL PETER HERSHISER** [3760] (1891 – 1967) son of Franklin and Mary Belle (Miller) Hershiser married twice; first to Ruth Arlene Van Liew and later to Josephine Johnson Valentine. Samuel was a farmer. **SCOTT DAVID HERSHISER** Sixth great grandson of progenitor Nicholas Kegg. **SHANE ISAAK HERSHISER** Seventh great grandson of progenitor Nicholas Kegg. **SHIRLEY A. HERSHISER** [3760A] (1935 – 2020) daughter of Almon and June (Hart) Hershiser married twice. Shirley married Louis Paul Kimble with whom she was mother of (4). Later, she married Eugene O. Roeder. Shirley was a loving and caring person who was always taking care of others, putting their needs in front of her own. **SKILER LYNN HERSHISER** Sixth great granddaughter of progenitor Nicholas Kegg. **SUSAN KAY HERSHISER** Fourth great granddaughter of progenitor Nicholas Kegg. **THOMAS HERSHISER** Fifth great grandson of progenitor Nicholas Kegg. **TRACEY LYNN HERSHISER** Sixth great granddaughter of progenitor Nicholas Kegg. **VELMA LUCILLE HERSHISER** [3761] (1908 – 1979) daughter of William and Pearl (Fast) Hershiser, married Lee Stahl Wilcox with whom she was mother of (3). Velma had been a schoolteacher at Billman School in Richmond Township. **VERNICE M. HERSHISER** [3762] (1893 – 1983) daughter of Lawrence and Sarah (Fink) Hershiser, married Harry Claten Steiert. Vernice was a retired bookkeeper for the Willard Area hospital and several other retail businesses. **VIRGIL PERRY HERSHISER** [3762A] (1913 – 1985) son of Chester and Estella (Hutchison) Hershiser, married Lucille Alberta Rang with whom

---

[3754] p.4A The Advertiser-Tribune (OH) Mar 14, 1979, obtained by D. Sue Dible [3755] Library clipping/Norwalk Reflector (OH) obtained by D. Sue Dible [3756] Willard Times Junction (OH) Dec. 29, 2021 [3757] p.11 Mansfield News Journal (OH) Nov 12, 1962 [3758] p.10 Mansfield News Journal (OH) May 4, 1940 [3759] p.6 Norwalk Reflector (OH) Nov 28, 1980, obtained by D. Sue Dible [3760] p.12 Mansfield News Journal (OH) July 6, 1967 [3760A] News Journal (OH) Dec. 18, 2020 [3761] Library obituary clipping obtained by D. Sue Dible [3762] p.4 Norwalk Reflector (OH) Feb 11, 1983, obtained by D. Sue Dible [3762A] p.4 Norwalk Reflector (OH) July 17, 1985, contributed by D. Sue Dible

he was father of (3). Virgil was a retired farmer and had been a guard at R.R. Donnelley and Sons, retiring in 1974.   **WILBUR EARL HERSHISER** [3763] (1917 – 1979) son of Chester and Estelle (Hutchison) Hershiser, married DonnaBelle Mae Pollock with whom he was father of (6). A retired farmer, Wilbur was a member of the Richmond United Methodist Church.   **WILLIAM JOHN HERSHISER** Fourth great grandson of progenitor Nicholas Kegg.   **WILLIAM THOMAS HERSHISER** [3764] (1882 – 1939) son of Franklin and Mary Belle (Miller) Hershiser, married Vesta Pearl Fast with whom he was father of (4). William spent his entire life on the farm on which he was born. He was a member of the United Brethren church and a former township trustee and school board member.
YVONNE EILEEN HERSHISER Fifth great granddaughter of progenitor Nicholas Kegg.

HERSOM

GERALD GENE HERSOM (1955 – 1985) aka "Jerry" son of Eugene and Ramona Jean (Wylie) Hersom.   **JEFFREY RALPH HERSOM** Sixth great grandson of progenitor Nicholas Kegg. **RAYMOND E. HERSOM** aka "Ray", Sixth great grandson of progenitor Nicholas Kegg.

HERTZENBERG

KRISTEN ANN HERTZENBERG Sixth great granddaughter of progenitor Nicholas Kegg.
LAUREN MICHELLE HERTZENBERG Sixth great granddaughter of progenitor Nicholas Kegg.

HERZOG

BETH E. HERZOG Sixth great granddaughter of progenitor Nicholas Kegg.
EMILY MAURINE HERZOG Seventh great granddaughter of progenitor Nicholas Kegg.
FRANK ROBERT HERZOG [3764A] aka "Pete" (1944 – 2017) son of Frank and Marjorie (Wire) Herzog, married Margaret Sims with whom he was father of (2). Pete was a Staff Sergeant in the Army Reserves for six years and a middle school teacher for 37 1/2 years. He volunteered at the Historic Forks of the Wabash and was active with the Indiana Junior Historical Society. Pete enjoyed traveling, gardening, splitting wood and spending time with his family.   **JAMES MILAN HERZOG** [3764B] (1940 – 2013) son of Frank and Marjorie (Wire) Herzog, married Patricia L. Bruns with whom he was father of (3). James served in the U.S. Navy as a statistician at the Great Lakes Exam Center, Ill. He was a Certified Professional Engineer employed by General Electric, in Fort Wayne, and then by Anchor Hocking, in Lancaster as a Project Engineer, where he was awarded patents for his work in the closure division. He was honored as a Senior Fellow for contribution to the success of the sealing machine business within the packaging group. He retired as a Senior Design Engineer after 30 years with Anchor Hocking / Crown Cork & Seal. He was an avid photographer who had recorded family celebrations with photos, slides, movies and videos since he was in high school. He also enjoyed gardening and sharing his photography.   **JAMES QUENTIN HERZOG** Seventh great grandson of progenitor Nicholas Kegg.
SCOTT R. HERZOG Sixth great grandson of progenitor Nicholas Kegg.
TANYA MARIE HERZOG Sixth great granddaughter of progenitor Nicholas Kegg.
THOMAS MILAN HERZOG Sixth great grandson of progenitor Nicholas Kegg.
TIMOTHY M. HERZOG aka "Tim", Sixth great grandson of progenitor Nicholas Kegg.

[3763] p2 Norwalk Reflector (OH) June 12, 1979, obtained by D. Sue Dible [3764] p.20 Mansfield News Journal (OH) Jan12,1939 [3764A] Myers Funeral Home (IN) [3764B] Fort Wayne Newspapers (IN) Oct. 25, 2013

HESS

BARRY E. HESS Fifth great grandson of progenitor Nicholas Kegg.   **BENJAMIN J. HESS** (3764C) (1944 – 2017) son of Randy and Shelli (Lafferty) Hess. Ben had been a chef for various restaurants. He loved to write poetry and was an avid reader and sports fan, having cheered for the Eagles. He loved music and had a passion for composing rap music. He had played ice hockey as a goalie for many teams, including the Lancaster Firebirds, Hershey Jr. Bears and the Holy Name Jets.   **CORINE HESS** Eighth great granddaughter of progenitor Nicholas Kegg.   **DUSTIN DELANY HESS** Sixth great grandson of progenitor Nicholas Kegg.   **DWAYNE LEE HESS** Sixth great grandson of progenitor Nicholas Kegg.   **GARY JOSEPH HESS** (3765) (1953 – 1999) son of Herbert and Doris (Owens) Hess. Gary graduated from Vo-Tech and completed master's studies at Fairmont West Virginia State Teachers College, with his last teaching position in Long Island, NY. He is also remembered for public singing at many public affairs, including sports events at the Point Stadium.   **GRAYSON ALEXANDER HESS** Seventh great grandson of progenitor Nicholas Kegg.   **IAN MICHAEL HESS** Eighth great grandson of progenitor Nicholas Kegg.   **IISA HESS** Eighth great granddaughter of progenitor Nicholas Kegg.   **JENNA ELIZABETH HESS** Sixth great granddaughter of progenitor Nicholas Kegg.   **JOHN ANDREW HESS** Sixth great grandson of progenitor Nicholas Kegg.   **JOHN JASON HESS** Sixth great grandson of progenitor Nicholas Kegg.   **KELLEN HESS** Eighth great grandchild of progenitor Nicholas Kegg.   **LIAM HESS** Eighth great grandson of progenitor Nicholas Kegg.   **MARYANN HESS** Fifth great granddaughter of progenitor Nicholas Kegg.   **REBECCA HESS** Seventh great granddaughter of progenitor Nicholas Kegg.   **RYAN HESS** Seventh great grandson of progenitor Nicholas Kegg.   **STACY LEE HESS** Sixth great grandson of progenitor Nicholas Kegg.

HETZ

CAMILLA HETZ (3765A) (1949 – 2018) daughter Edward and Beulah (Garlitz) Hetz married James Joseph LeClaire with whom she was mother of (1). Camilla was employed at Hunter Douglas.   **CHARLES E. HETZ** Fifth great grandson of progenitor Nicholas Kegg.   **CHARLES HETZ** Sixth great grandson of progenitor Nicholas Kegg.   **EDITH FERN HETZ** Fourth great granddaughter of progenitor Nicholas Kegg.   **EDWARD CHARLES HETZ** (3766) (1918 – 1996) son of William and Mamie (Durst) Hetz, married Beulah Grace Garlitz with whom he was father of (2). Edward was a member of the Mount Zion United Methodist Church and Grantsville Post 214 American Legion. He was a retired roads construction worker and a U.S. Army veteran of World War II.   **STACEY HETZ** Sixth great granddaughter of progenitor Nicholas Kegg.   **TRAVIS C. HETZ** Sixth great grandson of progenitor Nicholas Kegg.

HETZEL

ALEXANDER IAN HETZEL Seventh great grandson of progenitor Nicholas Kegg.   **AMANDA ERIN HETZEL** Seventh great granddaughter of progenitor Nicholas Kegg.   **BEN HETZEL** Seventh great grandson of progenitor Nicholas Kegg.   **DELLA LEONA HETZEL** (3766A) (1932 – 2015) daughter of Francis and Ruth (Knouf) Hetzel, married Victor Paul Evenson with whom she was mother of (4). Being an Air Force wife, she lived in several places: Shreveport, LA; Homestead AFB, FL; K.I. Sawyer AFB, MI; Burns Flat, OK; Riverside, CA and eventually, they moved to Topeka. Della worked for Fleming, Co., GMD and retired after 26 years as a Human Resources Payroll Clerk. She was a member of Southwest Christian Church. She was a member of Strato-Jet Square Dance Club for 25 years. Della enjoyed trail riding and working with the horses. She was a member of Nisqually Backcountry Horsemen Club.   **FRANCES N. HETZEL** Fifth great granddaughter of progenitor

---

(3764C) Lebanon Daily News (PA) Mar 3, 2008 (3765) Johnstown Tribune-Democrat (PA) Mar 5, 1999, obtained by D. Sue Dible (3765A) Newman Funeral Homes (MD) obtained by D. Sue Dible (3766) p.4 Cumberland Times News (MD) July 20, 1996 (3766A) Topeka Capital-Journal (KS) May 13, 2015

Nicholas Kegg. **GARY ALLEN HETZEL** Sixth great grandson of progenitor Nicholas Kegg.
MATTHEW HETZEL Seventh great grandson of progenitor Nicholas Kegg.
MATTHEW IVAN HETZEL Sixth great grandson of progenitor Nicholas Kegg.
MELANIE ANNE HETZEL Seventh great granddaughter of progenitor Nicholas Kegg.
ROBERTA HETZEL Fifth great granddaughter of progenitor Nicholas Kegg.
RUTH E. HETZEL Fifth great granddaughter of progenitor Nicholas Kegg.

HEWETT

CHRISTINA LYNN HEWETT Seventh great granddaughter of progenitor Nicholas Kegg.
KIMBERLY ANN HEWETT Seventh great granddaughter of progenitor Nicholas Kegg.

HIBBARD

MIKE HIBBARD Seventh great grandson of progenitor Nicholas Kegg.
TABITHA M. HIBBARD Seventh great granddaughter of progenitor Nicholas Kegg.

HICKEY

PAUL HICKEY Seventh great grandson of progenitor Nicholas Kegg.

HIGDAY

JAMES LAIRD HIGDAY [3766B] (1922 – 1999) son of Robert and Bertha (Laird) Higday married twice; first to Gloria Marie Woods with whom he was father of (2). Later, he married Ann Frazzini. James served in the Army Air Force as a pilot during World War II. He retired as president of Public Service Company of Colorado. He was a former president of the Colorado Jaycees.
VICTORIA LYNN HIGDAY aka "Vicky", Sixth great granddaughter of progenitor Nicholas Kegg.

HIGGINS

DONNA HIGGINS Sixth great granddaughter of progenitor Nicholas Kegg. **HANNAH HIGGINS** Sixth great granddaughter of progenitor Nicholas Kegg. **MARTIN HIGGINS** Sixth great grandson of progenitor Nicholas Kegg.

HIGGINSON

CHRISTOP HIGGINSON Sixth great grandson of progenitor Nicholas Kegg. **JASON D. HIGGINSON** Sixth great grandson of progenitor Nicholas Kegg. **JEFFREY A. HIGGINSON** Sixth great grandson of progenitor Nicholas Kegg. **SARA M. HIGGINSON** Sixth great granddaughter of progenitor Nicholas Kegg.

HILL

ALEX HILL Seventh great grandson of progenitor Nicholas Kegg. **ASHLEY HILL** Seventh great granddaughter of progenitor Nicholas Kegg. **BENJAMIN HILL** Fifth great grandson of progenitor Nicholas Kegg. **CAMERON BRUNK HILL** Eighth great grandson of progenitor Nicholas Kegg. **CAROL BERNICE HUMPHREY HILL** [3767] (1936 – 2020) daughter of Orson and Velma (Thompson) Hill. Clarence Humphrey (her birth father) left for Wichita Falls, Texas when Carol was just

---

[3766B] Rocky Mountain News (CO) Jan 24, 1999 [3767] Corvallis Gazette-Times (OR) Mar. 15, 2020

six months old. He never returned. Her mother married Orson Hill who was the only father Carol knew. Carol married Myron Bacigalupi with whom she was mother of (2). Later, she married Kenton L. Smith. An active Navy wife, she endured long separations from her deployed husband. She worked as a counselor for weight watchers and enjoyed bowling. Carol was active in various organizations, but her love was working in a Yarn Shop in the village where she taught knitting.   **CHESS HILL** Fifth great grandson of progenitor Nicholas Kegg.   **FORBES HILL** Seventh great grandson of progenitor Nicholas Kegg.   **JAMES E. HILL** Sixth great grandson of progenitor Nicholas Kegg.   **JESSE HILL** Sixth great grandson of progenitor Nicholas Kegg.   **MARY JANE HILL** (1836 -?) daughter of William and Catherine (Knouf) Hill, married Michaelis H. Galvin with whom she was mother of (3). **MICHAEL HILL** Sixth great grandson of progenitor Nicholas Kegg.   **NATHAN HILL** Seventh great grandson of progenitor Nicholas Kegg.   **ROBYN GAYL HILL** Seventh great granddaughter of progenitor Nicholas Kegg.   **TARA KELLEY HILL** Sixth great granddaughter of progenitor Nicholas Kegg.   **WILLIAM JAY HILL** Seventh great grandson of progenitor Nicholas Kegg. **WILLIAM ORSON MICHAEL HILL** [3768] (1943 – 1973) son of Orson and Velma (Thompson) Hill married Dianna Gail Day with whom he was father of (2). William was employed as a mechanic. A Nascar driver for the past 10 years, he was a member of the International Association of Mechanics and Autoworkers Union Local 1173, Pleasant Hill.   **WANETA MARY HILL** [3769] (1935 – 2000) daughter of Curtis and Dorothy (Crouse) Hill married Bruce L. Phenicie with whom she was mother of (4). Waneta was employed as a press operator for Brazeway Inc.

HILLARD

MAX HILLARD Eighth great grandson of progenitor Nicholas Kegg.

HILLEGAS

ANNIE HILLEGAS Fifth great granddaughter of progenitor Nicholas Kegg.
ANTHONY HILLEGAS Sixth great grandson of progenitor Nicholas Kegg.
BARBARA J. HILLEGAS Fifth great granddaughter of progenitor Nicholas Kegg.
BETTY HILLEGAS [3770] (1921 – 2002) daughter of Stanford and Elizabeth (Holler) Hillegas. Betty dedicated her life as a Christian Missionary teacher, teaching at Bethany Orphanage, this later becoming Bethany Christian School for 50 years. She was awarded teacher of the year for Wolfe County.
CAROLYN R. HILLEGAS Fourth great granddaughter of progenitor Nicholas Kegg.
CHARLES CLYDE HILLEGAS Fourth great grandson of progenitor Nicholas Kegg.
CLYDE HENRY HILLEGAS [3770A] (1903 – 1986) son of George and Elizabeth (May) Hillegas married twice, first to Edna Naoma Bowman with whom he was father of (2). Later, he married Dorothy Ella Herbert with whom he was father of (3). Clyde retired from Ponfeigh Coal Co., where he had been employed as a coal miner. In addition, he had been employed as an auto salesman for Bruckman Olds of Somerset.   **DAVID WESLEY HILLEGAS** Fourth great grandson of progenitor Nicholas Kegg. **DEREK HILLEGAS** Sixth great grandson of progenitor Nicholas Kegg.   **DIANE R. HILLEGAS** Fifth great granddaughter of progenitor Nicholas Kegg.   **DORIS HILLEGAS** [3771] (1920 – 1998) daughter of Stanford and Elizabeth (Holler) Hillegas, married Edward J. Will. Doris was a former salesclerk at Straub Bros., Bedford, Fairfoot Shoe Factory and for Salisbury Undergarment in Salisbury. Member St. John's United Church of Christ in Salisbury and attended St. John the Baptist Catholic Church in New Baltimore.   **EDWARD E. HILLEGAS** [3771A] (1904 – 1991) son of George and Elizabeth (May) Hillegas, married Pauline A. Trent with whom he was father of (2). Edward had been employed in highway construction.

[3768] Concord Transcript (CA) April 10, 1973 [3769] The Daily Telegram (MI) Jan 29, 2000 [3770] Daily American (PA) Nov 9, 2002/Myersdale Library transcribed by Jessica Orr [3770A] Daily American (PA) July 11, 1986/ Myersdale Library transcribed by Jessica Orr [3771] Daily American (PA) Feb 23, 1998/Myersdale Library transcribed by Jessica Orr [3771A] New Republic (PA) Oct 31, 1991, contributed by D. Sue Dible

ELIZABETH ANN HILLEGAS Fourth great granddaughter of progenitor Nicholas Kegg. **GALE LEROY HILLEGAS** [3772] (1923 – 1999) aka "Mike", son of Stanford and Elizabeth (Holler) Hillegas, married Jane Gundrum with whom he was father of (2). Gale was a member of St. John's United Church of Christ, Salisbury, where at one time he served as choir director, deacon, elder and Consistory president. He was a U.S. Army veteran of Korean Conflict, member of Salisbury American Legion, Post 459. Member of Salisbury Lions Club for 31 years, served as past president and past secretary. Member of Tub Mill Arts and was an avid lover of music. Gale played shortstop for the Salisbury Cardinals when the team won the Southern Somerset County baseball championship in 1948. He retired maintenance man for Somerset State Hospital, has also been employed as a housepainter. **GEORGE ELMER HILLEGAS** [3772A] (1874 – 1954) son of Henry and Juliana (Turner) Hillegass married Elizabeth May with whom he was father of (7). George was employed as a miner. **HAROLD JAY HILLEGAS** [3772B] aka "Jay" (1928 – 2013) son of Clyde and Edna (Bowman) Hilegas, married Delores Schatz with whom he was father of (3). A U.S. Navy veteran of WWII. Jay was a member of Jennerstown United Methodist Church, Pennsylvania Golf Course Owners Assocation, Mountain Valley and Pittsburgh Golf Course Superintendents Associations and USWA. Former member of Boswell Lions Club. Retired employee of U.S. Steel Corp., with 26 years of service. Jay was the owner and operator of Oakbrook Golf Course for 49 years. **HELEN EUDORA HILLEGAS** [3773] (1919 – 2012) daughter of Jesse and Olla (Wagner) Hillegas, married Andrew J. Krnach with whom she was mother of (8). **J.C. HILLEGAS** Fifth great grandson of progenitor Nicholas Kegg.
JAMES MICHAEL HILLEGAS (1943 – 1943) son of Marcus and Ruth (Harclerode) Hillegas.
JAMES PAUL HILLEGAS Fourth great grandson of progenitor Nicholas Kegg.
JANET K. HILLEGAS Fourth great granddaughter of progenitor Nicholas Kegg.
JEAN ELIZABETH HILLEGAS Fourth great granddaughter of progenitor Nicholas Kegg.
JESSE U. HILLEGAS [3773A] (1897 – 1986) son of George and Elizabeth (May) Hillegas, married Olla Fern Wagner with whom he was father of (3). Jesse retired from Goodyear after 32 years' service.
JESSIE HILLEGAS Fifth great granddaughter of progenitor Nicholas Kegg.
JOHN MICHAEL HILLEGAS Fourth great grandson of progenitor Nicholas Kegg.
JON RUSSELL HILLEGAS Fourth great grandson of progenitor Nicholas Kegg.
KATHY HILLEGAS Fifth great granddaughter of progenitor Nicholas Kegg. **KURTIS HILLEGAS** Sixth great grandson of progenitor Nicholas Kegg. **LARRY V. HILLEGAS** Sixth great grandson of progenitor Nicholas Kegg. **LUANNE MARIE HILLEGAS** Fifth great granddaughter of progenitor Nicholas Kegg. **MARCUS THEODORE HILLEGAS** [3773B] (1901 – 1978) son of George and Elizabeth (May) Hillegas, married Ruth E. Harclerode with whom he was father of (5). Marcus retired from Queen City Dairy Company. **MARIAH HILLEGAS** Sixth great granddaughter of progenitor Nicholas Kegg. **MARLA B. HILLEGAS** Fourth great granddaughter of progenitor Nicholas Kegg. **MARY M. HILLEGAS** [3773C] (1900 – 1996) daughter of George and Elizabeth (May) Hillegas, married Dr. Harold Melvin Couchenour with whom she was mother of (2). Mary was A homemaker, she was a member of the First United Methodist Church, Speedster Club and the Homebuilders Club. **PATRICIA A. HILLEGAS** Fifth great granddaughter of progenitor Nicholas Kegg. **PAUL EVERETT HILLEGAS** [3774] (1921 – 2010) son of Jesse and Olla (Wagner) Hillegas, married Dorothy Loreta Bouldin with whom he was father of (2). Paul was a U.S. Navy veteran of WWII. Paul was assigned to the Navy Lighter-Than-Air squadrons in California where he participated in aerial submarine surveillance along our coast. **R. DEAN HILLEGAS** Fourth great grandson of progenitor Nicholas Kegg. **RICHARD HILLEGAS** aka "Dick", 4th great grandson of progenitor Nicholas Kegg. **ROBERT HILLEGAS** Fifth great grandson of progenitor Nicholas Kegg. **ROBERT C. HILLEGAS** [3775] (1923 – 2010) aka "Bob", son of Clyde and Edna (Bowman) Hillegas married twice; first to Helen L. Goughenour with whom he was father of (3). Later, he married Patricia Nipps Porias. Bob was a U.S.

[3772] Daily American (PA) June 24, 1999/Myersdale Library transcribed by Jessica Orr [3772A] p.13 - Cumberland Times (MD) Oct 20, 1954 [3772B] Hoffman Funeral Homes (PA) [3773] Reed Funeral Home, OH [3773A] p.D8 - Akron Beacon Journal (OH) April 17, 1986 [3773B] The Republic (PA) Aug 24, 1978, contributed by Jessica Orr Meyersdale Library [3773C] News Republic (PA) Oct 3, 1996, contributed by Kerry L. Miller Meyersdale Library [3774] Press-Enterprise (CA) Aug 15, 2010 [3775] Tribune-Democrat (Johnstown, PA) Dec 10, 2010

Army veteran of World War II, having served in the European Theater of Operations and participated in the Battle of the Bulge. He also received an award for excellence in athletics from the Army. After the Army, Bob moved to Ohio and served 10 years with the Selective Service. He was the owner and operator of Wolfsburg Auto Service, Columbus, Ohio, and a retired appraiser for State Farm Auto Insurance. Member and past commander of the VFW in New Lexington, Ohio, was a 32nd Degree Shriner in Columbus, Ohio, and an Exhausted Rooster for the New Lexington Jaycees. Also, a member of Belmont United Methodist Church, Johnstown, and Jerome Post 802, American Legion. Bob also enjoyed golfing and hunting. **RODNEY HILLEGAS** Fifth great grandson of progenitor Nicholas Kegg.
RUSSELL HILLEGAS Sixth great grandson of progenitor Nicholas Kegg.
SHERRY LOUISE HILLEGAS [3775A] (1950 – 2008) daughter of Clyde and Dorothy (Herbert) Hillegas. Sherry worked as a registered nurse in the oncology department of Johns Hopkins Hospital, Baltimore, and also worked as a certified dialysis nurse. She was a former member of First United Methodist Church, Somerset. **STANFORD ALBERTUS HILLEGAS** [3775B] (1895 – 1987) son of George and Elizabeth (May) Hillegas, married Elizabeth C. Holler with whom he was father of (4). Stanford was a retired highway construction foreman. - **TERRY M. HILLEGAS** Fifth great grandson of progenitor Nicholas Kegg. **TOLVA MAXINE HILLEGAS** [3775C] (1917 – 2003) daughter of Stanford and Elizabeth (Holler) Hillegas, married Homer C. Gnaney with whom she was mother of (4). Tolva was a retired postal worker for the U.S. Postal Service. After her retirement, she sold Avon for 20 years. She was a member of the Salisbury Fireman's Auxiliary, American Legion Auxiliary and also was a member of St. John's United Church of Christ and the TTT Class. Mrs. Gnagey played the piano and loved music. She was a devoted mother and grandmother and was very faithful to her church.
WESTON HILLEGAS Sixth great grandson of progenitor Nicholas Kegg.

HILLEGASS

ALBERT L. HILLEGASS Fifth great grandson of progenitor Nicholas Kegg.
ALLEN W. HILLEGASS Fifth great grandson of progenitor Nicholas Kegg.
ALVIN L. HILLEGASS [3776] (1953 – 1953) son of Dalton and Thelma (Turner) Hillegass.
AMBER L. HILLEGASS Sixth great granddaughter of progenitor Nicholas Kegg.
ANDREW JACKSON HILLEGASS [3777] (1859 – 1931) aka "A. J.", son of Henry and Juliana (Turner) Hillegass married twice; first to Sebelda Hoon with whom he was father of (3). Later, he married Ida Catherine Zeigler with whom he was father of (5). A. J. spent most of his time in the service of the church. It was his work and his qualities of Christian brotherhood those who knew him recognized.
ANNA LOIS HILLEGASS [3778] (1953 – 2005) daughter of Dalton and Thelma (Turner) Hillegass married twice, was mother of (1). **ANNA M. HILLEGASS** [3779] (1898 – 1965) daughter of Andrew and Ida (Zeigler) Hillegass married twice; first to Arthur McVicker with whom she was mother of (1). Later, she married Frederick M. Shoemaker with whom she was mother of (4). Anna was a retired schoolteacher. She was a member of Milligans Cove Christian Church and the Ladies Bible Class of Buffalo Mills Methodist Church. **ANNA MARY HILLEGASS** [3780] (1862 – 1900) daughter of Henry and Juliana (Turner) Hillegass, married Henry Frederick Turner with whom she was mother of (9).
BARRY LYNN HILLEGASS [3781] (1957 – 2021) son of Evan and Helen (Kerr) Hillegass was father of (1). He married Kimberly (Werner) Sciranko. Barry was a certified electrician and was employed by Standard Acoustical in Hagerstown, Maryland. He also worked at the concession stand business with his family. Barry enjoyed going to the Bedford County Dirt Drag Races, hunting, wood working, and spending time with his family. **BETTY LOU HILLEGASS** Fifth great granddaughter of progenitor Nicholas Kegg. **BRIAN LEE HILLEGASS** Fifth great grandson of progenitor Nicholas Kegg.

[3775A] Hauger-Zeigler Funeral Home (MD) [3775B] Daily American (PA) Sep 11, 1987 contributed by Winnie Nichols Meyersdale Library [3775C] Newman Funeral Home Inc. (PA) [3776] p.11 – Evening Times (MD) Apr 14, 1953 [3777] p.4 - Bedford Gazette (PA) Sep 4,1931 [3778] Press of Atlantic City (NJ) June 27, 2005 [3779] The Cumberland News (MD) June 23,1965 [3780] Bedford Gazette (PA) Sept 14, 1900 [3181] Bedford Gazette (PA) Aug 5, 2021

CHARLES LEE HILLEGASS [3781A] (1939 – 2021) aka "Charlie" son of Delbert and Bertha (Turner) Hillegass. **CLARENCE ARNOLD HILLEGASS** [3781B] (1927 – 1998) son of Delbert and Bertha (Turner) Hillegass married twice, first to Helen Marie Hewitt with whom he was father of (2). Later he married Evelyn Maxine Bishop. Clarence was a machinist and an Air Force veteran.
CONNIE S. HILLEGASS 5th great granddaughter of progenitor Nicholas Kegg.
CORA EDITH HILLEGASS [3782] (1891 – 1960) daughter of Andrew and Sebelda Hoon, married Harvey Theodore Meyers with whom she was mother of (4). Cora was a member of Mt. Lebanon United Church of Christ. **DAVID AARON HILLEGASS** Fifth great grandson of progenitor Nicholas Kegg.
DAVID LEE HILLEGASS Fifth great grandson of progenitor Nicholas Kegg.
DAVID W. HILLEGASS (1960 – 1960) son of Dalton and Thelma (Turner) Hillegass.
DIANE HILLEGASS Fifth great granddaughter of progenitor Nicholas Kegg.
DONNA HILLEGASS Fifth great granddaughter of progenitor Nicholas Kegg.
GALEN RAY HILLEGASS [3783] (1952 – 1987) son of Evan and Helen (Kerr) Hillegass, married Claudia Cogswell with whom he was father of (2). Galen was a member of the U.S. Air Force, attaining the rank of Master Sergeant. **GEORGE ELMER HILLEGASS** [3784] (1874 – 1954) son of George and Juliana (Turner) Hillegass, married Elizabeth May with whom he was father of (7). His death was attributed directly to the storm following "Hurricane Hazel". **HARRY E. HILLEGASS** (1929 – 1972) son of Delbert and Bertha Pearl (Turner) Hillegass. **HELEN G. HILLEGASS** Fourth great granddaughter of progenitor Nicholas Kegg. **HENRIETTA HILLEGASS**. (1864 –?) daughter of Henry and Juliana (Turner) Hillegass. **JAMES DALE HILLEGASS** Fifth great grandson of progenitor Nicholas Kegg. **JOHN M. HILLEGASS** Fifth great grandson of progenitor Nicholas Kegg.
JOSIAH HENRY HILLEGASS [3785] (1907 – 1979) aka "Joe", son of Andrew and Ida (Zeigler) Hillegass, married Leona Eliza Bartlett with whom he was father of (2). Joe retired after 43 years' service with the A. Polsky Company. He was a member of the Good-year Heights United Methodist Church, Loyalty Lodge No. 645 F.&A.M., Yusef Khan Grotto, and the Polsky's 20 Year Club.
LEONA MAE HILLEGASS [3786] (1945 – 2000) daughter of Dalton and Thelma (Turner) Hillegass, married four times. **LOUIS RAY HILLEGASS** [3787] (1925 – 1978) son of Delbert and Bertha Pearl (Turner) Hillegass, married Janet Woolf with whom he was father of (1).
MARIE CATHERINE HILLEGASS [3788] (1867 – 1928) aka "Katie", daughter of Henry and Juliana (Turner) Hillegass, married John Clay with whom she was mother of (3). **MARY HILLEGASS** [3789] (1905 – 1975) daughter of Andrew and Ida (Zeigler) Hillegass, married Albert Munzert. Mary was a member of Zion Lutheran Church, Hollidaysburg. **MARY BERTHA HILLEGASS** Fifth great granddaughter of progenitor Nicholas Kegg. **NELLIE MAE HILLEGASS** [3790] (1933 – 1937) daughter of Delbert and Bertha Pearl (Turner) Hillegass. **NORA LYDIA HILLEGASS** [3791] (1891 – 1956) daughter of Andrew and Sebelda (Hoon) Hillegass, married John Russell Shoop. Nora was a member of the Reformed Church. **OLIVE MADOLYN HILLEGASS** [3792] (1899 – 1981) daughter of Andrew and Ida (Zeigler) Hillegass, married C. Lloyd Sternberg. Olive was a member of the First United Methodist Church of Cuyahoga Falls and the XYZ Club of the Church. She was also a member of the Falls Chapter No. 245 O.E.S. **PAULA SUE HILLEGASS** [3793] (1953 – 2021) aka "Zoots" or "Sotch" daughter of Evan and Helen (Kerr) Hilligass was mother of (1). Paula worked for her father and stepmother at the local racetrack, Bedford County Fair, and for Mae's Diner, where she was a waitress and cook. Paula loved the Pittsburgh Steelers, doing crossword puzzles and getting her nails done.
PAULINE E. HILLEGASS [3794] (1901 – 1965) daughter of Andrew and Ida (Zeigler) Hillegass, married Vilgaude Otto Dossett with whom she was mother of (2). Pauline was employed in the sales accounting department of Firestone. She was a member of Christ Methodist Church and its Wesleyan Service Guild.

[3781A] dignitymemorial.com/obituaries Largo, FL [3781B] p.5 - St. Petersburg Times (FL) May 7, 1998 [3782] Bedford Gazette (PA) Aug 13, 1960 [3783] p.3 Bedford Inquirer (PA) July 17, 1987 [3784] p.13 - Cumberland Times (MD) Oct 20, 1954 [3785] Akron Public Library obituary clipping obtained by D. Sue Dible [3786] News & Observer (Raleigh, NC) July 9, 2000 [3787] Washington Post/Ancestry.com Historical Newspapers 1851-2003 [3788] Bedford Gazette (PA) Sept. 21, 1928 [3789] Bedford County Historical Society obituary obtained by D. Sue Dible [3790] Johnstown Daily Tribune (PA) Dec 27, 1937 obtained by D. Sue Dible [3791] Bedford Gazette (PA) Oct 4, 1956 [3792] Akron Public Library obituary clipping obtained by D. Sue Dible [3793] Bedford Gazette (PA) May 26, 2021 [3794] Akron Public Library obituary clipping obtained by D. Sue Dible

PETER ALBERT HILLEGASS [3795] (1870 – 1899) son of Henry and Juliana (Turner) Hillegass.
SAUNDRA HILLEGASS Fifth great granddaughter of progenitor Nicholas Kegg.
SARAH A. HILLEGASS, (1866 –?) daughter of Henry and Juliana (Turner) Hillegass.
SHAWN P. HILLEGASS Sixth great grandson of progenitor Nicholas Kegg.
SHELLY L. HILLEGASS Sixth great granddaughter of progenitor Nicholas Kegg.
SHERRI A. HILLEGASS Fifth great granddaughter of progenitor Nicholas Kegg.
TAMMY MARIE HILLEGASS Sixth great granddaughter of progenitor Nicholas Kegg.
TERRY WAYNE HILLEGASS Fifth great grandson of progenitor Nicholas Kegg.
TODD EUGENE HILLEGASS (1967 – 1967) son of Evan and Helen (Kerr) Hillegass.
VICKI LYNN HILLEGASS Fifth great granddaughter of progenitor Nicholas Kegg.

HILLENBRAND

OLIVIA HILLENBRAND Eighth great granddaughter of progenitor Nicholas Kegg.
TAYLOR HILLENBRAND Eighth great granddaughter of progenitor Nicholas Kegg.

HILLMAN

BRITTENY RENEE HILLMAN Seventh great granddaughter of progenitor Nicholas Kegg. **JAYNE L. HILLMAN** Sixth great granddaughter of progenitor Nicholas Kegg. - **JOHN JAY HILLMAN** Sixth great grandson of progenitor Nicholas Kegg. **JOHN RYAN HILLMAN** Seventh great grandson of progenitor Nicholas Kegg.

HILLSKOTTER

MICHAEL DENNIS HILLSKOTTER Seventh great grandson of progenitor Nicholas Kegg.
MICHELLE DENISE HILLSKOTTER Seventh great granddaughter of progenitor Nicholas Kegg.

HIMES

ASHLEY HIMES Sixth great granddaughter of progenitor Nicholas Kegg. **CARY J. HIMES** aka "Woody", Fifth great grandson of progenitor Nicholas Kegg. **CINDY HIMES** Fifth great granddaughter of progenitor Nicholas Kegg. **JOSEPH HIMES** Sixth great grandson of progenitor Nicholas Kegg. **JOY M. HIMES** Sixth great granddaughter of progenitor Nicholas Kegg.
KAYDENCE HIMES Seventh great granddaughter of progenitor Nicholas Kegg.
KORTNEY HIMES Seventh great granddaughter of progenitor Nicholas Kegg.
STEPHEN DOUGLAS HIMES [3795A] (1953 – 2008) son of Charles and Freda (Daley) Himes, married Joy Robey with whom he was father of (2).

HIMLIN

MATTHEW P. HIMLIN Sixth great grandson of progenitor Nicholas Kegg.

HINDALL

PATSY ANN HINDALL [3796] (1934 – 2011) daughter of Harold and Edna (Houck) Hindall, married Elmer R. Bollander with whom she was mother of (5). Patsy was of the Baptist faith. **GARY LYNN HINDALL** Fifth great grandson of progenitor Nicholas Kegg. **LETA JEAN HINDALL** [3796A] aka "Jean" (1925 – 2017) daughter of Harold and Linda (Houck) Hindall, married William Musgrave. Leta

---

[3795] The Bedford Gazette (PA) Dec 22, 1899 [3795A] Covenant Funeral Service (VA) [3796] Turner Funeral Homes (FL) [3796A] Courier (OH) Aug 31, 2017

was employed as a legal secretary at Marathon Oil Company. She was a member of the First Presbyterian Church, Blanchard Valley Hospital Auxiliary, and an associate member of the Findlay Elks Lodge #75. Jean enjoyed playing cards and the card game Mahjong. **TROY LYNN HINDALL** Sixth great grandson of progenitor Nicholas Kegg.

HINEN

CHLOE HINEN Eighth great granddaughter of progenitor Nicholas Kegg.

HINES

JONATHAN HINES Sixth great grandson of progenitor Nicholas Kegg. **ROBERT HINES** Sixth great grandson of progenitor Nicholas Kegg. **WILLIAM HINES** Sixth great grandson of progenitor Nicholas Kegg.

HINISH

KENTON HINISH Seventh great grandson of progenitor Nicholas Kegg. **KEYAN HINISH** Seventh great grandson of progenitor Nicholas Kegg.

HINKLE

HOLDEN NICHOLAS HINKLE Sixth great grandson of progenitor Nicholas Kegg.

HINNEBUSCH

BECKY HINNEBUSCH Seventh great granddaughter of progenitor Nicholas Kegg.
CONNER HINNEBUSCH Eighth great grandson of progenitor Nicholas Kegg.
JASON HINNEBUSCH aka "Jay", Seventh great grandson of progenitor Nicholas Kegg.
STEPHEN J. HINNEBUSCH Seventh great grandson of progenitor Nicholas Kegg.

HIPP

BETH A. HIPP Fifth great granddaughter of progenitor Nicholas Kegg. **JAMES RONALD HIPP** [3796B] (1933 – 1999) son of Joseph and Ann Marie (Kegg) Hipp, married Patricia Money with whom he was father of (5). James retired from the car shop of Bethlehem Steel and U-Haul. **JOAN MARIE HIPP** aka "Joanne", Fourth great granddaughter of progenitor Nicholas Kegg. **JODY HIPP** Fifth great grandson of progenitor Nicholas Kegg. **JUSTIN HIPP** Sixth great grandson of progenitor Nicholas Kegg. **KAITLYN RENEE HIPP** Sixth great granddaughter of progenitor Nicholas Kegg. **KEITH ALAN HIPP** Fifth great grandson of progenitor Nicholas Kegg. **MARJORIE S. HIPP** Fifth great granddaughter of progenitor Nicholas Kegg. **MARK J. HIPP** Fifth great grandson of progenitor Nicholas Kegg. **BRIAN GERALD HIPP-VAUGHT** Fifth great grandson of progenitor Nicholas Kegg.

HIRSCH

MELISSA S. HIRSCH Sixth great granddaughter of progenitor Nicholas Kegg.

[3796B] p.A13 -Tribune Democrat (PA) May 16, 1999

HITCHINS

BECKY HITCHINS Seventh great granddaughter of progenitor Nicholas Kegg.
MICHELE HITCHINS Seventh great granddaughter of progenitor Nicholas Kegg.

HITE

ALICE LOUISE HITE [3797] (1928 – 1996) daughter of Walter and Thelma (Mallory) Hite, married Richard J. Green with whom she was mother of (2). **ANGELA MICHELE HITE** Sixth great granddaughter of progenitor Nicholas Kegg. **BEATRICE ANN HITE** Fourth great granddaughter of progenitor Nicholas Kegg. - **BARRY J. HITE** Sixth great grandson of progenitor Nicholas Kegg. **DANIEL C. HITE** Sixth great grandson of progenitor Nicholas Kegg. **DOROTHY REBECCA HITE** (1915 – 1989) daughter of Lorenzo and Gertrude (Cessna) Hite, married Ralph Wesley Shannon with whom she was mother of (2). **EILEEN KAY HITE** Fourth great granddaughter of progenitor Nicholas Kegg. **EVELYN PAULINE HITE** [3798] (1913 – 1999) daughter of Lorenzo and Gertrude (Cessna) Hite married twice; first to Franklin Morgan Nowell, and later to John Stephen Vargo. Evelyn was first to volunteer and serve in 1942 in the newly formed Women's Army Corps. She served during World War II and was discharged as a major. **GAELYN CAER HITE** Seventh great granddaughter of progenitor Nicholas Kegg. **GERTRUDE L. HITE** [3799] (1930 – 2001) aka "Trudy", daughter of Walter and Thelma (Mallory) Hite married three times; first to John Kinghorn with whom she was mother of (1). She married David Riggs with whom she was mother of (2) and later, married Matthew Paul Himlin with whom she was mother of (1). Trudy was remembered for her kindness and touched the lives of many.
JENNIFER LYNN HITE Seventh great granddaughter of progenitor Nicholas Kegg.
JESSICA LEONE HITE Seventh great granddaughter of progenitor Nicholas Kegg.
JODI LYNNETTE HITE Seventh great granddaughter of progenitor Nicholas Kegg.
KATHERINE P. HITE [3799A] (1907 – 1995) daughter of Lorenzo and Gertrude (Cessna) Hite married twice, first to Evan Francis Bridgewater with whom she was mother of (1), later, she married Dallas Wilbur Heim. Katherine worked as a buyer and clerk for Martin Schwartz during the 1930's and 1940's. Later, she worked side by side with Dallas as co-owner of Heim's Drycleaners in Pittsburgh from 1947 to 1972. She was active in church and charity work. **LOUISE CHARLOTTE HITE** [3800] (1897 – 1959) daughter of Lorenzo and Gertrude (Cessna) Hite, was mother of (1) and later, married Edwin Stoler Bossler with whom she was mother of (3). Louise was a member of the Grove Avenue Methodist Church, the lady's missionary unit of the church and a charter member of Fortnightly Reading Club. **MARGARET RUTH HITE** (1909 – 1996) daughter of Lorenzo and Gertrude (Cessna) Hite, married Robert Prosser Fevner and later, married Donald Douglas Griffith. **NANETTE M. HITE** Sixth great granddaughter of progenitor Nicholas Kegg. **NELLIE GRACE HITE** [3801] (1900 – 1901) daughter of Lorenzo and Gertrude (Cessna) Hite. **OPAL FERN HITE** [3802] (1922 – 1994) aka "Fern", daughter of Walter and Mildred (McGunigale) Hite married Sterling James Logue, she married Charles Arthur Gildersleeve with whom she was mother of (1). Last, she married Robert H. Hovey. Fern was a bookkeeper and homemaker. **PAUL HITE** Sixth great grandson of progenitor Nicholas Kegg. **RETA MAE HITE** (1910 – 1978) daughter of Lorenzo and Gertrude (Cessna) Hite, married George Joseph Pavlick with whom she was mother of (2). **SHELLEY LOUISE HITE** Sixth great granddaughter of progenitor Nicholas Kegg **WALTER CLYDE HITE** [3803] (1904 – 1957) son of Lorenzo and Gertrude (Cessna) Hite married twice; first to Mildred Irene McGunigale with whom he was father of (1). Later, he married Thelma Lillian Mallory with whom he was father of (3).
WALTER CLYDE HITE [3803A] (1933 – 2015) son of Walter and Thelma (Mallory) Hite married twice, first to Marian Anderson with whom he was father of (4) later he married Shirley Gates. Walter served as

---

[3797] Tribune Democrat (PA) July 12, 1996 [3798] Johnstown Tribune (PA) Nov 10, 1999, obtained by James Thomas Rosenbaum [3799] San Diego Union-Tribune (CA) Feb 6, 2001 [3799A] Tribune-Democrat (PA) May 20, 1995 [3800] Rootsweb obituary transcribed by Frederick D. Royer [3801] Bedford Gazette (PA) May 3, 1901 [3802] Statesman Journal (Salem, OR) June 26, 1994 [3803] p.27 - San Diego Union (CA) Feb 11, 1957 [3803A] Mohave Daily News (AZ) Mar. 29, 2015

an Army Medic during the Korean War. He retired from AT&T. His love of horse racing brought him back to San Diego every summer where he worked the Solana Gate at the Del Mar racetrack for 20 years. He was a lifetime member of the Bullhead City Elks Lodge. He loved horse racing, sports, shuffleboard, fishing, poker and beer.

HOCKENBERRY

ALICE PEARL HOCKENBERRY (3804) (1882 – 1954) daughter of Daniel and Amanda (Kegg) Hockenberry, married George Marion Brantner with whom she was mother of (3). **CORNELIA OLIVE HOCKENBERRY** (3805) (1906 – 1971) daughter of Emory and Emma (Clark) Hockenberry, married Samuel Floyd Snyder with whom she was mother of (3). Cornelia belonged to Bedford Springs Chapter No. 41, of the Order of the Eastern Star, and was a cedarette with Tall Cedars of Lebanon Lodge No. 27 in Everett. She was a member of the Shake Spring Church of the Brethren.
DANIEL ANTHONY HOCKENBERRY (3806) (1900 – 1963) son of William and Carrie (Mellott) Hockenberry, married Rose Kathryn Seel. Dan owned and operated a Las Vegas Motel until he retired.
DANIEL F. HOCKENBERRY Fifth great grandson of progenitor Nicholas Kegg.
DANIELLE HOCKENBERRY Seventh great granddaughter of progenitor Nicholas Kegg.
DAVID B. HOCKENBERRY Fifth great grandson of progenitor Nicholas Kegg.
DENNIS HOCKENBERRY Sixth great grandson of progenitor Nicholas Kegg.
DON HOCKENBERRY Sixth great grandson of progenitor Nicholas Kegg.
DOUGLAS D. HOCKENBERRY (3806A) (1968 – 2015) son of Duane and Donna (Beegle) Hockenberry married twice. He was father of (2) before his marriage to Michelle Redmond with whom he was father of (1). Doug was a logger working and cutting timber all over the country. He enjoyed working outdoors, hunting, fishing and hunting mushrooms with his brothers. **DUANE A. HOCKENBERRY** (3807) (1937 – 2018) son of Emory and Helen (Miller) Hockenberry, married Donna Beegle with whom he was father of (4). Over Duane's career, he was employed as a heavy equipment operator and later owned and operated his own truck, which he drove coast-to-coast with his wife. He also later worked for Bollman's Charter Service. Duane enjoyed fishing, hunting, reading books and collecting farm tractors.
ELDA MARJORY HOCKENBERRY (3808) (1912 – 2001) daughter of Emory and Emma (Clark) Hockenberry, married William Stanley Bollman with whom she was mother of (3). Elda was employed by the former Lion Manufacturing Company of Everett for 29 years, where she served as president of the Amalgamated Union. With her husband, Elda purchased her first school bus, beginning their involvement in the transportation business. Elda drove the school bus for about 10 years and was involved in the management of the business. In 1962, they started Bollman Charter Service, for which Elda conducted many tours throughout the country. She was a member of the American Bus Association and the Bedford County Chamber of Commerce. She was a member and past Worthy Matron of the Bedford Springs Chapter 41 of the Order of the Eastern Star. **EMILY JANE HOCKENBERRY** Fifth great granddaughter of progenitor Nicholas Kegg. **EMORY C. HOCKENBERRY** (3809) (1917 – 1993) son of Emory and Emma (Clark) Hockenberry, married Helen R. Miller with whom he was father of (2). Emory had worked construction for H.J. Williams, was an owner/operator for Wilson Freight Lines, and retired as a driver for Continental Freight Lines. He was a member of Teamsters Local 453, Cumberland; and the Improved Order of the Redmen, Wambic Tribe 507.
EMORY JACOB HOCKENBERRY (3810) (1879 – 1961) son of Daniel and Amanda (Kegg) Hockenberry, married Emma Jane Clark with whom he was father of (5). In 1903, Emory met with a serious accident. While delivering a load of coal at a house in Alliance he was struck by a limb of a large tree, under which he had halted the team. The limb broke from the trunk and struck Emory, breaking his back. Luckily, he fully recovered. **ESPIE HAYES HOCKENBERRY** (3811) (1877 – 1964) son of

---

(3804) p.2 - Chronicle Express (NY) Oct 28, 1954 (3805) Bedford Inquirer (PA) May 28, 1971 (3806) The Billings Gazette (MT) March 22, 1963 (3806A) Bedford Gazette (PA) Sept 29, 2015 contributed by Bob Rose (3807) Bedford Gazette (PA) Aug 27, 2018, obtained by Bob Rose (3808) p.3 - Bedford Inquirer (PA) May 11, 2001, obtained by Bob Rose (3809) Bedford Gazette (PA) Oct 11, 1993 (3810) BOOR Obits, p. 228, 229 obtained by Duke Clark (3811) Rodman Public Library obituary obtained by D. Sue Dible

Daniel and Amanda (Kegg) Hockenberry, married Amelia Urmson with whom he was father of (3). Espy was a retired master plumber. He was a member of the Moose Lodge and belonged to the Modern Woodmen of America.   **ETTA A.H. HOCKENBERRY** (born abt.1896) daughter of William and Carrie (Mellott) Hockenberry.   **HARRY FRANKLIN HOCKENBERRY** [3812] (1888 – 1973) son of Daniel and Amanda (Kegg) Hockenberry, married Flossie Mellott with whom he was father of (8).

HARRY FRANKLIN HOCKENBERRY [3813] (1924 – 2003) son of Harry and Flossie (Mellott) Hockenberry married twice; first to Frances Irene Taylor with whom he was father of (6). Later, he married Mable R. Dively. Harry was a self-employed truck driver who also owned and operated his East Providence Township cattle farm. He enjoyed hunting and caring for his livestock.

HAZEL LEONE HOCKENBERRY [3813A] (1921 – 2008) daughter of Harry and Flossie (Mellot) Hockenberry, married Charles Harrison Coleman with whom she was mother of (4). Hazel worked as a seamstress at Lion Manufacturing in Everett. She was a homemaker who enjoyed cooking, canning, gardening and quilting and especially enjoyed spending time with her family.   **JEAN HOCKENBERRY** Fifth great granddaughter of progenitor Nicholas Kegg.   **JESSIE MAE HOCKENBERRY** [3814] (1916 – 2008) daughter of Harry and Flossie (Mellott) Hockenberry, married William Melvin Shaffer with whom she was mother of (2). Jessie enjoyed cooking, gardening, quilting and spending time with her family and friends.   **LEE E. HOCKENBERRY** [3814A] (1929 – 2004) son of Harry and Flossie (Mellot) Hockenberry, married Phyllis Steckman with whom he was father of (1). Lee owned and operated his own backhoe service, which he enjoyed immensely, for many years, Hockenberry Construction Company. Previously he was a bulk milk hauler, and enjoyed hunting and was a CB radio enthusiast.

LORRAINE GAYNELL HOCKENBERRY [3814B] (1925 – 2017) daughter of Emory and Emma (Clark) Hockenberry, married Woodrow W. Vaughn. During World War II, Lorraine worked at Letterkenny Army Depot driving munitions trucks where she met her husband, Woodrow Vaughn. She was a homemaker during her married years. After the death of her husband in 1995, Lorraine became a tour escort for Bollman Bus Service, where she traveled as far as Alaska and Australia while leading large groups of people on tours. During this time, she had seen more of the United States than most people can imagine. Lorraine had a strong love for the Lord.   **MABEL HOCKENBERRY** [3815] (1911 – 1965) daughter of Harry and Flossie (Mellott) Hockenberry, married Albert Dale Layton with whom she was mother of (5).   **MARSHA HOCKENBERRY** Fifth great granddaughter of progenitor Nicholas Kegg.

MARY CARRIE HOCKENBERRY (1873 – 1884) daughter of Daniel and Amanda (Kegg) Hockenberry.   **MAXINE HOCKENBERRY** [3815A] (1926 – 2017) daughter of Harry and Flossie (Mellot) Hockenberry, married Theodore Daniel Snyder. Maxine enjoyed shopping, dancing, listening to country music and outings with the girls. She was employed as a cook over the years at various local restaurants.   **MINNIE VIOLA HOCKENBERRY** [3816] (1891 – 1955) daughter of Daniel and Amanda (Kegg) Hockenberry, married Lawrence Homer Burket with whom she was mother of (1). Minnie taught in the area schools for some time and was a member of the Church of the Brethren.

MYRTLE MAY HOCKENBERRY [3817] (1887 – 1975) daughter of Daniel and Amanda (Kegg) Hockenberry, married David Calhoun with whom she was mother of (6). Myrtle was a member of the Mt. Union United Church of Christ and the Bedford Chapter No. 41, order of Eastern Star.

NAOMI LUCY HOCKENBERRY [3818] (1881 – 1949) daughter of Daniel and Amanda (Kegg) Hockenberry, married Marshall Edward Bequeath with whom she was mother of (1).

PAUL E. HOCKENBERRY [3819] (1905 – 1969) son of Espie and Amelia (Urmson) Hockenberry, married Regina Teresa Maue. Paul retired as purchasing agent and senior vice president of Industries Supply Co.   **PENNY HOCKENBERRY** Fifth great granddaughter of progenitor Nicholas Kegg.

RALPH D. HOCKENBERRY (1908 – 1909) son of Espie and Amelia (Urmson) Hockenberry.

[3812] Bedford Gazette (PA) Dec 1, 1973, obtained by Duke Clark [3813] p.3 - Bedford Inquirer (PA) Jan 24, 2003, obtained by Bob Rose [3813A] Cumberland Times News (MD) May 16, 2008 [3814] Bedford Inquirer (PA) Jan 2, 2009, obtained by Bob Rose [3814A] p.3 - Bedford Inquirer (PA) Apr 16, 2004 contributed by Bob Rose [3814B] Bedford Gazette (PA) June 26, 2017 contributed by Bob Rose [3815] Bedford County Historical Society obituary obtained by D. Sue Dible [3815A] Akers Funeral Home (PA) [3816] Bedford Gazette (PA) Jan 27, 1955 [3917] Bedford Gazette (PA) June 24, 1975, obtained by Duke Clark [3818] Everett Public Library obituary obtained by D. Sue Dible [3819] Rodman Public Library obituary obtained by D. Sue Dible

ROGER C. HOCKENBERRY Fifth great grandson of progenitor Nicholas Kegg.
ROGER W. HOCKENBERRY aka "Hawk", Fifth great grandson of progenitor Nicholas Kegg.
ROSS FRANKLIN HOCKENBERRY (3820) (1908 – 1950) son of Emory and Emma (Clark) Hockenberry. **SAMUEL DANIEL HOCKENBERRY** (3821) (1919 – 1990) son of Harry and Flossie (Mellott) Hockenberry, married Betty Jane Brown with whom he was father of (2). Samuel retired as a plant foreman from New Enterprise Stone & Lime Co., after 36 years of service.
TEHYA MOON HOCKENBERRY Seventh great granddaughter of progenitor Nicholas Kegg.
TRISTAN HOCKENBERRY Seventh great granddaughter of progenitor Nicholas Kegg.
ULYSSIS RUE HOCKENBERRY (1885 – 1887) son of Daniel and Amanda (Kegg) Hockenberry.
VIOLA E. HOCKENBERRY (3821A) (1913 – 2003) daughter of Harry and Flossie (Mellott) Hockenberry, married John William Cornell with whom she was mother of (1). Viola was a homemaker who enjoyed caring for her family. She was employed as a seamstress at Lion Manufacturing in Everett for over 20 years. **WILLIAM WILSON HOCKENBERRY** (3822) (1872 – 1950) son of Daniel and Amanda (Kegg) Hockenberry, married Carrie Mellott with whom he was father of (2). William was a farmer by occupation.

HODGE

JOHN WILLIAM HODGE (3823) (1926 – 1996) son of Edward and Doris (Huddy) Hodge was an Army veteran of WWII serving in the Second Infantry Division.

HODGSON

DENISE MICHELLE HODGSON Sixth great granddaughter of progenitor Nicholas Kegg.

HOEL

JACK HOEL (born abt. 1925) son of William and Lillian (Burritt) Hoel.

HOESTERY

CADE HOESTEREY Seventh great grandson of progenitor Nicholas Kegg.

HOFACKER

HERMAN A. HOFACKER Sixth great grandson of progenitor Nicholas Kegg.
HOPE MCKELVEY HOFACKER Sixth great granddaughter of progenitor Nicholas Kegg.
MELVIN R. HOFECKER (3824) (1919 – 1944) son of Clayton and Mary Etta (Kegg) Hofecker. Melvin was employed at the Air Reduction Sales Company when he was inducted into the Army and went overseas where he was killed in action in the South Pacific. **RUSSELL N. HOFECKER** (3825) (1916 – 1924) son of Clayton and Mary Etta (Kegg) Hofecker. Russell was a grade pupil at the Cypress school and was a member of the Sunday School of the Park-avenue U.B. Church when he contracted meningitis that took the 8-year-olds life. **TINA L. HOFECKER** Fifth great granddaughter of progenitor Nicholas Kegg.

(3920) The Bedford Gazette (PA) March 31, 1950 (3821) Bedford Inquirer (PA) May 4, 1990, obtained by Duke Clark (3821A) p.3 - Bedford Inquirer (PA) July 18, 2003, contributed by Bob Rose (3822) The Bedford Gazette (PA) June 23,1950 (3823) Dayton Daily News (OH) May 7, 1996 (3824) Johnstown Tribune-Democrat (PA) Oct 14, 1944, obtained by D. Sue Dible (3825) Johnstown Tribune-Democrat (PA) June 30, 1924, obtained by D. Sue Dible

HOFFMAN

BRIAN SCOTT HOFFMAN Sixth great grandson of progenitor Nicholas Kegg. **CODY HOFFMAN** Seventh great grandson of progenitor Nicholas Kegg. **DAMIAN LEE HOFFMAN** Sixth great grandson of progenitor Nicholas Kegg. **DAVID HOFFMAN** Seventh great grandson of progenitor Nicholas Kegg. **DAVID KEYS HOFFMAN** Sixth great grandson of progenitor Nicholas Kegg. **DEIRDRE HOFFMAN** Seventh great granddaughter of progenitor Nicholas Kegg. **DONNA HOFFMAN** Fifth great granddaughter of progenitor Nicholas Kegg. **ERIKA HOFFMAN** Sixth great granddaughter of progenitor Nicholas Kegg. **HAROLD RAY HOFFMAN** Fifth great grandson of progenitor Nicholas Kegg. **JAMIE LYNN HOFFMAN** Sixth great granddaughter of progenitor Nicholas Kegg. **JARED HOFFMAN** Seventh great grandson of progenitor Nicholas Kegg. **JOHN HOFFMAN** Fifth great grandson of progenitor Nicholas Kegg. **KARL GEORGE HOFFMAN** (1949 – 1996) son of Harold and Josephine (Stewart) Hoffman, married Patti S. Rosenberg with whom he was father of (1). **KARAL EDWIN HOFFMAN** Fifth great grandson of progenitor Nicholas Kegg. **KAY HOFFMAN** Fifth great granddaughter of progenitor Nicholas Kegg. **MARGARET HOFFMAN** Fifth great granddaughter of progenitor Nicholas Kegg. **MARK TODD HOFFMAN** Sixth great grandson of progenitor Nicholas Kegg. **MARY REBECCA HOFFMAN** Fifth great granddaughter of progenitor Nicholas Kegg **NATE HOFFMAN** Seventh great grandson of progenitor Nicholas Kegg. **NEVAN HOFFMAN** Seventh great grandson of progenitor Nicholas Kegg. **NICK HOFFMAN** Seventh great grandson of progenitor Nicholas Kegg. **NOLAN HOFFMAN** Seventh great grandson of progenitor Nicholas Kegg. **PAMELA ROSE HOFFMAN** Sixth great granddaughter of progenitor Nicholas Kegg. **SUSAN HOFFMAN** Sixth great granddaughter of progenitor Nicholas Kegg. **WENDY HOFFMAN** Sixth great granddaughter of progenitor Nicholas Kegg. **WILLIAM R. HOFFMAN** Fifth great grandson of progenitor Nicholas Kegg.

HOFFMIRE

EMMA CORA HOFFMIRE [3826] (1888 – 1966) daughter of Isaac and Emma (Kegg) Hoffmire, married Fred D. Olmstead with whom she was mother of (2). Emma was a member of Eastern Star and the Past Matrons Club.

HOLADAY

KATHLEEN HOLADAY Fifth great granddaughter of progenitor Nicholas Kegg.
MARIANNE HOLADAY Fifth great granddaughter of progenitor Nicholas Kegg.
RICHARD HOLADAY Fifth great grandson of progenitor Nicholas Kegg.

HOLCOMB

JOSHUA T. HOLCOMB Sixth great grandson of progenitor Nicholas Kegg.
NATASHA GWEN HOLCOMB Sixth great granddaughter of progenitor Nicholas Kegg.

HOLLAND

AMY NOEL HOLLAND Sixth great granddaughter of progenitor Nicholas Kegg. **DAVIS HOLLAND** Eighth great grandson of progenitor Nicholas Kegg. **DRAY E. HOLLAND** Seventh great grandson of progenitor Nicholas Kegg. **JACOB HOLLAND** Seventh great grandson of progenitor Nicholas Kegg. **JAMES JEFFREY HOLLAND** Sixth great grandson of progenitor Nicholas Kegg.

[3826] The Daily Oklahoman (OK) Aug 8, 1966

JAMES JEROMY HOLLAND Sixth great grandson of progenitor Nicholas Kegg.
JESSICA HOLLAND Eighth great granddaughter of progenitor Nicholas Kegg.
MICHELLE HOLLAND Seventh great granddaughter of progenitor Nicholas Kegg.
NATHAN HOLLAND Seventh great grandson of progenitor Nicholas Kegg.
PAUL HOLLAND Seventh great grandson of progenitor Nicholas Kegg.

HOLLENBECK

ED HOLLENBECK Sixth great grandson of progenitor Nicholas Kegg.
ELIZABETH EDWEEN HOLLENBECK Sixth great granddaughter of progenitor Nicholas Kegg.
GARY LYNN HOLLENBECK Fifth great grandson of progenitor Nicholas Kegg.
GARY LYNN HOLLENBECK JR. Sixth great grandson of progenitor Nicholas Kegg.
JAN P. HOLLENBECK Fifth great grandson of progenitor Nicholas Kegg.   **JUDY HOLLENBECK** [3827] (1942 – 2006) daughter of William Percival and Eleanor (Embs) Hollenbeck married twice, first to Johnnie Wayne Elam with whom she was mother of (3). Later, to Larry Lee Conway with whom she was mother of (2). Judy was a Registered Nurse and was formerly employed by Borgess Medical Center in Kalamazoo for 18 years. She was a member and Deacon of the First Reformed Church of Decatur, member of the Michigan Nurses Assoc., Log Cabin Quilters of Kalamazoo, the Scarlett O'Hatters of the Red Hat Society of Decatur, and BSF and CBS Bible Studies   **KATHRYN NELL HOLLENBECK** Fifth great granddaughter of progenitor Nicholas Kegg.   **LARRY HOLLENBECK** Fifth great grandson of progenitor Nicholas Kegg.   **MILDRED G. HOLLENBECK** (1910 – 1990) daughter of Edwin and Nellie (Bray) Hollenbeck, married Hermuth W. Regner with whom she was mother of (3).
PATSY ANN HOLLENBECK Fifth great granddaughter of progenitor Nicholas Kegg.
REBECCA ELEANOR HOLLENBECK Sixth great granddaughter of progenitor Nicholas Kegg.
SALLY HOLLENBECK Fifth great granddaughter of progenitor Nicholas Kegg.
STACEY ANN HOLLENBECK Sixth great granddaughter of progenitor Nicholas Kegg.
STEPHANIE RENEE HOLLENBECK Sixth great granddaughter of progenitor Nicholas Kegg.
THEODORE LEO HOLLENBECK Sixth great grandson of progenitor Nicholas Kegg.
VICKI HOLLENBECK Fifth great granddaughter of progenitor Nicholas Kegg.
WILLIAM EDWIN HOLLENBECK Fifth great grandson of progenitor Nicholas Kegg.

HOLLIGER

ETHAN HOLLIGER Seventh great grandson of progenitor Nicholas Kegg.
SETH HOLLIGER Seventh great grandson of progenitor Nicholas Kegg.

HOLLINGER

JANICE LOUISE HOLLINGER Fifth great granddaughter of progenitor Nicholas Kegg.
SUSAN JO HOLLINGER Fifth great granddaughter of progenitor Nicholas Kegg.

HOLLINGSHEAD

NATHAN SEAN HOLLINGSHEAD Seventh great grandson of progenitor Nicholas Kegg.

HOLLINGSWORTH

MAKAYLA ANN HOLLINGSWORTH Eighth great granddaughter of progenitor Nicholas Kegg.

[3827] Kalamazoo Gazette (MI) Aug 22, 2006

HOLLIS

GARY LEE HOLLIS Fifth great grandson of progenitor Nicholas Kegg. **MICAH HOLLIS** Sixth great grandson of progenitor Nicholas Kegg. **TAMMY LEE HOLLIS** Fifth great granddaughter of progenitor Nicholas Kegg.

HOLLNAGEL

JAYMES D. HOLLNAGEL aka "Jay", Eighth great grandson of progenitor Nicholas Kegg. **JESSICA HOLLNAGEL** Eighth great granddaughter of progenitor Nicholas Kegg.

HOLLOMAN

CHRYSTAL ANNE HOLLOMAN Sixth great granddaughter of progenitor Nicholas Kegg.
JAMES CLAYTON HOLLOMAN Fifth great grandson of progenitor Nicholas Kegg.
MATTHEW C. HOLLOMAN [3828] (1979 – 2015) aka "Matt", son of James and Deborah (Horner) Holloman. Matt was affiliated with the Sons of the American Legion Plymouth Post 447 and was a member of the Cleveland Browns Backers. He was a former Mickey Mart employee in Plymouth.

HOLLOWAY

TERRY HOLLOWAY Seventh great grandson of progenitor Nicholas Kegg.

HOLLOWINSKI

ELLIE RAY HOLLOWINSKI Seventh great granddaughter of progenitor Nicholas Kegg.

HOLORAN

CONNER W. HOLORAN Eighth great grandson of progenitor Nicholas Kegg.
KELLY M. HOLORAN Eighth great granddaughter of progenitor Nicholas Kegg.

HOLSINGER

KELLY KRISTINE HOLSINGER Seventh great grandson of progenitor Nicholas Kegg.

HOLSTEIN

SANDRA NICOLE HOLSTEIN Sixth great granddaughter of progenitor Nicholas Kegg.
VICTORIA ELIZABETH HOLSTEIN Sixth great granddaughter of progenitor Nicholas Kegg.

HOLT

CANDICE M. HOLT Sixth great granddaughter of progenitor Nicholas Kegg. **CHRISTOPHER A. HOLT** Sixth great grandson of progenitor Nicholas Kegg. **CONSTANCE HOLT** aka "Connie", Sixth great granddaughter of progenitor Nicholas Kegg. **LEAH HOLT** Sixth great granddaughter of progenitor Nicholas Kegg. **MATTHEW HOLT** Sixth great grandson of progenitor Nicholas Kegg. **TARA HOLT** Sixth great granddaughter of progenitor Nicholas Kegg.

[3828] Norwalk Reflector (OH) Jan 15, 2015

HOLTZ

DARIN J. HOLTZ Sixth great grandson of progenitor Nicholas Kegg. **DONALD LEE HOLTZ** Fifth great grandson of progenitor Nicholas Kegg. **DUSTIN ALEXANDER HOLTZ** [3829] (1977 – 1999) son of Donald Lee Holtz was killed on his birthday when the car he was a passenger hit a tree. **HEATHER LYNN HOLTZ** Sixth great granddaughter of progenitor Nicholas Kegg. **PATRICK HOLTZ** Sixth great grandson of progenitor Nicholas Kegg.

HOLZSCHUHER

KATIE HOLZSCHUHER Seventh great granddaughter of progenitor Nicholas Kegg.

HON

CORINNA A. HON Sixth great granddaughter of progenitor Nicholas Kegg. **KENNETH L. HON** Sixth great grandson of progenitor Nicholas Kegg. **TODD R. HON** Sixth great grandson of progenitor Nicholas Kegg.

HONTS

HEATHER HONTS Seventh great granddaughter of progenitor Nicholas Kegg. **JESSE KURT HONTS** Sixth great grandson of progenitor Nicholas Kegg. **JOHN STACY HONTS** Sixth great grandson of progenitor Nicholas Kegg. **JOHN LESTER HONTS** Seventh great granddaughter of progenitor Nicholas Kegg. **RICKY LEE HONTS** (1957 – 2001) son of Lester and Peggy (Gibbens) Honts married Cheryl Hall with whom he was father of (1).

HONEYCUTT

RANDY HONEYCUTT Eighth great grandson of progenitor Nicholas Kegg.
TAMMY GENNE HONEYCUTT Seventh great granddaughter of progenitor Nicholas Kegg.

HOOD

EDWARD SCOTT HOOD [3830] (1966 – 2009) son of Edward and Darlene (Smith) Hood, married Karen B. Jenkins with whom he was father of (2). **KEVIN HOOD** Sixth great grandson of progenitor Nicholas Kegg. **LUKE HOOD** Seventh great grandson of progenitor Nicholas Kegg. **ZACHARY HOOD** Seventh great grandson of progenitor Nicholas Kegg.

HOOK

DEBRA JEAN HOOK Seventh great granddaughter of progenitor Nicholas Kegg.
MARK HOOK Sixth great grandson of progenitor Nicholas Kegg.

HOOKER

BENJAMIN HOOKER Seventh great grandson of progenitor Nicholas Kegg.
BRIDGETT DAWN HOOKER (1953 – 1953) daughter of Pryce and Patricia (Owens) Hooker.
DANA HOOKER Seventh great granddaughter of progenitor Nicholas Kegg. **DARREN HOOKER** Seventh great grandson of progenitor Nicholas Kegg. **DENNIS HOOKER** Seventh great grandson of

---

[3829] Herald Palladium (MI) May 27, 2000 [3830] The Washington Post (DC) May 19, 2009

progenitor Nicholas Kegg. **JAIRUS HOOKER** Seventh great grandson of progenitor Nicholas Kegg. **JAKE HOOKER** Seventh great grandson of progenitor Nicholas Kegg. **JOE HOOKER** Seventh great grandson of progenitor Nicholas Kegg. **LOGAN HOOKER** Seventh great grandson of progenitor Nicholas Kegg. **PATRICK HOOKER** Seventh great grandson of progenitor Nicholas Kegg. **TRAVIS HOOKER** Seventh great grandson of progenitor Nicholas Kegg.

HOOPER

ALANA HOOPER Seventh great granddaughter of progenitor Nicholas Kegg. **ALLEN HOOPER** Sixth great grandson of progenitor Nicholas Kegg. **KAREN HOOPER** Sixth great granddaughter of progenitor Nicholas Kegg. **WILLIAM GERALD HOOPER** Sixth great grandson of progenitor Nicholas Kegg.

HOOPES

PATRICIA ANN HOOPES Fifth great granddaughter of progenitor Nicholas Kegg.

HOOVER

ALEXA MARIE HOOVER Seventh great granddaughter of progenitor Nicholas Kegg. **ALLISON HOOVER** Seventh great granddaughter of progenitor Nicholas Kegg. **ANDREA HOOVER** Seventh great granddaughter of progenitor Nicholas Kegg. **CHARLES HOOVER** [3831] (1954 – 2022) aka "Jack", son of Robert and Delores (Rice) Hoover married Melanie Jane Whisel with whom he was father of (2). Jack loved his career as a farmer, working on machinery and combining in the fall with his brother on the Hoover Brothers Farms that they owned and operated. Jack was a social member of the Everett American Legion and enjoyed riding his Harley and had previously been part of some motorcycle clubs. **DON HOOVER** Sixth great grandson of progenitor Nicholas Kegg. **DOROTHY GRACE HOOVER** [3832] (1921 – 1985) daughter of Harrison and Susanna (Morris) Hoover, married Albert Vaughn Sparks with whom she was mother of (2). Dorothy was a former employee of Erie Frequency of Carlisle. She was a member of Farm Women's Group #9. **DUANE DALE HOOVER** [3833] (1918 – 1995) son of Harry and Jessie (Kegg) Hoover, married Lois Eldine Kitchens with whom he was father of (2). Duane spent many years as a deputy stock inspector in addition to operating the family ranch near Otter, Montana. He enjoyed ranch life, the outdoors, playing horseshoes and watching baseball. Duane involved with the country churches and family bible studies. He was also a member of the Montana Stockgrower's Association. **DYLAN E. HOOVER** Seventh great grandson of progenitor Nicholas Kegg. **ELIZABETH JOAN HOOVER** [3834] (1916 – 1981) aka "Bette", daughter of Harry and Jessie (Kegg) Hoover, married Albert J. Wilson. Bette taught shorthand at KBU. During World War II, Bette served in military intelligence with the Women's Army Corps. **EVELYN VIRGINIA HOOVER** [3835] (1917 – 1964) daughter of Harrison and Susanna (Morris) Hoover, married Ray E. Firebaugh. **HARRY F. HOOVER** Fifth great grandson of progenitor Nicholas Kegg. **HAZEL PAULENE HOOVER** [3836] (1915 – 1975) daughter of Harrison and Susanna (Morris) Hoover, married Clarence Angus Martin with whom she was mother of (2). **HILLARY HOOVER** Seventh great granddaughter of progenitor Nicholas Kegg. **HOWARD H. HOOVER** (1961 - 1983) son of Robert and Delores (Rice) Hoover. **ISAAC JAMES HOOVER** Seventh great grandson of progenitor Nicholas Kegg. **JACK ADAMS HOOVER** [3837] (1919 – 2002) son of Harrison and Susanna (Morris) Hoover married three times; first to Ruth Lois Salkeld, then to Leona Felton. Later, he married Eva Hengst Manspeaker. **JANICE E. HOOVER** Fifth great granddaughter of progenitor Nicholas Kegg.

[3831] Bedford Gazette (PA) Feb 21, 2022 [3832] Bedford County Historical Society (PA), book 69, p. 172 obtained by D. Sue Dible [3833] Casper Star-Tribune (WY) Oct 26, 1995 [3834] Spokane Chronicle (WA) Oct 13, 1981 [3835] Bedford County Genealogical Society obituary obtained by D. Sue Dible [3836] Duke Clark Obituary collection p. 2719 [3737] Altoona Mirror (PA) April 10, 2002

JEAN MARY HOOVER [3838] (1917 – 1996) daughter of Harry and Jessie (Kegg) Hoover, married Robert Henry Haraldson with whom she was mother of (2). Jean was schooled in a one-room schoolhouse in Montana and later moved with her family to Sheridan, Wyo., where she graduated from high school. She worked for Mountain States Telephone Co., in Sheridan, Fort Collins, Colo. and Denver. In Denver she met Robert Haraldson. They were engaged in 1943, before he went to serve in World War II. When he returned in 1945, they were married. They spent their honeymoon in Spokane and remained here for more than 50 years. She had worked at The Crescent for five years and then for Dodson's Jewelers for 10 years. She and her husband were members of Fourth Memorial Church and taught Sunday school for many years. They later were among the group that started Northview Bible Church, where they also taught Sunday school and were involved with home Bible studies. **JIM HOOVER** Sixth great grandson of progenitor Nicholas Kegg. **KATHLEEN HOOVER** Fifth great granddaughter of progenitor Nicholas Kegg. **KELLY ELIZABETH HOOVER** Seventh great granddaughter of progenitor Nicholas Kegg. **LANDON HOOVER** Seventh great grandson of progenitor Nicholas Kegg. **MARCELINE OLIVIA HOOVER** Eighth great granddaughter of progenitor Nicholas Kegg. **MARISSA NICOLE HOOVER** Seventh great grandchild of progenitor Nicholas Kegg. **MARJORIE REBECCA HOOVER** Fourth great granddaughter of progenitor Nicholas Kegg. **MARK HOOVER** Fifth great grandson of progenitor Nicholas Kegg. **MARY L. HOOVER** Fifth great granddaughter of progenitor Nicholas Kegg. **MATTHIAS GORDON HOOVER** Sixth great grandson of progenitor Nicholas Kegg. **MICHAEL HOOVER** aka "Mike", Fifth great grandson of progenitor Nicholas Kegg. **MIKE HOOVER** Fifth great grandson of progenitor Nicholas Kegg. **NANCY HOOVER** Fifth great granddaughter of progenitor Nicholas Kegg. **NICOLE RENEE HOOVER** Seventh great granddaughter of progenitor Nicholas Kegg. **PHIL HOOVER** Sixth great grandson of progenitor Nicholas Kegg. **REBECCA A. HOOVER** Fifth great granddaughter of progenitor Nicholas Kegg. **ROBERT MARCUS HOOVER** [3839] (1956 – 1998) aka "Mark", son of Robert and Delores (Rice) Hoover. Mark was employed at the family farm at Everett RD 1 and was an avid hunter. **ROCHELLE HOOVER** Sixth great granddaughter of progenitor Nicholas Kegg. **RUTH C. HOOVER** Fifth great granddaughter of progenitor Nicholas Kegg. **WALTER CHARLES HOOVER** Sixth great grandson of progenitor Nicholas Kegg. **WILLIAM JAMES HOOVER** Sixth great grandson of progenitor Nicholas Kegg.

HOPE

MATTHEW LEE HOPE Sixth great grandson of progenitor Nicholas Kegg. **RYAN LEE HOPE** Sixth great grandson of progenitor Nicholas Kegg. **TIFFANI HOPE** Sixth great granddaughter of progenitor Nicholas Kegg.

HOPKINS

MARY HOPKINS Sixth great granddaughter of progenitor Nicholas Kegg. **MATTHEW HOPKINS** Sixth great grandson of progenitor Nicholas Kegg. **MICHAEL HOPKINS** Sixth great grandson of progenitor Nicholas Kegg. **ROBERT ANDREW HOPKINS** Sixth great grandson of progenitor Nicholas Kegg. **ROBERT L. HOPKINS** Sixth great grandson of progenitor Nicholas Kegg. **THEODORE D. HOPKINS** Sixth great grandson of progenitor Nicholas Kegg. **WILLIAM T. HOPKINS** Sixth great grandson of progenitor Nicholas Kegg.

HORAN

RYAN HORAN Eighth great grandson of progenitor Nicholas Kegg. **TRACEY HORAN** Eighth great granddaughter of progenitor Nicholas Kegg.

[3838] p.B2 - Spokesman-Review (WA) Aug 30, 1996 [3839] Bedford County Historical Society (PA) book 81, p.58; obtained by D. Sue Dible

HORN

ADDISON HORN Sixth great granddaughter of progenitor Nicholas Kegg. **JEFFREY L. HORN** Fifth great grandson of progenitor Nicholas Kegg. **KIRSTEN MACKENZIE HORN** Sixth great granddaughter of progenitor Nicholas Kegg. **LEVI JONATHAN HORN** Sixth great grandson of progenitor Nicholas Kegg. **MIRANDA HORN** Sixth great granddaughter of progenitor Nicholas Kegg. **RYAN SCOTT HORN** [3840] (1986 – 2003) son of Jeffrey and Amy (Rose) Horn. Ryan was an employee at Hoss's Restaurant, Bedford. He was affiliated with Christ Victory Church, New Buena Vista. He was a hunter and fisherman and was going into the 11th grade when he sustained fatal injuries in an auto accident.

HORNE

JANET BUSHNELL HORNE Fourth great granddaughter of progenitor Nicholas Kegg.
KENNETH JEFFREY HORNE Fourth great grandson of progenitor Nicholas Kegg.
MICHAEL S. HORNE Sixth great grandson of progenitor Nicholas Kegg. **TALAN R. HORNE** Seventh great grandson of progenitor Nicholas Kegg. **VANESSA L. HORNE** Sixth great granddaughter of progenitor Nicholas Kegg.

HORNER

BETTY LOU HORNER Fifth great granddaughter of progenitor Nicholas Kegg.
CHERLY HORNER Fifth great granddaughter of progenitor Nicholas Kegg. **LORN L. HORNER** Fifth great grandson of progenitor Nicholas Kegg. **VICKY HORNER** Sixth great granddaughter of progenitor Nicholas Kegg.

HORST

CAROL I. HORST [3841] (1965 – 1991) daughter of James and Katharine (Luntar) Horst.
HERBERT M. HORST Fifth great grandson of progenitor Nicholas Kegg.
JAMES RICHARD HORST Fifth great grandson of progenitor Nicholas Kegg. **JOSEPH F. HORST** Sixth great grandson of progenitor Nicholas Kegg. **MATTHEW J. HORST** Sixth great grandson of progenitor Nicholas Kegg. **RICHARD HARLEY HORST** Fifth great grandson of progenitor Nicholas Kegg. **RONALD JOSEPH HORST** Fifth great grandson of progenitor Nicholas Kegg.

HORTON

DENA K. HORTON Sixth great granddaughter of progenitor Nicholas Kegg.
DOUGLAS R. HORTON Seventh great grandson of progenitor Nicholas Kegg.
RICHARD D. HORTON Sixth great grandson of progenitor Nicholas Kegg.

HORWATH

JENNIFER HORWATH Fifth great granddaughter of progenitor Nicholas Kegg.
THEODORE HORWATH aka "Teddy", Fifth great grandson of progenitor Nicholas Kegg.

[3840] Bedford Inquirer (PA) July 4, 2003, obtained by Ed Rose shared by Bob Rose [3841] p.11 St. Louis Post Dispatch (MO) Sep 24, 1991

HORWEDEL

CHRISTINE HORWEDEL Sixth great granddaughter of progenitor Nicholas Kegg.
DANIEL J HORWEDEL Sixth great grandson of progenitor Nicholas Kegg. **DARIC HORWEDEL** Sixth great grandson of progenitor Nicholas Kegg. **DAVID CHARLES HORWEDEL** Fifth great grandson of progenitor Nicholas Kegg. **JAMES EDWIN HORWEDEL** Fifth great grandson of progenitor Nicholas Kegg. **JON PATRICK HORWEDEL** Fifth great grandson of progenitor Nicholas Kegg. **KEN HORWEDEL** Sixth great grandson of progenitor Nicholas Kegg.
KRISTA HORWEDEL Sixth great granddaughter of progenitor Nicholas Kegg.
LEOTA PEARL HORWEDEL (born abt. 1919) daughter of Pearley and Esther (Dean) Horwedel.
LEWIS CHARLES HORWEDEL [3842] (1918 – 1984) aka "Charles", son of Pearley and Esther (Dean) Horwedel married Ouida Jean Lovett with whom he was father of (5). Charles was a World War II veteran serving in the U.S. Army. He was employed by the Vista Unified School District.
MICHAEL NEAL HORWEDEL Fifth great grandson of progenitor Nicholas Kegg.
ROBERT JAYSON HORWEDEL Sixth great grandson of progenitor Nicholas Kegg.
TANYA HORWEDEL Sixth great granddaughter of progenitor Nicholas Kegg.
TERRENCE JAY HORWEDEL [3843] (1948 – 2013) aka Terry, son of Charles and Ouida (Lovett) Horwedel married M.E. Youngdah with whom he was father of (1). Later, he married Lucinda Shayron Campbell.

HOSKINS

JACKSON HOSKINS Ninth great grandson of progenitor Nicholas Kegg. **NATE HOSKINS** Ninth great grandson of progenitor Nicholas Kegg.

HOTTMAN

AVA LYNN HOTTMAN [3844] (1950 – 2006) daughter of Elwood and Barbara (Liming) Hottman. Ava worked 23 years with the Ohio Environmental Protection Agency where she last served as Assistant Environmental Administrator of the Division of Surface Water. She began working at the Ohio EPA in 1976 in the Water Quality Planning Program. **BETHLYN HOTTMAN** Sixth great granddaughter of progenitor Nicholas Kegg. **BRANDON HOTTMAN** Seventh great grandson of progenitor Nicholas Kegg. **CATHERINE ANN HOTTMAN** Sixth great granddaughter of progenitor Nicholas Kegg.
DAVID HOTTMAN Sixth great grandson of progenitor Nicholas Kegg.
DENNIS MARSHALL HOTTMAN Fifth great grandson of progenitor Nicholas Kegg.
DOUG HOTTMAN Sixth great grandson of progenitor Nicholas Kegg. **ELAINE M. HOTTMAN** Sixth great granddaughter of progenitor Nicholas Kegg. **ELLEN ANN HOTTMAN** Sixth great granddaughter of progenitor Nicholas Kegg. **GREGG PATRICK HOTTMAN** [3845] (1951 – 1999) son of Elwood and Barbara (Liming) Hottman. Gregg was a graduate of The Ohio State University;
JANET HOTTMAN Sixth great granddaughter of progenitor Nicholas Kegg.
JARRETT M. HOTTMAN Seventh great grandson of progenitor Nicholas Kegg.
JEFFREY T. HOTTMAN Sixth great grandson of progenitor Nicholas Kegg. **JULIA HOTTMAN** Sixth great granddaughter of progenitor Nicholas Kegg. **MICHAEL W. HOTTMAN** Sixth great grandson of progenitor Nicholas Kegg. **NORMAN DELANO HOTTMAN** [3846] (1936 – 2000) son of Glenn and Evelyn (Crevison) Hottman, married Charlotte A. Miller with whom he was father of (3). Norman retired from Tokheim Corp. and Gasboy Limited of Canada as president. He began his employment with Tokheim in 1972 as sales manager of the Detroit district, working his way up as assistant general sales manager, general sales manager, eastern regional vice president and director of

---

[3842] Times Advocate (Escondido, CA) Feb 17, 1984 [3843] The Sacramento Bee (CA) June 9, 2013 [3844] The Courier (OH) Feb 28, 2006 [3845] Courier/GenealogyBuff/ Misc. Hardin County, Ohio Obituaries [3846] The News-Sentinel (IN) Dec 13, 2000

sales western region. He was a member of Kenton, Ohio Elks Lodge 157 where he served as exulted ruler in 1970. **PATRICIA HOTTMAN** Sixth great granddaughter of progenitor Nicholas Kegg.
RACHELLE HOTTMAN Seventh great granddaughter of progenitor Nicholas Kegg.
TERRY SUE HOTTMAN Sixth great granddaughter of progenitor Nicholas Kegg.

HOTZ

JENNA DAWN MARIE HOTZ Seventh great granddaughter of progenitor Nicholas Kegg.

HOUCK

EDNA BERNITA HOUCK [3847] (1904 – 1997) daughter of Charles and Gertrude (Arnold) Houck, married Harold Lehr Hindall with whom she was mother of (3). Edna was a homemaker.
MABEL MAXINE HOUCK [3848] (1907 – 1983) daughter of Charles and Gertrude (Arnold) Houck, married Ovis Roderick Monroe with whom she was mother of (2). Mabel was a member of the Jehovah's Witness church. **MARY MARIE HOUCK** [3849] (1905 – 1977) aka "Marie", daughter of Charles and Gertrude (Arnold) Houck married twice; first to Adam F. Rettig with whom she was mother of (2). Later, she married Herbert Gardner Tuthill. A housewife, Marie attended Jehovah's Witnesses Kingdom Hall, Lima.

HOUGH

JEAN E. HOUGH [3850] (1918 – 1990) daughter of Samuel and Gertrude (Beaver) Hough, married George F. Smith with whom she was mother of (1). **MARGARET ANN HOUGH** [3851] (1910 – 1989) daughter of Samuel and Gertrude (Beaver) Hough, married Roy Ernest Bloom with whom she was mother of (1). **ROBERT TYLER HOUGH** Seventh great grandson of progenitor Nicholas Kegg.

HOUP

KAMERON HOUP Eighth great grandson of progenitor Nicholas Kegg. **KAYLIN HOUP** Eighth great granddaughter of progenitor Nicholas Kegg. **TYLEN HOUP** Eighth great grandson of progenitor Nicholas Kegg.

HOUSE

JENNIFER LYNNE HOUSE Sixth great granddaughter of progenitor Nicholas Kegg.

HOUSER

CHRISTOPHER HOUSER Seventh great grandson of progenitor Nicholas Kegg. **MARY HOUSER** aka "Mimi", Fifth great granddaughter of progenitor Nicholas Kegg. **ROBERT BOOSE HOUSER** Fifth great grandson of progenitor Nicholas Kegg. **ROBERT CORBIN HOUSER** Sixth great grandson of progenitor Nicholas Kegg.

HOUSEWORTH

ANDREA KAY HOUSEWORTH Seventh great granddaughter of progenitor Nicholas Kegg.

[3847] p.9 - St. Petersburg Times (FL) Apr 16, 1997obtained by D. Sue Dible [3848] Muncie Public Library obituary obtained by D. Sue Dible [3849] p.A6 - Findlay Courier (OH) May 4, 1977, obtained by D. Sue Dible [3850] p.5 Pittsburgh Post-Gazette (PA) Aug 29, 1990 [3851] Pittsburgh Post-Gazette (PA) Aug 16, 1989

HOUSTON

DIANE C. HOUSTON Sixth great granddaughter of progenitor Nicholas Kegg.
JOANNA L. HOUSTON Sixth great granddaughter of progenitor Nicholas Kegg.

HOWARD

CALVIN FRANK HOWARD [3852] (1922 – 1981) son of Earl and Edna (Skode) Howard, married Ruth Cannon with whom he was father of (3). Calvin was a veteran of World War II, having served in Korea. He entered the military in 1940 and retired in 1961 as a major in the Air Force. He had received the American Campaign Medal, American Defense Medal Service Medal, World War II Victory Medal, the American Occupation Medal, Korean Service Medal and the United Nations Service Medal. He was a member of Arthur Butler Post 359 of East Syracuse. **CHARLOTTE EDNA HOWARD** [3853] (1925 – 2009) daughter of Earl and Edna (Skode) Howard married twice; first to Rudolph R. Gelenser with whom she was mother of (1). Later, she married Edward J. Urban. As a young woman, Charlotte was an avid equestrian. Her expansive career covered state government, administration at the John Hall Foundation and later, Diocesan Publications in New Cumberland. She was also a long-time member of West Shore Country Club. **LISA DIANE HOWARD** Sixth great granddaughter of progenitor Nicholas Kegg. **NANETTE D. HOWARD** [3854] (1961 – 1997) daughter of Maj. Calvin and Ruth (Cannon) Howard, married David E. Pizio with whom she was mother of (2). Nanette worked for several years at the family business, Captain Ahab's Restaurant, DeWitt. **PAMELA M. HOWARD** Sixth great granddaughter of progenitor Nicholas Kegg. **PATRICIA ANN HOWARD** [3855] (1932 – 1974) daughter of William and Madeline (Ingram) Howard, married George M. Williamson with whom she was mother of (1). Patricia was a member of St. John's Lutheran Church, Belleville, where she was a teacher in the church Sunday School, a youth advisor in the church, a former member of the church council and co-founder of the church library. She belonged to the LCW. Patricia was a past president of the Belleville Civic Club, a former Girl Scout leader in Belleville, a past president of the Mifflin County Society for Retarded Children and a member of the Registry of Medical Technologists of the American Society of Clinical Pathologists. A registered medical technologist, she worked at Lewistown Hospital.
STEPHEN C. HOWARD Sixth great grandson of progenitor Nicholas Kegg.
WILLIAM H. HOWARD [3856] (1895 – 1971) son of William and Laura (Gump) Howard, married Madeline (Ingram with whom he was father of (1). William had served in the U. S. Army and was a veteran of World War I. He was a charter and life member of the Frank P. Hommon Post No. 24, American Legion at Huntingdon and belonged to the F. and A.M., Everett Lodge No. 524. For 28 years he served as a resource's investigator for the Department of Public Instruction, retiring in 1960. In later years he was employed as a reservations clerk at the Huntingdon Motor Inn.

HOWARTH

ANDREW HOWARTH Sixth great grandson of progenitor Nicholas Kegg. **AUSTIN HOWARTH** Seventh great grandson of progenitor Nicholas Kegg. **CARRIE HOWARTH** Sixth great granddaughter of progenitor Nicholas Kegg. **JASON HOWARTH** Sixth great grandson of progenitor Nicholas Kegg. **NANCY LORRAINE HOWARTH** Fifth great granddaughter of progenitor Nicholas Kegg.

[3852] p.C2- Syracuse Post Standard March 4, 1981 [3853] p.A6 - Patriot-News (PA) Dec 15, 2009 [3854] p. B4 Syracuse Post Standard (NY) April 3, 1997 [3855] Daily News (Huntingdon, PA) June 26, 1974 [3856] p.2 Daily News (PA) Nov. 4, 1971

HOWSARE

CAROL J. HOWSARE Sixth great granddaughter of progenitor Nicholas Kegg.
JOHN R. HOWSARE Sixth great grandson of progenitor Nicholas Kegg.
KIMBERLY S. HOWSARE Sixth great granddaughter of progenitor Nicholas Kegg.

HOWSER

DUANE MITCHELL HOWSER Seventh great grandson of progenitor Nicholas Kegg.
JAMES ALAN HOWSER Seventh great grandson of progenitor Nicholas Kegg.
VICTOR LEE HOWSER Seventh great grandson of progenitor Nicholas Kegg.

HRUSKOCY

AMY CHRISTINE HRUSKOCY Sixth great granddaughter of progenitor Nicholas Kegg.

HSU

SAMUEL HSU Eighth great grandson of progenitor Nicholas Kegg.

HUBBARD

BARBARA SUE ANN HUBBARD [3857] (1945 – 1977) daughter of Lowell and Barbara (Wyckoff) Hubbard, married Gaylord E. Garrison with whom she was mother of (2). Barbara was active in the Bessie Ellison PTA. She was also a Cub den mother. A former elementary school teacher, Mrs. Garrison had taught at St. Francis Xavier and Spring Garden schools. **JON L. HUBBARD** Fifth great grandson of progenitor Nicholas Kegg. **ROBERT STEPHEN PORTER HUBBARD** (1948 – 1968) son of Lowell and Barbara (Wyckoff) Hubbard a Navy Seaman was a Vietnam casualty, killed in Thua Thien Republic of Vietnam.

HUBBLE

BETH HUBBLE Sixth great granddaughter of progenitor Nicholas Kegg. **HARLEY JOE HUBBLE** Sixth great grandson of progenitor Nicholas Kegg. **KATIE HUBBLE** Seventh great granddaughter of progenitor Nicholas Kegg. **MEG HUBBLE** Sixth great granddaughter of progenitor Nicholas Kegg. **SARAH LYNN HUBBLE** Sixth great granddaughter of progenitor Nicholas Kegg.

HUBLER

HARRY JOHN HUBLER Fourth great grandson of progenitor Nicholas Kegg. **HELENE MAXINE HUBLER** Fourth great granddaughter of progenitor Nicholas Kegg. **HOWARD C. HUBLER** Fourth great grandson of progenitor Nicholas Kegg. **JACQUELYN HUBLER** Fourth great granddaughter of progenitor Nicholas Kegg.

HUDAK

AMY HUDAK Sixth great granddaughter of progenitor Nicholas Kegg. **CAROL ANN HUDAK** Fifth great granddaughter of progenitor Nicholas Kegg. **JEFFREY LEE HUDAK** Fifth great grandson of progenitor Nicholas Kegg. **JOAN HUDAK** Fifth great granddaughter of progenitor Nicholas Kegg.

[3857] St. Joseph News-Press/Gazette (MO) Nov 7, 1977

KATIE HUDAK Sixth great granddaughter of progenitor Nicholas Kegg.

HUDDY

ANN LOUISE HUDDY Fifth great granddaughter of progenitor Nicholas Kegg.
BARBARA ALICE HUDDY (3858) (1948 – 1993) daughter of George and Jeanette (Reeves) Huddy, married James Elliott with whom she was mother of (3). Barbara had worked as a nurse at Doctors Hospital in Lanham, Meridian Nursing Home in Silver Spring and Lorien Nursing Home in Columbia. Her hobbies included bowling and travel. **BILLIE JO HUDDY** Fifth great granddaughter of progenitor Nicholas Kegg. **CARL MILLS HUDDY** (1913 – 1994) son of Charles and Edith (Mills) Huddy, married twice; first to Ruby Ethel Richards with whom he was father of (4). Later, he married Galena Rose Bond. **CARL RICHARD HUDDY** Fifth great grandson of progenitor Nicholas Kegg.
CAROL RENEE HUDDY Sixth great granddaughter of progenitor Nicholas Kegg.
CARON SUE HUDDY (1944 – 1944) daughter of Virgil and Verna (Wooley) McConaha Huddy.
CHARLES WILLIAM HUDDY (3859) (1938 – 2010) aka "Bill", son of Virgil and Verna (Wooley) McConaha Huddy, married twice; first to Katherine Georgia Dewitt with whom he was father of (1). Later, he married Mary Lou Vanmeter with whom he was father of (3). Millwright by trade, Bill enjoyed working, hunting, and attending gun shoots. He especially loved the hills of his childhood and returned to them upon his retirement. **DANIEL JAMES HUDDY** aka "Danny", Sixth great grandson of progenitor Nicholas Kegg. **DAVID R. HUDDY** Sixth great grandson of progenitor Nicholas Kegg.
DENISE ROSE HUDDY Sixth great granddaughter of progenitor Nicholas Kegg.
DOMINIK HUDDY Seventh great grandson of progenitor Nicholas Kegg.
DOROTHY M. HUDDY (1924 – 1992) daughter of Charles and Edith (Mills) Huddy married Edward Conley. **EDWARD LEROY HUDDY** Fifth great grandson of progenitor Nicholas Kegg.
GARRETT ANDREW HUDDY Sixth great grandson of progenitor Nicholas Kegg.
GEORGE EARL HUDDY (1914 – 1982) son of Charles and Edith (Mills) Huddy, married Jeanette Reeves with whom he was father of (3). **GEORGE MICHAEL HUDDY** aka "Mike", Sixth great grandson of progenitor Nicholas Kegg. **HAZEL HUDDY** (1902 – 1904) daughter of John and Leah (Kline) Huddy. **IVALUE SUE HUDDY** (3860) (1906 – 2001) daughter of Lorenzo and Grace (Figgins) Huddy, married Wiley Maxwell Ryan with whom she was mother of (5).
JACQUELINE MARIE HUDDY Seventh great granddaughter of progenitor Nicholas Kegg.
JAMES HUDDY Sixth great grandson of progenitor Nicholas Kegg. **JAMES EDWIN HUDDY** (3861) (1908 – 1969) son of Lorenzo and Grace (Figgins) Huddy, married Lena Estella Wolf. James was a World War II veteran and served as a machinist's mate in the Seabees. **JAMES ROLAND HUDDY** (1934 – 2008) son of Thomas and Nellie (Campbell) Huddy, married Nancy Carole Taylor with whom he was father of (2). **JANE HUDDY** (1948 – 1948) daughter of William and Ada (Rife) Huddy.
JENNIE LUCILLE HUDDY (3862) (1909 – 2009) aka "Lucille", daughter of James and Margaret (Emish) Huddy, married Herbert Wayne Walker with whom she was mother of (1). Lucille was a member of Immanuel United Methodist Church, a past, longtime, Sunday school teacher and was a devoted and loving mother, grandmother and great-grandmother. **JOHN HUDDY** Sixth great grandson of progenitor Nicholas Kegg. **JOHN HUDDY** Sixth great grandson of progenitor Nicholas Kegg.
JOHN EDWARD HUDDY (3863) (1946 – 1947) son of William and Ada (Rife) Huddy.
JOHN PARKER HUDDY Sixth great grandson of progenitor Nicholas Kegg.
JOSHUA DAVID HUDDY Seventh great grandson of progenitor Nicholas Kegg.
JUDITH AGNES HUDDY (1937 – 1937) daughter of Charles and Edith (Mills) Huddy.
JUDITH KAY HUDDY aka "Judy", Fifth great granddaughter of progenitor Nicholas Kegg.
KELLI HUDDY Sixth great granddaughter of progenitor Nicholas Kegg. **KELLY LYNN HUDDY** Sixth great granddaughter of progenitor Nicholas Kegg. **KEVIN D. HUDDY** Sixth great grandson of

---

(3858) Washington Post (DC) July 21, 1993 (3859) Toledo Blade (OH) July 8, 2010 (3860) Athens, OH obit book; Findlay library obtained by D. Sue Dible (3861) Athens Messenger (OH) Feb 9, 1969 (3862) Logan Daily News (OH) Mar 6, 2009 (3863) p.6 Logan Daily News (OH) Oct 6, 1947

progenitor Nicholas Kegg. **LAUREN CATHERINE HUDDY** Sixth great granddaughter of progenitor Nicholas Kegg. **LEAH ELIZABETH HUDDY** (1904 – 1985) daughter of John and Leah (Kline) Huddy, married John Patrick Casey with whom she was mother of (2).
LILLIAN FLORENCE HUDDY [3864] (1920 – 2001) daughter of James and Margaret (Emish) Huddy married twice; first to Jack Morgan Wilson with whom she was mother of (1). Later, she married Fred Hamner Hall. Lillian was a charter and life member of Pandorian Club, Nelsonville, Ohio. Lillian was a member of Northwest United Methodist Church and Twig #25, Children's Hospital, Columbus Women's Club, Columbus Dental Auxiliary, Tri-Village Lions Auxiliary and a former member of Columbus Damenchor and Swiss Club. **LORENZO DOW HUDDY** [3865] (1904 – 1976) son of Lorenzo and Grace (Figgins) Huddy, married Vivian Paulina Willison with whom he was father of (1).
LYNSI ELIZABETH HUDDY Seventh great granddaughter of progenitor Nicholas Kegg.
MARGARET LOUISE HUDDY (1915 – 1916) daughter of James and Margaret (Emish) Huddy.
MARK ANTHONY HUDDY Sixth great grandson of progenitor Nicholas Kegg.
MARK HAMILTON HUDDY Fifth great grandson of progenitor Nicholas Kegg.
MATTHEW DOW HUDDY Sixth great grandson of progenitor Nicholas Kegg.
MILDRED J. HUDDY [3866] (1911 – 2006) daughter of Lorenzo and Grace (Figgins) Huddy, married Charles D. Campbell with whom she was mother of (4). Mildred attended the Church of God in Laurel Run and Newark. **NICHOLAS DAVID HUDDY** Seventh great grandson of progenitor Nicholas Kegg. **PAULINE FRANCIS HUDDY** (1920 – 1988) daughter of Charles and Edith (Mills) Huddy married twice; first to Ben Mason, later she married Darrell King Figgins.
RANDAL SCOTT HUDDY Sixth great grandson of progenitor Nicholas Kegg. **REBECCA HUDDY** aka "Becky", Sixth great granddaughter of progenitor Nicholas Kegg. **RICK HUDDY** Fifth great grandson of progenitor Nicholas Kegg. **ROBERT E. HUDDY** Fifth great grandson of progenitor Nicholas Kegg. **RONA ELEANOR HUDDY** (1930 – 1994) daughter of Thomas and Nellie (Campbell) Huddy, married Gail Gerald Lonberger with whom she was mother of (4).
SARA PAIGE HUDDY Seventh great granddaughter of progenitor Nicholas Kegg.
STEVEN DOW HUDDY Fifth great grandson of progenitor Nicholas Kegg.
SUSAN J. HUDDY Sixth great granddaughter of progenitor Nicholas Kegg. **TANNER HUDDY** Seventh great grandson of progenitor Nicholas Kegg. **TERRY HUDDY** Sixth great grandson of progenitor Nicholas Kegg. **THOMAS ALONZO HUDDY** [3867] (1903 – 1985) son of Lorenzo and Grace (Figgins) Huddy, married Nellie Etta Campbell with whom he was father of (4).
THOMAS LEE HUDDY Fifth great grandson of progenitor Nicholas Kegg.
TRACE RICHARD HUDDY Sixth great grandson of progenitor Nicholas Kegg.
TRACY ANN HUDDY Seventh great granddaughter of progenitor Nicholas Kegg.
WILLIAM CHARLES HUDDY Seventh great grandson of progenitor Nicholas Kegg.
WILLIAM EDWARD HUDDY (1916 – 1992) son of Charles and Edith (Mills) Huddy married twice; first to Virginia Mae Hillyer and later, to Ada Rife. William was father of (5).

HUDSON

ANNA MARGARET HUDSON Sixth great granddaughter of progenitor Nicholas Kegg.
CATHERINE HUDSON Sixth great granddaughter of progenitor Nicholas Kegg.
CONNER HUDSON Seventh great grandson of progenitor Nicholas Kegg. **GARRETT HUDSON** Seventh great grandson of progenitor Nicholas Kegg. **JAMES HUDSON** Sixth great grandson of progenitor Nicholas Kegg. **SEAN HUDSON** Seventh great grandson of progenitor Nicholas Kegg.
THOMAS RALPH HUDSON JR. Seventh great grandson of progenitor Nicholas Kegg.
THOMAS RALPH HUDSON Sixth great grandson of progenitor Nicholas Kegg.
WILLIAM HUDSON aka "Bill", Sixth great grandson of progenitor Nicholas Kegg.

[3864] GenLookups.com Ohio Obituary and Death Notice Archive - Page 937 [3865] p.10 Athens Messenger (OH) Aug 29, 1932 [3866] Athens Messenger (OH) Aug 2, 2006 [3867] p.14 The Athens Messenger (OH) April 24, 1929

WILLIAM HUDSON Seventh great grandson of progenitor Nicholas Kegg. **WILLIAM C HUDSON** (3867A) aka "Bill" (1947 – 2008) son of William and Marjorie (Jones) Hudson, married Susan A. Marto. Bill worked as a machinist for the former Robertshaw Controls, New Stanton. He was a founding member of the Westmoreland County Vietnam Veterans Association, and a member of the VFW, American Legion and a lifetime member of the NRA. He was a veteran of the Vietnam War, having served in the Army.

HUEGEL

MATILDA HUEGEL Eighth great granddaughter of progenitor Nicholas Kegg.

HUFF

REBA HUFF Fourth great granddaughter of progenitor Nicholas Kegg.

HUFFER

MASON HUFFER Seventh great grandson of progenitor Nicholas Kegg.

HUFFNER

MARY BETH HUFFNER Sixth great granddaughter of progenitor Nicholas Kegg.
PATRICIA JANE HUFFNER Sixth great granddaughter of progenitor Nicholas Kegg.

HUFNAGEL

KATIE HUFNAGEL Sixth great granddaughter of progenitor Nicholas Kegg.
MARIA HUFNAGEL Sixth great granddaughter of progenitor Nicholas Kegg.

HUGGINS

CHLOE ISABELLE HUGGINS Seventh great granddaughter of progenitor Nicholas Kegg.
LUKE MILO HUGGINS Seventh great grandson of progenitor Nicholas Kegg.
SEAN RICHARD HUGGINS Seventh great grandson of progenitor Nicholas Kegg.

HUGHES

AMANDA HUGHES Seventh great granddaughter of progenitor Nicholas Kegg.
MISTY HUGHES Seventh great granddaughter of progenitor Nicholas Kegg.

HULBERT

ALAN LEE HULBERT Sixth great grandson of progenitor Nicholas Kegg. **ANDREW JOHN HULBERT** Sixth great grandson of progenitor Nicholas Kegg. **ASHLEY HULBERT** Seventh great granddaughter of progenitor Nicholas Kegg. **BRADLEY HULBERT** aka "Brad", Seventh great grandson of progenitor Nicholas Kegg. **BRANDON HULBERT** Seventh great grandson of progenitor Nicholas Kegg. **CHAYNE HULBERT** Seventh great grandson of progenitor Nicholas Kegg. **CHEYENNE HULBERT** Seventh great granddaughter of progenitor Nicholas Kegg. **CHRISTOPHER ANDREW HULBERT** Seventh great grandson of progenitor Nicholas Kegg.

(3867A) Clement Pantalone Funeral Home Inc.

DARLENE J. HULBERT Fifth great granddaughter of progenitor Nicholas Kegg.
DONNA IRENE HULBERT [3867B] (1938 – 2001) daughter of Winfield and Sylvia (Karnatz) Hulbert married three times, first to Lawrence Arthur Spoerry with whom she was mother of (4). Later, she married Bud Swigert. After his death, she married Donald Eugene Vannatta. Donna was head cashier at Daugherity's Supermarket in Adel before retiring and a member of Adel United Methodist Church and American Legion Auxiliary. **GEORGE A. HULBERT** Sixth great grandson of progenitor Nicholas Kegg. **GEORGE R. HULBERT** 5th great grandson of progenitor Nicholas Kegg.
JAMES HULBERT Sixth great grandson of progenitor Nicholas Kegg. **JOAN HULBERT** aka "Jo", Fifth great granddaughter of progenitor Nicholas Kegg. **LOIS JEAN HULBERT** 5th great granddaughter of progenitor Nicholas Kegg. **LORUS WINFIELD HULBERT** [3868] (1930 – 1994) son of Winfield and Sylvia (Karnatz) Hulbert, married Merla Maxine Silsby with whom he was father of (3). Lorus attended school at Coon Rapids, Iowa. After graduation he went to Montana to live with Aunt Irene and Uncle Glen York. In October 1950, he enlisted in the Air Force and after basic training was sent to Germany to serve until his discharge in November 1953. He worked at the cement plant in Superior. Lorus belonged to VFW Post 7830 and the Wagon Wheelers Square Dance Club.
MARILYN K. HULBERT Sixth great granddaughter of progenitor Nicholas Kegg.
MAX EUGENE HULBERT Sixth great grandson of progenitor Nicholas Kegg.
MELISSA HULBERT Seventh great granddaughter of progenitor Nicholas Kegg.
MILDRED HULBERT aka "Chris", Sixth great granddaughter of progenitor Nicholas Kegg.
MYRON EUGENE HULBERT [3868A] (1932 – 2014) son of Winfield and Sylvia (Karnatz) Hulbert, married Marjorie June Nelson with whom he was father of (3). Myron loved working on cars, tractors, farm equipment, camping, hunting and fishing. After high school he worked at the Union Pacific Railroad from 1951 to 1953 in Wyoming as a welder; He served in the Korean War on the 38th Parallel in the 2nd Infantry Division. Myron farmed with his brother, Lorus, after the service. He worked for the City of Mankato, REA, John Deere, Jewell Implement and Dubuque Packing House. In 1984 he opened Hulbert Repair. After closing Hulbert Repair he worked at Becker Electric and Mankato Livestock.
REX ALAN HULBERT Sixth great grandson of progenitor Nicholas Kegg.
SHAUNEE MAXINE HULBERT Seventh great granddaughter of progenitor Nicholas Kegg.
SHELDON HULBERT Seventh great grandson of progenitor Nicholas Kegg.
UNA IRENE HULBERT (1910 – 1967) aka "Irene", daughter of Clarence and Bessie (Dwiggans) Hulbert married twice; first to Mr. Shultz and later to Glenn William York.
WILLIAM HENRY HULBERT (1906 – 1906) son of Clarence and Bessie (Dwigans) Hulbert.
WINFIELD ARTHUR HULBERT [3868B] (1908 – 1994) son of Clarence and Bessie (Dwigans) Hulbert married twice, first to Sylvia Christine Karnatz with whom he was father of (5). Later, he married Tamera Elaine Lovell with whom he was father of (2) He worked at a locker plant for Garst & Thomas Seed Corn Company, at a foundry in Perry and on construction.

HULL

ALEAH HULL Sixth great granddaughter of progenitor Nicholas Kegg. **ARON MATTHEW HULL** Seventh great grandson of progenitor Nicholas Kegg. **ATIRA J. HULL** Seventh great granddaughter of progenitor Nicholas Kegg. **CAROL ANN HULL** Fifth great granddaughter of progenitor Nicholas Kegg. **CHERYL RAYE HULL** Fifth great granddaughter of progenitor Nicholas Kegg. **CLAYTON HULL** Sixth great grandson of progenitor Nicholas Kegg. **CORY HULL** Sixth great grandson of progenitor Nicholas Kegg. **JACOB ELIJAH HULL** Sixth great grandson of progenitor Nicholas Kegg. **JEREMIAH D. HULL** Seventh great grandson of progenitor Nicholas Kegg. **KEITH ALLEN HULL** Fifth great grandson of progenitor Nicholas Kegg. **KEVIN ROY HULL** [3868C] (1967 – 2015) son of Leroy and Betty Mae (Barnes) Hull, married Hollie Ann Buckner with whom

---

[3867B] Des Moines Register (IA) Jan 14, 2001 [3868] FindAGrave Memorial#41371011 Originally Created by: TLC [3868A] Superior Express (NE) Dec 18, 2004 [3868B] obituary obtained from Find A Grave 43758922 Created by: Jan Plambeck [3868C] Tribune Chronicle (OH) March 17, 2015

he was father of (4). Kevin was a U.S. Navy veteran. He enjoyed biking, photography and fishing. **KYLE HULL** Sixth great grandson of progenitor Nicholas Kegg. **LARRY LEE HULL** (3869) (1948 – 2020) son of Leroy and Betty Mae (Barnes) Hull married Jane Marie Wilson with whom he was father of (2). Later he married Nancy Olds Jamieson and Lastly Donna aka "Darlene". Following high school graduation, Larry worked at Wolf's Sunoco, Salem Stamping Sales at GM. He also owned and operated OK Welding Division. He drove trucks for Warren Scrap, Haliburton, and Cortland Truck Service. In 1981, Larry owned and operated Cortland Insurance Agency providing insurance for many Cortland residents. He also was the owner of Hull's Home Improvement. Larry was involved in numerous clubs, Bazetta/Cortland Optimist, Cortland Rotary, Cortland Men's Club, and the Cortland Moose. He enjoyed camping, hunting, boating, fishing. **MELANIE HULL** Seventh great granddaughter of progenitor Nicholas Kegg. **MICHELE HULL** Sixth great granddaughter of progenitor Nicholas Kegg. **MONIQUE CORIN HULL** aka "Bubbles", Sixth great granddaughter of progenitor Nicholas Kegg. **SIERRA HULL** Sixth great granddaughter of progenitor Nicholas Kegg. **SYDNEY HULL** Ninth great granddaughter of progenitor Nicholas Kegg. **TRACEY LYNN HULL** Sixth great granddaughter of progenitor Nicholas Kegg. **TYLER HULL** Eighth great grandson of progenitor Nicholas Kegg.

HULTS

ANDREW HULTS Seventh great grandson of progenitor Nicholas Kegg.
KILEY RYANN HULTS Eighth great granddaughter of progenitor Nicholas Kegg.

HUMMEL

CARSON EDWARD HUMMEL Fifth great grandson of progenitor Nicholas Kegg. **ELIZABETH JANE HUMMEL** Fifth great granddaughter of progenitor Nicholas Kegg. **EMILY RAE HUMMEL** Sixth great granddaughter of progenitor Nicholas Kegg. **HENRY JOSHUA HUMMEL** (3869A) aka "Ben" (1919 – 2012) son of Daniel and Sarah (Turner) Hummel, married Loretta Catherine Rounds with whom he was father of (2). Henry served in the Army Air Force during WW II, enlisting in 1942, where he attended armament and gunnery school at Lowry Field in Denver, Colo. In 1943, he was assigned to Dutch Air Force Base, and he was also stationed at the Flexible Gunner School at Tyndall Field in Florida, where he served under Commander Queen Wihelmina. In 1945, Henry was transferred to Laredo Air Force Base in Laredo, Texas. Corporal Henry J. Hummel was discharged in 1945 in Tampa, Fla. After the war, in 1946, Ben worked as an auto body technician in LaVale, Cumberland, and McCoole. Eventually, he designed and built his own body shop on Rt. 40. For six years he was an Auto Body Instructor at Allegany Vo. Tech College. He retired from body work after 31 years of service. Henry had many hobbies, including hunting, fishing, reading, writing poetry, which he wrote many poems for his wife, and he enjoyed playing the fiddle, banjo and organ. Henry was an excellent carpenter, having designed and built much of his home, including stonework, woodwork and specialty cabinets. He was known for storytelling-the kind of stories that remind us of where we come from and for giving advice with the wisdom of experience. He believed one could achieve whatever one determined to do. He was known for his sense of humor, wit, and gratitude for those who cared for others. He was a member of the Mt. Zion United Methodist Church, Grantsville Post 214, American Legion and Post 8826 Walker-Harris, V.F.W., Salisbury, Pa. **JANE HUMMEL** (3870, 3871) (1923 – 1966) daughter of Daniel and Sarah (Turner) Hummel, married Robert N. Davis with whom she was mother of (1). Jane was a member of St. Stephen's Catholic Church, the Confraternity of Christian Wives and Mothers, auxiliary to Grantsville Fire Company, American Legion Auxiliary and Grantsville Cemetery Committee. She was president of the Casselman Valley Homemakers Club. **JOSEPH GERALD HUMMEL** aka "Joey", Sixth great grandson of progenitor Nicholas Kegg. **LINDA MARIE HUMMEL** Fifth great granddaughter of

---

(3869) Tribune Chronicle (OH) March 8, 2020 (3869A) Cumberland Times News (MD) Nov 24, 2012 (3870) Fresh Eggs: A Western Maryland Childhood page 105 by Alice Lorraine FaithTrafford Publishing (3871) Republican (PA) Sep 15, 1966, Myersdale Library transcribed by Abby Bowman

progenitor Nicholas Kegg. **MARGARET ALMIRA HUMMEL** Fourth great granddaughter of progenitor Nicholas Kegg. **RACHAEL DIANE HUMMEL** Sixth great granddaughter of progenitor Nicholas Kegg.

HUMPHREY

ALICE LUCILLE HUMPHREY [3872] (1940 – 2007) daughter of William and Edna (Baker) Humphrey, married Ted Roesner with whom she was mother of (4). Alice was a special woman who dealt with life's adversities with amazing strength and a beautiful smile. She was a woman with great faith in God and well known for many years for her spiritual attributes. Alice was remembered for her generosity and kindness to all. **ANDREW HUMPHREY** Sixth great grandson of progenitor Nicholas Kegg. **CAROL JEAN HUMPHREY** Fifth great granddaughter of progenitor Nicholas Kegg. **CHRISTINE HUMPHREY** Sixth great granddaughter of progenitor Nicholas Kegg. **DAVID DEAN HUMPHREY** Sixth great grandson of progenitor Nicholas Kegg. **KEITH ANDREW HUMPHREY** (1948 – 1948) son of Ardyn and Aretha (Kroger) Humphrey. **LAURA ELIZABETH HUMPHREY** Sixth great granddaughter of progenitor Nicholas Kegg. **LYNN M. HUMPHREY** Fifth great granddaughter of progenitor Nicholas Kegg. **MARK WILLIAM HUMPHREY** Sixth great grandson of progenitor Nicholas Kegg. **MELISSA HUMPHREY** Sixth great granddaughter of progenitor Nicholas Kegg. **NEIL HUMPHREY** Sixth great grandson of progenitor Nicholas Kegg. **RITA ANN HUMPHREY** Fifth great granddaughter of progenitor Nicholas Kegg. **SHAY ANNE HUMPHREY** Sixth great granddaughter of progenitor Nicholas Kegg. **ZACK HUMPHREY** Sixth great grandson of progenitor Nicholas Kegg.

HUNT

CANDACE MAE HUNT Sixth great granddaughter of progenitor Nicholas Kegg.
CONSTANCE HUNT [3872A] aka "Connie" (1945 – 2023) daughter of Charles and Margaret (Perdew) Hunt married Mr. McKee with whom she was mother of (2). Connie had been employed as manager at Buchanan Lumber Company. She later managed Whitetail Wetlands bed & breakfast in New Paris.
COURTNEY HUNT Ninth great granddaughter of progenitor Nicholas Kegg. **DAVID LEE HUNT** Sixth great grandson of progenitor Nicholas Kegg. **JONATHAN HUNT** Seventh great grandson of progenitor Nicholas Kegg. **MARGARET HUNT** Fifth great granddaughter of progenitor Nicholas Kegg. **MELANIE HUNT** Ninth great granddaughter of progenitor Nicholas Kegg.
MILDRED J. HUNT Fifth great granddaughter of progenitor Nicholas Kegg. **ROBERT LEE HUNT** Sixth great grandson of progenitor Nicholas Kegg. **ROBIN MICHELE HUNT** Sixth great granddaughter of progenitor Nicholas Kegg. **SAMUEL JAMES HUNT** Sixth great grandson of progenitor Nicholas Kegg. **SONDRA KAY HUNT** Sixth great granddaughter of progenitor Nicholas Kegg. **ZACHARY HUNT** Ninth great grandson of progenitor Nicholas Kegg.

HUNTER

EDWIN L HUNTER [3872B] (1921 – 2017) son of Edwin and Geneva (Crevison) Hunter married twice, first to Ann Lewis with whom he was father of (1). Later, he married Nancy Hamlin Coccia. Ed owned and operated the Warrensburg Laundry. He was very proud to have served his country in the U.S. Marine Corps with duty in the 1st Battalion, 3rd Marine Division during World War II. He was an active member of the First Congregational Church in Port St. Lucie, Marine Corps League (Jack Ivy Detachment No. 666), American Legion Post No. 318 and the Port St. Lucie Elks No. 2658. Ed was an avid golfer.

[3872] The Knoxville News-Sentinel (TN) Feb 16, 2007 [3872A] Bedford Gazette (PA) Jan 18, 2023 [3872B] The Post Star (Glens Falls, NY) Mar 2, 2017

HARRY BRADFORD HUNTER Sixth great grandson of progenitor Nicholas Kegg.
JOHN ALFRED HUNTER Sixth great grandson of progenitor Nicholas Kegg. **SHARON HUNTER** (3872C) (1942 – 2014) daughter of Edwin and Ann (Lewis) Hunter married twice, first to Arthur Birmann Klussendorf with whom she was mother of (2). Later she married Richard Tar. A career in real estate working with Najer Realty and later with Rondack Realty, where she was the Warrensburg sole assessor from 1977 through 1981. In 1981, Sharon continued her career by working as a right-of-way aide for the New York State Department of Transportation (DOT) when there were fewer than 40 professional women at the main DOT office. While working full-time, she earned her bachelor's degree from the College of St. Rose in Albany. After the death of her husband, Sharon traveled extensively with her friend, Bob Cross, on his Nordic tug, "At Last," fulfilling a dream to live on a boat. She enjoyed being a member of the Hudson River Piecemakers Quilting Guild and spending time teaching her friends to quilt.
SUSAN JANE HUNTER (1953 – 2010) daughter of John and Carol (Casey) Hunter married Kayo Parsley with whom she was mother of (2).

HURD

DARLENE HURD Sixth great granddaughter of progenitor Nicholas Kegg.
HALEY GRACE HURD Eighth great granddaughter of progenitor Nicholas Kegg.
JOHN RICHARD HURD Sixth great grandson of progenitor Nicholas Kegg.
JOHN RICHARD HURD Seventh great grandson of progenitor Nicholas Kegg.
MACKENZIE PEYTON HURD Eighth great granddaughter of progenitor Nicholas Kegg.
MARLENE HURD Sixth great granddaughter of progenitor Nicholas Kegg.
NEDRA VIRGENE HURD Sixth great granddaughter of progenitor Nicholas Kegg.
RYAN EVAN HURD Seventh great grandson of progenitor Nicholas Kegg.

HURLEY

NOAH JOSEPH HURLEY Seventh great grandson of progenitor Nicholas Kegg.

HUSSEY

BETTY LEE HUSSEY (1920 – 1968) daughter of Lowell and Vera (Knittle) Hussey, married Clarence Glen Haessig with whom she was mother of (2). **LOWELL CARSON HUSSEY** (3872D) (1922 – 1987) son of Lowell and Vera (Knittle) Hussey married Lolita L. Frledenberg. Lowell was vice president of Bank of America.

HUSTER

BARRY JON HUSTER (3872E) aka "B.J." (1947 – 2021) son of Harry and Lysbeth (McCollough) Huster married Sharon Morris with whom he was father of (3). Later, he married Sandra Lee Taylor.
BETH ANN HUSTER Sixth great granddaughter of progenitor Nicholas Kegg.
DANA LYNETTE HUSTER Sixth great granddaughter of progenitor Nicholas Kegg.
HARRY EUGENE HUSTER (3872F) (1921 – 1999) son of Harry and Edith (McDaniel) Huster, married Lysbeth Ann (McCollough) Brandimarte with whom he was father of (2). Harry had been display director of both Jones and Hartley's department stores. He later became the buyer for Jones Men's Department in the downtown and Middletown Mall stores. Before his retirement, he had been employed for 12 years as the executive vice president and artist in residence at the Drulane Manufacturing Co. in Fairmont. He served two terms on the Marion County Senior Citizen Board of Directors and was currently serving as a

---

(3872C) Post Star (NY) Aug 19, 2014 (3872D) Los Angeles Times (CA) Nov 20, 1987 (3872E) Faith Chapel Funeral Homes - South Chapel (FL) Aug. 30, 2021, obtained by D. Sue Dible (3872F) www.genlookups.com p. 981 West Virginia Obituary and Death Notice Archive

member of the board of directors of the 8th Air Force Historical Society, West Virginia Chapter. Harry had been a former member of the B.P.O.E. No. 294, Fairmont Moose No. 9, and the American Legion Post No. 17. He enjoyed swimming and walking, was an avid motorcyclist, loved camping in visiting campgrounds across the United States, and was an artist and creative woodworker. He was in the U.S. Air Force during World War II with the 8th Air Force in London, England. Harry flew 25 bombing missions over Germany. **JASON BRADLEY HUSTER** Sixth great grandson of progenitor Nicholas Kegg. **LYNDA LEIGH HUSTER** Fifth great granddaughter of progenitor Nicholas Kegg.

HUSTON

CASSANDRA JANEEN HUSTON Sixth great granddaughter of progenitor Nicholas Kegg. **JENNIFER HUSTON** Sixth great granddaughter of progenitor Nicholas Kegg. **JESSICA HUSTON** Sixth great granddaughter of progenitor Nicholas Kegg.

HUTCHINS

GENENE LEE HUTCHINS Fifth great granddaughter of progenitor Nicholas Kegg.

HUTCHISON

DELIAH HUTCHISON Seventh great granddaughter of progenitor Nicholas Kegg.
GRAHAM FREDERICK HUTCHISON [3873] (1906 – 1971) son of Hugh and Mabel (Graham) Hutchison, married Ingeborg Strangfeld with whom he was father of (2). Col. Hutchison served as an enforcement agent with the U.S. Treasury Department and was a practicing attorney in Washington before entering the service in 1943. He served as an intelligence officer on the staff of General Eisenhower at SHAEF (Supreme Headquarters Allied Expeditionary Force) in London. He parachuted in with a battalion of hand-picked men, landing behind German lines in the early morning hours of D-Day to disrupt German communications and was seriously injured by shrapnel from enemy fire. Col. Hutchison was discharged with a combat disability after spending several years in hospitals as a result of his injuries. He received numerous decorations and citations. After his discharge, Col Hutchison entered the shipyard business in Miami and was owner of the North Miami Beach Yacht Basin and Boat Repair. He was active in civic affairs, serving as president of the South Florida improvement Association; a director of the Port Security council; President of Florida counter-intelligence Division of the Dade County Civil Defense Council; A member of the Crime Commission of Greater Miami Beach; and president of the North Miami Beach Chamber of Commerce. Tiring of the metropolitan area, Graham sold out his interest in the Miami area and toured Florida looking for a secluded spot for retirement. He found what he wanted on a wooded hill near the little town of Lake Geneva, built a home and moved his family. He came out of retirement in 1970 to accept an appointment by Gov. Claude Kirk as Justice of the Peace District 4, Clay County. A position which he held at the time of his death. **JAMES HUTCHISON** aka "Luke" Sixth great grandson of progenitor Nicholas Kegg. **JOHNATHON HUTCHISON** Sixth great grandson of progenitor Nicholas Kegg. **MARK ELLIS HUTCHISON** [3874] (1953 – 1998) son of Graham and Ingeborg (Strangfeld) Hutchison, married Kathy Matthews with whom he was father of (2). Mark worked in manufacturing and attended Olivet Evangelical Free Church. **RAYMOND MULAND HUTCHISON** (1930 – 1979) son of Otto and Cleora (Wehrle) Hutchison. **ROBERT DALE HUTCHISON** (1912 – 1980) son of Hugh and Mabel (Graham) Hutchison. **RODERICK HUTCHISON** Fifth great grandson of progenitor Nicholas Kegg.

[3873] Bradford County Telegraph Dec 9, 1971, FindAGrave# 82065251 Created by: Ann [3874] Herrick Public Library Film Number 007594933 Michigan Obituaries, 1820-2006

HUTSON

GAGE HUTSON Seventh great grandson of progenitor Nicholas Kegg.
GREGORY CHRISTOPHER HUTSON aka "Chris", Sixth great grandson of progenitor Nicholas Kegg. **ISABELLE HUTSON** Seventh great granddaughter of progenitor Nicholas Kegg.
KADEN HUTSON Seventh great grandson of progenitor Nicholas Kegg. **LAURA LEE HUTSON** Sixth great granddaughter of progenitor Nicholas Kegg. **PIPER HUTSON** Seventh great granddaughter of progenitor Nicholas Kegg.

HUTTON

DONALD PATRICK HUTTON aka "Pat", Sixth great grandson of progenitor Nicholas Kegg. **MICHAEL K. HUTTON** Sixth great grandson of progenitor Nicholas Kegg.
MILFORD KENNEDY HUTTON [3874A] aka "Don" (1933 – 2015) son of Thomas and Jeanne (Kennedy) Hutton, married Frieda Jo Davis with whom he was father of (3). Don retired as an engineer for Conoco. He attended Oklahoma A&M in Stillwater where he was a boxer in the ROTC and received a bachelor's degree in engineering. **SHARA ELAINE HUTTON** Sixth great granddaughter of progenitor Nicholas Kegg.

HYDE

ALEXANDRA ELYSE HYDE Eighth great granddaughter of progenitor Nicholas Kegg. **COLLEEN B. HYDE** Fifth great granddaughter of progenitor Nicholas Kegg. **DUSTIN HYDE** Sixth great grandson of progenitor Nicholas Kegg. **JAKE HYDE** Sixth great grandson of progenitor Nicholas Kegg. **JENNIFER HYDE** Sixth great granddaughter of progenitor Nicholas Kegg. **JOSEPH HYDE** Sixth great grandson of progenitor Nicholas Kegg. **JOSEPH ROBERT HYDE** Fifth great grandson of progenitor Nicholas Kegg. **KATHLEEN ELIZABETH HYDE** Eighth great granddaughter of progenitor Nicholas Kegg. **LARRY HYDE** Fifth great grandson of progenitor Nicholas Kegg. **LUKE HYDE** aka "Shorty", Sixth great grandson of progenitor Nicholas Kegg. **MARTIN PATRICK HYDE** aka "Marty" Fifth great grandson of progenitor Nicholas Kegg. **MEGAN HYDE** Sixth great granddaughter of progenitor Nicholas Kegg. **RICHARD D. HYDE** Fifth great grandson of progenitor Nicholas Kegg. **RICHARD E. HYDE** [3874B] aka "Dick" (1930 – 2005) son of William and Ida (Suder) Hyde, married Cecelia Jacalyn Quigley with whom he was father of (6). Dick served 4 years in the U.S. Air Force. He retired after 35 years at American Can Company, Hammond as a tool and dye maker. He assisted in starting the Portage Pop Warner and coached Biddy Basketball and Baseball for many years. Dick also coached softball for the Boy Scouts Troop 220 for St. Frances Catholic Church, Lake Station and was an avid Notre Dame Fan. **ROBERT W. HYDE** Fourth great grandson of progenitor Nicholas Kegg. **SAMANTHA RENEE HYDE** Seventh great granddaughter of progenitor Nicholas Kegg. **SHEILA MARIE HYDE** Fifth great granddaughter of progenitor Nicholas Kegg. **TIM HYDE** Sixth great grandson of progenitor Nicholas Kegg.
TINA HYDE Sixth great granddaughter of progenitor Nicholas Kegg.

HYLLESTED

KRISTINA RAE HYLLESTED Sixth great granddaughter of progenitor Nicholas Kegg.

HYSELL

JACOB HYSELL Eighth great grandson of progenitor Nicholas Kegg.

[3874A] Oklahoma Welcome (OK) June 15, 2015 [3874B] Times (IN) Aug 23, 2005

HYZER

AMY KATHERINE HYZER Fifth great granddaughter of progenitor Nicholas Kegg. **LIBBY HYZER** Fifth great granddaughter of progenitor Nicholas Kegg. **MARTHA LEIGH HYZER** [3875] (1960 – 1995) daughter of Keith and Nancy (Stuckey) Hyzer did secretarial work over the years and was a talented author of articles in the Pioneer Press newspapers and other publications including the Chicago Tribune. Martha's work appeared in the Woman News, Travel and Sunday Magazine sections. Her most memorable one was an illustrated essay titled "Courage is the Thing" that ran Aug. 9, 1992, in the magazine. One of her articles describes having overcome a drinking problem, of having fought writer's block, of the bravery of her Australian shepherd dog, and of those who found getting out of bed in the morning being an act of courage. "Ultimately," she wrote, "we face our demons alone; with luck, it strengthens us Her other writings ranged from technical articles to stories for children. Martha was an original member of the Rockford Dance Company.

ICKES

PATRICK ICKES Fifth great grandson of progenitor Nicholas Kegg. **TRAVIS ICKES** Fifth great grandson of progenitor Nicholas Kegg. **WENDY ICKES** Fifth great granddaughter of progenitor Nicholas Kegg.

IMGRUND

JENNIFER DAWN IMGRUND Seventh great granddaughter of progenitor Nicholas Kegg. **MICHAEL GREGORY IMGRUND** Seventh great grandson of progenitor Nicholas Kegg.

IMLER

BARRY A. IMLER Seventh great grandson of progenitor Nicholas Kegg.
BERNARD PHREY IMLER [3876] (1902 – 1969) son of Lebbeus and Clara (Kegg) Imler married Catherine Shoemaker. **DIANA M. IMLER** Seventh great granddaughter of progenitor Nicholas Kegg.
DONALD ALTON IMLER Seventh great grandson of progenitor Nicholas Kegg.
DONALD L. IMLER Fifth great grandson of progenitor Nicholas Kegg.
ELIZABETH MYRTLE IMLER [3877] (1926 – 2003) daughter of Orvis and Clara (Lydic) Imler, married Franklin L. Howard. **GARY K. IMLER** Seventh great grandson of progenitor Nicholas Kegg. **GARY L. IMLER** Sixth great grandson of progenitor Nicholas Kegg. **IRMA H. IMLER** [3878] (1930 – 1994) daughter of Orvis and Clara (Lydic) Imler. Irma retired from GTE Phillips. **JERRY IMLER** Sixth great grandson of progenitor Nicholas Kegg. **JERRY IMLER** Seventh great grandson of progenitor Nicholas Kegg. **JUDY IMLER** Sixth great granddaughter of progenitor Nicholas Kegg. **LENA IMLER** Seventh great granddaughter of progenitor Nicholas Kegg. **MAKENNA IMLER** Eighth great granddaughter of progenitor Nicholas Kegg. **MARIAN H. IMLER** [3879] (1932 – 2008) daughter of Orvis and Clara (Lydic) Imler, married Elmer Nyiri with whom she was mother of (8). **MARY LUCILLE IMLER** (born abt.1901) daughter of Lebbeus and Clara (Kegg) Imler married twice; first to Lester Clyde Yost and later, to Harvey Harry Ketcham. **ORVIS CHARLES IMLER** (1902 – 1954) son of David and Mertle (Beegle) Imler, married Clara Lydic with whom he was father of (3). Orvis was employed by P.R.R. Car Shop. **TERRY L. IMLER** Fourth great grandson of progenitor Nicholas Kegg. **TINA B. IMLER** Sixth great granddaughter of progenitor Nicholas Kegg.

[3875] Chicago Tribune (IL) June 21, 1995 [3876] Altoona Tribune (PA) Dec 25, 1923 [3877] Bedford Gazette (PA) Dec 5, 2003, obtained by D. Sue Dible [3878] Altoona Mirror (PA) Aug 20, 1994 [3879] Altoona Mirror (PA) Oct 14, 2008

INGALLS

J. JACOB INGALLS Eighth great grandson of progenitor Nicholas Kegg.

INGRAM

STEVEN LEE INGRAM Sixth great grandson of progenitor Nicholas Kegg.

INMAN

CARMEN ERSILL INMAN [3880] (1909 – 2000) daughter of Harvey and Rose (Knouf) Inman, married George Turbett. Carmen was an executive council member for the State of Iowa. **ILA JUNE INMAN** [3881] (1920 – 2010) daughter of Harvey and Rose (Knouf) Inman, married Robert Wallace Ainley with whom she was mother of (2). Ila enjoyed reading, needlepoint, gardening, cooking, traveling and spending time with friends and family. She was employed as a cooking demonstrator for Oster Small Kitchen Appliances.

IRIZARRY

EMMA ELIZABETH IRIZARRY Seventh great granddaughter of progenitor Nicholas Kegg.

IRVIN

CAROLYN G. IRVIN Sixth great granddaughter of progenitor Nicholas Kegg.
CHARLES REID IRVIN Sixth great grandson of progenitor Nicholas Kegg.
JAYNE IRVIN Sixth great granddaughter of progenitor Nicholas Kegg.

IRVING

ALEXA IRVING Eighth great granddaughter of progenitor Nicholas Kegg. **CALEB IRVING** Eighth great grandson of progenitor Nicholas Kegg. **ELAYNA IRVING** Eighth great granddaughter of progenitor Nicholas Kegg. **MAIZY GRACE IRVING** Eighth great granddaughter of progenitor Nicholas Kegg. **PARKER IRVING** Eighth great grandson of progenitor Nicholas Kegg.

IRWIN

DAVID MICHAEL IRWIN Eighth great grandson of progenitor Nicholas Kegg.
DEBORAH ANN IRWIN Seventh great granddaughter of progenitor Nicholas Kegg.
DEBORAH JEAN IRWIN Eighth great grandson of progenitor Nicholas Kegg. **HEALY I. IRWIN** (1952 – 1952) Healy was born and died under alias surname (MOTT). Healy was a daughter of Joseph and Grace Ann (Arrants) Irwin. **JACQUELINE ANNETTE IRWIN** Seventh great granddaughter of progenitor Nicholas Kegg. **JOSEPH V. IRWIN** Seventh great grandson of progenitor Nicholas Kegg.
JEFFREY MICHAEL IRWIN Seventh great grandson of progenitor Nicholas Kegg.
SARAH IRWIN Seventh great granddaughter of progenitor Nicholas Kegg.

ISON

ANDREW ISON Sixth great grandson of progenitor Nicholas Kegg.

[3880] p.A6 - Vero Beach Press Journal (FL) Nov 14, 2000 [3881] Daily Journal Franklin (IN) Mar 5, 2010

IVANCICH

ANTHONY PAUL IVANCICH Sixth great grandson of progenitor Nicholas Kegg.
KRISTIN MARIE IVANCICH Sixth great granddaughter of progenitor Nicholas Kegg.
NATALIE ANNE IVANCICH Sixth great granddaughter of progenitor Nicholas Kegg.

JACKSON

AMY MARIE JACKSON Sixth great granddaughter of progenitor Nicholas Kegg. **ANDREW D. JACKSON** Seventh great grandson of progenitor Nicholas Kegg. **CHARLES R. JACKSON** Seventh great grandson of progenitor Nicholas Kegg. **CHERI MAE JACKSON** Sixth great granddaughter of progenitor Nicholas Kegg. **CHRISTINA JACKSON** Sixth great granddaughter of progenitor Nicholas Kegg. **DANIEL RICHARD JACKSON** (1951 – 1992) son of Richard and Laura (Wells) Jackson. **DANNY JACKSON** Sixth great grandson of progenitor Nicholas Kegg. **DARLENE LENORA JACKSON** Fifth great granddaughter of progenitor Nicholas Kegg. **DAVID WELLS JACKSON** [3882] (1942 – 2010) son of Richard and Laura (Wells) Jackson, married Debra Ann Mielke with whom he was father of (5). David loved and lived life to the fullest. He enjoyed traveling and spending time with his family and friends. Additional interests include drawing, cooking, airplanes, boating and cars. David retired from American Airlines in 1995 after 30 years of service. He then began a new career selling cars at Five Star Ford. **DEBORAH JACKSON** Sixth great granddaughter of progenitor Nicholas Kegg. **DENNIS JACKSON** Sixth great grandson of progenitor Nicholas Kegg. **ELLA JACKSON** Seventh great granddaughter of progenitor Nicholas Kegg. **GRACE JACKSON** Seventh great granddaughter of progenitor Nicholas Kegg. **GREG JACKSON** Seventh great grandson of progenitor Nicholas Kegg. **LAURINDA JACKSON** Seventh great granddaughter of progenitor Nicholas Kegg. **MADELAINE JACKSON** Seventh great granddaughter of progenitor Nicholas Kegg. **MATTHEW JACKSON** Seventh great grandson of progenitor Nicholas Kegg. **RACHEL JACKSON** Seventh great granddaughter of progenitor Nicholas Kegg. **ROMANA A. JACKSON** Fifth great granddaughter of progenitor Nicholas Kegg. **SANDRA KAY JACKSON** (1944 – 1951) daughter of Richard and Laura (Wells) Jackson. **SARAH SUSANN JACKSON** Sixth great granddaughter of progenitor Nicholas Kegg. **SHEILA JACKSON** Sixth great granddaughter of progenitor Nicholas Kegg. **SHIRLEY JOANNE JACKSON** Fifth great granddaughter of progenitor Nicholas Kegg. **TODD JACKSON** Seventh great grandson of progenitor Nicholas Kegg.

JACOB

DENISE JACOB Sixth great granddaughter of progenitor Nicholas Kegg. **DENNIS L. JACOB** [3883] (1941 – 1973) son OF Edwin and Veda (Rice) Jacob, married Carolyn Kay Merrell with whom he was father of (3). **JEFFREY JACOB** Sixth great grandson of progenitor Nicholas Kegg. **MICHAEL ANN JACOB** [3884] (1963 – 1964) daughter of Dennis and Carolyn (Merrell) Jacob. **ROBERT E. JACOB** Fifth great grandson of progenitor Nicholas Kegg. **RONALD JACOB** Fifth great grandson of progenitor Nicholas Kegg.

JAFFE

BENJAMIN JAFFE Fifth great grandson of progenitor Nicholas Kegg. **BRUCE A. JAFFE** Fifth great grandson of progenitor Nicholas Kegg.

[3882] Fort Worth Star-Telegram (TX) Aug 18, 2010 [3883] p.23B - Omaha World Herald (NE) March 25, 1973 [3884] p.30 - Omaha World Herald (NE) Mar 17, 1964

JAGERSON

GLORIA SUE JAGERSON Fifth great granddaughter of progenitor Nicholas Kegg.

JAMAIL

JACOB BRYANT JAMAIL Seventh great grandson of progenitor Nicholas Kegg.

JAMES

ALYSSA NICOLE JAMES Eighth great granddaughter of progenitor Nicholas Kegg.
ANGELA JAMES Seventh great granddaughter of progenitor Nicholas Kegg. **BRANDY JAMES** Fifth great granddaughter of progenitor Nicholas Kegg. **CHRIS JAMES** Seventh great grandson of progenitor Nicholas Kegg. **DANIEL E. JAMES** Sixth great grandson of progenitor Nicholas Kegg. **DAVID JAMES** Sixth great granddaughter of progenitor Nicholas Kegg. **DAVID JAMES** Fifth great grandson of progenitor Nicholas Kegg. **DENNIS JAMES** Sixth great grandson of progenitor Nicholas Kegg. **DIANNA JAMES** Sixth great granddaughter of progenitor Nicholas Kegg.
DONALD E. JAMES [3885] (1939 – 2019) son of Carl and Margaret (Ott) James, married Nancy Lewis with whom he was father of (2). Donald was employed for 32 years by the Murry's Steaks Company as a Driver/Salesman and was well known in the community as "The Murry Man." Donald also was a Ham Radio Operator. He had a love of flying RC airplanes and would enjoy afternoons flying his models and attending air shows in the region. **DORIS JAMES** Sixth great granddaughter of progenitor Nicholas Kegg. **HAROLD OTT JAMES** Fifth great grandson of progenitor Nicholas Kegg.
HAZEL ROBERTA JAMES [3886] (1935 – 1993) aka "Bobbi", daughter of Carl and Margaret (Ott) James married twice; first to James Joseph Rosage with whom she was mother of (1). Later, she married Jack Byron Faust. Bobbi had worked as a timekeeper for Hedstrom Corp. **INFANT JAMES** (1969 – 1969) daughter of Donald and Nancy (Lewis) James. **JAY ANDREW JAMES** Seventh great grandson of progenitor Nicholas Kegg. **JOEL LEE JAMES** [3887] (1969 – 1980) aka "Joey", son of John and Barbara (Boyle) James would have been a fifth-grade student at Everett Elementary School.
JOHN E. JAMES Sixth great grandson of progenitor Nicholas Kegg. **JOHN GLENN JAMES** Seventh great grandson of progenitor Nicholas Kegg. **JOHN GRANVILLE JAMES** [3888] (1920 – 2001) son of Glenn and Mary (Ditch) James married twice; first to Dorothy Mae Ritchey with whom he was father of (9). Later, he married Barbara Jean Boyle with whom he was the father of (9). John was a lifetime dairy farmer. **JOHN PAUL JAMES** Fifth great grandson of progenitor Nicholas Kegg. **KELLY JAMES** Sixth great granddaughter of progenitor Nicholas Kegg.
KRISTINA LYNN JAMES Seventh great granddaughter of progenitor Nicholas Kegg. **MARGARET JAMES** aka "Dolly", Fifth great granddaughter of progenitor Nicholas Kegg. **MARGARET ANN JAMES** Fifth great granddaughter of progenitor Nicholas Kegg.
MARK JAMES Sixth great grandson of progenitor Nicholas Kegg. **MARY JO JAMES** Fifth great granddaughter of progenitor Nicholas Kegg. **MICHAEL JAMES** Fifth great grandson of progenitor Nicholas Kegg. **OTTIS R. JAMES** [3889] (1884 – 1900) son of John and Emma (Kegg) James was thrown, or fell, from his horse, alighting upon his head. He was found unconscious sometime afterward by a passerby and taken to his home. It is not known how the accident occurred as no one was near when it happened. The injured boy never regained consciousness. **ROBIN LYNN JAMES** [3890] (1981 – 2008) daughter of Dennis and Dorothy (Foor) James was mother of (3). Robin had a loving and caring sense of humor, great smile, and enthusiasm for life. **TERRY JAMES** Sixth great grandson of progenitor Nicholas Kegg. **TERRY EILEEN JAMES** Sixth great granddaughter of progenitor Nicholas Kegg. **TIM JAMES** Sixth great grandson of progenitor Nicholas Kegg.

[3885] Bedford Gazette (PA) Jan 7, 2019, obtained by Bob Rose [3886] Everett Public Library obtained by D. Sue Dible [3887] Bedford County Historical Society (PA), book 7-page 2459 obtained by D. Sue Dible [3888] p.3 - Bedford Inquirer (PA) Nov 2, 2001, obtained by Bob Rose [3889] The Bedford Gazette (PA) Nov 16, 1900 [3890] Bedford County Historical Society, book 99, p 125 obtained by D. Sue Dible

TODD JAMES Sixth great grandson of progenitor Nicholas Kegg. **TODD E. JAMES** Sixth great grandson of progenitor Nicholas Kegg. **TRACEY J. JAMES** [3891] (1982 – 1995) daughter of Terry and Mary Jane (Weicht) James. **TRAVIS JAMES** Seventh great grandson of progenitor Nicholas Kegg.

JAMETSKI

JAMES LEE PAUL JAMETSKI [3892] (1992 – 2008) son of Larry and Angela (Urick) Jametsky. **LAWRENCE PAUL JAMETSKI** Sixth great grandson of progenitor Nicholas Kegg. **TORI JAMETSKI** Sixth great granddaughter of progenitor Nicholas Kegg.

JANOSKI

ELIZABETH JANOSKI Sixth great granddaughter of progenitor Nicholas Kegg.
KIMBERLY LYNN JANOSKI Fifth great granddaughter of progenitor Nicholas Kegg.
KRISTINE A. JANOSKI Fifth great granddaughter of progenitor Nicholas Kegg.
MICHAEL JANOSKI Sixth great grandson of progenitor Nicholas Kegg.
MICHAEL F. JANOSKI Fifth great grandson of progenitor Nicholas Kegg.

JANSEN

GRANT JANSEN Seventh great grandson of progenitor Nicholas Kegg.
SHANNA JANSEN Seventh great granddaughter of progenitor Nicholas Kegg.

JANSON

ALLISON LAURA JANSON Fifth great granddaughter of progenitor Nicholas Kegg. **AMBER LISA JANSON** Fifth great granddaughter of progenitor Nicholas Kegg. **CATHERINE AMANDA JANSON** Fifth great granddaughter of progenitor Nicholas Kegg. **INFANT JANSON** (1891 – 1891) daughter of Augustus and Clara (Kegg) Janson. **IRA AUGUST JANSON** (1893 – 1896) son of Augustus and Clara (Kegg) Janson. **MARILYN PATRICIA JANSON** (1932 – 1933) daughter of John and Gladys (Hawkins) Janson. **WILLIAM RICHARD JANSON** Fourth great grandson of progenitor Nicholas Kegg.

JANSSEN

CRAIG R. JANSSEN Seventh great grandson of progenitor Nicholas Kegg. **DELANY MABEL JANSSEN** Eighth great granddaughter of progenitor Nicholas Kegg. **DEREK JANSSEN** Seventh great grandson of progenitor Nicholas Kegg. **JONAH PATRICK JANSSEN** Eighth great grandson of progenitor Nicholas Kegg. **SHELBY JANSSEN** Seventh great granddaughter of progenitor Nicholas Kegg.

JARBOE

LAURA JARBOE Sixth great granddaughter of progenitor Nicholas Kegg.
LINDSAY JARBOE Sixth great granddaughter of progenitor Nicholas Kegg.

[3891] Bedford Inquirer (PA) Dec15, 1995 [3892] Bonney-Watson funeral Home (WA) obituary obtained by D. Sue Dible

JARRETT

DEAN JARRETT Fifth great grandson of progenitor Nicholas Kegg.
SCOTT JARRETT Fifth great grandson of progenitor Nicholas Kegg.

JASIONOWSKI

ALEXANDER JAMES JASIONOWSKI Seventh great grandson of progenitor Nicholas Kegg.
EVIE JASIONOWSKI Seventh great granddaughter of progenitor Nicholas Kegg.

JEFFERS

STEPHANIE JEFFERS Sixth great granddaughter of progenitor Nicholas Kegg.

JEFFRIES

PATRICK JEFFRIES Seventh great grandson of progenitor Nicholas Kegg.
SARA JEFFRIES Seventh great granddaughter of progenitor Nicholas Kegg.

JENKINS

CATHERINE JENKINS Seventh great granddaughter of progenitor Nicholas Kegg.
HOMER JENKINS Seventh great grandson of progenitor Nicholas Kegg.
HOMER SYLVESTER JENKINS [3893] (1927 – 1987) son of Eugene and Kathryn (Duvall) Jenkins, married Orawan Suttisaragara with whom he was father of (3).   **ROBERT JENKINS** Seventh great grandson of progenitor Nicholas Kegg.

JENNINGS

EMILY KATHERINE JENNINGS Sixth great granddaughter of progenitor Nicholas Kegg.

JENSEN

BRAXTON JENSEN Seventh great grandson of progenitor Nicholas Kegg.
TAYA JENSEN Seventh great granddaughter of progenitor Nicholas Kegg.

JESKO

CARYN MICHELE JESKO Fifth great granddaughter of progenitor Nicholas Kegg.
CASSI A. JESKO Fifth great granddaughter of progenitor Nicholas Kegg.   **CHAD JESKO** Fifth great grandson of progenitor Nicholas Kegg.   **CHARLES MICHAEL JESKO** Fifth great grandson of progenitor Nicholas Kegg.   **DAVID ALAN JESKO** (1952 – 2013) son of Paul and Kathryn (Ferrell) Jesko, married Caroline with whom he was father of (2).   **DAVID ALAN JESKO** Fifth great grandson of progenitor Nicholas Kegg.   **GEORGE R. JESKO** aka "Ronnie", Fourth great grandson of progenitor Nicholas Kegg.   **GREGORY RONALD JESKO** Fifth great grandson of progenitor Nicholas Kegg.   **KAREN PATRICIA JESKO** [3893A] aka "Patti" (1939 – 2011) daughter of Paul and Kathryn (Ferrell) Jesko, married Edward Wensing with whom she was mother of (2).   **KATHY JESKO** Fifth great granddaughter of progenitor Nicholas Kegg.   **KENNY JESKO** Sixth great grandson of

---

[3893] FindAGrave Memorial# 25790698 Created by: Marie Graham [3893A] Plain Dealer (OH) June 23, 2011

progenitor Nicholas Kegg.   **KEVIN JESKO** Fifth great grandson of progenitor Nicholas Kegg.
PATRICIA KIM JESKO aka "Patty", Fifth great granddaughter of progenitor Nicholas Kegg.
PAUL KENNETH JESKO aka "P.J.", Fourth great grandson of progenitor Nicholas Kegg.
ROBERT JESKO Fifth great grandson of progenitor Nicholas Kegg.   **ROBERT RICHARD JESKO** [3894] (1936 – 2008) aka "Dick", son of Paul and Kathryn (Ferrell) Jesko, married Carolyn Ann Saville with whom he was father of (2).   **SCOTT ERIC JESKO** Fifth great grandson of progenitor Nicholas Kegg.   **SHARON JESKO** Fourth great granddaughter of progenitor Nicholas Kegg.
TERRI LYNN JESKO Fifth great granddaughter of progenitor Nicholas Kegg.   **TROY A. JESKO** Fifth great grandson of progenitor Nicholas Kegg.   **TYLER JESKO** Fifth great grandson of progenitor Nicholas Kegg.   **WILLIAM KIM JESKO** Fourth great grandson of progenitor Nicholas Kegg.

JEWELL

BRIAN KEITH JEWELL Fifth great grandson of progenitor Nicholas Kegg.
DENISE LYNN JEWELL Fifth great granddaughter of progenitor Nicholas Kegg.
HANNA JEWELL Sixth great granddaughter of progenitor Nicholas Kegg.   **KAYRA JEWELL** Sixth great granddaughter of progenitor Nicholas Kegg.   **KEEGAN JEWELL** Seventh great grandson of progenitor Nicholas Kegg.   **LINCOLN JEWELL** Seventh great grandson of progenitor Nicholas Kegg.   **NOAH HOWARD JEWELL** Sixth great grandson of progenitor Nicholas Kegg.
TROY JEWELL Sixth great grandson of progenitor Nicholas Kegg.
TROY MICHAEL JEWELL Fifth great grandson of progenitor Nicholas Kegg.

JEWETT

FRANCES R. JEWETT (1894 – 1949) daughter of William and Julia (Cagg) Jewett, married William Dorance Nowell with whom she was mother of (1).

JIMMERSON

MARK ALLEN JIMMERSON Seventh great grandson of progenitor Nicholas Kegg.
MONTE LEE JIMMERSON Seventh great grandson of progenitor Nicholas Kegg.

JOBE

CHARLENE JOBE Sixth great granddaughter of progenitor Nicholas Kegg.   **SEAN JOBE** Sixth great grandson of progenitor Nicholas Kegg.   **THOMAS JOBE** Sixth great grandson of progenitor Nicholas Kegg.   **TIM JOBE** Sixth great grandson of progenitor Nicholas Kegg.

JOERSZ

DOUGLAS SCOTT JOERSZ [3895] (1963 – 1985) son of Donald and Shirley (Swank) Joersz. Douglas was a farm employee.   **KAREN JOERSZ** Sixth great granddaughter of progenitor Nicholas Kegg.
PHILLIP JOERSZ Sixth great grandson of progenitor Nicholas Kegg.   **WANDA JOERSZ** Sixth great granddaughter of progenitor Nicholas Kegg.

JOHN

KATIE JOHN Sixth great granddaughter of progenitor Nicholas Kegg.

[3894] p.A9 - Ann Arbor News (MI) Oct 15, 2008   [3895] Tri-City Herald (Pasco, Washington) Oct 1, 1985

JOHNS

JULIE ANN JOHNS (3896) (1943 – 1944) daughter of Julian and Helena (Bing) Johns.
KIMBERLY ANN JOHNS Sixth great granddaughter of progenitor Nicholas Kegg.

JOHNSON

ANN JOHNSON Sixth great granddaughter of progenitor Nicholas Kegg.
ABIGAIL JEANNE JOHNSON Eighth great granddaughter of progenitor Nicholas Kegg.
ALAINA JOHNSON Eighth great granddaughter of progenitor Nicholas Kegg.
ALANNA JOHNSON Sixth great granddaughter of progenitor Nicholas Kegg. **ALEXIA JOHNSON** Eighth great granddaughter of progenitor Nicholas Kegg. **ALLAN ANDREW JOHNSON JR.** Seventh great grandson of progenitor Nicholas Kegg. **ALTA MARGUERITE JOHNSON** (3896A) (1889 – 1999) daughter of Edward and Effie Pearl (Johnson)Johnson married three times, first to Jack Childers with whom she was mother of (12). Later she married Paul Tedrow and divorced. Later married Bill Arrington. **BENJAMIN JOHNSON** Seventh great grandson of progenitor Nicholas Kegg.
BERKELEY JOHNSON Seventh great granddaughter of progenitor Nicholas Kegg.
BILL JOHNSON Sixth great grandson of progenitor Nicholas Kegg.
BRENT ANDREW JOHNSON Sixth great grandson of progenitor Nicholas Kegg.
BRITTANY JOHNSON Seventh great granddaughter of progenitor Nicholas Kegg.
BRITTANY ANNE JOHNSON Seventh great granddaughter of progenitor Nicholas Kegg.
CALEB JOHNSON Sixth great grandson of progenitor Nicholas Kegg. **CAROLL E. JOHNSON** (3897) (1936 – 2018) aka "Dipper", son of William Orlo and Esther (Beymer) Johnson married Beverly with whom he was father of (5). Dipper joined the tire business for 25 years. He later joined Iowa Realty as a Realtor, where he retired after 20 years. He was the President of Iowa Tire Dealers Association, Des Moines Soap Box Derby, and a member of The Elks Lodge in West Des Moines.
CECIL NEIL JOHNSON (1901 – 1952) aka "Neil", son of Edward and Effie (Johnson) Johnson, married Olive Estella Beymer with whom he was father of (3). **CECIL NEIL JOHNSON** (3897A) (1924 – 2001) son of Cecil and Olive (Beymer) Johnson, married Darlene Pine with whom he was father of (1). Cecil served in the U.S. Army during W.W. II, landing at Normandy Beach on D-Day. He worked for Kinnison Truck Lines for 20 years as a bookkeeper and dispatcher. He then worked for Bud Barr for 3 years. Cecil was a member of the First Christian Church and American Legion Lorraine Post #67, both in Red Oak. **CHRISTOPHER LEE JOHNSON** (died 1979) son of Jerry and Carole (Lombard) Johnson.
CODY JOHNSON Sixth great grandson of progenitor Nicholas Kegg. **DEBBIE JOHNSON** Fifth great granddaughter of progenitor Nicholas Kegg. **DEBBIE JOHNSON** Sixth great granddaughter of progenitor Nicholas Kegg. **DENNIS DUANE JOHNSON** Fifth great grandson of progenitor Nicholas Kegg. **DONALD E. JOHNSON** (3897B) (1918 – 2010) son of Elmer and Hazel (Shrock) Johnson, married Vera R. O'Brien. Donald was a Seaman First Class in the Navy from 1944 to 1946. After the war, he worked for Westinghouse and then moved to Sacramento, Calif., where he worked as an aeronautical engineer on the McClellan Air Force Base. He was a member of the Masons, Scottish Rite, and the Elks. He was an avid sailor, hiker, golfer, and bridge player. **DONALD EUGENE JOHNSON** aka "Gene", Fifth great grandson of progenitor Nicholas Kegg. **DUANE DAY JOHNSON** (3898) (1909 – 2001) aka "Doc", son of Edward and Effie (Johnson) Johnson, married Doris Autumn (Pettis) O'Grady with whom he was father of (1). Doc was raised in Ringgold County and farmed most of his life. As a young man he worked herding sheep in the mountains of Idaho. Doc joined the Army in August of 1942 and received his basic training at Fort Douglas, Utah. He served his country during World War II fighting in France and Germany. He served with the 319th Infantry as Staff Sergeant and fought in the Battle of the Bulge. During his combat duty he was wounded three times: once in Tincry, France and again in

---

(3896) p.2 Columbus Dispatch (OH) Feb 10, 1944 (3896A) genealogybuff Iowa Obituary and Death Notices Archive – p.298 (3897) Hamiltons Funeral Home (IA) obtained by D. Sue Dible (3897A) Sellergren-Lindell-DeMarce Funeral Home (IA) (3897B) The Sacramento Bee (CA) May 30, 2010 (3898) Ringgold County, Iowa Obituary Collection-32

Douripat, France. He was also wounded during a combat mission in Luxembourg. He received one service stripe, two overseas service bars from the American Campaign and the European-African-Middle Eastern Theater. He received three Bronze Battle Stars, a World War II Victory Medal Purple Heart with two oak leaf clusters. He returned to the family farm when the war was over. Doc served in several civic, fraternal and veteran organizations including the Kellerton American Legion, Post #676 and the Ringgold County Commission of Veterans Affairs. He served on the Election Board for several years and as a trustee of Athens Township. Doc was also a member of IOOF lodge. Doc enjoyed family gatherings.
EDWIN JOHNSON Fifth great grandson of progenitor Nicholas Kegg. **EFFIE PEARL JOHNSON** (1877 – 1967) daughter of William and Sarah (Laird) Johnson, married Edward Johnson with whom she was mother of (8). **ELISABETH RENEE JOHNSON** Eighth great granddaughter of progenitor Nicholas Kegg. **ELIZABETH JOHNSON** Sixth great granddaughter of progenitor Nicholas Kegg. **ELVIN GENE JOHNSON** Fifth great grandson of progenitor Nicholas Kegg.
FRANCINE JOHNSON Seventh great granddaughter of progenitor Nicholas Kegg.
GERALD LEROY JOHNSON [3898A] aka "Bill" (1911 – 2007) son of Edward and Effie Pearl (Johnson) Johnson was married twice, first to Ethel A. Buckley with whom he was father of (2). Later he married Helen (Dollarhide) Fithian. As a young man, Bill first traveled west when he and two of his brothers hopped a ride aboard a freight train. Bill served in the US Army in Normandy during WWII. For most of his adult life, Bill made his living as a long-haul truck driver. One of Bill's greatest enjoyments was spending time with his grandchildren outdoors, where he loved to fish and camp.
GLENN EDWIN JOHNSON [3899] (1934 – 2020) son of Wayne and Bessie (Stanley) Johnson married Kathryn "Ruth" Johnson with whom he was father of (1). Later he married Janice (Hartlein) Downey. Glenn served in the U.S. Army from 1955 to 1957 in Communications. After exiting the Army, he attended a technical school for TV repair in Des Moines. He worked as a TV Repair Technician until he transferred to Emporia, KS to become Manager of Cablevision. **GREGORY E. JOHNSON** Sixth great grandson of progenitor Nicholas Kegg. **HOWARD JOHNSON** Sixth great grandson of progenitor Nicholas Kegg. **JACK JOHNSON** (1949 – 1949) son of Perry and Donna (Tindle) Johnson. **JAN MARIE JOHNSON** (1953 – 1971) daughter of Perry and Donna (Tindle) Johnson, married Eddie Eugene Overholser. **JANET JOHNSON** Sixth great granddaughter of progenitor Nicholas Kegg. **JAY JOHNSON** Sixth great grandson of progenitor Nicholas Kegg.
JEFFREY GLEN JOHNSON Sixth great grandson of progenitor Nicholas Kegg.
JENNIFER MICHELLE JOHNSON Sixth great granddaughter of progenitor Nicholas Kegg. **JERALD JOHNSON** Fifth great grandson of progenitor Nicholas Kegg. **JERRY LEE JOHNSON** Sixth great grandson of progenitor Nicholas Kegg. **JIL JOHNSON** Sixth great granddaughter of progenitor Nicholas Kegg. **JIM JOHNSON** Sixth great grandson of progenitor Nicholas Kegg.
JOE JOHNSON Sixth great grandson of progenitor Nicholas Kegg. **JOHN JOHNSON** Sixth great grandson of progenitor Nicholas Kegg. **JON MICHAEL JOHNSON** aka "Mike", Sixth great grandson of progenitor Nicholas Kegg. **KAREN JOHNSON** Sixth great granddaughter of progenitor Nicholas Kegg. **KAREN JOHNSON** (1941 – 1941) daughter of Charles and Joyce (Wallace) Johnson. **KARIN L. JOHNSON** Fifth great granddaughter of progenitor Nicholas Kegg.
KENNETH MAX JOHNSON Fifth great grandson of progenitor Nicholas Kegg.
KEVIN JOHNSON Sixth great grandson of progenitor Nicholas Kegg. **LAURIE JOHNSON** Fifth great granddaughter of progenitor Nicholas Kegg. **LESA JOHNSON** Sixth great granddaughter of progenitor Nicholas Kegg. **LINDA JOHNSON** Sixth great granddaughter of progenitor Nicholas Kegg. **LLOYD JOHNSON** Fifth great grandson of progenitor Nicholas Kegg.
LOIS VIRGINIA JOHNSON (1916 – 1997) daughter of Edward and Effie (Johnson) Johnson, married Harry Franklin Epps with whom she was mother of (2). **LUCILLE EMMA JOHNSON** (1909 – 1994) aka "Tillie", daughter of Melburn and Axie Pearl (Brandenburg) Johnson married twice; first to Autin Paul Raine with whom she was mother of (2). Later, she married Eldon Luther Eichelberger.

[3898A] Idaho Press Tribune (ID) Feb. 10, 2007 [3899] Armstrong Funeral Homes (IA) obtained by D. Sue Dible

MABEL JEANETTE JOHNSON (3900) (1907 – 1968) daughter of Melburn and Axie Pearl (Brandenburg) Johnson, married Oscar Vernon Hanlin. **MAE VALIER JOHNSON** (1906 – 1999) daughter of Edward and Effie (Johnson) Johnson, married Leonard Edward Morrow with whom she was mother of (4). **MARCIE KAY JOHNSON** Sixth great granddaughter of progenitor Nicholas Kegg. **MARCUS JOHNSON** Seventh great grandson of progenitor Nicholas Kegg. **MARK JOHNSON** Sixth great grandson of progenitor Nicholas Kegg. **MELANIE JOHNSON** Sixth great granddaughter of progenitor Nicholas Kegg. **MILDRED MARIE JOHNSON** (3900A) (1902 – 1979) daughter of Melburn and Axie Pearl (Brandenburg) Johnson married twice; first to Noel Sherman Smith with whom she was mother of (6). Later, she married Charles Ross Baker. Mildred worked as a registered nurse, a schoolteacher and a licensed psychologist. **MITCHELL JOHNSON** Sixth great grandson of progenitor Nicholas Kegg. **MORGAN JOHNSON** Seventh great granddaughter of progenitor Nicholas Kegg. **PAT JOHNSON** Sixth great grandson of progenitor Nicholas Kegg. **PACHIA JOHNSON** Sixth great granddaughter of progenitor Nicholas Kegg. **PATRICIA JOHNSON** Sixth great granddaughter of progenitor Nicholas Kegg. **PAUL JOHNSON** Sixth great grandson of progenitor Nicholas Kegg. **PEGGY JOHNSON** Sixth great granddaughter of progenitor Nicholas Kegg. **PERRY BEYMER JOHNSON** (3900B) (1927 – 2010) son of Cecil and Olive (Beymer) Johnson, married Donna Marie Tindle with whom he was father of (7). Perry enlisted in the US Army right after graduation. He was stationed in Alaska for two years. He took correspondence courses to repair radios and TVs and started driving a semi-truck for Kinnison Trucking of Red Oak. Perry purchased the Diagonal Café from Wilbur and Josephine Maudlin. Together with his wife, they ran the café until 1974. **RANDY JOHNSON** Sixth great grandson of progenitor Nicholas Kegg. **RICKY LYNN JOHNSON** (3901) (1957 – 1960) son of William and Lois (Blubaugh) Johnson was riding in the back seat of the car when the door came open and he fell and struck his head on the pavement. He was dead upon arrival at the hospital. **ROGER JOHNSON** Sixth great grandson of progenitor Nicholas Kegg. **RON JOHNSON** Fifth great grandson of progenitor Nicholas Kegg. **RONALD JOHNSON** Fifth great grandson of progenitor Nicholas Kegg. **RONNIE LEE JOHNSON** Sixth great grandson of progenitor Nicholas Kegg. **ROXANNE JOHNSON** aka "Roxie" Fifth great granddaughter of progenitor Nicholas Kegg. **SCOTT JOHNSON** Sixth great grandson of progenitor Nicholas Kegg. **SEAN A. JOHNSON** Seventh great grandson of progenitor Nicholas Kegg. **SEIGEL L. JOHNSON** (1905 – 1978) son of Melburn and Axie Pearl (Brandenburg) Johnson, married Beulah A. Thompson, later married Ethel Lucille (Buck) Burk. **SHANE TIMOTHY JOHNSON** Eighth great grandson of progenitor Nicholas Kegg. **SHARON LEE JOHNSON** Fifth great granddaughter of progenitor Nicholas Kegg. **SHAWN JOHNSON** Seventh great grandson of progenitor Nicholas Kegg. **SHELBY JOHNSON** Seventh great granddaughter of progenitor Nicholas Kegg. **SUSAN JOHNSON** Sixth great granddaughter of progenitor Nicholas Kegg. **TAMMY JOHNSON** Sixth great granddaughter of progenitor Nicholas Kegg. **TERRI L. JOHNSON** Sixth great granddaughter of progenitor Nicholas Kegg. **THERON MERLE JOHNSON** Fifth great grandson of progenitor Nicholas Kegg. **TRAVIS JOHNSON** Sixth great grandson of progenitor Nicholas Kegg. **VALERY E. JOHNSON** Sixth great granddaughter of progenitor Nicholas Kegg. **WAYNE RAY JOHNSON** (1909 – 1993) son of Edward and Effie (Johnson) Johnson, married Bessie Emmaline Stanley with whom he was father of (2). **WILLIAM ORLO JOHNSON** (1904 – 1948) son of Edward and Effie (Johnson) Johnson, married Esther Martha Beymer with whom he was father of (4). **WILLIAM ORLO JOHNSON** (3902) (1928 – 2000) aka "Bill", son of William and Esther (Beymer) Johnson married twice; first to Nina Ruth Holtzman with whom he was father of (1). Later, he married Lois Lavon Blubaugh with whom he was father of (5). His greatest joy was spending time with his loved ones, watching TV, reading good westerns, and working at the trolley garage in Creston, Iowa. **WINIFRED ETHEL JOHNSON** (3902A) (1915 – 2004) daughter of Elmer and Hazel (Shrock) Johnson

---

(3900) p.20 Newark Advocate (OH) May 28, 1968 (3900A) Oregon Obituary obtained from Find A Grave# 133818331 (3900B) Watson - Armstrong Funeral Home (IA) (3901) Mount Ayr Record-News (IA) Nov 24, 1960, transcribed by Sharon R. Becker (3902) GenLookups.com Iowa Obituary and Death Notices Archive - Page 288 (3902A) Paris News (TX) March 31, 2006

married twice; first to Charles Porter Baker with whom she was mother of (3). Later, she married James Thayer York.

JOHNSTEN

CHRISTIAN JOHNSTEN Fifth great grandson of progenitor Nicholas Kegg. **CHRISTINA M. JOHNSTEN** Fifth great granddaughter of progenitor Nicholas Kegg. **DAVID JOHNSTEN** Fourth great grandson of progenitor Nicholas Kegg. **JENNIFER A. JOHNSTEN** Fifth great granddaughter of progenitor Nicholas Kegg. **RICHARD JOHNSTEN** Fourth great grandson of progenitor Nicholas Kegg.

JOHNSTON

CHRISTOPHER JOHNSTON Sixth great grandson of progenitor Nicholas Kegg. **JACKLYN L. JOHNSTON** Sixth great granddaughter of progenitor Nicholas Kegg. **JENNA JOHNSTON** Seventh great granddaughter of progenitor Nicholas Kegg. **JOSEPH JOHNSTON** Sixth great grandson of progenitor Nicholas Kegg. **NIKKI LEAH JOHNSTON** Sixth great granddaughter of progenitor Nicholas Kegg. **RYAN JOHNSTON** Sixth great grandson of progenitor Nicholas Kegg. **SARAH JOHNSTON** Sixth great granddaughter of progenitor Nicholas Kegg. **TIM JOHNSTON** Sixth great grandson of progenitor Nicholas Kegg.

JOINER

JAMES MARK JOINER Seventh great grandson of progenitor Nicholas Kegg.

JONES

ADDIE JONES Eighth great granddaughter of progenitor Nicholas Kegg.
ALBERT ELLSWORTH JONES [3903] (1898 – 1956) son of Malcolm and Estella (Ohr) Jones married Myrtle M. Bowles with whom he was father of (1). **ALBERT ELLSWORTH JONES JR.** (1921 – 1994) son of Albert and Mina Louise (Kelly) Jones with whom he was father of (2). Albert was a WWII veteran receiving both the Silver Star and Purple Heart. **ALEX JONES** Seventh great grandson of progenitor Nicholas Kegg. **ALEXANDER ARTHUR JONES** Seventh great grandson of progenitor Nicholas Kegg. **AMIE JONES** Sixth great granddaughter of progenitor Nicholas Kegg.
ANNA MARGARET JONES (1953 – 1953) daughter of Robert and Anna (Chalfant) Jones. **BENJAMIN KEGG JONES** [3904] (1869 – 1912) son of John and Eliza (Kegg) Jones, a merchant of Baltimore, Maryland. **BRIEN ARTHUR JONES** Sixth great grandson of progenitor Nicholas Kegg. **CAITLIN JONES** Sixth great granddaughter of progenitor Nicholas Kegg. **CANDACE ANN JONES** aka "Candy", Sixth great granddaughter of progenitor Nicholas Kegg. **CAROL MARIE JONES** [3905] (1942 – 2020) daughter of Alvin and Helen (Kegg) Jones married Charles Clem Miller with whom she was mother of (2). Carol enjoyed sewing, crocheting, pulling weeds and making pots of chili and pot pie for the whole family to enjoy together. **CHARLES CALHOUN JONES** [3905A] aka "Chuck" (1940 – 2013) son of Charles and Marjorie (Calhoun) Jones, married Patricia Jean Diehl with whom he was father of (3). Chuck was a member of the armed services serving first as a Captain in the US Army and later as a Captain in the US Air force. Chuck was a financial advisor, a wealth manager, and a legacy planner. He held many professional designations from the American College, where he served on the Board of Directors and was one of six honorees in The American College Hall of Fame. Chuck served many organizations during his lifetime leaving a lasting impression on those who served with him.

[3903] The Philadelphia Inquirer (PA) March 23, 1956 [3904] p.11 Sun (Baltimore, Maryland) Jan 21, 1912 [3905] Bedford Gazette (PA) June 19, 2020, obtained by Bob Rose [3905A] Kansas City Star (MO) May 3, 2013

CHRISTOPHER ANDREW JONES Seventh great grandson of progenitor Nicholas Kegg.
CORA L. JONES [3906] (1866 - 1946) daughter of John and Eliza (Kegg) Jones.
COURTLAND JONES Seventh great grandson of progenitor Nicholas Kegg.
COURTNEY R. JONES [3907] (1988 – 1988) daughter of Thomas and Maryann (Hess) Johnes.
DAKOTA JONES Eighth great grandchild of progenitor Nicholas Kegg. **DAVID WALTER JONES** Sixth great grandson of progenitor Nicholas Kegg. **DONALD M. JONES** [3908] (1876 – 1930) son of John and Eliza (Kegg) Jones was employed as a surveyor. **EDWIN T. JONES** (abt 1904 -?) son of Thomas and Lillie (Major) Jones. **ELISE JONES** Fifth great granddaughter of progenitor Nicholas Kegg. **ELLIOTT JONES** Sixth great grandson of progenitor Nicholas Kegg. **EMILY M. JONES** Fourth great granddaughter of progenitor Nicholas Kegg. **ERIC JONES** Fifth great grandson of progenitor Nicholas Kegg. **ERIC PAUL JONES** Sixth great grandson of progenitor Nicholas Kegg.
FREDERICK JONES [3909] (1861 – 1954) aka "Fred", son of John and Eliza (Kegg) Jones married twice; first to Minnie B. Davis. Later, he married Minnie Belle Vermillion. Fred was employed as an oil well driller having worked for both Pure Oil Co., and Dawes Arboretum. **GARY R. JONES** Sixth great grandson of progenitor Nicholas Kegg. **GLENN RAYMOND JONES** Fourth great grandson of progenitor Nicholas Kegg. **HANNAH JONES** Seventh great granddaughter of progenitor Nicholas Kegg. **HELEN ELIZABETH JONES** (1926 – 1999) daughter of Ernest and Flora (May) Jones.
JAMES ALBERT JONES [3910] (1948 – 1980) son of Robert and Anna (Chalfant) Jones. James graduated from East Bay High School and earned his degree in commercial art from Florida State University. A professional Boy Scout executive with the Allegheny Council in Pittsburgh, he worked in management for Kresge Co. (K.Mart) and Jamesway in Pennsylvania, New York and West Virginia. He lived and worked in both Pittsburgh and Stahlstown at various times between 1970 and 1977. James just completed management training for the National Truck Stops of America Chain, when he died.
JANICE MARIE JONES Sixth great granddaughter of progenitor Nicholas Kegg. **JESSIE JONES** [3911] (1870 – 1944) daughter of John and Eliza (Kegg) Jones, married Charles C. Porter with whom she was mother of (1). Jessie had been choir mother at Emanuel Episcopal Church and was chairman of the choir chapter for twenty-five years. In the period in which she was choir mother, Jessie made all vestments for members of the choir. In addition, she taught one of the classes in the Sunday school.
JOHN EVAN JONES (1906 – 1995) aka "Jack", son of John and Nellie (Gump) Jones, married Valerie C. Green with whom he was father of (2). **JOHN WILLIAM JONES** (1876 -?) son of John and Eliza (Kegg) Jones, married Lydia with whom he was father of (2). **JUDITH DIANE JONES** Fifth great granddaughter of progenitor Nicholas Kegg. **KATHRYN LYNN JONES** aka "Kathy", Seventh great granddaughter of progenitor Nicholas Kegg. **KEVIN M. JONES** Eighth great grandson of progenitor Nicholas Kegg. **LAWRENCE W. JONES** Fifth great grandson of progenitor Nicholas Kegg.
MALCOLM SINCLAIR JONES [3912] (1872 – 1935) son of John and Eliza (Kegg) Jones married Estella Valencia Ohr with whom he was father of (1). Malcolm was an outstanding swimmer, athlete and amateur baseball player and pitcher. He declined an offer to enter the ranks of professional baseball in those times. **MARGARET LUCILLE JONES** (1917 – 1991) aka "Mimi", daughter of Thomas and Lillie (Major) Jones married three times; first to Elmer Riggs with whom she was mother of (2). She married Jack Raymond Tillery with whom she was mother of (1). She married Mr. Tower.
MARILYN ELAINE JONES Fifth great granddaughter of progenitor Nicholas Kegg.
MARJORIE CHRISTY JONES aka "Christe", Sixth great granddaughter of progenitor Nicholas Kegg.
MARY ALMA JONES [3913] (1859 – 1916) daughter of John and Eliza (Kegg) Jones.
MARY ALMA JONES (abt 1907 -?) daughter of John and Lydia Jones, married John Osborne Crawford. **MATTHEW JONES** Sixth great grandson of progenitor Nicholas Kegg.
MELANIE JEAN JONES [3914] (1949 – 2016) daughter of Robert and Anna (Chalfant) Jones. Melanie retired after 35 years as a second-grade teacher for Riverview Schools. She was a member of the

---

[3906] The Cumberland News (MD) Oct 21, 1946 [3907] Oakland Press (MI) Dec 20, 1988 [3908] p.11 - Cumberland Evening Times (MD) March 12, 1930 [3909] The Newark Advocate (OH) Oct 9, 1954 [3910] Latrobe Bulletin (PA) Nov 7, 1980 [3911] p.7 - The Cumberland Evening Times (MD) March 6, 1944 [3912] Cumberland Evening Times (MD) Aug 1, 1935 [3913] Cumberland Times (MD) June 9, 1916 [3914] Tampa Bay Times (PA) June 12, 2016

Riverview United Methodist Church, as well as a member of the Eastern Star.

MILDRED JANE JONES [3915] (1900 – 1953) daughter of John and Lydia Jones, married Lewis Richard Cannon with whom she was mother of (4).   **MYRTLE IRENE JONES** Fourth great granddaughter of progenitor Nicholas Kegg.   **PAMELA JONES** Sixth great granddaughter of progenitor Nicholas Kegg.
RALPH MILLER JONES [3916] (1947 – 2009) son of Robert and Anna (Chalfant) Jones.
RICHARD W. JONES Sixth great grandson of progenitor Nicholas Kegg.   **ROBERT G. JONES** Sixth great grandson of progenitor Nicholas Kegg.   **ROBERTA LOUISE JONES** [3917] (1946 – 1981) aka "Bobbie", daughter of Robert and Anna (Chalfant) Jones, married Paul Eckart Gonzalez. Bobbie was a member of the Board of Directors for the Women's Survival Center and a freelance writer.
ROGER JONES Fifth great grandson of progenitor Nicholas Kegg.   **SALLY JONES** Fifth great granddaughter of progenitor Nicholas Kegg.   **SHIRLEY VIRGINIA JONES** (1922 – 2001) daughter of Harold and Ada (Calhoun) Jones.   **SOPHIA JONES** Eighth great granddaughter of progenitor Nicholas Kegg.   **SOPHIE JONES** Seventh great granddaughter of progenitor Nicholas Kegg.
SUSAN KAY JONES [3917A] (1949 – 2014) daughter of Frank and Patricia (Fisher) Jones. Susan completed Flight Attendant Training with TWA Airlines. In 1972 she moved with her family to Scottsdale, where she attended Arizona State University, pursuing a degree in music therapy. Susan enjoyed crocheting, playing the piano, oil painting, and reading travel books and cookbooks. Her happiest times were those spent with her family and keeping in touch with long-distance relatives.
STACY A. JONES Sixth great granddaughter of progenitor Nicholas Kegg.
STEPHANIE ANN JONES Sixth great granddaughter of progenitor Nicholas Kegg.
STEVEN DOUGLAS JONES Fifth great grandson of progenitor Nicholas Kegg.
SUZANNE ELIZABETH JONES Seventh great granddaughter of progenitor Nicholas Kegg.
WENDY ANN JONES Sixth great granddaughter of progenitor Nicholas Kegg.

JONTZ

BRADLEY RICHARD JONTZ [3917B] (1958 – 2013) son of Robert and Shirley (Porter) Jontz graduated with a BA in Education from Missouri State University and ultimately received his master's in psychology from Burlington College in Burlington, VT. His work took him to Tucson, AZ, Miami, FL, and ultimately Las Vegas, NV.   **COURTNEY LYNN JONTZ** Sixth great granddaughter of progenitor Nicholas Kegg.   **ERIN JONTZ** Sixth great granddaughter of progenitor Nicholas Kegg.
GREGG R. JONTZ Fifth great grandson of progenitor Nicholas Kegg.
MICHAEL JONTZ Sixth great grandson of progenitor Nicholas Kegg.

JORDAN

SETH JORDAN Fifth great grandson of progenitor Nicholas Kegg.   **SHANE JORDAN** Fifth great grandson of progenitor Nicholas Kegg.   **SPENCER JORDAN** Fifth great grandson of progenitor Nicholas Kegg.

JORGENSEN

CODY JORGENSEN Seventh great grandson of progenitor Nicholas Kegg.

[3915] Washington Post (D.C.) March 12, 1953 [3916] Tampa Tribune (FL) Sep 3, 2009 [3917] The Tampa Times (FL) Nov 4, 1981 [3917A] Bedford Gazette (PA) Jan 7, 2014, contributed by Bob Rose [3917B] Johnson Family Funeral Home (IA)

JOSLEN

JANE ELLEN JOSLEN Fifth great granddaughter of progenitor Nicholas Kegg.
JERRY WAYNE JOSLEN Fifth great grandson of progenitor Nicholas Kegg.
RUTH ANN JOSELEN Fifth great granddaughter of progenitor Nicholas Kegg.

JOZENS

GEORGE FREDERICK JOZENS Sixth great grandson of progenitor Nicholas Kegg.
JONATHON THOMAS JOZENS Sixth great grandson of progenitor Nicholas Kegg.
JOSHUA WILLIAM JOZENS Seventh great grandson of progenitor Nicholas Kegg.
LISA JEAN JOZENS Sixth great granddaughter of progenitor Nicholas Kegg.
STEPHEN CHARLES JOZENS Sixth great grandson of progenitor Nicholas Kegg.

JUDAY

BENJAMIN TODD JUDAY Sixth great grandson of progenitor Nicholas Kegg. **HUNTER JUDAY** Seventh great granddaughter of progenitor Nicholas Kegg. **MARGARET JUDAY** aka "Peggy", Fifth great granddaughter of progenitor Nicholas Kegg. **PAMELA KAY JUDAY** "Pam", Fifth great granddaughter of progenitor Nicholas Kegg. **PATRICIA L. JUDAY** Fifth great granddaughter of progenitor Nicholas Kegg. **PATRICK JUDAY** Fifth great grandson of progenitor Nicholas Kegg.
PAUL FRANCES JUDAY Fifth great grandson of progenitor Nicholas Kegg.
PAUL FRANCIS JUDAY Sixth great grandson of progenitor Nicholas Kegg.
PAUL FRANCIS JUDAY Seventh great grandson of progenitor Nicholas Kegg.
PAULETTE J. JUDAY Fifth great granddaughter of progenitor Nicholas Kegg.
PENNY MARIE JUDAY Fifth great granddaughter of progenitor Nicholas Kegg.
PERRY ALAN JUDAY [3918] (1953 – 2000) son of Paul and Margery (Pfenning) Juday, married Alice Lorene Rollen. Perry was a mobile home repairman, Pentecostal and an Army veteran.
PHILLIP BRIAN JUDAY Fifth great grandson of progenitor Nicholas Kegg.

JULIUS

CHERYL LYNN JULIUS Sixth great granddaughter of progenitor Nicholas Kegg.
DONNA IRENE JULIUS [3918A] (1950 – 2013) daughter of Donald and Irene (Kegg) Julius married twice, first to Kenneth James Spafford with whom she was mother of (4). Later she married Gregory Franklin Godwin with whom she was mother of (1). Donna spent her life dedicated to her family, her love of horticulture, the arts, and her ever-present wanderlust. She was employed as the Greenhouse Manager by Dammann's Lawn and Garden at 30th and Franklin for over 20 years, where she shared her love of nature and growing plants with anyone who came in contact with her. She especially loved caring for and growing hostas, daylilies, and orchids. Donna was a supporter of the Indianapolis Arts Community, and religiously patronized the IRT, Indianapolis Opera, Beef and Boards, and Dance Kaleidoscope; as well as many of the local live theatre companies. **JOAN JULIUS** Fifth great granddaughter of progenitor Nicholas Kegg. **RICKEY BRYANT JULIUS** [3918B] (1956 – 2012) son of Donald and Irene (Kegg) Julius married three times; first to Cindy Sappington with whom he was father of (1). He married Pamela Darlene Clarke and last to Sandra Lee Martin. Rickey was employed at Fibertek, Inc. of Herndon, VA. He enjoyed spending time on his John Deere tractor mowing grass. **WINDY LEILANI JULIUS** 5th great granddaughter of progenitor Nicholas Kegg.

[3918] p.7 - St. Petersburg Times (FL) Dec 20, 2000 [3918A] Indianapolis Star (IN) March 5, 2013 [3918B] Washington Post (DC) July 31, 2012

JUSTICE

CHRIS JUSTICE Eighth great grandson of progenitor Nicholas Kegg.

KALDIS

ALEXANDER KALDIS Seventh great grandson of progenitor Nicholas Kegg. **KRISTINA KALDIS** Seventh great granddaughter of progenitor Nicholas Kegg. **NICHOLAS KALDIS** Seventh great grandson of progenitor Nicholas Kegg.

KALFAS

JENNIFER KALFAS Seventh great granddaughter of progenitor Nicholas Kegg.
JESSICA KALFAS Seventh great granddaughter of progenitor Nicholas Kegg.

KALINOWSKI

PATRICIA MARIA KALINOWSKI Sixth great granddaughter of progenitor Nicholas Kegg.
SUSAN MARIA KALINOWSKI (1949 – 1949) daughter of Frank and Athalone (Streight) Kalinowski.

KALLESTAD

ELIZABETH KALLESTAD Sixth great granddaughter of progenitor Nicholas Kegg.
JOHN M. KALLESTAD Sixth great grandson of progenitor Nicholas Kegg.
STEPHEN KALLESTAD Sixth great grandson of progenitor Nicholas Kegg.

KALLUNKI

KAREN KALLUNKI Fifth great granddaughter of progenitor Nicholas Kegg.

KALWITZ

CARRIE ANN KALWITZ Fifth great granddaughter of progenitor Nicholas Kegg.
CHRISTINE MARGARET KALWITZ Fifth great granddaughter of progenitor Nicholas Kegg.

KAMHOLZ

NADINE KAMHOLZ Fifth great granddaughter of progenitor Nicholas Kegg.

KANE

DAWN KANE Seventh great granddaughter of progenitor Nicholas Kegg.
HOLLY KANE Seventh great granddaughter of progenitor Nicholas Kegg.

KANN

ABIGAIL ELIZABETH KANN Sixth great granddaughter of progenitor Nicholas Kegg.
RACHEL KANN Sixth great granddaughter of progenitor Nicholas Kegg.

KANTNER

ANDREW B. KANTNER Fifth great grandson of progenitor Nicholas Kegg.
CHRISTOPHER KANTNER Fifth great grandson of progenitor Nicholas Kegg. **JOSIE KANTNER** Fifth great granddaughter of progenitor Nicholas Kegg. **JULIE KANTNER** Fifth great granddaughter of progenitor Nicholas Kegg.

KAPALKO

JENNIFER KELLY LOUISE KAPALKO Seventh great granddaughter of progenitor Nicholas Kegg.
KYLE LONA MONROE KAPALKO Eighth great grandson of progenitor Nicholas Kegg.

KAPINOS

DANIEL A. KAPINOS Seventh great grandson of progenitor Nicholas Kegg.
DUSTIN A. KAPINOS Seventh great grandson of progenitor Nicholas Kegg.
EMMA KAPINOS Eighth great granddaughter of progenitor Nicholas Kegg.

KAPPEL

DAVID ARTHUR KAPPEL Sixth great grandson of progenitor Nicholas Kegg.
KATHERINE KAPPEL Sixth great granddaughter of progenitor Nicholas Kegg.
KRISTINE E. KAPPEL aka "Kris", Sixth great granddaughter of progenitor Nicholas Kegg.

KARAS

CONSTANTINA ANGELA KARAS [3919] (1966 – 2015) daughter of Angelo and Donna (Vlasaty) Karas. Constantina was employed as a domestic housekeeper.

KARNOSH

RICHARD KARNOSH Seventh great grandson of progenitor Nicholas Kegg.

KARNS

HARRY STUDEBAKER KARNS (1911 – 1911) son of Harry and Bessie (Nycum) Karns.
JASON KARNS Sixth great grandson of progenitor Nicholas Kegg. **JEFFREY N. KARNS** Sixth great grandson of progenitor Nicholas Kegg. **JESSE KARNS** Sixth great grandson of progenitor Nicholas Kegg. **JOHN KARNS** Seventh great grandson of progenitor Nicholas Kegg.
JUDITH LYNN KARNS aka "Judy", Fifth great granddaughter of progenitor Nicholas Kegg.
KIRBY LEE KARNS Fifth great grandson of progenitor Nicholas Kegg. **LINFORD A. KARNS** Sixth great grandson of progenitor Nicholas Kegg. **LOGAN KARNS** Sixth great grandson of progenitor Nicholas Kegg. **MARK F. KARNS** Sixth great grandson of progenitor Nicholas Kegg.
MASON FIELD KARNS [3919A] (1936 – 2022) son of John and Belva Ruth (Hart) Karns married Betty Jo Newkirk with whom he was father of (1). **MELINDA KARNS** Seventh great granddaughter of progenitor Nicholas Kegg. **PEGGY BESS KARNS** Fifth great granddaughter of progenitor Nicholas Kegg. **ROBERT JOHN KARNS** (1934 – 1934) son of John and Belva (Hart) Karns.
TAMARA MARIE KARNS Seventh great granddaughter of progenitor Nicholas Kegg.

[3919] Roselawn Memorial Park (KS) [3919A] Enid Buzz (OK) Sep 20, 2022

KARR

COURTNEY KARR Seventh great granddaughter of progenitor Nicholas Kegg.
DANNY DEAN KARR Sixth great grandson of progenitor Nicholas Kegg. **HOLLY KAY KARR** Seventh great granddaughter of progenitor Nicholas Kegg. **KARISSA SUE KARR** Seventh great granddaughter of progenitor Nicholas Kegg. **LELAND EUGENE KARR** Sixth great grandson of progenitor Nicholas Kegg. **LINDSEY KARR** Seventh great granddaughter of progenitor Nicholas Kegg. **VALERIE KAY KARR** [3919B] (1968 – 2018) daughter of Corwin and Shirley (Sickels) Karr married Brent Lloyd Fletchall with whom she was mother of (1). Valarie had worked as a nurse and later was the head housekeeper for the Mount Ayr Inn.

KARTERMAN

DON SCOTT KARTERMAN Sixth great grandson of progenitor Nicholas Kegg.
JACK MONROE KARTERMAN [3920] (1909 – 1989) son of John and Glenna (Combs) Karterman, married Edith J. Bailey with whom he was father of (2). Jack spent four years in the National Guard in Washington. He had been employed at Seattle First National Bank when he removed to Alaska where he went to work for Lucky Shot Mine and remained there until the mine closed during World War II. He had worked as a timekeeper, radio operator, postmaster, truck driver, and assisted in assaying and surveying. Jack began working for the Alaska Railroad in 1941 and remained there until his retirement. He was a warehouseman and superintendent of stores, hotels, commissaries and housing. At the time of his retirement, he was a procurement and supply officer. Jack enjoyed Boy Scouts and earned the wood badge. He also enjoyed fishing and duck hunting.

KASALES

ETHAN KASALES aka "E.B.", Sixth great grandson of progenitor Nicholas Kegg.

KASSA

EASTON KASSA Ninth great grandson of progenitor Nicholas Kegg. **SHANE KASSA** Eighth great grandson of progenitor Nicholas Kegg. **SHANELLE KASSA** Eighth great granddaughter of progenitor Nicholas Kegg.

KASTL

ANGELA KASTL Sixth great granddaughter of progenitor Nicholas Kegg.

KASTNER

CLAIRE KASTNER Sixth great granddaughter of progenitor Nicholas Kegg. **DAVID WILLIAM KASTNER** Fifth great grandson of progenitor Nicholas Kegg. **JEFFREY KASTNER** Sixth great grandson of progenitor Nicholas Kegg. **LAURA KASTNER** Sixth great granddaughter of progenitor Nicholas Kegg. **MIKAELA KASTNER** Eighth great granddaughter of progenitor Nicholas Kegg. **STEVEN MICHAEL KASTNER** Fifth great grandson of progenitor Nicholas Kegg.

[3919B] Record News (Mount Ayr, IA) May 16, 2018, obtained by D. Sue Dible [3920] Anchorage Daily News (AK) Sep 21, 1989

KAUCHAK

ALYSSA KAUCHAK Seventh great granddaughter of progenitor Nicholas Kegg.
CHLOE KAUCHAK Seventh great granddaughter of progenitor Nicholas Kegg.
JAMES DAVID KAUCHAK Sixth great grandson of progenitor Nicholas Kegg.
JULIE KAUCHAK Sixth great granddaughter of progenitor Nicholas Kegg.
KRISTYN KAUCHAK Sixth great granddaughter of progenitor Nicholas Kegg.
KYRSTIN KAUCHAK Seventh great granddaughter of progenitor Nicholas Kegg.

KAUFMAN

KAREN ELAYNE KAUFMAN Sixth great granddaughter of progenitor Nicholas Kegg.
KATHLEEN GAYLE KAUFMAN Sixth great granddaughter of progenitor Nicholas Kegg.
STEPHANIE KAY KAUFMAN Seventh great granddaughter of progenitor Nicholas Kegg.
STEVEN LYNN KAUFMAN Sixth great grandson of progenitor Nicholas Kegg.
STEVEN LYNN KAUFMAN JR. Seventh great grandson of progenitor Nicholas Kegg.

KAUFFMAN

AMY KAUFFMAN Sixth great granddaughter of progenitor Nicholas Kegg. **BETH KAUFFMAN** Sixth great granddaughter of progenitor Nicholas Kegg. **ISAAC KAUFFMAN** Seventh great grandson of progenitor Nicholas Kegg. **KARA KAUFFMAN** Seventh great granddaughter of progenitor Nicholas Kegg. **KIP KAUFFMAN** Sixth great grandson of progenitor Nicholas Kegg. **LOIS KAUFFMAN** Fifth great granddaughter of progenitor Nicholas Kegg.

KAYLOR

RHONDA ANN KAYLOR Seventh great granddaughter of progenitor Nicholas Kegg.

KEALY

ELLIE LINEA KEALY Seventh great granddaughter of progenitor Nicholas Kegg.

KEATON

CHAD M. KEATON Sixth great grandson of progenitor Nicholas Kegg.
MADDISON KAYLYNN KEATON Seventh great granddaughter of progenitor Nicholas Kegg.

KEEFER

ANTHONY BRANDON KEEFER Sixth great grandson of progenitor Nicholas Kegg.
THADDEUS WARREN KEEFER, aka "Thad", Sixth great grandson of progenitor Nicholas Kegg.

KEELER

LORI A. KEELER Sixth great granddaughter of progenitor Nicholas Kegg.

KEENAN

GARY KEENAN Fifth great grandson of progenitor Nicholas Kegg. **GREGORY KEENAN** Fifth great grandson of progenitor Nicholas Kegg. **JANE ANN KEENAN** Fifth great granddaughter of progenitor Nicholas Kegg. **JOHN PATRICK KEENAN** Fifth great grandson of progenitor Nicholas Kegg. **NANCY KEENAN** Fifth great granddaughter of progenitor Nicholas Kegg.

KEENER

MADISON MARIE KEENER Seventh great granddaughter of progenitor Nicholas Kegg. **MICHAEL KEENER** Seventh great grandson of progenitor Nicholas Kegg. **MORGAN KEENER** Seventh great granddaughter of progenitor Nicholas Kegg.

KEES

ALISHA KEES Eighth great granddaughter of progenitor Nicholas Kegg. **CANDACE DAWN KEES** Ninth great granddaughter of progenitor Nicholas Kegg. **CHARLOTTE NOELLE KEES** Ninth great granddaughter of progenitor Nicholas Kegg. **D.J. KEES** Eighth great grandson of progenitor Nicholas Kegg.

KEESY

LOA BELLE KEESY [3921] (1889 – 1974) daughter of Emery and Ida (Hershiser) Keesy, married Robert Earl Sterling with whom she was mother of (2). Loa was a member of the First United Methodist Church, Kings Daughters Sunday School Class, the Missionary Society, and a life member of the WCTU.

KEEVER

BRETT KEEVER Sixth great grandson of progenitor Nicholas Kegg. **DANA KEEVER** Sixth great granddaughter of progenitor Nicholas Kegg. **DEANNE KEEVER** Sixth great granddaughter of progenitor Nicholas Kegg. **JEFF KEEVER** Sixth great grandson of progenitor Nicholas Kegg.

KEGERREIS

BRIAN KEGERREIS Seventh great grandson of progenitor Nicholas Kegg.
LEAH KEGERREIS Seventh great granddaughter of progenitor Nicholas Kegg.

KEGG

ADA MARIE KEGG (1917 – 1917) daughter of Thomas and Ada (Young) Kegg. **ADAM KEGG** Fifth great grandson of progenitor Nicholas Kegg. **ADAM EMERICK KEGG** Sixth great grandson of progenitor Nicholas Kegg. **ADAM KYLE KEGG** Fifth great grandson of progenitor Nicholas Kegg. **ADAM RUSSELL KEGG** Sixth great grandson of progenitor Nicholas Kegg. **ADDIE KEGG** Seventh great granddaughter of progenitor Nicholas Kegg. **AHIMAZ KEGG** (1853 – 1854) son of Sebastian and Elizabeth (Zembower) Kegg. **ALAINA KEGG** Seventh great granddaughter of progenitor Nicholas Kegg. **ALAN LESLIE KEGG** Fourth great grandson of progenitor Nicholas Kegg. **ALBERT G. KEGG** (1915 – 1915) son of George and Olive (Cheuvront) Kegg. **ALBERT JAMES KEGG** [3922] (1907 – 1907) son of Walter and Alcinda (Imler) Kegg. **ALDEN FRANK KEGG** [3923] (1908 – 1958) son of Henry and Elizabeth (Kaufmann) Kegg, married Ruth C. Thompson with whom he was father of (1). **ALEXANDRIA D. KEGG** aka "Ali", Sixth great granddaughter of progenitor Nicholas Kegg. **ALGIE VERNON KEGG** [3924] (1907 – 1984) son of

---

[3921] Willard, OH Library obituary clipping obtained by D. Sue Dible [3922] The Bedford Gazette (PA) Nov 22,1907 [3923] p.7 - Charleroi Mail (PA) Dec. 31, 1958 [3924] p.19B Indianapolis Star (IN) June 24, 1984

John and Margaret (Miller) Kegg married twice; first to Pauline Boyd and later to Opal V. (Slater) Bradberry. Algie had been a machinist with the former P.R. Mallory & Co. Inc., 39 years. He was a member of Veritis Masonic Lodge and Mallory Pin Club and was a former member of Brightwood Methodist Church, all in Indianapolis. **ALICE KEGG** [3925] (1908 – 1959) daughter of Henry and Elizabeth (Kaufmann) Kegg, married Raymond Charles Keller. Alice was employed in the First National Bank of Pittsburgh. **ALICE AMELIA KEGG** [3926] (1863 – 1918) daughter of Emanuel and Lucetta (Quinn) Kegg married twice; first to David Lemay with whom she was mother of (1). Later, she married John William McMahan with whom she was mother of (2). **ALICE JEANETTE KEGG** (1860 – 1937) daughter of Joseph and Nancy (Green) Kegg, married Oren C. Wyckoff with whom she was mother of (1). **ALLISON KEGG** Sixth great granddaughter of progenitor Nicholas Kegg.
ALLISON JEANETTE KEGG aka "Alli", Sixth great granddaughter of progenitor Nicholas Kegg.
ALLISON RENEE KEGG Sixth great granddaughter of progenitor Nicholas Kegg.
ALMA ELIZABETH KEGG [3927] (1895 – 1977) daughter of George and Mary Amanda (McDaniel) Kegg married twice; first to Walter G. Calhoun with whom she was mother of (4). Later, she married Lewis Edward Rodabaugh with whom she was mother of (2). Alma was employed by the Star Beacon newspaper. **ALTHEA REBECCA KEGG** Fourth great granddaughter of progenitor Nicholas Kegg.
AMANDA KEGG aka "Mandy", Sixth great granddaughter of progenitor Nicholas Kegg.
AMANDA KEGG (1849 – 1857) daughter of Sebastian and Elizabeth (Zembower) Kegg.
AMANDA LEE KEGG [3928] (1850 – 1927) daughter of John and Mary (Swartz) Kegg, married Daniel Webster Hockenberry with whom she was mother of (10). **AMIE NICOLE KEGG** Fifth great granddaughter of progenitor Nicholas Kegg. **AMY RUTH KEGG** [3929] (1965 – 2019) daughter of Dave and Rita (Kennedy) Kegg, married John Rodney Cox with whom she was mother of (3). Amy received a bachelor's in communications from Grand Canyon University. She had a caring soul and cherished raising her children. She was a former member of Jesus People U.S.A. Amy enjoyed working with children, painting, and art. She most of all loved spending time with her family.
ANDREA LAVERNE KEGG Fifth great granddaughter of progenitor Nicholas Kegg.
ANDREW KEGG (born abt. 1766) son of progenitor Nicholas Kegg. **ANDREW KEGG** (1838 – 1859) son of Sebastian and Elizabeth (Zembower) Kegg. **ANDREW CARNEGIE KEGG** [3930] (1898 – 1952) son of Walter and Maryetta (Clark) Kegg married twice; first to Janet and later to Garnet Lagretta Scandrol. **ANDREW JACKSON KEGG** [3931] (1838 – 1876) son of Benjamin and Elizabeth (Pennell) Kegg, married Mary Ann Suter with whom he was father of (8). Andrew was a civil war veteran whose military service was researched extensively by his 3rd cousin/3 times removed, former Lieutenant colonel U.S.M.C. Stephen Sayko as transcribed as follows; Andrew Jackson Kegg was born on April 20, 1838, in Rainsburg, Bedford County, Pennsylvania. At age 27, on September 1, 1862, he joined for duty, and was mustered into service as a private in Company C, 2nd Regiment Potomac Home Brigade, Maryland Infantry. He enlisted at Cumberland, Maryland for three years' service. On the Muster Rolls for Company C from September 1862 through April 1863, he is listed as "Present". On a Special Muster Roll for April 10, 1863, he is listed as being absent sick in the hospital in Cumberland, Maryland. On the Company Muster Roll for May and June 1863, his status was not provided. On all Company Muster Rolls from July 1863 through June 1864, he is listed as "Present". On the Company Muster Rolls for July and August 1864 he is listed as absent sick in Cumberland, Maryland. Additional information provided on Regimental Returns notes that during this period that he was left behind as worn out and not fit for duty. During September 1864, with the mustering out of the regiment's original enlistees, Andrew was transferred to Company A of the new organization now designated as the Veteran Battalion, 2nd Regiment, Potomac Home Brigade. On the Company C Muster-out Roll at Cumberland, Maryland dated September 29, 1864, it is noted that he was last paid to June 30, 1864. He is listed as being 23 years old and the remarks note him as a "Recruit". Comment: He is still listed as a recruit because he did not enlist during the period August-October 1861. The Descriptive Book for Company A gives his age as 26 years

---

[3925] p.6 - The Charleroi Mail (PA) Feb 10, 1959 [3926] p.7 - Fort Wayne News Sentinel Jun 11, 1918 [3927] p.15-The Star Beacon (Ohio) April 5, 1977, obtained by D. Sue Dible [3928] Bedford County Historical Society obituary obtained by D. Sue Dible [3929] Erlewein Mortuary & Crematory in Greenfield (IN) [3930] p.40 Pittsburgh Press (PA) Mar 23, 1952 [3931] researched & written by Stephen Sayko

old and his height as five feet five inches. He is also described as having a dark complexion, hazel eyes, and dark hair. His occupation prior to enlisting was clerk and his birthplace listed as Rainsburg, Pennsylvania. It is also noted that he was enlisted by John Weir at Cumberland on September 1, 1862, for a three-year term. On the Company A Muster Roll for September and October 1864 he is listed as "Present" and noted his enlistment was on September 1, 1862, at Cumberland, Maryland for three years' service. On the November and December 1864 Company Muster Rolls through February 1865, he is listed as "Present". On the March and April 1865 Company Muster Rolls he is listed as "Absent" with the remarks "Detached at Provost Marshal Office Cumberland, Maryland". Andrew was mustered out of service on May 29, 1865. On the Company Muster-out Roll dated May 29, 1865, at Camp Bradford, Baltimore, Maryland it is noted that he was last paid to February 28, 1865, and was owed an additional $8.41. He was also due $100.00 bounty. Also noted was that he owed the U.S. $1.30 for lost equipment. Although not noted on his company's muster rolls, Regimental Returns list him as serving as an orderly assigned to a General Courts Martial Board at New Creek, Va. from November 1863 to March 1864 and as an orderly assigned to a General Courts Martial Board at Piedmont, Va. during February and March 1864. During April 1864 he was assigned as the company clerk and continued in this capacity through June 1864.

Comment: It appears that his civilian occupation as a clerk was responsible for him being assigned similar duties within his regiment during much of his service.

After his discharge from Federal service, Andrew Jackson Kegg remained in Cumberland, Maryland for a brief period prior to returning to Bedford County, Pennsylvania. He remained in Bedford County to 1870 working with his father. He subsequently relocated to Somerset County for a period and finally returned to Cumberland, Allegany County, Maryland where he died of consumption on January 2, 1876. He is buried in Rose Hill Cemetery in Cumberland. Although Andrew was in poor health after his military service due to an asthmatic condition and other complications, he never applied for a federal pension for a service-related disability, however on October 18, 1881; his widow Mary Ann (Suter) Kegg applied for a widow's pension (Application # 286962). At some point this application was approved and she was granted a widow's pension (Certificate # 253326). At the time of her death on December 19, 1905 at age 70, she was receiving $12.00 a month. Mary Ann, who was born in 1836 in Springfield, Ohio and Andrew were married April 20, 1859, in Cumberland, Maryland. Their union produced eight children, five of which were listed in his widow's pension application as living in 1888: Emma K. Kegg (1863), John P. Kegg (1865), Walter W. Kegg (1868), Viola W. Kegg (1873), William E. Kegg (1876). Their three deceased children were: Benjamin F. Kegg (1860-1862), Jennette Kegg (1861-1862), Lydia A. Kegg (1870-1887).   **ANDREW M. KEGG** Fifth great grandson of progenitor Nicholas Kegg.
ANNA CATHERINE KEGG Fifth great granddaughter of progenitor Nicholas Kegg.
ANNA ELIZABETH KEGG [3932] (1830 – 1899) daughter of Boston and Maria Kegg, married David Routsong with whom she was mother of (6).   **ANNA ELIZABETH KEGG** [3933] (1906 – 1906) daughter of John and Elizabeth (Corley) Kegg.   **ANNA MARGARET KEGG** [3934] (1863 – 1931) daughter of Andrew and Susanna (Lukens) Kegg, married David J. Mentzer with whom she was mother of (5).   **ANNA MARY KEGG** (1809 – 1859) daughter of John and Catherine (Faehr) Kegg married twice; first to Andrew Turner with whom she was the mother of (7). Later, she married Frederick Turner.
ANTHONY THOMAS KEGG Sixth great grandson of progenitor Nicholas Kegg.
ARTHUR HEROLD KEGG (1895 – 1907) son of George and Rhoda (Jones) Kegg.
AUBREY KEGG Sixth great granddaughter of progenitor Nicholas Kegg.
AUDALINE MARGARET KEGG [3935] (1921 – 2003) aka "Peg", daughter of Levi and Vera (Straley) Kegg married four times; first to Herbert Leo Dulabhan, then to William George Dulabahn. She married Ernest Homer Cunningham with whom she was mother of (1). Later, she married Paul West.

[3932] Traverse City Record Eagle (MI) Feb 21, 1899 [3933] Bedford Gazette (PA) Oct. 5, 1906 [3934] Bedford Gazette (PA) Aug 21, 1931 [3935] Akron Beacon Journal (OH) Dec31, 2003

AUDREY AUMAE KEGG Fifth great granddaughter of progenitor Nicholas Kegg. **BABY KEGG** (1958 – 1958) son of Russell and Francis (Kendall) Kegg. **BALEIGH KEGG** Seventh great granddaughter of progenitor Nicholas Kegg. **BARBARA JEAN KEGG** Fifth great granddaughter of progenitor Nicholas Kegg. **BARBARA SUE KEGG** Fifth great granddaughter of progenitor Nicholas Kegg. **BARRY KENNETH KEGG** Fifth great grandson of progenitor Nicholas Kegg. **BEATRICE KEGG** (1913 – 1985) daughter of George and Mary (Gilles) Kegg, married Henry Lythgoe with whom she was mother of (2). **BECKY JANE KEGG** Fifth great granddaughter of progenitor Nicholas Kegg. **BENJAMIN KEGG** Seventh great grandson of progenitor Nicholas Kegg. **BENJAMIN FRANKLIN KEGG** [3936] (1815 – 1900) son of Solomon and Elizabeth (Shuman) Kegg, married Elizabeth Pennell with whom he was father of (7). Benjamin conducted the Barnum Hotel on Baltimore Street, Cumberland, Md., during the Civil War, until 1886 when he returned to Friends Cove. In 1872 he went back to Cumberland and took charge of a hotel. Three or four years later he returned to Colerain township and took up his residence on his farm there. **BENJAMIN FRANKLIN KEGG** (1860 – 1862) son of Andrew and Mary Ann (Suter) Kegg. **BERNICE FAYE KEGG** [3937] (1932 – 2012) daughter of Chalmer and Martha (Bowser) Kegg, married John Nodich with whom she was mother of (4). Bernice was employed as a manager with United Telephone, Bell Telephone and later AT&T. She was a member of the Palisades Republican Club as well as the North Penn Women's Republican Club and a member of the Pioneers. Bernice enjoyed traveling, playing cards and games. Most of all, she enjoyed spending time with her grandchildren. **BERTHA BELLE KEGG** [3938] (1892 – 1989) daughter of John and Isabella (Alexander) Kegg, married James Melvin Sewell Livengood with whom she was mother of (4). **BESSIE LOUISE KEGG** [3939] (1924 – 1989) daughter of Walter and Hazel (Moon) Kegg married twice; first to George Nelson Armstrong later, she married Maurice Walter Heffner with whom she was mother of (3). Bessie was a homemaker. She was a member of Lafayette Congregational Church and formerly served as an art director with Camp Tawa in Lafayette. **BETH ALICE KEGG** (1952 – 1995) daughter of George and Dorothy (Gwaltney) Kegg married twice; first to Richard Lynn Galbreath and later, to Ron Duke Carpenter. Beth had been employed as a nurse. **BETSY LYNN KEGG** Fourth great granddaughter of progenitor Nicholas Kegg. **BETTY ANN KEGG** Fourth great granddaughter of progenitor Nicholas Kegg. **BETTY JANE KEGG** Third great granddaughter of progenitor Nicholas Kegg. **BETTY LOUISE KEGG** [3940] (1936 – 2018) daughter of Charles and Laura (Drake) Kegg married Leonard Laverne Morey with whom she was mother of (3). **BEVERLY JOAN KEGG** Fourth great granddaughter of progenitor Nicholas Kegg. **BLANCHE ELEANOR KEGG** [3941] (1880 – 1965) daughter of James and Elsie (Baker) Kegg married twice; first to Clarence A. Harshman and later, to Charles Frederick Pugh with whom she was mother of (1). **BOSTON KEGG JR.** (1801 – 1872) son of Sebastian and Maria (Roof) Kegg, married Maria with whom he was father of (8). **BRADLEY KEGG** Sixth great grandson of progenitor Nicholas Kegg. **BRENDA KAY KEGG** Fifth great granddaughter of progenitor Nicholas Kegg. **BRIAN ALAN KEGG** Fifth great grandson of progenitor Nicholas Kegg. **BRIAN E. KEGG** Sixth great grandson of progenitor Nicholas Kegg. **BRIAN GARY KEGG** Fifth great grandson of progenitor Nicholas Kegg. **BRIAN KEITH KEGG** [3942] (1960 - 2020) son of Charles and Shirley Joan (Caldwell) Kegg. **BRIAN RICHARD KEGG** Sixth great grandson of progenitor Nicholas Kegg. **CADIE KEGG** [3943] (1969 – 1969) daughter of Richard and Iva (Martin) Kegg. **CALEB JAMES KEGG** Sixth great grandson of progenitor Nicholas Kegg. **CAMERON JAMES KEGG** Seventh great grandson of progenitor Nicholas Kegg. **CAMILLE C. KEGG** Fourth great granddaughter of progenitor Nicholas Kegg. **CARL CHESTER KEGG** Fourth great grandson of progenitor Nicholas Kegg. **CAROL KEGG** Fifth great granddaughter of progenitor Nicholas Kegg. **CAROLINE E. KEGG** (1821 – 1899) daughter of Jacob and Eve Smith Kegg, married Peter A. Lininger with whom she was mother of (9).

[3936] The Bedford Gazette (PA) Jan 4, 1901 [3937] Shelly Funeral Home, Warrington, PA [3938] The South Bend Tribune (IN) Jan 13, 1989 [3939] Lima News (OH) Apr 1989 obtained by D. Sue Dible [3940] dignitymemorial.com [3941] Oakland Tribune (CA) June 7, 1965 [3942] The Sacramento Bee (CA) Jan. 17, 2021 [3943] Siskiyou Daily News (CA) Nov 19, 1969

CARRIE ELLA KEGG (3944) (1878 – 1957) daughter of Nathaniel and Catherine (Bowser) Kegg, married Charles Kuckuck with whom she was mother of (2). **CARRIE MAY KEGG** (3945) (1872 – 1917) daughter of Levi and Emily (Calhoun) Kegg, married Albert W. Millin with whom she was mother of (5). Carrie was a very religious woman. **CARSON RILEY KEGG** Seventh great grandson of progenitor Nicholas Kegg. **CATHERINE ANN KEGG** (1833 – 1845) daughter of Nicholas and Elizabeth (Turner) Kegg. **CATHERINE KEGG** (3946) (1812 – 1905) aka "Katie" daughter of Solomon and Elizabeth (Shuman) Kegg, married Isaac Diehl with whom she was mother of (5). Catherine was a most devoted Christian woman and a constant reader of her German Bible.
CATHERINE LUCILLE KEGG (3947) (1918 – 1968) daughter of Walter and Hazel (Moon) Kegg married twice; first to Kenneth A. Brown with whom she was mother of (3). Later, she married Larry L. Miller with whom she was mother of (2). **CATHERINE MYERS KEGG** (1798 – 1832) daughter of Christopher Myers and Miss Kegg/Adopted by her aunt and uncle, Peter and Eve (Harclerode) Kegg; Catherine married David Border with whom she was mother of (4). **CATHIE SUE KEGG** Fifth great granddaughter of progenitor Nicholas Kegg. **CECELIA JANE KEGG** (1861 – 1878) daughter of John and Susannah (Crow) Kegg, married Joel Thomas Simcox with whom she was mother of (1). **CECELIA MARIE KEGG** (3948) (1893 – 1979) daughter of William and Elizabeth (Harbrant) Kegg. Cecelia was a member of St. Joseph's Catholic Church. She retired employee of Galliker Dairy Co. **CHALMER CURTIS KEGG** (3949) (1910 – 2002) son of Chester and Jennie (Rawlings) Kegg, married Martha Helena Bowser with whom he was father of (11). Chalmer was a member of St. John's United Church of Christ and was a lifelong farmer and carpenter. **CHARLES KEGG** (abt 1866 -?) son of Jacob and Elizabeth (Maxfield) Kegg. **CHARLES KEGG** Fifth great grandson of progenitor Nicholas Kegg. **CHARLES E. KEGG** (3950) (1915 – 2005) aka "Whitey", son of John and Bessie (Gross) Kegg, married Elizabeth R. Cover with whom he was father of (3). "Whitey" spent every morning walking through the 8th ward. He worked at the Shaffer Ice Company in Hornerstown doing various tasks, eventually having his own delivery route. He oversaw the horses and "broke" many teams of western mustangs to pull the wagons. He retired from Bethlehem Steel Corp., after 37 1/2 years of service, where he was a schedule clerk for the open-hearth bricklayers. **CHARLES EUGENE KEGG** Fifth great grandson of progenitor Nicholas Kegg. **CHARLES MELVIN KEGG** Fourth great grandson of progenitor Nicholas Kegg. **CHARLES O. KEGG** (3951) (1916 – 1939) son of Louis and Eva (Webb) Kegg, was employed as a truck driver for the Auto Body Supply Company. Charles was fatally stabbed in the heart with a penknife following an argument over a box of matches outside the restaurant of Bernard Kotchin at 207 Broad Street. **CHARLES ROBERT KEGG** (3952) (1933 – 2001) son of Charles and Laura (Drake) Kegg, married Shirley Joan Caldwell with whom he was father of (2). **CHARLES WILLIAM KEGG** (3953) (1911 – 1954) son of Henry and Elizabeth (Kaufmann) Kegg, married Helen Belle Wright with whom he was father of (1). Charles was associated with the Hosdreg Manufacturing Co. in Deming. **CHARLOTTE M. KEGG** (3954) (1902 – 1983) daughter of Benjamin and Flora (Templin) Kegg, married Murl Wallace Stallsmith. **CHERYL L. KEGG** Fifth great granddaughter of progenitor Nicholas Kegg. **CHESTER GLEN KEGG** (3955) (1909 – 1927) aka "Glenn", son of Chester and Jennie (Rawlings) Kegg. Glenn, a highly respected young man who died the result of injuries he received in a motorcycle accident near his home. **CHRISTENA KEGG** (3956) (1848 – 1926) aka "Christe", daughter of William and Mary (Naus) Kegg, married Hiram Wise with whom she was mother of (6). **CHRISTENA KEGG** (3956) (1848 – 1926) aka "Christe", daughter of William and Mary (Naus) Kegg, married Hiram Wise with whom she was mother of (6).
CHRISTIAN RAYMOND KEGG Fifth great grandson of progenitor Nicholas Kegg.
CHRISTIE L. KEGG Fifth great granddaughter of progenitor Nicholas Kegg.

(3944) Johnstown Tribune Democrat (PA) Apr 8, 1957, obtained by D. Sue Dible (3945) p 574 Herald of Gospel Liberty, Volume 109 June 14, 1917 (3946) Bedford Gazette (PA) Oct 27, 1905 (3947) Bellefontaine Examiner (OH) Feb 19, 1968, obtained by D. Sue Dible (3948) Tribune-Democrat (PA) Nov 21,1979, obtained by D. Sue Dible (3949) Bedford Inquirer (PA) March 1, 2002 (3950) Tribune Democrat (PA) Nov 29, 2005 (3951) Microfilm Johnstown Public Library obtained by D. Sue Dible (3952) p.24 Sacramento Bee (CA) Oct 24, 1953 (3953) p.2 - The Chronicle Telegram (OH) Feb 23, 1954 (3954) p.2 - Salem News (OH) Jan 24,1983 obtained by D. Sue Dible (3955) Bedford Gazette (PA) Sept 16, 1927 (3956) p.8 - Kenton Democrat (OH) Sept 24, 1926, obtained by D. Sue Dible

CHRISTINA LYNN KEGG aka "Christy", Sixth great granddaughter of progenitor Nicholas Kegg.
CHRISTINE KEGG Sixth great granddaughter of progenitor Nicholas Kegg.
CHRISTOPHER KEGG Sixth great grandson of progenitor Nicholas Kegg.
CHRISTOPHER A. KEGG Fifth great grandson of progenitor Nicholas Kegg. **CHRISTY KEGG** Fifth great granddaughter of progenitor Nicholas Kegg. **CLARA MAY KEGG** (1868 – 1952) daughter of Levi and Mary Elizabeth (Mower) Kegg, married Lebbeus L. Imler with whom she was mother of (2). Clara was a dressmaker in Queens, N.Y. **CLARE FRANKLIN KEGG** [3957] (1910 – 1968) aka "Buster", son of George and Mabel (McClelland) Kegg, married Frances Elizabeth Wernert with whom he was father of (2). Buster was an assistant postal station supervisor, employed in the Post Office for more than 30 years. He was a member of Zenobia Shrine, Scottish Rite, and Pyramid Lodge, F & AM. **CLAUD GERALD KEGG** (1913 – 1914) son of Samuel and Idella (Diehl) Kegg. **CLAYTON DAVID KEGG** Seventh great grandson of progenitor Nicholas Kegg.
CLIFFORD WILLIAM KEGG [3958] (1888 – 1956) son of Harrison and Idella (Randels) Kegg married twice; first to Eleanor Hart and later, to Margaret Catherine (Stack) Grinn. Clifford was employed by a house trailer delivery firm in Elkhart, entered the hospital from complications resulting from injuries sustained in an auto accident a month earlier where he had sustained broken ribs. They apparently were not of a serious nature at the time. However, his physician said complications resulted and his death was due to pulmonary effusion, fluid in his chest cavity. Clifford was a member of the Eagles lodge and Veterans of Foreign Wars in Warsaw. He was a World War I veteran.
CODY LESTER ENOCH KEGG Seventh great grandson of progenitor Nicholas Kegg.
COLLEEN MABEL KEGG [3959] (1927 – 2016) daughter of William and Alma (Suter) Kegg, married Robert Eugene Hollis with whom she was mother of (2). Colleen was a homemaker and a member of the St. John United Church of Christ in Bedford. She is also a member of the Bedford American Legion Post #113 Ladies Auxiliary. Colleen was a wonderful and loving mother, grandmother, sister, aunt and friend.
CONNER KEGG Fifth great grandson of progenitor Nicholas Kegg. **CONRAD EUGENE KEGG** [3960] (1893 – 1955) aka "Gene", son of Judson and Ethel (Haines) Kegg, married Catherine Lovina Provance with whom he was father of (3). Gene was a retired captain of the Wabash Fire department. He joined the local fire force in 1921 and served 32 years with the department. Gene was a member of the Masonic lodge and the Indiana Fireman's association. **CORA AMANDA KEGG** (1892 – 1906) daughter of John and Margaret (Miller) Kegg. **CORA C. KEGG** (1864 – 1885) daughter of Josiah and Henrietta (Wonders) Kegg. **CRYSTAL LEE KEGG** Seventh great granddaughter of progenitor Nicholas Kegg. **COURTNEY KEGG** Sixth great granddaughter of progenitor Nicholas Kegg.
CYNTHIA LEE KEGG Fifth great granddaughter of progenitor Nicholas Kegg.
CYNTHIA MARIE KEGG Sixth great granddaughter of progenitor Nicholas Kegg.
DANIEL BURTON KEGG aka "Dan", Sixth great grandson of progenitor Nicholas Kegg.
DANIEL HARRISON KEGG Sixth great grandson of progenitor Nicholas Kegg.
DANNIE VAUGHN KEGG (1944 – 2001) son of Jack and Betty (Rittenhouse) Kegg married twice; first to Eileen Plumb and later to Brenda K. Garrett. **DAVID KEGG** Fourth great grandson of progenitor Nicholas Kegg. **DAVID IRWIN KEGG** Fifth great grandson of progenitor Nicholas Kegg.
DAVID MICHAEL KEGG Fifth great grandson of progenitor Nicholas Kegg.
DAVID MICHAEL KEGG Sixth great grandson of progenitor Nicholas Kegg.
DAVID RANDALL KEGG Sixth great grandson of progenitor Nicholas Kegg.
DAVID SANFORD KEGG [3961, 3962] (1824 – 1876) son of Solomon and Elizabeth (Shuman) Kegg, married Margaret Robison with whom he was father of (5). David was a clothier by trade. David's signature is on the last will and testament of his grandfather Sebastian Kegg. Sometime after 1850 the surname picked up the letter (S) changing Kegg to Keggs. David's descendants continue to use the surname Keggs.

[3957] p.24-Toledo Blade (OH) obtained by D. Sue Dible [3958] Warsaw Times - Union (IN) Jun 18, 1956 [3959] Louis Geisel Funeral Home Bedford, PA [3960] Wabash Public Library obituary obtained by D. Sue Dible [3961] p62 San Francisco Municipal Reports for the Fiscal Year 1876 [3962] Commemorative Biographical Record, Wayne & Holmes County, OH Beers 1889

DELILAH CATHERINE KEGG (3963) (1919 – 1983) daughter of George and Olive (Cheuvront) Kegg married twice; first to James Alston Rummer and later, to Charles Elbert Minear with whom she was mother of (4). **DIANE LYDIA KEGG** (3964) (1946 – 1950) daughter of Thomas and Blanche (Pimentel) Kegg. **DIANE LYNNE KEGG** Fifth great granddaughter of progenitor Nicholas Kegg. **DOLORES AUDREY KEGG** Fourth great granddaughter of progenitor Nicholas Kegg. **DONALD CHARLES KEGG** (3965) (1898 – 1971) son of Judson and Ethel (Haines) Kegg married twice; first to Eva Marie Olinger with whom he was father of (1). Later, he married Alice Inez Vantilburg. Donald had been employed as plant manager at Metal Forming Corp. in Elkhart. **DONALD T. KEGG** Fifth great grandson of progenitor Nicholas Kegg. **DONALD WAYNE KEGG** (3966) (1956 – 2022) son Hohn and Evelyn (Linder) Kegg, married Darrell C. Miller. Donald retired as an I.T. specialist for the University of Cincinnati Health. **DOROTHY BERNADEAN KEGG** (3967) (1910 – 1979) daughter of Samuel and Idella (Diehl) Kegg, married Paul Leslie Dively with whom she was mother of (3). Dorothy was a retired employee of the Lions Manufacturing Company in Everett after 20 years of employment. She was a member of the Friends Cove United Church of Christ. **DOROTHY D. KEGG** (3968) (1924 – 2014) daughter of William and Barbara (Lubomski) Kegg, married Paul J. Balint with whom she was mother of (1). **DREWZILLIA A. KEGG** (1851 – 1870) daughter of Joseph and Nancy (Green) Kegg, married Richard P. Pottenger with whom she was mother of (1). **DUANE M. KEGG** Fifth great grandson of progenitor Nicholas Kegg. **DUSTIN SEAN KEGG** Sixth great grandson of progenitor Nicholas Kegg. **DYAN MICHELLE KEGG** Fifth great granddaughter of progenitor Nicholas Kegg. **EDDIE KEGG** (3969) (1881 – 1885) son of Nathaniel and Catherine (Bowser) Kegg. **EDGAR WILLIAM KEGG** aka "Bill", Fifth great grandson of progenitor Nicholas Kegg. **EDGAR WILLIAM KEGG** aka "Eddie", Sixth great grandson of progenitor Nicholas Kegg. **EDITH MAE KEGG** (3970) (1900 – 1963) daughter of William and Cora (Shaffer) Kegg, married Ernest Henry Williams with whom she was mother of (2). The wife of a rancher, Edith was a member of the Pythian Sisters of Yreka and the Shasta Valley Garden club. She was active in community affairs and was an avid fisherwoman and hunter. **EDNA W. KEGG** (3971) (1881 – 1961) daughter of George and Mary (Williams) Kegg, married Albert Calhoun. A graduate of Juanita College, Edna also completed a theological course at Defiance College, O. She followed a teaching career for many years, and among the schools in which she taught were Calhoun Warriors Ridge, Clark and Bunker Hill as well as many others. Her prime interest was centered in religious activities. She was a member of the First Congregational Christian Church of Everett and served as a deaconess in the church organization. Edna taught a Sunday School Class for more than thirty years and served not only as a teacher but as a counselor for the members. In recognition of her completion of 30 years of perfect attendance at Sunday school, Edna was presented a Bible from the Holy Lands, and this was one of her prized possessions. She was instrumental in promoting leadership training classes in the community and aided other worthwhile programs for the betterment of the area. She was active in the work of the WCTU. **EFFIE MAE KEGG** (1885 -?) daughter of Samuel and Ida (Hart) Kegg married three times; first to James Bruce Reed with whom she was mother of (2). She married Frederick James Bithell with whom she was mother of (1). Later, she married Mr. Walker. **ELENORA KEGG** (1858 – 1910) aka "Norah", daughter of Jacob and Elizabeth (Maxfield) Kegg married twice; first to George Brown. Later, she married James Gunson Bragg with whom she was mother of (3). **ELIANA MARIE KEGG** Seventh great granddaughter of progenitor Nicholas Kegg. **ELIJAH TREVOR KEGG** Seventh great grandson of progenitor Nicholas Kegg. **ELIZA JENNIE KEGG** (3972) (1840 – 1902) daughter of Benjamin and Elizabeth (Pennell) Kegg, married John William Jones with whom she was mother of (8). **ELIZABETH KEGG** Fifth great granddaughter of progenitor Nicholas Kegg. **ELIZABETH KEGG** (born abt.1790) daughter of John and Catherine (Faehr) Kegg.

(3963) Daily Californian (CA) May 2, 1983, obtained by D. Sue Dible (3964) p.35 Sacramento Bee (CA) July 27, 1950 (3965) The Elkhart Truth (IN) Oct. 13, 1971, obtained by D. Sue Dible (3966) Cincinnati Enquirer (OH) Jan 3, 2022 (3967) Duke Clark Bedford County obituary clipping collection (3968) Pittsburgh Post-Gazette (PA) Feb 26, 2014 (3969) Microfilm Johnstown Public Library obtained by D. Sue Dible (3970) p.11 Medford Mail Tribune (OR) July 30, 1963 (3971) Duke Clark Obituary Collection pg. 625 (3972) Cumberland Times (MD)USGenWeb Project contributed by Charles Often

ELIZABETH KEGG (born abt.1803) daughter of Sebastian and Maria (Roof) Kegg, married David Smith Jr. **ELIZABETH KEGG** [3973] (1846 – 1846) daughter of Nicholas and Elizabeth (Turner) Kegg. **ELIZABETH KEGG** (1855 – 1933) daughter of Sebastian and Elizabeth (Zembower) Kegg married twice; first to Henry C. Smith with whom she was mother of (7). Later, she married Samuel B. Morris with whom she was mother of (3). **ELMER CHESTER KEGG** [3974] (1884 – 1969) son of John and Rachel (Faulkner) Kegg. Elmer had retired from George Kistner and Sons. **EMANUEL KEGG** (1822 – 1863) son of John and Rachael (Myers) Kegg was recognized with Distinguished Service in Co. K, 18th Reg. Calvary Regiment PA. Two original civil war letters from Emanuel Kegg to his brother Josiah Kegg were auctioned on ebay. The seller states: he can make some of it out. The first from Camp Fairfax, Virginia dated April 7th, 1863. This letter was written in fountain pen & ink, refers to some long overdue pay, camp movements, about one man getting shot and one wounded, also talks about getting revolvers and new sabers and he says "old Abe has paid his boys at last - now we feel like fighting for the union and for the government", sending money & boots home to his family. The second letter was from Camp McClellan, Nov. 24 (no year written) also in fountain pen, but the ink was very faded. This letter makes reference to drilling 3 times a day, having coffee and bread but no sugar, and beef(?) that would last a week if they didn't eat much at a time, and sharing with another camp, calvary regiments, marching orders, soldiers going every which way, east, west. **EMANUEL S. KEGG** [3975] (1835 – 1921) aka "Emil", son of Jacob and Eve (Smith) Kegg married twice; first to Lucetta (Quinn) Penilm with whom he was father of (3). Later he married Nancy E. Glancy. Emil was employed as a contractor. He was a member of the Knights of Pythias. **EMMA IVANILLA KEGG** [3976] (1864 – 1938) daughter of John and Susannah (Crow) Kegg married twice; first to James Franklin Williams with whom she was mother of (3). Later, she married John William Sanders with whom she was mother of (3).
EMMA SMITH KEGG (1860 – 1888) daughter of Solomon and Sarah (Brant) Kegg, married Isaac Burr Hoffmire with whom she was mother of (1). **EMORY CLYDE KEGG** (1915 – 1915) son of Samuel and Idella (Diehl) Kegg. **ENOS KEGG** (1851 – 1858) son of Sebastian and Elizabeth (Zembower) Kegg. **ERNEST R. KEGG** [3977] (1879 – 1904) son of Samuel and Ida (Hart) Kegg worked for Harry Pruner at Maple Park. He was fatally injured on the Pennsylvania Railroad at Stony Bridge.
ESTHER NAOME KEGG [3978] (1896 – 1972) daughter of Rev. Philip and Elizabeth (Stanfield) Kegg, married Warren Ross Nusbaum with whom she was mother of (1). Esther was a member of Castle United Methodist Church, its Missionary Circle and Delta Alpha Klan. **ETHEL M. KEGG** [3979] (1897 – 1953) daughter of Henry and Elizabeth (Kaufmann) Kegg married Charles Arthur Reed with whom she was mother of (2). **ETTA LOUISE KEGG** Fifth great granddaughter of progenitor Nicholas Kegg. **ETTA M. KEGG** [3980] (1868 – 1935) daughter of Simon and Sarah (May) Kegg, married Horace W. Palmer. **EUNICE PAULINE KEGG** [3981] (1898 – 1992) daughter of John and Laura (Raby) Kegg, married Lyman S. Baird with whom she was mother of (1). **EVANGELINE KEGG** (1862 – 1863) daughter of Joseph and Nancy (Green) Kegg. **EVE KEGG** (abt 1795 -?) daughter of Peter and Susan (Koons) Kegg, married Abraham Heist. **EVELYN ELIZABETH KEGG** [3982] (1898 – 1944) daughter of Walter and Bessie (Galbreth) Kegg, married Emory Yeager Brown with whom she was mother of (1). Evelyn had at one time been employed with the Ligonier Refrigerator Company.
EVELYN MARTHA KEGG [3983] (1912 – 1950) aka "Eva", daughter of Louis and Eva (Webb) Kegg, married Mr. Castagnola with whom she was mother of (2). **EVERETT ALLEN KEGG** [3984] (1923 – 1993) aka "Bud", son of Walter and Hazel (Moon) Kegg, married Mildred Louise Robson with whom he was father of (1). Everett retired after 28 years as a salesman with National Life & Accident Insurance Co. He was a member of Indian lake Community Church, Indian Lake Men's Club, Indian Lake Lions Club of Russells Point, and was an associate member of the Indian Lake Chamber of Commerce. He was

---

[3973] Bedford County PA Archives, Vol 5, p 90 obtained by Bob Rose [3974] The Elkhart Truth (IN) Jun 30, 1969, obtained by D. Sue Dible [3975] p.16 - Fort Wayne News Sentinel (IN) July 7, 1921 [3976] p.12 Medford Mail Tribune (OR) Mar 6, 1938 [3977] Cambria Freeman (Ebensburg, Pa.) USGenWeb Project contributed by Patti Millich [3978] p.22 - The Elkhart Truth (IN) Oct 23, 1972, obtained by D. Sue Dible [3979] p.2 - Charleroi Mail (PA) Nov. 24, 1953 [3980] Mansfield News Journal Sep 4, 1935, obtained by D. Sue Dible [3981] Alumni News Massachusetts Institute of Technology Published as a part of the issue of July 1922 page 125 [3982] Library obituary clipping obtained by D. Sue Dible [3983] Johnstown Tribune (PA) May 24, 1950 obtained by D. Sue Dible [3984] Bellefontaine Examiner (OH) Jul 12, 1993 obtained by D. Sue Dible

an Army veteran of World War II, where he served in the Medical Corps. **FANNIE H. KEGG** [3985] (1877 – 1893) daughter of Simon and Sarah (May) Kegg. **FLORA KEGG** (1865 – 1865) daughter of Solomon and Sarah (Brant) Kegg. **FLORENCE B. KEGG** [3986] (1903 – 1958) daughter of Henry and Elizabeth (Kaufmann) Kegg, married Boyd Emery Smith. Florence was employed as secretary to the production manager of the American Brake Shoe Co. **FLOYD REED KEGG** aka "Casey", Fourth great grandson of progenitor Nicholas Kegg. **FOREST EUGENE KEGG** [3987] (1901 – 1967) son of James and Mary (McNalley) Kegg. **FRANK KEGG** Fifth great grandson of progenitor Nicholas Kegg. **FRANK CHEUVRONT KEGG** Fourth great grandson of progenitor Nicholas Kegg.
FRANK THOMAS KEGG Sixth great grandson of progenitor Nicholas Kegg. **FRANKLIN L. KEGG** [3988] (1914 – 1991) son of Louis and Eva (Webb) Kegg, married Edith F. Gallagher with whom he was father of (3). **FRANKLIN PIERCE KEGG** [3989] (1853 – 1901) son of John and Christena (Diehl) Kegg, married Mary Catherine Wilson with whom he was father of (5). Franklin was in the employ of the Cambria Iron company. **FRANKLIN SAMUEL KEGG** [3990] (1879 – 1953) aka "Frank", son of Nathaniel and Catherine (Bowser) Kegg, married Alpha Matilda Gardner. Frank had been employed at Bethlehem Steel Company. He was a member of Beulah EUB Church and Jr. Order of Mechanics. **FRED EMERY KEGG** [3991] (1879 – 1918) son of John and Susannah (Crow) Kegg, married Minnie E. Rohrer. Fred was a prosperous farmer. He was a kind and considerate neighbor and stood well among the people. **FREDERICK CHARLES KEGG** (1944 – 1944) son of Charles and Klara (Bednarik) Kegg. **GARY CHALMER KEGG** [3992] (1941 – 2000) son of Chalmer and Martha (Bowser) Kegg, married Norma Darlene Rose with whom he was father of (2). Gary had been employed by Merck Pharmaceutical Co., for more than 37 years, managing mechanical employees. He was a member of Sellerimille Moose Lodge and the Bucks Mont Two Cylinder Club and won many honors for his work in restoring antique tractors, particularly John Deere models. **GENEVIEVE ELIZABETH KEGG** [3993] (1905 – 1984) daughter of William and Elizabeth (Harbrant) Kegg, married Emerson Weaver.
GEORGE ALBERT KEGG [3994] (1853 – 1861) son of Andrew and Susanna (Lukens) Kegg. **GEORGE ALBERT KEGG** [3995] (1881 – 1963) son of Samuel and Ida (Hart) Kegg, married Olive May Cheuvront with whom he was father of (6). **GEORGE ALBERT KEGG** [3996] (1927 – 1991) son of Thomas and Ada (Young) Kegg, married Dorothy F. Gwaltney with whom he was father of (4). George retired from the Chrysler Corp. He enjoyed golfing, fishing and hunting. He was a member of the Masons and the Elks in Indiana. **GEORGE ELMER KEGG** [3997] (1875 – 1920) son of Levi and Emily (Calhoun) Kegg, married Mabel E. McClelland with whom he was father of (3).
GEORGE ERMEL KEGG (1946 – 1999) son of George William Kegg, married Charlotte Frances Algeo with whom he was father of (2). **GEORGE IRVIN KEGG** [3998] (1893 – 1971) son of John and Margaret (Miller) Kegg married twice; first to Alice May Schrock with whom he was father of (2). Later, he married Mary K. Gilles, with whom he was father of (2). George was a retired carpenter.
GEORGE MYLES KEGG Fourth great grandson of progenitor Nicholas Kegg. **GEORGE S. KEGG** Sixth great grandson of progenitor Nicholas Kegg. **GEORGE SAMUEL KEGG** [3999] (1916 – 2000) son of George and Olive (Cheuvront) Kegg, married Marie Helen Winters with whom he was father of (5). George retired after 33 years from the Firestone Rubber Co., where he had been employed as a millwright. He was a member of the Church of Christ in Uniontown. He was also a member of the Portage Lakes Lodge 752 Free and Accepted Masons. **GEORGE SAMUEL KEGG** Fifth great grandson of progenitor Nicholas Kegg. **GEORGE VINCENT KEGG** Seventh great grandson of progenitor Nicholas Kegg. **GEORGE W. KEGG** (1858 – 1895) son of Sebastian and Elizabeth Zembower) Kegg married twice; first to Mary Elizabeth Williams with whom he was father of (3). Later, he married Mary Amanda McDaniel with whom he was father of (1).

[3985] Richland Shield & Banner (OH) March 11, 1893, obtained by D. Sue Dible [3986] Chronicle Telegram (Elyria, OH) Apr 1, 1958 [3987] Microfilm Johnstown Public Library obtained by D. Sue Dible [3988] The Philadelphia Inquirer (PA) Dec 30, 1991 [3989] Bedford Gazette (PA) Oct 25, 1901 [3990] Johnstown Tribune Democrat (PA) Feb 5, 1953, obtained by D. Sue Dible [3991] Yreka Journal (CA) Nov 6, 1918 contributed by Helen Easton [3992] Bedford Inquirer (PA) Nov 10, 2000 obtained by Bob Rose [3993] Johnstown Tribune Democrat (PA) August 26, 1984, obtained by D. Sue Dible [3994] Vol 34 p3 Bedford Inquirer (PA) May 10, 1861 [3995] Akron Beacon Journal (OH) Jan 30, 1963, obtained by D. Sue Dible [3996] p.8F - Portland Press Herald (OR) May 31, 1991, obtained by D. Sue Dible [3997] The Blade (Toledo, Ohio) obtained by D. Sue Dible [3998] Sarasota Herald-Tribune (FL) Jun 5, 1971 [3999] p.D8 - Akron Beacon Journal (OH) Jan 7, 2000

GEORGE WASHINGTON KEGG (1840 – 1841) son of John and Rachael (Myers) Kegg.
GINGER MARIE KEGG Fifth great granddaughter of progenitor Nicholas Kegg. **GRACE KEGG** [3999A] (1917 – 2007) daughter of James and Ophelia (Price) Kegg married Roy J. Baughman with whom she was mother of (2). Grace was a graduate of Everett High School, a homemaker and a member of the New Bedford Domestic Science Club and the New Bedford Presbyterian Church. She enjoyed crosswords, Scrabble and reading. **GRACE MARIE KEGG** [4000] (1886 – 1959) daughter of Harrison and Idella (Randels) Kegg, married Thomas Allen Gordon with whom she was mother of (2).
GUY FRANKLIN KEGG [4001] (1918 – 1970) son of Chester and Jennie (Rawlings) Kegg, married Gladys Leone Beegle with whom he was father of (4). Guy was employed as a machinist for the Humble Oil Company and a veteran of World War II. He was a member of the American Legion post at Everett and St. Marks Lutheran Church. **HANNAH KEGG** Sixth great granddaughter of progenitor Nicholas Kegg. **HANNAH KEGG** Sixth great granddaughter of progenitor Nicholas Kegg.
HANNAH KEGG (born abt.) daughter of Sebastian and Maria (Roof) Kegg, married George (sp?) Kerchner/Kauffman. **HANNAH L. KEGG**, (died bef 1891) daughter of Jacob and Eve (Smith) Kegg.
HARRIET JEAN KEGG Fourth great granddaughter of progenitor Nicholas Kegg.
HARRISON FREMONT KEGG [4002] (1857 – 1926) aka "Horace", son of Joseph and Nancy (Green) Kegg, married Idella Randels with whom he was father of (3). Horace had a finger sawed off at the lesh factory in 1885 and later worked as a RR freight conductor. Horace was best known as the big bass drummer in the Warsaw Cornet Band. On Nov 11, 1915, Earle H. Davenport wrote a column that appeared on page 7 in The Northern Indianian transcribed as follows; I've heard a lot of music in my life time, you kin bet, And if everything turns out right, I hope to hear more yet; But of all the bands that I have heard, in this glorious land, There's none, sez I, that stands ace high, with the Warsaw Cornet Band. They had no great director who wore medals on his breast, It was just made up of hum town boys, the ones who played the best, But when they played old "Thirty-one" I tell ya, it was grand, They didn't take back seats for none, that Warsaw Cornet Band. John Lathrop was the leader, played a silver belled cornet, And say! by Jing! he could make it ring; I seem to hear him yet. If only you could have heard him, I know you'd understand Why my thoughts go back on memory's track to the Warsaw Cornet Band. Hugh Hanna, he played alto horn, believe me he could play. There ain't no one could beat him, no matter what you say; "Skip" Millice played the snare drum, and played with either hand, Say, they warn't none but artist in the Warsaw Cornet Band. Charley Downs played the "tuby," and I never envied him. Fer the horn was big, and round, and fat, and Charley then was slim, 'Twas such a load to carry I couldn't understand How Charley could stand marchin' with the Warsaw Cornet Band. Horace Kegg played the big bass drum and my, how he could beat it; The folks I used to know to hum loved to see Old Kegg mistreat it; But his boom-boom--boom-boom-boom, most certainly was grand. They couldn't do without Old Kegg in that Warsaw Cornet Band. Charley Funk played the clarinet, and he could make it toot, While "Stubby" Sharp starred as well, at playin' on the flute. They entered in all the tournyments and won on every hand. The best on in the county was the Warsaw Cornet Band. Eli Snyder was drum major, majestic one, at that, With skill he juggled a baton, and wore a high fur hat, When e'er the band was on parade, Eli was in command. With him in front they war't afraid that Warsaw Cornet Band.

But all them days is past and gone, that band don't play no more,
The players have all gone to rest, their playin' days are o'er,
But somehow I feel that somewhere, in some far better land.
Someday I'll hear the music of the Warsaw Cornet Band.

[3999A] The Vindicator (Youngstown, OH) July 26, 2007 [4000] Akron-Summit County Public Library obituary obtained by D. Sue Dible [4001] p.6 - Cumberland Times (MD) May 6, 1970 [4002] p.3-Warsaw Union (IN) Dec. 15, 1926

HARRY KEGG Fifth great grandson of progenitor Nicholas Kegg.   **HARRY KEGG** (1854 – 1940) son of Andrew and Susanna (Lukens) Kegg, married Emma Claire McGregor. Harry was a retired carpenter.   **HARRY KEGG** [4003,4004] (1870 – 1924) son of Jacob and Elizabeth (Maxfield) Kegg married twice; first to Mary Garver and later, to Nellie Nye. Harry was a barber. It was 1901, his wife Nellie had been out of town. Harry smiled ear to ear, happy to relate to a newspaper reporter that his wife was returning home from a trip and that he would not have to eat baker's bread or wash his own dishes anymore for the summer. When Harry died there were no heirs, both wives had preceded him. Harry had left real estate and personal property valued at about $10,000 that created an attack on his Last Will and Testament. Harry's sister Minnie stated that the sole heirs are his two sisters, Minnie E. Brown, Ida Shrock; two brothers, John C. Kegg and Walter M Kegg two nieces, Helen Bragg and Bonnie Slagle and a nephew Morris D Bragg and that the estate should be divided into five equal parts, each of the brothers and sisters receiving one share and one share being divided among the nieces and nephew. Filing an action in Circuit Court to prevent the probate of the Will based on the claim that Harry was of unsound mind at the time it was executed; he was subject to undue influence and the will was unduly executed Stated in the complaint that the day before his death, Harry changed the will excluded his sisters and nephew and nieces.   **HARRY KEGG** (1893 – 1939) son of James and Elsie (Baker) Kegg, married Loretta C. Ambrose with whom he was father of (2).   **HARRY A. KEGG** [4005] (1921 – 1970) aka "Bud", son of Louis and Eva (Webb) Kegg, married Ruth Miller with whom he was father of (3). Harry was employed at 14-inch mill, Johnstown Plant, Bethlehem Steel Corp. He was a veteran of World War II.   **HARRY EARL KEGG** [4006] (1892 – 1912) son of Benjamin and Flora (Templin) Kegg. Harry died a result of lockjaw, following an injury received in attempting to stop a runaway horse when he ran a splinter into his foot.   **HARRY FRANKLIN KEGG** [4007] (1889 – 1918) son of John and Margaret (Miller) Kegg, married Gertrude E. Wise with whom he was father of (1).   **HARRY LEROY KEGG** [4008] (1891 – 1971) son of Nathaniel and Catherine (Bowser) Kegg. Harry was a veteran of World War I. a member of Loyal Order of Moose; Menoher Post, VFW; and Plummers and Steamfitters Union.   **HARRY RICHARD KEGG** [4009] (1968 – 1987) son of Donald and Hazel (Yohn) Kegg. Harry was employed by SEPCO.   **HARVEY E. KEGG** (1892 – 1893) son of Nicholas and Hester (Diehl) Kegg.   **HARVEY GEORGE KEGG** Fourth great grandson of progenitor Nicholas Kegg.   **HARVEY NICHOLAS KEGG** [4010] (1909 – 1973) son of John and Mary Etta (Shaffer) Kegg, married Ruth Marie Robson with whom he was father of (6). Harvey was a self-employed bread delivery man.   **HAYDEN KEGG** Sixth great grandson of progenitor Nicholas Kegg.   **HAZEL HESTER KEGG** [4011] (1913 – 1995) daughter of Chester and Jennie (Rawlings) Kegg, married Ernst Frederick Boettcher with whom she was mother of (3).   **HAZEL MARIE KEGG** [4012] (1904 – 1982) daughter of James and Mary (McNalley) Kegg, married Arthur George Parks with whom she was mother of (3).
HEATHER KEGG Fifth great granddaughter of progenitor Nicholas Kegg.
HEATHER COLLEEN KEGG Fifth great granddaughter of progenitor Nicholas Kegg.
HEATHER R. KEGG Sixth great granddaughter of progenitor Nicholas Kegg.
HELEN CATHERINE KEGG [4013] (1911 – 1933) daughter of John and Bessie (Gross) Kegg was mother of (1).   **HELEN L. KEGG** Fourth great granddaughter of progenitor Nicholas Kegg.
HENRY KEGG (born abt. 1760) son of progenitor Nicholas Kegg, married Catherine Miller. No children were born to this union.   **HENRY KEGG** (1835 – 1843) son of John and Rachael (Myers) Kegg. His original tombstone is located inside the Pioneer Historical Society. The inscription on the front slate; Henry Kagg 1838 - 1845 7 years 5 months.   **HENRY C. KEGG** (1861 – 1892) son of Levi and Mary (Mower) Kegg.   **HENRY ELMER KEGG** (1886 – 1881) son of Nicholas and Hester (Diehl) Kegg.

[4003] Ligonier Leader (IN) July 18, 1901 [4004] Warsaw Union (IN) May 13, 1925 [4005] p.10 – Tribune-Democrat (PA) Jun10,1970, obtained by D. Sue Dible [4006] p.190-The Mahoning Dispatch Index obtained by D. Sue Dible [4007] Microfilm Johnstown Public Library obtained by D. Sue Dible [4008] Tribune-Democrat (PA) Jun 4,1971 obtained by D. Sue Dible [4009] Patriot-News (PA) Feb 27, 1987 [4010] Microfilm Johnstown Public Library obtained by D. Sue Dible [4011] p.5 - York Daily Record (PA) Sept 12, 1995 [4012] Washington Post (DC) Jul 11, 1982 [4013] Microfilm Johnstown Public Library obtained by D. Sue Dible

HENRY FRANKLIN KEGG [4014] (1866 – 1916) son of Josiah and Henrietta (Wonders) Kegg, married Elizabeth Catherine Kaufmann with whom he was father of (6). Henry was a well-known stone cutter. **HENRY L. KEGG**, (died bef. 1920) son of Jacob and Eve (Smith) Kegg, married Nancy E. (nee unknown). Harry was employed as a printer and pressman. His wife is listed as a widow, in the 1920 census residing as an inmate Marion County Poorhouse Asylum. **HENRY ROY KEGG** [4015] (1919 – 1920) son of Roy and Margaret (Carson) Kegg. **HORACE VIRGIL KEGG** [4016] (1877 – 1945) son of James and Laura (Steiner) Kegg, married Cora Delia Christy with whom he was father of (2). Over his lifetime Horace was proprietor of H. V. Kegg Jeweler specializing in watch repair. Later, he was employed as a Night Shipper Lockhart Inn McKees Rocks, Steel plant and, a production clerk at an iron mill. **HOWARD KEGG** (1885 – 1885) son of James and Elsie (Baker) Kegg. **HOWARD E. KEGG** [4017] (1910 – 1997) aka "Jack", son of John and Margaret (Miller) Kegg married twice; first to Emma M. Schultz with whom he was father of (1). Later, he married Ethel Irene Hofecker. Jack was a life member of Solomon Run Volunteer Fire Co.; S.O.A.R. and Good Fellowship Club of U.S. Steel Retirees.
IAN M. KEGG Sixth great grandson of progenitor Nicholas Kegg. **IDA KEGG** [4018] (1899 – 1969) daughter of William H. G. and Allie (Blanchard) Kegg, married Russell Jabez Nall with whom she was mother of (1). **IDA BELLE KEGG** [4019] (1863 – 1956) daughter of Jacob and Elizabeth (Maxfield) Kegg, married Elder Samuel S. Shrock with whom she was mother of (3). **IDA C. KEGG** [4020] (1880 – 1936) daughter of Franklin and Mary (Wilson) Kegg, married Adolph James Mintzer with whom she was mother of (2). Ida was a member of the Woman's Beneficial Union and the Ladies Auxiliary to the Moose. **IDA E. KEGG** [4021] (1916 – 1978) daughter of Russell and Bertha (Moore) Kegg married twice; first to Charles James Ehrenfeld and later, to Lloyd H. Chilcot. **IDA MARIE KEGG** [4022] (1924 – 1989) daughter of Charles and Rose (Park) Kegg, married Carl P. Trownson with whom she was mother of (3). Ida was employed by Children's Hospital Medical Center and was a member of Eastern Star, Ellet Chapter. **IDA MAY KEGG** [4023] (1918 – 1962) daughter of Louis and Eva (Webb) Kegg married twice; first to Herbert Andrew Stouffer with whom she was mother of (2). Later, she married Frank Hernandez. **INFANT KEGG** (1938 – 1938) child of Edgar and Gladys (Porter) Kegg. **INFANT KEGG** (1878 – 1878) child of John and Rachel (Faulkner) Kegg. **INFANT KEGG** (1892 – 1892) child of Judson and Ethel (Haines) Kegg. **INFANT KEGG** (1916 – 1916) daughter of Paul and Ruth (Neely) Kegg. **INFANT KEGG** (1920 – 1920) daughter of James and Ophelia (Price) Kegg. **INFANT KEGG** (1923 – 1923) son of Louis and Eva (Webb) Kegg. **INFANT KEGG** (1940 – 1940) daughter of Harvey and Ruth (Robson) Kegg. **INFANT KEGG** (1907 – 1907) son of George and Mabel (McClelland) Kegg. **IRVIN KEGG** aka "Chip", Fifth great grandson of progenitor Nicholas Kegg. **J. DOUGLAS KEGG** (1941 – 2003) son of Jack and Betty (Rittenhouse) Kegg married Patti Sue Gay, Terry L. Neman and Linda Cheryl Jackson. **JACK EUGENE KEGG** [4024] (1916 – 1976) son of Conrad and Catharine (Provance) Kegg married twice; first to Lois Lesie Henry. Later, he married Betty Jayne Rittenhouse with whom he was father of (7). Jack was the owner and operator of Jack Kegg's Plumbing and Heating. He was a member of American Legion Post 110. **JACK EUGENE KEGG JR.** [4025] (1949 – 2013) son of Jack and Betty Jayne (Rittenhouse) Kegg, married Katherine Louise Henney with whom he was father of (3). Jack served in the U.S. Army's 101st Airborne Division and was deployed to Vietnam for three tours of duty as a door gunner. He was a proud member of American Legion Post 381 in Rome City. **JACOB KEGG** Sixth great grandson of progenitor Nicholas Kegg. **JACOB KEGG** [4026] (1796 – 1858) son of Peter and Susan (Koons) Kegg, married Eve Smith with whom he was father of (14). Jacob was a carpenter and cabinetmaker. He was pardoned in 1841 by Gov. Corwin after being sentenced to a 3-year term for alleged forgery. The records detailed a description of his appearance; Jacob was 5' 7", hazel eyes, dark hair getting gray, dark complexion, scar on thumb of left

---

[4014] Charleroi Mail (PA) Nov. 3, 1916 [4015] Charleroi Mail (PA) March 26, 1920 [4016] The Pittsburgh Press (PA) Oct 14, 1945 [4017] Microfilm Johnstown Public Library obtained by D. Sue Dible [4018] New York Times (NY) Oct 26, 1969 [4019] Adventist Archives p.27 Review and Herald 1956 [4020] Johnstown Tribune (PA) Jan 27, 1936, obtained by D. Sue Dible [4021] Johnstown Tribune Democrat (PA) May 14, 1978, obtained by D. Sue Dible [4022] p.D11 - Akron Beacon Journal (OH) Oct 30, 1989 [4023] Johnstown Tribune-Democrat (PA) Oct 17, 1962, obtained by D. Sue Dible [4024] The Elkhart Truth (IN) Jan. 7, 1976, obtained by D. Sue Dible [4025] KPC News (IN) Mar 20, 2013 [4026] p.33 Micofilm Richland County men served time in the Ohio Penitentiary

hand, small scar above right eyebrow, low forehead, large nose, tolerable large eyebrows.

JACOB KEGG, (born abt. 1799) son of Sebastian and Elizabeth (Roof) Kegg. Jacob was father of (1). **JACOB KEGG** (4027) (1829 – 1895) son of John and Rachael (Myers) Kegg, married Evalia McEldowney with whom he was father of (1). A Civil War veteran, Jacob enlisted in 1861, served in Co. D 55th regiment and was discharged in 1864. **JACOB KEGG** (1840 – 1841) son of Nicholas and Elizabeth (Turner) Kegg. **JACOB CEDRIC KEGG** (4028) (1905 – 1957) son of Walter and Bessie (Galbreth) Kegg, married Marguerite Barker with whom he was father of (2). Jacob was employed as a drug store pharmacist. **JACOB S. KEGG** (4029) (1833 – 1911) son of Jacob and Eve (Smith) Kegg, married Elizabeth Maxfield with whom he was father of (11). Jacob was employed as a wagonmaker.
JACOB T. KEGG aka "Jake" Seventh great grandson of progenitor Nicholas Kegg. **JAMES KEGG** Sixth great grandson of progenitor Nicholas Kegg. **JAMES F. KEGG** (4030) (1906 – 1963) son of James and Mary (McNalley) Kegg, married Maud A. Stedman with whom he was father of (1). James was employed as supervisor for the patrol department of Johnstown Plant, Bethlehem Steel Co.
JAMES HARRY KEGG (1918 – 1988) son of Harry and Loretta (Ambrose) Kegg, married Delphine E. Fucciolo. **JAMES HENRY KEGG** (4031) (1875 – 1960) son of Franklin and Mary (Wilson) Kegg married twice; first to Mary A. McNalley with whom he was father of (4). Later, he married Cressey Louise Dudley. **JAMES HEZEKIAH KEGG** (1867 – 1872) son of John and Mary (Miller) Kegg.
JAMES J. KEGG Fourth great grandson of progenitor Nicholas Kegg. **JAMES KEVIN KEGG** Fourth great grandson of progenitor Nicholas Kegg. **JAMES MADISON KEGG** (1855 – 1925) son of Joseph and Nancy (Green) Kegg, married Elsie V. Baker with whom he was father of (6).
JAMES MILTON KEGG (4032) (1845 – 1927) son of Benjamin and Elizabeth (Pennell) Kegg married twice; first to Laura Lavinia Steiner with whom he was father of (1). Later, he married Margaret Elizabeth Stivers. James was a Union troop drummer boy, Maryland regiment during the civil war. Later, he was a grocer, and proprietor of the Farmers Exchange. 1913, James owned the large frame building on East Pitt Street, intending to go out of business when fire completely destroyed the building.
JAMES MILTON KEGG (4033) (1907 – 1976) son of Horace and Cora (Christy) Kegg, married Venice Augusta Zerrenner with whom he was father of (1). James was an Elk's Lodge member for thirty-five years and a member of no. 794, Santa Ana. **JAMES STANLEY KEGG** (4034) (1885 – 1946) son of George and Mary (Williams) Kegg, married Ophelia Price with whom he was father of (6).
JAMES WILLIAM KEGG (1945 – 2018) son of William and May (Nunn) Kegg.
JAMIE LEIGH KEGG Sixth great granddaughter of progenitor Nicholas Kegg. **JAY KEGG** (4035) (1889 – 1910) son of William and Rosa (Sorrells) Kegg was murdered. His body was found floating in the Arkansas River some distance below Fort Smith. **JEAN LANORE KEGG** Fifth great granddaughter of progenitor Nicholas Kegg. **JEANNE SHIRLEY KEGG** Fourth great granddaughter of progenitor Nicholas Kegg. **JEFFREY P. KEGG** Sixth great grandson of progenitor Nicholas Kegg.
JENNA KEGG Fifth great granddaughter of progenitor Nicholas Kegg. **JENNETTE KEGG**, (1861 – 1862) daughter of Andrew and Mary Ann (Suter) Kegg. **JENNETTE LA SETTE KEGG** (1895 – 1987) daughter of Judson and Ethel (Haines) Kegg married twice; first to Jean Frederick Schmalzreid with whom she was mother of (3). Later, she married Walter Francis Vantilburg.
JENNIE MARY KEGG (4036) (1868 – 1927) daughter of Nathaniel and Catherine (Bowser) Kegg, married Robert Nelson Ferrell with whom she was mother of (9). Jennie was a member of the Central Christian church. **JENNIFER KEGG** Sixth great granddaughter of progenitor Nicholas Kegg.
JENNIFER COLLEEN KEGG Sixth great granddaughter of progenitor Nicholas Kegg.
JERICA MARY KEGG Fifth great granddaughter of progenitor Nicholas Kegg. **JEROB KEGG** Fifth great grandson of progenitor Nicholas Kegg. **JESSE EARL KEGG** (1927 – 1996) son of Jesse and Thelma (Young) Kegg, married Rita Jane Pafford with whom he was father of (2).
JESSE JAMES KEGG Sixth great grandson of progenitor Nicholas Kegg.

(4027) Vol XXIV p3 Bedford Gazette (PA) Aug 29, 1856 (4028) p.15 Indianapolis Star (IN) Mar 6, 1957 (4029) Ligonier Leader (IN) Sep 6, 1911, obtained by D. Sue Dible (4030) Microfilm Johnstown Public Library obtained by D. Sue Dible (4031) Washington Post (DC) Jan 23, 1960 (4032) Bedford Gazette (PA) Feb 11, 1927 (4033) Santa Ana Orange County Register Jan 29, 1976 (4034) Microfilm Johnstown Public Library obtained by D. Sue Dible (4035) p.1 Arkansas Gazette June 21, 1910 (4036) The Morning Herald (PA) Jan 27, 1927

JESSE TRAHERN KEGG Fifth great grandson of progenitor Nicholas Kegg.
JESSICA ELIZABETH KEGG Sixth great granddaughter of progenitor Nicholas Kegg.
JESSICA MARIE KEGG Sixth great granddaughter of progenitor Nicholas Kegg. **JILLIAN KEGG** Fifth great granddaughter of progenitor Nicholas Kegg. **JOAN KEGG** Fourth great granddaughter of progenitor Nicholas Kegg. **JOANNE LOUISE KEGG** Fifth great granddaughter of progenitor Nicholas Kegg. **JOB KEGG** (1843 – 1858) son of Sebastian and Elizabeth (Zembower) Kegg. **JOENE ADAMAE KEGG** [4037] (1921 – 1999) daughter of George and Olive (Cheuvront) Kegg married twice; first to Walter Moffett with whom she was mother of (2). Later she married Mr. Calhoun; Joene was a homemaker. **JOHANNA LENORA KEGG** [4038] (1920 – 1998) aka "Joan", daughter of Conrad and Catharine (Provance) Kegg, married Merle Victor Rawson. Joan retired from LaGrange County Hospital as a registered nurse and was a member of Mount Zion Lutheran Church in LaGrange.
JOHN KEGG Fifth great grandson of progenitor Nicholas Kegg. **JOHN KEGG** Sixth great grandson of progenitor Nicholas Kegg. **JOHN KEGG** (abt 1832 – bef 1850) son of John and Christena (Diehl) Kegg, married Mary Ann Swartz with whom he was father of (1). **JOHN KEGG** (1768 – 1831) son of progenitor Nicholas Kegg, married Catherine Faehr with whom he was father of (8). **JOHN KEGG** [4039] (1791 – 1846) son of Sebastian and Maria (Roof) Kegg, married Rachael Myers with whom he was father of (11). **JOHN KEGG** (abt 1800 -?) son of Peter and Susan (Koons) Kegg. **JOHN KEGG** [4040] (1812 – 1855) son of John and Catherine (Faehr) Kegg, married Christena Mary Diehl with whom he was father of (7). **JOHN KEGG** (abt 1841 – bef 1891) son of Jacob and Eve (Smith) Kegg.
JOHN BRADLEY KEGG [4041] (1978 – 1978) son of John and Judy (Grubb) Kegg. **JOHN C. KEGG** [4042] (1868 – 1945) son of Jacob and Elizabeth (Maxfield) Kegg, married Laura Raby with whom he was father of (1). John was the proprietor of a grocery store. **JOHN DAVID KEGG** Sixth great grandson of progenitor Nicholas Kegg. **JOHN EARLEY KEGG** [4043] (1870 – 1916) son of Nathaniel and Catherine (Bowser) Kegg, married Bessie Bell Gross with whom he was father of (5). John was employed on the Structural plant of the Cambria Steel Company. He was a member of Dale Council, Jr. O. U. A. M. and Trinity Lutheran Church. **JOHN GEORGE KEGG** aka "Johnny" Sixth great grandson of progenitor Nicholas Kegg. **JOHN HOMER KEGG** [4044] (1901 – 1978) son of John and Margaret (Miller) Kegg, married Elsie Elizabeth Hofecker with whom he was father of (1). **JOHN O. KEGG** [4045] (1852 – 1940) son of Boston and Maria Kegg married twice; first to Rachel Faulkner with whom he was father of (3). Later, he married Isabella Alexander with whom he was father of (1). John was a retired blacksmith. **JOHN RUSSELL KEGG** (1881 – 1884) son of John and Susannah (Crow) Kegg. **JOHN STEVEN KEGG** [4046] (1863 – 1934) son of Josiah and Henrietta (Wonders) Kegg, married Margaret Harriet Miller with whom he was father of (9). John was a retired farmer. **JOHN T. KEGG**, (born abt. 1866) son of Joshua and Sarah (Bierly) Kegg. **JOSEPH KEGG** (born abt.1831) aka "Josiah", son of Jacob and Eve (Smith) Kegg, married Lucetia (Wilson) Locklin with whom he was father of (2). **JOSEPH LEE KEGG** Fifth great grandson of progenitor Nicholas Kegg. **JOSEPH S. KEGG** [4047] (1822 – 1873) son of Jacob and Eve (Smith) Kegg, married Nancy E. Green with whom he was father of (8). Joseph was a farmer. **JOSHUA KEGG** Sixth great grandson of progenitor Nicholas Kegg. **JOSHUA KEGG** (born abt. 1815) son of John and Catherine (Faehr) Kegg. **JOSHUA A. KEGG** (1833 – 1851) son of Nicholas and Elizabeth (Turner) Kegg. **JOSHUA ALAN KEGG** Fifth great grandson of progenitor Nicholas Kegg. **JOSHUA REED KEGG** [4048] (1843 – 1919) son of John and Christena (Diehl) Kegg married twice; first to Sarah C. Bierly with whom he was father of (1). Later, he married Susan Earnest. **JOSIAH KEGG** [4049] (1831 – 1902) son of John and Rachael (Myers) Kegg, married Henrietta Wonders with whom he was father of (5). Josiah was a stone mason by trade.
JOYCE ELAINE KEGG Fourth great granddaughter of progenitor Nicholas Kegg.

[4037] Review Journal (NV) Dec 24, 1999 [4038] p.11 - News-Sentinel (IN) Sept 14, 1998 [4039] Bedford County Pennsylvania Archives, Volume 6, Page 61obtained by Bob Rose [4040] Bedford Gazette (PA) Nov 28, 1902 [4041] UBCN. Jun 1978 obtained by Duke Clark [4042] pg. 2 - The Elkhart Truth (IN) Feb 13, 1945, obtained by D. Sue Dible [4043] Microfilm Johnstown Public Library obtained by D. Sue Dible [4044] Tribune-Democrat (PA) May 2,1978, obtained by D. Sue Dible [4045] p.2 - The Elkhart Truth (IN) May 21, 1940, obtained by D. Sue Dible [4046] Microfilm Johnstown Public Library obtained by D. Sue Dible [4047] "A History of Knox County, Ohio, "Chapter XXXIX Morgan Township p366 [4048] Bedford County Genealogical Society obituary obtained by D. Sue Dible [4049] The Bedford Gazette (PA) Jan 24, 1902

JUDSON DOUGLAS KEGG [4050] (1865 – 1915) son of Emanuel and Lucetta (Quinn) Kegg, married Ethel Lenora Haines with whom he was father of (4). Judson had been employed as a brakeman, a Nickel Plate switchman later, a locomotive fireman of the Big Four system. **JULIA ANNE KEGG** Fourth great granddaughter of progenitor Nicholas Kegg. **JULIANNA KEGG** [4051] (1806 – 1890) daughter of John and Catherine (Faehr) Kegg, married William Blackburn with whom she was mother of (5). **JUSTUS KEGG** Sixth great grandson of progenitor Nicholas Kegg. **KAITLIN ALYSE KEGG** Sixth great granddaughter of progenitor Nicholas Kegg. **KARA KEGG** Sixth great granddaughter of progenitor Nicholas Kegg. **KAREN ANNETTE KEGG** Fourth great granddaughter of progenitor Nicholas Kegg. **KARI LEE KEGG** Fifth great granddaughter of progenitor Nicholas Kegg. **KATELYN MARIE KEGG** Sixth great granddaughter of progenitor Nicholas Kegg. **KEHLI KEGG** Sixth great granddaughter of progenitor Nicholas Kegg. **KENNETH CLARENCE KEGG** [4052] (1915 – 1964) son of William and Barbara (Lubomski) Kegg, married Hildegarde Elizabeth Daniels with whom he was father of (1). Ken was the owner of Kegg Television Shop in Perrysville. He was a member of several Masonic bodies, the American Radio Relay League and Allegheny County Rifle Club. **KERRY SUE KEGG** Sixth great granddaughter of progenitor Nicholas Kegg. **KIMBERLY KEGG** Sixth great granddaughter of progenitor Nicholas Kegg. **KIRA LYNN KEGG** Seventh great granddaughter of progenitor Nicholas Kegg. **KRISTIN MARIE KEGG** Fifth great granddaughter of progenitor Nicholas Kegg. **KRISTINE KEGG** Fifth great granddaughter of progenitor Nicholas Kegg. **KRISTY KEGG** Fifth great granddaughter of progenitor Nicholas Kegg.
LARRY RAYMOND KEGG Fourth great grandson of progenitor Nicholas Kegg.
LAURA LEE KEGG Sixth great granddaughter of progenitor Nicholas Kegg. **LAUREN KEGG** Seventh great granddaughter of progenitor Nicholas Kegg. **LENA MARGARET KEGG** [4053] (1911 – 1987) daughter of Benjamin and Flora (Templin) Kegg, married Albert K. Barnes with whom she was mother of (8). Lena was a member of First Christian Church. **LEO-CADIE KEGG** Fifth great granddaughter of progenitor Nicholas Kegg. **LEONA E. KEGG** [4054] (1912 – 1991) daughter of James and Ophelia (Price) Kegg, married Laban B. Monn with whom she was mother of (3). Leona was a registered nurse, retired from the obstetric unit at Jameson Memorial Hospital.
LEONORA NETTIE KEGG (1877 – 1976) daughter of James and Elsie (Baker) Kegg married twice; first to Clarence Bayley Savage with whom she was mother of (2). Later, she married William Chandos Young. **LEOTA MAY KEGG** (1895 – 1918) daughter of Walter and Maryetta (Clark) Kegg, married William J. Giesy with whom she was mother of (1). **LESLIE ANN KEGG** [4055] (1993 – 1993) daughter of Tony and Julie (Campbell) Kegg. **LEVI KEGG** [4056] (1821 – 1907) son of Solomon and Elizabeth (Shuman) Kegg, married Mary Elizabeth Mower with whom he was father of (4). Levi was a tailor by trade. He was a veteran, having served in Company D. 101st Regiment, Penna., Infantry.
LEVI KEGG [4057, 4058] (1844 – 1921) son of Sebastian and Elizabeth (Zembower) Kegg, married Emily Calhoun with whom he was father of (5). On September 23, 1863, Levi enlisted in the PA infantry, 149th Regiment also known as the "Bucktails". He was discharged on November 6, 1864. **LEVI J. KEGG** [4059] (1898 – 1949) son of Benjamin and Flora (Templin) Kegg, married Vera Evaline Straley with whom he was father of (2). Levi served in California, Utah, Texas and Hawaii with the U.S. Army for 21 years. After his retirement he made his home in Washington, D.C. **LEVI RANDOLF KEGG** [4060] (1847 – 1894) son of Benjamin and Elizabeth (Pennell) Kegg, married Mary Maria Ramsey. Levi was a veteran, having served in Co.H. 2nd Patomac Home Regiment, Maryland Infantry. He was employed as a tinsmith. **LINDA CATHERINE KEGG** Fourth great granddaughter of progenitor Nicholas Kegg. **LISA ANN KEGG** Fifth great granddaughter of progenitor Nicholas Kegg. **LIZZIE KEGG** (1864 – 1880) daughter of Jacob and Elizabeth (Maxfield) Kegg.

[4050] p.12-The Fort Wayne Daily News March 29, 1915 [4051] Morning Tribune (Altoona, Pa) Nov 17, 1890, contributed to USGenWeb Archives by Michael Caldwell [4052] North Hills News Record (PA) July 29, 1964 [4053] The Vindicator (Youngstown, Ohio) Dec 10, 1987 [4054] p.5 New Castle News (PA) Feb 28, 1991 [4055] Patriot-News (PA) June 9, 1993 [4056] p.6 - Evening Times (MD) Jan 12, 1907 [4057] p.795 Herald of gospel liberty, Volume 107, Issues 1-26 By General Convention of the Christian Church [4058] NARA T289 Civil War Pensions [4059] p.6-Alliance Review (OH) June 3, 1949, obtained by D. Sue Dible [4060] The Evening Times (MD) Feb 27, 1894

LORI JEAN KEGG Fifth great granddaughter of progenitor Nicholas Kegg. **LOUIS T. KEGG** [4061] (1889 – 1965) son of Franklin and Mary (Wilson) Kegg married twice; first to Eva Webb with whom he was father of (7). Later, he married LauraBelle Mallory. Louis was employed as an automobile salesman. He was a member of First EUB Church and Retired Men's Club of Johnstown. **LUCAS KEGG** Sixth great grandson of progenitor Nicholas Kegg. **LUCY ANN KEGG** [4062] (1862 – 1945) daughter of Joseph and Lucretia (Wilson) Kegg, married Henry F. B. Stichter with whom she was mother of (7). Lucy united with the Mennonite Church in her youth and remained faithful until death. **LUCY MAY KEGG** (1895 – 1982) daughter of William and Elizabeth (Harbrant) Kegg married twice. first to Harry Frederick Cobaugh and later to Ralph Douglas Wilbert. **LYDIA A. KEGG** [4063] (1870 – 1887) daughter of Andrew and Mary Ann (Suter) Kegg. Lydia was 17 years old and planned to be married in October upon her 18th birthday. She died of typhoid fever. **MABEL ARVILLA KEGG** [4064] (1919 – 1988) daughter of Chester and Jennie (Rawlings) Kegg married twice; first to William Frank Hite with whom she was mother of (2). Later, she married Harry E. Cornell. Mabel was a member of St. John's United Church of Christ, Bedford. **MABEL E. KEGG** [4065] (1891 – 1965) daughter of Benjamin and Flora (Templin) Kegg, married Charles David Venable with whom she was mother of (2). Mabel had been employed as a hospital cook. **MABEL IRENE KEGG** [4066] (1886 - 1979) daughter of Nathaniel and Catherine (Bowser) Kegg, married Frederick W. Mintmier with whom she was mother of (1). Mabel was a member of Trinity Lutheran Church. **MARCELYN F. KEGG** [4067] (1947 – 1990) daughter of Franklin and Edith (Gallagher) Kegg was mother of (3). **MARGARET KEGG** (born abt. 1802) daughter of Peter and Eve (Harclerode) Kegg, married Mr. (sp) Otto Ott or Otts. **MARGARET KEGG** (born abt. 1795) daughter of John and Catherine (Faehr) Kegg, married Jacob Knouf with whom she was mother of (8). **MARGARET KEGG** [4068] (1843 – 1910) daughter of John and Rachael (Myers) Kegg, married William Henry Stuckey. **MARGARET IRENE KEGG** (1904 – 1992) aka "Marge", daughter of John and Margaret (Miller) Kegg married three times; first to William Edward Ray with whom she was mother of (3). Later she married Mr. Lane and George S. Greene. **MARGARET VIRGINIA KEGG** [4069] (1850 – 1923) daughter of Benjamin and Elizabeth (Pennell) Kegg, married Henry Clay Metzler. **MARGUERITE ANNA KEGG** [4070] (1902 – 1980) daughter of William and Elizabeth (Harbrant) Kegg, married Nelson William Riffle. Marguerite was a member of St. Joseph's Catholic Church, and ladies auxiliary to Post 294, American Legion. **MARIA KEGG** (abt 1818 -) daughter of John and Catherine (Faehr) Kegg married Jacob Snider. **MARIA BARBARA MYERS KEGG** [4071, 4072] (1802 – 1887) aka "Barbara", daughter of Mr. and Mrs. Christopher Myers, the 9-year-old was adopted in 1811 by her maternal Uncle Peter and Aunt Eve (Harclerode) Kegg, married Henry Hershiser with whom she was mother of (6). **MARIAN WINNIFRED KEGG** [4073] (1932 – 2007) daughter of William and Alma (Suter) Kegg, married Leon Charles Bowser with whom she was mother of (1). Marian was a member of the Huber Heights United Methodist Church and was a housewife. **MARIE ROGET KEGG** [4074] (1973 – 1993) daughter of John and Sharon (Brower) King Kegg, married Rajendra Navnit Panchal with whom she was mother of (1). Marie was a waitress at Vandenberg Officers Club and Maranatha Christian Fellowship Church. **MARILYN RANDOLPH KEGG** Fifth great granddaughter of progenitor Nicholas Kegg. **MARK KEGG** Fifth great grandson of progenitor Nicholas Kegg. **MARK AARON KEGG** Fifth great grandson of progenitor Nicholas Kegg. **MARY ADA KEGG** [4075] (1878 – 1948) daughter of Samuel and Ida (Hart) Kegg married twice; first to Mr. Markle and later to Arch W. Martin. **MARY ANN KEGG** Fifth great granddaughter of progenitor Nicholas Kegg. **MARY ANN KEGG** (1806 – 1881) daughter of Peter and Eve (Harclerode) Kegg, married Simon Snider Stuckey IV with whom she was mother of (10).

[4061] Johnstown Tribune Democrat (PA) June 21, 1965, obtained by D. Sue Dible [4062] Missionary Church Gospel Herald Sep 1945 [4063] Cumberland Times (MD) Sept 08, 1887 [4064] Bedford County Historical Society bk 68, p 90 Mar 2, 1988, obtained by D. Sue Dible [4065] p.8 - Salem News (OH) March 26,1965, obtained by D. Sue Dible [4066] Johnstown Tribune Democrat (PA) Dec 5, 1979, obtained by D. Sue Dible [4067] The Philadelphia Inquirer (PA) Dec 27, 1990 [4068] Bedford Gazette (PA) Apr 22, 1910 [4069] The Bedford Gazette (PA) Jan 12, 1923 [4070] Johnstown Tribune Democrat (PA) June 3, 1980, obtained by D. Sue Dible [4071] p. 457 HISTORY OF SENECA COUNTY. CHAPTER XVII. CLINTON TOWNSHIP AND TIFFIN [4072] p. 7, col. 5-Seneca Advertiser (OH) Sep 15, 1887, obtained by D. Sue Dible [4073] Louis Geisel Funeral Home, PA [4074] Modesto Bee (CA) June 2, 1993 [4075] Plain Dealer (OH) Mar 27, 1948, obtained by D. Sue Dible

MARY ANN KEGG (4076) (1825 – 1901) daughter of John and Rachael (Myers) Kegg married twice; first to James Bowles with whom she was mother of (1). Later, she married William Barnes.
MARY ANN KEGG (1833 – 1833) daughter of Nicholas and Elizabeth (Turner) Kegg.
MARY ANNE KEGG (1942 – 2011) daughter of George and Dorothy (Christensen) Kegg married Mr. Bell with whom she was mother of (1) Mary Anne was employed as a nurse. **MARY CATHERINE KEGG** (1851 – 1864) daughter of John and Christena (Diehl) Kegg. **MARY E. KEGG** (1848 – 1850) daughter of Joseph and Nancy (Green) Kegg. **MARY E. KEGG** (4077) (1892 – 1973) daughter of Levi and Emily (Calhoun) Kegg, married James Harrison Hershberger with whom she was mother of (6). Mary was a member of the Everett First United Church of Christ. **MARY ELIZABETH KEGG** (4078) (1843 – 1908) aka "Molly", daughter of Benjamin and Elizabeth (Pennell) Kegg, married John Weir with whom she was mother of (1). **MARY ELIZABETH KEGG** (4079) (1906 – 2005) daughter of Samuel and Idella (Diehl) Kegg, married Glenn Beegle with whom she was mother of (3). Mary graduated in 1929 from J. C. Blair Memorial Hospital in Huntingdon and through a career spanning 35 years, did early private and general duty at Timmins Hospital, the Sipes Hospital and Bedford County Memorial. During the six years before retirement, she was a part-time relief nurse with Donahoe Manor. She was a former member of the J.C. Blair Alumni and the Bedford Hospital Aux. and RSVP. She was a member of St. John's UCC Church. **MARY ELLEN KEGG** (4080) (1874 – 1945) daughter of Simon and Sarah (May) Kegg, married William Paul Kyner with whom she was mother of (2). **MARY ETTA KEGG** (1896 - ?) daughter of John and Margaret (Miller) Kegg married twice; first to Clayton E. Hofecker with whom she was mother of (2). Later, she married Dr. John Miles Evans Brown. **MARY JANE KEGG** (4081) (1877 – 1922) daughter of Franklin and Mary (Wilson) Kegg, married Harry McClure Owens with whom she was mother of (7). Mary was a member of Trinity Evangelical Church. **MARY JANE KEGG** (4082) (1855 – 1922) aka "Mollie", daughter of Jacob and Eve (McEldowney) Kegg, married Rueben Diehl with whom she was mother of (2). **MARY LOIS KEGG** (1923 – 1924) daughter of James and Ophelia (Price) Kegg. **MARY MARIE KEGG** (4083) (1859 – 1944) daughter of Boston and Maria Kegg, married Orpheus Longworth Prentice with whom she was mother of (5). Mary was a schoolteacher. At 34 years old she was pronounced insane. **MARY MYERS KEGG** (1804 -?) daughter of Mr. and Mrs. Christopher Myers, the 7-year-old was adopted in 1811 by her maternal Uncle and Aunt, Peter and Eve (Harclerode) Kegg, married Joseph Border with whom she was mother of (1). **MARYANN KEGG** (abt 1805 -?) daughter of Sebastian and Maria (Roof) Kegg, married Benjamin Bisaline. **MATILDA KEGG** (4084) (1835 – 1907) daughter of Boston and Maria Kegg, married Samuel Elton Bodle with whom she was mother of (7). **MATTHEW KEGG** Sixth great grandson of progenitor Nicholas Kegg.
MATTHEW KEGG Seventh great grandson of progenitor Nicholas Kegg. **MATTHEW G. KEGG** Fifth great grandson of progenitor Nicholas Kegg. **MAURA KEGG** Fifth great granddaughter of progenitor Nicholas Kegg. **MAYME R. KEGG** (4085) (1886 – 1911) daughter of Nicholas and Katherine (Rock) Kegg, married Daniel S. Fielding with whom she was mother of (1). **MAZAYA KEGG** Sixth great granddaughter of progenitor Nicholas Kegg. **MELISSA KEGG** Fifth great granddaughter of progenitor Nicholas Kegg. **MELISSA KEGG** Sixth great granddaughter of progenitor Nicholas Kegg.
MERLE ELWOOD KEGG (4086) (1919 – 1989) son of Samuel and Idella (Diehl) Kegg, married Mary Pauline May with whom he was father of (2). Merle was a retired woodworker and had been an employee of Exact Level of Manns Choice for 15 years. He was known locally for his hobby of building guitars and clocks. **META ALICE KEGG** (1863 – 1906) daughter of John and Susannah (Crow) Kegg married James Franklin Russell. **MICHAEL KEGG** Sixth great grandson of progenitor Nicholas Kegg. **MICHAEL KEGG** Fifth great grandson of progenitor Nicholas Kegg. **MICHAEL E. KEGG** (4087) (1964 – 1964) son of Russell and Sharon (Frankhouser) Kegg.

(4077) Duke Clark Obituary collection pg. 1963 (4078) The Evening Times (MD) Jan 13, 1908 (4079) p.3 - Bedford Inquirer (PA) Oct 21, 2005, obtained by Bob Rose (4080) Cashmere Valley Record (WA) July 5, 1945, obtained by D. Sue Dible (4081) Tribune-Democrat (PA) Jan 5, 1922 (4082) Bedford Gazette (PA) April 14, 1922 (4083) Tribune (Seymour, Indiana) Sep 8, 1944 (4084) p. 20 - The Fort Wayne Journal Gazette (IN) May 19, 1907 (4085) p.5 - Evening News (CA) Mar 16, 1911 (4086) p.3 - Bedford Inquirer (PA) Dec 29, 1989 (4087) Akron Beacon Journal (OH) Nov 1, 1964, obtained by D. Sue Dible

MICHAEL P. KEGG Fifth great grandson of progenitor Nicholas Kegg. **MICHAEL RAY KEGG** Fifth great grandson of progenitor Nicholas Kegg. **MICHAEL ZACHARY KEGG** Seventh great grandson of progenitor Nicholas Kegg. **MIKAYLA KEGG** Seventh great granddaughter of progenitor Nicholas Kegg. **MINNIE BELL KEGG** [4088] (1870 – 1933) daughter of Simon and Sarah (May) Kegg. **MINNIE E. KEGG** [4089] (1873 – 1958) daughter of Jacob and Elizabeth (Maxfield) Kegg, married Eugene Orlando Brown. Minnie was a member of the First Presbyterian Church. **MIRIAM HILL ETHYL KEGG** Fourth great granddaughter of progenitor Nicholas Kegg. **MIRVINE MUNCASTER KEGG** (1889 – 1892) son of Walter and Maryetta (Clark) Kegg. **MYLES JOSEPH KEGG** [4090] (1899 – 1967) son of John and Margaret (Miller) Kegg married twice; first to Henrietta Stanffer. Later, he married Nellie M. Jenkins with whom he was father of (2). **MYRON J. KEGG** [4091] (1905 – 1960) son of Benjamin and Flora (Templin) Kegg, married Doris Dewan with whom he was father of (1). Myron was employed as a trucker. **MYRTLE M. KEGG** [4092] (1881 – 1970) daughter of John and Rachel (Faulkner) Kegg, married Charles Derry Bridge with whom she was mother of (1). Myrtle was a 75-year member of the United Brethren Church, affiliated with the First Christian Church at Edwardsport. **NANCY CAROLE KEGG** Fourth great granddaughter of progenitor Nicholas Kegg. **NATHAN KEGG** Sixth great grandson of progenitor Nicholas Kegg. **NATHANIEL KEGG** [4093] (1841 – 1929) son of John and Christena (Diehl) Kegg, married Catherine Elizabeth Bowser with whom he was father of (8). Nathaniel enlisted in the 138th Regiment, P. V. I., and served throughout the Civil War. **NICHOLAS KEGG** [4094] (1842 – 1863) son of Nicholas and Elizabeth (Turner) Kegg. **NORA KEGG** Fifth great granddaughter of progenitor Nicholas Kegg. **ONA VIVIAN KEGG** [4095] (1898 – 1955) son of William and Cora (Shaffer) Kegg, married Mildred Grace Mort with whom he was father of (3). Ona was a rancher. He was associated with the Yreka Congregation of Jehovah Witnesses. **PATRICIA RUTH KEGG** Fourth great granddaughter of progenitor Nicholas Kegg. **PAUL ALLEN KEGG** Fifth great grandson of progenitor Nicholas Kegg. **PAUL DAVID KEGG** Sixth great grandson of progenitor Nicholas Kegg. **PAUL PRESTON KEGG** [4096] (1892 – 1964) son of Rev. Philip and Elizabeth (Stanfield) Kegg, married Ruth C. Neely with whom he was father of (2). Paul was a carpenter/house builder. He had worked for Kistner and Sons as a supervisor. Paul was a member of the Castle EUB Church, and Kane Lodge F & AM. **PEARL MARIE KEGG** (1912 – 1977) daughter of George and Alice (Schrock) Kegg, married Edwin Monroe Ashley with whom she was mother of (1). **PEGGY ANN KEGG** [4097] (1934 – 1973) daughter of Theodore and Carolina (Engel) Kegg. **PETER KEGG** [4098, 4099] (1779 – 1831) son of progenitor Nicholas Kegg was married twice; first to Susan Koons with whom he was father of (5). Later, he married Eve Harclerode with whom he was father of (2) and adopted (5) of his deceased sisters' children. Peter was a logger by trade. **PHEBY JANE KEGG** (1860 -?) daughter of Joseph and Lucretia (Wilson) Kegg. **PHILLIP P. KEGG** [5000] (1854 – 1919) son of Boston and Maria Kegg, married Elizabeth Jane Stanfield with whom he was father of (3). Philip had united with the St. Joseph conference of the United Brethren church and had begun preaching, although his ordination did not take place until 1890. He was assigned to charges at Walkerton, Kewanna, Macy, Donaldson, Urbana, again at Kewanna and then to Wakarusa, where his active ministry ended. Rev. Philip conducted a store and was a part time farmer for a period of 10 years. Later, he was employed by Contractor G. C. Kistner until his health failed to such an extent that he was no longer able to perform manual labor. **PHYLLIS KEGG** Fourth great granddaughter of progenitor Nicholas Kegg. **PHYLLIS JANE KEGG** Fifth great grandson of progenitor Nicholas Kegg. **POLLY KEGG** [5001] (born abt. 1809) daughter of Sebastian and Maria (Roof) Kegg, married John Lichtenwalter.

[4088] Mansfield News (OH) Dec 11, 1933 [4089] Library obituary obtained by D. Sue Dible [4090] Johnstown Daily Tribune (PA) Feb 18, 1967 obtained by D. Sue Dible [4091] p.8 - Salem News (OH) Nov 30, 1960 obtained by D. Sue Dible [4092] The Vincennes Sun-Commercial (IN) Oct 26, 1970 [4093] Bedford County Genealogical Society obituary obtained by D. Sue Dible [4094] Vol 7 p4 Bedford Gazette (PA) Oct 2, 1863 [4095] Siskiyou Daily News Genealogical Society Siskiyou County obtained by Jennifer Bryan (4096) p.3 - The Elkhart Truth (IN) June 22, 1964 obtained by D. Sue Dible [4097] p.14 Pittsburgh Post-Gazette (PA) March 10, 1973 [4098] Bedford County Orphans Court Nov 7, 1811 [4099] Bedford County Last Will & Testament/ Church of the Latter Day Saints Records (Utah) [5000] p.2 - Elkhart Truth (IN) Feb 11, 1919 [5001] Boston Kegg/Bedford County Last Will & Testament/ Church of the Latter Day Saints Records

RACHEL MYERS KEGG (1807 – 1884) daughter of Mr. and Mrs. Christopher Myers, the 4-year-old was adopted in 1811 by her maternal Uncle and Aunt, Peter and Eve (Harclerode) Kegg, married Joel McDaniel with whom she was mother of (3). **RALPH WILMONT KEGG** [5002] (1916 – 1992) son of Chester and Jennie (Rawlings) Kegg, married Helen Frances Grimes with whom he was father of (2). Ralph was a former employee of the May and Bigley Pin Mill for 10 years and was a retired farmer in the Dutch Corner area. **RANDALL S. KEGG** Fifth great grandson of progenitor Nicholas Kegg. **RANDI LEE KEGG** Sixth great granddaughter of progenitor Nicholas Kegg. **RAY A. KEGG** Fifth great grandson of progenitor Nicholas Kegg. **RAYMOND KEGG** (1904 – 1904) son of Walter and Maryetta (Clark) Kegg. **RAYMOND LEE KEGG** (1938 – 1991) son of Charlie and Laura (Drake) Kegg, married Flora Belle Schubert with whom he was father of (3). **REBECCA KEGG** aka "Becky", Sixth great granddaughter of progenitor Nicholas Kegg. **REBECCA KEGG** [5003] (1830 – 1912) daughter of Solomon and Elizabeth (Shuman) Kegg, married Emanuel Joseph Beegle with whom she was mother of (6). Rebecca was well known in Friend's Cove where she spent the greater part of her life. She was a member of the Lutheran Church and was a highly respected citizen. **REBECCA KEGG** [5004] (1833 – 1918) daughter of John and Rachael (Myers) Kegg married twice; first to George Day with whom she was mother of (1). Later, she married Jacob Sherk. **REBECCA JANE KEGG** [1354] (1841 – 1908) daughter of Sebastian and Elizabeth (Zembower) Kegg, married Simon S. Bussard with whom she was mother of (4). **RELA M. KEGG** [5005] (1896 – 1966) daughter of Nicholas and Katherine (Rock) Kegg, married Lionel Everard Pedley with whom she was mother of (3). **RENEE L. KEGG** Fifth great granddaughter of progenitor Nicholas Kegg. **RHEMA BESSIE KEGG** [5006] (1891 – 1961) daughter of Joseph and Ruth (Riegle) Kegg, married Harry Elmer Williams. Rhema attended the First Christian church, was a member of the Ladies Auxiliary to the Brotherhood of Railway Trainmen, the Daughters of American the Rebekah lodge, the Theodore Wells Woman's Relief Corps No. 355, and the Ladies Auxilliary No. 3, Railway Veterans. **RHUE ELLIE KEGG** (1857 – 1861) daughter of Andrew and Susanna (Lukens) Kegg. **RICHARD PAUL KEGG** [5007] (1939 – 1943) son of Paul and Louise (Miller) Kegg. Richard was 4 years old when his clothing ignited from a fire in the kitchen stove while his mother was feeding the chickens on the Kegg farm. His brother's cries attracted the attention of his mother, who beat out the flames, but not until her son had suffered first and second degree burns about the entire body. **RICHARD SOLOMON KEGG** [5008] (1914 – 1990) aka "Dick", son of James and Ophelia (Price) Kegg married twice; first to Mary Margaret Ringla with whom he was father of (2). Later, he married Patricia Yount. **RICHARD WAYNE KEGG** [5009] (1938 – 1959) son of William and Alma (Suter) Kegg. **RICK KEGG** Sixth great grandson of progenitor Nicholas Kegg. **ROBERT KEGG** aka "Bob", Fourth great grandson of progenitor Nicholas Kegg. **ROBERT ANTHONY KEGG** Sixth great grandson of progenitor Nicholas Kegg. **ROBERT C. KEGG** (1887 – 1920) son of James and Elsie (Baker) Kegg. **ROBERT FRANCIS KEGG** aka "Bobby", Sixth great grandson of progenitor Nicholas Kegg. **ROBERT FRANKLYN KEGG** (1946 – 1959) son of Benjamin and Mary (Floyd) Kegg. **ROBERT HOWARD KEGG** [5010] (1913 – 2007) aka "Bob", son of Russell and Bertha (Moore) Kegg was father of (2). Bob retired from Bethlehem Steel Corp., plate mill, after 45 years' service. He was a 70-year plus member of the F.O.E. 778, where he was a former president and trustee, and attended the First Christian Church. **ROBERT JOHN KEGG** Fourth great grandson of progenitor Nicholas Kegg. **ROBERT LEA KEGG** [5011] (1932 – 1975) aka "Gee", son of Myron and Doris (Dewan) Kegg, married Donna Jean Coleman with whom he was father of (3). His body was donated to the Case Western Reserve University Medical Center. **ROBERT RUSSELL KEGG** [5012] (1912 – 1987) son of James and Mary (McNalley) Kegg, married Helen Edith Braud. **ROBERT THOMAS KEGG** (1920 – 1989) son of Harry and Loretta (Ambrose) Kegg, married Stella Menghi. **ROBERT THOMAS KEGG** Seventh great grandson of progenitor Nicholas Kegg.

[5002] Bedford Gazette (PA) Apr 26, 1992 obtained by D. Sue Dible [5003] Bedford Gazette (PA) Feb 23, 1912 [5004] p. 11- col. 2 Freeport Journal Standard (IL) April 24, 1918 [5005] Eureka Humboldt Standard (CA) Mar 2, 1966 [5006] Bellefontaine Examiner (OH) May 20, 1961, obtained by D. Sue Dible [5007] Bedford Gazette (PA) Dec. 23, 1943 [5008] p.C-3 Indianapolis Star (IN) Oct 29, 1990 [5009] Duke Clark obituary clipping collection [5010] Tribune-Democrat (PA) Apr 8, 2007 [5011] Salem News (OH) Feb10,1975 obtained by D. Sue Dible [5012] p.30 Times-Picayune (New Orleans, Louisiana) Feb 23, 1941

ROCKFORD ERIK KEGG (5013) (1956 – 1972) son of Jack and Betty (Rittenhouse) Kegg. The 15-year-old was pronounced dead on arrival at the LaGrange Hospital with severe brain damage, the result of a one-car accident on LaGrange CR500E a mile and a half south of U.S. 20. According to police, Rockford's friend lost control of his car due to the excessive speed as he started around a slight curve. The car veered across to the west side of the road and hit a tree head-on. Rockford was thrown partly out of the car. **ROGER W. KEGG** Fifth great grandson of progenitor Nicholas Kegg.
ROMAINE MANON KEGG (5014) (1908 – 1986) daughter of Samuel and Idella (Diehl) Kegg, married Francis Marion Hershberger with whom she was mother of (2). Romaine was a registered nurse and worked at the old Timmins Hospital and had also done a lot of private duty nursing. After her retirement she did volunteer work for the RSVP. **ROSAN KEGG** (abt 1834 -?) daughter of Nicholas and Elizabeth (Turner) Kegg. **RUTH KEGG** (1890 – 1890) daughter of Joseph and Ruth (Riegle) Kegg.
RUTH KATHERINE KEGG (1906 – 1907) daughter of William and Elizabeth (Harbrant) Kegg.
RUTH LOUISA KEGG (5015) (1889 – 1963) daughter of Rev. Philip and Elizabeth (Stanfield) Kegg, married Ezra Jack Eisenhour with whom she was mother of (2). **RYAN E. KEGG** Fifth great grandson of progenitor Nicholas Kegg. **RYAN JOSEPH KEGG** Sixth great grandson of progenitor Nicholas Kegg. **RYAN PATRICK KEGG** Seventh great grandson of progenitor Nicholas Kegg.
SAMUEL KEGG (born abt. 1845) son of William and Mary (Naus) Kegg. **SAMUEL KEGG** (1845 – 1923) son of John and Christena (Diehl) Kegg. **SAMUEL EDMUND KEGG** (5016) (1857 – 1949) son of John and Mary (Miller) Kegg, married Ida Catherine Hart with whom he was father of (9). **SAMUEL EMMETT KEGG** (5017) (1887 -?) son of Samuel and Ida (Hart) Kegg a veteran, Co. D. Third Dev. Batt. 155 Depot Brigade, honorably discharged Feb 1, 1919, Camp Dis. N.J., was later employed as a blacksmith. Samuel was the original fighting Kegg, a boxer who could always be found in the corner of his younger brothers, Lemon and Orange. There were times Samuel substituted for his brothers. **SAMUEL L. KEGG** (1901 – 1929) son of John and Bessie (Gross) Kegg. **SARA KEGG** Fifth great granddaughter of progenitor Nicholas Kegg. **SARAH KEGG** Seventh great granddaughter of progenitor Nicholas Kegg. **SARAH KEGG** Sixth great granddaughter of progenitor Nicholas Kegg. **SARAH A. KEGG** (1844 – 1907) daughter of William and Mary (Naus) Kegg married twice; first to Squire Martin with whom she was mother of (2). Later, she married Thomas Wilson Arnold with whom she was mother of (2). **SARAH ANN KEGG** (1837 – 1841) daughter of John and Rachael (Myers) Kegg. **SARAH CATHERINE KEGG** (5018) (1851 – 1928) daughter of Benjamin and Elizabeth (Pennell) Kegg, married H. Virgil Porter with whom she was mother of (5).
SARAH FLORENCE KEGG (abt 1860 -?) daughter of Jacob and Elizabeth (Maxfield) Kegg.
SAVANNAH GRACE KEGG Sixth great granddaughter of progenitor Nicholas Kegg.
SCOTT RICHARD KEGG Fifth great grandson of progenitor Nicholas Kegg.
SCOTT WILLIAM KEGG Fifth great grandson of progenitor Nicholas Kegg. **SEAN KEGG** Seventh great grandson of progenitor Nicholas Kegg. **SEBASTIAN KEGG** (5019, 5020) (1767 – 1851) aka "Boston", son of progenitor Nicholas Kegg, married twice Maria Elizabeth Roof with whom he was father of (8). Later, he married Mary Ann Finemore with whom he was father of (3).
SEBASTIAN KEGG (5021, 5022) (1811 – 1876) son of Jacob Kegg, married Elizabeth Zembower with whom he was father of (12). **SHANNON KEGG** Seventh great granddaughter of progenitor Nicholas Kegg. **SHANNON KEGG** (1859 – 1859) daughter of John and Mary (Miller) Kegg.
SHANNON LEE KEGG Sixth great grandson of progenitor Nicholas Kegg.
SHELBY RENEE KEGG Sixth great granddaughter of progenitor Nicholas Kegg. **SILAS KEGG** (1854 – 1955) son of John and Mary (Miller) Kegg. **SILAS HENRY KEGG** (abt 1856 -?) son of Jacob and Elizabeth (Maxfield) Kegg. **SIMON KEGG** (1836 – 1859) son of Sebastian and Elizabeth (Zembower) Kegg. **SKYLER JORDON KEGG** Sixth great grandson of progenitor Nicholas Kegg.
SOLOMON KEGG (abt 1788 – bef 1870) son of Sebastian and Maria (Roof) Kegg married Elizabeth

---

(5013) The Elkhart Truth (IN) July 10, 1972, obtained by D. Sue Dible (5014) Bedford Gazette (PA) Oct 22, 1986 (5015) South Bend Tribune (IN) April 9, 1963 (5016) Cleveland Necrology File, Reel #044., obtained by D. Sue Dible (5017) Sandusky Star Journal (OH) Feb 15, 1916 (5018) Cumberland Evening Times (MD) June 12, 1928 (5019) Philadelphia Inquirer (PA) April 10, 1830 (5020) p.3 - Bedford Gazette (PA) Dec 4, 1835 (5021) Bedford County (PA) Last Will & Testament/The Church of Jesus Christ of Latter-day Saints (5022) The Bedford Gazette (PA) Feb 2, 1900

Shuman with whom he was father of (9). Later, he married Margaret Mowry. Solomon had been employed as a shoemaker. **SOLOMON J. KEGG** (1833 – 1883) son of Boston and Maria (nee unknown) Kegg, married Sarah A. Brant with whom he was father of a daughter they named Flora. She died within three months and the couple adopted Emma Smith. **SOLOMON W. KEGG** [5023] (1846 – 1927) son of Sebastian and Elizabeth (Zembower) Kegg. He married Amanda Williams. Solomon was a man of business ability and was a great benefit to the community in which he lived. A highly respected citizen, he was appointed Guardian of the minor children of the late Jackson Mills.
SONYA SUE KEGG Sixth great granddaughter of progenitor Nicholas Kegg. **SOPHIA A. KEGG** (1857 – 1882) daughter of Levi and Mary (Mower) Kegg. **STACEY LAYNE KEGG** Sixth great granddaughter of progenitor Nicholas Kegg. **STACY LEE KEGG** Sixth great granddaughter of progenitor Nicholas Kegg. **STEPHEN RICHARD KEGG** (1964 – 1972) aka "Steve" son of Richard and Linda (Conway) Kegg. **STEPHEN ROCKFORD KEGG** aka "Rocky", sixth great grandson of progenitor Nicholas Kegg. **STEVE KEGG** Fifth great grandson of progenitor Nicholas Kegg. **STEVEN EDWARD KEGG** Fourth great grandson of progenitor Nicholas Kegg.
SUSANNAH ELIZABETH KEGG (1824 – 1865) daughter of Jacob and Eve (Smith) Kegg, married Israel Rice with whom she was mother of (6). **SYLVIA S. KEGG** [5024] (1887 – 1913) daughter of Joseph and Ruth (Riegle) Kegg, married Adrian Gorrell Cook. **TERESA L. KEGG** Fifth great granddaughter of progenitor Nicholas Kegg. **THEODORE EDGAR KEGG** [5025] (1929 – 1943) son of Theodore and Carolina Mildred (Engel) Kegg. **THOMAS KEGG** (1846 – 1846) son of Joseph and Nancy (Green) Kegg. **THOMAS A. KEGG** aka "T", Fifth great grandson of progenitor Nicholas Kegg. **THOMAS ALAN KEGG** Sixth great grandson of progenitor Nicholas Kegg.
THOMAS EDWARD KEGG [5026] (1884 – 1946) son of Harrison and Idella (Randels) Kegg, married Ada Day Young with whom he was father of (3). Tom inherited the railroad lure from his father and had been employed as a locomotive engineer on the Big Four. **THOMAS JOSEPH KEGG** aka "Tommy", Sixth great grandson of progenitor Nicholas Kegg, served in the Gulf War. **TINY KEGG** (1876 – 1877) daughter of John and Susannah (Crow) Kegg. **TRENT ZACHARY KEGG** Fifth great grandson of progenitor Nicholas Kegg. **TRINITY KEGG** Seventh great grandchild of progenitor Nicholas Kegg. **TRISTON KEGG** Seventh great granddaughter of progenitor Nicholas Kegg. **TWIN KEGG** (1883 – 1883) child of Samuel and Ida (Hart) Kegg. **TWIN KEGG** (1883 – 1883) child of Samuel and Ida (Hart) Kegg. **TWINS KEGG** (abt 1911 -?) children of William and Cora (Shaffer) Kegg. **VALERIE ANN KEGG** Seventh great granddaughter of progenitor Nicholas Kegg.
VESTA VIRGINIA KEGG [5027] (1915 – 1988) daughter of Chester and Jennie (Rawlings) Kegg, married William Rosenzweig. **VICTORIA ANN KEGG** Sixth great granddaughter of progenitor Nicholas Kegg. **VIDA TIAM KEGG** Fifth great granddaughter of progenitor Nicholas Kegg. **VINCENT SCOTT KEGG** Fifth great grandson of progenitor Nicholas Kegg.
VIOLETTE MIGNOTTE KEGG [5028] (1885 – 1904) daughter of Nicholas and Katherine (Rock) Kegg. **VIRGINIA LEA KEGG** (1926 – 2002) daughter of George and Olive (Cheuvront) Kegg, married Ralph Sundey with whom she was mother of (3). **WALTER KEGG** Sixth great grandson of progenitor Nicholas Kegg. **WALTER EVERETT KEGG** [5029] (1900 – 1954) son of Joseph and Ruth (Riegle) Kegg, married Hazel Moon with whom he was father of (4). Walter was secretary for the Bellafontaine Fraternal Order of Eagles. **WALTER MAXFIELD KEGG** [5030] (1875 – 1965) son of Jacob and Elizabeth (Maxfield) Kegg married twice; first to Bessie Ethel Galbreth with whom he was father of (3). Later, he married Lucy Hinderer. Walter operated a barber shop in Ligonier for many years.
WALTER WEDDLE KEGG [5031, 5032] (1867 – 1951) son of Andrew and Mary Ann (Suter) Kegg, married Maryetta Clark with whom he was father of (10). Walter was in the contracting business, a plasterer to be more exact. He left Cumberland as a young man and worked on the construction of several of Pittsburgh's largest buildings. Walter suffered a skull fracture when a North Side garage owner was

---

[5023] Bedford Gazette (PA) May 27, 1927 [5024] Library obituary clipping obtained by D. Sue Dible [5025] p.18 Pittsburgh Press (PA) Dec 30, 1943 [5026] Anderson Daily Bulletin (IN) May 24, 1968 [5027] p.15 York Daily Record (PA) Aug 17, 1974 [5028] Bedford Gazette (PA) Feb 26, 1904 [5029] Bellafontaine Examiner (OH) Jan 15, 1954, obtained by D. Sue Dible [5030] Ligonier Leader (IN) Nov 3, 1965, obtained by D. Sue Dible [5031] The Pittsburgh Press Thursday, October 4, 1951 [5032] Cumberland Evening Times (MD) Oct 5, 1951

backing a car out of the garage when a woman called to him to stop. He found Walter lying on the walk behind and a few feet from his car. Walter's first question when picked up was: "What happened?" Walter was unable to tell Homicide Detectives John Stack and James Rimmel, who interviewed him at the hospital whether he had been hit or had fallen before he passed away. **WESLEY KEGG** Sixth great grandson of progenitor Nicholas Kegg. **WILLIAM KEGG** son of William Cagg, Grandson of progenitor Nicholas Kegg. **WILLIAM KEGG** [5033] (abt 1798 – 1828) son of Peter and Susan (Koons) Kegg. **WILLIAM KEGG** [5034, 5035, 5036, 5037] (abt 1823 – 1847) son of Solomon and Elizabeth (Shuman) Kegg was a farmer who enlisted for the duration of the Mexican war. His age upon enlisted was 24 years. Various Company Muster Rolls note that he was absent sick in the hospital at Puebla as of August 8, 1847. On the January-February Muster Roll it is noted that he died at Puebla, Mexico (no date given). On a War Department Adjutant General's Office document dated December 19, 1847, it is noted that he died about Sept 1, 1847. **WILLIAM KEGG** (1831 – 1853) son of Nicholas and Elizabeth (Turner) Kegg. **WILLIAM KEGG** [5038] (1951 – 1951) son of Paul and Louise (Miller) Kegg. **WILLIAM A. KEGG** (1821 –?) son of John and Rachael (Myers) Kegg, married Mary Helen Naus with whom he was father of (9). William enlisted in Co. E., Reg. 10 Ohio Calvary when Lincoln called for a volunteer army from each state. William never returned from battle. **WILLIAM A. KEGG** (1830 – 1893) son of Jacob and Eve (Smith) Kegg, married Lillian Mary Rhoades. William was a veteran of Co. A, 59th Indiana Infantry. **WILLIAM ALDEN KEGG**, aka "Billy", Fifth great grandson of progenitor Nicholas Kegg. **WILLIAM ALONZO KEGG** [5039] (1859 – 1891) son of Emanuel and Lucetta (Quinn) Penilm Kegg married and had children. William was a carpenter. **WILLIAM CAGG/KEGG.** (1762 – 1817) son of progenitor Nicholas Kegg married and was father of (5). The descendants of William are the only known part of this tree to spell their surname Cagg as it originally appeared in census records. **WILLIAM DREW KEGG** Seventh great grandson of progenitor Nicholas Kegg.
WILLIAM E. KEGG [5040] (1855 – 1901) son of Jacob and Elizabeth (Maxfield) Kegg, married Altha Alsie Beckwith. For several years William was a valued and trustworthy employee of Gerberand Treasli's blacksmith shop. At about 23 years of age he moved to Jefferson, Ohio married and returned to Jefferson where he was employed in a dry goods, boot and shoe store, in which he later became a partner. **WILLIAM EDGAR KEGG** [5041] (1875 – 1945) son of Andrew and Mary Ann (Suter) Kegg, married Josephine Rohman with whom he was father of (4). William retired from work with the baking company. He was a member of the SS Peter and Paul Catholic church. **WILLIAM FRANK KEGG** aka "Billy", Fourth great grandson of progenitor Nicholas Kegg. **WILLIAM H. KEGG** [5042] (1868 – 1941) son of Josiah and Henrietta (Wonders) Kegg. **WILLIAM HOWARD KEGG** [5043] (1868 – 1943) son of John and Mary (Miller) Kegg, married Elizabeth J. Harbrant with whom he was father of (7). William was a former employee of the Penn Traffic Company. He was a member of St. John's Reformed Church. **WILLIAM JASON KEGG** Sixth great grandson of progenitor Nicholas Kegg.
WILLIAM JENNINGS KEGG (1908 – 1987) son of William and Elizabeth (Harbrant) Kegg, married May Lillian Nunn with whom he was father of (2). **WILLIAM JOHN KEGG** [5044] (1891 – 1955) son of Walter and Maryetta (Clark) Kegg married twice; first to Barbara Lubomski with whom he was father of (2). Later, he married Rose Marie Klasnick. **WILLIAM VARE KEGG** [5045] (1926 – 1974) son of Charles Orange Kegg and Rose (Park) Kegg, married Ruth Robinson Kegg with whom he was father of (2). A retired Air Force staff sergeant, William served with the Air Force for 22 years and was a veteran of both World War II and the Korean War. After retirement he was a driver for an auto transport company. William was a member of the Denison Church of Jesus Christ of Latter-Day Saints. **WILLIAM W. KEGG** (born abt. 1850) son of Joseph and Nancy (Green) Kegg.

[5033] Ohio Repository (Canton) July 11, 1828 [5034] p.116 History of Bedford, Somerset, and Fulton Counties, Pennsylvania : with illustrations and biographical sketches of some of its people [5035] The Regimental Descriptive Book of the 2nd Pennsylvania Volunteer Infantry obtained by Stephen Sayko [5036] Bedford Gazette (PA) Jan 25, 1901 [5037] National Archives obtained by Stephen Sayko [5038] Bedford Gazette (PA) May 7, 1951 [5039] Fort Wayne Sentinel (IN) Apr 22, 1891 [5040] Ligonier Leader (IN) Dec 5, 1901 [5041] Cumberland Evening Times (MD) Dec. 27, 1945 [5042] Cumberland Evening Times (MD) Jan 29, 1941 [5043] Daily Tribune (Johnstown, PA) Feb 4, 1943 [5044] Pittsburgh Post-Gazette (PA) September 26, 1955 [5045] Sherman Public Library obituary clipping (TX)obtained by D. Sue Dible

WILLIAM WATSON KEGG [5046] (1873 – 1898) son of Nathaniel and Catherine (Bowser) Kegg.
WOODROW PHILIP KEGG [5047] (1913 – 1993) son of William and Elizabeth (Harbrant) Kegg. Woodrow retired from Bethlehem Steel Corp. Army veteran of World War II, a member of St. John Gaulbert Church, American Legion, and Oakland Volunteer Fire Co. **ZACHARY KEGG** Seventh great grandson of progenitor Nicholas Kegg. **ZACHARY AARON KEGG** aka "Zak", Sixth great grandson of progenitor Nicholas Kegg. **ZACHERY KEGG** Sixth great grandson of progenitor Nicholas Kegg. **ZACHERY KEGG** Sixth great grandson of progenitor Nicholas Kegg.

KEGGS

BEATRICE KEGGS [5048] (1907 – 2001) daughter of Robert and Tempest (Wortman) Keggs, married Clyde Theodore Hannah with whom she adopted (1). Beatrice was the first woman to be elected to her community's school board. At her church, Beatrice was a choir mother and Sunday school teacher. She also was a Girl Scout leader, a Y-teen and band parent. **CHARLES W. KEGGS** [5049] (1858 – 1938) aka "Chas", son of David and Margaret (Robison) Kegg/s, married Sarah Jane Speck with whom he was father of (4). **DAVID KEGGS** (abt 1850 –?) son of David and Margaret (Robison) Kegg/s.
EVA A. KEGGS [5050] (1854 – 1937) daughter of David and Margaret (Robison) Kegg/s married Peter W. Biggs with whom she was mother of (3). Her life was an extremely active one and her sunny smile and kindly deeds won for her a large circle of friends. **FLOYD CHARLES KEGGS** Fifth great grandson of progenitor Nicholas Kegg. **GEORGE WESLEY KEGGS** [5051] (1844 – 1926) son of David and Margaret (Robison) Kegg/s, married Malinda Loula King with whom he was father of (2). George was a veteran of the Union Army having served in the Civil War. **HEATHER IRIS KEGGS** Sixth great granddaughter of progenitor Nicholas Kegg. **JARED KEGGS** Sixth great grandson of progenitor Nicholas Kegg. **KARL KEGGS** Fourth great grandson of progenitor Nicholas Kegg. **LOVINA KEGGS** (born abt. 1847) daughter of David and Margaret (Robison) Kegg/s.
MARY L. KEGGS [5052] (1868 – 1956) daughter of George and Malinda (King) Keggs married twice; first to Robert H. Hartman with whom she was mother of (2). Later, she married William T. Cain. Mary had been a lifelong member of the First Methodist Church. **MATTHEW J. KEGGS** Sixth great grandson of progenitor Nicholas Kegg. **ROBERT H. KEGGS** (1875 – 1953) son of George and Malinda (King) Keggs, married Tempest C. Wortman with whom he was father of (1). Robert had been employed on the Railroad as a brakeman. **SARENA HARRIET KEGGS** [5053] (1921 – 1997) aka "Sparky", daughter of Harry and Anna (Viergot) Keggs, married Ruben Kallunki with whom she was mother of (1). Sparky was a homemaker. She helped organize the Friendship Station in Plymouth Township, she was a member of the Corvette Club of Michigan and enjoyed car racing.
SHIRLEY ELAINE KEGGS (1960 -2021) daughter of Lloyd and Iris (Reed) Kegg married Skip Hampton with whom she was mother of (2). Shirley loved people and made friends with everyone she met. She would give the shirt off her back to help anyone in need and took time to make others feel important. She would often make cakes and cookies in celebration of co-worker's birthdays, anniversaries or graduations. If someone had something to celebrate, Shirley was the one to get the celebration started. Shirley was employed at the eye bank obtaining cornea donations. She had previously worked with special needs children and coached youth football. Shirley was a big fan of the New England Patriots.

[5046] Daily Tribune (Johnstown, PA) Dec 29, 1898 obtained by D. Sue Dible [5047] The Tribune Democrat (PA) Jun 7,1993 obtained by D. Sue Dible [5048] GenealogyBuff/ Brown County, Indiana Obituary Collection-88 [5049] Shreve News (OH) Oct 6, 1938, obtained by D. Sue Dible [5050] Shreve News (OH) Dec 16, 1937, obtained by D. Sue Dible [5051] p.20 Lexington Leader (KY) Nov 14, 1926 [5052] Big Sandy News (KY) Oct 18, 1956 [5053] p.A6 Westland Observer (MI) May 8, 1997

www.ingramcontent.com/pod-product-compliance
Lightning Source LLC
Chambersburg PA
CBHW081148290426
44108CB00018B/2475